Classic and Contemporary Studies in Social Psychology

Classic and Contemporary Studies in Social Psychology

A Text-Reader

Todd D. Nelson

California State University, Stanislaus

Los Angeles | London | New Delhi
Singapore | Washington DC | Melbourne

FOR INFORMATION:

SAGE Publications, Inc.
2455 Teller Road
Thousand Oaks, California 91320
E-mail: order@sagepub.com

SAGE Publications Ltd.
1 Oliver's Yard
55 City Road
London EC1Y 1SP
United Kingdom

SAGE Publications India Pvt. Ltd.
B 1/I 1 Mohan Cooperative Industrial Area
Mathura Road, New Delhi 110 044
India

SAGE Publications Asia-Pacific Pte. Ltd.
3 Church Street
#10-04 Samsung Hub
Singapore 049483

Copyright © 2019 by SAGE Publications, Inc.

Printed in the United States of America

ISBN 978-1-4833-7005-7

This book is printed on acid-free paper.

Certified Sourcing
www.sfiprogram.org
SFI-00453

SFI label applies to text stock

Acquisitions Editor: Lara Parra
Editorial Assistant: Zachary Valladon
Production Editor: Olivia Weber-Stenis
Copy Editor: Colleen Brennan
Typesetter: C&M Digitals (P) Ltd.
Proofreader: Lawrence W. Baker
Cover Designer: Anupama Krishnan
Marketing Manager: Katherine Hepburn

18 19 20 21 22 10 9 8 7 6 5 4 3 2 1

Contents

12 | Groups   **385**

1

History of Social Psychology

The roots of social psychology stretch almost as far back as the beginning of psychology. Many mark 1879 as the beginning of the field of psychology, because that was when Wilhelm Wundt opened the first laboratory (in Leipzig, Germany) for experiments in psychology. He also published an influential early textbook in psychology (Wundt, 1897), delineating the areas of study for this new field. Interestingly, one of the first textbooks with the title *Social Psychology* was written not by a psychologist but by a sociologist (Ross, 1908b). Perhaps it was the times, or an artifact of early sociological writing, but Ross (1908a) defined social psychology in a unique way. He said social psychology "studies the psychic planes and currents that come into existence among men in consequence of their association" (p. 577). McDougall (1908) said that social psychology must "show how, given the native propensities and capacities of the individual human mind, all the complex mental life of the individual mind, all the complex mental life of societies is shaped by them and in turn reacts upon the course of their development and operation in the individual" (p. 18). Allport (1924) said that social psychology is "the science which studies the behavior of the individual in so far as his behavior stimulates other individuals, or is itself a reaction to their behavior; and which describes the consciousness of the individual in so far as it is a consciousness of social objects and social reactions" (p. 12). I focus on these textbook definitions because when a field is just getting started, textbooks provide a sort of blueprint for the field, setting the parameters of the proper areas of study and those areas that fall outside of the purview of scientists in that fledgling field. The three earliest texts in social psychology, although containing chapters that differ in what the authors perceive as the proper areas of study, all generally focus on some common elements in their definition of the field. They highlight the importance of the individual (as opposed to large groups, as studied by sociologists) and how that person influences and is influenced by his social world. Most social psychologists today would agree that social psychology is "an attempt to understand and explain how the thought, feeling, and behavior of individuals are influenced by the actual, imagined, or implied presence of others" (Allport, 1985, p. 3). In this chapter, we briefly cover an incomplete overview of some of the main historical developments in social psychology (for more thorough reviews, see Jones, 1985; Kruglanski & Stroebe, 2012). It is important for scientists in all fields to develop a solid understanding of the history of research and theory in their field, so the work they do and the directions they want to take their research will be built on the established research and make clear connections to that research. In so doing, we work to build a reliable foundation of empirically supported knowledge on which we can advance science.

BEHAVIORISM AND WORLD WAR II

From the turn of the 19th to the 20th century, until approximately 1960, behaviorism dominated psychology. Watson (1925), reacting against what he perceived to be the unscientific methods used by early psychologists (e.g., introspection), said that psychology should concern itself solely with observable behavior. In so doing, we can meet the standards of the scientific method and will attain respect as a legitimate scientific field. He called this new approach "behaviorism," and it was very influential across nearly all subfields of psychology. From its inception, social psychology was going to be at odds with behaviorism, in that social psychology dealt with a number of cognitive aspects of life (e.g., the self, attitudes). Recall that behaviorism says that psychology should not deal with any aspect of cognition because it is not observable.

Moreover, as social psychology developed over the decades, a number of the studies revealed what we now regard as an axiom in social psychology: What is important to know in predicting behavior is how the person perceives or construes the environment. In contrast, behaviorism says that if we want to predict behavior, we need to understand the lawful relations between the stimuli in the environment and behavior. In essence, strict behaviorists say that a certain stimulus will always (or usually) elicit a given behavior in people. But social psychologists disagree (Nelson, 1998). Consider this example:

Suppose you get a speeding ticket. For some people, that experience is devastating and it causes a lot of anxiety, fear, and sadness and can do so for weeks afterward. On the other hand, other people toss the ticket in the backseat and have already essentially forgotten about it as the police car leaves the scene. Same stimulus, different construals of the stimulus. Similarly, a given piece of art viewed by 10 people will evoke 10 different reactions in those people. Same stimulus, different perceptions of it, which cause different thoughts, feelings, and behaviors in response to the stimulus.

Not too long after social psychology came into being, World War II started and consumed Europe. The rise of Nazi Germany threatened all of Europe and, indeed, the world. It sounds strange to say, but Adolf Hitler indirectly contributed to the growth of psychology (and social psychology as well) in the United States. The reason is that many scientists fled their homes in Europe to escape Hitler's invading forces and genocidal regime. The German school of thought in psychology known as Gestalt (you might remember its motto: The whole is greater than the sum of its parts) came over with those scientists. Among the many luminary scientists to make their new home in the United States was the social psychologist Karl Lewin. Lewin's (1951) field theory (in a nutshell: Behavior is a function of the person and the environment: $B = f[p \times e]$) and his other research became so influential that he is widely regarded as the father of modern American social psychology. Lewin was also a very strong advocate for the position that research should have real-world applications, and it should aim to solve social problems, such as housing, discrimination, poverty, and so on. This approach was also very influential on the field, spawning a professional society (the Society for the Psychological Study of Social Issues) and several applied journals, and changing the way many researchers approach their experiments for generations.

BALANCE AND DISSONANCE

In the 1940s and 1950s, Fritz Heider was conducting studies and writing about the need for cognitive consistency. Heider said that people strive to have consistency among their attitudes, behaviors, and their relationships. Consistency here simply refers to consistent attitudes, consistent values, and commonality among those attitudes, behaviors, and attitudes held by people in one's life. Inconsistency, Heider said, is uncomfortable, and one will seek to restore what he called "balance" among those disparate elements, by either changing an attitude or, in some cases, dropping a relationship (Heider, 1958).

Heider's balance theory was very influential and provided the basis for perhaps the most famous theory in all of social psychology: cognitive dissonance theory, conceived by Leon Festinger (1957). Festinger said that when people hold two inconsistent cognitions, or one cognition that is incompatible with a behavior, people feel a negative arousal, and that negative feeling motivates the individual to restore cognitive consistency as soon as possible. Now, the way that this usually happens, according to the theory, is that the individual changes one of the cognitions, to bring it in line with the other. In the case of an incompatible thought and behavior, because the behavior is often harder to change, the cognition is changed. For example, suppose a person is talking negatively about friend A on the phone to friend B. After hanging up with friend B, the individual feels cognitive dissonance. Why? Because the individual was talking disparagingly about a friend. Those two things are inconsistent. In this case, it is hard

to "un-ring the bell" in terms of the negative talk that just happened, and the person may try to resolve the dissonance by saying to herself: "I just said negative things about friend A. I am not the kind of person who does that to her friends. But if I just did that, maybe that means that friend A isn't really my friend anymore." A statement like that (changing the way she thinks about friend A) brings her thoughts in line with the disparaging behavior, and the dissonance is eliminated. Although Festinger conducted research on the theory for only about 10 years, the theory was extremely influential and still is to this day.

SOCIAL COGNITION: EXPLICIT AND IMPLICIT

In the mid-1970s, researchers turned their attention to understanding further how people make judgments, how they think of themselves in relation to others, and how they think others think about them (metacognition). This approach[1] was known as the social cognition approach in social psychology, and it quickly rose to popularity (Carlson, 2013; Fiske & Taylor, 1984; Hamilton, 1976). We won't get into details here (see just-cited references for detailed review), considering we discuss this in the social cognition chapter of our book. But research in social cognition has discovered that people are not very rational in their decision making (Kahneman, Slovic, & Tversky, 1982), and in general, people will tend to care more about making the fastest decision, not the accurate one (Fiske & Taylor, 1984).

All the decisions and cognitive activity social cognition researchers were examining were concerned with explicit cognition, that is, cognition that occurs in consciousness, that we are aware of and can direct. Research in cognitive psychology, however, found that

---

[1]Carlson (2013) makes a compelling argument that social cognition is both a content area and an approach in social psychology.

there is another, equally important type of cognition that can have strong effects on our conscious thoughts and behavior. In 1970, Warrington and Weiskrantz found that individuals with amnesia respond equally well (compared with people without amnesia) on a memory test when given a certain kind of memory test. That is, on explicit memory tests (e.g., free recall; given a blank piece of paper, your job is to write what you just saw moments ago), people with amnesia perform significantly worse than people without amnesia. But on memory tests that are deemed implicit, there will be an initial list of words and then a test list of words composed of partial words, such as c_t, and the job of the respondent is to fill in the missing letter to complete the original word from the list. This early research heralded in a new era of research on this fascinating concept of implicit memory (Graf & Schacter, 1985; Roediger, 1990). Implicit cognition refers to a past experience that we are unaware of that can influence our overt thoughts, feelings, and behavior (Greenwald & Banaji, 1995). Although that sounds a lot like Freud's concept of the unconscious, it is not, in that it has none of his psychoanalytic assumptions and it doesn't refer to the unconscious. Research on implicit social cognition has increased dramatically since the early 1990s (Gawronski & Payne, 2010) and continues today, with much research focusing on implicit prejudice and stereotyping (Dasgupta, 2009).

SOCIAL COGNITIVE NEUROSCIENCE

Developments in neuroimaging in the 1990s led to more researchers becoming interested in understanding how the brain reacts in real time to a stimulus. In turn, are certain parts of the brain more active doing certain cognitive tasks? If we then are able to ascertain what parts of the brain are used

in first impressions, for example, then are those parts of the brain the same parts used for social perception, attribution, or even in correcting those first impressions? This new area of study is called social cognitive neuroscience (SCN; Ochsner & Lieberman, 2001). This denotes the three levels of analysis, emphasizing cognition as the common language between social psychology and neuroscience. The methodology used in this research is neuroimaging, specifically, functional magnetic resonance imaging (fMRI). The fMRI is essentially a giant very powerful magnet, and when activated, it detects changes in the oxygen level in the hemoglobin in your brain's blood. The pattern of activation tells us what parts of the brain are being used from moment to moment. What we get is a real-time "movie" of how the brain is responding to not only a static stimulus but a changing one, like a video. SCN research is still relatively young, and there is much that we have yet to learn using fMRI. For example, some research suggests that the amygdala (brain structure most often associated with fear) is activated when perceiving photos of outgroups (Forbes, Cox, Schmader, & Ryan, 2011). The thinking was that the outgroup is associated with the unknown, which leads us to experience fear, and this is at the root of outgroup prejudice. But subsequent research indicated it wasn't that simple and that sometimes the amygdala didn't get activated with the presentation of a photo of the outgroup (Richeson, Todd, Trawalter, & Baird, 2008). So, much more research is needed to understand the more nuanced relationship between the amygdala activation and prejudice (Kubota & Phelps, 2015). Research on social cognitive neuroscience shows no signs of slowing down, and more and more researchers are learning more every day and are developing increasingly sophisticated models about the workings of the brain and how its component parts work in daily social life (Dore, Zerubavel, & Ochsner, 2015).

INTRODUCTION TO READING 1.1

Triplett (1898)

Back in 1898, when Triplett did his famous study of bicycle race times, social psychology wasn't even a field yet (some put it at the publication of McDougall's [1908] text, whereas others put it at Allport's [1924] text). But most social psychologists regard Triplett's (1898) paper as describing the first social psychology experiment, because it looks at how our behavior can change when we are interacting with another person. In the paper you are about to read, Triplett discusses two studies, one an archival analysis of bicycle race records and another an experiment involving turning fishing rod reels alone and in competition with someone else. The two studies showed that sometimes, when people do a task alone, they perform it more accurately and faster than when they do it with another person (e.g., a competitor). But he also found that sometimes people do that task faster when they are competing against another person and slower when doing it by themselves. You'll see that Triplett (and others after him, for the next 60 or so years) struggled to explain these confusing results. This paper may be a tougher read than most other papers in this volume, because of its level of detail and because of the time in which it was written (today's journal reviewers and editors stress clarity in writing). But as you read, think critically about how he is conducting his analyses (bike race times) and designing and conducting the fishing rod experiment, and see if you have ways to improve what Triplett did. Enjoy the paper!

Reading 1.1

THE DYNAMOGENIC FACTORS IN PACEMAKING AND COMPETITION.

By Norman Triplett, Indiana University.

This paper gives some facts resulting from a study in dynamogenic stimulation carried on in the Psychological Laboratory of Indiana University and their application to explain the subject of Pacemaking and Competition.

> Sounds complicated. It is a shame that Triplett doesn't define it.

The work has been done under the direction of Dr. W. L. Bryan and Dr. J. A. Bergstrom, to both of whom I am greatly indebted for the help rendered throughout its progress.

A copy of the official bicycle records made up to the close of the season of 1897 was obtained from the Racing Board of the League of American Wheelmen, and from these records certain facts are given, which, with the help of the chart showing the times made for certain distances by professionals in the three kinds of races principally dealt with, will make clearer the discussion following. The lower curve of the chart represents the record for the distances given in the unpaced efforts against time. The middle curve the paced race against time, and the upper curve the best time made in competition races with pacemaker.

> This famous study, regarded as the first study in social psychology, is in fact an example of archival research. Triplett is examining bicycle records. He is not conducting an experiment.

The definition of these races may be given as follows: The unpaced race against time is an effort by a single individual to lower the established record. No pacemaker is used; the only stimulation of the rider being the idea of reducing his own or some other man's former time.

The paced race against time is also a single effort to make a record. It differs only in the fact that a swift multicycle, such as a tandem or "quod" "makes the pace" for the rider. If he has well trained pacers and is skillful in changing crews as they come on, so as to avoid losing speed, the paced man may reduce the mark for the distance ridden. The two kinds of efforts described are not really races but are called so for convenience. Both are run with a flying start.

The third or paced competition race is a real race. Here, besides keeping up with the pace-maker, is the added element of beating the other contestants. No records are given for the unpaced competition race. This race will, however, be referred to in the course of this paper. It is often called a "loafing" race from the fact that the riders hang back and try to make pace-makers of each other, well knowing that a contestant starting out to make the pace can not win.

VALUE TO BE GIVEN THESE RECORDS.

In presenting these records it is with the feeling that they have almost the force of a scientific experiment. There are, it is computed, over 2,000 racing wheelmen, all ambitious to make records. The figures as they stand to-day have been evolved from numberless contests, a few men making records which soon fall to some of the host who are pressing closely behind. Reductions now made, however, are in general small in amount. Were all the men engaged in racing to make an effort to reduce the time in the kinds of races named, it is probable that the records already made would stand or be but very little reduced while the present leaders and their closest competitors would again assert their superiority, each in his own style of race. Regarding the faster time of the paced races, as derived from the records, it may be asked whether the difference is due to pacing or to the kind of men who take part; and whether the argument ascribing the difference noted to pacing or competition should have less validity from the fact that different men hold the records in the different races. Men fast at one kind of racing are found to be comparatively slow at another. It is for this reason, perhaps, that Michael refuses to meet any one in an unpaced contest. The racer finds by experience that race in which he is best fitted to excel and specializes in that. The difference in time, therefore, between the paced and unpaced race, as shown by the records, is a measure of the difference between the experts in the two classes of racers. It seems probable that the same amount of difference exists relatively between the averages of the classes they represent. A striking practical proof that the difference between the paced and unpaced trials noted in the records is due to pacing, is found in the paced and unpaced time of some individual racers, given later, in which the difference in time corresponds closely to that of the records. The fact may be mentioned, too, that wheelmen themselves generally regard the value of a pace to be from 20 to 30 seconds in the mile.

DISCUSSION OF RECORDS.

Since the records of unpaced efforts against time, shown on the lower curve of the chart, are given only to 25 miles, comparisons with the other races are made for the same distance.

As is readily seen the time made here is much slower than in the paced race against time. The various factors advanced in explanation are given in detail in the following pages but the fact itself deserves attention at this point.

Not so fast, Norman. Almost only counts in horseshoes and hand grenades.

Lower curve, unpaced-against time. Middle curve, paced-against time. Upper curve, paced competition race.

Chart I

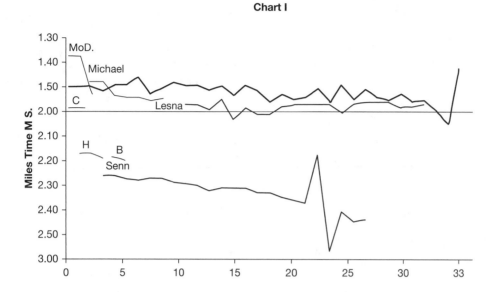

It has been stated that the value of a pace is believed by racing men to be worth to the racer from 20 to 30 seconds in the mile, depending on the individual. The difference between the paced and unpaced race against time is, it is seen from these figures, somewhat greater.

	Average time per mile		Gain over unpaced	Gain percent. over	Gain percent. Competition
	Min.	Sec.	Sec.	unpaced	over paced.
25 miles unpaced against time,	2	29.2			
" " paced " "	1	55.5	34.4	22.9	
" " paced competition	1	50.35	39.55	26.4	3.5

The paced record from the 3rd to the 10th mile inclusive, is held by Michael. His average gain per mile over Senn, the unpaced champion, is 34 seconds. From the 11th mile upward, a different man, Lesna, holds the paced records. Evidently the pace is not worth so much to him for his average gain per mile is only 29.7 seconds, and a portion of this apparent gain is really due to the increasing exhaustion of the unpaced man, Senn.

That the ability to follow a pace varies with the individual is well known. As a rule the rider who is fast with a pace is slow without it, and the converse is believed to be true. This is the reason why the same man can never hold records in both paced and unpaced races. Walter Sanger is one of the fastest unpaced riders on the track, but he can ride only a few seconds better with the very best pacemakers, while Michael, whose ability as a "waiter" is almost marvellous, would fall a comparatively easy victim, his rivals think, in an unpaced race. Success in paced racing presupposes a well trained force of pacers. The last named rider has confessedly enjoyed greater advantages than his competitors in this respect.

The regularity with which he rides is seen in his paced record from 3 to 10 miles. His average rate for these 8 miles was 1 min. 53 sec. with a mean variation of less than .8 second. Other evidences of the constancy of the gain from a pace may be seen through all the records, the time for

20 miles professional, unpaced is			49 min.	20 sec.
25 "	"	paced "	49 "	8.4 "
20 "	amateur,	unpaced "	52 "	17 "
25 "	"	paced "	51 "	57.2 "
80 "	professional, unpaced "		3 hr. 54 "	53 "
100 "	"	paced "	3 " 52 "	14 "

Showing in these cases again in favor of the pace of practically 25%. However, ratios between records made by different men, even though they are the product of many riders and entitled to great consideration, have not the absolute certainty that the paced and unpaced time of the same man would have. Data on this point is difficult to obtain, however, as trackmen seldom follow both kinds of racing but specialize in that for which they are best fitted. The best times for one mile of two prominent racers who are good at both games have, however, been secured and are here given.

Arthur Gardiner, one mile, unpaced,				2 min.	3.8 sec
"	"	"	" paced by 2 quods,	1 "	39.6 "
Earle Kiser,	"	"	unpaced,	2 "	10 "
"	"	"	" paced,	1 "	42 "

The gain, in the case of the first, of the paced over the unpaced, is 24.2 seconds, nearly 20 percent. The second gains 28 seconds, nearly 22 percent., or within nine-tenths of one per cent. of the difference between the official paced and unpaced records made by different men.

Dr. E. B. Turner, F. R. C. S., England, in 1889, began a scientific study of the Physiology of Pacing and Waiting races, lasting over three years. He was a racing man himself and in his investigations made many tests on himself and others. Some figures showing the difference in time made by him at different distances, paced and unpaced, are given. In comparing them with the records of to-day it must be remembered that the wheel then used was heavy and fitted with cushion tires so that the time made in trials is slow as compared with the time made with the modern pneumatic wheel, and in consequence the value of the pace expressed in percent., appears small. It is seen that as between distances paced and unpaced, his average gain per mile for the different trials varies all the way from 11.8 seconds to 20 seconds.

The upper curve of the chart shows the records made in paced competition races. Here, besides beating the record, the racer is intent on defeating his rivals. This race is started from the tape and in consequence is slightly slower for the first two or three miles than the time in the paced race against time with flying start. Thereafter the better time made witnesses to the power and lasting effect of the competitive stimulus. For 25 miles the time in this race averages 5.15 seconds per mile, or 3.5 percent. faster than the paced race against time. From the 3rd to the 10th mile the same man, Michael,[2] holds the record in both races. His time in the competition miles averages over 5 seconds faster than his paced miles against time. The fact that the same racing crews were used in both races suggests that in the latter race they also were responsive to the competition stimulus.

Distance in Miles.	Details of Pacing	Time.		Gains for paced over unpaced trial.		Average gain per mile.	Per-cent gain.
		Min.	Sec.	Min.	Sec.	Sec.	
1	4 Pacemakers	2	37.6				
1	No "	2	49.4		11.8	11.8	7.
3	5 "	8	6.6				
3	No "	8	57.8		51.2	17.	9.5
3	No "	9	7.	1	.4	20.	11.7
4	1 tandem "	11	31.				
4	No "	12	2.4		.53	13.25	7.33
5	Several "	14	5.8				
5	" "	13	50.4				
5	No "	15	23.8	1	.18	15.6	8.4
5	No "	15	37.2	1	31.4	18.25	9.8
5	Alt. laps "	16	38.4	2	32.6	30.5	15.3
10	Several "	31	18.4				
10	No "	33	17.2	1	58.8	11.8	6.
25	Numerous "	71	15.8				
25	Shared "	85	21.8	14	6.	36.	16.5
25	" "	81	16.4	10	.6	24.	

[2] Since this article was written Michael's time in paced competition racing has been lowered. On June 17, 1898, E. A. McDuffie in his race with Taylor broke all records up to 30 miles. His time was 55 :09 1-5, which is r min. 23 4-5 seconds faster than Michael's time for that distance. This increases the gain over the paced race against time to 8 seconds per mile.

In his treatise on the "Physiology of Waiting and Pacemaking in Speed Competitions," Dr. Turner asserts that the causes operating to produce the differences noted between paced and unpaced races are directly due to the physiological effects of bodily and mental exercise. Stated briefly: the man who in a given distance does the greater amount of muscular work burns up the greater amount of tissue and in consequence his blood is more loaded with waste products and he excretes more urea and uric acid than the man who does a less amount in the same time. This excretion of nitrogenous products as shown by his experiments is directly proportional to the amount of work done. The blood, surcharged with the poisonous matter, benumbs the brain and diminishes its power to direct and stimulate the muscles, and the muscles themselves, bathed by the impure blood, lose largely their contractile power. He asserts further, that phosphoric acid is the principal product of brain work, and that carbonic acid, lactic acid and uric acid are excreted in greater quantities during brain work. Therefore, the man racing under conditions to produce brain worry will be most severely distressed.

> Interesting early attempt to explain the difference in racing times between bikers riding by themselves (unpaced) and by themselves with a pace maker (paced). Turner believes that whoever works their muscles harder will end up with muscle waste products in their blood, which clouds their thinking, and ability to skillfully operate their muscles, and thus their overall performance is diminished.

The production of phosphoric acid by brain work is, however, in dispute. Some observers have found the phosphates diminished, whilst others have found them present in larger quantities during intellectual labor. As James says it is a hard problem from the fact that the only gauge of the amount is that obtained in excretions which represent other organs as well as the brain. Dr. Turner's tables of results bear him out, however, in the assertion that a less amount of waste matter was excreted on days when little or no exercise was taken, a greater amount when pacers were used, and the greatest amount when he made his own pace.

> So, Turner asserts that performance on the bike will be worst when unpaced, and better when riding with a pace maker.

Basing his position on these physiological facts he states his thesis thus: "Given two men of equal calibre, properly trained and racing on a fair course, it is impossible (bar falls and similar accidents) for one of them to lead, make fast running and win the race; and the easier the track, the lighter and better the machines ridden, and the faster the time of the race—the longer the distance by which the one following will win." This is known by every rider and accounts for the "loafing" in unpaced competition races, as no man, unless decidedly superior to his competitors, dares to set the pace.

THEORIES ACCOUNTING FOR THE FASTER TIME OF PACED AND COMPETITION RACES.

> We won't evaluate in detail the several theories put forth to try to explain the difference in bicycle race times. But this is a good opportunity to explain that, when doing research, one starts with a particular theory, from which one obtains specific hypotheses (testable predictions), and then designs an experiment to test those predictions. Now, in archival research like Triplett's, the results are already known, and the researcher then tries to explain the data with "the best theory" (the most parsimonious — simplest, with fewest assumptions).

Of the seven or eight not wholly distinct theories which have been advanced to account for the faster time made in paced as compared with unpaced competitive races and paced races against time as against unpaced races against time, a number need only be stated very briefly. They are grouped according to their nature and first are given two mechanical theories.

SUCTION THEORY.

Those holding to this as the explanation assert that the vacuum left behind the pacing machine draws the rider following, along with it. Anderson's ride of a mile a minute at Roodhouse, Ill., with the locomotive as pacemaker, is the strongest argument in its favor. Those maintaining this theory believe that the racer paced by a tandem is at a disadvantage as compared with the racer paced by a quod or a larger machine, as the suction exerted is not so powerful.

THE SHELTER THEORY.

This is closely related to the foregoing. Dr. Turner accepts it as a partial explanation of the aid to be gained from a pace, holding that the pacemaker or the leading competitor serves as a shelter from the wind, and that "a much greater amount of exertion, purely muscular, is required from a man to drive a machine when he is leading than when he is following, on account of the resistance of the air, and the greater the amount of wind blowing the greater the exertion, and conversely, the greater the shelter obtained the less the exertion."

This is the theory held, in general, by racers themselves. One of the champion riders of the country recently expressed this common view in a letter, as follows: "It is true that some very strong unpaced riders do not have any sort of success in paced racing. The only reason I can give for this is just simply that they have not studied the way to follow pace so as to be shielded from the wind. No matter which way it blows there is always a place where the man following pace can be out of the wind."

ENCOURAGEMENT THEORY.

The presence of a friend on the pacing machine to encourage and keep up the spirits of the rider is claimed to be of great help. The mental disposition has been long known to be of importance in racing as in other cases where energy is expended. It is still as true as in Virgil's time that the winners "can because they think they can."

THE BRAIN WORRY THEORY.

This theory shows why it is difficult for the leader in an unpaced competition race to win. For "a much greater amount of brain worry is incurred by making the pace than by waiting" (following). The man leading "is in a fidget the whole time whether he is going fast enough to exhaust his adversary; he is full of worry as to when that adversary means to commence his spurt; his nervous system is generally strung up, and at concert pitch, and his muscular and nervous efforts act and react on each other, producing an ever increasing exhaustion, which both dulls the impulse-giving power of the brain and the impulse-receiving or contractile power of the muscles."

THEORY OF HYPNOTIC SUGGESTIONS.

A curious theory, lately advanced, suggests the possibility that the strained attention given to the revolving wheel of the pacing machine in front produces a sort of hypnotism and that the accompanying muscular exaltation is the secret of the endurance shown by some long distance riders in paced races. Notice that Michael was able to make the last mile of his great 30 mile competition race the fastest of all and one of the fastest ever ridden.

THE AUTOMATIC THEORY.

This is also a factor which favors the waiting rider, and gives him a marked advantage. The leader, as has been noted, must use his brain to direct every movement of his muscles. As he becomes more distressed it requires a more intense exertion of will power to force his machine through the resisting air. On the other hand, the "waiter" rides automatically. He has nothing to do but hang on. "His brain having inaugurated the movement leaves it to the spinal cord to continue it and only resumes its functions when a change of direction or speed is necessary."— (Lagrange.) When he comes to the final spurt, his brain, assuming control again, imparts to the muscles a winning stimulus, while the continued brain work of the leader has brought great fatigue.

These facts seem to have a large foundation in truth. The lesser amount of fatigue incurred in paced trials is a matter of general knowledge. It is a common experience with wheel men, and within that of the writer, that when following a lead on a long ride the feeling of automatic action becomes very pronounced, giving the sensation of a strong force pushing from behind. Of course the greater the distance ridden the more apparent becomes the saving in energy from automatic riding, as time is required to establish the movement. It may be remembered, in this connection, that while the average gain of the paced over the unpaced record is 34.4 seconds, the difference between them for the first mile is only 23.8 seconds.

As between the pacer and the paced, every advantage seems to rest with the latter. The two mechanical factors of suction and shelter, so far as they are involved, assist the rider who follows. So the psychological theories, the stimulation from encouragement, the peculiar power induced by hypnotism, and the staying qualities of automatic action, if of help at all, directly benefit the paced rider. The element of disadvantage induced by brain action, on the contrary, belongs more especially to the rider who leads.

THE DYNAMOGENIC FACTORS.

The remaining factors to be discussed are those which the experiments on competition, detailed in the second part hereof, attempt to explain. No effort is made to weaken the force of the foregoing factors in accounting for the better time of paced races in comparison with unpaced races of the same type, but the facts of this study are given to throw whatever additional light they may.

This theory of competition holds that the bodily presence of another rider is a stimulus to the racer in arousing the competitive instinct; that another can thus be the means of releasing or freeing nervous energy for him that he cannot of himself release; and, further, that the sight of movement in that other by perhaps suggesting a higher rate of speed, is also an inspiration to greater effort. These are the factors that had their counterpart in the experimental study following; and it is along these lines that the facts determined are to find their interpretation.

This theory might explain those instances where the presence of another biker made one ride faster (compared to when one biked alone).

OTHER FORMS OF RACING.

A few brief statements, mostly quoted from Dr. Turner's treatise, are given to show the value of a pacemaker in other forms of racing: "Foot racing differs from cycle racing in that it involves a much greater muscular effort. At each stride the whole body must be lifted and projected seven feet or more. The exertion is much the same whether the competitor makes his own pace or follows. "So the leader" and "waiter" commence their final spurt under more equal conditions than those which obtain in a cycle race, and a much smaller degree of superiority in the leading man enables him to run the spurt out of his opponent and win.

In ice skating the conditions are closely similar to those in wheel races, and a pacemaker is of nearly as much use as on the cycle track.

In a boat race the crews do not wait behind each other, but struggle for the lead, and when they have obtained it "wait in front." The reasons for this are good:

(1) If a boat be clear in front it may take its opponent's water and wash it.

(2) The crew leading can see the others and regulate its pace accordingly.

(3) The actual physical labor involved in propelling a boat is very great, and therefore the laws of exercise already treated of apply.

(4) The length of a racing eight is 50 feet or more, and the time necessary to pass is too great to permit of waiting.

For similar reasons there is not the slightest advantage in waiting in a swimming race.

In horse racing a pacemaker is of use, but is not the overwhelming advantage it is in cycle racing. A good horse can run out an inferior, just as a good man can on foot; but in big races a stable companion is generally started to make running, when the favorite is a good stayer, in order that he may have a fast run race, without being put to the disadvantage of himself making the pace. This is especially true of distance races.

Kolb, from his study of the respiration and pulse curves resulting from a maximum effort in the various kinds of races, asserts that in cycling and skating, where great speed is attained by the use of special groups of muscles, it is the pulse rate that is largely increased, while in boat racing, running, wrestling and heavy gymnastics, the respiration is chiefly affected. If this claim is established it may furnish a reason why the pacemaker or competitor has greatest value in cycle and skating races. In these, where the ratio between power and speed is high, the outflow of nervous energy necessary in spurting has large expression. In the other class, while the energy made available by the competitive instinct, is probably the same, it is limited in its results by the respiratory need.

PART II.

From the laboratory competitions to be described, abstraction was made of nearly all the forces above outlined. In the 40 seconds the average trial lasted, no shelter from the wind was required, nor was any suction exerted, the only brain worry incident was that of maintaining a sufficiently high rate of speed to defeat the competitors. From the shortness of the time and nature of the case, generally, it is doubtful if any automatic movements could be established. On the other hand, the effort was intensely voluntary. It may be likened to the 100 yard dash—a sprint from beginning to end.

DESCRIPTION OF APPARATUS.

The apparatus for this study consisted of two fishing reels whose cranks turned in circles of one and three-fourths inches diameter. These were arranged on a Y shaped frame work clamped to the top of a heavy table, as shown in the cut. The sides of this frame work were spread sufficiently far apart to permit of two persons turning side by side. Bands of twisted silk cord ran over the well lacquered axes of the reels and were supported at C and D, two meters distant, by two small pulleys. The records were taken from the course A D. The other course B C being used merely for pacing or competition purposes. The wheel on the side from which the records were taken communicated the movement made to a recorder, the stylus of which traced a curve on the drum of a kymograph. The direction of this curve corresponded to the rate of turning, as the greater the speed the shorter and straighter the resulting line.

METHOD OF CONDUCTING THE EXPERIMENT.

A subject taking the experiment was required to practice turning the reel until he had become accustomed to the machine. After a short period of rest the different trials were made with five-minute intervals between to obviate the possible effects of fatigue.

A trial consisted in turning the reel at the highest rate of speed until a small flag sewed to the silk band had made four circuits of the four-meter course. The time of the trial was taken by means of a stop-watch. The direction of the curves made on the drum likewise furnished graphic indications of the difference in time made between trials.

LIMITS OF ERROR.

Frequent trials of the machinery showed very small errors. In each regular trial the flag travelled 16 meters. For ten test trials the average number of turns of the reel necessary to send it over this course was found to be 149.87, with a mean variation of .15, showing that the silk band did not slip to any appreciable extent. If 40 seconds be taken as the average time of a trial (which is not far wrong), .15 of a turn will be made in .04 second.

Care was also exercised to have the kymograph maintain, so far as possible, a uniform rate of turning. When fully wound up it would run for nearly three hours. The actual running time in taking the six trials of a subject was about 4 minutes, or 40 seconds per trial. In testing, the drum was rotated during 4 minutes. The time necessary to repeat this amount of rotation was found, by trials, to be 4 minutes and 3 seconds, thus showing a retardation in each trial of about one-eightieth of the former trial as shown on the drum. The direct time of trials was taken with a stop-watch. It is from records thus taken that the tables given are composed. The drum curves, however, are important as giving a graphic representation of whatever changes occurred during the progress of the trial. The stylus, responding immediately to every change in rate of turning, gives clearly: indications of the force of competition, of the effects of adverse stimulation, fatigue, and other phenomena. The tendency of the retardation of the drum would be to diminish all these effects by one-eightieth an amount not appreciable to the eye.

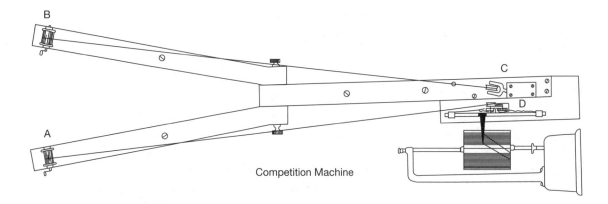

Competition Machine

STATEMENT OF RESULTS.

In the course of the work the records of nearly 225 persons of all ages were taken. However, all the tables given below, and all statements made, unless otherwise specified, are based on the records of 40 children taken in the following manner: After the usual preliminaries of practice, six trials were made by each of 20 subjects in this order: first a trial alone, followed by a trial in competition, then another alone, and thus alternating through the six efforts, giving three trials alone and three in competition. Six trials were taken by 20 other children of about the same age, the order of trials in this case being the first trial alone, second alone, third a competition trial, fourth alone, fifth a competition, and sixth alone.

By this scheme, a trial of either sort, after the first one, by either of the two groups, always corresponds to a different trial by the opposite group. Further, when the subjects of the two groups come to their fourth and sixth trials, an equal amount of practice has been gained by an equal number of trials of the same kind. This fact should be remembered in any observation of the time made in trials by any group.

During the taking of the records, and afterwards in working them over, it was seen that all cases would fall into two classes:

First. Those stimulate—

1   to make faster time in competition trials,

2   in such a way as to inhibit motion.

Second. The small number who seemed little affected by the race.
The three tables which follow are made up from the records of the 40 subjects mentioned. The classification was in general determined by the time record as taken by the watch.

The first table gives the records of 20 subjects who, on the whole, were stimulated positively. The second table contains IO records of subjects who were overstimulated. The third table shows the time of IO subjects who give slight evidence of being stimulated.

The probable error used in the tables is that for a single observation : $r = .6745 - \sqrt{\dfrac{\sum v^2}{n-1}}$.

Its magnitude is large from the nature of the case. To ascertain how large this should properly be, the individual differences of the subjects of Group A in Table I were eliminated in the following manner : The average of the six trials made by each subject was taken as most fairly representing him. With this as a basis the six trials were reduced to percentages—thus doing away with peculiarities due to age and disposition. By this means the probable errors of this group for the six trials in order were 2.57, 1.43, 1.81, 2.24, 1.11, 1.55. A similar reduction should be made in the probable error of all the tables.

In the tables, A represents a trial alone, C a trial in competition.

TABLE I.   Subjects Stimulated Positively.

GROUP A.

	Age.	A.	C.	A.	C.	A.	C.
Violet F.	10	54.4	42.6	45.2	41.	42.	46.
Anna P.	9	67.	57.	55.4	50.4	49.	44.8

(Continued)

TABLE I. (Continued)

	Age.	A.	C.	A.	C.	A.	C.
Willie H.	12	37.8	38.8	43.	39.	37.2	33.4
Bessie V.	11	46.2	41.	39.	30.2	33.6	32.4
Howard C.	11	42.	36.4	39.	41.	37.8	34.
Mary M.	11	48.	44.8	52.	44.6	43.8	40.
Lois P.	11	53.	45.6	44.	40.	40.6	35.8
Inez K.	13	37.	35.	35.8	34.	34.	32.6
Harvey L.	9	49.	42.6	39.6	37.6	36.	35.
Lora F.	11	40.4	35.	33.	35.	30.2	29.
Average	11	47.48	41.88	42.6	39.28	38.42	36.3
P. E.		6.18	4.45	4.68	3.83	3.74	3.74
Gains			5.6	.72	3.32	.86	2.12

GROUP B.

	Age.	A.	A.	C.	A.	C.	A.
Stephen M.	13	51.2	50.	43.	41.8	39.8	41.2*
Mary W.	13	56.	53.	45.8	49.4	45.	43.*
Bertha A.	10	56.2	49.	48.	46.8	41.4	44.4
Clara L.	8	52.	44.	46.	45.6	44.	45.2
Helen M.	10	45.	45.6	35.8	46.2	40.	40.
Gracie W.	12	56.6	50.	42.	39.	40.2	41.4
Dona R.	15	34.	37.2	36.	41.4	37.	32.8
Pearl C.	13	43.	43.	40.	40.6	33.8	35.
Clyde G.	13	36.	35.	32.4	33.	31.	35.
Lucile W.	10	52.	50.	43.	44.	38.2	40.2
Average	11.7	48.2	45.68	41.2	42.78	39.	39.82
P. E.		5.6	4.	3.42	3.17	2.89	2.84
Gains			2.52	4.48	1.58	3.78	.82

*Left-handed

IX-35

TABLE II. Subjects Stimulated Adversely.

GROUP A.

	Age.	A.	C.	A.	C.	A.	C.
Jack R.	9	44.2	44.	41.8	48.	44.2	41.
Helen F.	9	44.	51.	43.8	44.	43.	41.2
Emma P.	11	38.4	42.	37.	39.6	36.6	32.
Warner J.	11	41.6	43.6	43.4	43.	40.	38.
Genevieve M.	12	36.	36.	32.6	32.8	31.2	34.8
Average	10.4	40.84	43.32	39.72	41.48	39.	37.4
P. E.		2.41	3.57	3.25	3.85	3.55	2.52

GROUP B.

	Age.	A.	A.	C.	A.	C.	A.
Hazel M.	11	38.	35.8	38.2	37.2	35.	42.
George B.	12	39.2	36.	37.6	34.2	36.	33.8
Mary B.	11	50.	46.	43.4	42.	48.	36.8
Carlisle B.	14	37.	35.4	35.	33.4	36.4	31.4
Eddie H.	11	31.2	29.2	27.6	27.	26.8	28.8
Average	11.8	39.08	36.48	36.36	34.76	34.4	34.56
P. E.		4.61	4.07	3.89	3.71	5.33	3.45

TABLE III. Subjects little affected by competition.

GROUP A.

	Age.	A.	C.	A.	C.	A.	C.
Alber P.	13	29.	28.	27.	29.	27.	28.6
Milfred V.	17	36.4	29.	29.4	30.2	30.2	32.2
Harry V.	12	32.	32.	32.6	32.6	32.6	31.6
Robt. H.	12	31.4	31.4	32.2	35.4	35.	32.4
John T.	11	30.2	30.8	32.8	30.6	32.8	31.8
Average	13	31.8	30.24	30.8	31.56	31.5	31.3
P. E.		1.9	1.13	1.71	1.7	2.06	1.05

(Continued)

TABLE III. (Continued)

GROUP B.

	Age.	A.	A.	C.	A.	C.	A.
Lela T.	10	45.	37.4	36.8	36.	37.2	38.
Lura L.	11	42.	39.	38.	37.	37.	38.
Mollie A.	13	38.	30.	28.	30.	30.2	29.6
Anna F.	11	35.	31.8	32.4	30.	32.	30.4
Ora R.	14	37.2	30.	29.	27.8	28.4	26.8
Average	11.8	39.44	33.64	32.84	32.16	32.96	32.16
P. E.		3.11	2.88	3.03	2.75	2.69	3.71

The 20 subjects given in Group A and Group B, of Table I, in nearly all cases make marked reductions in the competition trials. The averages show large gains in these trials and small gains or even losses for the succeeding trials alone. The second trial for Group A is a competition, for Group B a trial alone. The gain between the first and second trials of the first group is 5.6 seconds, between the first and second trials of the second group, 2.52 seconds. The latter represents the practice effect—always greatest in the first trials, the former the element of competition plus the practice. The third trial in Group A—a trial alone—is .72 seconds slower than the preceding race trial. The third trial in Group B—a competition—is 4.48 seconds faster than the preceding trial alone. The fourth trials in these two groups are on an equality, as regards practice, from an equal number of trials of the same kind. In the first case the gain over the preceding trial is 3.32 seconds. In the latter there is a loss of 1.58 seconds from the time of the preceding competition trial. In like manner there is an equality of conditions in regard to the sixth trial of these groups, and again the effect of competition plainly appears, the competition trial gaining 2.12 seconds, and the trial alone losing .82 seconds with respect to the preceding trial. These are decided differences. Curve No. 1 in Chart II is a graphical representation of them.

The 20 subjects whose records are given in Table II are of interest. With them stimulation brought a loss of control. In one or more of the competition trials of each subject in this group the time is very much slower than that made in the preceding trial alone. Most frequently this is true of the first trial in competition, but with some was characteristic of every race. In all, 14 of the 25 races run by this group were equal or slower than the preceding trial alone. This seems to be brought about in large measure by the mental attitude of the subject. An intense desire to win, for instance, often resulting in over-stimulation. Accompanying phenomena were labored breathing, flushed faces and a stiffening or contraction of the muscles of the arm. A number of young children of from 5 to 9 years, not included in our group of 40, exhibited the phenomena most strikingly, the rigidity of the arm preventing free movement and in some cases resulting in an almost total inhibition of movement. The effort to continue turning in these cases was by a swaying of the whole body.

This seems a most interesting fact and confirmatory of the probable order of development of the muscles as given by Dr. Hall and others. In the case of those sufficiently developed to have the fast forearm movement, fatigue or overstimulation seemed to bring a recurrence to the whole arm and shoulder movement of early childhood, and if the fatigue or excitement was sufficiently intense, to the whole body movement, while younger children easily fell into the swaying movement when affected by either of the causes named.

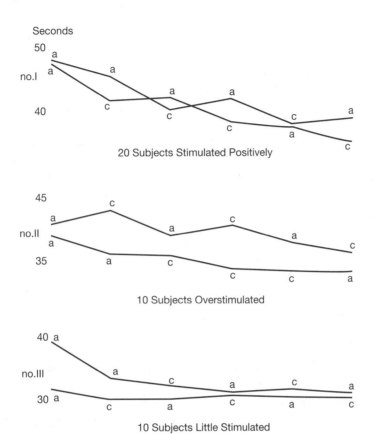

20 Subjects Stimulated Positively

10 Subjects Overstimulated

10 Subjects Little Stimulated

It reminds one of the way in which fatigue of a small muscle used in ergographic work, will cause the subject to attempt to draw on his larger muscles, or, of the man who moves to the city and acquires the upright carriage and springing step of the city-bred man, who, when greatly fatigued, insensibly falls into the old "clodhopper" gait. This tendency to revert to earlier movements and also old manners of speech, as Hopfner has shown in his "Fatigue of School Children," is common, when, for any reason, the centers of control are interfered with. It may be said, therefore, that in the work under consideration the chief difference between this group and the large group in Table I, was a difference in control; the stimulation inhibiting the proper function of the motor centers in the one case, and reinforcing it in the other. This, at least, seemed apparent from the characteristics exhibited by the two classes. Observation of the subjects of this class under trial, and careful scrutiny of their graphic records, show how decided gains were sometimes lost by the subject "going to pieces" at the critical point of the race, not being able to endure the nervous strain. Yet there exists no sharp line of division between subjects stimulated to make faster time and those affected in the opposite way. In some instances the nervous excitement acted adversely in every race trial, while in others, a gain in control, enabled the subject to make a material reduction in the last competition. A. B., one of three adults affected adversely, is an athletic young man, a fine tennis and hand-ball player, and known to be stimulated in contests of these kinds. It was noticed that in his competition trials time was lost because of his attempt to take advantage of the larger muscles of the arm and shoulder. After many trials and injunctions to avoid the movement he gained sufficient control to enable him to reduce the time in the competitions.

A. V., an adult of nervous organization, went half through his race with a great gain over his trial alone, but seeing his antagonist pushing him closely, broke down and lost the most of the gain made in the first half. The time of the trial alone was 38.6 seconds, that of the competition was 37.2 seconds. A comparison of the time in which the halves of the trials were made was computed in the following way: On the ordinate of the graph is measured the distance the stylus travels across the drum during 150 turns of the reel—the number in a trial. The distance on the abscissa between the ordinates running through the ends of the curve of any trial gives the time of the trial.

Parallel abscissas were drawn at the extremities of the curves, and a third one-half way between them. Half of the turns made in a trial were thus on each side of this middle line, and the times in which these turns were made were proportional to the segments of this line made by the curve intersecting it. By this means it was found that A. V. made the first 75 turns in his competition trial in 15 seconds, the second half in 22.2 seconds. By the same means, each half of the preceding trial alone was 19.3 seconds-an exception to the rule that the last half is slower because of fatigue.

Other curves when worked out in this way gave similar results. The time record, therefore, it must be seen, is not always a true index to the amount of stimulation present. Had the trials consisted of but half as many turns the effect of competition as it appears in the tables would have been shown much more constantly. Table II would have been a smaller group if indeed any necessity existed for retaining it.

A comparison of the time made by the different groups shows that the subjects of Table I are much slower than those of Table II, and that a still greater difference exists between this group and the subjects found in Table III. It may be said that they are slower because of greater sluggishness of disposition, and that the reductions made are largely a result of the subjects warming up. This, indeed, may be a part of the cause for it, but as the larger reductions coincide with the competition trials this cannot be held to completely account for it. A glance over the individual records discovers some facts which furnish a plausible partial explanation, when taken in connection with the following fact. The age at which children acquire control of the wrist movements, a large factor in turning the reel with speed, was found to be about 1.1 years in general, although a few of 9 and 10 years had this power. Now, of the 20 subjects composing Table I, 7 are 10 years of age or younger, while two others, age 13, are left-handed and being compelled to use the right hand are slow in consequence. So, here are 9 subjects, a number nearly equal to the group in Table II or Table III, who had a reason for being slow. Were these omitted from the count, the time of the initial trial would be found not to vary materially from that of Table II.

Besides the lack of muscular development of the younger subjects mentioned above, many of the subjects of Table I seemed not to have proper ideals of speed. The desire to beat, if it did nothing else, brought them to a sense of what was possible for them. The arousal of their competitive instincts and the idea of a faster movement, perhaps, in the contestant, induced greater concentration of energy.

The subjects in Table III, are a small group who seemed very little affected by competition. They made very fast time, but they are older than the average; their muscular control was good, and they had the forearm movements. Practice gains while somewhat apparent at first in some cases, are, as shown by curve No. 3 of the chart, on the whole, less in amount. Their drum records show fewer fluctuations and irregularities, and less pronounced fatigue curves at the end.

These seems to be a striking analogy between these subjects and those racing men who are fast without a pace, but can do little or no better in a paced or competition race.

OBSERVATIONS ON THE WORK.

Energy Fluctuations. Among the many personal differences shown by the various subjects, nervous peculiarities were of great interest. A number exhibited the marked periodicity of energy discovered by Dr. Lombard, and described by him in the AMERICAN JOURNAL OF PSYCHOLOGY. It was especially prominent in the cases of L. P. and H. F., both bright children of an exceedingly nervous temperament, a rapid period being succeeded by one of apparent fatigue, thus alternating to the end of the trial. It was noticeable both in trials alone and in competition. In both subjects the phenomenon became less marked in the course of the trials. Both were much affected by the stimulation. The first making gains in her races, the second, almost helpless from nervous agitation in her first competition, does better in the second, and succeeds in making a substantial reduction in her third race, although a large part of the gain made in the first half of the trial is lost in the second.

Kolb in his "Physiology of Sport" asserts that in every physical contest involving a maximum effort there will be fluctuations of energy, and says that all oarsmen are familiar with the "hills" in the boat race, one being encountered in the second minute, the other at the end of the sixth minute. Long distance runners also experience the ebb and flow of strength markedly.

Effects from Age. It seems probable that one who is amenable to the stimulation of competition in childhood will be susceptible during his whole life; like the race horse that retains his desire to run long after the ability is lacking. The age at which the instinct develops was not ascertained. Two boys of 5 years possessed it to a marked degree. The one defeated in their race, according to his mother, felt badly about it all day. Adult subjects displayed the same differences of stimulation as in the case of children. It might be inferred from the records taken that the effect is greatest in early life and diminishes with advancing years. The practice effect, however, is greatest among the young, as they do not have the skill in the use of the hand that comes later. With adults, owing to their greater muscular control, practice counts for much less. So it was that the latter more surely made reductions in their competition trials, but smaller ones.

People differ greatly, as was noted, in the degree in which they are stimulated, but for the same individual it seems to be a constant force.

Two girls who were trained till the gain from practice was a small matter, in a ten days' trial showed remarkable uniformity in making reductions in their race trials. From the shortness of the period, in these cases, half the usual number of turns, and the skill acquired, the reductions were, however, small in amount. The averages for the ten days are as follows:

This is an important point. Triplett is saying that some people react differently to the presence of others in biking (some ride faster, some ride slower), but that within one person, their particular reaction to the presence of another is always the same (e.g., always fast or always slow—relative to their time when biking alone). The main finding in his study of bike race times was that for some people, they rode faster (compared to their bike time alone) when they were riding against another person. But for others, the presence of another rider causes them to ride slower (relative to their bike time alone). He (and researchers in social psychology for the ensuing 60 years) couldn't explain these mixed results, and it wasn't until Zajonc's 1965 Drive Theory that we had a robust explanation for these mixed results.

	a	c	a	c	a	c
Bessie V.	15.8	14.9	15.3	14.65	15.3	14.55
Helen F.	18.45	17.5	18.52	17.22	18.02	16.77

Each subject had 30 competitions. Out of this number the time for the first subject was reduced in 24 or four-fifths of the entire number. It was equal to the preceding trial in two cases. The second was faster in her race trials in 25 of the 30 or five-sixths of all, and in two cases equalled the preceding record. Of the three remaining trials, the pain from a blister on the hand caused one to be made in slower time.

In the race trials of the 40 subjects a portion of the reduction when made might in some cases be attributed to encouraging remarks. For instance, the racer would be told to "keep on, you are ahead," or "just one more round," in order to steady him. In the extended trial of the two subjects under discussion, however, some preliminary words to arouse the desire to beat were used, but after the start not a word was spoken. Whatever effect appeared was purely that of competition.

SEX DIFFERENCES.

Some small differences were found in the motor rate between the sexes, corresponding in general to the results exhibited in Dr. W. L. Bryan's study of "Motor Ability." For this grouping, the averages only for which are given, all cases were taken in which a trial alone was succeeded by a trial in competition.

At 10 years of age the boys begin faster than the girls, but both sexes are practically together on the competition trial. The greater speed of the boys, as Dr. Bryan has pointed out, is largely a result of their greater knack or skill in doing things, attributable to their more active life.

At 11 the boys are distinctly ahead, and, as noted before, a year's time has brought a large increase in speed, as at about this age a free use of the wrist movement is gained. At 12 the boys are slower than at 11, and have no advantage over the girls. A difference appears again at 13 in favor of the boys. In the case of adults a slight margin of difference on the side of the males is seen.

With this table the mean variation was used.

TABLE IV.

Age.	MALES.			FEMALES		
	Cases.	A.	C.	Cases.	A.	C.
10	5	41.88	41.6	13	46.83	41.4
		4.34	5.52		3.76	2.98
11	14	35.76	34.36	25	40.3	37.89
		4.37	5.1		5.2	4.47
12	14	38.1	35.7	19	38.39	35.77
		3.92	2.75		6.11	4.

Age.	MALES.			FEMALES		
	Cases.	A.	C.	Cases.	A.	C.
13	7	34.1	32.94	15	39.65	36.24
		7.13	4.81		5.3	5.1
Adults	45	31.35	29.	14	32.77	29.24
		3.17	3.29		2.8	2.56

As to the amount of stimulation the odds are apparently with the female sex. The proportion of girls influenced by competition is greater. Of the 40 subjects, 14 or 36.6 percent. were boys, 26 or 63.4 percent. were girls. In the group of those who were susceptible and influenced positively were 28.6 percent. of the boys and 61.5 percent. of the girls. In the group influenced negatively were 35.7 percent. of the boys and 19.2 percent. of the girls, and in the group not influenced 35.7 percent. of the boys and 19.2 percent. of the girls were found. These figures are deduced from the grouping made on the basis of the time record. An inspection of the graphs indicates that six in Table III were somewhat stimulated, although it is not made evident from the watch record. Were these subjects, consisting of 5 girls and 1 boy, to be transferred to their proper table the result would show that 100 percent. of the girls and 71 percent. of the boys showed stimulation.

The gross amount of the effect of competition is also greater in girls. When they were stimulated and had control they made greater gains than the boys and when over-stimulated their losses were greater than those made by the boys. The 16 girls of Table I gained the average sum of 10 seconds in their competition trials, while the four boys of this group gained an average sum of 8.15 seconds. In Table II the 5 girls lost 3 seconds each, in the course of their competition trials, while the 5 boys lost less than 1 second each.

INFLUENCES AFFECTING THE TIME OF SUCCEEDING TRIALS ALONE.

It is a well-known fact, that some wheelmen, who in private practice can go very fast, fail to distinguish themselves when the real race is run in the presence of the public. The weakening effect of nervous agitation has been ascribed as the cause. On the other hand, Manouvrier, in his dynamometric studies found that this subject increased the energy of his movement when spectators were present. This is a common observation. The boy can turn better handsprings when wishing to impress the girls with a sense of his accomplishments. The football team play better ball under the stimulation of the home crowd. Other examples could be instanced showing how people respond to various social stimulations.

In the records of the 40 subjects found in the three groups discussed above, there are 80 cases wherein a competition trial is followed by a trial alone. Of these, 45 were made in faster time than the preceding competition trial. Several facts seem to contribute to this result.

First, greater facility in turning naturally follows from the practice gained in former trials. In general, spectators were not permitted during the trials alone, but in a few cases visitors were present. The effect of this would be to stimulate the subject in a trial alone. Then, too, the competition element entered into the trials alone and it was found advisable in some cases to keep from the subject the time made, as there was a constant desire to beat his own or his friend's records, and thus make all the trials competitive. The competition feeling seemed present all the time. It is felt, therefore, that succeeding trials alone are not really non-competitive trials.

In addition, the competition trial was a pattern for after trials, giving a higher ideal of speed and a hint of what was possible for the subject. Fere remarks that it was his own experience, and that of a majority of experimenters in dynamometrie, "that the second trial was in general stronger than the first, the first trial having the effect of reinforcing the idea of the movement." The same thing seems peculiarly true of the kind of work under discussion. The subject comes to a succeeding trial alone with a reinforced image of the movement. The over-excitement of the former race is gone, but somewhat of its stimulating effect, it may be, remains and in consequence more than half of the cases equal or exceed the former competitive trial.

PART III.

THE IDEA OF MOVEMENT.

We are led to believe that in the laboratory competitions detailed in Part II of this article, besides the bodily presence of a competitor, the idea of his movement, whether gained from sight or sound, had a stimulating effect on the racer. Some subjects followed with the eyes the course of the flags during the race and directed their exertions accordingly. Others seemed to be spurred on by the sound of the other machine, gaining some idea of the speed from the noise it made. Either seemed to possess equal power as a stimulus.

A favorite psychological principle with Fere, whose "Sensation et Mouvement" describes the most important work done in the field of Dynamogeny, is that "the energy of a movement is in proportion to the idea of that movement." He gives an experiment illustrating the subject as follows:

"If we ask the subject to look attentively at the movements of Hexion, which we make with our hand, at the end of a few minutes he declares that he has the sensation of the same movement being made in his own hand, even though it may be entirely unmoved. And soon, indeed, his hand begins irresistibly to execute rhythmic movements of Hexion. Or, if instead of letting the experiment come to this point, the subject is stopped at the moment where he commences to have the sensation of movement, and a dynamometer is placed in his hand, it is shown that the energy of his effort is increased one-fourth to one-half." Before the experiment the normal dynamometric force of the right hand was 23 kg., of the left, 15 kg. After seeing the experimenter make 20 fiexions, the pressure for the subject's right hand was 46 kg., or double the former record. The left hand showed a slightly diminished force. An attempt was made to verify Fere's work with the ergograph. The subject was required to make maximum finger lifts corresponding to the beats of a metronome. After a series of lifts, the signal was given by the operator raising the index finger as if with the effort of lifting. Of 12 subjects tried, 8 made an increase when taking the time from the finger. The amount of increase seemed to be in proportion to the attention bestowed on the lifted finger of the operator. Two, who noticeably gave little attention to the straining of the finger except as a mere signal for lifting, made no gain whatever. Five maximum lifts of E. J., immediately preceding the substitution of the finger movement, averaged 17.2 millimeters in height, with a mean variation of .6 m. m. The first five efforts made at the sight of the finger movement averaged 19.1 m. m., mean variation .7 m. m., again of 11 percent. P. M. G., toward the end of an exhaustion curve, of which the last five lifts averaged 7.2 m. m., made five lifts, taking the cue from the finger, of an average height of 11.4 m. m., after which the energy of his efforts again began to decrease.

EFFECT OF A HIGHER RATE ON COUNTING.

An experiment on vocalization was made wherein a higher rate was suggested to the subject.

Ten subjects took the work described below on six successive days. Each was required to count aloud from 1 to 20 and repeat, as rapidly as articulation permitted, for 5 seconds. Three trials were made. The operator now counted at a faster rate and asked the subject to follow that rate. Three trials of this kind were made. This may be called Programme A.

Programme B differed from this merely in the one particular that the operator did no counting, but the three preliminary trials alone were followed instead by three similar trials alone—the intervals between trials, however, remaining the same.

Five subjects began with Programme A and five with Programme B, alternating each day, so that in the course of the six days each person had three experiences with each programme. The average sum counted by each subject during the series of trials is given below. Dividing by nine will give the average number counted in a single trial of that kind.

	PROGRAMME A.			PROGRAMME B.		
Cases.	No. alone.	After a higher rate is given.	Gain.	No. alone.	Alone. No rate given.	Gain.
10	288.4	307.6	19.2	287.	288.5	1.5

The difference between the averages of the first two columns, 19.2, is the average gain of the ten subjects after they have had given them the idea of a faster rate of counting. Under this programme each individual makes a gain, under the other, where no higher rate is given, seven make smaller gains, three lose, and the average gain is but 1.5.

The principle of ideomotor action has wide application in human life. In the cases cited the observance of motion in another became a stimulus to greater effort. It may, however, have the opposite effect. A correspondence of rhythm of movement seems necessary to make it of aid. Two boys jumping together, or one following immediately at the sight of the other's jump, will not cover the distance possible in jumping alone, because the swaying of the body, and swinging of the arms, not being synchronous or rhythmic become a distraction. So one soon becomes fatigued when walking with a person out of step.

CONCLUDING STATEMENT.

From the above facts regarding the laboratory races we infer that the bodily presence of another contestant participating simultaneously in the race serves to liberate latent energy not ordinarily available. This inference is further justified by the difference in time between the paced competition races and the paced races against time, amounting to an average of 5.15 seconds per mile up to 25 miles. The factors of shelter from the wind, encouragement, brain worry, hypnotic suggestion, and automatic movement, are common to both, while the competitors participate simultaneously in person only in the first.

In the next place the sight of the movements of the pacemakers or leading competitors, and the idea of higher speed, furnished by this or some other means, are probably in themselves dynamogenic factors of some consequence.

POST-ARTICLE DISCUSSION

As we discussed earlier, the mixed results that Triplett found went unexplained until Zajonc (1965) convincingly presented his drive theory of social facilitation. Zajonc suggested that the mere presence of others increases our physiological arousal, which, in turn, causes us to make the dominant response (essentially a default response/behavior). The dominant response will be the "correct" (performance-enhanced) one when the task is something that the person has done a lot (well-learned) or when the task is easy. But on tasks that are difficult or not well-learned, the dominant response will be "incorrect" and performance will be impaired. Zajonc has shown that the thing that initiates this process is the "mere presence" of others, and that the process even happens in simple lifeforms, such as cockroaches (see our discussion of the Zajonc, Heingartner, & Herman, 1969, experiment with cockroaches in Chapter 12: Groups).

When you read the Triplett paper, did you think of ways to improve the methods he used for each study? Were there any limitations or confounds in the studies? I know that paper was a bit different to read compared to reading more contemporary research papers, and in some places it is quite detailed and not an easy read, but I hope you were able to appreciate the historic nature of the paper and also the glimpse into how early psychologists tried to experimentally understand behavior. This paper illustrates how two different research methodologies (experiment and archival data analysis) can converge on the same finding, lending added confidence in the research conclusions.

THINGS TO THINK ABOUT

1. In attempting to explain his findings, Triplett uses words like *instinct*. This is not very scientific and is much more of a speculation on his part. To be fair, psychology was in its infancy as a science (social psychology didn't even exist yet!) and didn't have a lot of sophisticated scientific methods. How might these types of explanations for behavior have contributed to the birth and popularity of behaviorism?

2. In your opinion, which of the several other alternative theories put forth best account for the bicycle race data? Why?

3. Thinking about Zajonc's drive theory explanation of Triplett's results, what is it about the "mere presence" of others that initiates social facilitation effects?

4. Do the results of Triplett's experiment with the fishing rods support or not support his explanations for the bicycle races?

5. In what ways might Triplett have improved his methodology or analysis for his fishing rod experiment? If such changes were made, are you confident he would still obtain the same findings? Why?

INTRODUCTION TO READING 1.2
LAPIERE (1934)

When Allport (1924) wrote one of the first textbooks in social psychology, he helped outline the parameters of study for the field. In this text, he included the study of attitudes. This has continued to be a core area of research and theory for social psychologists for good reason. If we are in the business of predicting future behavior (based on experiment data), then attitudes would be an invaluable tool in that regard. The reason is that it makes intuitive sense: attitudes (an evaluation of something) *should* guide behavior. If I have a positive attitude toward a brand called "Joe's chili," it should make sense that the next time I am in the supermarket and I need to buy a can of chili, I will be highly likely to choose—from all the other brands of chili—a can of Joe's chili. Similarly, if it is an election year, and I know that you have a positive attitude toward candidate X, I can predict with a high degree of accuracy that you will vote for candidate X.

The article you are about to read, "Attitudes vs. Actions," by LaPiere (1934), is an early study of attitudes. Specifically, LaPiere once traveled the United States with a Chinese couple and noticed that despite a strong anti-Chinese prejudice in America at the time, they had no trouble getting a hotel room. A couple of months later, when LaPiere was traveling back that way again, he phoned the hotel to ask if they could accommodate an important Chinese gentleman. The hotel replied with a strong "No." This led to his idea to study the relationship between attitudes and behaviors. When you read this article, remember that it is written differently than research papers are written today; it is more of a first–person narrative than an objective, structured report. Also, be thinking about what you liked about the way he did his study and how you might improve on it if you were to do it. Enjoy the article!

Reading 1.2

Attitudes vs. Actions

Richard T. LaPiere

By definition, a social attitude is a behaviour pattern, anticipatory set or tendency, predisposition to specific adjustment to designated social situations, or, more simply, a conditioned response to social stimuli[1]. Terminological usage differs, but students who have concerned

It needs to be noted that this is one of the very early definitions of "attitude," and as such, it has been revised over the ensuing decades. Social psychologists today define an attitude as an evaluation of something along dimensions of "favor" "unfavor" or "good" "bad."

themselves with attitudes apparently agree that they are acquired out of social experience and provide the individual organism with some degree of preparation to adjust, in a well-defined way, to certain types of social situations if and when these situations arise. It would seem, therefore, that the totality of the social attitudes of a single individual would include all his socially acquired personality which is involved in the making of adjustments to other human beings.

But by derivation social attitudes are seldom more than a verbal response to a symbolic situation. For the conventional method of measuring social attitudes is to ask questions (usually in writing) which demand a verbal adjustment to an entirely symbolic situation. Because it is easy, cheap, and mechanical, the attitudinal questionnaire is rapidly becoming a major method of sociological and socio-psychological investigation. The technique is simple. Thus from a hundred or a thousand responses to the question "Would you get up to give an Armenian woman your seat in a street car?" the investigator derives the "attitude" of non-Armenian males towards Armenian females. Now the question may be constructed with elaborate skill and hidden with consummate cunning in a maze of supplementary or even irrelevant questions yet all that has been obtained is a symbolic response to a symbolic situation. The words "Armenian woman" do not constitute an Armenian woman of flesh and blood, who might be tall or squat, fat or thin, old or young, well or poorly dressed – who might, in fact, be a goddess or just another old and dirty hag. And the questionnaire response, whether it be "yes" or "no," is but a verbal reaction and this does not involve rising from the scat or stolidly avoiding the hurt eyes of the hypothetical woman and the derogatory states of other street-car occupants. Yet, ignoring these limitations, the diligent investigator will jump briskly from his factual evidence to the unwarranted conclusion that he has measured the "anticipatory behavior patterns" of non-Armenian males towards Armenian females encountered on street cars. Usually he does not stop here, but proceeds to deduce certain general conclusions regarding the social relationships between Armenians

Not necessarily. You can develop an attitude by reading about something, hearing about it, or seeing it. You don't have to directly experience the object. However, research does show that people will hold their attitude with more conviction if they have had direct experience with the attitude object.

LaPiere is suggesting that when we ask people their attitudes about a given issue, we are not learning how the individual would really behave with regard to the attitude object, once they come into contact with it. It turns out that this question, about the consistency between attitudes and behavior, will be a recurring issue throughout history in social psychological research.

TABLE I.   **Distribution of Results from Questionnaire Study of Establishment "Policy" Regarding Acceptance of Chinese as Guests**

Replies are to the Question: "Will You Accept Members of the Chinese Race as Guests in Your Establishment?"

	Hotels, etc., Visited		Hotels, etc., not Visited		Restaurants, etc., Visited		Restaurants, etc., not Visited	
Total	47		32		81		96	
	1*	2*	1	2	1	2	1	2
Number replying	22	25	20	12	43	38	51	45
No	20	23	19	11	40	35	37	41
Undecided: depend upon upon circumstances	1	2	1	1	3	3	4	3
Yes	1	0	0	0	0	0	0	1

*Column (1) indicates in each case those responses to questionnaires which concerned Chinese only. The figures in columns (2) are from the questionnaires in which the above was inserted among questions regarding Germans, French, Japanese, etc.

and non-Armenians. Most of us have applied the questionnaire technique with greater caution, but not I fear with any greater certainty of success.

Some years ago I endeavored to obtain comparative data on the degree of French and English antipathy towards dark-skinned peoples.[2] The informal questionnaire technique was used, but, although the responses so obtained were exceedingly consistent, I supplemented them with what I then considered an index to overt behavior. The hypothesis as then stated *seemed* entirely logical. "Whatever our attitude on the validity of 'verbalization' may be, it must be recognized that any study of attitudes through direct questioning is open to serious objection, both because of the limitations of the sampling method and because in classifying attitudes the inaccuracy of human judgment is an inevitable variable. In this study, however, there is corroborating evidence on these attitudes in the policies adopted by hotel proprietors. Nothing could be used as a more accurate index of color prejudice than the admission or non-admission of colored people to hotels. For the proprietor must reflect the group attitude in his policy regardless of his own feelings in the matter. Since he determines what the group attitude

TABLE II. Distribution of Results Obtained from Actual Experience in the Situation Symbolized in the Questionnaire Study

Conditions	Hotels, etc.		Restaurants, etc.	
	Accompanied by Investigator	Chinese not so Accompanied at Inception of Situation*	Accompanied by Investigator	Chinese not so Accompanied at Inception of Situation
Total	55	12	165	19
Reception very much better than investigator would expect co have received had he been alone, but under otherwise similar circumstances	19	6	63	9
Reception different only to extent of heightened curiosity, such as investigator might have incurred were he alone but dressed in manner unconventional to region yet not incongruous	22	3	76	6
Reception "normal"	9	2	21	3
Reception perceptibly hesitant and not to be explained on other than "racial" grounds	3	1	4	1
Reception definitely, though temporarily, embarrassing.	1	0	1	0
Not accepted	1	0	0	0

*When the investigator was not present at the inception of the situation the judgments were based upon what transpired after he joined the Chinese. Since intimately acquainted with them it is probable that errors in judgment were no more frequent under these conditions than when he was able to witness the inception as well as results of the situation.

is towards Negroes through the expression of that attitude in overt behavior and over a long period of actual experience, the results will be exceptionally free from those disturbing factors which inevitably affect the effort to study attitudes by direct questioning."

But at that time I overlooked the fact that what I was obtaining from the hotel proprietors was still a "verbalized" reaction to a symbolic situation. The response to a Negro's request for lodgings might have been an excellent index of the attitude of hotel patrons towards living in the same hotel as a Negro. Yet to ask the proprietor "Do you permit members of the Negro race to stay here?" does not, it appears, measure his potential response to an actual Negro.

All measurement of attitudes by the questionnaire technique proceeds on the assumption that there is a mechanical relationship between symbolic and non-symbolic behavior. It is simple enough to prove that there is no *necessary* correlation between speech and action, between response to words and to the realities they symbolize. A parrot can be taught to swear, a child to sing "Frankie and Johnny" in the Mae West manner. The words will have no meaning to either child or parrot. But to prove that there is no *necessary* relationship does not prove that such a relationship may not exist. There need be no relationship between what the hotel proprietor says he will do and what he actually does when confronted with a colored patron. Yet there may be. Certainly we are justified in assuming that the verbal response of the hotel proprietor would be more likely to indicate what he would actually do than would the verbal response of people whose personal feelings are less subordinated to economic expediency. However, the following study indicates that the reliability of even such responses is very small indeed.

Beginning in 1930 and continuing for two years thereafter, I had the good fortune to travel rather extensively with a young Chinese student and his wife.[3] Both were personable, charming, and quick to win the admiration and respect of those they had the opportunity to become intimate with. But they were foreign-born Chinese, a fact that could not be disguised. Knowing the general "attitude" of Americans towards the Chinese as indicated by the "social distance" studies which have been made, it was with considerable trepidation that I first approached a hotel clerk in their company. Perhaps that clerk's eyebrows lifted slightly, but he accommodated us without a show of hesitation. And this in the "best" hotel in a small town noted for its narrow and bigoted "attitude" towards Orientals. Two months later I passed that way again, phoned the hotel and asked if they would accommodate "an important Chinese gentleman." The reply was an unequivocal "No." That aroused my curiosity and led to this study.

In something like ten thousand miles of motor travel, twice across the United States, up and down the Pacific Coast, we met definite rejection from those asked to serve us just once. We were received at 66 hotels, auto camps, and "Tourist Homes," refused at one. We were served in 184 restaurants and cafes scattered throughout the country and treated with what I judged to be more than ordinary consideration in 72 of them. Accurate and detailed records were kept of all these instances. An effort, necessarily subjective, was made to evaluate the overt response of hotel clerks, bell boys, elevator operators, and waitresses to the presence of my Chinese friends. The factors entering into the situations were varied as far and as of often as possible. Control was not, of course, as exacting as that required by laboratory experimentation. But it was as rigid as is humanly possible in human situations. For example, I did not take the "test" subjects into my confidence fearing that their behavior might become

---

Critics of the attitude-behavior link say that attitudes are simply—as LaPiere states it here—abstract ideas that one has about an issue or object. The critic says that they bear no regular relation to how the person will react to or behave with the attitude object in real life. As such, they say it is fruitless to study attitudes. Social psychologists, however, say that attitudes are more consequential than mere abstract ideas. The reason we study attitudes is that they do in fact guide behavior across situations. Thus, if we know what one's attitude is about a given attitude object, we can predict how the person will behave in the future with regard to that object. For example, if I know you have a very positive attitude toward Diet Mountain Dew, I can predict with some confidence that the next time you are shopping for soda, you are highly likely to purchase Diet Mountain Dew.

As you may know, in the United States at that time, there was a very strong anti-Chinese prejudice. This prejudice actually goes back to the 1800s, when Chinese were a large part of the labor force that helped build the inter-state railroad system, but they were treated horribly by their employers.

self-conscious and thus abnormally affect the response of others towards them. Whenever possible I let my Chinese friend negotiate for accommodations (while I concerned myself with the car or luggage) or sent them into a restaurant ahead of me. In this way I attempted to "factor" myself out. We sometimes patronized high-class establishments after a hard and dusty day on the road and stopped at inferior auto camps when in our most presentable condition.

In the end I was forced to conclude that those factors which most influenced the behavior of others towards the Chinese had nothing at all to do with race. Quality and condition of clothing, appearance of baggage (by which, it seems, hotel clerks are prone to base their quick evaluations), cleanliness and neatness were far more significant for person to person reaction in the situations I was studying than skin pigmentation, straight black hair, slanting eyes, and flat noses. And yet an air of self-confidence might entirely offset the "unfavorable" impression made by dusty clothes and the usual disorder to appearance consequent upon some hundred miles of motor travel. A supercilious desk clerk in a hotel of noble aspirations could not refuse his master's hospitality to people who appeared to take their request as a perfectly normal and conventional thing, though they might look like tin-can tourists and two of them belong to the racial category "Oriental." On the other hand, I became rather adept at approaching hotel clerks with that peculiar crab-wise manner which is so effective in provoking a somewhat scornful disregard. And then a bland smile would serve to reverse the entire situation. Indeed, it appeared that a genial smile was the most effective password to acceptance. My Chinese friends were skillful smilers, which may account, in part, for the fact that we received but one rebuff in all our experience. Finally, I was impressed with the fact that even where some tension developed due to the strangeness of the Chinese it would evaporate immediately when they spoke in unaccented English.

The one instance in which we were refused accommodations is worth recording here. The place was a small California town, a rather inferior auto-camp into which we drove in a very dilapidated car piled with camp equipment. It was early evening, the light so dim that the proprietor found it somewhat difficult to decide the genus *voyageur* to which we belonged. I left the car and spoke to him. He hesitated, wavered, said he was not sure that he had two cabins, meanwhile edging towards our car. The realization that the two occupants were Orientals turned the balance or, more likely, gave him the excuse he was looking for. "No," he said, "I don't take Japs!" In a more pretentious establishment we secured accommodations, and with an extra flourish of hospitality.

To offset this one flat refusal were the many instances in which the physical peculiarities of the Chinese served to heighten curiosity. With few exceptions this curiosity was considerably hidden behind an exceptional interest in serving us. Of course, outside of the Pacific Coast region, New York, and Chicago, the Chinese physiognomy attracts attention. It is different, hence noticeable. But the principal effect this curiosity has upon the behavior of those who cater to the traveler's needs is to make them more attentive, more responsive, more reliable. A Chinese companion is to be recommended to the white traveling in his native land. Strange features when combined with "human" speech and action seems, at times, to heighten sympathetic response, perhaps on the same principle that makes us uncommonly sympathetic towards the dog that has a "human" expression in his face.

What I am trying to say is that in only one out of 251 instances in which we purchased goods or services necessitating intimate human relationships did the fact that my companions were Chinese adversely affect us. Factors entirely unassociated with race were, in the main, the determinant of significant variations in our reception. It would appear reasonable to conclude that the "attitude" of the American people, as reflected in the behavior of those who are for pecuniary reasons presumably most sensitive to the antipathies of their white clientele, is anything but negative towards the Chinese. In terms of "social distance" we might conclude that native Caucasians are not averse to residing in the same hotels, auto-camps, and "Tourist Homes" as Chinese and will with complacency accept the presence of Chinese at an adjoining table in restaurant or cafe. It does not follow that there is revealed a distinctly "positive" attitude towards the Chinese, that whites prefer the Chinese to other whites. But the facts as gathered certainly preclude the conclusion that there is an intense prejudice towards the Chinese.

Yet the existence of this prejudice, very intense, is proven by a conventional "attitude" study. To provide a comparison of symbolic reaction to symbolic social situations with actual reaction to real social situations, I "questionnaired" the establishments which we patronized during the two year period. Six months were permitted to lapse between the time I obtained the overt reaction and the symbolic. It was hoped that the effects of the actual experience with Chinese guests, adverse or otherwise, would have faded during the intervening time. To the hotel or restaurant a questionnaire was mailed with an accompanying letter purporting to be a special and personal plea for response. The questionnaires all asked the same question, "Will you accept members of the Chinese race as guests in your establishment?" Two types of questionnaire were used. In one this question was inserted among similar queries concerning Germans, French, Japanese, Russians, Armenians, Jews, Negroes, Italians, and Indians. In the other the pertinent question was unencumbered. With persistence, completed replies were obtained from 128 of the establishments we had visited; 81 restaurants and cafes and 47 hotels, auto-camps, and "Tourist Homes." In response to the relevant question 92 percent of the former and 91 percent of the latter replied "No." The remainder replied "Uncertain; depend upon circumstances." From the woman proprietor of a small auto-camp I received the only "Yes," accompanied by a chatty letter describing the nice visit she had had with a Chinese gentleman and his sweet wife during the previous summer.

A rather unflattering interpretation might be put upon the fact that those establishments who had provided for our needs so graciously were, some months later, verbally antagonistic towards hypothetical Chinese. To factor this experience out responses were secured from 32 hotels and 96 restaurants located in approximately the same regions, but uninfluenced by this particular experience with Oriental clients. In this, as in the former case; both types of questionnaires were used. The results indicate that neither the type of questionnaire nor the fact of previous experience had important bearing upon the symbolic response to symbolic social situations.

It is impossible to make direct comparison between the reactions secured through questionnaires and from actual experience. On the basis of the above data it would appear foolhardy for a Chinese to attempt to travel in the United States. And yet, as I have shown, actual experience indicates that the American people, as represented by the personnel of hotels, restaurants, etc., are not at all averse to fraternizing with Chinese within the limitations which apply to social relationships between Americans themselves. The evaluations which follow are undoubtedly subject to the criticism which any human judgment must withstand.

Margin notes:

This main finding of the study by LaPiere was that the prejudiced attitudes of the white hotel and restaurant owners against Chinese people did not at all predict how they would react to the two real Chinese people when they sought accommodations in the hotel or eat at the restaurant. That is, the couple was served and granted hotel accommodations in all but 1 of 251 instances. This astonishing finding seems to suggest a low correlation between attitudes and behavior.

He is saying that you'd never know that there is an intense prejudice against Chinese people based on the behavior of the white owners of the restaurants and hotels owners they visited.

This is a smart inclusion to this paper: another study in which LaPiere seeks to verify the strong anti-Chinese prejudice among those very hotel and restaurant owners they visited. If this is confirmed, it provides objective support for the main finding of a vast difference between one's attitudes and one's behavior.

Wow! 92% of restaurant owners and 91% of hotel owners replied on a questionnaire that NO they would not serve a Chinese couple.

But the fact is that, although they began their travels in this country with considerable trepidation, my Chinese friends soon lost all fear that they might receive a rebuff. At first somewhat timid and considerably dependent upon me for guidance and support, they came in time to feel fully self-reliant and would approach new social situations without the slightest hesitation.

The conventional questionnaire undoubtedly has significant value for the measurement of "political attitudes." The presidential polls conducted by the *Literary Digest* have proven that. But a "political attitude" is exactly what the questionnaire can be justly held to measure; a verbal response to a symbolic situation. Few citizens are ever faced with the necessity of adjusting themselves to the presence of the political leaders whom, periodically, they must vote for—or men may meet and adjust in some way one to the other.

The questionnaire is probably our only means of determining "religious attitudes." An honest answer to the question "Do you believe in God?" reveals all there is to be measured. "God" is a symbol; "belief" a verbal expression. So here, too, the questionnaire is efficacious. But if we would know the emotional against. Especially is this true with regard to the president, and it is in relation to political attitudes towards presidential candidates that we have our best evidence. But while the questionnaire may indicate what the voter will do when he goes to vote, it does not and cannot reveal what he will do when he meets Candidate Jones on the street, in his office, at his club, on the golf course, or wherever two responsiveness of a person to the spoken or written word "God" some other method of investigation must be used. And if we would know the extent to which that responsiveness restrains his behavior it is to his behavior that we must look, not to his questionnaire response. Ethical precepts are, I judge, something more than verbal professions. There would seem little to be gained from asking a man if his religious faith prevents him from committing sin. Of course it does—on paper. But "moral attitudes" must have a significance in the adjustment to actual situations or they are not worth the studying. Sitting at my desk in California I can predict with a high degree of certainty what an "average" business man in an average Mid-Western city will reply to the question "Would you engage in sexual intercourse with a prostitute in a Paris brothel?" Yet no one, least of all the man himself, can predict what he would actually do should he by some misfortune find himself face to face with the situation in question. His moral "attitudes" are no doubt already stamped into his personality. But just what those habits are which will be invoked to provide him with some sort of adjustment to this situation is quite indeterminate.

It is highly probable that when the "Southern Gentleman" says he will not permit Negroes to reside in his neighborhood we have a verbal response to a symbolic situation which reflects the "attitudes" which would become operative in an actual situation. But there is no need to ask such a question of the true "Southern Gentleman." We knew it all the time. I am inclined to think that in most instances where the questionnaire does reveal non-symbolic attitudes the case is much the same. It is only when we cannot easily observe what people do in certain types of situations that the questionnaire is resorted to. But it is just here that the danger in the questionnaire technique arises. If Mr. A adjusts himself to Mr. B in a specified way we can deduce from his behavior that he has a certain "attitude" towards Mr. B and, perhaps, all of Mr. B's class. But if no such overt adjustment is made it is impossible to discover what A's adjustment would be should the situation arise. A questionnaire will reveal what Mr. A writes or says when confronted with a certain combination of words. But not what he will do when he meets Mr. B. Mr. B is a great deal more than a series of words. He is a man and he acts.

Funny you mention the *Literary Digest*, LaPiere. For years, the *Digest* was renowned for its accurate polling of U.S. citizens when it comes to their political views, and specifically who they plan to vote for in the next presidential election. Between 1916 and 1936, it had accurately predicted the winner of the presidential election based on its polling. However, for the 1936 poll, the *Digest* poll predicted an overwhelming win for the Republican, Alfred Landon. But it turned out that some spunky Democrat named Franklin D. Roosevelt won in a landslide. How could the *Digest* have gotten it so wrong (by the way, it was so disgraced by that fiasco, it went out of business in 2 years)? Its polling methods were to blame: the *Digest* sampled 10 million people, from its subscriber list (a little over 2 million people). These are people who are rich enough to have a magazine subscription during the Great Depression. They also sampled from automobile registration records and telephone registries. Who has enough money during the Depression to be able to afford a car and/or a phone? Republicans. So the *Digest* essentially only sampled Republicans.

LaPiere is making the case here, in this last section of his paper, against the idea that attitudes and behavior are connected (based on the results of his study).

His action is not necessarily what Mr. A. "imagines" it will be when he reacts verbally to the symbol "Mr. B."

No doubt a considerable part of the data which the social scientist deals with can be obtained by the questionnaire method. The census reports are based upon verbal questionnaires and I do not doubt their basic integrity. If we wish to know how many children a man has, his income, the size of his home, his age, and the condition of his parents, we can reasonably ask him. These things he has frequently and conventionally converted into verbal responses. He is competent to report upon them, and will do so accurately, unless indeed he wishes to do otherwise. A careful investigator could no doubt even find out by verbal means whether the man fights with his wife (frequently, infrequently, or not at all), though the neighbors would be a more reliable source. But we should not expect to obtain by the questionnaire method his "anticipatory set or tendency" to action should his wife pack up and go home to Mother, should Elder Son get into trouble with the neighbor's daughter, the President assume the status of a dictator, the Japanese take over the rest of China, or a Chinese gentleman come to pay a social call.

Only a verbal reaction to an entirely symbolic situation can be secured by the questionnaire. It may indicate what the responder would actually do when confronted with the situation symbolized in the question, but there is no assurance that it will. And so to call the response a reflection of a "social attitude" is to entirely disregard the definition commonly given for the phrase "attitude." If social attitudes are to be conceptualized as partially integrated habit sets which will become operative under specific circumstances and lead to a particular pattern of adjustment they must, in the main, be derived from a study of humans behaving in actual social situations. They must not be imputed on the basis of questionnaire data.

The questionnaire is cheap, easy, and mechanical. The study of human behavior is time consuming, intellectually fatiguing, and depends for its success upon the ability of the investigator. The former method gives quantitative results, the latter mainly qualitative. Quantitative measurements are quantitatively accurate; qualitative evaluations are always subject to the errors of human judgment. Yet it would seem far more worthwhile to make a shrewd guess regarding that which is essential than to accurately measure that which is likely to prove quite irrelevant.

> LaPiere is making a good point—if we are to believe that attitudes are accurate predictors of behavior, we need to determine the degree of correlation between their attitude and how that person subsequently behaves with regard to the attitude object.

NOTES

1. See Daniel D. Droba, "Topical Summaries of Current Literature," *The American Journal of Sociology*, 1934, p. 513.
2. "Race Prejudice: France and England," *Social Forces*, September, 1928, pp. 102–111.
3. The results of this study have been withheld until the present time out of consideration for their feelings.

POST-ARTICLE DISCUSSION

The results of this paper were quite a surprise to social psychologists, considering the importance they placed on attitudes and their ability to predict future behavior. However, they maintained their trust in the attitude–behavior link over the ensuing decades, until the publication of a paper by Wicker (1969). This paper got a lot of attention because it made the claim that, after careful analysis of the literature, Wicker suggested that there was a very poor relationship between attitudes and behavior. This devastating critique of one of the cornerstones of social psychology led to several years of social psychologists attempting to justify the attitude–behavior link but also wondering if the critics might be right. This time, roughly 1969 to 1975, is known as "the crisis of confidence."

Researchers supporting the attitude–behavior link fought back against the critics by arguing that single behaviors are affected by a number of factors that may be irrelevant to one's attitude. Thus, the single behavior wouldn't be a reliable indicator of a particular attitude. However, as Fishbein and Ajzen (1974) and others (Eagly & Chaiken, 1993) have noted, if we aggregate multiple behaviors together into a composite index, the correlation between the attitude and behavior composite increases substantially. For example, using a single-behavior measure, the correlation between attitude and behavior in one study was .13. But when multiple behaviors were composed into an index, the attitude–behavior link jumped to .65 (Fishbein & Ajzen, 1974). Other researchers found the same pattern of results. In one case, grouping 14 single behaviors into one overall behavioral index brought the attitude–behavior correlation from a low of .12 to .62 (Weigel & Newman, 1976).

How do we explain the dramatic results of LaPiere (1934), that despite the strong anti-Chinese prejudice during the time, only 1 of 250 hotels and restaurants refused service to a Chinese couple? One possibility is that prejudiced people may be reluctant to show their prejudices due to norms of civility (Campbell, 1963, as cited in Eagly & Chaiken, 1993). On the one hand, that makes intuitive sense, but then consider the time and remember that racial prejudice was something that people were not afraid to publicly show. Racism was not only "normal," it was institutionalized in Jim Crow laws segregating public facilities (Jones, 1997). So, how would YOU explain the lack of correlation between attitudes and behavior in this study?

THINGS TO THINK ABOUT

1. Do you think that researchers would obtain the same results today? Why or why not?

2. Are attitudes a good predictor of future behavior?

(Continued)

(Continued)

3. How might you have worked to standardize the methods by which the stereotyped target would approach and interact with hotel and restaurant staff/owners?

4. What variables, besides race, might influence how one is treated by hotel and restaurant owners?

5. Can you think of another area where people might appear to say one thing but do another (i.e., their attitudes don't match their behavior)?

2

Research Methods

A social psychologist, like any other scientist, utilizes a specific set of procedures to examine the phenomena of interest to him. This is otherwise known as the **scientific method**. The scientific method is a way of understanding the natural world. It is a set of assumptions and procedures that guide the way we gather data, and they specify the conditions under which we can trust the data that are obtained. For example, one principle of the scientific method is standardization. It stipulates that, in an experiment, all aspects of the experiment are the same for all experimental conditions except the levels of the independent variables. Doing this helps the researcher make the assertion that, if she obtains differences on the dependent variable between experimental conditions, then those must have been caused by the differences in the independent variable between the conditions, because each group was exposed to the same procedures and stimuli in all other respects. In this chapter, we discuss further how social psychologists conduct their research. Of course, this is by no means meant to be an exhaustive review, and those interested in a more complete discussion are advised to consult other detailed sources (e.g., Aronson, Brewer, & Carlsmith, 1985; Aronson, Ellsworth, Carlsmith, & Gonzales, 1990; Reis & Judd, 2000).

TYPES OF STUDIES

Descriptive

One of the first questions researchers need to ask is what type of data they are seeking. Do we merely want to ask questions of the subjects? Do we merely want to describe people, or a person, or an interaction? This basic type of research is termed *descriptive research* and encompasses very simple methods such as surveys, or case studies, or naturalistic observation (whereby a subject is observed but is unaware of being observed; for example, people-watching in a mall). It is important to note that these studies do not manipulate variables, and they don't allow us to make any cause–effect statements about behavior. But these types of studies are good places to get ideas for experiments.

Correlations

Another source for experiment ideas is correlational research. Remember that a correlation is the naturally occurring relationship between any two variables. For example, there is a strong positive correlation between physical violence and ice cream sales. Huh? Does that mean that eating a lot of ice cream makes you more likely to hit someone? Or is it the other way around?

Hitting someone makes you crave a nice bowl of rocky road ice cream? Both of those seem unlikely. Perhaps a third explanation would make more sense. What do the two have in common? They both increase in the summer. So, perhaps it is the case that this third variable, summer, causes an increase in both, and in so doing, causes an artificial correlation between ice cream sales and rates of physical violence. This illustrates one of the problems with correlational research: the so-called third variable problem whereby two variables are correlated only because they are linked to a third variable that is the reason for elevations in those two variables (Brewer, 2000). Correlations tell us that two variables are related but not *how* they are related. You may have heard the axiom "Correlation does not equal causation." That is unfortunate, because more often than not, social psychologists are seeking to discover the causes of behavior in a given situation. If the goal of science in general is to explain and predict observed phenomena, then it would be best to be able to know what tends to reliably cause a particular behavior (or thought, or feeling) to occur. So, just like descriptive research, correlational studies are good points for researchers to get ideas for experiments that will help reveal causation.

Experiments

The great majority of research in social psychology comes in the form of experiments. There is a good reason for that. Experiments are the only way that we can establish cause and effect relationships between variables. Experiments allow researchers to examine the influence of one variable (or several) on the individual, and by holding other variables constant, we can establish the causal influence (if any) of that variable on behavior. We are seeking to discover if there is a causal effect of the independent variable(s) (IV; the variables the experimenter manipulates) on the dependent variable(s) (DV; the variables the experimenter measures).

In the smallest, simplest type of experiment design, a 2 × 2, there are two independent variables, with two levels of each variable. This forms four experimental conditions. Subjects are *randomly selected* (everyone in the population of interest has an equal chance of being selected for the experiment) and then *randomly assigned* (each subject has an equal chance of being assigned to any of the experiment conditions) to one of the four experimental conditions. Remember, an IV is something that the experimenter manipulates. We cannot manipulate aspects of the subject, such as their gender, religion, socioeconomic status. Those are termed *subject variables*. Suppose our variables are mood and comfort. For mood, we will assign people to either experience happiness or anger. For comfort, we will assign people to either a high comfort or low comfort condition. We write this design like this: it is a 2 (mood: happy vs. anger) × 2 (comfort: high vs. low) between-subjects design. The between-subjects designation says that each subject is exposed to one level of each of the variables. In a within-subjects design, all the subjects are exposed to all levels of all variables. So, if we hold all variables constant, and only vary those we want to vary (the IVs), then to the extent that we find differences between the experimental groups on their answers on the dependent variable (in this example, let's say the DV is expectations for future success on a task), we can say with some confidence that the different levels of the IV are the cause of the differences on the DV.

THEORY AND HYPOTHESES

Good research must be based on a theory. The goal of the research is to develop data that speak to the theory either in terms of support or no support. A theory is an integrated set of principles that explains and predicts some phenomenon. In psychology, we can't say that our data "prove" a theory (as one can in some other sciences), because we are dealing with humans and humans are messy. There will always be outliers in any experiment, testing any theory. We never get to 100% perfect results all the time, but we can get very close. We set very high standards for accepting that there is a true cause and effect relationship between two variables. This is the statistical likelihood that the results are due to chance. We say that we will only consider a finding a reliable and causal factor in changing the DV when there is less than a 5% chance that that change is due to random error. The hypotheses we derive from the theory are testable predictions about what we believe will happen in a given situation, with certain factors present. For example, given the theory of cognitive dissonance (Festinger, 1957), we might make a prediction about what a person will do when they say one thing that is incompatible with a behavior that they just performed. If we find evidence that the prediction was not supported, and assuming we didn't have any major flaws in our design, method, or statistical power, we would say that the theory is thus not supported. If the theory continues to bring no supportive data, it will be abandoned in favor of a different, ideally more parsimonious (accounts for the most data with the fewest assumptions) theory. This is what we refer to as the "self-correcting nature of science."

DOING EXPERIMENTAL RESEARCH: FURTHER CONSIDERATIONS

Suppose you are ready to start recruiting your subjects for your experiment. First, how many subjects do you need? Researchers can get a fairly exact number (N) for their study from a computer statistical program. A rough rule of thumb I used to use was to strive for about 20 per experiment condition for between-subjects designs. Too few subjects, and one will not have the statistical power to find an effect if it is there (Type II error—incorrectly believing there is no effect when there is one). On the other hand, if you have too many subjects, tiny effects may look significant erroneously (Type I error—incorrectly believing there is a significant finding when there is none in reality).

Second, how and who do we recruit? Ideally we would like to have our results generalize to the entire world, but that isn't possible because of cross-cultural differences. So we (researchers in the United States) will restrict our population to people in the United States.[1] How do we find our sample (the group of people from the population who do the experiment)? We randomly select them from the population. This means that everyone in the population has an equal chance to be selected for the experiment. This, as you might guess, is an ideal that no one ever reaches. First, not everyone in the United States is reachable. Some are homeless, some are institutionalized, some are ill, some live off the grid, and so on. Ideally we would like the sample to be a small

[1]But even a country can have important regional differences that can affect our ability to generalize our results, depending on the nature of our research. For example, research on aggression has shown significant differences between people in the northern United States and those in the southern United States in their acceptance and even expectation of physical violence as a response to threats to one's (or their family's) honor (Cohen & Nisbett, 1994).

representation of the population. So, according to that, I would want to have equal proportions of subjects as in the population according to their race, gender, religion, education level, age, and so on. You can guess that this is very labor-intensive, expensive, and nearly impossible to accomplish. So, instead, what we do is recruit subjects from introductory psychology classes on campus. Are college students a representative sample of the entire U.S. population? No, but they are the closest we can practically get. There are legitimate criticisms of this approach (Sears, 1986). However, psychologists generally have made the case that the differences between the college sophomore and other adults in the population are not significant enough to warrant concern.

Third, once we have our sample, we need to randomly assign (each person has an equal chance of being in any of the experiment conditions) each person to an experimental condition. Doing this ensures an equal distribution of people in each condition. Based on probability, we get a roughly equal proportion of people who are tired, hungry, excited, confused, and any other idiosyncrasies, distributed in each condition. In so doing, we have experiment conditions made of equal groups. So when they are exposed to the IV, the differences we see on the DV (if any) are due to the IV and not to individual differences between people.

Fourth, how do researchers overcome the problem of the artificiality of the lab? This is a big problem that can interfere with the potential generalizability of the research findings to the population. An experiment is worthless if it only explains behavior that happens in the lab room of the researcher. We want our lab results to be able to predict behavior in the real world. There are two ways researchers have tried to solve this issue. First is something called mundane realism. This is where the researcher tries to make the lab room physically look like a real-world setting. The idea is that if the room looks like the real world, subjects will forget the artificiality of the situation and will be more likely to behave as they would in the real world. The problem with this approach is that it is expensive, labor-intensive, and impractical, given that most researchers share lab space. An alternate solution is that researchers strive for psychological realism. The idea here is to have the IV be especially strong, such that it is psychologically and emotionally involving. The stronger the IV punch, the more the subject will react naturally. This does seem to work, and it is good advice for all researchers. One of the reasons most experiments fail is that their IVs are too weak. But if our IVs are strong enough, and the data still fail to support the hypotheses, we will know it is not the strong IVs but something else (e.g., too few subjects, poor measures, reactive topic, etc.).

INTRODUCTION TO READING 2.1

Aronson et al. (1990)

Nearly all psychology experiments, by necessity, have to employ a bit of deception in order for the experiment to work. That is, participants need to be kept in the dark about the specific purpose of the experiment, so that such knowledge doesn't influence their behavior and thus render worthless any data obtained from the participants. The deception takes the form of a "cover story," a sort of vague explanation of the purpose of the study (e.g., a study on racial prejudice might be called a study of social issues). The degree of deception also varies from mild (such as the kind I just mentioned) to strong, as in the case of Milgram's (1963) infamous obedience experiments, where subjects really believed they were hurting (or killing) another man in the next room. At the end of experiments, researchers should debrief the subjects, telling them about the true purpose of the study and why they needed to be deceived. Different researchers have different opinions on how to debrief. For the more mild types of deception, some experimenters may elect to hand out a short debriefing sheet to the participants at the end of the

study. These sheets explain the study and purpose of deception, as well as provide contact information and even some references for those interested in learning more about the topic.

With experiments that involve more deception, it is important to do a face-to-face debriefing. This part of the experiment has a number of considerations that are detailed in the chapter you are about to read. Debriefing should be done a certain way, with careful attention to make sure that the subject doesn't feel worse (e.g., gullible for believing your cover story) than they did when they started the experiment. The debriefing is an opportunity for the subject to learn more about the study and also, importantly, an opportunity for the experimenter to learn from the subject about how the experiment appears to the subject. In my view, this chapter, written by a prominent social psychologist, should be required reading for all social psychologists as they learn research methods. I remember it having a big impact on me after I read it, and I hope you enjoy it too!

Reading 2.1

The Postexperimental Interview

Elliot Aronson, Phoebe C. Ellsworth, J. Merrill Carlsmith, and Marti Hope Gonzales

The experiment does not end when the data have been collected. The experimenter will want to determine the subjects' reactions to the procedure and to provide them with a full explanation of the experiment. The postexperimental interview is not an unimportant "add-on"; rather, it provides the investigator with an invaluable opportunity to find out what the experiment meant to the individual subjects. It is an opportunity for the subjects to comment freely about how the experiment struck them, why they responded as they did, the alternatives they considered, and all other facets of their individual responses. This is the time for us to determine whether the subjects interpreted their experience as we intended. More important, the postexperimental interview provides the experimenter with an opportunity to fulfill an obligation to the subject: to explain all aspects of the procedure fully,

This is the key point of this chapter: The postexperimental interview (aka "debriefing") is an extremely important tool when constructing your experiment and a very useful tool that one should strive to always include as part of your experiment. In experiments involving deception, it is crucial that the experimenter do a post-experimental interview.

to explore the meaning of the experience for the subject and the experimenter, and to discuss the scientific importance of the results.

If any deception has been employed, the experimenter now can verify that the subject believed the version of events presented in the cover story, or discover whether the subject had some doubts. If the subject *did* entertain any suspicion, the experimenter can systematically probe for further information needed to judge whether the suspicion was specific enough and accurate enough to raise questions about the validity of the data collected from that subject.

Whether or not deception is used, the experimenter should give the subject a full explanation of the experiment and make certain that the subject completely understands the purposes and the procedures before leaving the laboratory. If the experiment has involved any disquieting events, the experimenter can explain why those events were essential. If any deception has been involved, it is almost always best if the subject is informed of the deception and the reasons why it was necessary.[1]

It is impossible to exaggerate the importance of the postexperimental interview. A poorly conducted debriefing can be the most distressing part of the whole experiment, making the subject feel like an object or—worse yet—like a fool. Accordingly, the postexperimental interview should never be approached lightly.

Some researchers have suggested that caring, sensitive experimenters are born and not made—as if any potentially good experimenter has an intuitive sense of what constitutes a considerate debriefing. Moreover, they suggest, if potential experimenters do not know the difference between a glib and cavalier debriefing and one that is respectful and caring, then they shouldn't be experimenters in the first place. We disagree. We believe that this aspect of the experiment is as much a skill as is each of the preceding phases, and that a great deal of effort should go into teaching these skills. The art and skill of debriefing should be as important a part of research training as learning to find or create settings, to manipulate the independent variable, to measure the dependent variable, and to analyze the data. Therefore, we have devoted this chapter to a discussion of the "whys" and "how tos" of conducting the postexperimental interview.

The two major purposes of the interview are closely interwoven. For the remainder of this chapter we will focus our attention on debriefing following an experiment involving deception. Many of these remarks are equally applicable to the experiment with no deception, but the issues are *especially* critical when deception is involved.

---

[1] Even the standard of full and honest disclosure is only a guideline, not an absolute rule. In some cases, such disclosures may create feelings of confusion, anxiety, or persistent self-doubt that may be more dangerous for the subject than ignorance of the whole truth. In research with children, for example, the child may not be able to understand the explanation and may be made to feel confused and uncertain about an event that might have seemed vaguely interesting but not particularly important. Or the child may remember only that the experimenter lied. One good way to deal with this problem is to explain the experiment to a parent who knows the child well and so is in a better position to decide what to say about the experiment.

Other dangers may arise in experiments involving adult subjects. If a personality test is administered, for example, it may often be unwise to reveal the subjects' scores to them or even to disclose the purpose of the test. Personality tests may have a reliability that suffices for large group experiments, but that should not be trusted for individual assessments. Even in experiments in which most subjects do receive a complete explanation, it may not be the best thing for some individuals. If a subject completely misunderstands the instructions and behaves inappropriately throughout the experiment, it may be very difficult to explain the experiment without making the subject feel like an idiot. These, and others like them, are delicate cases; the experimenter must always be sensitive to peculiarities of the procedures or of individual subjects that might raise questions about the advisability of complete debriefing. Like all other general rules in this book, the rule of full and honest disclosure has exceptions.

Sidenotes:

A main reason for debriefing is to find out if participants were suspicious or interpreted the procedures, questionnaires, or purpose of the experiment differently or in a way that might bias their responses.

Experimenters have a responsibility to do a professional, ethical, and thorough post-experimental debriefing.

Aronson and colleagues rightly point out the importance of learning how to do a proper debriefing, and that this is a skill that can be learned and taught.

CONDUCTING THE POSTEXPERIMENTAL INTERVIEW

If the experiment has involved deception, the experimenter must (1) probe gently to determine the precise nature of any suspicions the subject may have and (2) explain the deception in a considerate and gradual manner. In practice, these two aims are mutually consistent and can be realized simultaneously by the same general procedure.

Probing for Suspicion

In probing for suspicion, it is important to utilize a series of questions, introduced gradually. Why the need to move gradually? Why not simply ask if the subject suspected deception on the part of the experimenter? For a variety of reasons, subjects may be unresponsive to direct questions. First, a person who *did* guess the hypothesis might hesitate to admit it, out of a misplaced desire to spare the experimenter. Second, regardless of their feelings for the experimenter, most people are reluctant to admit that they can be fooled easily. Consequently, a subject who is suddenly told that deception was involved may imply that he or she suspected it all along. Thus, an abrupt procedure might fail to reveal some of the truly suspicious subjects, while falsely exaggerating the number of apparently suspicious subjects. As a result, the experimenter may be led to make inappropriate changes or to abandon a perfectly viable procedure. Moreover, abruptly stating that deception has been used is a harsh technique that could add unnecessarily to the subject's discomfort and elicit justifiable anger.

The best way to begin a postexperimental interview is to ask if the subject has any questions. If the subject has none, the experimenter should ask if the entire experiment was perfectly clear in its overall purpose and if all aspects of the procedure made sense. The subject can then be told that people react to things in different ways and that the experimenter would find it helpful to hear about the subject's feelings about and reactions to the experiment, the reasons for the subject's responses, and so on. Then, the experimenter should ask specifically whether the subject found any aspect of the procedure odd, confusing, or disturbing. Such a discussion may take a considerable length of time

By this point in the interview, the subject is likely to have revealed any doubts or suspicions. Moreover, the experimenter should have all the information needed to discover whether the subject misunderstood the directions or failed to share the experimenter's assumptions about the meaning of the treatment. If no suspicions have been voiced, the experimenter can continue: "Do you think there may have been more to the experiment than meets the eye?" This question is almost a dead giveaway. Even a previously unsuspicious subject will probably begin to suspect that the experimenter was concealing something. In our experience, many subjects will take this opportunity to say that they did feel that the experiment, as described, appeared too simple, or too complex, or not ideally designed to test the hypothesis, or something. This is desirable. Whether or not the subjects really were suspicious, this question allows them to indicate that they are not completely naive; it gives them a chance to see themselves as less gullible than they otherwise might. The experimenter should immediately ask them to say some more about their suspicions, to elaborate on their questions about the procedure. The experimenter can then ask how these questions might have affected their behavior. From the subjects' answers to these questions, the experimenter can judge the extent to which their suspicions are likely to have affected their responses.

Debriefing is a gradual process, involving many questions, designed to allow the participant to feel comfortable in revealing their thoughts about the purpose of the experiment, and any suspicions they may have had about aspects of the experiment.

There is no set time allotment for debriefings. However, the experimenter should allow sufficient time to do a relaxed, thorough interview at the end of each experiment session. So, for example, the experiment could take 20 minutes, and the experimenter would then allow for another 10–25 minutes for debriefing (the exact timing of each session and debriefing can be better estimated during pilot-testing of the experiment).

Key question. Allows participants—even if they were not suspicious—to "save face" and not feel naïve or gullible about being deceived by the experimenter.

When determining the criteria under which one will discard a participant's responses, it is important to have that done before running the experiment (OK to do during pilot testing).

Absolutely always debrief participants individually. Even if they were run in groups. The debriefing process is a conversation between the experimenter and each unique, particular participant. If one tried to debrief pairs or groups, their responses could influence the responses of others in the group, and the information the experimenter obtained would be worthless.

This is important to remember. When deception is used, it is important to do a post-experiment interview. But it is important to do it CORRECTLY, or else it is very easy for the participant to feel naïve, gullible, or embarrassed for believing the deceptive cover story about the experiment.

When deception is a part of the experiment, it is important during debriefing to clearly communicate to the participant that deception was necessary and that it is important that all participants believe the deception, or else the experiment wouldn't work. So the experimenter must stress that the participant shouldn't feel gullible because our job is to make sure ALL people believe the deception.

This is a fairly conservative technique; it will tend to overestimate the number of suspicious subjects, since some subjects may not arrive at any accurate suspicion until they have been exposed to a hint that deception may have been involved and have been forced by direct questioning to consider the nature of that deception. The criteria for excluding subjects' data should be rigid and should be set down before the experiment begins; an appropriate time is between the pilot subjects and the first "real" subject. And, of course, the decision to eliminate any particular subject from the data analysis should be made without knowledge of how that subject responded on the important measures.

Incidentally, it should be apparent that one implication of these recommendations is that subjects should be debriefed individually, even when two or more subjects have participated in the experiment. In the first place, it is difficult, if not impossible, to make accurate assessments of two subjects' reactions to the experiment if they are interviewed simultaneously. If one subject voices a suspicion, there is strong social pressure on the other to concur. Together, the two subjects are likely to arrive at a common interpretation of the experiment, which may not reflect what either of them felt at the time. Thus debriefing subjects in groups defeats the experimenter's purpose of making precise determinations of the degree of suspicion felt by each subject. In addition, this procedure defeats another primary purpose of the debriefing: the protection of the subject's feelings of competence through gradual revelation of the hypothesis. If two subjects are debriefed together, the less suspicious one may feel gullible and inferior when the other first voices any suspicions. The one who is slower to perceive the gist of the experimenter's gradual revelation of the purpose of the study may feel stupid and naive when the other understands it more quickly. The experimenter's remarks to the effect that most subjects typically believe the cover story will be vitiated if the subject sees another person whose perceptions differed. This kind of experience in group debriefing can make a subject feel foolish, and we have more than once heard students who have been debriefed in this way (not in our experiments) complain that "the debriefing was the worst part of the experiment."

Revealing Deception

When deception has been employed, debriefing in and of itself can cause subjects considerable embarrassment. Most people do not enjoy learning that they have been duped. Thus, even subjects who are perfectly convinced that the experimenter obtained no satisfaction deceiving them may *still* feel foolish, simply because they have been successfully deceived. For that reason, extreme care should be used in revealing the specifics of the deceptive techniques employed.

Once the experimenter has a full understanding of the subject's perception of the experiment, the debriefing process should be continued. Thus, the experimenter might say something like this: "You are on the right track; we were interested in some problems that we couldn't discuss with you in advance. One of our major concerns in this study is. . . ." The experimenter should continue by describing the problem being studied, specifying the reasons for its importance and explaining clearly exactly how the subject was deceived and why the deception was necessary. Further, the experimenter can reduce subjects' embarrassment by explaining that a great deal of time and effort went into constructing a situation that would be credible to everyone. By doing so, the experimenter assures the subjects that being duped or taken in does not in any way reflect on their perspicacity; rather, it is an indication that the experimenter had done his or her job right, and that the cover story was a credible one. The experimenter should include this information in the debriefing so that the subjects will realize that they were taken in by the effectiveness of the *situation* and *not* because of any gullibility or naivete of their own. Moreover, before terminating the experimental session, the experimenter should be certain that the subject fully understands all this.

A similar procedure is in order when the experimental treatments induce the subjects to behave in a "negative" manner—for example, to conform in the Asch experiment. Clearly, if the experiment is designed to produce this kind of behavior, and it is a good experiment, most subjects will be manifesting the unflattering behavior at least some of the time. The experimenter should point this out to each subject, stressing the fact that the person is not extreme in this direction; rather, the experimental operations must have been extremely powerful, since they induced the same kind of behavior from most of the people who served as subjects.

There is little doubt about the goal of the debriefing process. Most investigators would agree with Herbert Kelman's (1968, p. 222) recommendation that "in general, the principle that a subject ought not to leave the laboratory with greater anxiety or lower self-esteem than he came in with is a good one to follow." How can we be sure that this goal has been achieved? It is sometimes difficult to tell whether the subject still feels uncomfortable after the debriefing. It is conceivable that some subjects might feel that they must act like "good sports" or help the experimenter save face and so may pretend to be in good spirits while remaining in inner turmoil. The experimenter should not be taken in by such pretenses but rather should go out of his or her way to make it easy for the subject to express any misgivings about the experiment. A good way of getting a subject to reveal any lingering disturbances or uncertainty about the experiment is to solicit suggestions for improving the experiment. If subjects still feel uneasy about their behavior in the experiment, or uncertain of any of the things the experimenter said, it is invariably easier for them to attribute these doubts to some hypothetical future subject than to admit personal concern. For example, consider an experiment in which the treatment involves creating a feeling of temporary low self-esteem in the subject by administering a fake personality test and then revealing the "results" that portray the subject as a weak, unattractive person. At the end of the session, the experimenter will of course assure the subject that the negative personality description was made up long before the subject ever took the test, that the same description is given to all subjects in the negative condition, and that the subject would have been given the same feedback no matter what responses were made on the test. At this point, the subject might ask, "But what happens if you get a person who just happens to really correspond to the description you gave?" This might be the hypothetical question it appears to be. But as psychologists, we know that it is possible that this subject is expressing some personal anxiety and, although realizing that the test was a fake, is still concerned about the possible accuracy of the description. The experimenter should take such a statement as a cue for extra tact and extra time spent reassuring the subject. In describing how the hypothetical future subject might be dealt with, the experimenter might point out that the negative personality description was comprised of vague generalities that sound plausible and applicable to all subjects. The experimenter might even read over some of the items, pointing out that *everyone* believes that a person "feels shy in new situations" or "sometimes hurts people without meaning to" or whatever the negative statements might be. If the subject has really been expressing her own worries, the extra information should be reassuring, and she will have been spared the necessity of admitting personal concern openly.

This is another key important point: The experimenter must strive to do everything he/she can to make sure that the participant leaves the experiment feeling no worse than when they started the experiment. For example, in experiments where a negative mood is induced in some subjects, those persons may be asked to rate how funny they find various comics at the end of the study, in order to put them in a good mood.

The timing of the debriefing is frequently a relevant factor in the experimenter's attempt to prevent the subject from experiencing unpleasant aftereffects. Some experimenters prefer to wait until after all subjects have completed their participation in the experiment before informing any of them of the true nature of the research. The explanation of the experiment is often accomplished en masse through the use of a printed communication. This procedure has certain economic and methodological advantages, that is, it saves time and makes it impossible for a subject to reveal the experimenter's description of the experiment to any future subject. There may be some experimental circumstances in which delayed mass debriefing can be employed without ill effects. However, we do not recommend this kind of shortcut debriefing when there is any chance that a deception or its revelation might be painful for the subject. Moreover , even if no discomfort is likely to ensue, other aspects of an experiment may make it wise to debrief the subject immediately after the session. In a typical study of opinion change, for example, the subject's opinion may have changed because, in the experiment, a particular point of view was attributed to a prestigious person. It would be a breach of ethics for the experimenter to allow this changed opinion to affect the subject's behavior after leaving the laboratory. Clearly, the sooner the subject is debriefed, the better.

In addition, in many experimental situations, the subjects are students, and, as mentioned previously, one of the reasons for students to volunteer (and a major rationale for using them) is the educational value of the experience. If the experimenter personally provides a clear and detailed explanation of the experiment as soon as it ends, allows the subjects to ask questions, and spends time clearing up any ambiguities that may remain, the subject receives maximum educational benefit from the experience.

Our student experimenters have sometimes complained to us that it is impossible to provide the sort of careful, sensitive debriefing we recommend because the subjects aren't interested in listening to it. It is hard to establish rapport with a person who is gathering up books, mumbling monosyllabic answers, and glancing at the clock every five seconds. Unfortunately, not many subjects expect a full explanation of the experiment or a serious concern about their own reactions, perhaps because they so rarely get them. Thus, it is important to tell the subject at the outset that you are going to sit down and discuss the experiment in detail, and that this is one of the most important parts of the experiment. It is a good idea to say how long it will take. And in scheduling the experimental sessions make sure you include enough time for the postexperimental interview. If you schedule the subject for one hour and the experiment itself takes 55 minutes, you cannot possibly conduct a thorough interview, nor can you expect the subject to be motivated to cooperate.

We have placed heavy emphasis on the obligations of the experimenter to provide immediate feedback to the subject. These obligations are real and comprise the strongest arguments for such feedback. But it is important to point out that by omitting the lengthy interview with the subject which we have recommended, the experimenter is deprived of an important heuristic experience. Nothing is a richer potential source of information about the strengths and weaknesses of an experiment than subjects' responses to detailed debriefing.

It is conceivable that in some circumstances, the experimenter may feel that the debriefing should not be complete. For example, the underlying theory, the conceptual variables, or the overall design of the experiment might be so complex that it is difficult and unnecessary to convey a complete picture of it to the subjects. In such cases the complete picture may be so intricate as to merely confuse the subjects about those aspects of the experiment that have

---

I agree with Aronson et al.—it is always advisable to do the debriefing with each participant immediately at the end of each experiment session (rather than wait to debrief all participants at once after all participants have been run in the study).

The thorough debriefing is an extremely important aspect of any experiment and essential to those involving deception. The responses of the participants can yield vital information that will serve to enhance the experiment.

most relevance to them. In these circumstances the experimenter might simplify the explanation, presenting only those aspects of the experiment which are easily explained and which are most pertinent to the subjects' own experience. It would be a mistake, however, to hold back aspects of the deception; to do so would violate the subjects' trust in the one part of the experiment where they have a right to expect perfect honesty.

How can we tell if the debriefing has been successful? Experimenters frequently ask the subjects to write down their reactions to the experiment after the debriefing is over. To some extent this procedure is designed to be a check on the effectiveness of the debriefing and to assess the fully informed subject's perceptions of the ethics of the experiment. It is difficult to know how much confidence to place in subjects' responses to such questions, since some people may be reluctant to criticize the study or to indicate discomfort, but at least on this superficial level, the results of postexperimental checks are very encouraging. For example, recall that Bibb Latane and Judith Rodin (1969) ran a study in which subjects overheard a woman in the next room fall down and cry out in pain. Although the subjects didn't realize it, the experimenter's true concern was with the question of how people would respond to the woman's distress. In most of the conditions, a majority of subjects did not respond at all—not even to the extent of calling out to ask whether the woman needed help. After the subjects had been debriefed and informed of the true purpose of the experiment, the experimenters asked them to fill out an anonymous questionnaire about their reactions to the experiment. Ninety percent of the subjects said that they had understood the true purpose of the experiment and that the use of deception was necessary to achieve this purpose. When asked about their personal reactions to the experiment and the *ethics* (as opposed to the necessity) of the deception, all of the subjects said that they would be willing to participate in similar experiments in the future and that the use of deception was justified. In addition, most of the subjects found the experiment interesting and stated that they were glad to have taken part. Although we cannot be sure that all subjects were telling the whole truth, it is unlikely that there was a great deal of unstated resentment. Moreover, it seems safe to assume that after the debriefing, most of the subjects felt that the experience had been worthwhile.

Enlisting the Subject's Aid

Because of demand characteristics inherent in conducting a direct assessment of subjects' perceptions and opinions about an experiment, it is often useful for the experimenter and instructive for the subject to make use of a more subtle measure: to enlist the subject's aid in improving the experiment. That is, before ending the debriefing, the experimenter can ask the subject for any suggestions about ways to improve the experimental procedure to make it more powerful, more credible, and more interesting for future subjects. This is the best way we know of for finding out about any of the negative aspects of the experiment. As we have pointed out repeatedly (see Chapter 9, for example), experimental subjects tend to be cooperative. In the worst circumstances, this may prevent them from admitting that the procedure caused them anguish, that the experiment had no meaning for them, or that it meant something other than what the experimenter thought it should mean. By specifically appealing to the subjects to help improve the experiment, the investigator can turn this cooperativeness to the advantage of the research and to the benefit of future subjects. In response to a genuine appeal, subjects may be only too pleased to cooperate by

Subjects love to be "good subjects" and do anything to help the experimenter. One great way they can do this is by giving their thoughts on how to improve the experiment.

criticizing the experiment. These criticisms often lead to improvement and are an indispensable aid to the experimenter, especially in the pilot stages of the research. In addition, this procedure often allows the subjects sufficient latitude to admit that they were (or still are) upset by the procedure or the deception; if this should occur, the experimenter knows that further efforts must be made to bring the subjects to a full understanding of the reasons for the procedure and an acceptance of their own responses to it.

Finally, the experimenter tries to convince the subjects *not to reveal anything* about the experiment. This is a serious problem, because even if only a few subjects have been tipped off, the results can be invalid. Moreover, it is sobering to reflect on the fact that it is almost impossible to screen out sophisticated subjects in advance. It is not easy to successfully swear all subjects to secrecy; often, the subjects are drawn from a single class or school, and there is consequently a strong likelihood that they have friends who might subsequently volunteer for the experiment. These friends are almost certain to press former subjects for information. The experimenter can conduct the experiment in a manner designed to minimize intersubject communication by recruiting subjects from a variety of contexts, by running the whole study in as short a time as possible, by checking to make sure that later subjects are not room-mates of early subjects (if a subject's roommate wants to participate, sign that person up for the next hour, so there will be no time for communication), and so on. In addition, the experimenter should attempt to forestall communication after the session, by graphically describing the waste of time and effort which result from including people who have prior knowledge about the procedure or the hypothesis of the experiment. In addition, the experimenter should provide a vivid account of the damage that can be done to the scientific enterprise by using data from such subjects. The experimenter should explain that because such information usually spreads rapidly, telling even one person might result in several subjects whose performance is either unusable or misleading.

The experimenter who has been sincere and honest in dealing with the subject during the postexperimental debriefing session can be reasonably confident that few subjects will break faith. To check on this, Aronson (1966) enlisted the aid of three undergraduates, each of whom approached three acquaintances who had recently participated in one of his experiments. The confederates explained that they had signed up for the same experiment, had noticed the friend's name on the sign-up sheet, and wondered what the experiment was all about. The experimenter had previously assured these confederates that their friends would remain anonymous. The results were encouraging. In spite of considerable urging, begging, and cajoling on the part of the confederates, none of the former subjects revealed the true purpose of the experiment; two of them went as far as providing the confederates with a replay of the cover story, but nothing else. Of course, not *all* experiments have given us such reason for optimism; some experimenters have found considerable leakage (e.g., Farrow, Lohss, Farrow, & Taub, 1975; Horka & Farrow, 1970; Lichtenstein, 1970; Walsh & Stillman, 1974). Differences in subjects' willingness to divulge information about an experiment could be a function of the nature of the deception employed; specifics of the experiment; when, where or by whom they were approached and asked for information; or the content, process, and degree of rapport established during the postexperimental session.

It will be easier for subjects to withstand pressure from curious friends if the experimenter gives them something to say. In urging the subjects to keep the true purpose of the experiment a secret, the experimenter can give examples of what they might say if asked about the experiment. For example, the experimenter can suggest that the task or some

---

At the end of debriefing, the experimenter needs to make clear to the participant the importance of not telling other potential participants about the details of the experiment (because if they knew about it before participating, any data obtained from them would be worthless).

This is an important point: If the experimenter is professional, and serious, and is honest and sincere in dealing with the participant, then the participant will be more likely to reciprocate by respecting the experimenter's admonition to not divulge experiment details to others (until after the whole study has concluded).

other superficial aspect of the procedure be described. Having something explicit to say spares the subjects the embarrassment of having to cut off friends with a prim, "I'd prefer not to discuss it," and also spares them the awkwardness of having to invent an innocuous description of the experiment.

What if the subject has been forewarned before entering the experimental room? That is, suppose that a subject *does* find out about the experiment from a friend who has participated previously. The new subject probably will not reveal this to the experimenter before the experiment, for fear of being disqualified from earning credit, money, points, love, or whatever incentive may have enticed the subject into the laboratory.[2] Moreover, if not prodded, the subject is unlikely to confess this after the experiment, because of reluctance to implicate the friend who, after all, broke a promise to the experimenter. Yet if the experimenter is unable to elicit this information, the results may be extremely misleading and the statement that no subjects were suspicious or sophisticated may be a serious error.

How can we be sure? Once again, the experimenter attempts to enlist the subject's cooperativeness, as well as the good will, which, it is to be hoped, has been built up during the postexperimental interview. First, as described above, the subject should be told clearly and forcefully the serious problems presented to science (and this particular research) if, unwittingly, the experimenter were to report erroneous data. The experimenter can then explain that although subjects are cautioned not to discuss the experiment, occasionally a former subject will reveal something by mistake. At this point, the experimenter can appeal to the subject to help out by mentioning now if she or he heard even a little about the experiment. The subject should, of course, be assured that the experimenter is uninterested in finding out *how* or *from whom* the information was transmitted. In the face of such a plea, few forewarned subjects will remain silent. We cannot overemphasize the importance of this kind of procedure as a safeguard against the artifactual confirmation of an erroneous hypothesis due to the misplaced cooperativeness of the subject. A truly cooperative subject will probably cooperate with the experimenter in this regard also and will respond to a direct plea from the experimenter.

DEBRIEFING FOLLOWING FALSE FEEDBACK TO SUBJECTS

Many of the suggestions we made earlier are aimed at helping the experimenter to achieve the goal of restoring the subjects' self-esteem and sense of well-being and of making the experiment a worthwhile experience for them. The experimenter should not assume, however, that following all these suggestions in preparing a standardized debriefing speech will automatically ensure success in returning the subjects to their pre-experimental state. Some experiments include false feedback to the subjects about their own abilities or performance. Such experiments require special care and caution in the postexperimental interview to ensure that the subjects not only understand that deception was involved but that they are also reassured

---

[2]Indeed, some researchers have taken advantage of subjects' tendencies to deceive experimenters about their knowledge. For example, David McMillen and James Austin (1971) were interested in the effects of having told a lie on people's willingness to help. When subjects were waiting to begin, a confederate entered the waiting room and told them about the alleged experiment. Fortunately for McMillen and Austin, and perhaps unfortunately for many other experimenters, 100 percent of the subjects—who were informed not only that the experiment involved taking a multiple-choice test, but also that most of the correct answers were "B"—lied to the experimenter and said they had heard nothing about the study!

Margin notes:

If the experimenter discovers this, he/she should discard this subject's session, and note for the record the reason why this subject's session was discarded.

A major component of psychological research is to educate participants (during debriefing) about the theory, design, hypotheses, and how they can find out more information about the experiment topic area. One efficient way to do this is to prepare a written debriefing with journal references and contact information for the experimenter. This sheet is given to all participants as they leave the session.

As discussed earlier, post-experimental debriefing is essential in studies that involve deception. If that deception also entailed telling the subject some negative evaluative information about themselves (e.g., that they did poorly on an IQ test), one has an ethical responsibility to make sure that the subject understands that this information was false, and that they understand WHY it was important to deceive them into believing the false information.

that what the experimenter said to them about their own performance is devoid of information value. Some research suggests that a simple debriefing may be inadequate to erase the beliefs about ability that are induced by false feedback during an experiment (Ross, Lepper, & Hubbard, 1975). Recall from Chapter 9 that these investigators gave subjects a series of notes, some ostensibly written by people who had actually attempted suicide, others by people simulating suicide notes. The subjects' task was to guess which of the notes were real and which were simulated. Independent of actual performance, some subjects were told that they had done very well (24 out of 25 correct). Other subjects were told that they had done poorly (10 out of 25 correct). During a full debriefing, all subjects were told clearly that the feedback they had received was unrelated to their performance and had been determined randomly before the experiment began. Nevertheless, when later asked a series of questions about whether they thought they were really good at discriminating real from fake suicide notes, subjects still showed residual effects of the experimental treatments. That is, subjects who were told that they were successful at the task (even though it was later clearly explained that they were not in fact successful) still believed that they would be more successful in the future than did control subjects. Similarly, subjects who were told that they had done badly still expected to do badly in the future, even after a full debriefing.

The mechanisms underlying this "perseverance" phenomenon are still not well understood, and speculation about them goes beyond our purpose here. Nevertheless, the demonstration is an important one for any experimenter who gives subjects false feedback about performance, personality, or anything else. Fortunately, Lee Ross and his colleagues were also able to show that a fuller debriefing, one that explicitly discusses the perseverance process, can successfully undo the results of the experimental treatment. A thorough understanding of this "process debriefing," as they term it, is important for any experimenter. Basically, it consists of not only indicating that the feedback was incorrect and discussing the reasons for this but also providing a full explanation of the tendency for people to maintain their distorted perceptions about their abilities at the task, even after the original information that created the perceptions has been discredited.

When false feedback is related not to subjects' performance on a specific experimental task but rather to more enduring personality characteristics, "undeceiving" subjects may be especially difficult. Elaine Walster and her colleagues (1967) found evidence that debriefing was not always immediately effective and that some kinds of subjects may behave as though they still believe the manipulation, even after a longer delay. Apparently, the situation these researchers used to induce low self-esteem in their subjects triggered all sorts of thoughts and memories that activated other *real* feelings of low self-esteem in some subjects, and these feelings could not easily be removed by debriefing. The subjects seemed to realize that the experimenter had been lying in suggesting that they were inferior people; nevertheless, their own reactivated feelings of inferiority led them to feel that the experimenter's characterization had unwittingly hit on the truth. It was as though the subjects said to themselves, "I know he didn't mean it, but it's true anyway." This kind of resistant residual effect presents a very serious problem, especially since at the present time we have no reliable means of identifying in advance the subjects for whom regular debriefing procedures are likely to be ineffective.

Each subject is unique, and it is important for the experimenter to be attuned to things the subject says in the post-experimental interview that would call for the experimenter to add new questions or follow a new line of questioning, in order to make sure each subject is as informed, feeling as good as possible, and educated about the purpose and rationale for deception in the experiment.

At the very least, the experimenter should make every effort to determine the needs of each individual subject and should try to tailor the debriefing session to meet these needs. The information provided should be redundant, especially for any individualized feedback the experimenter might have given the subject on the basis of false personality tests and the like.

The technique of gradually inducing the subject to recognize and describe the deception is probably one of the most effective means of ensuring that the subject fully understands it. A subject who is able to state the truth about an experiment is probably more likely to understand the truth than is one who simply hears it from the experimenter. If the debriefing session lasts longer than the experimenter expected, the next-scheduled subject should be canceled, so that the subject being debriefed doesn't leave with any remaining anxiety or confusion. Finally, the experimenter might do well to test the subject's understanding of the experiment in general and the treatment as it was applied in particular.

As we have pointed out repeatedly in this text, the experimental psychologist who concludes that research involving deception is the only valid method for elucidating the questions under study faces difficult ethical questions. Surely the quality and efficacy of the procedures used to explain the research and experimental procedures to the subject are indispensable for the justification of the use of such techniques. Research on this critical aspect of the entire experimental procedure is a welcome addition to our knowledge of how to carry it out most successfully and humanely.

POST-ARTICLE DISCUSSION

Often, when new experimenters are designing their studies, they may focus more on the design, materials, and procedure of the study and less on what happens when the data have been collected. The experiment is done, right? No. As you just read, the researcher has an ethical duty to inform the subject about the true purpose of the study and to explain why the experiment was conducted as it was. Ideally, this should be done face to face, with the experimenter taking time to answer any questions the subject has in a sensitive, clear manner. Debriefing should be an educational experience for the subject, and subjects can learn more about how research in psychology is designed and conducted and why some procedures need to be followed (e.g., deception).

I think one of the things about the Aronson et al. chapter that makes it so important is that it makes the point that debriefing is essential, it should be taken seriously, and researchers have an ethical obligation to learn how to do debriefings thoroughly and with sensitivity to their subjects. Researchers must make sure they are attentive to any concerns subjects may have. The researcher is in a power position and has to be sensitive to the subjects' position so that the subjects don't feel intimidated to not ask questions or to give false or socially desirable answers (when subjects give politically correct or other answers they think you want to hear but that may not reflect the subject's true position). Finally, the experimenter can learn a lot from the subject, in terms of ways to improve the experiment and how the experiment procedures are influencing subjects (in intended or unintended ways).

Even after having run several experiments during my undergraduate and graduate training, I remember reading this during my doctoral training and finding this chapter a revelation. I hope you enjoyed the chapter and have new insights about the ethical and scientific responsibilities that psychology researchers have when conducting research with human subjects.

THINGS TO THINK ABOUT

1. Do you think all social psychology experiment debriefing should be done face to face? Why or why not?

2. Some critics of social psychology experiments say that researchers should never deceive the subjects. Do you agree? Explain.

3. How long should a post-experiment interview (debriefing) last?

4. When debriefing, should you read a script to your subjects? Should you have them complete more questionnaires during the debriefing (e.g., to probe for suspicion)?

5. What can the experimenter do to ascertain whether the subject is in a worse state at the end of the experiment (compared to when they started), and, if so, how can the experimenter restore the subject's well-being or affective state?

INTRODUCTION TO READING 2.2
Dickerson et al. (1992)

This article is a bit different from the Aronson et al. chapter in that it doesn't specifically focus on research methods, but rather, it is an experiment showing how to induce cognitive dissonance in people and, in so doing, cause them to conserve their water usage. This paper is less of a discussion of ways to do research and more of an illustration of (1) a very clever methodology to (2) address a practical concern using (3) social psychological theory. As an example of a practical application of social psychological theory, cognitive dissonance theory was shown in a previous study to help increase condom use (Aronson, Fried, & Stone, 1991). Dickerson and her colleagues attempted in this experiment to apply the same principles to encourage water conservation.

The father of modern American social psychology, Kurt Lewin, famously said, "There is nothing so practical as a good theory." He was making the point that our research should inform us on how best to address real-world problems and make people's lives better. Science for science's sake has its place, but Lewin was more interested in finding ways for researchers to help solve daily problems in real life, as well as larger societal issues, such as poverty, prejudice, and justice. As I mentioned earlier, one of the features of the article you are about to read is that it addresses a real-world issue directly and (mini-spoiler) quite successfully! Finally, pay special attention to the creative method and the lengths to which the researchers go to obtain the data. Enjoy the article, and we will talk more afterward!

Reading 2.2

Using Cognitive Dissonance to Encourage Water Conservation[1]

CHRIS ANN DICKERSON

**RUTH THIBODEAU, ELLIOT ARONSON,[2]
AND DAYNA MILLER**

In a field experiment on water conservation, we aroused dissonance in patrons of the campus recreation facility by making them feel hypocritical about their showering habits. Using a 2×2 factorial design, we manipulated subject's "mindfulness" that they had sometimes wasted water while showering, and then varied whether they made a "public commitment" urging other people to take shorter showers. The "hypocrisy" condition—in which subjects made the public commitment after being reminded of their past behavior—was expected to be dissonance-arousing, thereby motivating subjects to increase their efforts to conserve water. The results were consistent with this reasoning. Compared to controls, subjects in the hypocrisy condition took significantly shorter showers. Subjects who were merely reminded that they had wasted water, or who only made the public commitment, did not take shorter showers than control subjects. The findings have implications for using cognitive dissonance as means of changing behavior in applied settings, especially those in which people already support the desired goal, but their behavior is not consistent with those beliefs.

Policy makers frequently attempt to modify behavior in a community, often by instituting information-based persuasive campaigns. These appear in various forms including broadcast announcements, newspaper advertisements, signs, mailings, and flyers. In recent years, drought has prompted administrators at the University of California at Santa Cruz (UCSC) to launch a major campaign of just this sort. Campus newspapers contained advertisements from the Water Conservation Office; flyers were posted on public bulletin boards and appeared in mailboxes. Specifically, the UCSC program encouraged people to think of water as a valuable resource and to adopt conservation-oriented behaviors such as flushing toilets less often, stopping the flow whenever possible while brushing teeth or washing dishes, and taking shorter, more efficient showers.

> Introduces the problem under investigation. Here it is a very applied (real-world, having real consequences in daily life) problem: water conservation. The issue: how best to design a persuasion message that is neither too weak nor too-heavy handed?

[1] The first author was supported by a National Science Foundation graduate fellowship while completing this research.
[2] Correspondence concerning this article should be addressed to Elliot Aronson, Psychology Board of Studies, Kerr Hall, University of California at Santa Cruz, Santa Cruz, CA, 95064.

The effectiveness of these types of persuasive messages and information campaigns is not certain. One experiment (Aronson & O'Leary, 1983) found that prominent signs asking people to take shorter showers produced mixed results. Indeed, if the message is too heavy-handed, it can even create a backlash. For example, although some subjects in the Aronson and O'Leary study reduced their water use, others showed their annoyance by sabotaging the signs and taking inordinately *long* showers. Moreover, even if people are initially persuaded by signs or flyers that conservation is worthwhile, there is controversy regarding the potency of such straightforward, and sometimes "coercive," appeals. They can produce attitude change, but the effects are frequently short-lived (Aronson, 1980).

Similarly, even when messages praising the value of water conservation are successful in changing people's attitudes, there is no guarantee that new attitudes will translate into new behaviors. Social psychologists have long been aware that the link between attitudes and behavior is problematic (e.g., Wicker, 1969). Thus, simply persuading people that conservation is beneficial might not result in reduced consumption. For example, Bickman (1972) interviewed 500 people about their attitudes concerning responsibility for removing litter. Although 94% of the subjects expressed favorable attitudes toward removing litter, only 2% actually picked up litter that had been intentionally left outside of the experimental setting by the experimenter.

We reasoned that a more effective means of promoting water conservation on campus might involve dissonance-generated self-persuasion, rather than informational or coercive appeals to save water. The motivating influence of cognitive dissonance has been shown to promote changes in attitudes as well as behavior (Aronson, 1969, 1980; Brehm & Wicklund, 1976; Freedman, 1965). Dissonance-related techniques have been utilized successfully in a number of applied situations: for example, to improve weight loss (Axsom & Cooper, 1981), reduce snake phobia (Cooper, 1980; Cooper & Axsom, 1982), and as a component of programs designed to promote energy conservation (e.g., Gonzales, Aronson, & Costanzo, 1988). Moreover, Pallak and his colleagues have demonstrated that dissonance-related interventions can produce enduring behavior change. Longitudinal studies have shown that a public commitment manipulation can cause people to reduce their energy consumption for six months or more (Pallak, Cook, & Sullivan, 1980; Pallak & Cummings, 1976; Pallak, Sullivan, & Cook, 1976).

As formulated by Festinger (1957), dissonance theory proposes that when a person holds two cognitions that are psychologically inconsistent, the person will experience cognitive dissonance, an unpleasant drive state akin to hunger or thirst. Once dissonance is aroused, an individual is motivated to reduce it, primarily through attitudinal or behavioral changes designed to reestablish consistency. Soon after Festinger's initial conceptualization, Aronson (1960, 1968) proposed that dissonance theory makes its clearest predictions when expectancies about the self are involved—that is, when people have done something that violates their self-concepts. Most of us share certain general beliefs about ourselves: for example, that we are good, moral, competent individuals. Therefore, choosing to engage in a behavior that is at odds with these important beliefs about the self should produce dissonance.

Given the central role of the self-concept in dissonance arousal, Aronson (1980) has argued that dissonance-related persuasion is likely to be much more effective than straightforward persuasive appeals. In a typical persuasion situation, such as those involving informational campaigns, people change their opinions because they have been convinced by an external source to do so. An unfortunate feature of this type of attitude change is that it is often

---

Another question: will one instance of water conversation change the person's water-conservation behaviors permanently?

The reasoning here is: get the person to publicly argue for the value of water conservation, then remind them of instances in their past where they didn't conserve water (induction of cognitive dissonance). The only way to reduce that dissonance is to engage in further water-conserving behaviors.

Dissonance reactions are strongest when they involve the self (violating one's own beliefs about their self).

Because it involves the self-concept, dissonance is predicted to 1) be more involving, and 2) be more long-lasting than other persuasion methods.

impermanent. For example, if I change my attitude because I hear a persuasive argument supporting one stance, I am likely to change it again if I hear a better argument supporting another position. There is very little of myself invested in the attitude.

In contrast, dissonance-generated persuasion is highly involving because it entails a challenge to a person's self-concept. Dissonance would occur, for example, if I believed I was a moral person, and then found myself in the uncomfortable position of having done something I considered immoral. To reduce this dissonance, I would need to rethink, or "justify," my actions in order to make them more consistent with my self-concept-typically through changes in relevant attitudes or behaviors. This subtle form of self-persuasion is powerful because the individual's self-concept is directly engaged in the process of attitudinal or behavioral change (Aronson, 1980).

Perhaps the most dramatic demonstration of dissonance-related persuasion is evidenced in the counter-attitudinal advocacy paradigm (e.g., Cohen, 1962; Festinger & Carlsmith, 1959; Nel, Helmreich, & Aronson, 1969). In this procedure, subjects are induced, under conditions of high choice or low incentive, to persuade others to believe something that they themselves do not believe. These subjects subsequently come to believe their own rhetoric; that is, they reduce dissonance by persuading *themselves* that their counter attitudinal statements were, in fact, a reflection of their true beliefs.

The counter-attitudinal advocacy paradigm, by definition, requires that experimenters induce people to defend a position that they were initially against. This requirement posed a problem for our effort to harness the power of the technique to promote water conservation. Conservation is an example of an "apple-pie and motherhood" issue that everybody already believes in, even though not everyone practices. Recently, however, Aronson and his colleagues (see Aronson, in press) have developed a modified version of the procedure so that it can be used in pro-attitudinal situations. The new technique involves creating feelings of hypocrisy. This is accomplished by inducing subjects to encourage other people to perform certain worthwhile behaviors. Subjects are then reminded that, on occasion, their own behavior has not been consistent with those goals. Essentially, subjects are confronted with the realization that they do not always practice what they preach. This realization is expected to generate dissonance because being a hypocrite would be inconsistent with most people's self-concepts as persons of integrity. As a result, subjects should be motivated to reduce dissonance by behaving in a manner more consistent with their espoused attitudes.

In an experiment on AIDS prevention, Aronson, Fried, and Stone (1991) explored the dissonance-arousing properties of this new procedure. Using a 2×2 factorial design, they induced feelings of hypocrisy regarding condom use. All subjects wrote pro-attitudinal speeches advocating condom use during all sexual encounters. Then, half the subjects simply rehearsed the arguments of the speech. The rest videotaped their prepared speeches, which they believed were going to be shown to high school students as part of an AIDS prevention program. Before taping their speeches, however, half the subjects were also reminded of the occasions when they had failed to use condoms in the past. Thus, all subjects believed that condom use was important, and all had composed a speech arguing that point. However, only those who both made a videotape and were reminded that they had engaged in unsafe sexual behavior were expected to feel hypocritical. These subjects were expected to reduce dissonance by strengthening their intentions to use condoms in the future. Aronson et al.'s (1991) results were consistent with this reasoning. Compared to subjects in the other conditions, those who

Introduction of hypocrisy.

received the hypocrisy manipulation expressed significantly greater intentions to increase their use of condoms, relative to their past behavior.

The results of this experiment are provocative in suggesting that a "hypocrisy" manipulation can arouse dissonance. Moreover, a follow-up experiment was conducted (Stone, Aronson, Crain, Winslow, & Fried, 1992), using a behavioral measure rather than self-reported behavioral intentions. Specifically, in each of the above conditions, subjects were subsequently given an opportunity to purchase condoms at a huge discount. Fully 83% of the subjects in the hypocrisy condition purchased condoms; this was a significantly greater percentage than in each of the other three conditions.

Did subjects, in fact, increase their condom use as a result of the hypocrisy manipulation? Obviously, it is impossible to know for sure. After all, one cannot follow people into the bedroom to observe their condom-using behavior. However, one *can* follow people into the shower-room—at least at public physical education facilities. The present experiment explores the utility of the hypocrisy-induction procedure in a field setting, using water conservation as the target behavior. In a conceptual replication of Aronson et al. (1991), public commitment endorsing water conservation was crossed with feedback intended to make subjects aware that they had wasted water in the past. After acknowledging that they supported conservation efforts, half the subjects agreed to help persuade other people to conserve water. Additionally, half the subjects were reminded that they did not live up to their own standards, and had sometimes been wasteful. The condition in which subjects both committed publicly to encourage other people to conserve and were reminded that they had wasted water was designed to make subjects feel hypocritical. These subjects were expected to reduce dissonance by reducing their water use while showering.

METHOD

Overview of the Procedure

Female swimmers were recruited as they exited the pool area, on their way to the locker room. A female experimenter (Experimenter 1), posing as a member of a campus water conservation office, approached each potential subject and asked if she could spare a few moments to help with a water conservation project. Then, depending on the experimental condition, subjects either answered some questions, signed a flyer, or both. Subjects were thanked for their participation, and their interaction with the first experimenter was terminated. However, unbeknown to subjects, a second female experimenter (Experimenter 2) was waiting in the shower room where she unobtrusively timed the length of each subject's shower and noted whether subjects turned the water flow off while soaping up.

Experimental Design

Two factors were manipulated: subjects' "mindfulness" of their sometimes wasteful showering habits, and subjects' "commitment" to pro-conservation behaviors. This 2 × 2 factorial design yielded the following conditions: 1) mindful-plus-commitment (hypocrisy), 2) mindful-only, 3) commitment only, and 4) unmindful/no commitment (no-treatment control). Our primary dependent variable was actual water use, as reflected in the length of subjects' showers. As a rougher measure of subjects' intentions to conserve water, we also noted whether subjects turned the shower off while applying soap, shampoo, or conditioner.

A "conceptual replication" refers to an experiment that tests the same hypothesis as a previous experiment, but uses different methods.

Hypothesis.

You might ask yourself: "why did they specifically seek out female swimmers for the experiment?" Remember that the goal of the experiment is to examine how the independent variables influence a person's water conservation. We'd ideally like to get a measure of their true conservation behaviors without the person being aware of it (so that the responses are most likely to be genuine). So how does one get a true assessment of a subject's water use without their knowledge? Sneak into their houses and hide somewhere in their bathrooms? Well that is illegal, so no. But we COULD have a research assistant approach people who are about to engage in some water-related activity (e.g., people at a gym taking a shower) and measure their shower water consumption.

The experiment requires that this experimenter employ a fair amount of deception, and acting talents!

Subjects

Participants in the study were 80 female swimmers who used the showers after exercising in the campus pool. Females were selected for this study because we intended to gather data only in the women's locker room. We used swimmers because pretesting indicated that swimmers could most reliably be expected to shower and shampoo before leaving the recreational facilities. Although the majority of swimmers used shampoo and/or soap when showering (to remove chlorine from their hair and skin), those few who simply rinsed off under the shower were excluded from the study in order to reduce extraneous within-group variance. This exclusion was minimal and did not occur with differential frequency in any of the treatment conditions.

And another reason they used swimmers. ☺

This is a good point that illustrates how one needs to be very specific in what is measured, and who qualifies as a participant. Here, not all female swimmers' shower data are used because some don't shampoo, and some just rinse. We want everyone to be standardized: to do the same behavior.

Experimental Setting

The particular configuration of the shower room is crucial to the design of this field study. The swimming pool and women's locker room are part of the same complex, with direct access to the showers available from poolside. The shower room is a large open room, approximately 15' wide by 25' long, without separate shower stalls or curtains. There are 13 showerheads, spaced along the walls of the shower room, and there are usually a number of people showering at any given time during operating hours. Typically, at least two or three other women were using the shower room at the same time as the subject and Experimenter 2. Frequently, there were more than five other women in the shower. These circumstances made it very easy to collect the dependent measures without attracting attention or arousing suspicion. Furthermore, it ensured that Experimenter 2's presence was unlikely to have detectable influence on the subject's behavior.

Procedure

While en route from the pool to the shower room, subjects were approached individually by Experimenter 1, who introduced herself as a representative of the campus water conservation office. After asking the subject if she had a few moments to spare, Experimenter 1 asked the subject whether she was on her way to the shower, and whether she was in favor of water conservation. If subjects answered "yes" to these questions, Experimenter 1 consulted a randomization chart and then introduced the experimental manipulations.

In the mindful-only treatment, she asked subjects to respond verbally to a "survey" consisting of a brief set of questions, such as: 1) When showering, do you ALWAYS turn off the water while soaping up or shampooing? 2) When you take showers, do you ALWAYS make them as short as possible, or do you sometimes linger longer than necessary? 3) In your view, about how long does it take an average person to shower and shampoo, without wasting any water? 4) About how long is your average shower at the Field House? These questions were designed to remind subjects that they had sometimes wasted water while showering.

In the commitment-only treatment, the subject was simply asked to help out with campus conservation efforts by printing her name with a thick black marking pen on a flyer that read: "Please conserve water. Take shorter showers. Turn showers off while soaping up. IF I CAN DO IT, SO CAN YOU!" Experimenter 1 explained that the flyer would be attached to posters that were being created for distribution around campus, and that they were intended to encourage other members of the campus community to conserve water. While making this

There are different ways to randomly assign a subject to an experimental condition. You could flip a coin, or use a random number table commonly found in the back of statistics textbooks (and close your eyes and point to a location on the table, open your eyes, and use that number to tell you to which condition you should assign the participant). The authors did something similar to the random number table here.

These help enhance the legitimacy of the cover story that the experimenter is a "water conservation officer."

request, Experimenter 1 drew subjects' attention to the large, colorful "sample" poster on display nearby, and mentioned that another poster was already in place outside of the women's locker room.

In the hypocrisy condition (mindful-plus-commitment), subjects first responded to the brief "mindfulness" survey, then signed the "commitment" flyer as outlined above.

The fourth condition served as a no-treatment control. In essence, the behavior of the subjects in this condition reflects a baseline response to the interventions instituted by the university in an effort to save water. Due to persisting drought conditions in California, UCSC had been quite actively promoting water conservation. Advertisements in the campus newspapers and flyers posted on public bulletin boards urged members of the campus community to reduce their water use. Most pertinent to this study, the university had posted a very large sign inside the actual shower room. The sign read: "Take Shorter Showers. Turn the Water Off While Soaping Up."

So, the mindful manipulation is designed to remind the subjects that they sometimes do not conserve water, while the commitment manipulation is designed to have the subject publicly proclaim that they always conserve water. This discrepancy creates the hypocrisy and, therefore, the cognitive dissonance that needs to be resolved.

Experimenters

Both experimenters were female students. The actions of the two experimenters were carefully coordinated. Experimenter 1 stood near a large door way leading from the pool deck into the athletic facilities complex. From this vantage point, she was able to intercept all female swimmers who were leaving the pool to enter the locker room. Experimenter 2 sat sunbathing by the pool, near the back door to the woman's locker room. This was approximately 30 feet from Experimenter 1's position. As Experimenter 1 began her interaction with the subject, Experimenter 2 watched, and made sure she could identify the subject later to collect the dependent measures.

As Experimenter 1 approached a potential subject, she asked the subject if she was on her way to the showers, and next, whether she could spare a few moments to participate in a water conservation project. If the subject answered yes to both, Experimenter 1 casually scratched her own knee before continuing the interaction. The knee scratch was a signal to Experimenter 2, who quickly entered the back door of the locker room, and began showering while waiting for the subject. This process enabled Experimenter 2 to remain unaware regarding which manipulation Experimenter 1 had delivered to the subject.

Experimenter 2 was already in the shower room, showering, when the subject entered. Several precautions were taken to guarantee that Experimenter 2 would not influence the subject's behavior. First, as noted above, the setting was a large shower room, and there were frequently a number of women showering. This reduced the possibility that Experimenter 2's presence had any noticeable effect on subjects. Additionally, since Experimenter 2 was often in the shower room for 10 to 15 minutes, she always brought shampoo, conditioner, a shaving razor, and a comb into the shower. These were used as necessary to make her showering appear as natural as possible. Finally, Experimenter 2 always left the water running during her shower. This was to avoid any possibility of influencing subjects to turn their own faucet on and off.

This is what one might call a "labor-intensive" experiment. One that involves having a research assistant take a shower (and casually observing the subject's water-conservation behavior) every time a new subject is taking a shower! That is a dedicated scientist!

Dependent Measures

Experimenter 2 wore a waterproof sports watch with stopwatch capacity, which she unobtrusively activated as soon as the subject turned on the shower. She also noted whether the subject turned off the shower while applying soap or shampoo. To assess water use accurately, the watch was stopped when the subject turned off the shower and was reactivated if the subject turned it back on to continue her shower.

RESULTS

Manipulation Checks

All subjects answered "yes" to the first question in the survey "Are you in favor of water conservation?"—thus indicating that their attitudes on this issue were positive. In the two conditions in which mindfulness was manipulated, subjects' answers to the brief set of questions confirmed that they were aware of their sometimes wasteful showering habits. That is, all subjects replied that: a) they did not always take the shortest possible showers; b) they sometimes lingered longer than necessary in the shower; and c) they did not always turn the shower off while soaping up or shampooing.

Shower Times

A two-way ANOV A was performed on subjects' shower times, measured in seconds (see Table I). No main effects for commitment or mindfulness were obtained, nor was the interaction of the two factors statistically significant, model $F(1,76) = 1.48$, $p < .26$. However, a planned comparison of mean shower times revealed a significant difference between the hypocrisy group ($M = 220.5$ sec) and the control group ($M = 301.8$ sec), $F(1,39) = 4.23$, $p < .05$. Means for the commitment-only ($M = 247. 7$) and mindfulness-only ($M = 248.3$) groups did not differ from each other, nor did either differ from the control or hypocrisy groups.

Turning Off the Shower

We also compared how often subjects in each condition turned off the shower while shampooing or soaping up. An overall chi square analysis yielded a marginally significant difference among all four groups on this dichotomous measure ($\chi^2 = 7.742$, $df = 3$, $p < .052$) (see Table 2). Next, a comparison of the hypocrisy and control groups revealed a significant difference in the expected direction, with hypocrisy subjects turning off the shower more often than control subjects ($\chi^2 = 4.912$, $df = 1$, $p < .027$).

The frequencies in the hypocrisy condition did not, however, differ from those in the mindful-only and commitment-only conditions. Indeed, the data from these three conditions were identical, with 14 out of 20 subjects in each group turning off the shower, compared to only 7 out of 20 in the control group ($\chi^2 = 7.742$, $df = 1$, $p < .005$).

TABLE I   Mean Shower Times (in seconds)

Condition	Mean	SD
Mindful-only	248.3	146.07
Commitment-only	247.7	104.05
Mindful/committed (hypocrisy)	220.5	100.62
Unmindful/uncommitted (control)	301.8	142.32

A manipulation check is an essential part of experiments. The experimenter is manipulating the Independent Variable(s) and is predicting that the different levels of the IV will have different effects on subjects' responses on the DV. But before we can have confidence in the results, we need to know that the IV had an impact on the participant. For example, if I was looking at the effects of anger and happiness on how people evaluated a story, I would need to randomly assign some to an angry mood induction condition and others to a happy mood induction condition. Immediately after the IV, I give participants a mood questionnaire in which they indicate the degree to which they are feeling various emotions. This will tell me if my manipulation of their moods worked.

TABLE 2   Frequency of Turning Off the Shower

Condition	Yes	No
Mindful-only	14	6
Commitment-only	14	6
Mindful/committed (hypocrisy)	14	6
Unmindful/uncommitted (control)	7	13

DISCUSSION

The first sentences of the discussion should tell the reader the main findings of the experiment and which (if any) hypotheses were correct.

The data from this experiment are consistent with our reasoning that higher levels of dissonance would be aroused for subjects in the hypocrisy condition, leading them to make greater efforts to conserve water than subjects in other conditions. Specifically, it was only subjects in this condition who took significantly shorter showers than subjects in the control condition. Unexpectedly, however, shower times for hypocrisy subjects were not significantly shorter than times for subjects in either the mindful or commitment conditions, both of which fell midway between times for hypocrisy subjects and controls. In addition, subjects in the mindful and commitment conditions were just as likely as those in the hypocrisy condition to turn the water off while showering. In all three conditions, this behavior occurred significantly more often than in the no-treatment condition.

Overall, this pattern of data suggests the possibility that subjects in all three groups were motivated to conserve water, although this effect was strongest for those in the hypocrisy condition. That is, rather than experiencing *no* dissonance, subjects in the mindful and commitment conditions might have experienced some feelings of hypocrisy, albeit of a milder sort than their counterparts in the hypocrisy group. Subjects in the former conditions were exposed to manipulations that could potentially arouse some feelings of hypocrisy. For example, in the commitment condition subjects signed a flyer that stated: "Take shorter showers . . . If I can do it, so can you!" For subjects who had wasted water in the past, this statement might have been experienced as somewhat hypocritical, even without the mindfulness manipulation to heighten its effect. Similarly, subjects in the mindful condition first affirmed their pro-conservation attitudes in the presence of the experimenter (recall that everyone answered "yes" to the initial question: "Are you in favor of water conservation?") and then were made aware of the discrepancy between their attitudes and behaviour—that is, the fact that they did not always take the shortest possible showers. This awareness could have aroused mild feelings of hypocrisy, or dissonance, for these subjects.

Why did subjects in these two conditions reduce dissonance by turning the water off, yet did not take shorter showers than controls? One possible reason is that turning the shower off is a fairly vivid and unambiguous way for subjects to demonstrate their commitment to conserve water. As such, it provides a natural "first step" for subjects who are motivated to conserve water, thus affording the clearest and most available route to dissonance reduction. Unlike hypocrisy subjects, however, subjects in the mindful and commitment groups did not take the additional step of significantly reducing the duration of their showers, relative to controls. This finding is consistent with our interpretation that hypocrisy subjects were experiencing the highest levels of dissonance and, as a result, were more motivated to act in accordance with their principles: both by turning off the shower *and* actually using less water. Finally, it should be noted that our primary dependent variable, length of shower, is a true measure of water conservation—unlike turning off the water, which is simply one method of potentially achieving that goal.

Could the effects found in the present experiment be due to some cause other than dissonance arousal? For example, could subjects have taken steps to conserve water simply because their pro-conservation attitudes were made salient by the experimental manipulations? Although our manipulations may have partly served to "prime" subjects' attitudes, we think it is unlikely that the shower-time results are due to the mere effects of attitude accessibility or salience. To begin with, subjects in all three experimental conditions were, in one way or another, reminded of their favorable attitudes toward water conservation prior to taking a shower. Yet, only subjects in the hypocrisy condition showed a significant reduction in their actual water use. In addition, data from the condom experiments discussed earlier (Aronson et al., 1991; Stone et al., 1992) do not support a "priming" interpretation of the present findings. The results of these studies, which employed similar manipulations and were conducted under more controlled laboratory conditions, reflected significantly greater dissonance arousal among hypocrisy subjects compared to all other experimental conditions.

Still, it could be argued that in the present study hypocrisy subjects might have experienced a more potent priming effect, given their exposure to both the mindful and commitment manipulations. While this alternative explanation cannot be ruled out, a close look at the details of the procedure makes this interpretation seem less plausible. Specifically, subjects in the hypocrisy condition were treated identically to those in the mindful condition except that the former also signed a leaflet advocating others to conserve water. This leaflet contained no new information above and beyond that already presented in the mindful condition; it simply restated methods of conserving water in the showers. (Indeed, this information is also posted conspicuously in the shower room itself and in other prominent locations within the adjacent locker room.) Thus, it seems doubtful that in the hypocrisy condition this redundant information—presented briefly and only seconds after the more extensive mindfulness manipulation— could have contributed appreciably to any "priming effect" produced by either of the manipulations alone. Rather, we would argue that the impact of signing the leaflet was that it made hypocrisy subjects uncomfortably aware of having preached something they did not always practice, thereby accounting for their greater motivation to conserve water. Future research is necessary, however, to determine conclusively whether these findings are best explained by dissonance arousal or are the effect of increased accessibility of attitudes via priming. In particular, laboratory studies based on the "misattribution of arousal" paradigm in dissonance research (e.g., Zanna & Cooper, 1974) would shed needed light on this issue.

Although a "priming" interpretation cannot be entirely ruled out, taken together with the findings of Aronson et al. (1991) and Stone et al. (1992) our results suggest that feelings of hypocrisy can be dissonance-arousing, thereby motivating people to bring their behavior into closer alignment with their espoused ideals. In addition, in recent years it has been proposed that individuals must produce "foreseeable aversive consequences" in order to experience dissonance (Cooper & Fazio, 1984; see also Thibodeau & Aronson, in press). Our findings cast doubt on this new formulation of dissonance theory. Any consequences resulting from complying with the experimenter's requests could only serve to promote water conservation—by encouraging other people to save water, and by helping the "Water Conservation Office" with a

Most researchers spend a fair amount of time in the discussion examining alternate explanations for their results, as do the current experimenters, in the following three paragraphs.

survey. Far from being an aversive consequence, saving water was something that all subjects in the present study already supported.

Finally, in the present experiment subjects experienced dissonance in a pro-attitudinal advocacy paradigm. This represents a new twist on the counter-attitudinal advocacy manipulation traditionally employed in dissonance research and opens up new opportunities for applying the theory in real-world settings. In particular, interventions along the lines of our hypocrisy manipulation may prove successful in motivating people to act in accordance with their already favorable attitudes toward a given issue, such as water conservation, condom use, recycling, etc. Clearly, using dissonance arousal as a strategy for changing behavior is somewhat more involved than simply hanging signs or posting flyers. As noted earlier, however, research suggests that changes in attitudes and behavior generated by cognitive dissonance tend to be more permanent and may also transfer to new situations, as compared to changes produced by other means of persuasion (Aronson, 1980). In the long run, then, dissonance-related persuasion may prove to be a cost-effective method for policy makers to employ in a variety of settings, especially those in which the goal is to produce higher levels of consistency between attitudes and beliefs.

REFERENCES

Aronson, E. (1960). *The cognitive and behavioral consequences of confirmation and disconfirmation of expectancies.* Application for Research Grant submitted to the National Science Foundation, Harvard University.

Aronson, E. (1968). Dissonance theory: Progress and problems. In R. Abelson, E. Aronson, W. McGuire, T. Newcomb, M. Rosenberg, & P. Tannenbaum (Eds.), *Theories of cognitive consistency: A sourcebook* (pp. 5–27). Chicago: McNally.

Aronson, E. (1969). The theory of cognitive dissonance: A current perspective. In L. Berkowitz (Ed.), *Advances in experimental social psychology* (Vol. 4, pp. 1–34). New York: Academic Press.

Aronson, E. (1980). Persuasion via self-justification: Large commitments for small rewards. In L. Festinger, (Ed.), *Retrospection on social psychology* (pp. 3–21). Oxford, UK: Oxford University Press.

Aronson, E. (in press). The return of the repressed: Dissonance theory makes a comeback. *Psychological Inquiry.*

Aronson, E., & Carlsmith, J. M. (1963). Effect of severity of threat on the valuation of forbidden behavior. *Journal of Abnormal and Social Psychology,* 66, 584–588.

Aronson, E., Fried, C., & Stone, J. (1991). Overcoming denial: Increasing the intention to use condoms through the induction of hypocrisy. *American Journal of Public Health,* 18, 1636–1640.

Aronson, E., & O'Leary, M. (1983). The relative effectiveness of models and prompts on energy conservation: A field experiment in a shower room. *Journal of Environmental Systems,* 12, 219–224.

Axsom, D., & Cooper, J. (1981). Reducing weight by reducing dissonance: The role of effort justification in inducing weight loss. In E. Aronson (Ed.), *Readings about the social animal* (3rd ed., pp. 181–196). San Francisco: Freeman.

Bickman, L. (1972). Environmental attitudes and actions. *Journal of Social Psychology,* 87, 323–324.

Brehm, J., & Wicklund, R. (1976). *Perspectives on cognitive dissonance.* Hillsdale, NJ: Lawrence Erlbaum Associates.

Cohen, A. (1962). An experiment on small rewards for discrepant compliance and attitude change. In J. Brehm and A. Cohen (Eds.), *Explorations in cognitive dissonance* (pp. 73–78). New York: Wiley.

Cooper, J. (1980). Reducing fears and increasing assertiveness: The role of dissonance reduction. *Journal of Experimental Social Psychology,* 16, 199–213.

Cooper, J., & Axsom, D. (1982). Effort justification in psychotherapy. In G. Weary and H. Mirels (Eds.), *Integrations of clinical and social psychology* (pp. 98–121). New York: Oxford.

Cooper, J., & Fazio, R. (1984). A new look at dissonance theory. In L. Berkowitz (Ed.), *Advances in experimental social psychology* (Vol. 17, pp. 229–265). New York: Academic Press.

Festinger, L. (1957). *A theory of cognitive dissonance*. Palo Alto, CA: Stanford University Press.

Festinger, L., & Carlsmith, J. M. (1959). Cognitive consequences of forced compliance. *Journal of Abnormal and Social Psychology, 58*, 203–210. Freedman, J. (1965). Long-term behavioral effects of cognitive dissonance. *Journal of Experimental Social Psychology, 1*, 145–155.

Gonzales, M., Aronson, E., & Costanzo, M. (1988). Using social cognition and persuasion to promote energy conservation: A quasi-experiment. *Journal of Applied Social Psychology, 18*, 1049–1066.

Nel, E., Helmreich, R., & Aronson, E. (1969). Opinion change in the advocate as a function of the persuasibility of the audience: A clarification of the meaning of dissonance. *Journal of Personality and Social Psychology, 12*, 117–124.

Pallak, M., Cook, D., & Sullivan, J. (1980). Commitment and energy conservation. In L. Bickman (Ed.), *Applied Social Psychology Annual* (Vol. 1, pp. 235–253). Beverly Hills: Sage Publications.

Pallak, M., & Cummings, W. (1976). Commitment and voluntary energy conservation. *Personality and Social Psychology Bulletin, 2*, 27–30.

Pallak, M., Sullivan, J., & Cook, D. (1976). *The long-term effects of commitment on voluntary energy conservation*. Presented at the meeting of the Midwestern Psychological Association, Chicago.

Stone, J., Aronson, E., Crain, L., Winslow, M., & Fried, C. (1992). *Creating hypocrisy as a means of inducing young adults to purchase condoms*. (In preparation.) University of California at Santa Cruz.

Thibodeau, R., & Aronson, E. (in press). Taking a closer look: Reasserting the role of the self-concept in dissonance theory. *Personality and Social Psychology Bulletin*.

Wicker, A. (1969). Attitudes versus actions: The relationship of verbal and overt behavioral responses to attitude objects. *Journal of Social Issues, 25*, 41–78.

Zanna, M., & Cooper, J. (1974). Dissonance and the pill: An attribution approach to studying the arousal properties of dissonance. *Journal of Personality and Social Psychology, 29*, 703–709.

POST-ARTICLE DISCUSSION

In social psychology, the concept of cognitive consistency has a long theoretical and empirical history. One of the early incorporations of this concept came with Fritz Heider's balance theory (Heider, 1958). Heider said that we are highly motivated to maintain balance (consistency) in our cognitions and in our relationships. If they become unbalanced, we are motivated to change something to make the situation balanced. For example, you have a friend, whom you like. Let's say your friend has another friend, whom you dislike. This triangle then becomes an imbalanced triad for you because of your dislike for your friend's friend. The stress and awkwardness of that other person in your life may be minor, in which case the imbalance isn't too strong and you will still keep your friend. But if that negative feeling is very strong, the imbalance will be so strong as to make you question whether being friends with your friend is worth all the hassle (the negative baggage of the other person in the picture).

Leon Festinger (1957)[1] expanded these ideas to formulate his influential cognitive dissonance theory. One might argue that Festinger's dissonance theory is the most famous or most influential in all of social psychology. Essentially, cognitive dissonance says that when people hold two inconsistent thoughts or an inconsistent thought and behavior, they feel a negative arousal (cognitive dissonance), which motivates the person to restore cognitive

[1] Although Festinger took his inspiration from Heider, Heider's book came out a year after Festinger's. The simple explanation is that Heider had been publishing articles about balance for many years prior to the publication of his 1958 book.

(Continued)

(Continued)

consistency by either changing one cognition or changing the way they think about the behavior.

The article you just read was coauthored by Elliot Aronson, who was a graduate student of Festinger's and later became a prominent advocate of cognitive dissonance theory in his research career. Aronson and his colleagues show in this paper that simply reminding people about their past failings in terms of water conservation (mindful only condition) or having them commit to trying to conserve water in the future (commitment only) was not enough to motivate behavior change. But when people say that conserving water is important and they publicly commit to do just that (by writing their name on the poster), they are reminded of how they have failed to conserve water. This failure creates dissonance. To eliminate the dissonance, they are motivated to bring their future water-conserving behavior in line with their public commitment, and in fact that is what they do. Cognitive dissonance is a powerful motive, and it can be used in productive ways to address social problems.

THINGS TO THINK ABOUT

1. When trying to get ideas for a good method to address a real-world problem like the one tackled in this paper (increasing water conservation), to what should researchers turn for inspiration?

2. Do you think that Experimenter 2 (the showering experimenter) may have caused the subjects to become suspicious in any way? Do you think Experimenter 1 questioning the subjects between the pool and the shower may have aroused any suspicion in the subjects? If so, how might you have designed it differently?

3. Why do you suppose the mindful-only or commitment-only conditions did not significantly alter water conservation compared to the control condition?

4. Can you think of other behaviors that this type of hypocrisy manipulation could affect such that it would have a positive effect on a real-world issue? For example, is there a way to design a hypocrisy manipulation into a commercial?

CHAPTER

3

Social Cognition

Social cognition is the application of concepts in cognitive psychology to our understanding of social interaction. Social cognition focuses on understanding the motivational, cognitive, and affective ways that people try to understand themselves and their social world (Fiske & Taylor, 2008; Kunda, 1999). If the goal of psychological science is to predict behavior in a given context, it is important to understand how individuals think about others in their social environment, about their relationship with others, and the influence of the social context on people.

Social cognition researchers seek to understand perceivers' conceptualizations of (a) themselves, (b) other people, and (c) the social context. These three elements simultaneously interact to produce social behavior. As you can imagine, this is a pretty daunting challenge and one that social psychologists are still working on. Social cognition research has revealed that people are not as rational as we might like to believe and that there are many sources of error and bias in social cognition that has tremendous influence on our social behavior. With a solid understanding of the limitations, biases, and shortcuts that occur in social cognition, people can be better equipped to think more critically about their social interactions and perhaps even be less prone to errors or prejudices in social cognition.

THE COGNITIVE MISER: EFFORTLESS THINKING

At any given moment, your brain is dealing with a lot of information: sensory, memory, biological, and what you're currently thinking about. Luckily, the brain is constructed such that it can easily multitask those varied types of input. However, researchers have learned over the decades that our consciousness has a limited capacity (Miller, 1956), and when we are asked to simultaneously analyze or think about different cognitive tasks, we tend to either fail at one or both, or we use a cognitive shortcut to finish one fast so that we can work on the other. For example, one study asked participants to form an impression of a target person while simultaneously reading a paragraph about Indonesia. Some participants were given a stereotype label of the target, whereas others were not given the label. Macrae, Milne, and Bodenhausen (1994) reasoned that if stereotypes act as cognitive capacity-saving devices, participants in the stereotype label condition should use that stereotype to form their impression of the target, and their recall for information about Indonesia should be more accurate (because they finished the target judgment task faster and had more time to then study and remember the paragraph information). This is precisely what the researchers found. People who were provided with the stereotype label were able to remember twice as many personality descriptors for the target, and they recalled more of the information from the paragraph, than did those participants who were not given a stereotype label.

Much research supports the idea that we tend to do whatever we can to conserve cognitive effort in social cognition. This is sometimes called the **cognitive miser** model (Taylor, 1981). The basic notion is that because we have a limited cognitive capacity to process information, we instead take shortcuts to arrive at a conclusion or judgment, *any* seemingly reasonable judgment, just so that we can quickly bring our thinking to a conclusion. We don't appear to be as concerned that we make an accurate judgment, just a fast one. As you can imagine, that often leads us to erroneous conclusions when we are trying to make decisions about the probability of an event, forming impressions about others, or interpreting the behavior of others. It is important to remember that many of these errors are a natural part of the limitations of our normal cognitive system. That is, many of these errors are not due to some shortcoming in the person's personality. However, there *are* some individual difference variables (sort of like a personality trait) that lead some people to be more likely to make these errors in judgment.

SCHEMAS

What do we do with all the information we take in from the world? Can we possibly organize or make sense of all the facts, rumors, ideas, and beliefs we form about our social world? It turns out that we do organize this information, with a cognitive tool known as a **schema**. A *schema* is a hierarchically organized cognitive structure that contains information about a stimulus and relations among its attributes (Cantor & Mischel, 1977; Fiske & Taylor, 1991; Hastie, 1981; Moskowitz, 2005; Taylor & Crocker, 1981). Schemas contain information, expectations, beliefs, values, probabilities, stereotypes, and more. A schema is useful in that it allows us to very quickly form a judgment, even on the basis of incomplete information. Schemas help us "fill in the blanks" in social perception.

Schemas are wonderful cognitive tools because, in a second, we "know" (well, at least we feel that we know) a lot about the person, her likely motives, behaviors, interests, and so forth. This helps us feel much less anxious going into that social interaction, because we can tailor our behavior accordingly, and we also feel as if we know what to expect from the other individual. The facilitation of social interactions is a major function of schemas.

Of course, the downside of schemas is that the information that comprises our schemas is not perfect (it is a biased database, so to speak). Therefore, the conclusions we make based on our schemas can be (and often are) incorrect. For the most part, however, there are usually no tangible negative consequences to that incorrect judgment, because we don't interact with the vast majority of people about whom we think using our various schemas. The benefit of coming up with a fast judgment about another person and feeling as if we know what to expect in social interactions with that individual far outweighs the negative consequences that one may suffer when using schemas to arrive at an embarrassing, incorrect judgment.

Schemas bias information processing at every stage of the memory process: attention, encoding, and retrieval. Schemas guide information processing in such a way that we pay more attention to information that is consistent with our schemas (Fiske, 1993), and we process that information more easily than we process schema-inconsistent information (Bargh & Thein, 1985; Srull, 1981; Wyer & Srull, 1994). Recall that stereotypes are part of schemas. Research shows that when we see information that is inconsistent with our stereotypes, we tend to misremember that stimulus in such a way as to make it consistent with our stereotype (Allport & Postman, 1947; Bodenhausen & Lichtenstein, 1987; Fiske & Neuberg, 1990; Rothbart, Evans, & Fulero, 1979).

Once we form an impression of someone, based on our schemas, it appears we are less open to revising that first impression (Wyatt & Campbell, 1951). When people form a schema, based on some information they receive, they tend to immediately formulate reasons, explanations, and other information that would support the development of that schema (Ross, Lepper, & Hubbard, 1975). By the time a person gets information that disconfirms the original information that led to the schema being created, the person has already gathered a lot of schema-consistent evidence, and the schema-inconsistent information is thus easily disregarded as a fluke, as irrelevant, or as just wrong (Anderson, Lepper, & Ross, 1980). So, what you've heard about first impressions, that is, that they are hard to break, is true (Wyer, 2010).

HEURISTICS: THE FAST TRACK TO DECISIONS

Every day, hundreds of times a day, we are faced with making decisions. Should I do my errands now or wait until tomorrow? Will I run into my boss at the gym again? Should I ask the attractive coworker to coffee? These decisions require us to take into account a number of variables, compile all the information we know about the situation at that moment, and attempt to arrive at the decision that will be most favorable to

us at that moment and in the future. Many of these decisions involve estimates of **probability**. Probability is the likelihood of an event occurring. Each of us has different standards for the initiation of action depending on the estimated probability of an event occurring (Carver & Scheier, 1981). For some, the probability of success needs to be very high before they will institute the behavior. For others, even a fairly low probability threshold is acceptable, because the anticipated reward is very high if the action brings about the desired goal (e.g., buying a lottery ticket).

With all the factors to consider, it can get pretty complicated trying to get an accurate estimate of the probability of an event. If we had to carefully deliberate each of these hundreds of probability estimates every day, we'd never get anything accomplished (Fiske & Taylor, 1991)! So, instead, our cognitive system uses various mental shortcuts called **heuristics** (Kahneman & Tversky, 1973; Nisbett, Krantz, Jepson, & Kunda, 1983; Tversky & Kahneman, 1974). Heuristics are cognitive rules of thumb that allow us to very quickly make judgments based on probability estimates. We know that the judgments we make with heuristics are likely not optimal (because they are made quickly, without a lot of careful thought), but they save an enormous amount of time and mental energy, so that is why we use them (Moskowitz, 2005).

EXPECTANCIES

One day, you are having lunch with your friend Armando, and you mention that you're going to a club with a mutual friend, named Charlie. "Charlie?" remarks Armando. "Yeah, . . . what?" you say, as you notice his face taking on a weird expression. "Well he's just . . . well, I don't wanna be mean, but he's a real jerk." Later that week, when you meet Charlie, you talk to him briefly, and after you leave the encounter, you think to yourself, "Armando was right—he really *is* a jerk!"

We've all had the experience of hearing some information about a person we're about to meet or a situation we're about to encounter and then developing some ideas about that person or situation. Psychologists refer to those ideas as **expectancies**. An expectancy is "a belief about a future state of affairs" (Olson, Roese, & Zanna, 1996, p. 211). In the fictional scenario from the previous paragraph, what happened was the perceiver went into the encounter with a negative expectation of what the other person (Charlie) would be like. What likely happens in these types of situations are two things: First, the negative expectation leads the perceiver to subtly (and nearly always nonconsciously) behave and say things that cause the target to say or do things that confirm the perceiver's expectation of the target (Kelley, 1950). This is known as a self-fulfilling prophecy, which we'll discuss shortly. The second process that occurs is that the expectation makes it more likely that the perceiver will pay attention to expectancy-confirming behavior from the target and to disregard or not pay attention to expectancy-disconfirming behavior. In so doing, the perceiver ends up with a very biased data set in his memory about the target. That is, his expectancies lead him to remember only expectancy-confirming behavior from the target. Later, when the perceiver is thinking about the personality characteristics of the target, the "available data" in the perceiver's memory confirm that the target mostly or only behaves in expectancy-confirming ways. This, of course, leads the perceiver to form a negative opinion of the target and may lead the perceiver to be less than enthusiastic about being around the other person! Another reason we're likely to feel that our expectancies are confirmed is that we often process information superficially or heuristically, and in those cases, we are much less likely to pay attention to expectancy-inconsistent information (Wilson, Lisle, Kraft, & Wetzel, 1989). Many studies show that in those instances where our expectancies are confirmed, we are very likely to remember those expectancy-confirming events (Harris & Rosenthal, 1985; Hastie, 1980; Olson et al., 1996).

SELF-FULFILLING PROPHECY

In a scene in the classic 1985 movie *The Breakfast Club*, Judd Nelson's character "Bender" (the "criminal") reveals to the other students in detention a glimpse of his home life and his relationship with his parents. He imitates his father talking to him: "'Stupid, worthless, no good, goddamn, freeloading son of a bitch. Retarded, big mouth, know-it-all, asshole, jerk.' [His mother chimes in] 'You forgot ugly, lazy, and disrespectful.'" In this brief scene, the power of self-fulfilling prophecies is revealed. A **self-fulfilling prophecy** is the process whereby a perceiver's expectations of a target eventually lead that target to behave in ways that confirm those expectations. In Bender's case, his parents think very poorly of him and expect him to amount to nothing in life. He likely has received that message directly and indirectly all his life, and, as a result, he starts behaving in ways that confirm their low expectations of him (frequently getting into trouble at school and with the police). Self-fulfilling prophecies are a special type of expectancy in that even subtle, nonverbal behavior from the perceiver can communicate an expectation that the target can discern, and this can affect the target's behavior accordingly.

COUNTERFACTUAL THINKING

When I was about 17, my coworker called me one night and asked if I wanted to go out with a few people from work. I agreed and began to drive the 7 or so miles from home to work. It was dark, around 8:45 p.m., as I drove about 30 mph down mostly residential streets toward my destination, the mall (I worked as a stockboy at a major department store). In a fraction of a second, my Firebird struck something. I immediately pulled over and got out of my car. Lying in the dark road was a black dog, mortally injured. A number of people came out of their houses, having heard a commotion. While some attended to the dog, a few others came up to me. One man put his arm around me, as he could see I was shaken up. I felt so bad for the dog and even worse that my car was the reason it was dying. The man with his arm around my shoulders told me, "There is nothing you could have done. No way to avoid it."

With that one sentence, I felt some relief. Why? Was he saying it is OK to kill a dog, or was I some heartless person? No. What he was doing, although I am sure he wasn't thinking about it in this way, was removing my natural tendency to blame myself for what happened and think about how I might have avoided the accident (Branscombe, Wohl, Owen, Allison, & N'gbala, 2003). Research has found that after an event has occurred, people tend to think about alternative outcomes to that event (Miller, Turnbull, & McFarland, 1990; Roese & Olson, 1995; Sanna, Chang, & Meier, 2001). Researchers refer to this as **counterfactual thinking.** Essentially, when we are thinking about these alternative outcomes, we're thinking about "what might have been." It is a learned inclination we develop around age 5 or 6 (Beck, Robinson, Carroll, & Apperly, 2006), in which we try to learn from an outcome, by trying to assure ourselves that

the choices we made that brought about the actual outcome were the best choices and that another possible choice wouldn't have yielded an even better outcome (in the event of a positive outcome). In the event of a negative outcome, counterfactual thinking may help us make better choices to avoid another negative outcome. Studies also suggest that the most common trigger for engaging in counterfactual thinking is the occurrence of a negative event (Roese, 1997; Roese & Olson, 1995).

Only sometimes do we find ourselves thinking about alternative outcomes to a positive event. For example, after getting soaked in a sudden rainstorm, you might say to yourself, "If only I had left work 5 or 10 minutes earlier, I would have made it to my car before it rained." We don't often try to mentally undo a positive event, because circumstances worked out in our favor, and we feel content that the choices we made that led to that positive outcome obviously must have been the right ones. Sometimes, though, we'll find ourselves congratulating our smart decisions by engaging in counterfactual thinking after positive outcomes. For example, "Wow, it is a good thing I avoided temptation to go out with my friends and party the night before the big exam and instead studied all night; otherwise, I wouldn't have received an A on the exam."

Work on schemas, heuristics, expectancies, and counterfactual thinking highlights the many pitfalls in our attempt to think rationally about the world and events in it. To the extent that we understand the biases in the way we think about other people, probability, and our own behavior, we will have a much better understanding of the way people think about themselves in social situations.

INTRODUCTION TO READING 3.1
Englich et al. (2006)

Retailers do something that is pretty smart. We, the consumers don't often think in depth about it, and it is likely many consumers don't think about it at all. But it puts more money in the pockets of the seller and takes money out of your pocket. What is this magic? It is pricing an item REALLY high, then drawing a line through the price on the price tag, putting a lower price, and calling it a "sale" or "discount." The initial high price is often called a "manufacturer's suggested retail price" (MSRP). The discount is often referred to as a "store price." This is meant to engender positive feelings for the store, for being on the side of the consumer and looking out for us against the big bad manufacturer's crazy high prices.

This works well. When we purchase an item that is "on sale," we feel like smart shoppers who got a good deal. In psychology, this is referred to as "anchoring." Here's how it works. Suppose a retailer wants to sell a shirt for $50, and the retailer prices it at $50. People will see little incentive to spend that much money on a shirt. They don't feel like they are spending wisely, and they believe the shirt is overpriced. Now, suppose the retailer prices the shirt at $85 (MSRP) and then crosses out that price on the price tag and puts a new price of $50. People will be much more inclined to spend $50 for the shirt, because they perceive it to be a much better deal (better value), and they are "saving money." In social influence research, a similar dynamic is referred to as "that's not all," whereby one makes a large request but then decreases the apparent size of the request with sales, coupons, discounts, or bonuses. In one

study that illustrates this, Burger (1986) set up a table on a campus with a sign that said he was selling cupcakes, but no prices were evident. He told half of the subjects the price was 75 cents. The other half were told $1, but before they could answer, he would say, "But I'll sell it to you for 75 cents." In the straight 75 cent condition, only 44% bought a cupcake. In the $1 down to 75 cent condition, 73% bought a cupcake. Wow!

Kurt Lewin, who many regard as the father of social psychology, famously said, "There is nothing so practical as a good theory." He meant that good research should have as its aim, a focus on applying a solution to a real-life problem. This takes us to our present paper. Englich, Mussweiler, and Strack investigated the application of anchoring in criminal sentencing. We know how pervasive anchoring is in our everyday thinking and how it can bias our judgments. But what happens when this cognitive error affects people's lives, as it can in decisions about length of sentencing.

As you read the experiments in this paper, think about what questions arise as you read the methods, and note them. How would you do things differently? Do you wonder why the researchers chose a particular design or research question? As always, pay attention to the results, noting which hypotheses were supported and if any predictions were not supported by the analyses. As always, note if it appears the researchers are making conclusions that go beyond the data. What conclusions can you draw from these four studies? Enjoy the paper, and we'll chat afterward!

Reading 3.1

Playing Dice With Criminal Sentences: The Influence of Irrelevant Anchors on Experts' Judicial Decision Making

Birte Englich

Thomas Mussweiler

Fritz Strack

Judicial sentencing decisions should be guided by facts, not by chance. The present research however demonstrates that the sentencing decisions of experienced legal professionals are influenced by irrelevant sentencing demands even if they are blatantly determined at random. Participating legal experts anchored their sentencing decisions on a given sentencing demand and assimilated toward it even if this demand came from an irrelevant source (Study 1), they were informed that this demand was randomly determined (Study 2), or they randomly determined this demand themselves by throwing dice (Study 3). Expertise and experience did not reduce this effect. This sentencing bias appears to be produced by a selective increase in the accessibility of arguments that are consistent with the random sentencing demand: The accessibility of incriminating arguments was higher if participants were confronted with a high rather than a low anchor (Study 4). Practical and theoretical implications of this research are discussed.

Keywords: *anchoring; sentencing decisions; experts; irrelevant anchors; decision making; selective accessibility*

> "God does not play dice with the universe."
>
> —Albert Einstein

Human judgment is often shaped by irrelevant influences. How we judge other people for example depends on the social category to which they belong (e.g., Bodenhausen, 1990), their physical attractiveness (Nisbett & Wilson, 1977), and whether or not we encounter them on a scary bridge (Dutton & Aron, 1974). Such influences from normatively irrelevant factors appear to be a fact of our mental lives (for an overview, see Wilson & Brekke, 1994).

One of the most intriguing instances of irrelevant influences on human judgment is that of a preceding judgment. Research on the so-called anchoring effect has demonstrated that a randomly chosen standard in a comparative judgment task may dramatically influence a subsequent absolute judgment of the same target. Indicating whether the percentage of African nations in the United Nations is higher or lower than an arbitrary

Definition of "anchoring effect"— the phenomenon being examined in this experiment.

number (the anchor) that has been determined by spinning a wheel of fortune (showing 65% or 10%), for example, influences subsequent estimates of this percentage (Tversky & Kahneman, 1974). Specifically, absolute judgments are assimilated toward the randomly chosen "anchor values." Such anchoring effects pervade a plethora of judgments (e.g., Epley & Gilovich, 2001; Northcraft & Neale, 1987) and are remarkably robust. Many findings indicate that clearly irrelevant numbers—even if they are blatantly determined at random—may guide numeric judgments that are generated under uncertainty (for an overview, see Chapman & Johnson, 2002; Epley, 2004; Mussweiler, Englich, & Strack, 2004; Mussweiler & Strack, 1999a).

ANCHORING IN COURT

This insight has important implications for many domains of human life. Specifically, these mechanisms seem to apply to decisions made by social institutions, decisions whose consequences may severely affect our lives. One example is the domain of legal decision making. Judges and juries have to decide the length of a defendant's prison term on the basis of uncertain and partially contradictory evidence. Therefore, judicial decisions are often judgments under uncertainty (see, e.g., Diamond, 1981; Ebbesen & Konecni, 1981; Hogarth, 1971; Partridge & Eldridge, 1974). Is it possible that such important judgments with far-ranging implications could be influenced by random numbers? Specifically, would a judge impose a longer prison term after being exposed to a higher number? Would this be the case even if the number is clearly irrelevant for the sentencing decision because it is randomly determined?

At first sight, this scenario seems highly unlikely. In fact, there is reason to believe that the laboratory findings that demonstrate influences of irrelevant and random anchors do not extend to the realm of judicial decision making. This is the case because legal decisions are distinct in a number of important ways. First of all, in the legal domain, a number of rules and prescriptions exist to minimize irrelevant influences on decision making. Typically, the penal code defines a set of criteria that needs to be met before a given deed qualifies as a crime. For example, the killing of another person is only seen as murder if the defendant killed the victim intentionally. Furthermore, the penal code and sentencing guidelines specify a range within which sentences for a crime have to fall. Finally, a large body of procedural rules prescribes how evidence must be gathered, presented, and processed. Hence, legal decision making appears to be more structured than those judgments for which influences from random anchors have been demonstrated in the laboratory. In addition, legal decision makers have been thoroughly trained in their specific domain of judgment and typically have considerable experience with related cases. A criminal judge who has spent several years studying criminal law and also has several years of professional experience may thus seem much better prepared to generate a sentence in a murder case than students are prepared to estimate the percentage of African nations in the United Nations. Finally, legal decision makers are likely to be more deeply involved in the decision process and to care more about the accuracy of the decision outcome. Making a judgment about the number of years a defendant has to spend in prison is

Authors' Note: This research was supported by the German Research Foundation (DFG). We would like to thank all participating legal experts, the German Postgraduate School of Administrative Sciences, and the Ministry of Justice of Baden-Württemberg. Thanks to Kirsten Soder, Viola Rost, Simone Dohle, and Thomas Dunlap for their indispensable practical support. Correspondence concerning this article should be sent to englich@psychologie.uni-wuerzburg.de.

Can you think of situations in life where a previous judgment can have an effect on a subsequent judgment? How about, for example, the amount a parent decides to give a child for allowance, depending on what amount they gave to an older sibling for their allowance?

One very important type of decision, made in legal cases, is how much time or fine a convicted criminal must pay for his or her crime. This is under investigation in the present experiment.

Question under investigation.

clearly more consequential than making a judgment about the percentage of African nations in the United Nations. In combination, all of these factors may work against a potential influence of random numbers on legal decisions.

At the same time however, some empirical findings suggest that even legal decisions may be open to anchoring influences under certain conditions. This seems to be the case for some specific types of anchors, namely, those that can be seen as providing relevant information about the legal decision at hand. Specifically, research in the civil context of damage awards shows clear effects of potentially relevant anchors: The higher a plaintiff's request in court, the higher the award that is obtained (Hastie, Schkade, & Payne, 1999; Malouff & Schutte, 1989; Marti & Wissler, 2000). In personal injury verdicts, the requested compensation systematically influences the compensation awarded by the jury as well as the judged probability that the defendant caused the plaintiff's injuries (Chapman & Bornstein, 1996).

Similar effects have been demonstrated in the criminal context. More specifically, it has been demonstrated that legal professionals who take the role of a judge in a realistic rape case are strongly influenced by the prosecutor's sentencing demand (Englich & Mussweiler, 2001). In addition, correlational evidence stemming from analyses of actual court files is suggestive of the same data pattern: Judges heavily weigh prosecution requests in their decisions (Englich, Mussweiler, & Strack, 2005). Furthermore, actual bail decisions were found to depend on whether the prosecution requested conditional bail or opposed bail (Dhami, 2003).

In all of these cases, a numeric value that is requested or suggested in court influences legal decisions. Notably, all of these anchors can be construed as providing valuable information for the legal decision at hand. For example, the compensation a party requests is likely to correspond to the actual damage that has been made. Thus, it cannot be ruled out that the anchors provided in these studies had some informational relevance.

Taken together, this research demonstrates that potentially relevant anchors may influence legal decisions. In combination with the basic research demonstrating that even completely irrelevant anchors influence judgments (Tversky & Kahneman, 1974), this applied work raises the question whether important judicial decisions may also be influenced by completely irrelevant numbers.

THE PRESENT RESEARCH

It thus remains unclear whether the influence of random numbers is limited to unstructured judgments for which people have little expertise, information, and motivation for accuracy or whether random numbers also influence more structured decisions that have important consequences and are made by experienced experts. The present research was designed to examine this question in the domain of legal decision making: Would the sentencing decisions of experienced legal professionals be influenced by irrelevant anchors even if the latter are determined at random? To find out, in four experiments we provided experienced legal professionals with realistic legal case materials and asked them to determine a sentence for the defendant. As is the case in actual trials, participating judges were exposed to a potential sentence (e.g., the sentencing demand of the prosecutor) before making their sentencing decision. In Study 1, the potential sentence stemmed from a source that—on normative grounds—should be irrelevant for the judge's decision, namely, from a journalist. In Study 2, the potential sentence was even more clearly irrelevant. Here, participants were informed that the given prosecutor's sentencing demand was determined at random. In Study 3, participants

Restatement of the research question being investigated.

Different types of irrelevant anchors that may or may not influence the sentences that the judges render in the experiments.

randomly determined this demand themselves by throwing a set of dice. Would their final sentences be influenced by these clearly irrelevant anchors?

In addition to examining this question, we wanted to explore the underlying psychological mechanisms of anchoring in the courtroom. In our past research, we have suggested that anchoring effects are produced by mechanisms of selective accessibility (Mussweiler et al., 2004; Mussweiler & Strack, 1999a, 1999b, 2000b; Strack & Mussweiler, 1997; for a related account, see Chapman & Johnson, 1999). More specifically, we assume that comparing the judgmental target to a provided anchor value increases the accessibility of anchor-consistent target knowledge. For example, considering a high sentencing demand as an anchor would selectively render accessible information that speaks for a high sentence (e.g., the defendant used force). Conceivably, using such easily accessible incriminating arguments as a basis for subsequent sentencing decisions leads to high sentences. From this perspective, higher sentences that follow from exposure to a high anchor are produced by a selectively increased accessibility of incriminating arguments. Past anchoring research outside the legal domain has provided substantial support for the selective accessibility notion (e.g., Mussweiler & Strack, 1999b, 2000b). Because all of this evidence was obtained with students who answered trivia questions about which they had little knowledge however, it remains unclear whether selective accessibility also plays a role in anchoring effects that are obtained in applied settings where experts have ample information about the judgment they make. In the present research, we set out to examine whether selective accessibility contributes to anchoring effects in sentencing decisions. Specifically, Study 4 exposed legal experts to randomly determined sentencing demands. Subsequently, we assessed the accessibility of incriminating and exculpatory arguments. If the selective accessibility mechanism is involved in how experts process these random sentencing anchors, incriminating arguments should be more accessible after exposure to a high anchor than after exposure to a low anchor.

In sum, the present research was designed to advance research on judgmental anchoring and research on judicial decision making in a number of important ways. First, we want to examine whether legal decision making is shaped by irrelevant influences. Second, we want to examine whether anchor values that are clearly irrelevant also influence judgments that are (a) structured by extensive norms and procedures, (b) made by experienced experts, and (c) pertain to a decision for which judges are professionally motivated to be accurate. Finally, we want to demonstrate that anchoring in information-rich settings involves a selective increase in the accessibility of anchor-consistent information.

STUDY 1

Rationale for experiment 1.

The goal of our first experiment is to examine whether a clearly irrelevant anchor influences the sentencing decisions of legal professionals. To ensure the social validity of the procedure, we focused on the potential influence of an irrelevant anchor to which judges may realistically be exposed during actual sentencing decisions.

In particular, we examined whether a sentencing anchor that is suggested by the media may influence judges' sentencing decisions. Clearly, the media often confront judges with potential sentencing anchors that—on normative grounds—should not influence their sentencing decisions. However, to the extent that judges process such normatively irrelevant anchors—so the selective accessibility model suggests—they may still have an effect on their sentencing decisions. Study 1 was designed to examine whether this is indeed the case. Specifically, we examined whether sentencing decisions would be influenced by an inquiry from a journalist that includes a potential sentencing anchor. Legal professionals were exposed to either a high or a low potential sentence in a case of alleged rape.

Method

Participants. We recruited 42 experienced legal professionals (28 men) at educational conferences for judges and prosecutors. Of these participants, 23 were judges and 19 were prosecutors. Note that in the German system of legal education, judges and prosecutors receive identical training and alternate between both positions in the first years of professional practice. On average, the legal professionals had 129.90 (SD = 105.87) months—more than 10 years—of professional experience in the courtroom. Participants' age ranged from 27 to 60 years, with a mean of 41.78 years (SD = 8.86). Men and women were equally distributed across experimental conditions.

Materials. Participants received realistic case material about an alleged rape. The materials were designed to include all the relevant information that is typically provided in actual court cases. To ensure that the material seemed realistic, it was designed in close collaboration with experienced trial judges. These judges worked through the material and supplemented it with information they believed was necessary to determine a sentence. This material was pretested in previous studies (Englich & Mussweiler, 2001), where it was judged to be complete and realistic by the participating legal experts.

The case material covered about four pages and consisted of brief descriptions of the incidence, the victim ("Sabine K."), and the defendant ("Peter F."). Furthermore, advisory opinions from a medico-legal and a psycho-legal expert and statements by the victim, the defendant, and two witnesses were provided. Participants took about 15 minutes to work through this material. The material included all the information (e.g., psychological consequences for the victim, resistance of the victim, threats by the assailant) that previous research has demonstrated to be important for an ascription of guilt in cases of rape (Krahé, 1991). For example, the consumption of alcohol by the victim and perpetrator was described as moderate (Schuller & Stewart, 2000), and further details—like the fact that the perpetrator used a condom (Hynie, Schuller, & Couperthwaite, 2003)—were revealed. In addition, participants had the relevant passages from the penal code at their disposal.

Procedure. Legal professionals participated in groups of up to 15. Participants were first handed the case materials, asked to work through them, and to put themselves in the role of the criminal judge in this specific case. Subsequently, they received the crucial questionnaire while keeping all the materials. In this questionnaire, participants were first instructed to imagine the following situation: During a court recess they receive a telephone call from a journalist who directly asks them, "Do you think that the sentence for the defendant in this case will be higher or lower than 1/3 year(s)?" (low/high anchor). About half of the participants were exposed to the high anchor, the other half to the low anchor. Participants were further instructed to imagine that to remain unbiased, they refuse to answer this question and instead bring the telephone call to a quick end. At a subsequent coffee break however, they meet a colleague with whom they start talking about the case. In the course of this conversation, they tell their colleague about the journalist's call. Embedded in this scenario participants

A note about pretesting: When one wants to be reasonably sure about how participants will perceive and interpret experimental stimuli, tasks, or measures, it is always a good idea to test it out on a separate group of subjects. It should be noted these participants are not in the "pilot testing" phase, but usually are a separate group of participants who are asked to respond to stimuli, tasks, or measures to be used in later experiments. For example, if we want to expose half of our participants to a photo of a "very attractive" woman compared to a photo of a "much less attractive" woman, we might take a lot of photos of various women and ask the pretesting subjects to rank each woman on her attractiveness on a scale from 1 (very unattractive) to 10 (very attractive). Then we'd take the photo that was ranked highest and the one ranked lowest and use those for our main experiment.

were asked, "What point of view would you represent to your colleague: Do you think that the sentence suggested by the journalist was too high, too low, or just right?" Participants indicated whether this potential sentence was too high, too low, or just right. Congruent with the standard anchoring procedure (Strack & Mussweiler, 1997; Tversky & Kahneman, 1974), this comparative anchoring question was included to ensure that participants do indeed process and consider the given anchor value. Subsequently, participants were asked to give their own sentencing decision. The sentencing decision was followed by a question about how certain the participant felt about the decision (1 = *not at all certain*, 9 = *very certain*) and by a rating of the quality of the presented case material. Specifically, participants indicated how realistic the provided case material was (1 = *not at all realistic*, 9= *absolutely realistic*). Finally, participants provided some demographic details.

Results and Discussion

Preliminary analyses. As in our previous research in which we used similar case materials (Englich & Mussweiler, 2001), participants judged the materials to be realistic, $M = 7.38$, $SD = 1.40$. This judgment did not depend on the anchoring condition, $t < 1$. The 19 prosecutors and 23 judges in our sample did not differ in the extent to which they judged the case material as realistic, $t < 1$. More important, the prosecutors and judges did not differ in the overall length of their sentences, $t < 1$. Furthermore, prosecutors and judges were similarly susceptible to anchoring influences in their sentencing decisions: There is no interaction between the anchoring condition and participants' legal profession, $F < 1$. Therefore, responses were collapsed across prosecutors and judges.

Sentencing decisions. Legal professionals' sentencing decisions for the identical legal case ranged from acquittal to 5 years in prison. An analysis of the mean sentencing decisions indicated that judges were clearly influenced by the potential sentence suggested by the journalist. Participants who had been exposed to the high sentencing anchor gave considerably higher sentences, $M = 33.38$ months, $SD = 9.65$, than participants who were confronted with a low anchor, $M = 25.43$, $SD = 10.49$, $t(40) = 2.56$, $p < .02$. Furthermore, participants felt fairly certain about their sentencing decision, $M = 6.02$, $SD = 2.04$, and certainty did not depend on the anchoring condition, $t < 1$.

Comparing the effects of relevant and irrelevant anchors. These findings indicate that sentencing decisions are influenced by clearly irrelevant sentencing anchors. A remaining open question is whether the magnitude of this influence differs from that of relevant sentencing anchors. To find out, we compared sentencing decisions in the present study with those obtained in one of our previous studies (Englich & Mussweiler, 2001, Study 2) in which legal professionals were confronted with the same materials and anchor values with the exception that these anchors represented the prosecutor's sentencing demand. A combined analysis of both studies revealed that sentencing decisions in both anchor conditions differed no matter whether this anchor was suggested by a journalist ($M = 25.43$ vs. $M = 33.38$) or the prosecutor ($M = 19.09$ vs. $M = 25.91$). In a 2 (anchor: high vs. low) ξ 2 (source: journalist vs. prosecutor) ANOVA, only the main effects for anchor, $F(1, 60) = 9.38$, $p < .01$, and source, $F(1, 60) = 8.19$, $p < .01$, reach significance, $F < 1$ for the interaction. This indicates that the magnitude of the resulting anchoring effect is independent of anchor relevance.

So it appears that the source of the recommending anchor is irrelevant . . . both equally affect sentencing recommendations by the legal professionals!

Interesting (and scary!)

Taken together, these results demonstrate that the sentencing decisions of experienced legal professionals may indeed be influenced by clearly irrelevant sentencing anchors. Although on normative grounds a potential sentence that is suggested by a journalist should not influence a final sentence in court, participants gave substantially higher sentences if they were exposed to a high rather than a low sentencing anchor. In fact, final sentences differed by about 8 months. Identical crimes were thus punished with strikingly divergent prison sentences depending on the sentencing anchor to which judges were exposed by the journalist.

In Study 2, we explored potential boundaries of this influence of irrelevant anchors. Would sentencing decisions by legal professionals be influenced even by anchors that were supposedly determined at random?

Question under investigation in experiment 2. Now, given the results of experiment 1, we might be thinking "well, if the source of the anchor is irrelevant, then the method by which an anchor is selected (even if random) may also influence final sentencing."

STUDY 2

Method

Participants. We recruited 39 legal professionals (18 women) during an educational conference; 37 were judges and 2 were prosecutors. Careful inspection of the 2 prosecutors' data in our sample reveals that neither their sentences nor their evaluations of the case materials differed from those of the judges in our sample. Therefore, we collapsed data for judges and prosecutors. On average, participants had 13.38 years ($SD = 8.58$) of professional experience in court. Participants' age ranged from 29 to 61 with a mean of 42.59 years ($SD = 9.44$).

Materials and procedure.   As in Study 1, participants were asked to put themselves in the role of a trial judge. This time, they had to find a sentence in a fictitious shoplifting case concerning a woman who had stolen some items from a supermarket for the 12th time. Again, the case material was compiled in close collaboration with legal professionals and consisted of brief descriptions of the incidence and the defendant ("Lena M."), an advisory opinion from a psycho-legal expert, and statements by the defendant and a witness. An independent protest using a different group of experienced legal professionals as participants ($N = 13$) demonstrated that these materials were judged to be complete ($M = 6.77$, $SD = 1.48$ on a 9-point rating scale with $1 = $ *not at all complete* and $9 = $ *absolutely complete*) and realistic ($M = 7.39$, $SD = 1.33$ on a 9-point rating scale with $1 = $ *not at all realistic* and $9 = $ *absolutely realistic*). Pretest participants were also asked to put themselves in the position of the trial judge in this case and to report their sentencing decision. Their mean sentence was $M = 5.62$ months ($SD = 2.57$).

After reading the case materials and the corresponding passages from the penal code, participants were handed the critical questionnaire in which they were asked to report their sentencing decision. As is the case in actual sentencing decisions in court, after working through the case material participants were asked to consider the sentencing demands of the prosecutor and the defense attorney before reporting their final decision. Participants were first confronted with a prosecutor's sentencing demand that was either high (9 months on probation) or low (3 months on probation). Instructions clearly pointed out that this demand had been determined at random, thus it did not represent any judicial expertise. Specifically, the instructions read,

For experimental purposes, the following prosecutor's sentencing demand was randomly determined, therefore, it does not reflect any judicial expertise: The prosecutor demands as a sentence for the accused Lena M. 3/9 months on probation. Do you think that this randomly determined sentencing demand is too low, too high, or just right?

Participants indicated whether they considered the randomly determined prosecutor's demand to be too low, too high, or just right. Subsequently, participants were confronted with the defense attorney's demand, which was always 1 month on probation, and again indicated whether they considered this demand to be too low, too high, or just right. Finally, participants reported their sentencing decision, indicated how certain they felt about their judgment (1 = *not at all certain*, 9 = *very certain*), answered the same question about the materials used in Study 1, and provided some demographic data.

Results and Discussion

Again, the case material was judged to be realistic, $M = 6.74$, $SD = 1.94$. Judges' sentencing decisions for the given shoplifting case varied between acquittal and 12 months on probation, with a mean sentence of 5.05 months ($SD = 3.18$). Further inspection of the given sentences reveals that they clearly depended on the prosecutor's sentencing demand, which was obviously determined at random. Specifically, judges who were exposed to the high demand gave higher sentences, $M = 6.05$ months, $SD = 3.07$, than judges who were exposed to the low demand, $M = 4.00$ months, $SD = 3.02$, $t(37) = 2.10$, $p < .052$. Again, participating legal professionals felt fairly certain about their sentencing decision, $M = 5.28$, $SD = 2.62$, and this certainty was independent of the anchoring condition, $t < 1.1$.

Comparing the effects of relevant and irrelevant anchors. To examine whether the magnitude of the obtained effect depends on the relevance of the given anchor, we compared the present findings with those of another study in which legal professionals ($N = 80$) were confronted with the same materials and anchor values with the exception that these anchors were relevant because they were suggested by the prosecutor (Englich, 2006). A combined analysis of both studies revealed that sentencing decisions in both anchor conditions differed no matter whether this anchor was blatantly selected at random ($M = 4.00$ vs. $M = 6.05$) or suggested by the prosecutor ($M = 4.10$ vs. $M = 6.98$). In a 2 (anchor: high vs. low) × 2 (source: random vs. prosecutor) ANOVA, only the main effect for anchor, $F(1, 115) = 26.82$, $p < .001$, reaches significance, $F(1, 115) = 1.16$, p 2 .3, for the main effect of source, $F < 1$ for the interaction. Thus, the magnitude of the resulting anchoring effect did not depend on anchor relevance.

These findings demonstrate that sentencing decisions of legal professionals may be influenced by a sentencing anchor even if this anchor is obviously determined at random.

The Influence of Expertise and Experience in Studies 1 and 2

In principle, one may expect that such random influences would be evident primarily in sentencing decisions by nonexpert judges. To the extent that professional expertise provides judges with alternative information that compensates for anchoring influences, experts may well show less bias from having processed a random anchor. The anchoring literature however suggests otherwise. Research on anchoring effects in the legal domain (e.g., Englich & Mussweiler, 2001) and beyond (e.g., Mussweiler, Strack, & Pfeiffer, 2000; Northcraft & Neale, 1987) has demonstrated that the judgments of experts are also open to anchoring influences. However, in all of these studies, anchors could be construed as relevant. Thus, it remains unclear whether experts may also be influenced by patently irrelevant anchors. A combined analysis of Studies 1 and 2 allows us to examine this question and to investigate whether the magnitude of anchoring differs for experts and nonexperts.

All participants in Studies 1 and 2 were experienced legal professionals, but they differed with respect to the specific fields of law in which their primary expertise lay. In Study 1, 24 participants were specialized in criminal law, whereas 18 were experts in other fields, such as civil law, administrative law, social law, and so on. Similarly, in Study 2, 17 participants were experts in criminal law and 22 were experts in other fields. The composition of our participant population thus allows us to differentiate between legal professionals who have specific expertise and long professional experience in the specific domain to which our legal cases pertained and those who had little specific expertise and professional experience in this domain.

In combination, Studies 1 and 2 included 41 experts in criminal law and 40 nonexperts. Although the sample sizes are too small to examine how expertise influenced sentencing decisions separately for the two studies, such an analysis is possible if the two studies are combined. To compare sentences across the different cases, we z-transformed the sentencing decisions.

As an examination of Figure 1 reveals, the sentencing decisions of experts and nonexperts in criminal law depended on the irrelevant sentencing anchors to similar degrees. In fact, a 2 (expert vs. nonexpert) × 2 (high vs. low anchor) ANOVA using the z-transformed sentencing decisions as the dependent variable only found a significant main effect of anchor, $F(1, 77) = 10.90$, $p < .001$, but no main effect of expertise and no interaction, all $Fs < 1$. Furthermore, simple effect analyses demonstrated that a significant anchoring effect occurs for experts,

FIGURE 1   Sentencing decisions (z values) of experts and nonexperts in criminal law who were confronted with a high versus low irrelevant sentencing anchor (combined analysis of Studies 1 and 2).

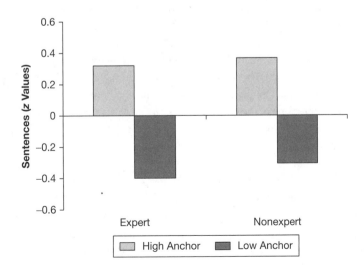

$t(39) = 2.45$, $p < .02$, and nonexperts, $t(38) = 2.23$, $p < .04$, alike. The only notable difference between the experts and nonexperts is that the experts felt more certain about their sentencing decision, $M = 6.88$, $SD = 1.60$, than the nonexperts, $M = 4.45$, $SD = 2.37$, $t(68.47) = 5.35$, $p < .001$. The certainty experienced by the judges however was unrelated to their susceptibility to the anchoring bias: In an additional analysis, the degree of bias is indicated by the distance between the prosecutor's initial demand and the judge's sentence and thus reflects the extent to which judges' sentences were assimilated toward the initial anchor. In fact, certainty and bias were uncorrelated, $r = .08$, $p > .5$. In combination with the higher certainty ratings of experts, this suggests that experts may mistakenly see themselves as less susceptible to biasing influences on their sentencing decisions.

STUDY 3

The results of Study 2 demonstrate that sentencing anchors that were blatantly determined at random influenced the sentencing decisions of legal professionals. There may however still remain some doubt whether the random nature of these anchors was fully accepted by our participants. To make absolutely sure that participants were fully aware of the fact that anchor values were randomly determined, we put randomization into the hands of our participants. In Study 3, participants randomly determined the sentencing anchors themselves by throwing a pair of dice. Would such anchors still influence sentencing decisions by legal experts?

Method

Participants. We recruited 52 legal experts (28 men) from a supplemental national postgraduate training program at the German University of Administrative Sciences in Speyer. Participants were junior lawyers from different German courts who had recently received their law degree and had acquired their first experiences as judges in court. Their ages ranged from 24 to 33 years with a mean of 27.5, $SD = 1.79$.

Materials and procedure. With the exception of the randomization procedure, materials and procedures were identical to those used in Study 2. This time, after working on the experimental materials, participants were told to randomly determine the prosecutor's sentencing demand themselves by throwing a pair of dice. The dice were loaded so that participants in Study 3 were confronted with exactly the same sentencing demands as participants in Study 2 (3 vs. 9 months on probation). Participants were informed that the experiment was a protest for a study on optimal questioning sequences in the courtroom, hence they should strictly follow the order of questions in the questionnaire. In addition, it was explained that the prosecutor's demand was determined at random to ensure that it did not influence participants' answers to the subsequent questions.

About half of the participants were handed a pair of dice that was loaded so that the dice always showed the numbers 1 and 2. The other half was given a pair of dice that was loaded so that the dice always indicated the numbers 3 and 6. After the dice had been thrown, participants were instructed to calculate the sum of the two dice and to fill in this sum as the prosecutor's sentencing demand in the questionnaire. Participants then worked on the sentencing questionnaire, which consisted of the same questions that were used in Study 2. This time,

---

If there is ever any doubt about the influence of an IV on a DV (as critics may have had about experiment 2—"were judges really aware of the random nature of the anchors?"), then another experiment may be necessary to explicitly address this criticism or doubt. Such is the case here with experiment 3, where the researchers want to make it even more obvious that the judges knew that the anchors were randomly determined.

we did not ask for additional ratings of the case materials because these materials had been extensively pretested in our previous research and in Study 2.

Results and Discussion

As in the previous studies, sentencing decisions for the identical crimes varied substantially, ranging from 1 month on probation to 12 months on probation with a mean sentence of 6.6 months, $SD = 3.57$. Overall, the sentencing decisions of the junior lawyers in Study 3 are thus similar to those of their more experienced colleagues who participated in Study 2.

Further analysis again revealed that sentencing decisions were influenced by the random sentencing anchors. Judges who were exposed to the high anchor gave higher final sentences, $M = 7.81$, $SD = 3.51$, than those who were confronted with a low anchor, $M = 5.28$, $SD = 3.21$, $t(50) = 2.71$, $p < .01$.[3] Participants felt moderately certain about their sentencing decisions, $M = 5.87$, $SD = 1.86$, and perceived certainty was independent of the anchoring condition, $t < .1$.

Anchors had an effect on sentencing decisions.

Comparing the effects of relevant and irrelevant anchors. We again compared the present findings with those of the other study with identical materials but relevant anchors (Englich, 2006). Again, sentencing decisions in both anchor conditions differed for anchors determined at random ($M = 5.28$ vs. $M = 7.81$) and suggested by the prosecutor ($M = 4.10$ vs. $M = 6.98$). In a 2 (anchor: high vs. low) × 2 (source: random vs. prosecutor) ANOVA, only the main effects for anchor, $F(1, 128) = 32.56$, $p < .001$, and source, $F(1, 128) = 4.54$, $p < .04$, reached significance, $F < 1$ for the interaction. No matter whether the anchor was determined by throwing dice or suggested by the prosecutor did judges assimilate their sentencing decisions to it to a similar degree.

Taken together, these findings demonstrate that even if legal experts randomly determined a sentencing anchor themselves by throwing a pair of dice, they were influenced by it. Judges assimilated their sentencing decisions toward these clearly irrelevant sentencing demands.

Comparing the Effects of High and Low Anchors to an Unanchored Control Group

Anchoring research typically compares the effects of high and low anchors without including an unanchored control group. This is done for at least three reasons. First, eliminating the preceding judgment in which judges consider the anchor makes it unclear whether potential differences in judgment are attributable to the absence of an anchor or to the absence of the preceding judgment task. Second, the fact that no anchor is provided in the experimental materials does not ensure that no anchor is used. It has been demonstrated that any number that is sufficiently accessible can serve as an anchor for numerical judgments (Mussweiler & Englich, 2005; Wilson, Houston, Etling, & Brekke, 1996). Judges who are not provided with an anchor value are thus likely to bring their own anchor into the experiment so that a no anchor control group is merely a self-anchored control group. Finally, most anchoring research is primarily interested in influences on the absolute magnitude of anchoring. Whether the low or the high anchor has a stronger effect is usually of minor importance. For all of these reasons, we have also followed the typical procedure of comparing judgments in a low and a high anchor condition in the present research.

At the same time, our pretesting data allow us to examine whether both anchors influence judges' sentencing decisions in Studies 2 and 3. To do so, we combined the data from both studies and examined whether the mean sentence that was given in the high versus low anchoring condition across both studies differed from the norm sentence that was given in our pretest. This analysis revealed that the combined mean sentence in the low anchor condition ($M = 4.73$, $SD = 3.16$) differed from the sentence given in the unanchored control condition ($M = 5.62$, $SD = 2.57$), $t(43) = 1.88$, $p < .07$. The combined mean estimate in the high anchor condition ($M = 7.06$, $SD = 3.41$) also differed from the unanchored sentence, $t(46) = 2.9$, $p < .01$. This supplemental analysis thus suggests that both anchors influenced sentencing decisions.

In combination, Studies 1 through 3 demonstrate that irrelevant and random numbers have powerful and robust effects on the sentencing decisions of legal professionals. In our final study, we attempt to shed light on the psychological mechanisms that contribute to this sentencing bias.

STUDY 4

Our previous research suggests that anchoring effects in other judgmental domains are produced by mechanisms of selective accessibility. Specifically, considering an anchor value selectively increases the accessibility of knowledge indicating that the target quantity may be similar to this anchor. Considering a high sentencing demand for example may selectively render those arguments accessible that imply a high sentence (e.g., the defendant used force). Study 4 was designed to examine whether such a selective accessibility effect would also be apparent for anchoring in sentencing decisions.

To do so, we developed a novel task as a measure of the expected selective accessibility consequences of judgmental anchoring. Specifically, we asked participants to categorize a series of arguments that were relevant for the present case as either incriminating or exculpatory as fast as possible.

Method

Participants. We recruited 57 legal experts (30 women) from a postgraduate training program for junior lawyers who had recently received their law degree and had acquired their first experiences as judges in court. Age ranged from 24 to 36, $M = 27.32$ years, $SD = 2.17$.

Procedures and materials. The case materials were identical to those used in Studies 2 and 3, and the procedures were largely similar to those of Study 3. Importantly, participants again determined the prosecutor's sentencing demand themselves by throwing a pair of dice. After working through all the materials and after indicating whether the prosecutor's and the defense attorney's demands were too high, too low, or just right, participants did not however report a sentencing decision. Instead, they worked on a categorization task that was designed to measure the accessibility of incriminating and exculpatory arguments.

In this categorization task, participants were exposed to a series of brief statements denoting incriminating and exculpatory arguments for the shoplifting case. For each of these statements, they had to indicate as fast as possible whether it corresponded to an incriminating or an exculpatory argument in the context of the present case. Participants thus categorized the given statements as incriminating or exculpatory by pressing either the right or the left

This is a fascinating idea, and it makes for an interesting experiment. Is it the case that the nature of an anchor (high vs. low) biases the types of arguments that are accessible to the subject when deciding on a sentencing recommendation?

If I am exposed to a high anchor, will that tend to bias me toward selectively giving more weight to incriminating evidence and less weight to exculpatory evidence?

Ctrl key on the computer board. The material consisted of 7 incriminating and 7 exculpatory arguments. These 14 arguments were pretested with a group of legal professionals ($N = 48$) who rated the relevance of each argument for the specific case. A selective accessibility effect should be most apparent for relevant arguments. Therefore, we selected the 4 incriminating arguments and 4 exculpatory arguments with the highest mean relevance ratings as our critical stimuli for the categorization task. The 4 critical incriminating arguments were previous convictions, violation of probation, persistent offender, and rapid subsequent offenses. The 4 critical exculpatory arguments were diminished responsibility, insignificance, kleptomania, and willingness to undergo therapy. The remaining 6 arguments that were of low relevance for the given case were used as filler items.

In the instructions to this task, participants were first informed about the ostensible purpose of the task, namely, to assess their current ability to concentrate by measuring their response latencies to material related to the case they had just worked on. Specifically, participants would be exposed to a series of brief statements that they should categorize as incriminating or exculpatory as fast and as accurately as possible. To that end, they should keep their left and right index fingers on the corresponding response keys throughout the task and should focus on a fixation point that was presented in the center of the computer screen. The fixation point was presented for 1,500 milliseconds and was overwritten by the target statement, which remained on the screen until participants had made their categorization decision. This sequence was repeated for all 14 statements. Presentation order was determined at random.

After completion of the categorization task, participants provided some demographic information, were debriefed and thanked for their participation. In the context of Study 4, we thus did not ask participants to provide sentencing decisions. The reason for this is that the categorization task we used to assess the accessibility of incriminating and exculpatory arguments simultaneously manipulated the accessibility of these arguments. Specifically, by presenting participants with anchor-consistent and anchor-inconsistent arguments, the categorization task provided them with judgment relevant information that is likely to directly influence subsequent judgments. In fact, previous research has demonstrated that manipulations of knowledge accessibility that are independent of the anchor manipulation influence target judgments (e.g., Chapman & Johnson, 1999; Mussweiler et al., 2000). In light of these findings, anchoring effects that were obtained subsequent to the categorization task would be difficult to interpret. Because of these ambiguities and because Studies 1 through 3 clearly demonstrated the judgmental influences that irrelevant anchors have in the judicial context, we focused exclusively on the selective accessibility consequences of irrelevant anchors in Study 4.

Results and Discussion

As suggested by Fazio (1990), we excluded response latencies that deviated by more than 3 standard deviations from the argument mean as outliers. The means given in Figure 2 provide substantial support for our hypothesis. As expected, incriminating arguments were categorized faster by participants who were exposed to a high rather than to a low sentencing demand, $t(55) = 2.03$, $p < .05$. In contrast, response latencies to exculpatory arguments did not depend on the anchoring condition, $t(55) < 1$. In a 2 (exculpatory vs. incriminating argument) × 2 (high vs. low anchor) mixed-model ANOVA with argument valence as a within factor and anchor as a between factor, this pattern produced a significant interaction effect,

$F(1, 55) = 5.23$, $p < .03$. In this analysis, none of the main effects reached significance, with $F < 1.5$, $p >$ for the main effect of the anchor on response times, and $F < 2.2$, $p > .1$ for the main effect of the argument valence showing slightly shorter reaction times for incriminating arguments.

These findings indicate that processing a random sentencing anchor leads to a selective increase in the accessibility of anchor-consistent arguments. Participants who were exposed to the high anchor were subsequently able to categorize incriminating arguments faster than participants who were exposed to a low sentencing anchor. Notably, categorizations of exculpatory arguments did not depend on the anchoring condition. Although this lack of an effect for exculpatory arguments is surprising at first sight, it is understandable in the light of research demonstrating that information with negative valence often carries more weight than information with positive valence (see Rozin & Royzman, 2001). In general, negative information receives more attention and seems to obtain priority in processing. This is apparent for example in the fact that negative words are detected more easily than positive words (Dijksterhuis & Aarts, 2003). The priority of negative information is also a potent influence on person judgment. For example, judgments about the moral qualities of a person are more strongly influenced by negative than positive deeds (Reeder & Brewer, 1979). In light of this research, it makes sense that our legal experts focused primarily on the incriminating arguments when processing the anchor value. This tendency is likely to be further strengthened by the fact that in the legal domain, judges' task is to determine whether the defendant is guilty beyond reasonable doubt. Because the defendant's guilt is primarily determined by the incriminating arguments, judges may focus more on incriminating than on exculpatory arguments. The extent to which judges focus on incriminating arguments however further depends on how compatible these arguments are with judges' processing objectives. Just as negative information is particularly attention grabbing if it is compatible with judges' processing objectives

The results from experiment 4, and illustrated in Figure 2 below, show that when one is exposed to a high anchor, they are faster at cognitively processing information consistent with a higher sentence. In this case, incriminating evidence that would support a higher sentence. It is almost as the individual is searching for information to justify the high anchor. We might also then assume that being exposed to a low anchor would make one predisposed to more quickly process information that is exculpatory, but the data don't support that prediction.

FIGURE 2

Response latencies (milliseconds) for categorizations of incriminating versus exculpatory arguments by judges who had been exposed to a high versus low sentencing demand (Study 4).

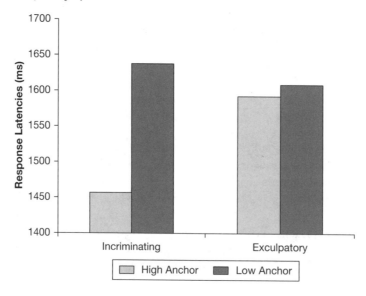

(Neumann & Strack, 2000), incriminating arguments will receive more attention if they are compatible with the hypothesis judges test while processing a given anchor. Incriminating arguments thus receive the most attention and are consequently most accessible if a high sentencing anchor was processed. As a consequence, the selective accessibility effect becomes apparent for these incriminating arguments.

GENERAL DISCUSSION

Judicial sentencing decisions should be guided by facts, not by chance. On normative grounds, the sentences that criminal judges impose should be immune to random influences. In the present research we have examined whether one particular random influence, namely, exposure to random numbers, has an effect on legal decisions. More specifically, we have investigated whether irrelevant anchor values that were obviously determined at random may influence sentencing decisions of legal professionals. Our results demonstrate that this is indeed the case. Using two different sets of case materials and different populations of legal experts as participants, our results demonstrate that blatantly irrelevant sentencing anchors influenced the sentencing decisions of legal experts. In Study 1, legal professionals were influenced by potential sentences that were suggested by a journalist's question during a telephone call—a source that clearly should be irrelevant on normative grounds. In the remaining three studies, the prosecutor's sentencing demands were even more clearly irrelevant. Specifically, in Study 2 participants were explicitly told that the provided sentencing demand was determined at random. Still, these potential sentences served as judgmental anchors and influenced the subsequent sentencing decisions of experienced legal professionals. Our final two studies went even further to ensure that sentencing demands were clearly irrelevant. Using a set of loaded dice, in Studies 3 and 4 our participants randomly determined the sentencing demands of the prosecutor themselves. Even though this procedure ensured that our participants were aware of the irrelevance of the sentencing demands, their sentencing decisions were dramatically influenced by them.

Notably, this influence of irrelevant anchors on sentencing decisions did not depend on judges' experience and expertise. Our analyses indicate that legal professionals who were experts in criminal law and had considerable experience in similar legal cases were influenced by irrelevant sentencing demands in much the same way as legal professionals who were experts in other aspects of law and had no actual experience with similar cases.

Furthermore, our analyses reveal that irrelevant sentencing anchors produce effects that are comparable in magnitude to those of relevant sentencing anchors. Thus, an anchor that participants randomly determined themselves by throwing a set of dice influences their sentencing decisions to a similar extent as the sentencing demand of a prosecutor.

Finally, the results of Study 4 suggest that these random influences on sentencing decisions involve mechanisms of selective accessibility. Considering a high irrelevant sentencing demand selectively makes incriminating arguments accessible. Because the final sentencing decision is then strongly influenced by those arguments that come to mind easily, this ultimately leads to higher sentencing decisions.

This research has a number of important implications for research on legal decision making as well as for research on judgmental anchoring. Research on legal decision making has repeatedly demonstrated that sentencing decisions are influenced by factors that—on normative grounds—are irrelevant and should thus not have any effect (e.g., Blair, Judd, & Chapleau,

Main finding of all 4 experiments. This is very interesting and has clear implications for the legal system. It illustrates that judges' sentencing decisions can often be swayed by irrelevant information.

2004; Lieberman, 2002). The present research demonstrates that sentencing decisions are even open to completely random influences. Random numbers may serve as anchors to which sentencing decisions are assimilated.

Previous research has shown that anchoring effects constitute a strong influence on legal decisions in general (e.g., Chapman & Bornstein, 1996; Hastie et al., 1999) and on criminal sentencing decisions in particular (Englich & Mussweiler, 2001). In this previous work however, the anchors that were given could be seen as providing relevant information about the judgment to be made. The present studies extend this work in at least two ways. First, they demonstrate that anchors that are clearly irrelevant because they were randomly determined still influence legal decisions. Second, they show that experienced experts in the specific sentencing domain are as susceptible to this influence as nonexperts. Thus, it is not only legal laypeople serving as jury members (e.g., Chapman & Bornstein, 1996) who are influenced by a given anchor. Experienced criminal judges who have worked on many related cases and have made many related sentencing decisions were still influenced by a sentencing demand that was determined by throwing a set of dice.

What are the implications of these findings for real-world court cases? Even though judges typically do not throw dice before making sentencing decisions, they are still constantly exposed to potential sentences and anchors during sentencing decisions. The mass media, visitors to the court hearings, the private opinion of the judge's partner, family, or neighbors are all possible sources of sentencing demands that should not influence a given sentencing decision. As the results of Study 1 demonstrate however, such authentic but normatively irrelevant anchors influence sentencing decisions as well as random anchors. Furthermore, random numbers that have been made accessible in an unrelated context may also be used as anchors for sentencing decisions. It has been demonstrated that numbers that were made accessible by extensive use in a prior task (Wilson et al., 1996) may influence judgments in much the same way as anchors that arise in the judgmental context itself. This suggests that sentencing decisions may also be influenced by irrelevant anchors that simply happen to be uppermost in a judge's mind when making a sentencing decision. The fact that random numbers may influence sentencing decisions—as our research demonstrates—suggests that irrelevant influences on sentencing decisions may be a widespread phenomenon.

In addition to these implications for legal decision making, the present studies also provide a number of important novel insights into the anchoring phenomenon. First, they demonstrate that the influence of random anchors is not limited to the psychological laboratory. To date, the influence of random anchors has only been demonstrated with judgments for which participants had little background knowledge, little experience, and little motivation to provide an accurate answer (Mussweiler & Strack, 2000a; Tversky & Kahneman, 1974). The judgments we examined in the present studies markedly differ from these earlier demonstrations. Specifically, the sentencing decisions we have focused on are more clearly structured in that decision criteria, procedural norms, and sentencing ranges are prescribed by the law. Furthermore, as legal professionals, our participants had received extensive training in the critical judgment domain, had considerable experience in making similar sentencing decisions, and were motivated to provide an accurate judgment. Still, they were influenced by random numbers even if they determined these numbers themselves by throwing dice.

Second, the present findings extend previous work examining anchoring influences on expert judgment in important ways. These previous studies (e.g., Joyce & Biddle, 1981;

What the findings mean for research on anchoring in social cognition.

Mussweiler et al., 2000; Northcraft & Neale, 1987; Wright & Anderson, 1989) have all examined the influence of anchors that may be seen as providing relevant information, such as the listing price of a house (Northcraft & Neale, 1987), a number provided by the experimenter (Joyce & Biddle, 1981), or a suggested selling price for a car (Mussweiler et al., 2000). As a consequence, these demonstrations of anchoring in expert judgment may simply be the result of experts' ability to make efficient use of relevant information. To our knowledge, evidence demonstrating that experts are influenced by truly irrelevant anchors has not been reported to date. In fact, one may well argue that experts are particularly likely to remain uninfluenced by irrelevant anchors. After all, experts have ample knowledge about the target domain that they could use to retrieve or construct a more relevant anchor. An experienced legal expert who has to determine a sentence in a case of rape for example may easily think back to similar cases and use the given sentences as anchors for the present sentencing decision. In this situation, a randomly determined number that is clearly irrelevant seems unlikely to have an effect. The present research however demonstrates that despite their experience and knowledge, expert judges are influenced by randomly determined anchors. In this respect, the present studies are the first to demonstrate that expert judgments are influenced by clearly irrelevant anchors. In addition, the present findings demonstrate that whereas experts are as susceptible to anchoring influences as novices, they feel more certain about their judgments. Expertise thus does make a difference. Ironically however, this difference is only apparent in the subjective not the objective quality of the judgment.

Furthermore, this research allows us to directly compare the magnitude of anchoring effects that are produced by relevant and irrelevant anchors. Previous research has demonstrated that anchors that are clearly irrelevant because they were selected at random influence judgments (e.g., Cervone & Peake, 1986; Mussweiler & Strack, 2000a; Tversky & Kahneman, 1974). The present studies demonstrate that such clearly irrelevant anchors produce anchoring effects of similar magnitude as clearly relevant anchors.

Finally, the present research provides important insights into the psychological mechanisms that underlie anchoring. We have suggested that anchoring effects are produced by a selective increase in the accessibility of anchor-consistent information about the judgmental target. Our previous research has supported this notion (for an overview, see Mussweiler & Strack, 2001). The results of Study 4 supplement this former work in two important ways. First, they suggest that selective accessibility also plays a role in anchoring effects in information-rich contexts where judges have ample knowledge about the judgmental target. One may well expect that exposure to an anchor value may only change the accessibility of target knowledge if judges rarely activate such knowledge. Knowledge that is at the core of judges' expertise however and that is consequently used on an almost daily basis may be so chronically accessible that it is difficult to further increase its accessibility by exposure to an anchor. The present findings however demonstrate that selective accessibility effects are also obtained for experienced judges who have ample background knowledge about the judgment to be made. This further emphasizes the ubiquity of the selective accessibility mechanism. Second, the results of Study 4 demonstrate that selective accessibility effects also result from exposure to randomly determined anchors. In this respect, the present findings suggest that selective accessibility may contribute to the effects of relevant and irrelevant anchors in a variety of judgmental settings.

Within and beyond the legal domain, irrelevant anchors may stem from different sources. They may be explicitly provided, subtly suggested, self-generated, simply coming to mind, or determined by throwing dice. As the present findings suggest, sentencing decisions may be influenced in all of these cases. God may not play dice with the universe—as Albert Einstein reassured us. But judges may unintentionally play dice with criminal sentences.

(drops mic)

NOTES

1. Congruent with the typical methodological approach to the study of anchoring effects, our analyses focused on judges' sentencing decisions and mostly ignored responses to the comparative anchoring question. Recent research has demonstrated that oftentimes anchoring effects occur no matter whether a comparative question is or is not asked. For example, subliminal presentation of an anchor value yields similar effects as including this value in a comparative question (Mussweiler & Englich, 2005). A supplemental analysis of our data indicates that answers to the comparative question and sentencing decisions were correlated, $r = .35$, $p < .03$. The more judges' answers to the comparative question imply a high sentence, the higher their actual sentencing decision.

2. Answers to the comparative anchoring question and sentencing decisions were again correlated, $r = .5$, $p < .001$.

3. As in Studies 1 and 2, answers to the comparative anchoring question and sentencing decisions were correlated, $r = .44$, $p < .001$.

REFERENCES

Blair, I. V., Judd, C. M., & Chapleau, K. M. (2004). The influence of afrocentric facial features in criminal sentencing. *Psychological Science, 15*, 674–678.

Bodenhausen, G. (1990). Stereotypes as judgmental heuristics: Evidence of circadian variations in discrimination. *Psychological Science, 1*, 319–322.

Cervone, D., & Peake, P. K. (1986). Anchoring, efficacy, and action: The influence of judgmental heuristics on self-efficacy judgments and behavior. *Journal of Personality and Social Psychology, 50*, 492–501.

Chapman, G. B., & Bornstein, B. H. (1996). The more you ask for, the more you get: Anchoring in personal injury verdicts. *Applied Cognitive Psychology, 10*, 519–540.

Chapman, G. B., & Johnson, E. J. (1999). Anchoring, activation, and the construction of values. *Organizational Behavior and Human Decision Processes, 79*, 1–39.

Chapman, G. B., & Johnson, E. J. (2002). Incorporating the irrelevant: Anchors in judgments of belief and value. In T. Gilovich, D. Griffith, & D. Kahneman (Eds.), *Heuristics and biases: The psychology of intuitive judgment* (pp. 120–138). Cambridge, UK: Cambridge University Press.

Dhami, M. K. (2003). Psychological models of professional decision making. *Psychological Science, 14*, 175–180.

Diamond, S. S. (1981). Exploring sources of sentence disparity. In B. D. Sales (Ed.), *The trial process: Perspectives in law and psychology* (Vol. 2, pp. 387–411). New York: Plenum.

Dijksterhuis, A., & Aarts, H. (2003). On wildebeests and humans: The preferential detection of negative stimuli. *Psychological Science, 14*, 14–18.

Dutton, D. G., & Aron, A. P. (1974). Some evidence for heightened sexual attraction under conditions of high anxiety. *Journal of Personality and Social Psychology, 30*, 510–517.

Ebbesen, E. B., & Konecni, V. J. (1981). The process of sentencing adult felons. In B. D. Sales (Ed.), *The trial process* (pp. 413–458). New York: Plenum.

Englich, B. (2006). *Order effects in the courtroom—The reason why the prosecution and the defense should change seats.* Unpublished manuscript, University of Würzburg.

Englich, B., & Mussweiler, T. (2001). Sentencing under uncertainty: Anchoring effects in the court room. *Journal of Applied Social Psychology, 31*, 1535–1551.

Englich, B., Mussweiler, T., & Strack, F. (2005). The last word in court—A hidden disadvantage for the defense. *Law and Human Behavior, 29*.

Epley, N. (2004). A tale of tuned desks? Anchoring as accessibility and anchoring as adjustments. In D. J. Koehler & N. Harvey (Eds.), *The Blackwell handbook of judgment and decision making* (pp. 240–256). Oxford, UK: Blackwell.

Epley, N., & Gilovich, T. (2001). Putting adjustment back in the anchoring and adjustment heuristic: Differential processing of self-generated and experimenter-provided anchors. *Psychological Science, 12,* 391–396.

Fazio, R. H. (1990). A practical guide to the use of response latency in social psychological research. In C. Hendrick & M. S. Clark (Eds.), *Research methods in personality and social psychology* (pp. 74–97). Newbury Park, CA: Sage.

Hastie, R., Schkade, D. A., & Payne, J. W. (1999). Juror judgment in civil cases: Effects of plaintiff's requests and plaintiff's identity on punitive damage awards. *Law and Human Behavior, 23,* 445–470.

Hogarth, J. (1971). *Sentencing as a human process.* Toronto, Canada: University of Toronto Press.

Hynie, M., Schuller, R. A., & Couperthwaite, L. (2003). Perceptions of sexual intent: The impact of condom possession. *Psychology of Women Quarterly, 27,* 75–79.

Joyce, E. J., & Biddle, G. C. (1981). Anchoring and adjustment in probabilistic inference in auditing. *Journal of Accounting Research, 19,* 120-145.

Krahé, B. (1991). Social psychological issues in the study of rape. In W. Stroebe & M. Hewstone (Eds.), *European review of social psychology* (Vol. 2, pp. 279–309). Chichester, UK: Wiley.

Lieberman, J. L. (2002). Head over the heart or heart over the head? Cognitive experiential self-theory and extralegal heuristics in juror decision making. *Journal of Applied Social Psychology, 32,* 2526–2553.

Malouff, J., & Schutte, N. S. (1989). Shaping juror attitudes: Effects of requesting different damage amounts in personal injury trials. *Journal of Social Psychology, 129,* 491–497.

Marti, M. W., & Wissler, R. L. (2000). Be careful what you ask for: The effects of anchors on personal injury damages awards. *Journal of Experimental Psychology: Applied, 6,* 91–103.

Mussweiler, T., & Englich, B. (2005). Subliminal anchoring: Judgmental consequences and underlying mechanisms. *Organizational Behavior and Human Decision Processes, 98,* 133–143.

Mussweiler, T., Englich, B., & Strack, F. (2004). Anchoring effect. In R. Pohl (Ed.), *Cognitive illusions—A handbook on fallacies and biases in thinking, judgment, and memory* (pp. 183–200). London: Psychology Press.

Mussweiler, T., & Strack, F. (1999a). Comparing is believing: A selective accessibility model of judgmental anchoring. In W. Stroebe & M. Hewstone (Eds.), *European review of social psychology* (Vol. 10, pp. 135–167). Chichester, UK: Wiley.

Mussweiler, T., & Strack, F. (1999b). Hypothesis-consistent testing and semantic priming in the anchoring paradigm: A selective accessibility model. *Journal of Experimental Social Psychology, 35,* 136–164.

Mussweiler, T., & Strack, F. (2000a). Numeric judgments under uncertainty: The role of knowledge in anchoring. *Journal of Experimental Social Psychology, 36,* 495–518.

Mussweiler, T., & Strack, F. (2000b). The use of category and exemplar knowledge in the solution of anchoring tasks. *Journal of Personality and Social Psychology, 78,* 1038–1052.

Mussweiler, T., & Strack, F. (2001). The semantics of anchoring. *Organizational Behavior and Human Decision Processes, 86,* 234–255.

Mussweiler, T., Strack, F., & Pfeiffer, T. (2000). Overcoming the inevitable anchoring effect: Considering the opposite compensates for selective accessibility. *Personality and Social Psychology Bulletin, 26,* 1142–1150.

Neumann, R., & Strack, F. (2000). Approach and avoidance: The influence of proprioceptive and exteroceptive cues on encoding of affective information. *Journal of Personality and Social Psychology, 79,* 39–48.

Nisbett, R. E., & Wilson, T. D. (1977). Telling more than we can know: Verbal reports on mental processes. *Psychological Review, 84,* 231–259.

Northcraft, G. B., & Neale, M. A. (1987). Expert, amateurs, and real estate: An anchoring-and-adjustment perspective on property pricing decisions. *Organizational Behavior and Human Decision Processes, 39,* 228–241.

Partridge, A., & Eldridge, W. B. (1974). *The second circuit sentencing study.* Washington, DC: Federal Judicial Center.

Reeder, G. D., & Brewer, M. B. (1979). A schematic model of dispositional attribution in interpersonal perception. *Psychological Review, 86,* 61–79.

Rozin, P., & Royzman, E. B. (2001). Negativity bias, negativity dominance, and contagion. *Personality and Social Psychology Review, 5,* 296–320.

Schuller, R. A., & Stewart, A. (2000). Police responses to sexual assault complaints: The role of perpetrator/complainant intoxication. *Law and Human Behavior, 24,* 535–551.

Strack, F., & Mussweiler, T. (1997). Explaining the enigmatic anchoring effect: Mechanisms of selective accessibility. *Journal of Personality and Social Psychology, 73,* 437–446.

Tversky, A., & Kahneman, D. (1974). Judgment under uncertainty: Heuristics and biases. *Science, 185,* 1124–1131.

Wilson, T. D., & Brekke, N. (1994). Mental contamination and mental correction: Unwanted influences on judgments and evaluations. *Psychological Bulletin, 116,* 117–142.

Wilson, T. D., Houston, C., Etling, K. M., & Brekke, N. (1996). A new look at anchoring effects: Basic anchoring and its antecedents. *Journal of Experimental Psychology: General, 4,* 387–402.

Wright, W. F., & Anderson, U. (1989). Effects of situation familiarity and financial incentives on use of the anchoring and adjustment heuristic for probability assessment. *Organizational Behavior and Human Decision Processes, 44,* 68–82.

POST-ARTICLE DISCUSSION

As we discussed earlier, one of the strengths of this paper is that it seeks to understand the limits of a cognitive bias that could have important effects on real-world decision making that can directly change the course of people's lives. Specifically, the researchers want to know if our susceptibility to the anchoring effect is controllable. If it is really important for you to NOT succumb to the anchoring effect, and try to be as objective and rational as possible, can you do it? We like to think that we have complete control over our cognitive output and the information that affects our decision making, but decades of social cognition research has instead revealed that our thinking is often biased and anything but rational (Kunda 1999; Kahneman, Slovic, & Tversky, 1982). In fact, one might say that "normal" cognition is rife with error and bias.

Curiously, in the legal field, the law appears to be unaware of this bias. For example, juries and judges often put a lot of weight on eyewitness testimony and memory, under the assumption that the witness was there at the crime scene so she must have the best information about the crime and perpetrator. As a result, tens of thousands of individuals are convicted of a crime based primarily or solely on eyewitness testimony (National Research Council, 2014). But much research suggests that, contrary to legal assumptions that our brains apparently work like flawless tape recorders, eyewitness memory is subject to all manner of biases and problems (Brewer & Wells, 2011).

Consider the research challenge the authors of these studies faced: how to design their experiments in a way that effectively addresses their goals of determining the extent to which irrelevant anchors bias sentencing decisions in legal professionals? So, for Study 1, who are our subjects? If you are the researcher, do you recruit college students (as is done in most studies) to make the judgments? Clearly no, because the purpose is to examine decision making among legal professionals. Next, how do you get the irrelevant anchor to the subject? What is one way in real life that judges might hear sentencing recommendations? Yes, reporters and news media might pose such opinions on the case. They clearly have no judicial expertise, and the legal professional knows that, so their opinions shouldn't influence the subject's decision, but they clearly did. What if (as in Study 2) we tell the legal professional that the prosecutor's recommendation (another main source of sentencing anchors) is purely randomly determined? Would that blatant, overt announcement of the irrelevant nature of the recommendation be enough to let the legal professional disregard it in their own sentencing? Again, the amazing answer appears to be no.

Recall that we have discussed that one of the main reasons a study fails to find an effect is that the IV is too weak. Researchers in this paper were concerned that perhaps the legal professionals in Study 2 didn't really appreciate the random nature of the sentencing recommendation from the prosecutor. So, in Study 3, they made this even clearer by having the subject randomly determine the sentencing anchors by rolling dice. Amazingly, high anchors (higher dice rolls) caused judges to give higher sentences, compared to those exposed to low anchors. Wow! Finally, the researchers examined the extent to which an anchor could bias cognitive accessibility to incriminating versus exculpatory evidence. The researchers address this via a clever response-latency method whereby, following the presentation of an anchor, participants were asked to make a judgment for each evidence item: Is this incriminating evidence or exculpatory evidence? (Participants hit Y or N key on the computer as fast as possible.) To the degree that participants hit the key faster, we would say that they are able to process that particular type of information faster. The speed in processing is thereby assumed to be caused by the prior anchor to which one was exposed. As you will recall, Study 4 indicated that exposure to a random high anchor made the participant able to categorize incriminating arguments faster. This, therefore, may be one reason, one cognitive avenue, by which the anchor biases sentencing recommendations in legal professionals.

This program of experiments nicely illustrates how researchers can address a problem from a number of angles, each study tackling a different aspect of the issue, such that, at the conclusion, we have a compelling series of conclusions and some replications within the experiments. The multiexperiment article has been the standard in social psychology for some time now (starting roughly in the late 1970s), and some argue that one of the benefits of this is that it advances science faster. Another major feature of these studies is that their conclusions are easily directly applied to a real-world context, and this practical application can change the way judges make their sentencing decisions, toward a more objective, less biased process. Kurt Lewin would be proud.

THINGS TO THINK ABOUT

1. To what degree do you believe that judges are influenced by media or public sentiment regarding an appropriate sentence for a defendant?

2. Study 1 found that the legal background and expertise of the outside sentence recommender had no differential effect on judges: They were equally influenced by experts and nonexperts. This was true in Study 2 even when subjects knew that the others' sentence was randomly determined. Study 2 showed that experts are more certain about their sentencing decision. Why do you suppose that is?

(Continued)

(Continued)

3. Study 3 revealed that legal experts who determined the sentencing guidelines by rolling dice were STILL influenced by those random anchors when they made their sentences. What do you think is going on here, when an expert is letting a serious decision be influenced by random numbers?

4. In Study 4, the researchers found that when subjects were asked to think about a high anchor, it facilitated their processing of incriminating evidence against the defendant. It is alarming to think that merely thinking about a high anchor number can bias our processing of subsequent information that may help (or hurt) the defendant when it comes to findings of guilt or innocence and sentencing. What do the results of these four studies suggest about the power of anchoring?

5. What are some ways judges could avoid being influenced by random anchors (or irrelevant anchors)?

6. How else might random anchors affect people in daily life?

INTRODUCTION TO READING 3.2
Medvec et al. (1995)

In social cognition, much research has focused on the interplay between the way we think and how we feel (Fiske & Taylor, 2008; Kunda, 1999). The way we think can be determined by how we feel, as when an employer decides between two applicants who are evenly qualified, but applicant A's interview was in the morning, and applicant B's interview was after lunch (during which the employer met up with a close relative she rarely sees). The employer hires applicant B because she has a more positive affective association with that person (to which she attributes better qualified applicant) compared to applicant A. Also, the way we think can determine how we feel, as in the case of counterfactual thinking. This is defined as *thinking about what might have been*. It is the "if only" situations we think about, usually after a negative event. For example, after a car accident, you may say, "If only I had left home 5 minutes earlier, I wouldn't have been hit by that truck."

There are two main routes whereby our cognitive undoing of an event influences our mood. First, the more ways we can mentally undo an event, the stronger our affective reaction will be to it. In my lectures, I use the *Titanic* to illustrate this. The loss of 1,500 people when the *Titanic* sunk was indeed a monumental tragedy. But what makes it even more tragic, and even haunting, is that there were so many aspects of that event, that if even one of them had happened, those people would not have died. I'll just list a few: The ship didn't have enough lifeboats for the number of passengers. The "watertight" compartments below decks were not watertight; their walls didn't go to the ceiling, and water just poured in from the iceberg tear into one compartment and into the next over the walls as if one were filling an ice cube tray. A nearby ship, the *Californian*, only 15 miles away, saw the distress rockets of the *Titanic* and did not turn around and go rescue the passengers. There are about 20 more things we could discuss, but you get the point.

The other major aspect of counterfactual thinking is that, when the event occurs, our affective reaction is determined by what almost happened but didn't. Exam grades are a good example to illustrate this. Suppose you just barely get a C on an exam. The most salient alternative outcome is "getting a D." But you didn't get a D, you got a C, so you feel good about that C. Now, what if you got the same C grade, but it was one point away from a B. Now, the most salient alternative outcome is "getting a B." But you didn't get that higher grade, and thus you feel negatively. In each case, it is the same grade—a C—but how you think about and feel about it is determined by the counterfactuals most prominent in your mind.

Now, if you want to experimentally study counterfactual thinking, what would be the best way to approach your design so that you have the best chance at testing your hypotheses? One of the first problems in any experiment is how to create the strongest IV possible. Perhaps one of the most common reasons an experiment may not yield significant results is that the IVs were too weak. So, we can certainly create negative outcomes in the lab for a subject and see how they generate counterfactuals. But these negative events are likely to be fairly mild (due to ethical constraints), so the motive to generate counterfactuals and the affective strength following those counterfactuals are likely to be weak.

In the first two of three studies, Medvec and her colleagues elected to study counterfactual thinking by examining the verbal counterfactuals and affective expressions in Olympic athletes on the winner's podium. This is a clever way to assess what has to be one of the strongest situations that can generate counterfactuals: a lifetime of training for one race or event. Anything less than first place would have to result in tremendous counterfactual thinking and negative affect, right? I won't ruin the surprise for you but instead ask that, as you read this outstanding paper, you still approach it with a critical eye and try to identify its strengths and weaknesses in design. Are there any limitations to the study that haven't been addressed? OK, now on to the paper. Enjoy, and we'll chat afterward!

Reading 3.2

When Less Is More: Counterfactual Thinking and Satisfaction Among Olympic Medalists

Victoria Husted Medvec

Scott F. Madey

Thomas Gilovich

One of the most intriguing phenonema social psychologists study is "counterfactual thinking." It is thinking about what might have been. We usually do this after a negative event has happened. The more we can mentally undo an event, the stronger our affective reaction to the event.

In this study, Medvec and her colleagues wondered how Olympic athletes would react when they win gold, win silver, or win bronze? Would they engage in counterfactual thinking?

This quote from the writing of William James, regarded as the father of American psychology, shows his prescience. He was a man ahead of his time, and much of what he wrote was later shown to be correct. Here he describes counterfactual thinking.

Research on counterfactual thinking has shown that people's emotional responses to events are influenced by their thoughts about "what might have been." The authors extend these findings by documenting a familiar occasion in which those who are objectively better off nonetheless feel worse. In particular, an analysis of the emotional reactions of bronze and silver medalists at the 1992 Summer Olympics—both at the conclusion of their events and on the medal stand—indicates that bronze medalists "tend to be happier than silver medalists. The authors attribute these results to the fact that the most compelling counterfactual alternative for the silver medalist is winning the gold, whereas for the bronze medalist it is finishing without a medal. Support for this interpretation was obtained from the 1992 Olympics and the 1994 Empire State Games. The discussion focuses on the implications of endowment and contrast for well being.

So we have the paradox of a man shamed to death because he is only the second pugilist or the second oarsman in the world. That he is able to beat the whole population of the globe minus one is nothing; he has "pitted" himself to beat that one; and as long as he doesn't do that nothing else counts. (James, 1892, p. 186)

James's (1892) observation represents an early statement of a fundamental principle of psychology: A person's objective achievements often matter less than how those accomplishments

Victoria Husted Medvec and Thomas Gilovich, Department of Psychology, Cornell University; Scott F. Madey, Department of Psychology, University of Toledo.

This research was supported in part by grants from the National Institute of Mental Health (MH45531) and the National Science Foundation (SBR9319558).

We would like to thank Todd Bickford, Theresa Buckley, Nancy De Hart, Deborah Fidler, Nina Hattiangadi, Allison Himmelfarb, Elena Jeffries, Danielle Kaplan, Talia Korenbrot, Renae Murphy, Sara Sirlin, and Shane Steele for their help in editing the videotapes and collecting data.

Correspondence concerning this article should be addressed to Thomas Gilovich, Department of Psychology, Uris Hall, Cornell University, Ithaca, New York 14853–7601.

are subjectively construed. Being one of the best in the world can mean little if it is coded not as a triumph over many, but as a loss to one. Being second best may not be as gratifying as perhaps it should.

Since James's time, of course, this idea has been both theoretically enriched and extensively documented. Social psychologists have shown that people's satisfaction with their objective circumstances is greatly affected by how their own circumstances compare with those of relevant others (Festinger, 1954; Suls & Miller, 1977; Taylor & Lobel, 1989). A 5% merit raise can be quite exhilarating until one learns that the person down the hall received an 8% increase. Psychologists have also demonstrated that satisfaction with an outcome likewise depends on how it compares with a person's original expectations (Atkinson, 1964; Feather, 1967, 1969). Someone who receives a 5% raise might be happier than someone who receives an 8% increase if the former expected less than the latter. Often it is the *difference* between the actual outcome and the expected outcome, or the actual outcome and the outcomes of others, that is decisive (Crosby, 1976; Olson, Herman, & Zanna, 1986).

More recently, psychologists have discovered a third way in which the determinants of satisfaction are relative. In particular, people seem to be greatly affected by how their objective outcomes compare to imagined outcomes that "might have been" (Kahneman & Miller, 1986; Kahneman & Tversky, 1982b; Markman, Gavanski, Sherman, & McMullen, 1993; Miller, Turnbull, & McFarland, 1990; Roese, 1994; Roese & Olson, in press). The intensity of people's reactions to events appears to be proportional to how easy it is to conjure up greater or lesser outcomes that "almost happened." An 8% return on one's investment might exceed expectations and yet be disappointing if one is reminded of an alternative investment one "almost" made that yielded a substantially higher return. The critical comparison in this case is a post computed response to what has occurred, rather than a precomputed representation of what seems likely, *ex ante,* to occur (Kahneman & Miller, 1986).

Most of the research on counterfactual thinking has held outcome constant and examined the reactions of people contemplating different counterfactual alternatives. For example, Kahneman and Tversky (1982b) asked their participants to imagine the reactions of two travellers who both missed their scheduled flights, one by 5 minutes and the other by 30 minutes. The outcome is the same—both must wait for the next flight-but it is easier to imagine a counterfactual world in which the first traveller arrives on time. Studies such as this have repeatedly shown that the same outcome can produce strikingly different reactions as a function of the ease of generating various counterfactual alternatives (Johnson, 1986; Kahneman & Miller, 1986; Kahneman & Tversky, 1982a, 1982b; Miller & McFarland, 1986; Miller et al., 1990; Turnbull, 1981; Wells & Gavanski, 1989).

We wished to take this a step further. We were interested in whether the effects of different counterfactual comparisons are sufficiently strong to cause people who are objectively *worse* off to sometimes feel better than those in a superior state. Moreover, we were interested not just in documenting isolated episodes in which this might happen, but in identifying a specific situation in which it occurs with regularity and predictability. The domain we chose to investigate was athletic competition.

We chose this domain of investigation because in athletic competition outcomes are typically defined with unusual precision. Someone finishes first, second, or third, for example, thereby earning a gold, silver, or bronze medal. With all else equal, one would expect the athletes' levels of satisfaction to mirror this objective order. We suspected, however, that all else

Let's say that whenever you are out driving, you never pick up hitchhikers. Let's further suppose that your friend Mark always picks up hitchhikers. Let's say that one day, you decide to pick up a hitchhiker and that person beats you and steals your car. Let's say that by some weird coincidence, the same thing happens to Mark on the same day. Who will feel worse: you or Mark? If we engage in counterfactual thinking in your case, it is fairly easy to mentally undo the bad event: if you had just stuck to your rule, you never would have been beaten and robbed. But your friend Mark cannot mentally undo his outcome so easily. He ALWAYS picks up hitchhikers, so . . . perhaps this bad event was bound to happen. So yes, you would feel worse. Have you ever wondered why people try to comfort someone in a tragic event by saying "there was nothing you could have done to prevent it"? They are trying to help the person not engage in counterfactual thinking, and in so doing, help them reduce/temper their pain/sadness.

One of the many strengths of this study is that it goes further than the common method of having subjects imagine counterfactual scenarios. There often is a difference in what we THINK we would do and what we actually do in a given situation. So, the researchers examined counterfactual thinking in Olympic athletes via videotapes of their interviews immediately after the event, analysis of their body language in the interviews, and also the affective reactions of the athletes on the winners podium.

One might think that Olympic athletes on the winning podium would be in a mood commensurate with their medal: gold=happiest, silver=second happiest, and bronze=third happiest. But if one considers the counterfactual thinking each medalist feels, the affective results are actually quite different. The key here is to remember that the individual's mood is affected primarily by what almost happened, but didn't happen.

is not equal—that the nature of athletes' counterfactual thoughts might cause their levels of satisfaction to depart from this simple, linear order.

Consider the counterfactual thoughts of bronze and silver medalists. What might their most compelling counterfactual thoughts be? One would certainly expect the silver medalist to focus on almost winning the gold because there is a qualitative difference between coming in first and any other outcome. Each event has only one winner, and to that victor belongs the considerable spoils that the modern commercial-athletic world bestows (R. H. Frank & Cook, 1995). Moreover, for the silver medalist, this exalted status was only one step away. To be sure, the silver medalist also finished only one step from winning a bronze, but such a downward social comparison does not involve much of a change in status (i.e., neither the bronze nor silver medalist won the event, but both won medals), and thus does not constitute as much of a counterfactual temptation.

In contrast, bronze medalists are likely to focus their counterfactual thoughts downward. Like the qualitative jump between silver and gold, there is a categorical difference between finishing third and finishing fourth. Third place merits a medal whereas the fourth-place finisher is just one of the field. This type of categorical difference does not exist in the upward comparison between second and third place.

A good way to study something is to examine it from multiple vantage points. This is sometimes referred to as the Multi-Method Matrix. To the degree that one gets converging results from, say, conceptual, behavioral, and affective (or cognitive) approaches to the issue, we can be confident in the results.

Because of this asymmetry in the direction of counterfactual comparison, the person who is objectively worse off (the bronze medalist) might nonetheless feel more gratified than the person who is objectively better off (the silver medalist). Like William James's (1892) pugilist, silver medalists may torment themselves with counterfactual thoughts of "if only . . ." or "why didn't I just . . . ." Bronze medalists, in contrast, may be soothed by the thought that "at least I won a medal." The net result is that with respect to athletic competition, there may be times when less is more.

We conducted three studies to examine this question. First, we analyzed the affective reactions of bronze and silver medalists as they won their medals in the 1992 Olympic games in Barcelona, Spain. Second, we had participants evaluate the Olympians' postcompetition interviews to see whether silver medalists seemed to be focused on the medal they almost won whereas third-place finishers appeared to relish the pleasure simply of being medalists. In the third study, we asked athletes themselves about the nature of their counterfactual thoughts.

STUDY I

In psychological research, experimentally coding behavior (in real life, or in the lab, or, as in this case, via videotape) entails the researcher starting out with an objective set of criteria (a "codebook") that the researcher sets prior to rating the behavior, which details how one should interpret or rate a particular behavior. Then, once the researcher has rated a particular behavior, we would want to compare it to the ratings of two or more other researchers who are using the same codebook to rate that particular behavior. To the degree the ratings are similar (inter-rater reliability), we can have confidence that the behavior is showing what the researchers are saying that it is showing.

We videotaped all of the National Broadcasting Company (NBC) coverage of the 1992 Summer Olympic games in Barcelona, Spain. From this footage, two master tapes were constructed. The first showed the immediate reactions of all bronze and silver medalists that NBC chose to televise at the time the athletes learned how they had finished. Thus, the tape shows Janet Evans as she touched the wall of the pool and discovered she had come in second, and Jackie Joyner-Kersey after she completed her last long jump and earned a bronze medal. The second tape consisted of all bronze and silver medalists whom NBC showed on the medal stand during the award ceremony. For example, this tape shows Matt Biondi receiving a silver medal for his performance in the 50-m freestyle, and the Lithuanian men's basketball team (in uniforms designed by The Grateful Dead) after they received their bronze medals.

Each tape was shown to a separate group of participants who were asked to rate the expressed emotion of each athlete. Because of the asymmetry in the likely counterfactual comparisons of the bronze and silver medalists, we expected those who finished third to be demonstrably happier than those who finished second.

Hypothesis.

Method

Participants. Twenty Cornell University undergraduates served as participants. Only people who indicated they were uninterested in and uninformed about sports were recruited. This ensured that their ratings would not be affected by any pre-existing knowledge about the athletes or their performance in the Olympic games.

Stimulus materials. The tape of the athletes' immediate reactions included shots of 23 silver and 18 bronze medalists. Not surprisingly, given NBC's main audience, most of these shots (25) were of Americans. To create the master tape, we simply copied all footage of the finish and immediate aftermath of all silver and bronze medal winners. These shots tended to be rather brief ($M = 14.4$ s; $SD = 8.3$ s), and we stayed with the scene for as long as NBC did. Because the issue of what footage to include involved minimal judgment, we did the editing ourselves.

This was not the case for the medal stand videotape. Here there were too many editing decisions to be made. Should a shot of the athlete *leaving* the medal stand be included? Should a certain "head and shoulders" shot on the medal stand be included or not? To eliminate the possibility of our expectations guiding these editorial decisions, we turned the job over to someone unaware of our hypothesis. We identified all medal stand shots of second- and third-place finishers in NBC's coverage, and asked our editor to copy those moments that best captured the emotion that the athletes appeared to be feeling. This resulted in a master tape of 20 silver and 15 bronze medal winners. The average length of each shot was 14.7 s, with an SD of 13.8 s. In this case fewer than half of the shots (15) were of American athletes.[1]

To avoid experimenter expectancy effects, researchers can turn the task over to someone unfamiliar with the hypotheses (or the conditions in which the participant was run) so that they cannot systematically bias the subject or procedures.

FIGURE 1   Mean happiness ratings.

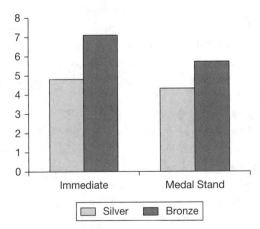

[1] The reason that Americans were not as overrepresented in this tape as they were in the other is that for many of our medal stand segments, it is the gold medal winner who is being featured by NBC and the silver and bronze medalists who are pictured incidentally. Thus, there were many instances in which NBC was focused on an American gold medalist, and we were able to capitalize on their ancillary coverage of a silver or bronze medalist from another country.

Two versions of each tape were created, with the order of presentation of the athletes varied across versions. Blank spaces were inserted between shots of the different athletes to provide participants with time to complete their ratings.

Procedure. Participants arrived at the laboratory in groups and were told that they would be watching a videotape of athletes from the 1992 Olympic games. They were informed that they were to rate the expressed emotions of each athlete on a 10-point "agony to ecstasy" scale. The participants were first asked to watch a few shots of athletes without making any ratings in order to give them an idea of the range of emotions shown on the tapes. After participants were familiar with the format of the videotape, the rating session commenced.

Five participants rated each version of each of the two videotapes. The tapes were shown without sound to eliminate the chance that commentators' remarks might affect their evaluations of the athletes' expressed emotions. A 1.5-inch (3.8 cm) strip of paper was affixed to the bottom of the video screen to occlude various graphics used by NBC to indicate the athlete's order of finish.

Results

Participants' ratings were highly reliable, for both the immediate-reactions videotape (Spearman-Brown index = .97) and the medal stand tape (Spearman-Brown index = .96). Thus, the ratings of all participants viewing the same tape were averaged to create an index of the happiness of each of the athletes. Preliminary analyses revealed no effect of order of presentation, so the data were collapsed across the two versions of each tape.

The mean happiness ratings are presented in Figure 1. As predicted, bronze medalists appeared happier on average than their counterparts who won silver medals. When assessing the athletes' immediate reactions, participants assigned the bronze medalists a mean happiness rating of 7.1 (SD = 2.0) but the silver medalists a mean rating of only 4.8 (SD = 1.9). When examining the athletes on the medal stand, participants assigned the bronze medalists a mean rating of 5.7 (SD = 1.7) and silver medalists a mean rating of only 4.3 (SD = 1.8).These data were analyzed with a 2 (type of medal: bronze vs. silver) × 2 (tape: immediate vs. medal stand) analysis of variance (ANOVA). This analysis revealed two significant main effects, but no interaction. The main effect of tape, $F(1, 72) = 4.78, p < .05$, indicates that the athletes on the whole looked happier immediately after their performances than when they were on the medal stand. More important, the main effect of type of medal, $F(1, 72) = 18.98, p < .001$, indicates that the athletes who finished third looked significantly happier than those who finished second.

There is a potential artifactual explanation of these results, however. In certain Olympic events, the competition is structured such that bronze medalists have just won a match or a game whereas silver medalists have just lost. A bronze medalist in wrestling, for example, would have just defeated the fourth place finisher, and the silver medalist would have just lost to the gold medal winner. We were concerned that being in the immediate aftermath of victory or defeat might have contaminated our comparison of bronze and silver medalists. Fortunately, most Olympic events (such as those in track, swimming, and gymnastics) are not structured in this way. In these events the athletes simply finish first, second, and third depending on how well they do.

To eliminate this "just won"–"just lost" artifact, we reanalyzed the data excluding all athletes involved in sports with this structure. This reduced our pool of 23 silver and 18 bronze

---

In this study, the subjects are rating the behavior of the athletes. In each rating, there are 5 raters, which is very good (the more raters the better).

Outstanding inter-rater reliability. This from a combination of having a clear codebook, good training for raters, and many raters.

Hypothesis confirmed.

All good scientists try to anticipate alternative explanations for one's results, and then do an experiment to show that the alternative explanation is not likely (and that one's prediction and theoretical explanation is more likely).

medalists in the immediate-reactions videotape to 20 and 15, respectively. Similarly, it reduced our pool of 20 silver and 15 bronze medalists in the medal-stand tape to 14 and 13, respectively. A 2 × 2 ANOVA of these data yielded the same significant main effect of type of medal as before, $F(1, 58) = 6.70$, $p < .02$. Bronze medalists appeared happier both immediately after their events ($M = 6.7$) and on the medal stand ($M = 5.6$) than their counterparts who had won silver medals ($Ms = 5.0$ and 4.7). Consistent with our thesis, impartial judges viewed bronze medalists as being happier than silver medalists, and this effect was not limited to those few events in which bronze and silver medalists were in the immediate aftermath of a victory or a defeat, respectively.[2]

Is there any other alternative interpretation of these data? Might these results be due to differences in the *ex ante* expectations of bronze and silver medalists rather than—as we propose—their *ex post* thoughts about what might have been? We think not. First of all, there is no reason to believe that bronze medalists as a whole tended to exceed their expectations or that silver medalists on average tended to fall short of theirs. To be sure, our sample of silver medalists probably entered the Olympics with higher expectations on average than our sample of bronze medalists, but they also *performed* better as well. There is certainly no compelling reason to believe that one group over or under-performed relative to their initial expectations.

This alternative interpretation can also be dismissed on empirical grounds. We obtained an unbiased measure of the athletes' likely expectations prior to the Olympics and then used a regression analysis to examine the effect of medal won (bronze or silver) after initial expectations were controlled statistically. The athletes' likely expectations were derived from *Sports Illustrated's* Olympic preview (Verschoth, 1992). *Sports Illustrated* predicted the likely bronze, silver, and gold medal winners of every Olympic event the week before the games began. Athletes who were expected to win gold, silver, or bronze medals were assigned expectation scores of 1, 2, and 3, respectively. Those not predicted to win a medal were assigned an expectation score of 4. As anticipated, the athletes in our samples who won silver medals were originally expected to do better ($M = 2.8$) than those who won bronze medals ($M = 3.0$), although not significantly so, $t < 1.0$. More important, however, is that a comparison of actual and anticipated performance argues against the claim that our results are due to differences in initial expectations of bronze and silver medalists. Silver medalists as a whole did better than anticipated (actual = 2.0; anticipated = 2.8), and therefore should have been relatively happy. Bronze medalists, on the other hand, performed on average exactly as expected (actual and anticipated = 3.0).

More formally, we entered the expected finish of each athlete into a regression equation that predicted the agony-ecstasy ratings from the medal won (silver or bronze), the medal predicted (gold, silver, bronze, or none), and the type of videotape segment (immediate reactions or medal stand). This analysis revealed that the effect of medal won remained significant

---

[2]One other aspect of the data should be noted. Because seven of the athletes pictured in the immediate-reactions videotape are also shown on the medal stand tape, the data are not all strictly independent and the ANOVA reported is not completely accurate. However, the results are not changed when this overlap is deleted from the analysis. We did this two ways: first, by keeping these athletes' immediate-reactions data and deleting their medal stand data; second, by deleting their immediate reactions and keeping their data from the medal stand. Regardless of which analysis we used to eliminate the redundancy, the bronze medalists were still rated significantly happier than the silver medalists.

when expectations were statistically controlled, $t(72) = 4.3$, $p < .0001$.[3] Silver medalists looked less satisfied with their performances than did bronze medalists, and they did so for reasons unrelated to how well they were expected to perform.

Discussion

Our first study highlights a reliable context—Olympic competition involving bronze and silver medal winners—in which those who perform better nonetheless feel worse. On the surface this result is surprising because an underlying premise of all serious athletic competition is that athletes should strive as hard as they can, and that the higher they finish the better they feel. When examined with an eye toward the athletes' counterfactual thoughts, however, our findings seem less surprising. To the silver medalist, the most vivid counterfactual thoughts are often focused on nearly winning the gold. Second place is only one step away from the cherished gold medal and all of its attendant social and financial rewards. Thus, whatever joy the silver medalist may feel is often tempered by tortuous thoughts of what might have been had she only lengthened her stride, adjusted her breathing, pointed her toes, and so on. For the bronze medalist, in contrast, the most compelling counterfactual alternative is often coming in fourth place and being in the showers instead of on the medal stand.

But can we confidently attribute these results to the athletes' counterfactual thoughts? Although the data from Study 1 are consistent with this claim, it is important to examine directly the proposed asymmetry in the athletes' counterfactual comparisons. The following two studies were designed to do exactly that. Do silver medalists tend to think about how they almost *won the* gold? Do bronze medalists focus on how close they came to missing out on a medal altogether? What exactly do athletes think about after they learn their medal standing?

STUDY 2

To examine the nature of Olympic medalists' counterfactual thoughts, we turned once again to NBC's coverage of the 1992 Summer Olympic games. NBC's sportscasters interviewed numerous medal winners immediately following their events, and from this footage we developed a master tape of all of NBC's interviews of bronze and silver medalists. Participants were shown the tape and asked to assess the extent to which the athletes seemed preoccupied with thoughts of how they *did* perform versus how they *almost* performed.

Method

Participants. Ten Cornell University students served as participants. As in the first study, we recruited students who considered themselves to be non-sports fans because we did not want any prior knowledge about the athletes to affect their ratings.

Stimulus materials. NBC interviewed 13 silver medalists and 9 bronze medalists immediately after their events, and these 22 interviews comprised the stimulus tape for this study. Two versions of the tape were created, with the order of presentation of the athletes varied across

---

[3]This effect remains significant when the athletes from the just won–just lost events are excluded and when the redundancy created by the 7 athletes who appear on both tapes is removed.

Margin notes

Remember: counterfactual thinking entails thinking about what might have been. One's perception of the event and also one's mood is determined by what almost occurred but didn't. For silver medalists, what almost happened is winning the gold, but they fell short. Leading them to feel worse than the bronze medalists.

Question underlying study 2. How might you design an experiment to assess the thoughts of the athletes?

For this study, subjects rated videos of the athletes to determine the extent to which the athlete talked about how they did versus how they almost performed.

the versions. The average length of each interview clip was 27 s ($SD = 14$ s). Blank spaces were inserted between the interviews to allow participants time to complete their ratings.

Procedure.   Participants arrived at the laboratory in groups and were told that they would be watching a videotape of athletes from the 1992 Olympic games. They were asked to watch and listen to each interview carefully and to rate each athlete's comments in two ways. First, they rated the apparent content of each athlete's thoughts on a 10-point scale ranging from "*at least 1 . . .*" (1) to "*/ almost. . . .*" (10). To clarify the meaning of this scale, participants were given an example of how a student who receives a B in a course could have various thoughts ranging from "at least I didn't get a C" to "I almost got an A."

Second, participants were asked to assess the extent to which the apparent content of the athlete's thoughts fell into three categories: (a) "Athlete seems focused on how he/she could have done worse; makes a comparison with one or more competitors who finished behind;" (b) "Athlete seems focused on how he/she could have done better; makes a comparison with one or more competitors who finished ahead;" (c) "Athlete seems focused on what he/she accomplished; no comparison to competitors." Participants were asked to indicate the percentage of the athlete's thoughts that seemed focused on each of the three categories. They could assign any number from 0 to 100% to each of the three categories, but the percentages they assigned had to add up to 100% for each athlete. The participants were asked to watch a number of clips without making any ratings so that they were aware of the types of comments they would be evaluating. Once participants were familiar with the format of the videotape and the rating scales, the rating session began.

Five participants rated each of the two versions of the videotape. As in the first study, a 1.5-inch (3.8 cm) strip of paper was affixed to the bottom of the video screen to occlude various graphics depicting the athlete's order of finish.

Results

The interrater reliability of participants' ratings was acceptably high (Spearman-Brown index = .74 and .93 for the first and second measures, respectively[4]), and so the ratings were averaged for each scale to create indices of the apparent thoughts of each athlete. Preliminary analyses of these data revealed no effect of order of presentation, so the data were collapsed across the two versions of the tape.

As predicted, silver medalists' thoughts were rated as being more focused on "I almost" than were those of bronze medalists. On the 10-point *"At least /"* to *"/ almost"* scale, participants assigned silver medalists' thoughts an average rating of 5.7 ($SD = 1.5$) and bronze medalists' thoughts an average rating of only 4.4 ($SD = 0.7$), $t(20) = 2.37$, $p < .03$.

The data from the second measure were less clear cut. First, participants thought that only a small percentage of the athletes' thoughts were focused downward on those they beat. The average assigned to this category was only 7.5% and did not differ between bronze and silver medalists. The percentages assigned to the other two categories conformed more closely to our predictions. Participants rated silver medalists as being more focused on upward comparisons ($M = 38\%$) than bronze medalists ($M = 20\%$), whereas bronze medalists were judged to be

This makes sense . . . for silver medalists, the thing that almost happened but didn't is winning gold. So it makes sense that they would be much more preoccupied with thoughts of "I almost" compared to bronze medalists.

---

[4]The .93 is the average Spearman-Brown index for the last two components of the second dependent measure, which, as we discuss in the main text, are the focus of our analysis.

more focused on their own performance ($M = 73\%$) than silver medalists ($M = 54\%$). Because these data are not independent (the percentage assigned to all categories must equal 100%), our test of significance was based on an index that combined the last two categories. Specifically, the percentage assigned to the category "looking upward" was subtracted from the percentage assigned to the category "focusing on one's own performance." As predicted, this index was higher for bronze medalists ($M = 53\%$) than for silver medalists ($M = 16\%$), although the difference was only marginally significant, $t(20) = 1.57, p < .15$.

Discussion

The results of the second study provide support for the hypothesized difference in the counterfactual thoughts of the bronze and silver medalists. Silver medalists seem to be focused on the gold medal they "almost" won, while bronze medallists seem content with the thought that "at least I did this well." This asymmetry can thus explain the observed differences in the athletes' expressed emotions in Study 1. This can be seen most clearly through an analysis that combines the data from Studies 1 and 2. Fifteen of the 22 athletes whose counterfactual thoughts were assessed in Study 2 were on the immediate-reactions videotape in Study 1 and thus were also rated on the agony-ecstasy scale. As we predicted, the two ratings correlated significantly: The more focused the athletes were on almost finishing higher, the less happy they seemed ($r = -.56, p < .05$)[5]. This relationship was also observed when the data for silver ($r = -.51$; $n = 10$) and bronze ($r = -.34; n = 5$) medalists were considered separately, although the sample sizes were then too small to yield statistical significance. Thus, by focusing on what they achieved, bronze medalists are rather happy; in contrast, a concern with what they failed to achieve makes the silver medalists seem less so.

In this study we did not have direct access to the athletes' thoughts; we had participants infer them on the basis of the athletes' comments. It is certainly possible, of course, that the athletes had various thoughts they did not verbalize. To overcome this limitation, we conducted a third study that examined bronze and silver medalists' own reports of their thoughts following an athletic competition.

STUDY 3

In designing Study 3, we sought an athletic forum with significant stakes where we could gain access to bronze and silver medalists immediately after their events. The 1994 Empire State Games provided such a forum. The Empire State Games have been a prominent amateur athletic event in New York State for the last 17 years. Athletes from across the state compete on a regional basis to qualify for the Empire State Games. Notable participants have included such athletes as Olympic gold medalists Dianne Roffe-Steinrotter and Jeff Blatnick and NBA basketball stars (and "Dream Team" members) Christian Laettner and Chris Mullin. In 1994, more than 5,000 athletes from across New York State competed in the 4-day event.

---

[5]We used the data from the immediate-reactions video tape in Study 1 rather than those from the medal stand tape simply because there was more overlap with the athletes interviewed in Study 2 for the former (15) than for the latter (7). Furthermore, 5 of the overlapping 7 from the medal stand tape also appeared on the immediate-reactions tape.

Margin notes:

As an aside, the term "marginally significant" has traditionally denoted significance results between $p > .05$ to $< .10$. In recent years, it has been somewhat controversial as to whether there even exists "marginal significance" with critics saying it is akin to "being kind of pregnant"—there is no such thing . . . one is either pregnant or not. Same with statistical significance: your results are either significant (i.e., $p < .05$) or not.

Hypotheses shown to be supported. Silver medalists think about almost winning the gold (but falling short, resulting in their negative mood). Bronze medalists think about performing well enough to be on the medal podium and not being in 4th place (resulting in a positive mood).

Basis for study 3.

Method

Participants. One hundred fifteen Empire State Game medalists participated in this study. All of the participants won bronze ($n = 55$) or silver ($n = 60$) medals in swimming or track events. The athletes competed in either the Scholastic Division (composed exclusively of students up to 12th grade; $n = 31$ males and 34 females) or the Open Division (consisting mainly of college students; $n = 25$ males and 25 females).

Procedure. The athletes were approached individually following their events and asked to rate their thoughts about their performance on the same 10-point scale used in Study 2. Specifically, they were asked to rate the extent to which they were concerned with thoughts of *"At least I . . ."* (1) versus *"I almost"* (10). Special effort was made to ensure that the athletes understood the scale before making their ratings. This was accomplished by mentioning how athletes might have different thoughts following an athletic competition, ranging from "I almost did better" to "at least I did this well."[6]

Results

As predicted, silver medalists' thoughts following the competition were more focused on "I almost" than were bronze medalists'. Silver medalists described their thoughts with a mean rating of 6.8 ($SD = 2.2$), whereas bronze medalists assigned their thoughts an average rating of 5.7 ($SD = 2.7$), $t(113) = 2.4, p < .02$.

Discussion

The data from this study are consistent with the findings from Study 2: Following a competition, silver medalists tend to focus more on what they failed to achieve than bronze medalists. This asymmetry in counterfactual comparisons explains why bronze medalists tend to be happier than silver medalists. While bronze medalists can find contentment in thinking "at least I won a medal," silver medalists are often confronted with an imagined outcome that *almost* occurred—a preferred outcome in which they are the winner and have the gold medal hanging around their neck. Imagining what might have been can lead those who do better to feel worse than those they outperform.

---

[6]We had hoped to include a question similar to the second measure used in Study 2 in which participants divided the athletes' thoughts into three categories by assigning the appropriate percentage to each. We thought this might be difficult for the athletes to do the moment they emerged from the heat of competition, however. We therefore tried to simplify matters by presenting the task spatially: The athletes were shown a plexiglass board in which we had carved a triple-pronged "pitchfork." The athletes were to distribute 10 metal tokens contained in the handle of the pitchfork into the categories represented by each prong. The three prongs were labeled "Who I Beat," "No Comparisons," and "Who Beat Me," and the athletes were told to apportion the tokens so as to represent the extent to which their thoughts were focused on each. Unfortunately, the measure proved to be exquisitely ineffective. Some athletes, particularly a number of shivering swimmers who had just emerged from the pool, seemed unable to comprehend it; others managed to dislodge the tokens; and the responses of still other athletes were contaminated by the comments of onlookers who found the device fascinating and offered unsolicited advice.

Margin notes:

This should be interesting . . . unlike the previous two studies, this one involves the researchers interviewing the athletes immediately after their competition.

Confirms results of study 2.

Silver medalists do better than bronze, yet feel worse, due to counterfactual thinking. Silver medalists focus on what they almost accomplished but didn't (being in first), and they therefore feel bad. The bronze medalists focus on what almost happened (being in fourth) but didn't (they are on the winner's podium in 3rd place) and thus they feel good.

GENERAL DISCUSSION

The purpose of this research was to examine whether there are reliable situations in which those who are objectively better off nonetheless feel worse than those in an inferior position. Athletics offered an ideal context in which to test this question for the same reason that it offers a useful context for investigating many psychological hypotheses—the availability of data of unusual objectivity and precision (Baumeister & Steinhilber, 1984; M. G. Frank & Gilovich, 1988;Gilovich, Vallone, & Tversky, 1985; Lau & Russell, 1980). In addition, athletics was chosen as the domain of investigation in this case because performance in athletics often yields a clearly defined rank order: Someone enters the record books as the first-, second-, or third-place finisher.

It should be clear, however, that the significance of the present results extends far beyond the playing field or the medal stand. There are many other situations in which the same processes documented here can likewise cause those who are better off to feel worse. A student who misses out on an A by one point and earns a B+ could easily feel less satisfied with the grade than someone who is in the middle of the pack of Bs. Or consider a person who correctly guesses all but one number in a lottery. Such an individual misses out on the jackpot, but usually wins a modest sum for coming close. The prize no doubt provides some enjoyment, but the knowledge of having just missed the jackpot is bound to come up from time to time and ruin otherwise blissful moments. More generally, as our opening quote from William James suggests, being one of the best may not be as satisfying as it might seem. The existence of a rival "best" can turn a gratifying appreciation of what one *is* into a disquieting focus on what one is *not*.

The hedonic impact of such a rival "best" raises the question of the extent to which social comparison processes rather than (or in addition to) counterfactual thoughts may have been responsible for our findings. We believe that our results are best situated in the research on counterfactual thinking for two reasons. First, we obtained evidence for the hypothesized asymmetry in the direction of counterfactual comparisons in Studies 2 and 3, but as yet no such evidence exists to support an asymmetry in the direction of social comparisons. Second, there is nothing in social comparison theory per se that would predict upward comparisons on the part of silver medalists and downward comparisons on the part of bronze medalists. Although such a pattern could certainly be made to fit with social comparison theory, it requires extra theoretical elements to do so. In contrast, the present pattern of results was originally derived from the work on counterfactual thinking and the psychology of "coming close" (Kahneman & Varey, 1990; Miller et al., 1990).

This does not mean, of course, that social comparison processes are never activated in the immediate aftermath of Olympic competition, or that such processes contributed nothing to the present findings. Social comparison processes and counterfactual thoughts are doubtless frequently intertwined. Social comparisons can be a source of counterfactual thoughts about "possible worlds" that one would not have otherwise, and counterfactual thoughts can make salient particular social comparisons that would otherwise remain hidden. Unfortunately, it is presently unclear how much of the asymmetry in counterfactual thinking we documented in this context was intertwined in this way with significant social comparisons.

Although the predicted findings were originally derived from previous research on counterfactual thinking, they also extend the work in this area in two important respects. First, as we stated at the outset, past research has held outcome constant and shown that the same outcome can give rise to very different reactions as a function of the counterfactual thoughts that are generated. Our results take this a step further: There are contexts in which people's counterfactual thoughts are sufficiently powerful to lead those who are objectively worse off to be reliably happier than those in a better position.

Our results also extend previous findings in this area by emphasizing the "automatic" or "imposed" nature of many counterfactual thoughts. Much of the recent work on counterfactual thinking has emphasized a person's ability to choose the most strategic counterfactual comparisons (Markman et al., 1993; Roese, 1994). "Counterfactual generation has functional value, and people tend to generate those counterfactuals that hold the greatest psychological value for them in a given situation" (Markman et al., 1993, p. 103). Downward comparisons (i.e., thinking about a worse outcome) are thought to provide comfort, whereas upward comparisons (i.e., thinking about a better outcome) are thought to improve future performance. Indeed, it has been shown that people who expect to perform again in the future are more likely to generate upward counterfactuals than those who expect to move on (Markman et al., 1993).

Although many counterfactual thoughts are doubtless strategically chosen in this way, such motivational considerations cannot account for the present findings. On the whole, the silver and bronze medalists at the Barcelona Olympics were at the peak of their athletic careers and therefore likely to continue to engage in similar high-level competitions in the future. From a motivational perspective, then, both groups should have made upward counterfactual comparisons in order to prepare for future contests. The asymmetry in counterfactual comparisons that we observed implies that many counterfactuals are imposed by the nature of the events experienced.

Indeed, Kahneman (in press) outlined a continuum of counterfactual thinking that ranges from "automatic" to "elaborative." Elaborative counterfactual processing is partly brought on through the exercise of choice, and its direction and intensity is influenced by the individual's motives and intentions. Automatic counterfactual thinking, in contrast, is "initiated by the occurrence of an event and . . . [is] . . . explainable largely in cognitive terms" (Kahneman, in press). The counterfactual thoughts that distinguish silver and bronze medalists shade toward the latter end of this continuum. Coming close to winning the gold, for example, appears to automatically activate frustrating images of having almost won it all.

We are not suggesting, of course, that finishing second or coming close to a cherished outcome always leads to less satisfaction than a slightly more modest performance. Finishing second is truly a *mixed* blessing. Performing that well provides a number of direct benefits that increase our well being—recognition from others, boosts to self-esteem, and so on. At the same time, it can indirectly lower satisfaction by the unfortunate contrast with what might have been. Thus, the inconsistent effect of finishing second is analogous to the "endowment" and "contrast" polarity that Tversky and Griffin (1991) claimed affects the hedonic significance of *all* experienced events. According to their analysis, any experience has a direct effect on well-being by what it brings to one's endowment—that is, the pleasure or pain derived from the event itself. But a person's experiences also have an indirect effect on well being by altering the adaptation level against which future experiences are contrasted. Their contrast (in which the event itself establishes a new standard against which future events are compared) is different than the one at work here (in which the events' proximity to a better outcome causes one to lose sight of what is and focus on what might have been). The core idea is the same, however. In both cases, the direct effect of the event itself is offset by a comparison process with the opposite effect, be it a comparison of future outcomes to the present, or the present outcome to a counterfactual alternative that was almost attained.

Tversky and Griffin (1991) have delineated some of the general rules that govern the relative weighting of endowment and contrast, and thus whether the net effect of a given event enhances or diminishes well being. They acknowledged, however, that the degree to which a given event evokes endowment and contrast can be highly idiosyncratic. As a consequence, when applied to a problem such as ours it can be difficult to predict exactly when those who are better off will nonetheless feel worse than those who are less fortunate.

Another unresolved issue, this one more tractable, concerns the duration of the effects we have documented here. We have established that bronze medalists are happier than silver medalists in the short run, but does this effect hold up over time? As yet there are no data to answer this question. Nevertheless, one of the most noteworthy features of life's near misses seems to be their durability. Consider the account of finishing second that Nicholson Baker (1991) provides his wife:

> [I] told her my terrible story of coming in second in the spelling bee in second grade by spelling *keep* 'c-e-e-p' after successfully tossing off *microphone,* and how for two or three years afterward I was pained every time a yellow garbage truck drove by on Highland Avenue and I saw the capitals printed on it, 'Help Keep Our City Clean,' with that impossible irrational K that had made me lose so humiliatingly . . .

Or consider the case of Abel Kiviat, the 1,500 m silver medalist in the 1912 Olympics in Stockholm. Kiviat had the race won until Britain's Arnold Jackson "came from nowhere" to beat him by one-tenth of a second. "I wake up sometimes and say, 'What the heck happened to me?' It's like a nightmare." Kiviat was 91 years old when he said this in an interview with the *Los Angeles Times* (cited in Tait & Silver, 1989, p. 351). It appears that thoughts about what might have been may plague us for a very long time.

A question for future researchers.

And this may be a clue toward the answer of the duration of counterfactual thinking. Most people likely have some event that for them may have resulted in a potentially more positive life outcome "if only" their choice had been different (or events had worked out differently). These "what ifs" and "If onlys" can haunt us a long time.

REFERENCES

Atkinson, J. W. (1964). *An introduction to motivation.* Princeton, NJ: Van Nostrand.

Baker, N. (1991).*Room temperature.* New York: Vintage.

Baumeister, R. F., & Steinhilber, A. (1984). Paradoxical effects of supportive audiences on performance under pressure: The home field disadvantage in sports championships. *Journal of Personality and Social Psychology, 47,* 85–93.

Crosby, F. (1976). A model of egoistical relative deprivation. *Psychological Review, 83,* 85–113.

Feather, N. T. (1967). Valence of outcome and expectation of success in relation to task difficulty and perceived locus of control. *Journal of Personality and Social Psychology, 7,* 372–386.

Feather, N. T. (1969). Attribution of responsibility and valence of success and failure in relation to initial confidence and task performance. *Journal of Personality and Social Psychology, 13,* 129–144.

Festinger, L. (1954). A theory of social comparison processes. *Human Relations, 7,* 117–140.

Frank, M. G., & Gilovich, T. (1988). The dark side of self and social perception: Black uniforms and aggression in professional sports. *Journal of Personality and Social Psychology, 54,* 74–85.

Frank, R.H., & Cook, P.(1995). *The winner-take-all society.* New York: Free Press.

Gilovich, T., Vallone, R. P., & Tversky, A. (1985). The hot hand in basketball: On the misperception of random sequences. *Cognitive Psychology, 17,* 295–314.

James, W. (1892). *Psychology.* New York: Holt.

Johnson, J. T. (1986). The knowledge of what might have been: Affective and attributional consequences of near outcomes. *Personality and Social Psychology Bulletin, 12,* 51–62.

Kahneman, D. (in press). Varieties of counterfactual thinking. In N. Roese & J. Olson (Eds.), *What might have been: The social psychology of counterfactual thinking*. Hillsdale, NJ: Erlbaum.

Kahneman, D., & Miller, D. T. (1986). Norm theory: Comparing reality to its alternatives. *Psychological Review, 93,* 136–153.

Kahneman, D., & Tversky, A. (1982a). The psychology of preferences. *Scientific American, 2,* 160–173.

Kahneman, D., & Tversky, A. (1982b). The simulation heuristic. In D. Kahneman, P. Slovic, & A. Tversky (Eds.), *Judgment under uncertainty: Heuristics and biases* (pp. 201-208). New York: Cambridge University Press.

Kahneman, D., & Varey, C. A. (1990). Propensities and counterfactuals: The loser that almost won. *Journal of Personality and Social Psychology, 59,* 1101–1110.

Lau, R. R., & Russell, D. (1980). Attributions in the sports pages: A field test of some current hypotheses about attribution research. *Journal of Personality and Social Psychology, 39,* 29–38.

Markman, K. D., Gavanski, I., Sherman, S. J., & McMullen, M. N. (1993). The mental simulation of better and worse possible worlds. *Journal of Experimental Social Psychology, 29,* 87–109.

Miller, D. T., & McFarland, C. (1986). Counterfactual thinking and victim compensation: A test of norm theory. *Personality and Social Psychology Bulletin, 12,* 513–519.

Miller, D., Turnbull, W., & McFarland, C. (1990). Counterfactual thinking and social perception: Thinking about what might have been. In L. Berkowitz (Ed.), *Advances in experimental social psychology* (Vol. 22, pp. 305–331). San Diego, CA: Academic Press.

Olson, J. M., Herman, P., & Zanna, M. P. (1986). *Relative deprivation and social comparison: The Ontario symposium* (Vol. 4). Hillsdale, NJ: Erlbaum.

Roese, N. J. (1994). The functional basis of counterfactual thinking. *Journal of Personality and Social Psychology, 66,* 805–818.

Roese, N. J., & Olson, J. M. (in press). *What might have been: The social psychology of counterfactual thinking*. Hillsdale, NJ: Erlbaum.

Suls, J. M., & Miller, R. L. (1977). *Social comparison processes: Theoretical and empirical perspectives*. New York: Wiley.

Tait, R., & Silver, R. C. (1989). Coming to terms with major negative life events. In J. S. Uleman & J. A. Bargh (Eds.), *Unintended thought* (pp. 351–382). New York: Guilford Press.

Taylor, S. E., & Lobel, M. (1989). Social comparison activity under threat: Downward evaluation and upward contacts. *Psychological Review, 96,* 569–575.

Turnbull, W. (1981). Naive conceptions of free will and the deterministic paradox. *Canadian Journal of Behavioural Science, 13,* 1–13.

Tversky, A., & Griffin, D. (1991). Endowment and contrast in judgments of well-being. In R. J. Zeckhauser (Ed.), *Strategy and choice* (pp. 297–318). Cambridge, MA: MIT Press.

Verschoth, A. (1992, July 22). Who will win what. *Sports Illustrated*.

Wells, G. L., & Gavanski, I. (1989). Mental simulation of causality. *Journal of Personality and Social Psychology, 56,* 161–169.

POST-ARTICLE DISCUSSION

Some people think that psychology is a collection of common-sense notions about behavior. They say that much of our experimental findings are intuitive and that we didn't really need to waste time studying what was an obvious conclusion. This Monday morning quarterbacking (what psychologists call "hindsight bias," i.e., overestimating the predictability of an outcome after the outcome has happened) is a stereotype psychology has to confront. We do it with science. That is, even though a result of an experimental question seems obvious from the start, good science requires that we conduct experiments to ascertain the degree to which the data support that assertion or prediction.

So it was with Milgram's obedience studies, Darley's helping behavior experiments, and many other examples in psychological research, where the "obvious" outcome turned out to be wrong and a counterintuitive finding was obtained. Those always make for particularly interesting studies, and the paper you just read is another example of such research. If you ask people, "Considering the three people on a winner's podium at the Olympics, who feels happiest, second happiest, and third happiest?" the "obvious" answer is that their affect coincides with their performance and the medal that they won. So, first place (gold) would feel the happiest, second place (silver) second happiest, and third place (bronze) the third happiest. But that isn't what the data revealed. Medvec's data showed that bronze felt the second happiest, and silver the third happiest (or, worst of the three). They explain this by making the case that the athletes engaged in counterfactual thinking.

As I mentioned in the introduction to this paper and in the margin notes, one of the strengths of this paper is that the researchers studied real-life counterfactual thinking in a situation where such thinking had a powerful influence on the subject's thoughts and feelings. These individuals trained nearly their whole lives for that one competitive performance. Whatever rank they place, their affect will be stronger than any experimental manipulation we could manage. This addresses one of the most common reasons an experiment fails to support its hypotheses: weak independent variables. There are no weak IVs in these experiments!

Another strength of this paper is that it reports a "program" of research, in which the researchers address a problem from a variety of directions and methods. This is not unique to this paper (and it is a common practice among researchers today), but the great thing about a paper like this is that one can see a progression of research questions being addressed in turn, and it is an interesting window into the mind of the researcher, and also an efficient way to advance science. So Study 1 revealed Olympic athletes' affect after their performance, and Study 2 examined the degree to which Olympic athletes engaged in counterfactual thinking after their performance. Is it possible that the athletes had nonverbalized thoughts about their performance? Study 3 sought the answer to that question.

These three studies nicely illustrate the power of field and experimental research to reveal the degree to which a particular type of thought process (counterfactual thinking) can influence the way we think about ourselves and our behavior and how we feel about our behavior. It can also reveal how such thoughts can help us learn from mistakes and motivate our goal-directed future behavior.

THINGS TO THINK ABOUT

1. Are there other groups (besides Olympic athletes) that would allow you to study counterfactual thinking?

2. What determines whether the direction of one's counterfactual thinking is upward or downward? For example, why did silver medalists focus upward instead of downward, and why did bronze medalists focus downward instead of upward?

3. In Study 1, why did the researchers reanalyze their results to eliminate the "just won" versus "just lost" artifact?

4. Do you think Study 3 was necessary? The authors say it was designed to assess whether athletes were holding back counterfactual thoughts that they didn't verbalize.

5. Why do the authors believe the results are best explained by counterfactual thinking and not social comparison?

6. Do you think that counterfactual thinking is automatic? Or, can it sometimes be (as Kahneman [1995] suggests) "elaborative" (consciously applied) and determined by one's motives?

7. What do you think about the duration of counterfactual thinking? Do some people mentally undo a particular negative event for years, or even the rest of their lives? If yes, what do you suppose makes that event different from all other negative events in the person's life that generated counterfactuals?

CHAPTER

4

The Self

One of the fundamental aspects of understanding how we think and behave is an understanding of ourselves. In that last word is the focus of this brief review: our self. But what is the "self" and how do we come to understand what that is, anyway? Like most concepts in psychology, the subject of the self was debated among the early philosophers, and it had its own chapter in William James's (1890) book *The Principles of Psychology*, which many say marked the formal establishment of the boundaries of psychology as a field. Although space precludes a discussion of the philosophy of the self (see Krueger, Heck, & Athenstaedt, 2018; Swann & Bosson, 2010, for a more extensive discussion), let us review some of the major themes and theories that have fascinated social psychologists for over 100 years.

THE SELF-CONCEPT

What do we mean when we think of "the self"? Most researchers would agree that a basic definition for **self-concept** is a system of affective and cognitive structures (schemas) about the self that brings coherence to each person's self-relevant experiences. Recall from the chapter on social cognition (Chapter 3) that a schema is a hierarchically organized mental structure that contains everything one knows about a given concept. Where do we obtain this self-concept? Because we are such social creatures, it may not surprise you to learn that much of the way we think about who we are is obtained from our interactions with other people. Cooley (1902) talked about this in terms of what he called a **looking glass self**. This is the idea that our sense of self stems from the information we get about us from other people. For example, suppose I think I am really funny. However, every time I tell a joke or make what I think is an amusing observation or otherwise funny statement, no one ever laughs. The constant lack of laughter and lack of feedback from others weigh heavily in my self-assessment and in shaping my self-concept. My self-concept then will influence how I define myself. Here, psychologists are talking about **self-identity**. Self-identity is one's self-definition of who he or she is. It includes one's personal attributes (characteristics, traits), self-concept, and membership in various groups. The self-concept is also formed by the way we compare our situations to those of others. This process, called **social comparison** (Festinger, 1954), helps us assess the appropriateness of our own feelings, thoughts, and behaviors. Through social comparison, we can evaluate ourselves, to get a measure of how we think we compare with others, and from this, we can determine our feelings of self-esteem (more on this later). Social comparison also helps us understand the commonality of our experiences with those of many others.

So, for example, if all your friends that you graduated from college with were now buying their first house, and you were still living at home with your parents or renting an apartment, you might feel like you weren't doing as well as your friends, and that might make you feel a bit dejected and negative about yourself. Although this sort of comparison (to people similar to oneself) is what Festinger (1954) said was best if you wanted to get a more accurate picture of how you are doing, it turns out that people tend to want to see themselves positively rather than accurately (Heck & Kreuger, 2015; Sedikedes & Gregg, 2003). This makes sense in light of the myriad ways we try to see ourselves in the best possible light rather than make an accurate assessment of who we are (Larson, 1977). Our brains may even be wired to see ourselves and the world in a positive light (Sharot, 2011). Whenever we want to feel good about ourselves, then, we can engage in **downward social comparison**; that is, we compare ourselves to someone who is not doing as well as we are. We are thus less inclined to engage in **upward social comparison**, that is, compare ourselves to people who are doing better than us, because we will feel worse about ourselves as a result.

MANY SELVES

In his landmark book *The Principles of Psychology*, James (1890) said that we have multiple selves. We have the **material self**, which is comprised of our body and our physical possessions. We have the **spiritual self**, which contains personality traits, attitudes, values, and beliefs. We also have the **social self**, which is the self that your friends, relatives, spouse, and others know. The point of this view is that the self is not a uniform construct; rather, it is multifaceted, containing aspects of our cognitions, our social interactions, and the literal physical self. We get feedback about each from moment to moment, and this lends to our overall conception of our self.

Markus and Nurius (1986) suggested that we have a number of **possible selves**. These are images we have in our mind of potential selves that we might be in the future, potential selves we want to avoid becoming in the future, and the selves we hope we will become. Each of these provides motivation for our behavior at any moment. For example, the reason you are in college is that you believe that getting a degree will bring you closer to a self you hope to be in the future and, at the same time, move you away from a feared self you do not want to become a reality (e.g., homeless). The number of potential future selves you have for yourself can also determine how you react when you receive information that one of those paths is no longer possible for you. Suppose you have 15 possible careers that you can see yourself doing after college, and one of them is lawyer. Let's further suppose that you take the LSAT, and the results show that there is no way you will get into any law school. No big deal, you still have 14 other possible selves you can explore. But suppose that you only have one possible future self: lawyer. Getting that negative LSAT score can then have a huge impact on you, because now it appears there is no future open, and, as a result, you may become depressed or even distraught (Niedenthal, Setterlund, & Wherry, 1992).

SELF-PRESENTATION

We all make conscious decisions each day, and multiple times a day, about how we will present ourselves to the world. That is, in our social world, we have different goals we want to accomplish. To accomplish those goals with different people in different situations, we may need to present a slightly different self to more smoothly navigate those interactions so that we move closer to our goals. For example, your goal with your spouse is to keep the relationship strong, happy, and growing together. So you present that committed spouse self to your husband or wife. At work, with your coworker friends, you want to show you are a team player, a fun person, and a hard worker, so you manage your behaviors to show those sides of yourself to them at any opportunity. You want your boss to see you as a hard worker, responsible, and worthy of promotion, so you are constantly looking for opportunities to engage in behaviors that will show your boss that side of you. These specific self-presentations are designed to create a specific impression of you for those different people in your social world. Social psychologists call this **strategic self-presentation**. Some researchers suggest that our tendency to be concerned about how we present ourselves to different people is hardwired in us like a personality trait, and they call this **self-monitoring** (Snyder, 1974).

SELF-MONITORING

Self-monitoring is the degree to which one is concerned with the self-presentation aspects of any situation. Snyder (1974) suggests that this functions much like a trait, always "on," and it guides behavior across situations. People who are high in self-monitoring are like social chameleons in that they change the self they present depending on with whom they are interacting. If you've ever seen the movie *Ferris Bueller's Day Off*, you have a good idea of what this looks like. Ferris is one way with his sister, a different Ferris with his friend Cameron, another way with his girlfriend, yet a different (and

almost infantile) Ferris with his parents, and still a different Ferris with his beleaguered school principal. On the other end of the spectrum are people who are low self-monitors. These people are not at all concerned with how they present themselves to others, and they therefore present the same self to everyone in all contexts. This has its positives (easy to remember how to present oneself), but it is outweighed by its negatives in that smooth social negotiation may be difficult. For example, say you are a person who likes to swear. Doing that is probably not going help you during a job interview. Doing that is not going to endear you to potential in-laws when meeting them for the first time. You get the idea. But somewhere in the middle, a moderate level of self-monitoring can be quite adaptive.

SELF-VERIFICATION

Research has revealed that we have a powerful need to have others see us the way we see ourselves (Swann, 2012; Swann & Read, 1981). If I think I am funny, I am motivated to get you to think I am funny and to hear your feedback that confirms that you think I am funny. If I get feedback from you indicating that you don't think I am funny, it makes me uncomfortable. Because now there is a disconnect with the impression I am putting forth (I'm a funny guy) and how others see me. This tendency is so strong that it can keep people in relationships that may be harmful or even abusive. In one study, researchers examined self-verification tendencies in people who were married or in long-term relationships (Swann, De La Ronde, & Hixon, 1994). Participants were first asked to complete a measure of their self-esteem. Then they were asked questions about how they viewed their partners and how they thought their partners viewed them.

Results indicated that for those high in self-esteem, the more positive they believed their spouses thought of themselves, the more committed they were to their partner. But, for those low in self-esteem, the picture was quite different. Those who thought their partner had a high opinion of them were *less* committed to their partner. One reason for this is that people with low self-esteem find it aversive to learn that there is a big gulf between how their partner views them and how they view themselves. That means that they have a lot of self-work to do before they are at the level their partner thinks they are. Also, it is unnerving (for people with low esteem) to have that discrepancy because they may think it is just a matter of time before their partner comes to his or her senses and sees them for who they really are (worthless, in their mind anyway) and breaks up with them.

Like waiting for the proverbial other shoe to drop. Even more intriguing and somewhat disturbing are the results concerning people with low self-esteem who have partners who also view them poorly. The data showed that low esteem partners were *more* committed to their partner when they thought the partner held a low view of them. People with low esteem think that their partner sees them for who they are, warts and all, and still loves them. They believe no one would ever love them (because people with low esteem think they are unlovable), so they should stay with this partner who claims to love them even though the partner may treat them poorly and may even abuse them. This strong self-verification motive may be one factor (not the only factor) that explains why some people stay in abusive relationships and why some keep returning to an abusive partner.

INTRODUCTION TO READING 4.1
Carney et al. (2010)

Imagine you're out hiking in the forest and you encounter a bear. Some experts advise raising your arms above your head and yelling loudly to attempt to cause the bear to retreat. That's the theory anyway (hope you won't have occasion to test it!). But this speaks to a fundamental aspect of behavior that appears to be common among many animals and, it turns out, humans too: One way that powerful and dominant animals and humans display their power is to make their bodies appear bigger.

In a fascinating line of research, Dana Carney, Amy Cuddy, and Andy Yap have explored an interesting question: If power is displayed by expanding one's body, is it possible to make nonpowerful people feel powerful by having them physically replicate those large postures and poses? For example, could

you take people with low self-esteem and have them behave in ways that people with high self-esteem behave, and would that cause the low-esteem persons to feel more positively about themselves?

Carney and colleagues examined this question in detail and presented their findings in the journal *Psychological Science*. Contrary to most articles in psychological journals these days, this article reports on only one experiment, and it is written in a concise manner. *Psychological Science* prefers to publish short, compact descriptions of research (in part due to publication limitations). So, this article is a bit unusual in that it reports only one study. But it is a very well done experiment and reports a novel line of research. Enjoy the paper, and we'll talk more afterward!

Reading 4.1

Power Posing: Brief Nonverbal Displays Affect Neuroendocrine Levels and Risk Tolerance

Dana R. Carney[1], Amy J.C. Cuddy[2], and Andy J. Yap[1]

[1]Columbia University and [2]Harvard University

Abstract

Humans and other animals express power through open, expansive postures, and they express powerlessness through closed, contractive postures. But can these postures actually cause power? The results of this study confirmed our prediction that posing in high-power nonverbal displays (as opposed to low-power nonverbal displays) would cause neuroendocrine and behavioral changes for both male and female participants: High-power posers experienced elevations in testosterone, decreases in cortisol, and increased feelings of power and tolerance for risk; low-power posers exhibited the opposite pattern. In short, posing in displays of power caused advantaged and adaptive psychological, physiological, and behavioral changes, and these findings suggest that embodiment extends beyond mere thinking and feeling, to physiology and subsequent behavioral choices. That a person can, by assuming two simple 1-min poses, embody power and instantly become more powerful has real-world, actionable implications.

Keywords

cortisol, embodiment, hormones, neuroendocrinology, nonverbal behavior, power, risk taking, testosterone

If animals make their bodies larger as a sign of power and dominance, do humans do the same?

Carney et al. answer that question by saying yes, humans do indeed do the same thing, and they suggest that these behaviors are rooted in evolutionary forces.

Here is one of the interesting main questions posed by the researchers for this experiment: if power makes one pose a certain way, can the reverse also work? That is, if you pose a person's body in the same manner that powerful people posture themselves, will that cause the person to feel more powerful?

The proud peacock fans his tail feathers in pursuit of a mate. By galloping sideways, the cat manipulates an intruder's perception of her size. The chimpanzee, asserting his hierarchical rank, holds his breath until his chest bulges. The executive in the boardroom crests the table with his feet, fingers interlaced behind his neck, elbows pointing outward. Humans and other animals display power and dominance through expansive non-verbal displays, and these power poses are deeply intertwined with the evolutionary selection of what is "alpha" (Darwin, 1872/2009; de Waal, 1998).

But is power embodied? What happens when displays of power are posed? Can posed displays cause a person to feel more powerful? Do people's mental and physiological systems prepare them to be more powerful? The goal of our research was to test whether high-power poses (as opposed to low-power poses) actually produce power. To perform this test, we looked at the effects of high-power and low-power poses on some fundamental features of having power: feelings of power, elevation of the dominance hormone testosterone, lowering of the stress hormone cortisol, and an increased tolerance for risk.

Corresponding Authors:

Dana R. Carney, Columbia University, Graduate School of Business, 717 Uris Hall, 3022 Broadway, New York, NY 10027-6902
E-mail: dcarney@columbia.edu

Amy J.C. Cuddy, Harvard Business School, Baker Library 449, Boston, MA 02163
E-mail: acuddy@hbs.edu

Power determines greater access to resources (de Waal, 1998; Keltner, Gruenfeld, & Anderson, 2003); higher levels of agency and control over a person's own body, mind, and positive feelings (Keltner et al., 2003); and enhanced cognitive function (Smith, Jostmann, Galinsky, & van Dijk, 2008). Powerful individuals (compared with powerless individuals) demonstrate greater willingness to engage in action (Galinsky, Gruenfeld, & Magee, 2003; Keltner et al., 2003) and often show increased risk-taking behavior[1] (e.g., Anderson & Galinsky, 2006).

The neuroendocrine profiles of the powerful differentiate them from the powerless, on two key hormones—testosterone and cortisol. In humans and other animals, testosterone levels both reflect and reinforce dispositional and situational status and dominance; internal and external cues cause testosterone to rise, increasing dominant behaviors, and these behaviors can elevate testosterone even further (Archer, 2006; Mazur & Booth, 1998). For example, testosterone rises in anticipation of a competition and as a result of a win, but drops following a defeat (e.g., Booth, Shelley, Mazur, Tharp, & Kittok, 1989), and these changes predict the desire to compete again (Mehta & Josephs, 2006). In short, testosterone levels, by reflecting and reinforcing dominance, are closely linked to adaptive responses to challenges.

Power is also linked to the stress hormone cortisol: Power holders show lower basal cortisol levels and lower cortisol reactivity to stressors than powerless people do, and cortisol drops as power is achieved (Abbott et al., 2003; Coe, Mendoza, & Levine, 1979; Sapolsky, Alberts, & Altmann, 1997). Although short-term and acute cortisol elevation is part of an adaptive response to challenges large (e.g., a predator) and small (e.g., waking up), the chronically elevated cortisol levels seen in low-power individuals are associated with negative health consequences, such as impaired immune functioning, hypertension, and memory loss (Sapolsky et al., 1997; Segerstrom & Miller, 2004). Low-power social groups have a higher incidence of stress-related illnesses than high-power social groups do, and this is partially attributable to chronically elevated cortisol (Cohen et al., 2006). Thus, the power holder's typical neuroendocrine profile of high testosterone coupled with low cortisol—a profile linked to such outcomes as disease resistance (Sapolsky, 2005) and leadership abilities (Mehta & Josephs, 2010)—appears to be optimally adaptive.

It is unequivocal that power is expressed through highly specific, evolved nonverbal displays. Expansive, open postures (widespread limbs and enlargement of occupied space by spreading out) project high power, whereas contractive, closed postures (limbs touching the torso and minimization of occupied space by collapsing the body inward) project low power. All of these patterns have been identified in research on actual and attributed power and its nonverbal correlates (Carney, Hall, & Smith LeBeau, 2005; Darwin, 1872/2009; de Waal, 1998; Hall, Coats, & Smith LeBeau, 2005). Although researchers know that power generates these displays, no research has investigated whether these displays generate power. Will posing these displays of power actually cause individuals to feel more powerful, focus on reward as opposed to risk, and experience increases in testosterone and decreases in cortisol?

In research on embodied cognition, some evidence suggests that bodily movements, such as facial displays, can affect emotional states. For example, unobtrusive contraction of the "smile muscle" (i.e., the zygomaticus major) increases enjoyment (Strack, Martin, Stepper, 1988), the head tilting upward induces pride (Stepper & Strack, 1993), and hunched postures (as opposed to upright postures) elicit more depressed feelings (Riskind & Gotay,

The relationship between testosterone and behavior (e.g. aggression or dominant behavior) is not a clear cut influence. Some evidence suggests that increased testosterone leads to increased aggressive or dominant behavior. Other evidence suggests that behaving in a dominant or aggressive way increases testosterone.

In addition to testosterone rising with competition, cortisol (a stress hormone) drops as power is achieved. The authors are building their case for the experiment here in the introduction.

This has been found in humans and animals. Those higher in power express it through expansive poses.

Here are the questions the researchers specifically seek to address in this study. Fascinating idea . . . if the powerful pose expansively, can we take a non-powerful person, have them pose expansively, and would they then FEEL more powerful?

This is the "facial feedback hypothesis"—says that when one's facial muscles are contracted in such a way as to form a smile, we'll feel happy, and when it is contracted to form a frown, we'll feel sad. And if you recall, this hypothesis is based on the James-Lange theory of emotion, which says that our subjective experience of emotion is based on our first physical response to the stimulus (so, for example, we feel happy because we notice we are smiling).

1982). Approach-oriented behaviors, such as touching, pulling, or nodding "yes," increase preference for objects, people, and persuasive messages (e.g., Briñol & Petty, 2003; Chen & Bargh, 1999; Wegner, Lane, & Dimitri, 1994), and fist clenching increases men's self-ratings on power-related traits (Schubert & Koole, 2009). However, no research has tested whether expansive power poses, in comparison with contractive power poses, cause mental, physiological, and behavioral change in a manner consistent with the effects of power. We hypothesized that high-power poses (compared with low-power poses) would cause individuals to experience elevated testosterone, decreased cortisol, increased feelings of power, and higher risk tolerance. Such findings would suggest that embodiment goes beyond cognition and emotion and could have immediate and actionable effects on physiology and behavior.

METHOD

Participants and overview of procedure

Forty-two participants (26 females and 16 males) were randomly assigned to the high-power-pose or low-power-pose condition. Participants believed that the study was about the science of physiological recordings and was focused on how placement of electrocardiography electrodes above and below the heart could influence data collection. Participants' bodies were posed by an experimenter into high-power or low-power poses. Each participant held two poses for 1 min each. Participants' risk taking was measured with a gambling task; feelings of power were measured with self-reports. Saliva samples, which were used to test cortisol and testosterone levels, were taken before and approximately 17 min after the power-pose manipulation.

Power poses

Poses were harvested from the nonverbal literature (e.g., Carney et al., 2005; Hall et al., 2005) and varied on the two non-verbal dimensions universally linked to power: expansiveness (i.e., taking up more space or less space) and openness (i.e., keeping limbs open or closed). The two high-power poses into which participants were configured are depicted in Figure 1, and the two low-power poses are depicted in Figure 2. To be sure that the poses chosen conveyed power appropriately, we asked 95 pretest participants to rate each pose from 1 (*very low power*) to 7 (*very high power*). High-power poses ($M = 5.39$, $SD = 0.99$) were indeed rated significantly higher on power than were low-power poses ($M = 2.41$, $SD = 0.93$), $t(94) = 21.03$, $p < .001$; $r = .99$.

To be sure that changes in neuroendocrine levels, powerful feelings, or behavior could be attributed only to the high-power or low-power attributes of the poses, we had 19 pretest participants rate the comfort, difficulty, and pain of the poses. Participants made all four poses (while wearing electrocardiography leads) and completed questionnaires after each pose. There were no differences between high-power and low-power poses on comfort, $t(16) = 0.24$, $p > .80$; difficulty, $t(16) = 0.77$, $p > .45$; or painfulness, $t(16) = -0.82$, $p > .42$.

To configure the test participants into the poses, the experimenter placed an electrocardiography lead on the back of each participant's calf and underbelly of the left arm and explained, "To test accuracy of physiological responses as a function of sensor placement relative to your heart, you are being put into a certain physical position." The experimenter then manually configured participants' bodies by lightly touching their arms and legs. As needed, the experimenter provided verbal instructions (e.g., "Keep your feet above heart level by putting them on

Predictions for this experiment.

Just a quick but important note about this. When you're doing an experiment and you're saying "this pose will make people feel powerful, and this other pose will make people feel less powerful", other researchers/critics will say "how do you know that?" That is why one needs to have empirical data to support your assertions. Here, the authors have earlier gathered such data in a smaller study conducted before this one (typically referred to as a "pretest").

Here, the authors want to rule out any confounds (like comfort, difficulty, or pain) that might influence the DV, and would ruin our ability to say that it was only the IV (poses) that influenced change in neuroendocrine levels and powerful feelings.

FIG. 1. The two high-power poses used in the study. Participants in the high-power-pose condition were posed in expansive positions with open limbs.

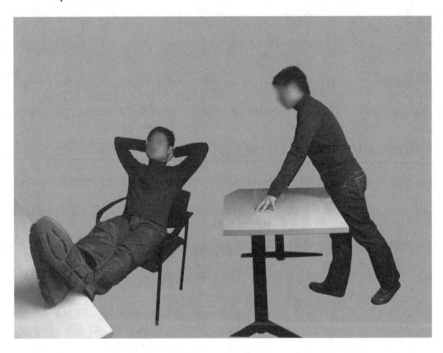

FIG. 2. The two low-power poses used in the study. Participants in the low-power-pose condition were posed in contractive positions with closed limbs.

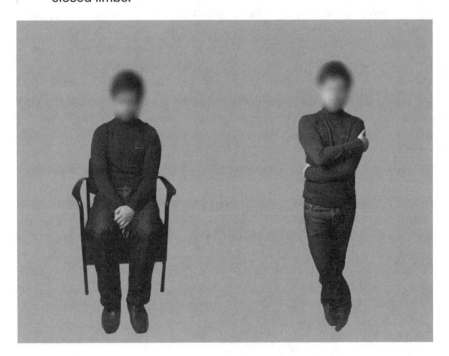

the desk in front of you"). After manually configuring participants' bodies into the two poses, the experimenter left the room. Participants were videotaped; all participants correctly made and held either two high-power or two low-power poses for 1 min each. While making and holding the poses, participants completed a filler task that consisted of viewing and forming impressions of nine faces.

Measure of risk taking and powerful feelings

After they finished posing, participants were presented with the gambling task. They were endowed with $2 and told they could keep the money—the safe bet—or roll a die and risk losing the $2 for a payoff of $4 (a risky but rational bet; odds of winning were 50/50). Participants indicated how "powerful" and "in charge" they felt on a scale from 1 (*not at all*) to 4 (*a lot*).

Saliva collection and analysis

Testing was scheduled in the afternoon (12:00 p.m.–6:00 p.m.) to control for diurnal rhythms in hormones. Saliva samples were taken before the power-pose manipulation (approximately 10 min after arrival; Time 1) and again 17 min after the power-pose manipulation ($M = 17.28$ min, $SD = 4.31$; Time 2).

Standard salivary-hormone collection procedures were used (Dickerson & Kemeny, 2004; Schultheiss & Stanton, 2009). Before providing saliva samples, participants did not eat, drink, or brush their teeth for at least 1 hr. Participants rinsed their mouths with water and chewed a piece of sugarfree Trident Original Flavor gum for 3 min to stimulate salivation (this procedure yields the least bias compared with passive drool procedures; Dabbs, 1991). Participants provided approximately 1.5 ml of saliva through a straw into a sterile polypropylene microtubule. Samples were immediately frozen to avoid hormone degradation and to precipitate mucins. Within 2 weeks, samples were packed in dry ice and shipped for analysis to Salimetrics (State College, PA), where they were assayed in duplicate for salivary cortisol and salivary testosterone using a highly sensitive enzyme immunoassay.

For cortisol, the intra-assay coefficient of variation (CV) was 5.40% for Time 1 and 4.40% for Time 2. The average interassay CV across high and low controls for both time points was 2.74%. Cortisol levels were in the normal range at both Time 1 ($M = 0.16$ μg/dl, $SD = 0.19$) and Time 2 ($M = 0.12$ μg/dl, $SD = 0.08$). For testosterone, the intra-assay CV was 4.30% for Time 1 and 3.80% for Time 2. The average interassay CV across high and low controls for both time points was 3.80%. Testosterone levels were in the normal range at both Time 1 ($M = 60.30$ pg/ml, $SD = 49.58$) and Time 2 ($M = 57.40$ pg/ml, $SD = 43.25$). As would be suggested by appropriately taken and assayed samples (Schultheiss & Stanton, 2009), men were higher than women on testosterone at both Time 1, $F(1, 41) = 17.40$, $p < .001$, $r = .55$, and Time 2, $F(1, 41) = 22.55$, $p < .001$, $r = .60$. To control for sex differences in testosterone, we used participant's sex as a covariate in all analyses. All hormone analyses examined changes in hormones observed at Time 2, controlling for Time 1. Analyses with cortisol controlled for testosterone, and vice versa.[2]

RESULTS

One-way analyses of variance examined the effect of power pose on post manipulation hormones (Time 2), controlling for baseline hormones (Time 1). As hypothesized, high-power poses caused an increase in testosterone compared with low-power poses, which caused a decrease in testosterone, $F(1, 39) = 4.29$, $p < .05$; $r = .34$ (Fig. 3). Also as hypothesized, high-power poses caused a decrease in cortisol compared with low-power poses, which caused an increase in cortisol, $F(1, 38) = 7.45$, $p < .02$; $r = .43$ (Fig. 4).

Also consistent with predictions, high-power posers were more likely than low-power posers to focus on rewards—86.36% took the gambling risk (only 13.63% were risk averse). In contrast, only 60% of the low-power posers took the risk (and 40% were risk averse), $\times 2$ $(1, N = 42) = 3.86$, $p < .05$; $\Phi = .30$. Finally, high-power posers reported feeling significantly more "powerful" and "in charge" ($M = 2.57$, $SD = 0.81$) than low-power posers did ($M = 1.83$, $SD = 0.81$), $F(1, 41) = 9.53$, $p < .01$; $r = .44$. Thus, a simple 2-min power-pose manipulation was enough to significantly alter the physiological, mental, and feeling states of our participants. The implications of these results for everyday life are substantial.

All analyses revealed success all around with respect to their hypotheses.

DISCUSSION

Our results show that posing in high-power displays (as opposed to low-power displays) causes physiological, psychological, and behavioral changes consistent with the literature on the effects of power on power holders—elevation of the dominance hormone testosterone, reduction of the stress hormone cortisol, and increases in behaviorally demonstrated risk tolerance and feelings of power.

These findings advance current understanding of embodied cognition in two important ways. First, they suggest that the effects of embodiment extend beyond emotion and cognition, to physiology and subsequent behavioral choice. For example, as described earlier, nodding the head "yes" leads a person to be more easily persuaded when listening to a persuasive appeal, and smiling increases humor responses. We suggest that these simple behaviors, a head nod or a smile, might also cause physiological changes that activate an entire trajectory of psychological, physiological, and behavioral shifts—essentially altering the course of a person's day. Second, these results suggest that any psychological construct, such as power, with a signature pattern of nonverbal correlates may be embodied.

These results also offer a methodological advance in research on power. Many reported effects of power are limited by the methodological necessity of manipulating power in a laboratory setting (e.g., complex role assignments). The simple, elegant power-pose manipulation we employed can be taken directly into the field and used to investigate ordinary people in everyday contexts.

Is it possible that our findings are limited to the specific poses utilized in this experiment? Although the power-infusing attribute of expansiveness and the poses that capture it require further investigation, findings from an additional study ($N = 49$) suggest that the effects reported here are not idiosyncratic to these specific poses. In addition to the poses used in the current report, an additional three high-power poses and an additional three low-power poses produced the same effects on feelings of power, $F(1, 48) = 4.38$, $p < .05$, $r = .30$, and risk taking, $\chi^2(1, N = 49) = 4.84$, $p < .03$, $\Phi = .31$.

By simply changing physical posture, an individual prepares his or her mental and physiological systems to endure difficult and stressful situations, and perhaps to actually improve confidence and performance in situations such as interviewing for jobs, speaking in public, disagreeing with a boss, or taking potentially profitable risks. These findings suggest that, in some situations requiring power, people have the ability to "fake it 'til they make it."

This is an important point. The authors here either tried to anticipate critics of the study, or are responding to a critique of an earlier draft of the paper (before it was submitted to the journal) in which the reviewer raises the issue of the findings being limited to a particular pose. To address this potential limitation, the authors conducted further research with other high and low power poses and found the same effects as with the previous poses. These new data support the main findings.

FIG. 3. Mean changes in the dominance hormone testosterone following high-power and low-power poses. Changes are depicted as difference scores (Time 2 – Time 1). Error bars represent standard errors of the mean.

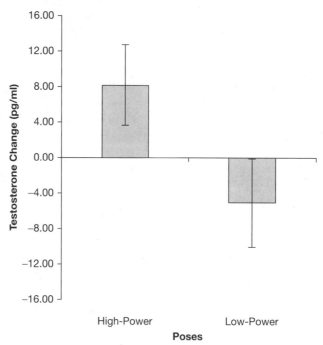

FIG. 4. Mean changes in the stress hormone cortisol following high-power and low-power poses. Changes are depicted as difference scores (Time 2 – Time 1). Error bars represent standard errors of the mean.

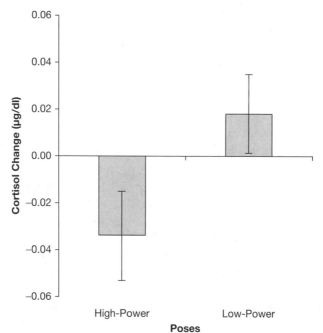

Over time and in aggregate, these minimal postural changes and their outcomes potentially could improve a person's general health and well-being. This potential benefit is particularly important when considering people who are or who feel chronically powerless because of lack of resources, low hierarchical rank in an organization, or membership in a low-power social group.

ACKNOWLEDGMENTS

We are gratefully indebted to the following individuals for their insight, support, and assistance with this research: Daniel Ames, Max Bazerman, Joe Ferrero, Alan Fiske and lab, Adam Galinsky, Deborah Gruenfeld, Lucia Guillory, Brian Hall, Bob Josephs, Brian Lucas, Malia Mason, Pranj Mehta, Michael Morris, Joe Navarro, Michael Norton, Thomas Schubert, Steve Stroessner, and Bill von Hippel.

DECLARATION OF CONFLICTING INTERESTS

The authors declared that they had no conflicts of interest with respect to their authorship or the publication of this article.

NOTES

1. The effect of power on risk taking is moderated by factors such as prenatal exposure to testosterone (Ronay & von Hippel, in press).
2. Cortisol scores at both time points were sufficiently normally distributed, except for two outliers that were more than 3 standard deviations above the mean and were excluded; testosterone scores at both time points were sufficiently normally distributed, except for one outlier that was more than 3 standard deviations above the mean and was excluded.

REFERENCES

Abbott, D.H., Keverne, E.B., Bercovitch, F.B., Shively, C.A., Mendoza, S.P., Saltzman, W., et al. (2003). Are subordinates always stressed? A comparative analysis of rank differences in cortisol levels among primates. *Hormones and Behavior*, *43*, 67–82.

Anderson, C., & Galinsky, A.D. (2006). Power, optimism, and the proclivity for risk. *European Journal of Social Psychology*, *36*, 511–536.

Archer, J. (2006). Testosterone and human aggression: An evaluation of the challenge hypothesis. *Neuroscience & Biobehavioral Reviews*, *30*, 319–345.

Booth, A., Shelley, G., Mazur, A., Tharp, G., & Kittok, R. (1989). Testosterone and winning and losing in human competition. *Hormones and Behavior*, *23*, 556–571.

Briñol, P., & Petty, R.E. (2003). Overt head movements and persuasion: A self-validation analysis. *Journal of Personality and Social Psychology*, *84*, 1123–1139.

Carney, D.R., Hall, J.A., & Smith LeBeau, L. (2005). Beliefs about the nonverbal expression of social power. *Journal of Nonverbal Behavior*, *29*, 105–123.

Chen, M., & Bargh, J.A. (1999). Consequences of automatic evaluation: Immediate behavioral predispositions to approach or avoid the stimulus. *Personality and Social Psychology Bulletin*, *25*, 215–224.

Coe, C.L., Mendoza, S.P., & Levine, S. (1979). Social status constrains the stress response in the squirrel monkey. *Physiology & Behavior*, *23*, 633–638.

Cohen, S., Schwartz, J.E., Epel, E., Kirschbaum, C., Sidney, S., & Seeman, T. (2006). Socioeconomic status, race, and diurnal cortisol decline in the Coronary Artery Risk Development in Young Adults (CARDIA) study. *Psychosomatic Medicine*, *68*, 41–50.

Dabbs, J.M. (1991). Salivary testosterone measurements: Collecting, storing, and mailing saliva samples. *Physiology & Behavior, 42*, 815–817.

Darwin, C. (2009). *The expression of the emotions in man and animals*. New York, NY: Oxford. (Original work published 1872).

de Waal, F. (1998). *Chimpanzee politics: Power and sex among apes*. Baltimore, MD: Johns Hopkins University Press.

Dickerson, S.S., & Kemeny, M.E. (2004). Acute stressors and cortisol responses: A theoretical integration and synthesis of laboratory research. *Psychological Bulletin, 130*, 355–391.

Galinsky, A.D., Gruenfeld, D.H., & Magee, J.C. (2003). From power to action. *Journal of Personality and Social Psychology, 87*, 327–339.

Hall, J.A., Coats, E.J., & Smith LeBeau, L. (2005). Nonverbal behavior and the vertical dimension of social relations: A meta-analysis. *Psychological Bulletin, 131*, 898–924.

Keltner, D., Gruenfeld, D.H., & Anderson, C. (2003). Power, approach, and inhibition. *Psychological Review, 110*, 265–284.

Mazur, A., & Booth, A. (1998). Testosterone and dominance in men. *Behavioral & Brain Sciences, 21*, 353–397.

Mehta, P.H., & Josephs, R.A. (2006). Testosterone change after losing predicts the decision to compete again. *Hormones and Behavior, 50*, 684–692.

Mehta, P.H., & Josephs, R.A. (2010). *Dual-hormone regulation of dominance*. Manuscript in preparation.

Riskind, J.H., & Gotay, C.C. (1982). Physical posture: Could it have regulatory or feedback effects on motivation and emotion? *Motivation and Emotion, 6*, 273–298.

Ronay, R., & von Hippel, W. (in press). Power, testosterone and risk-taking: The moderating influence of testosterone and executive functions. *Journal of Behavioral Decision Making*.

Sapolsky, R.M. (2005). The influence of social hierarchy on primate health. *Science, 308*, 648–652.

Sapolsky, R.M., Alberts, S.C., & Altmann, J. (1997). Hypercortisolism associated with social subordinance or social isolation among wild baboons. *Archives of General Psychiatry, 54*, 1137–1143.

Schubert, T.W., & Koole, S.L. (2009). The embodied self: Making a fist enhances men's power-related self-conceptions. *Journal of Experimental Social Psychology, 45*, 828–834.

Schultheiss, O.C., & Stanton, S.J. (2009). Assessment of salivary hormones. In E. Harmon-Jones & J.S. Beer (Eds.), *Methods in the neurobiology of social and personality psychology* (pp. 17–44). New York, NY: Guilford.

Segerstrom, S., & Miller, G. (2004). Psychological stress and the human immune system: A meta-analytic study of 30 years of inquiry. *Psychological Bulletin, 130*, 601–630.

Smith, P.K., Jostmann, N.B., Galinsky, A.D., & van Dijk, W.W. (2008). Lacking power impairs executive functions. *Psychological Science, 19*, 441–447.

Stepper, S., & Strack, F. (1993). Proprioceptive determinants of emotional and non-emotional feelings. *Journal of Personality and Social Psychology, 64*, 211–220.

Strack, F., Martin, L.L., & Stepper, S. (1988). Inhibiting and facilitating conditions of the human smile: A nonobtrusive test of the facial feedback hypothesis. *Journal of Personality and Social Psychology, 54*, 768–777.

Wegner, D.M., Lane, J.D., & Dimitri, S. (1994). The allure of secret relationships. *Journal of Personality and Social Psychology, 66*, 287–300.

POST-ARTICLE DISCUSSION

Well, was I right, or was I right? Cool study, huh? OK, so let's talk about it. Have you ever wondered, "Where do they get their ideas for experiments?" or thought to yourself (as is common among psychology students), "It seems like all the experiments have been done already. How can I come up with a new idea?" Well, no, it certainly isn't the case that all the experiments have been done already, and a good source for new experiment ideas is to look at the world around you through the lens of a scientist. I know, you are saying, "How do I do that?" One of my goals as a professor is to introduce students to the way that psychologists think scientifically about the world and how they experimentally test ideas about cognition and behavior. That is also the goal of this book. I hope that, by the end of the book, you will see the world through the eyes of a budding young scientist.

So let's take Carney and colleagues' (2010) observation about powerful people (and animals): They tend to have more expansive postures and broad body positions. That premise is not too controversial, and most researchers would agree with it. Now, recall from introductory psychology the "facial feedback" hypothesis. This hypothesis says that the reason we experience certain emotions is that we detect our facial muscles constricted in the same way as, say, a smile and that information tells us that we are smiling, so we must feel positively toward the thing we are looking at or thinking about. It (our smile) may even tell us that we find the stimulus humorous and that we should laugh. You'll recall this is derived from the James–Lange theory of emotion. Now, apply this hypothesis to powerful people. If powerful people exhibit certain expansive postures, is it the case that the process works in reverse? If we pose someone who is not high in power in those expansive postures, will that person say to herself, "My body is in a powerful posture, so I must have power. I feel powerful"?

One of the excellent features of this paper is the attention that the researchers pay to potential critics of their study and how the researchers attempt to address alternate explanations of the data. For example, the researchers acquired data on cortisol to further bolster the argument that posing in expansive postures is associated with more power and less stress (lower cortisol). Moreover, the researchers did a small separate test with a separate group of subjects to examine if the poses they put people in were considered powerful. People rated the poses on a self-report measure, and the researchers found that the poses they believed were more powerful were indeed perceived by subjects as more powerful (and the low-power poses were perceived by subjects as low power). Finally, a critic might say, "How do you know that changes in cortisol levels were affected only by the poses and not by other aspects of the situation, such as difficulty of the pose, pain associated with the pose, or discomfort?" To address this, the researchers obtained data from another pretest group of subjects that had participants in the high- and low-power pose conditions rate their feelings of comfort, pain, and whether they perceived the pose as difficult. The data showed there were no differences between high- and low-power conditions on these dimensions. That means that if differences in perceived power occurred between high- and low-power conditions, that could only be attributed to the pose itself and not anything else.

In addition to the novel and clever experimental questions examined by the researchers, this paper was included to show the reader an example of a paper that is well written, concise, direct, and clear and that highlights an elegant experiment design, with careful attention to competing interpretations of the data and doing the work necessary to rule out those alternate interpretations. I hope you enjoyed this paper as much as I have!

THINGS TO THINK ABOUT

1. What is it about making your body more "expansive" that might cause you to feel more powerful?

2. Why do you think testosterone levels rise in anticipation of competition and when one wins, but the levels of testosterone drop when one loses?

3. Are feelings of power incompatible with feeling stress?

4. Consider the premise of the experiments here: Doing something that powerful people do (having more expansive body displays) will cause one to feel more powerful. If true, could we expand this reasoning to other areas, such as self-esteem? So if you take a person with low self-esteem and ask him to do or say things that high self-esteem people do or say, will that cause the individual to feel higher self-esteem?

5. Why do you suppose the researchers also measured feelings of power by measuring cortisol and testosterone levels before and after the subjects did the posing? Wouldn't it be enough to just ask people about their feelings of power before and after?

6. Do you think that the power posing and the resultant feelings of power (and lower stress) can have lasting effects? How long do those feelings of power last? How would you design an experiment to address that question?

INTRODUCTION TO READING 4.2
Yap et al. (2013)

In 1990, my dissertation advisor, Galen Bodenhausen, published the results of a fascinating study that showed that whether one was more likely to stereotype another person in a social judgment depended on the alignment between the time of day he or she was making that judgment and his or her own circadian rhythm (Bodenhausen, 1990). One of the many fascinating things about these data was the idea that whether one stereotyped another person could be dependent on the time of day. This runs contrary to long-standing notions about prejudiced persons—that if one is prejudiced, one is prejudiced all the time and that, because being prejudiced is part of one's personality, it doesn't fluctuate from situation to situation. But yet Bodenhausen's results showed that stereotyping is dependent on situational factors such as the time of day (and its alignment with one's physiological arousal).

Studies like that and like the one you are about to read remind us that much of our behavior is strongly affected by situational influences. This influence tends to be underappreciated, and the job of the researcher is to explore such potential influences on our behavior. Yap and his colleagues report data that show that something as incidental as the size of our seat or our workspace can either cause our bodies to stretch out or constrict, and such differences in our body posture can have remarkable effects on a wide range of our behaviors. Another thing you'll note is that this article reports the results of four studies. Two are lab experiments and two are field studies. Recall from earlier readings in this book that it is always desirable to empirically approach a concept with multiple methods. To the degree that different methodologies all point to the same conclusion, we can have greater confidence in that conclusion.

Remember that no experiment is perfect, and there are bound to be limitations to the method or interpretations of any study. The choices that the experimenter makes may not be those you would make in terms of analyses or design. These are legitimate points for critique. So, as you would with any experiment paper, read this paper with a critical eye and note what, if any changes, you would make, and why. Let's talk about those afterward. Enjoy the paper!

Reading 4.2

The Ergonomics of Dishonesty: The Effect of Incidental Posture on Stealing, Cheating, and Traffic Violations

Andy J. Yap[1], Abbie S. Wazlawek[2], Brian J. Lucas[3], Amy J. C. Cuddy[4], and Dana R. Carney[5]

Abstract

Research in environmental sciences has found that the ergonomic design of human-made environments influences thought, feeling, and action. In the research reported here, we

[1]Sloan School of Management, Massachusetts Institute of Technology; [2]Columbia Business School, Columbia University; [3]Kellogg School of Management, Northwestern University; [4]Harvard Business School, Harvard University; and [5]Haas School of Business, University of California, Berkeley

examined the impact of physical environments on dishonest behavior. In four studies, we tested whether certain bodily configurations—or postures—incidentally imposed by the environment led to increases in dishonest behavior. The first three experiments showed that individuals who assumed expansive postures (either consciously or inadvertently) were more likely to steal money, cheat on a test, and commit traffic violations in a driving simulation. Results suggested that participants' self-reported sense of power mediated the link between postural expansiveness and dishonesty. Study 4 revealed that automobiles with more expansive driver's seats were more likely to be illegally parked on New York City streets. Taken together, the results suggest that, first, environments that expand the body can inadvertently lead people to feel more powerful, and second, these feelings of power can cause dishonest behavior.

Keywords

design, dishonesty, embodiment, human factors, nonverbal behavior, power, environmental effects, morality, social structure, social behavior

The ergonomics and physical geography of our everyday environments are powerful: They determine our social networks and relationships (Werner, Altman, & Brown, 1992), personal and interpersonal functioning (Altman, Taylor, & Wheeler, 1971), our workplace productivity (Knight & Haslam, 2010), and our subjective well-being (Kaplan & Kaplan, 2009; Leonard, 2012). The research reported here examined the impact of our environment on an important social behavior: dishonesty. Each day, our bodies are continually stretched and contracted by our working and living environments—by the seats and levers in our cars and by the furniture and work spaces in our homes and offices. Although we may pay very little attention to ordinary and seemingly innocuous shifts in our bodily posture, these subtle postural shifts can have a tremendous impact on our thoughts, feelings, and behavior (Damasio, 1994; Niedenthal, 2007; Niedenthal, Barsalou, Winkielman, Krauth-Gruber, & Ric, 2005).

Most central to the current research is the finding that expansive body postures lead to a psychological state of power (Bohns & Wiltermuth, 2012; Carney, Cuddy, & Yap, 2010; Fischer, Fischer, Englich, Aydin, & Frey, 2011; Huang, Galinsky, Gruenfeld, & Guillory, 2011). And power—whether caused by laboratory manipulations or real-world structural features—appears to be linked to increases in a wide range of dishonest behaviors (Boles, Croson, & Murnighan, 2000; Guinote, 2007; Keltner, Gruenfeld, & Anderson, 2003; Lammers, Stapel, & Galinsky, 2010; Lammers, Stoker, Jordan, Pollmann, & Stapel, 2011). Is it possible that expansive postures incidentally shaped by our environment could lead to dishonest behavior? This question was the focus of the current research.

The idea that the human body has the ability to shape the mind has piqued the interest of scholars for centuries. Darwin (1872/1904) and the father of experimental psychology,

Corresponding Authors:

Andy J. Yap, Sloan School of Management, Massachusetts Institute of Technology, 100 Main St., Cambridge, MA 02142
E-mail: andyyap@mit.edu

Dana R. Carney, Haas School of Business, University of California, Berkeley, 573 Bakar Faculty Building, Berkeley, CA 94720
E-mail: dcarney@berkeley.edu

Margin notes:

Here is the basis for this paper. The authors are suggesting (with citations to previous supporting evidence) that the certain environments can expand and contract our bodies, and this can, in turn, have tremendous influences on our thoughts, feelings, and behaviors.

This finding, explored in detail in our other paper in the Self section, is well-supported by the experimental evidence. Making the body wider, taller, or extending the limbs outward makes one feel more powerful. Try it!

Key question being addressed in this paper. It is an interesting one: can we be more prone to dishonesty by aspects of the environment that cause us to have more expansive postures?

Do you remember the James-Lange theory of emotion? It says that a stimulus causes a physiological change in our body, and that leads to the subjective experience of emotion.

William James (1884), were among the first to theorize about mind-body connections. But it was not until the 1970s that the bidirectional connection between bodily displays and psychological states was empirically demonstrated (Duclos et al., 1989; Laird, 1974; Rhodewalt & Comer, 1979; Riskind, 1983; Riskind & Gotay, 1982; Strack, Martin, & Stepper, 1988; Wells & Petty, 1980). For example, in a study using facial electromyography, Laird (1974) asked participants to furrow their eyebrows (i.e., frown) or clench their teeth (i.e., smile). When participants clenched their teeth, they reported more happiness and humor. Strack et al. (1988) later replicated and extended this work. Similarly, Wells and Petty (1980) demonstrated that participants who nodded their heads (in a motion of agreement) while listening to messages found the messages to be more persuasive than did participants who shook their heads (in a motion of disagreement).

> See also research on what is known as the "facial feedback hypothesis" (essentially the James-Lange notion that, for example, we "are in a good mood because we notice we are smiling").

POWERFUL POSTURES

Across humans and animals, power and dominance are expressed through expansive, open-bodied postures (which involve spreading out and occupying more space), whereas powerlessness and subordination are expressed through relatively more contractive, closed-bodied postures (Carney, Hall, & LeBeau, 2005; Darwin, 1872/1904; de Waal, 1998; Ellyson & Dovidio, 1985; Hall, Coats, & Smith LeBeau, 2005; Tiedens & Fragale, 2003; Weisfeld & Beresford, 1982). Research has also shown that these expansive nonverbal "power poses" may activate mental concepts and emotions associated with power and even go so far as to initiate a trajectory of physiological changes associated with a powerful state (Bohns & Wiltermuth, 2012; Carney et al., 2010; Carney et al., 2013; Huang et al., 2011). These studies demonstrated that when men and women engaged in expansive (as opposed to contractive) postures, they felt more powerful, engaged in more approach-oriented and risk-seeking behavior, and appeared to evidence a physiological buffer against pain and stress. Similarly, Riskind and Gotay (1982) demonstrated that slumped and constricted postures, compared with upright and confident postures, induced a state of helplessness and feelings of stress. Finally, Harmon-Jones and Peterson (2009) found that a supine body posture (i.e., lying down), compared with an upright body posture, reduced approach motivation.

> The authors are building the rationale for their experiments. If expansive poses make one appear more powerful, and feel more powerful, it is reasonable to assume one would also think one is indeed more powerful than others.

POWER AND DISHONEST BEHAVIOR

Regardless of how power is manipulated or observed in the lab or field, it is consistently related to dishonesty. For example, power is associated with cheating to improve one's odds of winning (Lammers et al., 2010), lying (Boles et al., 2000) , lying more easily (Carney et al., 2013), hypocrisy (Lammers et al., 2010), and infidelity (Lammers et al., 2011). According to Keltner et al. (2003), power activates the behavioral approach system, which causes powerful individuals to focus on rewards and act in a self-interested and goal-consistent manner (Galinsky, Gruenfeld, & Magee, 2003; Guinote, 2007; Inesi, 2010).

> Those higher in power are also more likely to view subordinates through the lens of stereotypes and prejudice (Fiske, 1993).

If expansive postures can lead to a state of power, and power can lead to dishonest behavior, this suggests something of real concern—that ordinary expanded (and contracted) nonverbal postures forced on us by our environments, which we happen or choose to be in, could impact our decisions and actions in ways that render us less (or more) honest.

THE FOCUS OF THE CURRENT RESEARCH ON THE ERGONOMICS OF DISHONESTY

We tested the hypothesis that expansive postures would lead to dishonest behaviors in four studies conducted in the field and the laboratory. The first was a field experiment that examined whether expansive (compared with contractive) postures employed in previous research (Bohns & Wiltermuth, 2012; Carney et al., 2010; Huang et al., 2011) would lead to stealing in an "overpayment" paradigm. The second experiment manipulated the expansiveness of work spaces in the lab and tested whether *incidentally* expanded bodies (shaped organically by the environment) increased dishonesty on a test. The third experiment examined if participants in a more expansive driver's seat would be more likely to hit-and-run when incentivized to go fast in a video-game driving simulation; we also tested the mediating role of sense of power in these effects. Finally, to extend results to a real-world context, we conducted an observational field study to test the ecological validity of the effect by examining whether automobile driver's seat size predicted the violation of parking laws in New York City. Consistent with recommendations from Simmons, Nelson, and Simonsohn (2012), we report how we determined our sample size, all data exclusions, all manipulations, and all measures used in the studies.

STUDY 1 (FIELD EXPERIMENT)

Method

Eighty-eight[1] community members (57 men, 31 women) were recruited from South Station train station in Boston, Massachusetts, and from outside a library at the city campus of Columbia University to participate in a study that ostensibly examined the relationship between stretching and impression formation. Participants were told they would receive $4 in return for participation. Postural expansiveness was manipulated using a procedure similar to that of Carney et al. (2010). We used a cover story about the effects of stretching on impression formation, and participants were randomly assigned to hold either an expansive or a contractive pose (Fig. 1) for 1 min while they formed impressions of faces shown to them by the experimenter. Next, to bolster the cover story, we had participants complete a survey on their impressions of a best friend.[2] Finally, although participants had been told they would receive $4 in payment, the experimenter handed them $8, which was comprised of three $1 bills and one $5 bill, fanned out (Fig. 2) and presented in such a way that participants would notice the "accidental" overpayment. The dependent measure was whether or not the participant kept the extra money. The experimenter coded for whether participants checked the money after they had received it.[3]

Results and discussion

Consistent with our theorizing, results from a chi-square analysis showed that participants who assumed the expansive pose, compared with the contractive pose, were significantly more likely to keep the extra money (i.e., to "steal by omission"), $\chi^2(1, N = 78) = 13.0$, $p < .001$, $\Phi = .41$. Seventy-eight percent of the expanded-posture participants kept the extra money, compared with 38% of contracted-posture participants.

FIG. 1. Poses employed by participants in Study 1.

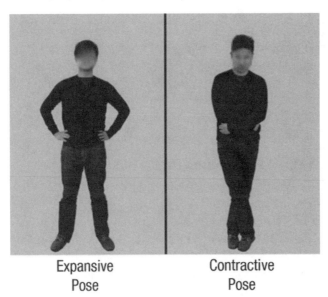

Expansive
Pose

Contractive
Pose

FIG. 2. Picture showing how money was presented to participants in Study 1.

Study 1 yielded initial evidence that expansive postures can lead to dishonest behavior. Participants in this experiment were explicitly instructed to assume a specific pose, yet the main focus of our research was posture imposed by the ergonomics of the environment. With this first experiment establishing the link between posture and dishonesty, Studies 2 through 4 investigated the impact of incidentally induced expansive (relative to contractive) postures on dishonest behavior. Participants in these studies were not explicitly instructed to assume specific poses, nor were they made explicitly aware that their posture was being manipulated. Instead, posture was naturally shaped by ordinary chairs and work spaces.

STUDY 2 (LABORATORY EXPERIMENT)

Method

In return for monetary compensation, 34 students[4] (14 men, 20 women) from Columbia University participated in a study that they were told examined how feng shui influences creativity.

Participants were seated in individual cubicles at desks with either a large (24 in. × 38 in.) or a small (12 in. × 19 in.) desk pad (Fig. 3). Participants saw only their own work space and not the work spaces of other participants. They were then instructed to complete two "creativity tasks."

The first was an anagram test on which, unbeknownst to participants, they would later have an opportunity to cheat. This cheating paradigm was adopted from Ruedy and Schweitzer (2010). Participants received a packet of papers in a manila folder and were allotted 4 min to unscramble 15 anagrams that were printed on the first page. They were incentivized by the experimenter's promise of $1 for every anagram solved. When time was called, participants were instructed to detach and retain the first page and return the folder and its remaining contents to the experimenter. Participants were unaware that an imprint of their test answers had been created by a sheet of carbonless copy paper hidden at the back of the folder.

Incidental posture was manipulated in the next task, which ostensibly measured inductive creativity. Participants were allotted 7 min to create a collage using materials that were placed around the edges of their desk pad. During the task, participants were allowed to use only the space on the desk pad. Posture was incidentally manipulated by the size of participants' desk pads. The large-desk-pad arrangement forced participants to stretch and reach for materials, thus incidentally imposing expansive postures. These participants also had chairs that were high enough to help them reach for the materials. In contrast, the small-desk-pad arrangement constrained participants' arm extensions because materials were within close reach, thus incidentally imposing contractive postures.

At the completion of the collage task, the experimenter, appearing very busy, rushed to each cubicle and handed participants the answer key for the anagram test. The experimenter explained that he had to manage another study in the adjacent lab and asked that each participant grade his or her own test. Participants were thus given an opportunity to alter their original answers in private. We used participants' number of altered answers, which we identified by comparing their self-graded tests with the carbon copies containing their original answers, as a measure of cheating.

Margin notes (left column):

Fascinating results! As we know from prior research, these expansive poses lead one to feel more powerful. So, this study suggests that those who feel more powerful are also more likely to "steal by omission." Why do you think there is that relationship between power and dishonesty?

Here in this result, the *p*-value was .001, meaning that the differences were profound and that the chances that these differences are not due to the IV are less than one in 1,000.

This is an important point. Though the authors found predicted differences in exp. 1, the subjects were aware of their posing, because the experimenters explicitly asked them to assume certain poses. If the posing is having an effect on the person, we need to know that it happens even when there is no external agent telling the person to pose, and indeed, when the subject is unaware that their body is in an expansive or contractive position. So that is why exps. 2–4 looked at environmental situations that naturally caused people to be in various poses, and examine its effects on dishonesty.

Cover story. By the way, "feng shui" is a Chinese philosophical system of creating a harmonious interaction between people and their environment. The way it is typically thought of in modern American usage is the arrangement of furniture, windows, open space, etc., in one's home to make the home the most spiritual and harmonious to one's personal energy.

Clever, right?

Here is the IV—different sized desk pads incidentally influencing one's posture.

Results and discussion

We hypothesized that expanded-posture participants would alter more of their answers, which would earn them more money. As predicted, a one-way analysis of variance (ANOVA) revealed that expanded-posture participants altered more answers ($M = 1.20$, $SD = 1.70$) than did contracted-posture participants ($M = 0.27$, $SD = 0.59$), $F(1, 29) = 4.04$, $p = .05$, $d = 0.73$.[5]

Studies 1 and 2 found consistent evidence that expansive postures, whether consciously posed or incidentally imposed, led to more dishonest behavior. In our third experiment, we examined whether driver's seat expansiveness led to more traffic violations in a driving simulation. Importantly, we also tested the mechanism underlying this effect. If expansive posture leads to a state of power, and power leads to increases in dishonest behavior, then the link between expansive posture and dishonest behavior should be mediated by participants' sense of power.

STUDY 3 (LABORATORY EXPERIMENT)

Method

Seventy-one students[6] (23 men, 48 women) from the University of California, Berkeley, were recruited to participate in a study that was ostensibly about physiology and video games. A realistic driving simulator was set up with a PlayStation 3 (Sony, Tokyo, Japan) and a Logitech Driving Force GT Racing Wheel (Logitech, Romanel-sur-Morges, Switzerland),

FIG. 3. Pictures showing the desk-space configurations for the expansive-posture (top row) and contractive-posture (bottom row) conditions of Study 2.

Expansive Contractive

Expansive

Contractive

Interesting! So, we have the first study in this series that shows that incidental posture (expansive vs. contractive) influences honesty.

Before you read ahead, put yourself in the researcher's position. How would you experimentally manipulate the expansiveness of a driver's seat?

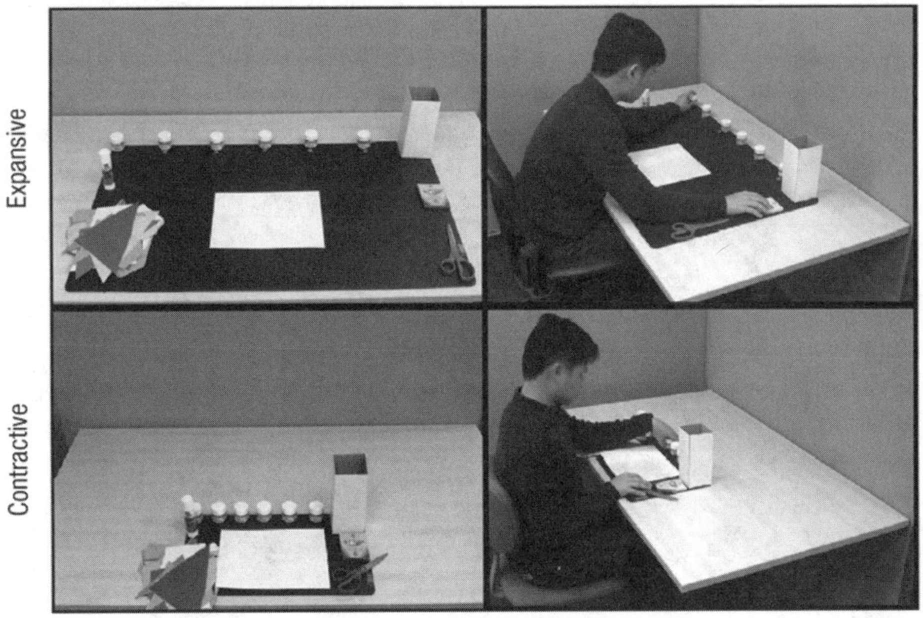

Clever solution to the problem of creating an expansive and contractive driver's seat!

The nice thing about this experiment (exp. 3) compared to the 4th study is that we can compare the same phenomenon in a controlled setting (exp. 3) and in a real-world setting (study 4). To the degree that the findings in each are the same, we can be even more confident in the hypothesis (and the theory from which it originated).

When one is trying to measure behavior when it isn't readily clear what the behavior is indicating, we employ "coders" of behavior using objective criteria (code book) that we have designed for the purposes of quantifying behavior. For example, if we are watching a video of participants interacting, and we want to code for number of friendly behaviors, we need a list of all behaviors we would consider friendly. Then have two or more coders watch the video, and each coder watches for how many behaviors he/she believes fit the criteria for "friendly" behavior. Then, we compare the coders' responses, and to the degree they match, we say we have "inter-rater reliability" (agreement). Typically an inter-rater reliability of .70 or higher is what we want. As you can see, the authors obtained a very high inter-rater reliability ($r = .95$).

Here, notice the author's wording. They didn't say "significant" differences between experiment conditions because the analyses revealed the differences were NOT statistically significantly different ($p = .087$). But the results are notable in that the small differences were in the expected direction.

which included a steering wheel and foot pedals. Participants were randomly assigned to sit in an expansive or contractive driver's seat (see Fig. 4 for a visual display of the setup).[7] Participants played the game *Need for Speed: Hot Pursuit*, which challenges players to race to the finish line as fast as possible. Participants were allotted one initial practice race to become accustomed to the game's controls. They were then offered a chance to win $10 if they could complete the same race within 5 min. Importantly, we implemented a rule that participants had to stop and count to 10 after a collision with any object in the race. Violation of this rule would shorten participants' total race time and thus help them to win the money. Rule violation—specifically, the number of times a participant hit an object and did not stop—served as our measure of cheating. Races were video recorded and coded by two research assistants for the number of hit-and-runs. Interrater reliability was determined by having the two coders rate the same sub-set of videos (10%). Once interrater reliability was established ($r = .95$), the remaining videos were divided equally between coders. After the race, participants reported how powerful they felt, using a Likert-type scale from 1 (*not at all*) to 5 (*extremely*).

Results and discussion

Consistent with our theorizing, results showed that being seated in an expansive seat lead participants to drive somewhat more recklessly (mean number of objects hit = 7.11, $SD = 8.51$) than being seated in a contractive seat did ($M = 4.33$, $SD = 3.60$), $F(1, 67) = 3.02$, $p = .087$. Importantly, participants in the expansive seat were more likely to hit-and-run (mean number of hit-and-runs = 6.31, $SD = 8.45$) than were those in the contractive seat ($M = 2.94$, $SD = 2.61$) after controlling for the number of objects hit, $F(1, 66) = 4.12$, $p = .046$, $d = 0.54$. The effect was significant when number of objects hit was not included as a covariate, $F(1, 67) = 4.81$, $p = .032$.[8]

We also predicted that participants' sense of power would mediate this effect. Bootstrapping analyses (Preacher & Hayes, 2004) based on 5,000 samples were conducted to estimate direct and indirect effects. The total effect of expansive posture on incidence of hit-and-runs (total effect = 3.37, $p = .03$) became non-significant when sense of power was included in the

FIG. 4. Pictures showing the driver's seat configurations for the expansive posture and contractive-posture conditions of Study 3.

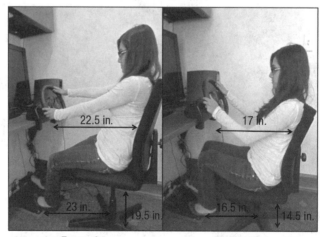

Expansive   Contractive

model (direct effect of expansive posture = 2.65, *p* = .09). Additionally, the total indirect effect (i.e., the difference between the total and direct effects) of expansive posture on incidence of hit-and-runs through sense of power was significant (point estimate = 0.72, bias-corrected bootstrap 95% confidence interval = [0.0197, 2.775])—the fact that zero fell outside the confidence interval indicated a significant mediation effect[9] (Fig. 5).

Three experiments yielded consistent evidence that expansive posture, whether posed consciously or shaped incidentally by one's desk space or driver's seat, can lead to dishonest behavior. Although the emergence of these effects in the lab may have been intriguing, to understand their generalizability and pervasiveness, we examined whether the same pattern of results would occur naturally—in the real world—in Study 4.

STUDY 4 (OBSERVATIONAL FIELD STUDY)

Having conducted three experiments, we thought it was critical to test the real-world generalizability of the incidental-posture effect. Thus, in Study 4, we used observational field-study methods to investigate whether drivers in expansive automobile seats were more likely than drivers in contractive seats to commit parking violations, an established measure of corrupt behavior in the economics literature (Fisman & Miguel, 2007). Specifically, we focused on double-parking—the parking of a car in an open lane such that adjacent, already parked vehicles are blocked in and active driving space is partially obstructed, which forces other drivers to maneuver through tighter spaces.

Method

Two hypothesis-blind research assistants recorded instances of double-parking on East–West streets between 116th Street and 102nd Street in New York City from 12 p.m. to 7 p.m. on weekdays. The research assistants recorded information about each double-parked vehicle as well as information about the legally parked adjacent vehicle (in the event that more than one legally parked vehicle was blocked in by the double-parked vehicle, information about the legally parked vehicle blocked most by the double-parked car was recorded). The legally parked vehicles served as our control sample. Data were recorded for a total of 126 automobiles.

FIG. 5. Results from Study 3: mediation model showing the effect of posture on incidence of hit-and-runs (a measure of rule violation), as mediated by sense of power. Values shown are unstandardized regression coefficients. On the lower path, the values below and above the arrow show results for when the mediator was included and was not included in the model, respectively.

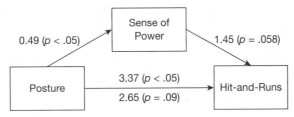

Now this is a bit tricky. The authors are predicting that the expansive seats are going to make people feel more powerful and that will then make them more likely to engage in dishonest (i.e., breaking the law) behavior. BUT, here they are not randomly assigned to the different types of seats, but they chose the seat (cars) themselves. So we may have a self-selection bias in that there may be differences between the groups (expansive vs. contractive seats) in the amount of law-breaking they do, but now we are not able to state it is due to our experimental manipulation of the IV on the DV, because there was no experimental manipulation of the IV. It could be that the differences are due to something else (i.e., personality factors) that cause people to choose one type of seat (or car) over another type, and THAT (personality) may be what is driving the obtained differences in law-breaking. This other possibility (personality) may be a confound.

Whenever one does research, one needs to try to identify potential outside variables (confounds) that might affect data collection. Here, we might ask the researcher why they chose this particular road (area), and why collect data from noon to 7pm (and why not on weekends)? Could there be something unusual about that location or those times that would either enhance double-parking or inhibit double-parking?

Measure of driver's seat (space) size. To create an index of the expansiveness of each auto-mobile's driver's seat, we calculated the volume of the space using information posted on respective car manufacturers' Web sites. Volume was computed by halving the product of the wheelbase (length between the front wheels and the back wheels), height, and width of the car (Fig. 6).

Measure of status of automobile brand. Because social status has been found to predict unethi-cal behavior (Piff, Stancato, Cote, Mendoza-Denton, & Keltner, 2012), we controlled for the status of vehicle brands by including it as a covariate in our analyses. To create an index of status, we conducted a study in which American participants ($N = 95$) rated the status of each of the observed vehicle brands using scales from 1 (*extremely low status*) to 7 (*extremely high status*). Responses were averaged to form a measure of vehicle status for each brand.

Small mini-study here just to obtain objective data on what one would call a high-status vs. low-status car. These data are then used to analyze experiment 4 data.

Results and discussion

Consistent with our theorizing, results from a binary logistic regression controlling for status[10] of cars indicated that vehicles with larger driver's seats were more likely to be double-parked, $b = 0.020$, $SE = 0.005$, $p < .001$. At 1 standard deviation above the mean in driver's seat size, the probability that the vehicle would be double-parked increased from 51% to 71%.

To account for the fact that drivers of lengthy cars might be more likely to double-park given the increased difficulty of finding large enough parking spots in a congested city such as New York, we controlled for status and car length in another regression. The relationship between driver's-seat size and double-parking remained marginally significant, $b = 0.015$, $SE = 0.009$, $p = .087$, despite the fact that length was strongly correlated with driver's seat size, $r = .83$, $p < .001$.

Although the results of this study provide some insights on the ecological validity of this phenomenon, the methodology has clear limitations (as is often the case with observational work). For example, we were unable to ascertain driver demographics, such as gender or body size, and drivers could not be randomly assigned to the conditions. Without professional appraisal of each car in our sample, we were also unable to accurately determine the cars' pres-ent value. However, when Study 4 is taken together with the three experiments, the package

FIG. 6. Schematic showing the dimensions of automobiles considered in the size computation in Study 4.

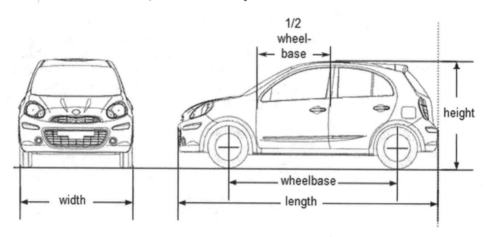

offers a more complete picture. It is important to note that Study 3 offset the limitations of Study 4 because in Study 3 participants were randomly assigned to expansive or contractive driver's seats, and vehicle attributes such as length and price were not an issue because the expansiveness of driver's seat was the only variable manipulated across conditions.

GENERAL DISCUSSION

Together, the results from these four studies provide multimethod evidence from both the lab and the real world that expansive postures incidentally shaped by the environment can lead to dishonesty. Studies 1 through 3 provided consistent evidence for the causal relationship between postural expansiveness and dishonest behavior. The use of different participant populations and real-world parking data suggests that the effect is ecologically valid.

Whereas researchers in design and human factors (Stokols, 1978; Werner et al., 1992) would not be surprised at our findings, very little research in psychology has ventured into the domain of ergonomics and social behavior. The current research suggests that catalysts for dishonesty could be lurking in people's ordinary, everyday environments—such as cars, workstations, and offices. Our bodies are perpetually enslaved by the structure of our physical spaces, and the findings reported here suggest that when our bodily postures are incidentally expanded by these spaces, we could be lured into behaving dishonestly.

That said, incidentally induced expansive postures could also produce beneficial effects, such as resilience against pain and stress, and bolster executive functioning, much as the research on social power has shown (Bohns & Wiltermuth, 2012; Carney et al., 2013; Smith, Jostmann, Galinsky, & van Dijk, 2008). The theoretical argument in Carney et al. (2013) is that power induces physiological changes that render people more willing and able to engage in all acts—whether honest or dishonest. Consistent with this idea, power does seem to promote ethical and socially responsible behaviors under certain conditions (e.g. Chen, Lee-Chai, & Bargh, 2001; DeCelles, DeRue, Margolis, & Ceranic, 2012). How do we reconcile these differences? There are some additionally useful theoretical ideas to consider.

Hirsh, Galinsky, and Zhong (2011) proposed that power could be a catalyst that reveals people's true selves. Recent research has also found that power enhances moral awareness among individuals with a strong moral identity but decreases moral awareness in those with a weak moral identity (DeCelles et al., 2012). Similarly, individuals with a communal relationship orientation are more socially responsible than those with an exchange relationship orientation, because power amplifies dominant dispositional cues (Chen et al., 2001).

Power can also shape a person by amplifying the dominant situational cue (Hirsh et al., 2011). Powerful individuals tend to focus on contextually activated goals (Guinote, 2007). They are more likely to cheat and take risks when the rewards, like those in the current research, are attractive (Anderson & Galinsky, 2006; Galinsky, Magee, Inesi, & Gruenfeld, 2006; Inesi, 2010; Lammers et al., 2010). However, when the most dominant contextual cue is to be cooperative, power should correspondingly promote behaviors that are more other-focused and less self-interested (Handgraaf, Van Dijk, Vermunt, Wilke, & De Dreu, 2008). Therefore, it seems that although power and expansive posture may lead to self-focused and dishonest behaviors, they do also lead to prosocial and socially responsible outcomes if the situational cues for such goals are salient.

One prescriptive point that could be offered from this work is that we may need to consider the science of ethics more holistically—taking into consideration not only the sometimes toxic

---

One of the great strengths of this paper, and a big reason why I wanted to include it in this reader is that it is a good example of research that uses multiple methods in multiple settings (lab and real world) to examine a psychological phenomenon. When we obtain experiment data from the lab that suggests support for a hypothesis (and, in turn, a theory), that is good. But, when we obtain similar results using multiple methods, and in different settings, our confidence in that finding is much stronger.

What are some practical applications of these findings in the real world?

Wait, didn't these studies just demonstrate that expansive postures led to a feeling of power, which increased dishonest behavior? Now we're reading that power also promotes ethical and responsible behavior? Which is it?

AHA! Here is a viable theory to reconcile the issue we just raised. Essentially, it says that power magnifies one's true self, so that if you are a dishonest person (or one with a "weak moral identity") and you feel powerful, you may be more likely to be dishonest (or break the law). If you have a strong moral center, then feeling powerful may lead you to be more ethical, helpful, and responsible.

effect of power itself, but also the nefarious impact of incentivizing the wrong things. Finally, the very ways in which offices and furniture are designed need examination and consideration. Future research could explore ways in which we could capitalize on even the simplest features of our physical environments, toward the goal of promoting ethical, prosocial, and healthy workplace behaviors.

AUTHOR CONTRIBUTIONS

All authors contributed to the study design. Data were collected by A. J. Yap, A. S. Wazlawek, and D. R. Carney's lab manager under the guidance of A. J. Yap. A. J. Yap and A. S. Wazlawek analyzed and interpreted the data under the supervision of D. R. Carney. A. J. Yap and D. R. Carney drafted the manuscript, and A. S. Wazlawek, B. J. Lucas, and A. J. C. Cuddy provided revisions. All authors approved the final version of the manuscript for submission.

ACKNOWLEDGMENTS

We thank Liza St. John, Erica Bragg, Kyonne Isaac, Amanda Bowling, Samantha Chu, and Dayna Stimson for data collection and research assistance. We also thank Adam Galinsky, Daniel Ames, Leanne ten Brinke, and members of the SNoB lab and PPIG for their insightful comments and suggestions.

DECLARATION OF CONFLICTING INTERESTS

The authors declared that they had no conflicts of interest with respect to their authorship or the publication of this article.

FUNDING

This research was supported by National Science Foundation CAREER Grant 1056194 to D. R. Carney.

NOTES

1. This study included two samples. Sample size was not predetermined, but the data were analyzed after the completion of each data-collection period. Both samples were subject to the same procedure with the exception that participants in one sample were administered the Regulatory Focus Questionnaire (Higgins et al., 2001) before the posture manipulation. We followed Schimmack's (2012) recommendation to combine data from these two samples into a single analysis. A meta-analytic approach to combining the samples was also undertaken to verify that our effect was as strong as it seemed when the raw data were combined. Toward that goal, the phi coefficients for effect size (which are equivalent to Pearson correlations for effect size in a 2×2 chi-squared analysis) were Fisher's z transformed, weighted by sample size, and then averaged. The average Fisher's z-transformed r value was then converted back into a Pearson r. The average effect-size r was .41, and the associated combined z value was 5.03, $p < .001$.
2. This survey was administered as part of our cover story. The data were not analyzed.
3. Eight participants did not count the money, and 2 reported awareness of our dishonesty measure. We made an a priori decision to exclude these participants from our analysis. Results remained significant when these participants were included, $\chi^2(1, N = 88) = 7.28, p = .007$.

4. We had aimed to recruit 40 participants, but because of logistical laboratory issues (i.e., an initially small subject population that was further reduced by competition for participants with two other researchers using the same dishonesty paradigm), we were able to recruit only 34 participants during the time frame for recruitment.

5. Debriefing checks revealed that 3 participants were aware of our dishonesty paradigm, so their data were excluded from analyses. One of these participants also altered the work-space layout without permission. One outlier whose number of altered answers was more than 3 standard deviations above the overall mean was also excluded. Results were not significant when these participants were included, $F(1, 33) = 0.29$, $p > .1$.

6. We had aimed to recruit between 70 and 80 participants; we stopped at 71 participants because the time frame for recruitment ended.

7. We asked participants to report on the difficulty of the task, using a 7-point Likert-type scale. Results revealed no significant difference between conditions.

8. Video recordings showed that 2 participants had problems maneuvering the car, which resulted in their repeatedly crashing into objects throughout the race. We made an a priori decision to exclude these participants. Results were not significant when these participants were included, $F(1, 69) = 0.50$, $p > .1$.

9. Bootstrapping analyses considering incidence of hit-and-run as a mediator between posture and sense of power as the outcome yielded marginally significant results. However, further analyses revealed that incidence of hit-and-run did not significantly predict sense of power for either expansive or contractive participants when analyzed separately.

10. There was no effect of status, $b = 0.45$, $SE = 0.34$, $p = .18$. When status was not included as a covariate, the effect remained significant, $b = 0.019$, $SE = 0.005$, $p = .001$.

REFERENCES

Altman, I., Taylor, D. A., & Wheeler, L. (1971). Ecological aspects of group behavior in social isolation. *Journal of Applied Social Psychology, 1,* 76–100.

Anderson, C., & Galinsky, A. D. (2006). Power, optimism, and risk-taking. *European Journal of Social Psychology, 36,* 511–536.

Bohns, V. K., & Wiltermuth, S. S. (2012). It hurts when I do this (or you do that): Posture and pain tolerance. *Journal of Experimental Social Psychology, 48,* 341–345.

Boles, T. L., Croson, R. T. A., & Murnighan, J. K. (2000). Deception and retribution in repeated ultimatum bargaining. *Organizational Behavior and Human Decision Processes, 83,* 235–259.

Carney, D. R., Cuddy, A. J. C., & Yap, A. J. (2010). Power posing: Brief nonverbal displays affect neuroendocrine levels and risk tolerance. *Psychological Science, 21,* 1363–1368.

Carney, D. R., Hall, J. A., & LeBeau, L. S. (2005). Beliefs about the nonverbal expression of social power. *Journal of Nonverbal Behavior, 29,* 105–123.

Carney, D. R., Yap, A. J., Lucas, B. J., Mehta, P. H., McGee, J. A., & Wilmuth, C. (2013). *Power buffers stress.* Unpublished manuscript, Haas School of Business, University of California, Berkeley.

Chen, S., Lee-Chai, A. Y., & Bargh, J. A. (2001). Relationship orientation as a moderator of the effects of social power. *Journal of Personality and Social Psychology, 80,* 173–187.

Damasio, A. (1994). *Descartes' error.* New York, NY: Grosset/Putnam.

Darwin, C. (1904). *The expression of emotions in man and animals.* London, England: Murray. (Original work published 1872)

DeCelles, K. A., DeRue, D. A., Margolis, J. D., & Ceranic, T. L. (2012). Does power corrupt or enable? When and why power facilitates self-interested behavior. *Journal of Applied Psychology, 97,* 681–689.

de Waal, F. (1998). *Chimpanzee politics: Power and sex among apes.* Baltimore, MD: Johns Hopkins.

Duclos, S. E., Laird, J. D., Schneider, E., Sexter, M., Stern, L., & Van Lighten, O. (1989). Emotion-specific effects of facial expressions and postures on emotional experience. *Journal of Personality and Social Psychology, 57,* 100–108.

Ellyson, S. L., & Dovidio, J. F. (1985). *Power, dominance, and nonverbal behavior.* New York, NY: Springer-Verlag.

Fischer, J., Fischer, P., Englich, B., Aydin, N., & Frey, D. (2011). Empower my decisions: The effects of power gestures on confirmatory information processing. *Journal of Experimental Social Psychology*, *47*, 1146–1154.

Fisman, R., & Miguel, E. (2007). Corruption, norms, and legal enforcement: Evidence from diplomatic parking tickets. *Journal of Political Economy*, *115*, 1020–1048.

Galinsky, A. D., Gruenfeld, D. H., & Magee, J. C. (2003). From power to action. *Journal of Personality and Social Psychology*, *85*, 453–466.

Galinsky, A. D., Magee, J. C., Inesi, M. E., & Gruenfeld, D. H. (2006). Power and perspectives not taken. *Psychological Science*, *17*, 1068–1074.

Guinote, A. (2007). Power and goal pursuit. *Personality and Social Psychology Bulletin*, *33*, 1076–1087.

Hall, J. A., Coats, E. J., & Smith LeBeau, L. (2005). Nonverbal behavior and the vertical dimension of social relations: A meta-analysis. *Psychological Bulletin*, *131*, 898–924.

Handgraaf, M. J. J., Van Dijk, E., Vermunt, R. C., Wilke, H. A. M., & De Dreu, C. K. W. (2008). Less power or powerless? Egocentric empathy gaps and the irony of having little versus no power in social decision making. *Journal of Personality and Social Psychology*, *95*, 1136–1149.

Harmon-Jones, E., & Peterson, C. K. (2009). Supine body position reduces neural response to anger evocation. *Psychological Science*, *20*, 1209–1210.

Higgins, E. T., Friedman, R. S., Harlow, R. E., Idson, L. C., Ayduk, O. N., & Taylor, A. (2001). Achievement orientations from subjective histories of success: Promotion pride versus prevention pride. *European Journal of Social Psychology*, *31*, 3–23.

Hirsh, J. B., Galinsky, A. D., & Zhong, C. B. (2011). Drunk, powerful, and in the dark: How general processes of disinhibition produce both prosocial and antisocial behavior. *Perspectives on Psychological Science*, *6*, 415–427.

Huang, L., Galinsky, A. D., Gruenfeld, D. H., & Guillory, L. E. (2011). Powerful postures versus powerful roles: Which is the proximate correlate of thought and behavior? *Psychological Science*, *22*, 95–102.

Inesi, M. E. (2010). Power and loss aversion. *Organizational Behavior and Human Decision Processes*, *112*, 58–69.

James, W. (1884). What is an emotion? *Mind*, *9*, 188–205.

Kaplan, S., & Kaplan, R. (2009). Creating a larger role for environmental psychology: The Reasonable Person Model as an integrative framework. *Journal of Environmental Psychology*, *29*, 329–339.

Keltner, D., Gruenfeld, D. H., & Anderson, C. (2003). Power, approach, and inhibition. *Psychological Review*, *110*, 265–284.

Knight, C., & Haslam, S. A. (2010). The relative merits of lean, enriched, and empowered offices: An experimental examination of the impact of workspace management strategies on well-being and productivity. *Journal of Experimental Psychology: Applied*, *16*, 158–172.

Laird, J. D. (1974). Self-attribution of emotion: The effects of expressive behavior on the quality of emotional experience. *Journal of Personality and Social Psychology*, *29*, 475–486.

Lammers, J., Stapel, D. A., & Galinsky, A. D. (2010). Power increases hypocrisy: Moralizing in reasoning, immorality in behavior. *Psychological Science*, *21*, 737–744.

Lammers, J., Stoker, J. I., Jordan, J., Pollmann, M., & Stapel, D. A. (2011). Power increases infidelity among men and women. *Psychological Science*, *22*, 1191–1197.

Leonard, P. (2012). Changing organisational space: Green? or lean and mean? *Sociology*, *47*, 333–349.

Niedenthal, P. M. (2007). Embodying emotion. *Science*, *316*, 1002–1005.

Niedenthal, P. M., Barsalou, L. W., Winkielman, P., KrauthGruber, S., & Ric, F. (2005). Embodiment in attitudes, social perception, and emotion. *Personality and Social Psychology Review*, *9*, 184–211.

Piff, P. K., Stancato, D. M., Cote, S., Mendoza-Denton, R., & Keltner, D. (2012). Higher social class predicts increased unethical behavior. *Proceedings of the National Academy of Sciences, USA*, *109*, 4086–4091.

Preacher, K. J., & Hayes, A. F. (2004). SPSS and SAS procedures for estimating indirect effects in simple mediation models. *Behavior Research Methods, Instruments, & Computers*, *36*, 717–731.

Rhodewalt, F., & Comer, R. (1979). Induced-compliance attitude change: Once more with feeling. *Journal of Experimental Social Psychology*, *15*, 35–47.

Riskind, J. H. (1983). Nonverbal expressions and the accessibility of life experience memories: A congruence hypothesis. *Social Cognition*, *2*, 62–86.

Riskind, J. H., & Gotay, C. C. (1982). Physical posture: Could it have regulatory or feedback effects on motivation and emotion? *Motivation and Emotion*, *6*, 273–298.

Ruedy, N. E., & Schweitzer, M. E. (2010). In the moment: The effect of mindfulness on ethical decision making. *Journal of Business Ethics, 95*, 73–87.

Schimmack, U. (2012). The ironic effect of significant results on the credibility of multiple-study articles. *Psychological Methods, 17*, 551–566.

Simmons, J. P., Nelson, L. D., & Simonsohn, U. (2012). *A 21 word solution.* Retrieved from http://ssrn.com/abstract=2160588

Smith, P. K., Jostmann, N. B., Galinsky, A. D., & van Dijk, W. W. (2008). Lacking power impairs executive functions. *Psychological Science, 19*, 441–447.

Stokols, D. (1978). Environmental psychology. *Annual Review of Psychology, 29*, 253–295.

Strack, F., Martin, L. L., & Stepper, S. (1988). Inhibiting and facilitating conditions of the human smile: A nonobtrusive test of the facial feedback hypothesis. *Journal of Personality and Social Psychology, 54*, 768–777.

Tiedens, L. Z., & Fragale, A. R. (2003). Power moves: Complementarity in dominant and submissive nonverbal behavior. *Journal of Personality and Social Psychology, 84*, 558–568.

Weisfeld, G. E., & Beresford, J. M. (1982). Erectness of posture as an indicator of dominance or success in humans. *Motivation and Emotion, 6*, 113–129.

Wells, G. L., & Petty, R. E. (1980). The effects of overt head movements on persuasion: Compatibility and incompatibility of responses. *Basic and Applied Social Psychology, 1*, 219–230.

Werner, C. M., Altman, I., & Brown, B. B. (1992). A transactional approach to interpersonal relations: Physical environment, social context and temporal qualities. *Journal of Social and Personal Relationships, 9*, 297–323.

POST-ARTICLE DISCUSSION

This series of studies is an excellent demonstration of using multiple methods to examine a particular concept. It also shows what researchers refer to as "programmatic" research, in that each study in the paper tries to address unanswered questions or limitations raised in the prior study but by using new methods and creative alternate designs. Recall in Study 1, Yap and his colleagues had people at a train station take either an expansive or a passive pose and then complete a questionnaire. Then they paid the subject for her time, and the question was, Would posing a certain way cause the subject to be dishonest by not telling the experimenter that she was paid too much?

In the other paper in this chapter, Carney et al. (2010) made the link between expansive body positions and feelings of power. This suggests that the environment's constricting one's physical body or allowing it to expand can cause one to experience a diminished sense of power or an increased sense of power. For example, consider the office chair you have at work: Are the ergonomics of the chair such that it causes you to slouch while you sit in it? If so, the chair is likely leading you to also feel less powerful. Do you sit in a tiny cubicle at work? That enclosed environment is also having that same negative effect on your sense of power. It is not a great revelation that those with more responsibilities and more actual power usually have bigger offices in a company.

Yap et al. also found evidence that body posture can affect one's honesty. Those with constricted body posture were less honest. Why do you suppose that is? What is

(Continued)

(Continued)

the link between honesty and feelings of power? If it is mostly the powerless who are dishonest, then how does one explain instances in corporate America where powerful people have been convicted of stealing from their company or some other illegal or unethical activity?

As I mentioned in the margin comments, one of the great strengths of this paper is that the authors used multiple methods to address the same problem. This is always the best approach in psychological experimentation because to the degree that multiple methods all converge on the same finding, we can say that the finding is not an artifact of the particular method or measures used, but the predicted effect is such a strong phenomenon that it will be revealed even with different methods and measures.

THINGS TO THINK ABOUT

1. Why does expanding our bodies make us feel powerful? Why would feeling powerful make one more likely to be dishonest or otherwise violate the law (e.g., drive recklessly)?

2. What are the pros and cons of doing research in the field? If you were the researcher, would you also have conducted field studies along with lab studies, or only lab experiments? Why?

3. For Study 1, the researchers didn't report any further information on how many participants checked the money (counted it, and therefore noticed the $5 bill). What other limitations or issues are there with Study 1?

4. For Experiment 2, do you think $1 for every anagram solved is a sufficiently strong motivation for participants to cheat? If not, how would you make their motive to cheat even stronger?

5. Consider the results in Experiment 3 that were "marginally significant." Recall that one of the main reasons an analysis fails to find an effect is that the independent variable is too weak. Another is that there really is no effect to be found. Which is going on here, and why?

6. What confounds (if any) do you think may be at play in Experiment 4? For example, what variables may be at play in those persons who have an expansive driver's seat? Would that be correlated with a bigger (and more expensive) car? If so, would that more expensive car be more likely to be owned by someone higher in socioeconomic status?

7. What are the practical applications of the main findings of this four-study package?

CHAPTER

5

Attitudes

From the early 1900s, when the field of social psychology was just being created, one of the things that these early social psychologists agreed on was that the study of attitudes must form an important cornerstone for the field (Allport, 1924). The reason for this was simple. We first agree that the goal of any science, including psychology, is to explain and predict phenomena. Thus, anything that would aid us in predicting future behavior would be useful to that endeavor. Now, attitudes can be defined as an evaluation of some attitude object (person, place, thing) along a continuum of good–bad, positive–negative, or similar variations. If a person has a very positive attitude toward, say, chocolate chip cookies, then I can predict with reasonable certainty that the next time that person needs to buy cookies, he or she will buy chocolate chip cookies. In other words, social psychologists have shown in their experiments that attitudes seem to guide future behavior, and that is why they are so important to the field: They help researchers predict future behavior. In this introduction, we briefly review some of the major topics of study when looking at attitudes. As with all introductions in this volume, this one is not meant to be comprehensive but rather a broad overview of select major subtopics in the study of attitudes.

ACQUISITION/FORMATION OF ATTITUDES

The first source of our attitudes comes from our early childhood and our parents or guardians (Sinclair, Dunn, & Lowery, 2005). Children trust their parents to instruct them about the world, and children internalize the attitudes that their parents explicitly and implicitly display (Allport, 1935; Eagly & Chaiken, 1993). However, some researchers contend that some attitudes are biologically based (Guastello & Guastello, 2008; Waller, Kojetin, Bouchard, Lykken, & Tellegen, 1990). For decades, most social psychologists approached the subject of the genetic basis of attitudes with much skepticism. However, the zeitgeist in the field has changed on this issue, to such an extent that Banaji and Heiphetz (2010) wrote, "Psychologists can no longer turn a blind eye to the fact that attitudes, like any other aspect of human nature and culture, have an evolutionary history" (p. 371).

In addition to the attitudes we acquire from our parents, we also are influenced by the evaluations our peers make. For example, a famous study by Newcomb (1943) examined political attitudes among upper-middle-class women. Some women indicated they planned to attend a small liberal arts college (Bennington College), and others had no plans to attend college. Newcomb found that 74% were Republican. After only 1 year of college, however, only 64% of the Bennington women were still Republican (75% of those who didn't attend were Republican). After 25 years, Newcomb found that 74% of the non-college women were still Republican, whereas only 40% of the Bennington women were Republican (Newcomb, Koenig, Flacks, & Warwick, 1967). Exposure to new ways of thinking and other attitudes from their college peers had a lasting impact on the Bennington women, causing them to make changes in their political views.

ATTITUDE MEASUREMENT

From the time that the earliest social psychologists focused on attitudes as a central area of study, they have also been occupied with understanding the best ways to measure attitudes.

Physiological Measures

One way researchers tried to ascertain attitudes is to assess changes in physiological arousal, such as heart rate, galvanic skin response, and blood pressure. The idea is that elevations in these measures would be correlated with stronger attitudes. This is similar to the logic behind the use of polygraph machines (lie detector tests). Most people get nervous when they tell lies, so the machine indicates changes in those physiological measures, and, theoretically, when the person lied. The problem with these types of measures is that they only show changes in physiological indices; they do not point to the underlying attitude or truth or falsehood of the statement that the person made. This is why, incidentally, lie detector machine results are not admissible in court.

A Direct Line to Attitudes?

A more elaborate approach to studying attitudes is called the "bogus pipeline" method (Jones & Sigall, 1971; Sigall & Page, 1971). Essentially, subjects are brought into the lab and hooked up to a device that looks a lot like a lie detector (polygraph) machine. They are told that it is a new device designed to tell the true attitudes that the subject has about the topics presented to them by the experimenter. After some further slight-of-hand on the part of the experimenter to make the subject believe in the capabilities of the machine, the experimenter then asks subjects to provide their attitudes toward a number of topics (e.g., race, politics, etc.). The reason this procedure gained a lot of attention is that it was purported to be a better way to assess true attitudes and to reduce socially desirable responding (politically correct but maybe not truthful answers) on the part of the subject. Did it work? Results from more than 31 studies suggest that it does work to reduce social desirability and enhance more truthful subject responses (Roese & Jamieson, 1993). Although this measure of attitudes was successful at what it set out to do, it is rarely used by today's experimental social psychologists because it is very labor intensive. Each session requires about 90 minutes, and the method requires a lot of acting (and deception) on the part of the experimenter.

The Questionnaire

So how do most researchers measure attitudes? The simplest and cheapest way possible, of course. That is the self-report questionnaire. There is an old saying in social science research, "If you want to know how people feel, ask them." That is exactly what this method does. Researchers typically present the subject with a printed series of questions or statements, to which the subject indicates his or her agreement or attitude.

To get an objective, quantitative and therefore measurable attitude, the subject circles a number along a number line (e.g., from 1 [strongly disagree] to 10 [strongly agree]) immediately below the statement, indicating the degree to which he agrees with the statement. This particular (and very popular) type of self-report questionnaire is called a Likert-type scale (Ray, 1951). This method of measuring attitudes is by far the most common, and the reason is that it is cheap (just the cost of making copies of the questionnaire), it is convenient (no need to fly in participants or put them up in hotels, as most subjects are college students participating in research in exchange for extra credit), and it is fast (often a researcher can pass out hundreds of questionnaires in large classes and get all their data in a matter of hours). The downside to self-report questionnaires is that sometimes the subject won't understand part of a question and, in the large classes, may not ask for help and instead just guess. Another problem is sometimes subjects want to present themselves in the most politically correct manner and so will not answer truthfully. Still another problem: Sometimes subjects are unwilling or unable to tell the researcher what their attitudes are on a given subject, especially if it is a socially sensitive one like race or politics or religion. Researchers have a number of ways to deal with these potential problems, and as a result, self-report questionnaires remain by far the most popular way to measure attitudes.

THE SEARCH FOR BALANCE

Balance Theory

In 1958, Fritz Heider published one of the most important books in social psychology. In it, he discusses his balance theory and how it makes the argument that people need balance or consistency among their cognitions. People need to feel like there is harmony or consistency among their values, attitudes, and beliefs, and when these are inconsistent, the person is motivated to restore balance in the form of cognitive consistency. This pertains to relationships, too. For example, suppose I (A) like my friend (O), and my friend likes her friend (P). Let's further suppose I don't like my friend's friend. Heider liked to diagram these situations in terms of relationship triads. If A, O, and P all liked each other, there would be harmony all around. But in the earlier scenario, you could write a plus sign (+) between me and my friend, and between my friend and her friend, but you'd need a minus sign (–) between me and my friend's friend. According to Heider, because this is an imbalanced triad and the imbalance is causing me discomfort, I need to do something about it. Do I like my friend enough to deal with the discomfort of my friend's friend occasionally? Is the discomfort of being around my friend's friend more than I find acceptable? If so, I may decide that my friendship with O is not worth the hassle, and I would end that friendship.

Cognitive Dissonance Theory

A year before Heider published his balance theory book, Leon Festinger published his theory of cognitive dissonance (1957). Building largely on Heider's work on balance theory,[1] Festinger said that when people hold two inconsistent thoughts or do a behavior that is inconsistent with a thought, people will feel uncomfortable. This discomfort is highly motivating, and the person will seek to get rid of this discomfort by changing

---

[1] Although Festinger's book came out a year before Heider's book, his theory built on Heider's earlier writing on balance theory.

one of the thoughts so that it is consistent with the other, or change the thought to make it consistent with the behavior. For example, Festinger talks about the dilemma that smokers face. They are engaging in a behavior that they know is harmful to their body. That should make them feel cognitive dissonance. How do they resolve it? He says that because it is very difficult for smokers to stop their smoking behavior, they need to change the way they think about smoking, to make it consistent with smoking. For example, if they thought that smoking hasn't been shown in experiments to cause cancer in humans, they could say it isn't harmful, and thus smoking isn't incompatible with their overall desire to preserve their life. Or perhaps they believe they are genetically able to resist any harmful effects of smoking because they have an uncle who smoked like a chimney his whole life and never got cancer. Festinger says that the motive to reduce cognitive dissonance is a powerful one, and it has wide-ranging effects on much of our behavior and attitudes. The theory has become one of the most studied and influential theories and has been supported by numerous experiments (Cooper, 2007; Dunning, 2015).

ATTITUDE CHANGE

In addition to studying how attitudes are formed, social psychologists are equally interested in investigating how those attitudes can be changed. This process, persuasion, is subject to the influence of personal, context, and message variables, and it is the combination of those that will determine the effectiveness of the persuasion message for that individual.

The Yale Approach

During World War II, the government commissioned Yale psychologist Carl Hovland to research the best ways to persuade the American public to do a number of things to help the war effort, such as conserve vital materials (rubber, silk, the best food) and buy war bonds to help fund the war. In a systematic program of research, Hovland and his colleagues found that three things are important in the persuasion process: the source, the message, and the audience (Hovland, Janis, & Kelly, 1953). Sources who are more attractive, credible, and knowledgeable are more persuasive. Messages that are designed to not appear to be too "pushy" (the "hard sell") are more persuasive. Audiences that are younger are more easily persuaded (because they haven't formed solid attitudes about the world yet), and audiences that are distracted (e.g., by a message with humor) are more easily persuaded. This program of research was invaluable and we learned much from it. Later, researchers sought to expand on this base by looking at the cognitive processes involved in persuasion.

The Elaboration Likelihood Model

During the late 1960s and early 1970s, social psychology was rocked by what many refer to as a "crisis of confidence" in a core tenet of its foundation: that attitudes predict behavior. Critics published devastating papers arguing that attitudes do a poor job of predicting future behavior, and therefore, the study of attitudes was essentially pointless (e.g., Wicker, 1971). After several years and many papers arguing the flaws in critics' papers, and also for the idea that when one aggregates situations the correlation from attitude to behavior is significantly higher, social psychology emerged from this crisis ready to again tackle the mysteries of attitudes and attitude change. In the early 1980s, Petty and Cacioppo (1986) published their elaboration likelihood model of persuasion, in which they argue that there are two routes to persuasion, depending on one's personal involvement in the issue. They say that if the issue is important to the recipient, he or she will take the "central route" in thinking about it. This means that the person will think very carefully about the persuasion message and will only change his or her attitude if the message presents logical, rational reasons why the new attitude should be adopted. On the other hand, if the issue is not that important to the recipient, he or she will take the "peripheral route" in which persuasion does not depend on logic or reason, but it can happen via "peripheral cues" such as celebrity of the source, distraction, and humor. This simple model appears to account nicely for how persuasion works in many contexts, and it has been supported by dozens of studies over the past several decades (O'Keefe, 2013).

INTRODUCTION TO READING 5.1
Festinger and Carlsmith (1959)

One of the more powerful psychological forces we experience in daily life is the desire to be consistent. It just makes life easier for us and for those around us. Consider how much more complicated things would be if your friend's attitudes about everything varied from day to day or even hour to hour. It would be exhausting trying to keep up. We also tend to have a less positive view of people who can't remain relatively consistent in their values and beliefs. In the 1940s and 1950s, Fritz Heider articulated the importance of cognitive consistency in his influential balance theory (Heider, 1946, 1958). Balance theory said, in part, that we all strive to maintain balance (cognitive consistency) between our values, attitudes, and beliefs. This striving for balance influences our relationships as well; we seek to be friends with people who share our values and beliefs.

Drawing from these ideas, Leon Festinger (1957) presented what can arguably be called the most influential theory in the history of social psychology: the theory of cognitive dissonance. The theory says that when we have two cognitively incompatible thoughts (or a thought that is incompatible with a behavior), we feel dissonance, a negative arousal state. We feel uncomfortable, and we are highly motivated to eliminate that dissonance. The theory says we can do this by making our thoughts (or thought and behavior) consistent. The way to do this is by changing one of your thoughts to match the other. As an illustration, Festinger (1957) discussed the dilemma faced by people who smoke. Smokers presumably have a positive attitude toward living and want to do things to prolong their life. However, they are doing a behavior they know is harmful to living long (smoking), and this should cause them to feel dissonance. How do smokers typically resolve this dissonance? Well, as most smokers will tell you, stopping smoking is very difficult. The easier route is to change the way they think about smoking. "Perhaps smoking isn't bad for you. Maybe the science isn't conclusive that it will hurt me." Or, "My uncle smoked and he lived to be 95, so smoking isn't bad for you." Once smokers change how they think about smoking ("It is not bad"), there is no inconsistency with their positive attitude toward life and not hurting themselves.

The paper you are about to read is perhaps the most famous experiment testing cognitive dissonance theory. Before you read it, let's put you in the researcher's seat. If you want to induce cognitive dissonance in an experiment subject (for the purposes of seeing how if and how subjects try to eliminate it), how would you do it? You would have to get the subject to have two incompatible attitudes (or attitude and behavior). It is not as easy as it might appear. Then, once the subject has dissonance, how can you provide the subject a way to eliminate it? They need a mechanism for changing their attitude. Stumped? I think you'll find Festinger and Carlsmith's solutions clever. Without further delay, let's read the Festinger and Carlsmith article. We'll chat afterward. Enjoy!

Reading 5.1

Cognitive Consequences of Forced Compliance

Leon Festinger and James M. Carlsmith[1]

WHAT happens to a person's private opinion if he is forced to do or say something contrary to that opinion? Only recently has there been any experimental work related to this question. Two studies reported by Janis and King (1954; 1956) clearly showed that, at least under some conditions, the private opinion changes so as to bring it into closer correspondence with the overt behavior the person was forced to perform. Specifically, they showed that if a person is forced to improvise a speech supporting a point of view with which he disagrees, his private opinion moves toward the position advocated in the speech. The observed opinion change is greater than for persons who only hear the speech or for persons who read a prepared speech with emphasis solely on elocution and manner of delivery. The authors of these two studies explain their results mainly in terms of mental rehearsal and thinking up new arguments. In this way, they propose, the person who is forced to improvise a speech convinces himself. They present some evidence, which is not altogether conclusive, in support of this explanation. We will have more to say concerning this explanation in discussing the results of our experiment.

Kelman (1953) tried to pursue the matter further. He reasoned that if the person is induced to make an overt statement contrary to his private opinion by the offer of some reward, then the greater the reward offered, the greater should be the subsequent opinion change. His data, however, did not support this idea. He found, rather, that a large reward produced less subsequent opinion change than did a smaller reward. Actually, this finding by Kelman is consistent with the theory we will outline below but, for a number of reasons, is not conclusive. One of the major weaknesses of the data is that not all subjects in the experiment made an overt statement contrary to their private opinion in order to obtain the offered reward. What is more, as one might expect, the percentage of subjects who complied increased as the size of the offered reward increased. Thus, with self-selection of who did and who did not make the required overt statement and with varying percentages of subjects in the different conditions who did make the required statement, no interpretation of the data can be unequivocal.

Recently, Festinger (1957) proposed a theory concerning cognitive dissonance from which come a number of derivations about opinion change following forced compliance. Since these derivations are stated in detail by Festinger (1957, Ch. 4), we will here give only a brief outline of the reasoning.

Let us consider a person who privately holds opinion "X" but has, as a result of pressure brought to bear on him, publicly stated that he believes "not X."

While this type of scenario—being forced to do or say something contrary to your own opinion—isn't very common in life, the researchers use this setup for their experiment to test basic ideas about Festinger's classic theory of cognitive dissonance. Specifically, how do people resolve incompatible thoughts (or a thought and behavior)?

Why do you suppose this happens?

Rather than getting into the weeds of the below numbered and detailed example, let us just define cognitive dissonance theory at its most fundamental: The theory says that when we hold two incompatible thoughts (or do a behavior that is incompatible with a thought), then we feel cognitive dissonance. This is a negative arousal that we are highly motivated to eliminate as soon as possible. The theory says that the way most people eliminate the incompatible thoughts is to change one to match the other. With an incompatible thought and behavior, since it is hard to un-ring a bell (the behavior has already been performed), we almost always change the incompatible attitude to match the behavior. Once the incompatible attitudes are matched, the dissonance disappears.

[1] The experiment reported here was done as part of a program of research supported by a grant from the National Science Foundation to the senior author. We wish to thank Leonard Hommel, Judson Mills, and Robert Terwilliger for their help in designing and carrying out the experiment. We would also like to acknowledge the help of Ruth Smith and Marilyn M. Miller.

1. This person has two cognitions which, psychologically, do not fit together: one of these is the knowledge that he believes "X," the other the knowledge that he has publicly stated that he believes "not X." If no factors other than his private opinion are considered, it would follow, at least in our culture, that if he believes "X" he would publicly state "X." Hence, his cognition of his private belief is dissonant with his cognition concerning his actual public statement.

2. Similarly, the knowledge that he has said "not X" is consonant with (does fit together with) those cognitive elements corresponding to the reasons, pressures, promises of rewards and/or threats of punishment which induced him to say "not X."

3. In evaluating the total magnitude of dissonance, one must take account of both dissonances and consonances. Let us think of the sum of all the dissonances involving some particular cognition as "D" and the sum of all the consonances as "C." Then we might think of the total magnitude of dissonance as being a function of "D" divided by "D" plus "C."

Let us then see what can be said about the total magnitude of dissonance in a person created by the knowledge that he said "not X" and really believes "X." With everything else held constant, this total magnitude of dissonance would decrease as the number and importance of the pressures which induced him to say "not X" increased.

Thus, if the overt behavior was brought about by, say, offers of reward or threats of punishment, the magnitude of dissonance is maximal if these promised rewards or threatened punishments were just barely sufficient to induce the person to say "not X." From this point on, as the promised rewards or threatened punishment become larger, the magnitude of dissonance becomes smaller.

4. One way in which the dissonance can be reduced is for the person to change his private opinion so as to bring it into correspondence with what he has said. One would consequently expect to observe such opinion change after a person has been forced or induced to say something contrary to his private opinion. Furthermore, since the pressure to reduce dissonance will be a function of the magnitude of the dissonance, the observed opinion change should be greatest when the pressure used to elicit the overt behavior is just sufficient to do it.

The present experiment was designed to test this derivation under controlled, laboratory conditions. In the experiment we varied the amount of reward used to force persons to make a statement contrary to their private views. The prediction [from 3 and 4 above] is that the larger the reward given to the subject, the smaller will be the subsequent opinion change.

PROCEDURE

Seventy-one male students in the introductory psychology course at Stanford University were used in the experiment. In this course, students are required to spend a certain number of hours as subjects (Ss) in experiments. They choose among the available experiments by signing their names on a sheet posted on the bulletin board which states the nature of the experiment. The present experiment was listed as a two-hour experiment dealing *with* "Measures of Performance."

During the first week of the course, when the requirement of serving in experiments was announced and explained to the students, the instructor also told them about a study that the

Just a quick note about "cover stories." In experiments, we don't want the subjects to know what we are investigating, or the real reason why we are doing things a certain way. If the subject DID know the reason why we are doing the study, he or she might change his or her behavior in order to "be a good subject" and give us the responses the subject thinks we want. That of course would result in garbage for data, and the whole study would be ruined. So instead, experimenters usually tell the subject a "cover story" about the purpose of the experiment. The cover story is generally an intentionally vague sentence or two. For example, instead of saying my study is really about racism, I might say that it is about "social attitudes."

psychology department was conducting. He explained that, since they were required to serve in experiments, the department was conducting a study to evaluate these experiments in order to be able to improve them in the future. They were told that a sample of students would be interviewed after having served as Ss. They were urged to cooperate in these interviews by being completely frank and honest. The importance of this announcement will become clear shortly. It enabled us to measure the opinions of our Ss in a context not directly connected with our experiment and in which we could reasonably expect frank and honest expressions of opinion.

When the S arrived for the experiment on "Measures of Performance" he had to wait for a few minutes in the secretary's office. The experimenter (E) then came in, introduced himself to the S and, together, they walked into the laboratory room where the E said:

> This experiment usually takes a little over an hour but, of course, we had to sche-
> dule it for two hours. Since we have that extra time, the introductory psychology
> people asked if they could interview some of our subjects. [Offhand and conversa-
> tionally.] Did they announce that in class? I gather that they're interviewing some
> people who have been in experiments. I don't know much about it. Anyhow, they
> may want to interview you when you're through here.

With no further introduction or explanation the S was shown the first task, which involved putting 12 spools onto a tray, emptying the tray, refilling it with spools, and so on. He was told to use one hand and to work at his own speed. He did this for one-half hour. The E then removed the tray and spools and placed in front of the S a board containing 48 square pegs. His task was to turn each peg a quarter turn clockwise, then another quarter turn, and so on. He was told again to use one hand and to work at his own speed. The S worked at this task for another half hour.

While the S was working on these tasks, the E sat, with a stop watch in his hand, busily making notations on a sheet of paper. He did so in order to make it convincing that this was what the E was interested in and that these tasks, and how the S worked on them, was the total experiment. From our point of view the experiment had hardly started. The hour which the S spent working on the repetitive, monotonous tasks was intended *to* provide, for each S uniformly, an experience about which he would have a somewhat negative opinion.

After the half hour on the second task was over, the E conspicuously set the stop watch back to zero, put it away, pushed his chair back, lit a cigarette, and said:

> O.K. Well, that's all we have in the experiment itself. I'd like to explain what this
> has been all about so you'll have some idea of why you were doing this. [E pauses.]
> Well, the way the experiment is set up is this. There are actually two groups in the
> experiment. In one, the group you were in, we bring the subject in and give him
> essentially no introduction to the experiment. That is, all we tell him is what he
> needs to know in order to do the tasks, and he has no idea of what the experiment
> is all about, or what it's going to be like, or anything like that. But in the other
> group, we have a student that we've hired that works for us regularly, and what
> I do is take him into the next room where the subject is waiting—the same room
> you were waiting in before—and I introduce him as if he had just finished being
> a subject in the experiment. That is, I say: "This is so-and-so, who's just finished

Now, for this experiment, the researchers want to have the subject do one or two really boring tasks for a long time. The cover story for this—the reason they are having the subject do this—is to measure "small motor performance" (e.g. hand-eye coordination). Sounds plausible to subjects.

They do this second boring task for another half-hour. Imagine if you did this . . . you'd likely be quite bored!

So, everyone does the boring tasks for 1 hour, then each subject is randomly assigned to one of three conditions. In the control condition, the subject is then escorted to a separate office where he or she is interviewed about the previous tasks he or she just completed. One of the key questions asked is if he or she enjoyed the tasks. (You can probably guess how he or she answered that question!) After that questionnaire, control condition subjects were debriefed and thanked for their participation, then dismissed.

Now the other, non-control group subjects were not interviewed at the end of the boring tasks but instead were asked to do the experimenter a favor. The experimenter said normally he has an assistant tell the next subject about the experiment, and how fun it is, but the assistant isn't there yet. So, would the subject agree to tell the next subject that the experiment was a lot of fun? (Subjects usually agreed.) For their efforts, the experimenter will pay them $1 (half of the subjects were told $1, the other half were told $20) or $20. Then the subject went to the secretary's office, where the next subject was waiting, and told that person the experiment was a lot of fun. Then, the experimenter brought the subject to the secretary's office, where he or she was interviewed about how much he or she enjoyed the tasks. After the subject completed the interview, he or she was thanked and dismissed.

the experiment, and I've asked him to tell you a little of what it's about before you start." The fellow who works for us then, in conversation with the next subject, makes these points: [The E then produced a sheet headed "For Group B" which had written on it: It was very enjoyable, I had a lot of fun, I enjoyed myself, it was very interesting, it was intriguing, it was exciting. The E showed this to the S and then proceeded with his false explanation of the purpose of the experiment.] Now, of course, we have this student do this, because if the experimenter does it, it doesn't look as realistic, and what we're interested in doing is comparing how these two groups do on the experiment—the one with this previous expectation about the experiment, and the other, like yourself, with essentially none.

Up to this point the procedure was identical for Ss in all conditions. From this point on they diverged somewhat. Three conditions were run, Control, One Dollar, and Twenty Dollars, as follows:

Control Condition

The E continued:

Is that fairly clear? [Pause.] Look, that fellow [looks at watch] I was telling you about from the introductory psychology class said he would get here a couple of minutes from now. Would you mind waiting to see if he wants to talk to you? Fine. Why don't we go into the other room to wait? [The E left the S in the secretary's office for four minutes. He then returned and said:] O.K. Let's check and see if he does want to talk to you.

One and Twenty Dollar Conditions

The E continued:

Is that fairly clear how it is set up and what we're trying to do? (Pause.) Now, I also have a sort of strange thing to ask you. The thing is this. [Long pause, some confusion and uncertainty in the following, with a degree of embarrassment on the part of the E. The manner of the E contrasted strongly with the preceding unhesitant and assured false explanation of the experiment. The point was to make it seem to the S that this was the first time the E had done this and that he felt unsure of himself.] The fellow who normally does this for us couldn't do it today—he just phoned in, and something or other came up for him—so we've been looking around for someone that we could hire to do it for us. You see, we've got another subject waiting [looks at watch] who is supposed to be in that other condition. Now, the professor_____, who is in charge of this experiment, suggested that perhaps we could take a chance on your doing it for us. I'll tell you what we had in mind: the thing is, if you could do it for us now, then of course you would know how to do it, and if something like this should ever come up again, that is, the regular fellow couldn't make it, and we had a subject scheduled, it would be very reassuring to us to know that we had somebody else we could call on who knew how to do it. So, if you would be willing to do this for us, we'd like to hire you to do it now and then be on call in the future, if something like this should ever happen again. We can pay you a dollar (twenty dollars) for doing this for us, that is, for doing it now and then being on call. Do you think you could do that for us?

If the S hesitated, the E said things like, "It will only take a few minutes," "The regular person is pretty reliable; this is the first time he has missed," or "If we needed you we could phone you a day or two in advance; if you couldn't make it, of course, we wouldn't expect you to come." After the S agreed to do it, the E gave him the previously mentioned sheet of paper headed "For Group B" and asked him to read it through again. The E then paid the S one dollar (twenty dollars), made out a hand-written receipt form, and asked the S to sign it. He then said:

> O.K., the way we'll do it is this. As I said, the next subject should be here by now. I think the next one is a girl. I'll take you into the next room and introduce you to her, saying that you've just finished the experiment and that we've asked you to tell her a little about it. And what we want you to do is just sit down and get into a conversation with her and try to get across the points on that sheet of paper. I'll leave you alone and come back after a couple of minutes. O.K.?

The E then took the S into the secretary's office where he had previously waited and where the next S was waiting. (The secretary had left the office.) He introduced the girl and the S to one another saying that the S had just finished the experiment and would tell her something about it. He then left saying he would return in a couple of minutes. The girl, an undergraduate hired for this role, said little until the S made some positive remarks about the experiment and then said that she was surprised because a friend of hers had taken the experiment the week before and had told her that it was boring and that she ought to try to get out of it. Most Ss responded by saying something like "Oh, no, it's really very interesting. I'm sure you'll enjoy it." The girl, after this listened quietly, accepting and agreeing to everything the S told her. The discussion between the S and the girl was recorded on a hidden tape recorder.

After two minutes the E returned, asked the girl to go into the experimental room, thanked the S for talking to the girl, wrote down his phone number to continue the fiction that we might call on him again in the future and then said: "Look, could we check and see if that fellow from introductory psychology wants to talk to you?"

From this point on, the procedure for all three conditions was once more identical. As the E and the S started to walk to the office where the interviewer was, the E said: "Thanks very much for working on those tasks for us. I hope you did enjoy it. Most of our subjects tell us afterward that they found it quite interesting. You get a chance to see how you react to the tasks and so forth." This short persuasive communication was made in all conditions in exactly the same way. The reason for doing it, theoretically, was to make it easier for anyone who wanted to persuade himself that the tasks had been, indeed, enjoyable.

When they arrived at the interviewer's office, the E asked the interviewer whether or not he wanted to talk to the S. The interviewer said yes, the E shook hands with the S, said good-bye, and left. The interviewer, of course, was always kept in complete ignorance of which condition the S was in. The interview consisted of four questions, on each of which the S was first encouraged to talk about the matter and was then asked to rate his opinion or reaction on an 11-point scale. The questions are as follows:

Key dependent variable:
attitude toward experiment.

1. Were the tasks interesting and enjoyable? In what way? In what way were they not? Would you rate how you feel about them on a scale from –5 to +5 where –5 means they were extremely dull and boring, +5 means they were extremely interesting and enjoyable, and zero means they were neutral, neither interesting nor uninteresting.

2. Did the experiment give you an opportunity to learn about your own ability to perform these tasks? In what way? In what way not? Would you rate how you feel about this on a scale from ϕ to 10 where 0 means you learned nothing and 10 means you learned a great deal.

3. From what you know about the experiment and the tasks involved in it, would you say the experiment was measuring anything important? That is, do you think the results may have scientific value? In what way? In what way not? Would you rate your opinion on this matter on a scale from ϕ to 10 where ϕ means the results have no scientific value or importance and 10 means they have a great deal of value and importance.

4. Would you have any desire to participate in another similar experiment? Why? Why not? Would you rate your desire to participate in a similar experiment again on a scale from –5 to +5, where –5 means you would definitely dislike to participate, +5 means you would definitely like to participate, and ϕ means you have no particular feeling about it one way or the other?

As may be seen, the questions varied in how directly relevant they were to what the *S* had told the girl. This point will be discussed further in connection with the results.

At the close of the interview the *S* was asked what he thought the experiment was about and, following this, was asked directly whether or not he was suspicious of anything and, if so, what he was suspicious of. When the interview was over, the interviewer brought the *S* back to the experimental room where the *E* was waiting together with the girl who had posed as the waiting *S*. (In the control condition, of course, the girl was not there.) The true purpose of the experiment was then explained to the *S* in detail, and the reasons for each of the various steps in the experiment were explained carefully in relation to the true purpose. All experimental Ss in both One Dollar and Twenty Dollar conditions were asked, after this explanation, to return the money they had been given. All *Ss,* without exception, were quite willing to return the money.

This section is also important
to include in the method section
of an experiment report.
We need to know how many
participants were discarded
from data analysis and the
specific reasons why their data
were discarded.

The data from 11 of the 71 Ss in the experiment had to be discarded for the following reasons:

1. Five Ss (three in the One Dollar and two in the Twenty Dollar condition) indicated in the interview that they were suspicious about having been paid to tell the girl the experiment was fun and suspected that that was the real purpose of the experiment.

2. Two Ss (both in the One Dollar condition) told the girl that they had been hired, that the experiment was really boring but they were supposed to say it was fun.

3. Three Ss (one in the One Dollar and two in the Twenty Dollar condition) refused to take the money and refused to be hired.

4. One S (in the One Dollar condition), immediately after having talked to the girl, demanded her phone number saying he would call her and explain things, and also told the *E* he wanted to wait until she was finished so he could tell her about it.

These 11 *Ss* were, of course, run through the total experiment anyhow and the experiment was explained to them afterwards. Their data, however, are not included in the analysis.

Summary of Design

There remain, for analysis, 20 Ss in each of the three conditions. Let us review these briefly: 1. *Control condition*. These Ss were treated identically in all respects to the Ss in the experimental conditions, except that they were never asked to, and never did, tell the waiting girl that the experimental tasks were enjoyable and lots of fun. 2. *One Dollar condition*. These Ss were hired for one dollar to tell a waiting *S* that tasks, which were really rather dull and boring, were interesting, enjoyable, and lots of fun. 3. *Twenty Dollar condition*. These Ss were hired for twenty dollars to do the same thing.

RESULTS

The major results of the experiment are summarized in Table 1 which lists, separately for each of the three experimental conditions, the average rating which the Ss gave at the end of each question on the interview. We will discuss each of the questions on the interview separately, because they were intended to measure different things. One other point before we proceed to examine the data. In all the comparisons, the Control condition should be regarded as a baseline from which to evaluate the results in the other two conditions. The Control condition gives us, essentially, the reactions of Ss to the tasks and their opinions about the experiment as falsely explained to them, without the experimental introduction of dissonance. The data from the other conditions may be viewed, in a sense, as changes from this baseline.

How Enjoyable the Tasks Were

The average ratings on this question, presented in the first row of figures in Table 1, are the results most important to the experiment. These results are the ones most directly relevant to the specific dissonance which was experimentally created. It will be recalled that the tasks were purposely arranged to be rather boring and monotonous. And, indeed, in the Control condition the average rating was −.45, somewhat on the negative side of the neutral point.

In the other two conditions, however, the Ss told someone that these tasks were interesting and enjoyable. The resulting dissonance could, of course, most directly be reduced by

TABLE 1   Average Ratings On Interview Questions For Each Condition

Question on Interview	Experimental Condition		
	Control (N = 20)	One Dollar (N = 20)	Twenty Dollars (N = 20)
How enjoyable tasks were (rated from −5 to +5)	−.45	+1.35	−.05
How much they learned (rated from 0 to 10)	3.08	2.80	3.15
Scientific importance (rated from 0 to 10)	5.60	6.45	5.18
Participate in similar exp. (rated from −5 to +5)	−.62	+1.20	−.25

The main results are the answers to the first question: How enjoyable were the tasks (the two boring tasks)? Now, think about what each subject in each condition went through. The control condition people just did some boring stuff and were asked "did you enjoy the tasks?" and of course, they are going to say NO. This is what they did with a −.45 rating on a scale of −5 to +5. Now, let's look at the $20 condition. Consider what happened: the subject thinks "this is boring," then finds him- or herself lying to another person saying "it was fun." This creates cognitive dissonance. However, the lie is effectively erased (or justified) by the $20 the subject is paid. He or she says to him or herself. "I think this is boring, but then I said it was fun. BUT I had a good reason to lie. . . . the $20, so I really still think it is boring." Which is what happened: they rated the tasks negatively (−.05). So whatever cognitive dissonance he or she might have started to have was eliminated by the $20 justifying the lie. Now the $1 group thought the tasks were boring, then they said they were fun to the next person. This creates cognitive dissonance. How can the subject eliminate it? Well, even back in 1957, $1 wasn't much money and not enough to justify telling that big lie. So he or she still had dissonance. Remember the way to get rid of dissonance is to change an attitude to match the other attitude. Subjects in this condition had a way to do that: in the interview. When asked how much they enjoyed the tasks, they thought something like, "I thought they were boring, but then I said they were fun. $1 doesn't justify the lie. So . . . maybe the tasks weren't boring actually. In fact, I liked them now that I think of it." In so doing, the subject's new attitude toward the tasks now matches the lie, and that wipes out the dissonance. This is exactly what happened: they rated the tasks relatively positively: +1.35.

persuading themselves that the tasks were, indeed, interesting and enjoyable. In the One Dollar condition, since the magnitude of dissonance was high, the pressure to reduce this dissonance would also be high. In this condition, the average rating was +1.35, considerably on the positive side and significantly different from the Control condition at the .02 level [2] ($t = 2.48$).

In the Twenty Dollar condition, where less dissonance was created experimentally because of the greater importance of the consonant relations, there is correspondingly less evidence of dissonance reduction. The average rating in this condition is only −.05, slightly and not significantly higher than the Control condition. The difference between the One Dollar and Twenty Dollar conditions is significant at the 0.3 level ($t = 2.22$). In short, when an S was induced, by offer of reward, to say something contrary to his private opinion, this private opinion tended to change so as to correspond more closely with what he had said. The greater the reward offered (beyond what was necessary to elicit the behavior) the smaller was the effect.

Desire to Participate in a Similar Experiment

The results from this question are shown in the last row of Table 1. This question is less directly related to the dissonance that was experimentally created for the Ss. Certainly, the more interesting and enjoyable they felt the tasks were, the greater would be their desire to participate in a similar experiment. But other factors would enter also. Hence, one would expect the results on this question to be very similar to the results on "how enjoyable the tasks were" but weaker. Actually, the results, as may be seen in the table, are in exactly the same direction, and the magnitude of the mean differences is fully as large as on the first question. The variability is greater, however, and the differences do not yield high levels of statistical significance. The difference between the One Dollar condition (+ 1.20) and the Control condition (−.62) is significant at the .08 level ($t = 1.78$). The difference between the One Dollar condition and the Twenty Dollar condition (−.25) reaches only the .15 level of significance ($t = 1.46$).

The Scientific Importance of the Experiment

This question was included because there was a chance that differences might emerge. There are, after all, other ways in which the experimentally created dissonance could be reduced. For example, one way would be for the S to magnify for himself the value of the reward he obtained. This, however, was unlikely in this experiment because money was used for the reward and it is undoubtedly difficult to convince oneself that one dollar is more than it really is. There is another possible way, however. The Ss were given a very good reason, in addition to being paid, for saying what they did to the waiting girl. The Ss were told it was necessary for the experiment. The dissonance could, consequently, be reduced by magnifying the importance of this cognition. The more scientifically important they considered the experiment to be, the less was the total magnitude of dissonance. It is possible, then, that the results on this question, shown in the third row of figures in Table 1, might reflect dissonance reduction.

The results are weakly in line with what one would expect if the dissonance were somewhat reduced in this manner. The One Dollar condition is higher than the other two. The difference between the One and Twenty Dollar conditions reaches the .08 level of significance on a two-tailed test ($t = 1.79$). The difference between the One Dollar and Control conditions is not impressive at all ($t = 1.21$). The result that the Twenty Dollar condition is actually lower than the Control condition is undoubtedly a matter of chance ($t = 0.58$).

---

[2] All statistical tests referred to in this paper are two-tailed.

How Much They Learned From the Experiment

The results on this question are shown in the second row of figures in Table 1. The question was included because, as far as we could see, it had nothing to do with the dissonance that was experimentally created and could not be used for dissonance reduction. One would then expect no differences at all among the three conditions. We felt it was important to show that the effect was not a completely general one but was specific to the content of the dissonance which was created. As can be readily seen in Table 1, there are only negligible differences among conditions. The highest t value for any of these differences is only 0.48.

DISCUSSION OF A POSSIBLE ALTERNATIVE EXPLANATION

We mentioned in the introduction that Janis and King (1954; 1956) in explaining their findings, proposed an explanation in terms of the self-convincing effect of mental rehearsal and thinking up new arguments by the person who had to improvise a speech. Kelman (1953), in the previously mentioned study, in attempting to explain the unexpected finding that the persons who complied in the moderate reward condition changed their opinion more than in the high reward condition, also proposed the same kind of explanation. If the results of our experiment are to be taken as strong corroboration of the theory of cognitive dissonance, this possible alternative explanation must be dealt with.

Specifically, as applied to our results, this alternative explanation would maintain that perhaps, for some reason, the Ss in the One Dollar condition worked harder at telling the waiting girl that the tasks were fun and enjoyable. That is, in the One Dollar condition they may have rehearsed it more mentally, thought up more ways of saying it, may have said it more convincingly, and so on. Why this might have been the case is, of course, not immediately apparent. One might expect that, in the Twenty Dollar condition, having been paid more, they would try to do a better job of it than in the One Dollar condition. But nevertheless, the possibility exists that the Ss in the One Dollar condition may have improvised more.

Because of the desirability of investigating this possible alternative explanation, we recorded on a tape recorder the conversation between each S and the girl. These recordings were transcribed and then rated, by two independent raters, on five dimensions. The ratings were, of course done in ignorance of which condition each S was in. The reliabilities of these ratings, that is, the correlations between the two independent raters, ranged from .61 to .88, with an average reliability of .71. The five ratings were:

1. The content of what the S said *before* the girl made the remark that her friend told her it was boring. The stronger the S's positive statements about the tasks, and the more ways in which he said they were interesting and enjoyable, the higher the rating.

2. The content of what the S said *after* the girl made the above-mentioned remark. This was rated in the same way as for the content before the remark.

3. A similar rating of the overall content of what the S said.

4. A rating of how persuasive and convincing the S was in what he said and the way in which he said it.

5. A rating of the amount of time in the discussion that the S spent discussing the tasks as opposed to going off into irrelevant things.

The mean ratings for the One Dollar and Twenty Dollar conditions, averaging the ratings of the two independent raters, are presented in Table 2. It is clear from examining the table that, in all cases, the Twenty Dollar condition is slightly higher. The differences are small, however, and only on the rating of "amount of time" does the difference between the two conditions even approach significance. We are certainly justified in concluding that the Ss in the One Dollar condition did not improvise more nor act more convincingly. Hence, the alternative explanation discussed above cannot account for the findings.

TABLE 2   Average Ratings of Discussion Between Subject and Girl

Dimension Rated	Conditions		
	One Dollar	Twenty Dollars	Value of *t*
Content before remark by girl (rated from 0 to 5)	2.26	2.62	1.08
Content after remark by girl (rated from 0 to 5)	1.63	1.75	0.11
Overall content (rated from 0 to 5)	1.89	2.19	1.08
Persuasiveness and conviction (rated from 0 to 10)	4.79	5.50	0.99
Time spent on topic (rated from 0 to 10)	6.74	8.19	1.80

SUMMARY

Recently, Festinger (1957) has proposed a theory concerning cognitive dissonance. Two derivations from this theory are tested here. These are:

1. If a person is induced to do or say something which is contrary to his private opinion, there will be a tendency for him to change his opinion so as to bring it into correspondence with what he has done or said.

2. The larger the pressure used to elicit the overt behavior (beyond the minimum needed to elicit it) the weaker will be the above mentioned tendency.

A laboratory experiment was designed to test these derivations. Subjects were subjected to a boring experience and then paid to tell someone that the experience had been interesting and enjoyable. The amount of money paid the subject was varied. The private opinions of the subjects concerning the experiences were then determined.

The results strongly corroborate the theory that was tested.

REFERENCES

FESTINGER, L. *A theory of cognitive dissonance.* Evanston, Ill: Row Peterson, 1957.

JANIS, I.L., & KING, B. T. The influence of role-playing on opinion change. *J. abnorm. soc. Psychol.,* 1954, 49, 211–218.

KELMAN, H. Attitude change as a function of response restriction. *Hum. Re/at.,* 1953, 6, 185–214.

KING, *B.* T., & JANIS, I. L. Comparison of the effectiveness of improvised versus non-improvised role-playing in producing opinion changes. *Hum. Relat.,* 1956, 9, 177–186.

POST-ARTICLE DISCUSSION

The article you just read is perhaps one of the most cited articles in social psychology. As we discussed in the introduction to this article, the reason for this is that it is the quintessential experiment supporting Festinger's very influential cognitive dissonance theory. You might have noticed a different "feel" to this article compared to many others in this book. It is written in a fairly plain, straightforward manner, the introduction and discussion are quite brief, and the method has an extraordinary amount of detail regarding the procedure and especially the dialogue used in the experiment. This is largely due to the time in which the experiment was done and the state of journals back then. Specifically, page space was not at such a premium in the 1950s compared to now, and as such, authors were free to submit single studies and free to engage in the luxury of detailing the dialogue used in an experiment. Today, authors would be told by journal editors to greatly truncate the dialogue or publish it as an appendix online, in order to meet very tight publication guidelines in most journals.

Regardless of those issues, a good rule of thumb for whether to include exact quoted dialogue in a research report is, "Is it essential to the experiment that these precise words be used?" Nearly all the time, the answer to that question is "No," in which case you would just describe what is being said to the subject, and it is left to the researcher how he or she wants to phrase it. Let us consider further how Festinger and Carlsmith designed their experiment. One problem they had was how to induce cognitive dissonance in their subjects. Remember, the point of the study was to see which conditions led to a feeling of dissonance and how subjects who felt dissonance eliminated that dissonance (if at all). The dissonance induction had to be something that everyone would experience. It wouldn't work if only some people felt that there was an inconsistency between their thoughts and their behavior (or between two thoughts/attitudes). So the choice of having everyone do a task that everyone would perceive as boring is an excellent idea. With that initial attitude established, it is a simple matter to have the subjects feel dissonance by asking them to do a behavior that directly contradicts their negative attitude about the tasks, that is, telling another subject that the tasks are a lot of fun. By the way, this is the "forced compliance" part of the article title. The researchers didn't really force the subjects to lie to the next subject; rather, they asked them to do it (subjects could stop the study any time they wanted). But every subject complied (which worked out well for the researchers).

Now, if we can create a way for the subject to explain away her lie to the next subject, that could eliminate the dissonance. For example, if I think of myself as a nice person, but I was asked by an authority figure to do a mean thing to someone, I wouldn't feel dissonance (good person but doing mean behavior), because I could explain away the mean behavior as being forced to do it by the authority figure. But if someone not in authority asked me to do it, I could no longer explain the mean behavior away, and I would likely feel dissonance. (Why was I mean? I was asked by a stranger to do it. That is not a good reason, so maybe that means that I really do have a mean streak and am not as nice as I thought I was.) In this case, I would change my attitude about myself to match the mean behavior.

In their experiment, Festinger and Carlsmith presented some subjects with a way to justify that lie: money. If you were paid enough to lie, then you could use that as a justification for the lie, and that would effectively eliminate (in your mind) the lie and eliminate any dissonance you felt. However, if the amount of money was insufficient to justify the lie, then you're stuck with the lie, and the dissonance remains. As the results indicated, $20 was enough to justify the lie for those in that condition, but those given $1 found that insufficient to justify the lie, and they felt dissonance. The next question for the researchers was "How can we set up a situation

(Continued)

(Continued)

whereby those still feeling dissonance (after the cash offer) can reduce it?" Remember that the theory says that when people feel dissonance, they are motivated to restore cognitive consistency between the incompatible attitudes or attitude and behavior. In this case, the subjects have a negative attitude (toward the tasks) and a positive behavior (saying tasks were fun). When trying to reconcile an attitude and behavior, the easiest path is to change one's attitude (because it is hard to undo a behavior) to make it consistent with the behavior.

In the experiment, the researchers give the subjects a chance to change their attitude toward the tasks by asking, at the end of the study, what their attitude is toward it. Here, the subjects have an opportunity to rethink their attitude toward the tasks, and, if need be, adjust it to match the behavior of saying it was fun. This was precisely what people in the $1 condition did. Remember that the control condition didn't feel dissonance, and what dissonance the subjects in the $20 condition may have felt was wiped away by the $20 justifying (and erasing, in their minds) the lie (saying it was fun), so they had no dissonance and thus no need to adjust their attitude toward the tasks (they said the tasks were boring). This was one of the first experiments to support Festinger's cognitive dissonance theory. Over the years, like most theories in science, subsequent data suggested ways to modify the theory and denote the limits and alternate mechanisms whereby dissonance may be created or reduced. However, it is good to remember and appreciate the elegance of this famous experiment and the simplicity of the design.

THINGS TO THINK ABOUT

1. Besides the boring tasks, what other ways could an experimenter induce an attitude in subjects?

2. Do you think that having detailed descriptions of dialogue in an experiment article is helpful to other researchers, or does it present unnecessary detail? Why?

3. Much of the literature on cognitive dissonance theory discusses "effort justification." The idea is that when one has dissonance, one can eliminate that dissonance by justifying the work (or behavior) they did. So how would that process go in the Festinger and Carlsmith experiment?

4. Can you think of other real-world examples of effort justification (e.g., relationships, joining elite groups)?

5. According to self-affirmation theory, one can reduce cognitive dissonance merely by affirming a positive part of oneself. Cognitive dissonance theory says that one has to change the relevant attitude to match the other attitude or behavior in the same domain, for dissonance reduction to occur. Meaning, if I have an attitude toward a brand of paper towels, and I do an inconsistent behavior toward that brand of paper towels, I must change my attitude toward that brand of paper towels to match the behavior in order for dissonance to be eliminated. Self-affirmation theory says that changing my attitude is not necessary and that I may just think, for example, "I may have incompatible attitudes, but I am a charitable (or honest, friendly, compassionate, etc.) person." What do you think of self-affirmation theory as an alternative explanation of how dissonance can be reduced?

6. Why do some country clubs charge tens of thousands in annual dues? (Does cognitive dissonance play a role here?)

INTRODUCTION TO READING 5.2
Wheeler et al. (2007)

In persuasion research, there have been several general approaches to understanding how people's attitudes can be changed. One of the earliest was the Yale program created in the 1940s by Hovland and his colleagues (Hovland et al., 1953). The U.S. government asked Hovland's team to come up with information on the best ways to persuade the American public to conserve materials for the war effort. Hovland's research showed the importance of the message, the source of the message, and the audience, and how the three interact to result in varying amounts of persuasion. Later, researchers focused not on the components of persuasion but rather the processes (or routes) to persuasion, as exemplified in the elaboration likelihood model by Petty and Cacioppo (1983, 1986) and Chaiken's heuristic-systematic model (Chaiken, 1980; Chaiken, Liberman, & Eagly, 1989).

In the paper you are about to read, the authors take a different approach to understanding persuasion. Whereas previous research focused on aspects of the persuasion message, or what is happening during the persuasion process, Wheeler and his colleagues examined whether cognitive processes that occur before the persuasion message is presented will influence the likelihood that the person will change his attitude on that topic. Similar

processes in psychology have been explored, such as the concept of priming, whereby exposure to a stimulus facilitates cognitive processing of that stimulus later. For example, being exposed to the word *nurse* will make one faster at recognizing related words (e.g., *hospital*) than if one wasn't first exposed to the prime of *nurse*. Wheeler and his colleagues predicted that if one has to do a lot of cognitive work, that will deplete one's later ability to generate counter-attitudinal arguments (against the persuasion message), and thus one will be vulnerable to the persuasion message. The authors further reason that if one normally generates a lot of arguments against a weak message and fewer against a strong persuasive message, then the effects of the prior heavy cognitive task should be most apparent in the weak argument conditions. This article by Wheeler et al. is another excellent example of clear writing; a thorough rationale; clever, simple, and effective experimental design; and careful post-analysis of competing views and interpretations of the data. Before you start reading, think about the following question, and we'll discuss it later: If the predictions are true, what are the implications for marketing, politics, or any other area that depends on effective persuasion? Enjoy the paper, and we'll talk afterward!

Reading 5.2

Resistance to persuasion as self-regulation:

Ego-depletion and its effects on attitude change processes

S. Christian Wheeler[a,*], Pablo Briñol[b], Anthony D. Hermann[c]

Received 21 August 2004; revised 1 December 2005
Available online 28 February 2006 Communicated by Spencer

Abstract

Counterarguing persuasive messages requires active control processes (e.g., generation and application of contradictory information) similar to those involved in other forms of self-regulation. Prior research has indicated that self-regulation ability is a finite resource subject to temporary depletion with use, and so engaging in self-regulatory tasks could impair individuals' ability to subsequently counterargue. Participants completed an initial task designed to deplete or not deplete their regulatory resources. Following the manipulation, participants read a message supporting a counterattitudinal policy. Results indicated that prior self-regulation reduced subsequent resistance, primarily when the message arguments were specious. Counterargument appears to be a self-regulatory process that can be undermined when self-regulatory resources have previously been diminished.
© 2006 Elsevier Inc. All rights reserved.

Keywords: Ego-depletion; Self-regulation; Resistance to persuasion; Attitude change; Acquiescence

People are often motivated to resist persuasion in order to hold correct attitudes, restore freedom, or maintain psychological consistency and sense of control (Wegener, Petty, Smoak, & Fabrigar, 2004). Resistance to persuasion is influenced by a wide variety of factors such as characteristics of the attitude under attack (e.g., its accessibility or importance, Fazio, 1995; Zuwerink & Devine, 1996), but also characteristics of the message recipient (e.g., motivation and ability to resist the persuasive appeal, Briñol & Petty, 2005; Briñol, Rucker, Tormala, & Petty, 2004; DeMarree, Wheeler, & Petty, 2005; Haugtvedt & Petty, 1992). Counterargument is the most extensively documented means of resistance, especially under conditions when processing motivation (Petty & Cacioppo, 1979) and ability (Wood, Rhodes, & Biek, 1995) are high, such as when one has ample resources to evaluate a personally relevant persuasive message. In this research, we sought to test the effects of a self-regulation construct, ego-depletion, on individuals' ability to resist counterattitudinal messages.

[a]518 Memorial Way, Stanford University, Stanford, CA 94305-5015, USA
[b]Universidad Autonoma de Madrid, Facultad de Psicologia, Carretera de Colmenar, Km. 15, 28049 Madrid, Spain
[c]Department of Psychology, Willamette University, 900 State Street, Salem, OR 97301, USA
* Corresponding author. Fax: +1 650 725 9932.
E-mail address: scwheeler@stanford.edu (S.C. Wheeler).

(margin note) Rationale for the study. This is usually presented in the first paragraph of an introduction.

The term ego-depletion refers to a state in which one's self-regulatory resources are diminished, and this diminishment is proposed to occur because acts of self-regulation and volition draw upon a single, limited intrapsychic resource (Muraven, Tice, & Baumeister, 1998). Theory in this area draws upon a strength metaphor, whereby exertion in one situation is followed by a period of reduced ability in a subsequent situation. Accordingly, any exertion of willpower or self-regulation in one task, so long as it is sufficiently demanding, should reduce any subsequent self-regulation on a second, seemingly unrelated task. This prediction has been supported across many experiments (e.g., Baumeister, Muraven, & Tice, 2000; Muraven et al., 1998; Schmeichel, Vohs, & Baumeister, 2003). Ego-depletion effects do not seem to be simply the result of the amount of effort required to complete the task. For example, avoiding thinking about a forbidden topic reduces subsequent self-regulatory ability, whereas solving equally challenging multiplications does not (Muraven et al., 1998; see also Muraven & Slessareva, 2003, experiment 3).

Resisting persuasion is another type of task that could draw on limited self-regulatory resources, and therefore, resistance processes could be impaired by preceding self-regulation. Counterarguing persuasive messages involves actively processing the message information, retrieving or generating new contradictory information, and applying it to the message content to refute it. All of these activities require the individual to engage in active control processes to defend the pre-existing attitude from attack. These processes match the criteria used to identify processes involving self-regulation—specifically, they involve engaging processes to reach a desired state (i.e., avoiding adopting a counterattitudinal position; Carver & Scheier, 1998) and overcoming a default or natural tendency (i.e., to acquiesce, Baumeister & Heatherton, 1996). If it is true that engaging in counterargument draws on the same limited resource as other self-regulatory processes, then engaging in self-regulatory tasks that deplete such a resource should impair the ability of individuals to subsequently resist counterattitudinal appeals.

When individuals are ego-depleted, their attitudes could be biased in an upward, acquiescent direction. Many studies have shown that self-regulation failure can increase acquiescence; individuals often "give in" to easier courses of action when their self-regulatory resources are depleted, even when they have the ability to guide their thoughts and action in more effortful, contrary ways (Baumeister & Heatherton, 1996). This type of acquiescence includes agreeing with positions forwarded by others. Acquiescence is often a default, passive, and low-effort response strategy (Hanley, 1965; Krosnick, 1991) that could be increased when individuals lack self-regulatory resources.

Unlike the myriad of experiments demonstrating reduced cognitive processing of persuasive messages under distraction or cognitive load (e.g., Petty, Wells, & Brock, 1976), the paradigm investigated in the present paper makes individuals' regulatory resource depleted, but does not restrict processing capacity at the time of persuasion. Additionally, given our self-regulatory framework, we predict that the depletion manipulation will inhibit the generation of counterarguments (i.e., unfavorable thoughts), rather than amount of thoughts generally. As a result, rather than reporting middling attitudes reflective of lack of attention to message arguments as shown in distraction experiments, ego-depleted participants could report acquiescent attitudes reflective of the types of agreement and "going along" shown in other self-regulation breakdowns.

The research in this paper was designed to test this hypothesis. Individuals were given a task shown in prior research to use and deplete regulatory resources. Following this task,

---

Unfortunately, this explanation is not really clear. The term "ego" has its origins in Freudian theory and has been used post-Freud to refer generally to one's self. Self-regulation refers to cognitive processes that one engages in to maintain your self. It is important when writing up a research manuscript that one endeavor to present concepts as clearly and plainly as possible, so that people not familiar with psychological terms will be able to understand what the paper is about.

Actually, there is much evidence from cognitive and social psychology that we do have a limited amount of cognitive energy to devote to whatever we are thinking of at a given moment. So it would follow that a cognitive task that is rather exhausting would leave the individual in a compromised state whereby he or she cannot devote his or her full cognitive attention to a subsequent cognitive task

Why do you think this is the case?

So here is the focus and proposition for the current study: if people are engaged in self-regulation processes (basically, cognitive work), that cognitive work will use up the limited cognitive resources we have at that time and make it harder for people to then engage in heavy cognitive work (like resisting persuasion) immediately thereafter.

In a nutshell: when we are experiencing "self-regulation failure," we are more likely to just agree to persuasion messages.

Interesting. Remember this, because the authors will need to experimentally defend this assertion.

they were presented with a message in favor of a counterattitudinal proposal. The quality of the message was varied such that some participants received strong and compelling counterattitudinal arguments whereas others received specious counterattitudinal arguments. Last, participants reported their attitudes and cognitive responses.

We predicted that ego-depletion would lead to higher levels of favorability in thoughts and attitudes. Additionally, however, the effects of ego-depletion on persuasion could deliver across the strong and weak message conditions. If the depletion of self-regulatory resources interferes with the generation of unfavorable cognitive responses, these effects on attitudes should be most observable under conditions in which counterargument naturally occurs most (i.e., when the counterattitudinal message contains specious arguments).[1] Hence, the effects of the depletion manipulation on persuasion could be larger in the weak, rather than the strong, argument condition. Thus, we predicted an ego-depletion by argument quality interaction on attitudes and cognitive responses such that individuals would distinguish between strong and weak arguments less when their self-regulatory resources were depleted. Additionally, we expected the depletion to be observed primarily when arguments were weak, when naturally occurring counterargument would be reduced by virtue of the limited self-regulatory resources available to the depleted participants.

METHOD

Participants

Sixty-eight student participants (24 males, 40 females, 4 declined to state) received $10 in exchange for their participation.

Procedure

Participants were run in groups of 2–8 in partitioned cubicles. Participants were randomly assigned to ego-depletion condition (with the experimenter blind to condition), and both ego-depletion conditions were represented in all experimental sessions.

Materials

Ego-depletion task. The ego-depletion task was the same as one used in previous self-regulation research (Baumeister, Bratslavsky, Muraven, & Tice, 1998). This task consists of two parts. In the first part, participants were instructed to cross out every "e" they could locate in a written passage. This task is relatively easy for participants and is used to establish a behavioral pattern that will be subsequently overridden or not. Participants had 5 min to complete this before the experimenter stopped them.

The second part of the task included the manipulation. Participants in the low-depletion condition repeated the first part, using the same rule that they had already learned. Participants in the high-depletion condition circled letters again but were instructed to cross out each "e" in

---

[1]The notion that counterargument (i.e., the generation of unfavorable thoughts) occurs primarily in response to weak arguments is supported by definition. Specifically, the recommended procedure for developing weak arguments includes pretesting the arguments among participants who are motivated to think to ensure that the arguments generate primarily unfavorable thoughts (Petty & Cacioppo, 1986).

Another point about clarity: Here, it is best to say "unfavorable thoughts about the persuasion message." A "counterargument" is precisely that.

This is a common component of persuasion research, because it allows the researcher to examine how his or her independent variable influences the subject's ability to distinguish between strong and weak persuasion messages.

Hypotheses.

the text, except when another vowel followed the "e" in the same word (e.g., "read") or when a vowel was one letter removed from the "e" in either direction (e.g., "vowel"). This latter rule required participants to override their established, habitual patterns and thus necessitated the exertion of self-regulatory resources. Both groups of participants had 5 min to complete the second part of the task.[2]

Counterattitudinal appeal. Participants were told that the university was considering implementing of mandatory comprehensive examinations in the upcoming academic year and wanted to first get students' reactions toward the policy. This policy is counterattitudinal to participants and was selected to motivate resistance to the message.

Manipulated within the message was the quality of the arguments (Petty & Cacioppo, 1986). Some participants read weak arguments, such as that the exams were desirable because they would permit students to compare their scores with students at other universities. Other participants read strong arguments, such as that the exams would lead to significant improvements in undergraduate education.

Attitude reports. Participants reported their attitudes toward the proposal along a series of 9-point semantic differential scales anchored by beneficial/harmful, good/bad, favorable/unfavorable, positive/negative, wise/foolish, and in favor/against ($a = .96$).

Cognitive responses. Participants listed the thoughts they had in response to the message using a thought-listing task (Cacioppo & Petty, 1981). Later, the computer presented them the thoughts they had listed and instructed them to indicate whether each thought was positive, negative, or neutral toward the proposal.

Additional measures. Three items measured the amount of effort, attention, and thought participants reported devoting to processing the persuasive message. These items were anchored by 1 = *not at all* and 9 = *very much.* Participants also reported their perceptions of message relevance along the same scale.

Additional items measured how much participants enjoyed the ego depletion task, how difficult they found the task, how tired they felt after the task, how interesting the task was, and how much effort they put into the task. These items were measured on 5-point scales anchored by 1 = *not at all* (e.g., enjoyable) and 5 = *very* (e.g., enjoyable).

RESULTS

Results were analyzed using a 2 (ego-depletion condition: depleted or not depleted) by 2 (argument quality: strong or weak) ANOVAs, except where noted.

> Ideally, here the researcher would provide evidence that this indeed was counterattitudinal to participants.

---

[2]The text used in both portions of the task was comprised of technical expositions excerpted from a statistics book and was unrelated to comprehensive exams. The photocopied passages were the same for both portions of the task, although copy quality was decreased for the depletion group in the second half of the task (see Baumeister et al., 1998).

Attitudes toward the proposal

Analyses of participants' attitudes yielded a significant main effect of argument quality, $F(1, 64) = 10.57$, $p < .002$, such that strong arguments ($M = 4.83$, $SD = 1.78$) were more persuasive than weak arguments ($M = 3.48$, $SD = 1.76$). Additionally, in partial support of our first hypothesis, there was a marginally significant main effect of ego-depletion, $F(1, 64) = 3.07$, $p < .08$, such that depleted participants ($M = 4.53$, $SD = 1.80$) tended to report more positive attitudes toward the proposal than did non-depleted participants ($M = 3.75$, $SD = 1.91$). Both of these effects were qualified by the predicted ego-depletion × argument quality interaction, $F(1, 64) = 5.04$, $p < .03$. Non-depleted participants were significantly more persuaded by strong arguments (M D 4.94, $SD = 1.78$) than by weak arguments ($M = 2.69$, $SD = 1.32$, $p < .0002$), whereas depleted participants did not distinguish between strong ($M = 4.74$, $SD = 1.83$) and weak ($M = 4.32$, $SD = 1.80$) arguments ($p < .48$). Looked at another way, depleted and nondepleted individuals were equally persuaded by strong arguments, ($p < .73$), but depleted individuals were significantly more persuaded by weak arguments than non-depleted individuals ($p < .006$).

Cognitive responses

A thought favorability index was computed as the difference between the number of favorable and unfavorable thoughts divided by the total number of thoughts.[3] Negative scores on this index indicate primarily unfavorable thoughts toward the proposal, whereas positive scores on this index indicate primarily favorable thoughts toward the proposal. Analyses of participants' cognitive responses yielded a significant main effect of argument quality, $F(1, 61) = 4.09$, $p < .05$, such that strong arguments ($M = .40$, $SD = .47$) led to relatively more favorable thoughts than weak arguments ($M = .63$, $SD = .45$). This effect was qualified by the predicted ego-depletion × argument quality interaction, $F(1, 61) = 7.52$, $p < .008$. Non-depleted participants generated relatively more favorable thoughts when they read strong arguments ($M =.29$, $SD = .52$) than when they read weak arguments ($M =.81$, $SD = .25$, $p < .001$), whereas depleted participants did not distinguish between strong ($M =.51$, $SD = .39$) and weak ($M =.43$, $SD = .54$) arguments ($p < .61$) in their cognitive responses. Looked at another way, depleted and non-depleted individuals generated similar thoughts in response to strong arguments, ($p = .17$), but depleted individuals generated significantly more favorable thoughts in response to weak arguments than did non-depleted individuals ($p < .02$). Hence, although all participants generated more unfavorable than favorable thoughts, the predicted interaction was obtained.

Evaluation of alternative hypotheses

Additional analyses tested whether these effects could be plausibly attributed to differential amounts of effort devoted to reading the proposal or to irrelevant features of the ego-depletion task. If the ego depletion manipulation made participants deliberately alter their effort toward evaluating the persuasive appeal, for example, this could be inconsistent with the ego-depletion account. Ego-depletion by argument quality ANOVAs on reported attention to the proposal message, reading effort, self-perceived thoughtfulness, and perceived relevance

---

[3]Three participants did not list any thoughts and so were excluded from the analysis.

of the message yielded no significant effects. These null results are inconsistent with the notion that depleted individuals voluntarily withheld effort in processing the persuasive appeal, relative to non-depleted individuals.

We also further examined cognitive responses to explore the extent to which the patterns of attitude change were attributable to differential levels of cognitive effort. Low levels of elaboration are typically associated with fewer cognitive responses reported in a thought-listing task and lower thought-attitude correlations (see Cacioppo & Petty, 1981; see Wegener, Downing, Krosnick, & Petty, 1995). Results indicated that individuals in the high ($M = 6.94$, $SD = 2.84$) and low ($M = 6.76$, $SD = 2.59$) depletion groups generated similar numbers of total thoughts, t (1, 66) = .27, $p < .79$, and the valence of these thoughts was correlated with attitudes equally in the high ($r = .73$) and low ($r = .78$) depletion groups, $z = .40$, $p < .65$. These patterns, too, are inconsistent with a differential elaboration account for the attitude change results.

A series of t tests were conducted to determine whether participants' perceptions of the high and low ego-depletion tasks differed significantly in ways that could account for the obtained attitude results. These analyses on feelings of being tired and on task enjoyment, effort, and interest also revealed no significant effects. These results are inconsistent with the notion that irrelevant features of the task such as its difficulty or inherent interest to participants were responsible for subsequent differences in information processing observed for the persuasive message.

DISCUSSION

This research supports the notion that self-regulatory resources are involved in resisting counterattitudinal messages and that such resistance can be thwarted by reduced self-regulatory capacity. More specifically, individuals who engaged in a task designed to reduce their self-regulatory resources reported more positive attitudes toward a counterattitudinal policy than those not so depleted. These effects occurred primarily among individuals who received weak and specious messages, and patterns of cognitive responding were consistent with the notion that depleted individuals generated more favorable cognitive responses than did individuals who were not depleted. Interestingly, these effects occurred despite high levels of processing effort on the part of depleted individuals that were equal to that of non-depleted individuals. These effects were also not due to differences in perceptions of the depletion tasks or of the difficulty of the depletion tasks.

These findings are important for several reasons. First, these findings expand our understanding of how situational factors can affect information processing and attitude change. Previous research has shown that factors such as time pressure or distraction in the present environment can interfere with the processing of persuasive messages (e.g., Petty et al., 1976). Our findings suggest that, even when individuals are free to take unlimited time to read self-relevant persuasive messages in a non-distracting environment, they may still fail to accurately assess the merit of and reject weak and specious arguments. Hence, the effects of prior situational variations may affect subsequent attitude change processes. Much like situational primes (e.g., DeMarree et al., 2005), efforts at self-regulation can affect judgment and behavior some time after the event has occurred. Nevertheless, although separated temporally, our depletion and persuasion tasks took place in succession and in the same setting. Future research is necessary to test the extent to which greater changes in context or greater time delays would affect these results.

Always start your discussion section with your main findings, either in the beginning or end of the first paragraph.

Main finding. The novel aspect of this is that it is one of the first pieces of evidence that shows that cognitive factors prior to the perception of the persuasion message can affect how people cognitive process the persuasion message.

Second, these findings provide and suggest critical links between the attitude change and self-regulation literatures, promoting novel ways of thinking about attitude change. Although research on other forms of mental control such as the suppression of thoughts (Wegner, 1994) and stereotypes (Macrae, Bodenhausen, Milne, & Jetten, 1994; von Hippel, Silver, & Lynch, 2000) has been guided by a self-regulatory framework, the attitude change literature has generally not. Nevertheless, there are a number of parallels between these two literatures. For example, high levels of self-focus have been shown to sometimes increase self-regulation of behaviors (Carver & Scheier, 1981; Duval & Wicklund, 1972), just as it has been shown to reduce stereotyping (among those motivated to resist doing so, Macrae, Bodenhausen, & Milne, 1998) and increase resistance to attitude change (Hutton & Baumeister, 1992, see, Briñol & Petty, 2005, for discussion of other roles self-focus can play in attitude change). Future research could examine whether additional antecedents, consequences, and parallel effects are shared between the attitudes and self-regulation literatures.

Third, the current findings also have potential implications for why people may engage in undesired behaviors. Previous research has shown that ego-depletion can increase the likelihood that people will engage in undesired behaviors (Vohs & Heatherton, 2000), and the present research shows that it can promote positive attitude shifts toward counterattitudinal policies, especially when justification for such policies are weak. This suggests the intriguing, albeit highly speculative, possibility that part of the reason individuals engage in undesired behaviors is because they lack the ability to successfully regulate the evaluative (i.e., approach and avoidance) responses they have to objects.

People's evaluative responses have been shown to shift as a function of their current goals (e.g., Ferguson & Bargh, 2004). For example, previous research has shown that objects and people are evaluated more favorably when they promote goal attainment than when they inhibit goal attainment (Ferguson & Bargh, 2004; Fitzsimons, 2004), and objects that do not facilitate goal attainment are devalued (Brendl, Markman, & Messner, 2003). These evaluative shifts are proposed to provide approach motivation that assists individuals in attaining their goals.

It is possible that the evaluative shifts in our study are a part of a more general tendency for ego-depletion to interfere with evaluative responding, and hence, approach and avoidance motivations to goal-relevant objects. If this were true, it could be that individuals who are ego-depleted or otherwise unskilled at self-regulation could exhibit weaker evaluative shifts regarding objects that facilitate or inhibit goal attainment. These hypotheses are clearly speculative and would involve more automatic processes than those likely to be at work in the present studies. Nevertheless, these kinds of extensions of self-regulation and attitude change research would lend additional insight into not only automatic evaluation processes, but also mechanisms behind and individual differences in self-control.

Locus and generality of effects

In our studies, we examined resistance to persuasion as the process of generating more unfavorable cognitive responses to the weak persuasive messages. According to our conceptualization, it is this process that was disrupted in the ego-depletion conditions of our studies, and comparison with the no-depletion control group supports this conclusion. Theorists have noted that in addition to this process definition, resistance could also be defined as an outcome

Interesting speculation, and something that future researchers could examine.

(i.e., no change following a persuasive appeal, Petty, Tormala, & Rucker, 2004; Wegener et al., 2004). Using this definition, one may wonder how the weak arguments condition of our study corresponds to a "baseline" condition.

To examine this issue, we collected additional data from the same relatively population. Participants read that the university was considering implementing comprehensive exams at their university the following year and that it wanted to first get students' reactions toward the policy. Participants reported their attitudes toward the exams in the absence of any arguments (the "baseline" condition) or after reading the same weak arguments presented to participants in our experiment. Results indicated that the "baseline" ($M = 3.95$, $SD = 1.92$) participants reported attitudes equivalent to those who read weak arguments ($M = 3.58$, $SD = 1.77$, $t(1, 103) = .77$, $p < .44$). These results are consistent with the notion that, in the absence of ego-depletion, participants who read weak arguments in favor of a policy are able to resist persuasion in the sense that exposure to the persuasive communication does not change their attitudes.

It is nevertheless important to remember, however, that our hypotheses concern resistance as a process, and not as an outcome. Under some conditions, it may be that exposure to weak arguments would lead to sufficient counterargument to lead to a "boomerang" effect (i.e., attitudes becoming more opposed to the proposal after reading the arguments). According to our process perspective, to the extent that this boomerang-inducing counterargumentation is disrupted by ego depletion, one might find both depleted and non-depleted individuals exposed to weak arguments differing from a no-message control group, such that depleted people were more favorable after reading the message and non-depleted people were more unfavorable after reading the message.

It is also important to note that we would not predict that ego depletion would necessarily always reduce resistance (as an outcome) to persuasive messages. Although the process of thoughtfully resisting persuasion (e.g., through generating unfavorable thoughts) appears to involve self-regulatory resources, other forms of resistance may not. For example, avoiding exposure to a boring advertisement would probably consume very little self-regulatory resources, but would presumably be effective in eliminating attitude change. In our studies, exposure to the persuasive message was relatively required, and so these types of lower-effort regulation strategies were not as available to participants.

Although our predictions were supported for the attitudinal issue of comprehensive exams, the extent to which these findings would occur for other attitude issues should be tested in future research. For example, students may have held only rather weak pre-existing attitudes toward comprehensive exams, and the observed effects of egodepletion may not have occurred for an attitude issue toward which individuals hold much stronger attitudes (e.g., abortion). On the other hand, if ego-depletion interferes with the generation of counterarguments, one might expect to observe larger ego-depletion effects for stronger attitudes, because counterargument is more likely to occur for strong than weak attitudes (see Petty & Krosnick, 1995) and should therefore be easier to detect under these conditions. Because self-regulation can be affected by motivation just as resistance to persuasion can (Muraven & Slessareva, 2003), ego-depletion seems most likely to lead to observable reductions in resistance under circumstances when motivation to resist is present but not sufficiently powerful to overwhelm the effects of egodepletion. Future research should examine whether and how attitude strength and extent of ego-depletion interact to affect resistance to persuasion.

This is why earlier I mentioned that it is always good to test your population to make sure that the baseline attitudes they have are indeed what you speculate (or hypothesize) they have when doing persuasion research.

Great idea for future research.

Implications

The present research has potential implications for many applied contexts. For example, marketing attempts could sometimes become more successful to the extent that individuals have been using their self-regulatory resources, especially when the appeals lack compelling support. One's resources may be more depleted at the end of the day because of the many independent acts of willpower required to navigate through social life (Baumeister & Heatherton, 1996). Similar to the lack of impulse control for behavior observed late at night (e.g., drinking, gambling, and overeating), failures of mental self-regulation might be also more likely to occur at the end of the day, making people more vulnerable to persuasion. More generally, populations may differ with respect to their resistance to persuasion. Dieters, individuals quitting smoking, and medical school students may all have lowered resistance to persuasion by virtue of their heavy self-regulatory demands.

Although prior self-regulation can have temporary deleterious effects on subsequent self-regulation, ego strength can improve with practice over the long term (e.g., Muraven, Baumeister, & Tice, 1999). Additional research in our labs is providing support for this factor's effect on persuasion as well. In one study, participants were instructed to think about the prior year while either suppressing thoughts and emotions about a specific person that was important to them during that period or not suppressing such thoughts. Following this depletion manipulation, participants read a message that contained either strong or weak arguments and advocated tuition increases at their school. Results indicated reduced effects of argument quality among those in the depletion condition, but this effect was moderated by their practice at mental control. More specifically, individuals who regularly engaged in mental control practices like yoga were not affected by the depletion manipulation. These results replicate those presented here with different manipulations, and they provide initial evidence regarding means by which individuals can increase their ability to resist influence by specious arguments under difficult conditions. Furthermore, these results further distinguish ego-depletion from other alternative mechanisms such as mental effort or difficulty, because chronic experience in self-regulation should not affect these types of processes.

Other theoretical frameworks

It is important to note that the self-regulatory processes uncovered in the present research are distinct from processes investigated in other paradigms. For example, Gilbert and colleagues (e.g., Gilbert, 1991) have argued that individuals automatically encode new statements in memory as true; disbelief of any new statement, even those blatantly labeled as false, requires additional cognitive effort. From this point of view, ego-depleted individuals simply may have had fewer cognitive resources available, and therefore, were more likely to believe any statement they read.

Although this alternative explanation may have some appeal on the surface, strong and weak arguments in this paradigm influence persuasion not because of varying degrees of (dis)belief, but rather because of the quality of support they provide the proposal. That is, non-depleted participants who rejected weak arguments, such as that comprehensive exams would enable them to compare their scores with students from other universities, did so not because they disbelieved that the statements were true (i.e., that they actually could compare their scores), but rather because the arguments did not provide a reasonable and valuable basis for the institution of comprehensive exams. Furthermore, additional data

So the authors are speculating that because people are using self-regulation during the day, they get cognitively exhausted and thus are more vulnerable to persuasion in the evening. A bold prediction!

While the current data don't speak directly to this, it certainly is an interesting avenue for future research.

Interesting findings, suggesting that those who regularly engage in behaviors that require mental concentration are less susceptible to subsequent ego-depletion and thus they were less susceptible to subsequent weak persuasion attempts.

(e.g., self-reported effort, cognitive responses) yielded nothing that suggests that depleted participants expended differential cognitive effort than non-depleted participants. In fact, participants were allowed all the time they needed to read and form an evaluation of the proposal.

Another line of research on the disrupt-then-reframe technique (Davis & Knowles, 1999; Fennis, Das, & Pruyn, 2004) shows that individuals are more likely to comply with a request when they are momentarily confused in some way (e.g., an unusual statement) and subsequently presented with a compelling argument. Davis and Knowles argued that the success of this technique relies on unexpected elements that disrupt individuals' typical interaction scripts, which in turn prompts them to attend to the details of the appeal (see also Erikson, 1964; Wegner & Vallacher, 1986). Although this technique is similar to ego-depletion in some respects, our ego-depletion manipulation did not involve confusing participants or disrupting their interaction scripts in any way, and attending to the details of weak arguments reduces their efficacy (see Knowles & Lynn, 2004 for more discussion of the differences between these two means of reducing resistance).

CONCLUSION

These findings provide further support for the ego-depletion framework and for the strength model in particular. This explicit link between the self-regulation and persuasion literatures has the potential to generate many provocative and novel findings and to enhance our understanding of both self-regulatory ability and resistance to persuasion. Thinking about resistance to persuasion as a self-regulatory process not only creates a linkage between two broad literatures, but also leads to the generation of many interesting hypotheses regarding the individuals in whom and the processes by which resistance to persuasion will operate.

REFERENCES

Baumeister, R. F., Bratslavsky, E., Muraven, M., & Tice, D. M. (1998). Ego depletion: Is the active self a limited resource? *Journal of Personality and Social Psychology, 74*(5), 317–338.

Baumeister, R. F., & Heatherton, T. F. (1996). Self-regulation failure: An overview. *Psychological Inquiry, 7*(1), 1–15.

Baumeister, R. F., Muraven, M., & Tice, D. M. (2000). Ego depletion: A resource model of volition, self-regulation, and controlled processing. *Social Cognition Special Issue: Social ignition: The interplay of motivation and social cognition, 18*(2), 130–150.

Brendl, C. M., Markman, A. B., & Messner, C. (2003). The devaluation effect: Activating a need devalues unrelated objects. *Journal of Consumer Research, 29*(4), 463–473.

Briñol, P., & Petty, R. E. (2005). Individual differences in persuasion. In D. Albarracin, B. T. Johnson, & M. P. Zanna (Eds.), *The handbook of attitudes and attitude change* (pp. 575–616). Hillsdale, NJ: Erlbaum.

Briñol, P., Rucker, D. D., Tormala, Z. L., & Petty, R. E. (2004). Individual differences in resistance to persuasion: The role of beliefs and meta-beliefs. In E. S. Knowles & J. A. Linn (Eds.), *Resistance and persuasion* (pp. 83–104). Mahwah NJ, Erlbaum.

Cacioppo, J. T., & Petty, R. E. (1981). Social psychological procedures for cognitive response assessment: The thought listing technique. In T. Merluzzi, C. Glass, & M. Genest (Eds.), *Cognitive assessment* (pp. 309–342). New York: Guilford.

Carver, C. S., & Scheier, M. F. (1981). *Attention and self-regulation: A control theory approach to human behavior*. New York: Springer.

Carver, C. S., & Scheier, M. F. (1998). *On the self-regulation of behavior*. New York, NY: Cambridge University Press.

Davis, B. P., & Knowles, E. S. (1999). A disrupt-then-reframe technique of social influence. *Journal of Personality and Social Psychology, 76*(2), 192–199.

DeMarree, K. G., Wheeler, S. C., & Petty, R. E. (2005). Priming a new identity: Self-monitoring moderates the effects of nonself primes on self-judgments and behavior. *Journal of Personality and Social Psychology, 89*(5), 657–671.

Duval, S., & Wicklund, R. A. (1972). *A theory of objective self-awareness.* New York: Academic Press.

Erikson, M. H. (1964). The confusion technique in hypnosis. *The American Journal of Clinical Hypnosis, 6*, 183–207.

Fazio, R. H. (1995). Attitudes as object-evaluation associations: Determinants, consequences, and correlates of attitude accessibility. In R. E. Petty & J. A. Krosnick (Eds.), *Attitude strength: Antecedents and consequences* (pp. 247–282). Hillsdale, NJ, England: Lawrence Erlbaum.

Fennis, B. M., Das, E. H. H. J., & Pruyn, A. T. H. (2004). "If you can't dazzle them with brilliance, baffle them with nonsense: Extending the *impact of the* disrupt-then-reframe technique of social influence. *Journal of Consumer Psychology, 14*(3), 280–290.

Ferguson, M. J., & Bargh, J. A. (2004). Liking is for doing: The effects of goal pursuit on automatic evaluation. *Journal of Personality and Social Psychology, 87*(5), 557–572.

Fitzsimons, G. M. (2004). The goal-dependent nature of interpersonal evaluations. Unpublished doctoral dissertation, New York University, New York.

Gilbert, D. T. (1991). How mental systems believe. *American Psychologist, 46*(2), 107–119.

Hanley, C. (1965). Personality item difficulty and acquiescence. *Journal of Applied Psychology, 49*(3), 205–208.

Haugtvedt, C. P., & Petty, R. E. (1992). Personality and persuasion: Need for cognition moderates the persistence and resistance of attitude changes. *Journal of Personality and Social Psychology, 63*(2), 308–319.

Hutton, D. G., & Baumeister, R. F. (1992). Self-awareness and attitude change: Seeing oneself on the central route to persuasion. *Personality and Social Psychology Bulletin, 18*(1), 68–75.

Knowles, E. S., & Lynn, J. A. (2004). Approach-avoidance model of persuasion: Alpha and Omega strategies for change. In E. S. Knowles & J. A. Lynn (Eds.), *Resistance and persuasion* (pp. 117–148). Mahwah, NJ: Erlbaum.

Krosnick, J. A. (1991). Response strategies for coping with the cognitive demands of attitude measures in surveys. *Applied Cognitive Psychology Special Issue: Cognition and Survey Measurement, 5*(3), 213–236.

Macrae, C. N., Bodenhausen, G. V., & Milne, A. B. (1998). Saying no to unwanted thoughts: Self-focus and the regulation of mental life. *Journal of Personality and Social Psychology, 74*(3), 578–589.

Macrae, C. N., Bodenhausen, G. V., Milne, A. B., & Jetten, J. (1994). Out of mind but back in sight: Stereotypes on the rebound. *Journal of Personality and Social Psychology, 67*(5), 808–817.

Muraven, M., & Slessareva, E. (2003). Mechanisms of self-control failure: Motivation and limited resources. *Personality and Social Psychology Bulletin, 29*(7), 894–906.

Muraven, M., Baumeister, R. F., & Tice, D. M. (1999). Longitudinal improvement of self-regulation through practice: Building self-control strength through repeated exercise. *Journal of Social Psychology, 139*(4), 446–457.

Muraven, M., Tice, D. M., & Baumeister, R. F. (1998). Self-control as a limited resource: Regulatory depletion patterns. *Journal of Personality and Social Psychology, 74*(3), 774–789.

Petty, R. E., & Cacioppo, J. T. (1979). Issue involvement can increase or decrease persuasion by enhancing message-relevant cognitive responses. *Journal of Personality and Social Psychology, 37*(10), 1915–1926.

Petty, R. E., & Cacioppo, J. T. (1986). *Communication and persuasion: Central and peripheral routes to attitude change.* New York: Springer.

Petty, R. E., & Krosnick, J. A. (Eds.). (1995). *Attitude strength: Antecedents and consequences.* Hillsdale, NJ, England: Erlbaum.

Petty, R. E., Tormala, Z. L., & Rucker, D. D. (2004). Resisting persuasion by counterarguing: An attitude strength perspective. In J. T. Jost, M. R. Banaji, & D. A. Prentice (Eds.), *Perspectivism in social psychology: The yin and yang of scientific progress* (pp. 37–51). Washington DC: American Psychological Association.

Petty, R. E., Wells, G. L., & Brock, T. C. (1976). Distraction can enhance or reduce yielding to propaganda: Thought disruption versus effort justification. *Journal of Personality and Social Psychology, 34*(5), 874–884.

Schmeichel, B. J., Vohs, K. D., & Baumeister, R. F. (2003). Intellectual performance and ego depletion: Role of the self in logical reasoning and other information processing. *Journal of Personality and Social Psychology, 85(1),* 33–46.

Vohs, K. D., & Heatherton, T. F. (2000). Self-regulatory failure: A resource-depletion approach. *Psychological Science, 11*(3), 249–254.

von Hippel, W., Silver, L. A., & Lynch, M. E. (2000). Stereotyping against your will: The role of inhibitory ability in stereotyping and prejudice among the elderly. *Personality and Social Psychology Bulletin, 26*(5), 523–532.

Wegener, D. T., Downing, J., Krosnick, J. A., & Petty, R. E. (1995). Measures and manipulations of strength-related properties of attitudes: Current practice and future directions. In: R. E. Petty & J. A. Krosnick, (Eds.), *Attitude strength: Antecedents and consequences* (pp. 455–487).

Wegener, D. T., Petty, R. E., Smoak, N. D., & Fabrigar, L. R. (2004). Multiple routes to resisting attitude change. In E. S. Knowles & J. A. Linn (Eds.), *Resistance and Persuasion* (pp. 13–38). Mahwah, NJ: Erlbaum.

Wegner, D. M. (1994). Ironic processes of mental control. *Psychological Review, 101,* 34–52.

Wegner, D. M., & Vallacher, R. R. (1986). Action identification. In R. M. Sorrentino & E. T. Higgins (Eds.), *Handbook of motivation and cognition: Foundations of social behavior* (pp. 550–582). New York, NY: Guilford Press.

Wood, W., Rhodes, N., & Biek, M. (1995). Working knowledge and attitude strength: An information-processing analysis. In R. E. Petty & J. A. Krosnick (Eds.), *Attitude strength: Antecedents and consequences* (pp. 283–313). Hillsdale, NJ: Erlbaum.

Zuwerink, J. R., & Devine, P. G. (1996). Attitude importance and resistance to persuasion: It's not just the thought that counts. *Journal of Personality and Social Psychology, 70*(5), 931–944.

POST-ARTICLE DISCUSSION

Past research has revealed that we have a finite amount of cognitive space with which to devote to any task we are currently working on. Whether it be the amount of information we can hold in short-term memory (Miller, 1956) or the fact that cognitive distraction or cognitive business leads people to be more likely to use a cognitive heuristic like a stereotype to make a social judgment (Macrae, Milne, & Bodenhausen, 1994), people can only think of a fixed number of things at one time. When consciousness is overloaded, we tend to forget information or we fail in our attempts to process information accurately. This suggests that when one is trying to do too much simultaneously, the system will falter. However, the authors of the paper you just read examine this from the standpoint of how the system handles two *sequential* cognitive tasks. Specifically, if the first task is very demanding (what the authors call "ego-depleting"), will the expenditure of that cognitive energy result in what we might call "cognitive fatigue" and make the person more susceptible to persuasion (because they cannot produce the requisite counterarguments to persuasion due to the fact that they are cognitive exhausted)?

Let's go over some of the predictions and findings. The authors reasoned that when people are normally (i.e., not under cognitive fatigue) exposed to a persuasion message, they automatically are able to formulate counterarguments to weak persuasion messages.

(Continued)

(Continued)

For example, suppose I say, "Ice cream is awful, and you shouldn't like it, because people aren't made to like cold foods." You might respond, "Huh?" and generate counterarguments. But what if I said the same thing ("Ice cream is bad, and you shouldn't like it") and presented various logical, science-based, rational arguments to support my position? Research shows that people generate far fewer counterarguments in the face of such strong persuasion messages. OK, now, the researchers predicted that if people are cognitively fatigued ("ego depleted"), they are just not going to be able to generate many counterarguments, no matter what persuasion message (strong vs. weak) is presented. But, if we compare the difference in counterarguments generated from non-ego-depleted to ego-depleted, you will note that the difference between the weak conditions will show a greater difference in counterarguments generated (many in non-depleted, few in depleted) compared to the strong message condition (few in non-depleted, few in depleted, so very little difference). This is precisely what their data showed. These data are fascinating in that they show how earlier cognitive work can have important implications for later cognitive processing, and this helps psychologists who study persuasion better understand the factors that influence persuasion and helps us understand the limitations of our cognitive system.

THINGS TO THINK ABOUT

1. Are there some types of cognitive activity that you think would be especially taxing (and result in maximum ego-depletion) compared to others that wouldn't be as draining? How would that difference influence subsequent persuasion processes?

2. The design is a 2 × 2 between-subjects design. Without doing a statistical power analysis, do you think the authors used enough subjects for this design? Why?

3. Do you think that men and women differ in their resistance to persuasion? Why or why not?

4. What do you think is happening in the ego-depleted condition that makes people susceptible to virtually any persuasion?

5. Do you think the authors did a good job addressing alternative theories? Explain.

6. Aside from what the authors discuss in the paper, what are some unanswered questions you have about the next steps for researchers in this area?

6

Social Perception

Social perception is the process by which we seek to know and understand others. Research in this area examines what it is about others that cause us to form certain inferences and conclusions about them, and it also encompasses the things we do to craft a certain impression in others' minds about us. What do you notice first about someone before you even talk to that person? Personality? Kindness? Usually these are hard to discern without first talking to the person. But what we do notice are the nonverbal features about the person, that is, the way the person looks.

NONVERBAL INFORMATION

Physical Appearance

How someone looks gives us a lot of information about who we think they are and what kind of person they are. It should be noted that we are talking about the use of stereotypes and schemas to guide most social perception based on physical appearance only. For example, suppose you see someone who has some tattoos and wears motorcycle boots, jeans, and a leather jacket. Based on the representativeness heuristic, you might conclude that the person probably rides a motorcycle and perhaps enjoys heavy metal music. Based on your stereotypes about people in those groups, you might further think that the person likes violence, or is violent, or has had trouble with the law. Maybe you further assume, based on your stereotypes, that the person smokes, drinks, or does drugs. Perhaps those conclusions lead you to avoid the person, and thus you may never see the person again in your life. But, what if you are completely wrong? What if that person is not like that and instead is someone you'd really get along with, and maybe even be best friends with? That is one of the major pitfalls of relying solely on stereotypes and schemas in social perception: Most of the time they lead to erroneous conclusions. But, as we discussed in the chapter on social cognition (Chapter 3), we don't really care about that. We would rather make a fast judgment than an accurate one, and stereotypes and schemas are perfect tools to accomplish that.

Emotions

Another major social inference (a guess) that we make about someone is how that person is feeling. We try to assess the intentions, expectations, and emotional state of others based on their expression of emotions. Darwin (1859) said that this ability should be very important for survival. Specifically, he said that we should be especially good at detecting signs of hostility over any other signs of friendly intent, because friendly intent won't threaten our survival, whereas hostility very much could threaten our survival. In a test of this idea, Hansen and Hansen (1988) had a group of 81 college student faces photographed. In one photograph, every face but one showed a happy expression, while one face showed an angry expression. The other photo showed the opposite. The researchers told the subjects to, as quickly as possible, find the one face that was showing a different feeling from the rest of the crowd. Results showed that, as Darwin predicted, those trying to find the one angry face in a sea of happy faces were especially adept and did it significantly faster than those trying to find the one happy face in a crowd of angry faces.

Research by Ekman and his colleagues (1987) investigated the degree to which our ability to identify emotion expression is innate or if it is something we need to learn. To answer this question, he had people from 10 countries look at six photos of people displaying distinct, basic emotions (fear, anger, surprise, happiness, sadness, and disgust). Before discussing the results, just a quick note about this methodology. This is used often in evolutionary psychology studies. The idea is that, to the degree that one finds consistency across cultures, it is supportive of the idea that the behavior is innate within humans, not something that must be learned. If there is great variability between cultures, that supports the idea that the behavior is a learned one, and not something that passes down through genetics (and the evolutionary process). The results of the study found that there was indeed great consistency across cultures in their agreement about what emotion was being displayed in each photo. Ekman et al. concluded that our perception of emotion is a universal and innate ability.

Eye Contact

You have heard the old cliché, "The eyes are the windows to the soul." Do people really put that much importance on eye contact in social perception? What can we learn (if anything) from different types of eye contact? When someone has good eye contact, we often infer that she is interested in what we have to say, that she has good social skills, and that she is polite. How about when someone evades eye contact? We might conclude a number of possible things about this person, including that he is shy, he is hiding something, he is ashamed, he is introverted, and so on. Finally, what do you think about a person who stares at you? In a romantic context, you might think the person is *very* interested in you or that the person is flirting with you. But, in the absence of a romantic context, it turns out that we interpret it the same way that many animals do: as a sign of hostility, challenge, or threat (Ellsworth & Carlsmith, 1973; Hinde & Rowell, 1962).

SCHEMAS

Recall from Chapter 3 that a schema is a hierarchically organized mental structure that contains everything we know about a concept. We use schemas to fill in the blanks of information that we get about something or someone. Schemas are great tools to help us come to a fast judgment about someone, which, as we have discussed in other chapters, is a primary goal for people. We are cognitively lazy, and we use mental shortcuts (heuristics) whenever possible to come to a fast decision about others. We are not really concerned about being accurate but being quick in our judgments (Kunda, 1999). For example, in one study, men and women were told about a child taking a test (Darley & Gross, 1983). Some were told she was from a high socioeconomic background, whereas others were told she came from a low socio-economic background. After watching a videotape of the girl taking an exam, they were asked about how well they thought she performed relative to her same-grade peers. Those who were told she was from a high socioeconomic background rated her performance as very high and well above her grade level. Those who were told she was from a low socioeconomic background rated her performance as much lower than her grade level. Both groups watched the same video, same stimulus, but their expectations (and stereotypes about different socioeconomic groups) were what guided their perceptions and colored their view of their social world, and the child in particular.

The Self-Fulfilling Prophecy

In another study, Rosenthal and Jacobson (1968) examined how the schemas and expectations of teachers can influence the performance of their students on their academic work. Researchers approached elementary school teachers and asked if they could administer a new test of intellectual ability to their students, in order to work out the bugs in its final development. It should be noted that the researchers got the approval from the administration first, after having told the administration what they really intended to investigate and how they planned to do it. The teachers were not told the true nature of the study (until after the study was finished), because that would have rendered the study pointless. The teachers agreed to the test, and their students took the test at the beginning of the school year.

After a month, the researchers return and tell the teachers that because the test is still in development, it is important that she not tell the kids their scores. The researcher tells the teacher that all but three kids performed at the level that is appropriate for their same-grade peers. (The researcher

earlier chose three names from the roster.) Those three, the researcher reveals, have vastly outperformed the class. They are early bloomers, little Einsteins. The researchers tell the teacher they would like to come back at the end of the school year to see how the kids performed on their academic work. Occasionally, they would like to sit in on the class and observe class activities. When the end of the school year comes, the teacher tells them that all the kids did fine work, but that, wow, those three little early bloomers greatly outperformed the rest of the class!

How did the researchers happen to pick the exact three kids who would do better than the rest of the class? Were they psychic? Something a bit less dramatic but still very interesting happened. When the researchers were watching the teacher interact with the students, they noticed that she would spend more time with those three who had scored higher on the test. The teacher would also say encouraging things to them such as, "I know you know this" or "You can do this." Those three children, in turn, picked up on these high expectations from the teacher and started working harder, studying harder, to live up to those high expectations. In so doing, the three kids outperformed the rest of the class. This phenomenon has come to be called "self-fulfilling prophecy." We define it as the phenomenon whereby a perceiver's expectations of a target lead the target to behave in ways that confirm those expectations. Since this initial study, it has been supported by many studies (Rosenthal, 1995).

FIRST IMPRESSIONS

You've probably heard that first impressions make a difference. They are important, but why? Researchers have discovered something referred to as the "primacy effect." Research on short-term memory shows that the information one first sees on a list of words is slightly more rehearsed and more likely to make it past short-term memory into long-term memory; this is the primacy effect. In person perception research, the first information we learn about someone will tend to bias all subsequent information we learn about the person. In a classic demonstration of this, Asch (1946) showed one group of people the following list of traits and asked them to form an impression of what kind of person this is: intelligent, skillful, industrious, determined, practical, cautious, and evasive. A second group were shown the same list of traits, but in reverse order, and were asked to form an impression of the person. The first group had a much more positive view of the person than the second. The main reason for this result was that the first information the first group got about this target was a list of positive traits, whereas the first information the second group got was a list of somewhat negative traits. The first information we receive tends to color or bias the way we see all subsequent information about the person.

In another study of first impressions, Rosenhan (1973) wanted to show the power of a psychiatric diagnostic label in terms of how it influences how the patient is perceived. He and several colleagues faked being schizophrenic and were admitted to a psychiatric hospital. According to plan, once admitted, they were to act normal. How long would it take the staff to realize they are not schizophrenic? It took up to 19 days for the staff to realize there was nothing wrong with these individuals. Rosenhan says that is because once someone has a label, all their subsequent behavior is seen through the lens of that label. For example, benign note-taking for their study was perceived as paranoid note-taking about people out to get the patient. First impressions are quite powerful!

INTRODUCTION TO READING 6.1
Kleck and Strenta (1980)

We all wonder how others perceive us. That is a major focus of social perception research. What are the factors that influence how we perceive others and how others perceive us? What is it about us that others use to form an impression of us? Research has shown that things like similarity between perceiver and target, stereotypes, perceiver motivation, cognitive availability, and mood can all have important effects on the impression we form even in those first few seconds of perceiving the other person (Jones, 1990). A question that psychologists have long wondered about is the question of how we think we are perceived by others. This is the heart of the paper by Kleck and Strenta that you are about to read.

One example of this is some fascinating research conducted by William Swann on "self-verification" (2012). Self-verification is the idea that we are highly motivated to have others see us as we see ourselves. In one study, Swann and his colleagues (1994) had high and low self-esteem individuals indicate how they thought their partner thought of them and how committed they were to their partner. For high self-esteem persons, everything was lovely. But for the low-self-esteem persons, it was a different story. When they believed that their partner put them on a pedestal and regarded them highly, it made them uncomfortable, and, in fact, they were less committed to the relationship. But, when persons with low self-esteem believed their partner also regarded (and treated) them poorly, they were more committed to that partner. These disparate findings for the persons with low self-esteem reflect the power of self-verification. This may be one (but certainly not the only) reason that people with low self-esteem stay in abusive relationships and why they keep returning to those abusive partners. They think "this is the only person who really sees the true me." Those with partners who regard them highly may be worried that their partner will someday realize that they are worthless and drop them.

So you see, the issues dealt with in social perception research concern fundamental aspects of social psychology. How we think of ourselves, how we think others view us, and how those thoughts (also referred to as "construals" or "perceptions") have a tremendous influence on the way we think about ourselves and others, and also on our feelings and behavior. The paper you are about to read follows this tradition. This article, by Kleck and Strenta, was chosen for two reasons: (1) It examines in detail how people perceive others with a potentially stigmatizing condition and how those with the condition *think* others are perceiving them. (2) The experimental methods used to address these questions are exceptional and clever. As you are reading the paper, consider carefully the sometimes intricate questions that are being asked of the subjects and, in light of those questions, how a researcher might design an experiment to reveal answers to those questions. Enjoy the paper, and we'll chat afterward!

Reading 6.1

Perceptions of the Impact of Negatively Valued Physical Characteristics on Social Interaction

Robert E. Kleck and Angelo Strenta

Individuals were led to believe that they were perceived as physically deviant in the eyes of an interactant. Following a brief discussion, they commented on those aspects of the interactant's behavior that appeared to be linked to the deviance. The experimental arrangements were such that the interactant did not, in fact, perceive them as deviant. Persons who thought that they possessed negatively valued physical characteristics found strong reactivity to the deviance in the behavior of their interactant, whereas those with a more neutrally valued characteristic did not. An expectancy/perceptual bias explanation was advanced to account for these results, though experimental demand could also be viewed as a plausible interpretation. Study 2 provided more definitive data on the demand aspects of the instructions used in the first study and reaffirmed that both the expectancy and the demand explanations were plausible. Study 3 used a new set of instructions explicitly devised to permit a test of the competing explanations. In addition to replicating the important findings of Study 1, the results of Study 3 in combination with those of Study 2 strongly undermine a demand interpretation of the original results. In a fourth study, persons who had observed the behavior of the interactants in Study 1 via videotape also perceived greater reactivity to an imputed negative form of deviance than to a neutral one. Data from this last study support the notion that the results of Studies 1 and 3 reflect the operation of an expectancy/perceptual bias mechanism and tend to rule out a self-fulfilling prophecy dynamic.

It is now well established that negatively valued deviant physical characteristics such as obesity (Maddox, Back, & Liederman, 1968), orthopedic disability (Kleck, 1969), and facial deformity (MacGregor, 1974) are important in determining some nontrivial social outcomes. Such physical characteristics affect, for example, the nature of the impressions we form of individuals having them (Kleinke, 1975), the causes we assign to these individuals' behavior (McArthur & Solomon, 1978), and whether we choose to affiliate with them or not (Snyder, Kleck, Strenta, & Mentzer, 1979).

Although a stigmatizing physical characteristic is important in determining some aspects of our responses to another individual, our own behavioral dispositions, contextual factors surrounding specific interactions, and non-physique-related characteristics of the deviant person also have an effect on our behavior. Wright (1960) has observed, however, that

This research was supported in part by National Institute of Mental Health Grant MH 29446 to the first author. The authors would like to thank Nannette J. Hart and Alice E. Watson, who served as confederates in Study 1, and Katherine R. Rackow and Sarah A. Riddle, who performed this task in Study 3.

Requests for reprints should be sent to Robert E. Kleck, Department of Psychology, Dartmouth College, Hanover, New Hampshire 03755.

physically deviant individuals often simply take it for granted that all of the behavior emitted by the persons interacting with them is causally linked to their own deviance. Davis (1961) and Goffman (1963) have likewise commented on the tendency for the physically stigmatized to articulate their interactions exclusively in terms of their stigma.

Considered in attribution theory terms, the tendency that Wright and others are postulating appears to make some sense. Kelley (1971), for example, argues that in attempting to arrive at some understanding of human action, the naive perceiver uses what he labels the principle of covariation. To the greatest possible extent, the perceiver systematically varies situations, people, and stimuli and observes when an effect in question occurs. When it comes to understanding the impact of a physical characteristic such as a missing arm on the behavior of others, the physically deviant individual is, however, at a particular disadvantage. That is, he or she cannot vary the presence or absence of the physical characteristic to test for its effects on others. In any face-to-face encounter, the characteristic is potentially implicated as a cause of the behavior of others, simply because it occurs in contiguity with those behaviors. Physically deviant individuals can still apply the principle of covariation to persons, and to the extent that their interactants treat them differently, they could conclude that the characteristic is not implicated. Interestingly enough, laboratory studies have shown that at least in initial encounters, the variability in behavior across physically normal individuals is less when they are interacting with a physically deviant person than when they are interacting with one who is physically normal (Kleck, 1968, 1969; Kleck, Ono, & Hastorf, 1966).

Attribution theory aside, we have little systematic evidence that persons who are physically deviant perceive this deviance as causally implicated in the behavior of others. The purpose of the first study reported in the present article, therefore, is to examine the likelihood that persons who possess deviant physical characteristics will see links between those characteristics and the behavior of an interactant. This question is examined under conditions in which the characteristic can, in fact, have no direct impact on the other's behavior. Thus, at some level, the experiment constitutes a test of Wright's (1960) proposition that physically deviant individuals will perceive a relationship between how they are treated and their physical characteristics, even when such a relationship does not objectively exist. The specific hypothesis being tested is that if the physical characteristic at issue is negatively valued (epilepsy or a facial scar), it will more likely be implicated in an interactant's behavior than if it is not stigmatizing (an allergy). The initial study also sought to explore the specific aspects of an interactant's behavior that would be attended to by a physically deviant individual when attempting to assess the nature of the impact of the deviance on an interactant's behavior. It was tentatively hypothesized that a person with an obvious physical defect (facial scar) would tend to focus on the gaze behavior of an interactant, whereas someone with a non obvious physical defect (epilepsy) would attend to nonverbal and verbal indicators of anxiety and tenseness.

STUDY 1

Method

Subjects. Subjects were 25 females enrolled in a coeducational college in the northeastern United States. Ten were unpaid volunteers from an introductory psychology course, and 15 were paid subjects recruited from campus dormitories. One subject had to be dropped, because she did not consent to have the scar material applied.

This is something that not only people with physical stigmas might think, but also those who are members of stereotyped groups. In the literature, this is referred to "attributional ambiguity." This refers to the idea that members of a stereotyped (or stigmatized) group have to constantly try to ascertain the reasons why people in non-stigmatized groups are acting a certain way toward the stigmatized person. For example, "Are they nice to me now because they don't want to appear prejudiced, or are they genuinely a nice person, and treating me nicely due to my individual characteristics as a person?" or "Do they dislike me because of who I am as a person, or because I am (stigmatized group name)?"

Special circumstance exists for those with a physical stigma, and this is the focus of the present research.

Rationale for the first experiment. It is quite an intuitive prediction, and somewhat surprising that little experimental evidence exists (at that time) to support the idea that people with physical stigmas would attribute others' behavior toward them as due in part to their physical stigma.

This too makes sense: if the target individual has a stigmatizing characteristic, he or she should be more likely to attribute others' behavior toward him or her as influenced by that characteristic, compared to target individuals with physical characteristics that are NOT stigmatized.

This is pretty specific: the question is—what aspects of the partner will target persons focus on when interacting with them? They predict that negative physically stigmatized persons will focus on the gaze of the partner (right? Like "are you staring at my scar?"), whereas those with non-negative physical characteristics would tend to focus on nonverbal or verbal indicators of anxiety.

Ok so here, the subjects think that their partner will read about their "stigmatizing" condition on p. 2 (epilepsy or allergy). But unknown to the subject, the experimenter removes p. 2 from the questionnaire before it is given to the interaction partner. So the partner never learns about any stigmatizing condition of the subject. But the point here is to make the subject THINK that the partner has read and now knows about the subject's condition.

This is one of my favorite aspects of this study, and why I really like it. It is a very simple yet very clever solution to the problem of creating a physical stigma for an individual (to see how others react to it, and how it influences how the subject interacts and perceives his or her partner's reaction to it), yet how to remove it before the interaction, so the subject thinks it is there but it isn't.

Solving another problem that plagues lab research: how to record behavior without having subjects be very suspicious.

Confederates. Each subject interacted with one of two persons who were presumed to be subjects like themselves. These two college-age females interacted with subjects in each of the experimental conditions described below. They were blind concerning the purposes of the study, the experimental manipulations, and the dependent measures. They were told only that they would be discussing a particular topic with a number of students and that part of their task was to be behaviorally consistent across the various interactions.

Procedure. When subjects arrived at the laboratory, they were given a set of written instructions that randomly assigned them to one of three conditions: allergy, epilepsy, or facial scar. These instructions informed them that they would be involved in a discussion with another female student and that the experimenter's interest was in whether that person's behavior would be affected by the physical condition attributed to them.

All subjects then completed a biographical questionnaire, which they presumed would be exchanged with the person with whom they were to interact. For the allergy and epilepsy groups, the second page of the questionnaire asked subjects to list any significant aspects of their medical history. The experimenter asked them to write either "a mild allergy that is under drug control" or "a mild form of epilepsy that is under drug control," depending on their random assignment to experimental conditions. The confederates actually saw only the first page of biographical information. Subjects in the facial scar condition were asked if a cosmetic preparation used to simulate facial disfigurement in dramatic productions could be applied to their face. As this material dries, it gives the appearance of a healed scar, the size and extent of which can be controlled by the application procedures. The scar was placed on the subject's right cheek between the ear and the corner of the mouth and was of a size to be clearly noticeable in face-to-face interaction. The experimenter gave the subject a small hand mirror to confirm that an authentic-looking scar had been placed on her face. As she put the mirror down, he informed her that he would have to put a moisturizer over the scar to keep it from cracking and peeling off. In the process of "moisturizing" the scar, the experimenter removed it without the subject's knowledge.

After cautioning subjects not to talk about their allergy, epilepsy, or facial scar unless the other person mentioned it, the experimenter then brought the confederate, who was in a waiting room down the hall, into the room where the interaction was to take place. Two chairs were placed near the center, and the confederate always took the same seat. The subject, who had come from an adjacent room, was asked to take the other chair, and both were told that additional instructions would be played to them over the speakers placed along one wall. The speaker cabinets also contained video cameras and microphones, which permitted the making of candid records of the interaction. The experimenter then went to an adjoining control room where he turned on the videotape equipment and the tape recorder, which contained the remaining instructions. These instructions specified the discussion topic (strategies people use in making friends) and asked the two participants to begin their interaction. The confederates had been instructed to initiate all discussions with the same comment but to not dominate the interaction.

After approximately 6 minutes, the experimenter entered the room and asked both individuals to return to separate rooms and complete the questionnaires that had been placed there. The questionnaire asked the subject to rate the confederate's behavior on five dimensions: amount of eye contact, degree of tenseness, amount of talking, degree of perceived patronization, and amount of liking for the subject as a person. In addition, she was asked to estimate how attractive the confederate found her to be and whether the confederate would have been more comfortable with a closer or more distant seating arrangement. All ratings were done on 14-point bipolar scales.

When the subject had completed this form, she was told that she and the other individual had been video taped and was asked to sign a release agreement allowing her part of the video-tape to be viewed by others. The subject was then given the opportunity to view and comment on the videotape made of the other interactant's behavior. A split-screen recording format had been used, and the side of the video monitor on which the subject appeared was masked so that she could see only her interactant (the confederate). She was first shown a brief segment of the interaction to familiarize her with the format and then saw and heard (over earphones) the entire interaction sequence. She was instructed to comment as the tape was played, on any aspect of the other person's behavior that she felt was responsive to the manipulated physical state (i.e., scar, allergy, or epilepsy), and her comments were tape-recorded. The experimenter reiterated that the manipulation may or may not have had an effect and that the subject should not feel compelled to find effects where none were evident.

At the conclusion of this commentary, the subject was asked to summarize her comments in writing and make any additional observations. The general nature of the research was explained to her, and any questions that she had concerning the procedures were answered in detail.

Results

The first set of dependent measures was derived from the verbal and written descriptions that subjects gave of the confederates' behavior. The verbal commentaries were transcribed and appended to the written summary. Two judges, unfamiliar with the general purposes of the study or the specific physical characteristics manipulated, rated each description on the extent to which the person giving it felt that the physical state attributed to them had affected the confederate's behavior. These ratings were made on a 14-point bipolar scale, and the reliability across the two judges for the entire sample was .85. An analysis of variance based on the average judge rating assigned to each subject revealed a significant treatment effect, $F(2, 21) = 10.43$, $p < .001$. Individual comparisons showed that scar and epilepsy condition subjects were both judged to have made statements reflecting a greater impact of their charac-teristics on the confederates than were allergy subjects, $t(14) = 4.62$, $p < .001$, and $t(14) = 3.28$, $p < .01$, respectively. Scar and epilepsy were not different from each other.

A preliminary content analysis of the commentaries suggested that only comments con-cerned with gaze behavior (e.g., eye contact, looking, watching) and tenseness (e.g., uncomfort-able, nervous, jittery) occurred with a frequency meriting statistical analysis. The experimenter and another person unfamiliar with the study independently coded the subjects' comments for the frequency with which these behaviors were seen as responsive to the manipulation of physical state. Interrater reliability coefficients were .98 for the gaze measure and .99 for tense-ness. Analyses of variance of these frequency counts revealed significant overall treatment effects for tenseness, $F(2, 21) = 3.72$, $p < .05$, and for gaze, $F(2, 21) = 5.61$, $p < .02$. Between-groups comparisons on the tenseness measure demonstrated that epilepsy subjects used such terms more frequently in describing the confederates' behavior than did allergy subjects, $t(14) = 2.33$, $p < .05$, but no other comparisons were significant. The same comparisons for the gaze measure revealed a significant difference only between the scar and allergy groups, $t(14) = 3.3$, $p < .01$, with the former making more references to gaze behavior than the latter.

DV. The authors are interested in finding out how someone with a stigmatizing condition that is either seen or unseen influences (or doesn't influence) the behavior of his or her interaction partner. For example, if I think you know that I have epilepsy, do I act defensively with you? Do I perceive all of your behavior with me to be influenced by your knowledge of my condition? Do I think that you find me less attractive because you know about my condition? Remember: in all the conditions, the confederate had NO knowledge of any stigma. The second page was removed in the unseen stigma condition, and the scar was removed in the physical stigma condition. This allows the researcher to purely assess how the subject's behavior does or doesn't influence his or her interaction partner.

This is an excellent addition to the method, in that it serves as a double-check against the impressions that the subject expressed in the earlier questionnaire. It gives the subject another, more explicit opportunity to really examine the behavior of the confederate, to ascertain any behavior that the subject perceives as being influenced by the subject's condition.

A good minimum inter-rater reliability is .70. .85 is even better.

Well this is interesting in that only the scar is a visible stigma, and epilepsy isn't a visible condition, yet they both differed significantly from allergy subjects in terms of their belief that their conditions had affected the confederate's behavior.

A multivariate analysis of variance, collapsed across confederates, was conducted for the seven dimensions on which subjects rated their interactant immediately following the encounter. This analysis yielded a significant main effect for experimental groups, $F(14, 30 = 2.95$, $p < .01$. Univariate analyses of variance conducted for each dependent measure demonstrated significant main effects for tenseness, $F(2, 21) = 15.59$, $p < .0001$; attraction, $F(2, 21) = 8.95$, $p < .002$; and liking, $F(2, 21) = 3.41$, $p = .05$. Specific between-groups comparisons for these three measures revealed the following pattern of results: Scar and epilepsy subjects perceived the confederate as significantly more tense than did allergy subjects, $t(14) = 6.08$, $p < .0001$, and $t(14) = 4.29$, $p < .001$, but scar and epilepsy groups did not differ from each other. Likewise, both scar and epilepsy subjects perceived that the confederate found them less attractive than did the allergy subjects, $t(14) = 3.79$, $p < .01$, and $t(14) = 2.26$, $p < .OS$, though on this measure, the scar and epilepsy groups themselves differed, with the former rating themselves as less attractive to the confederate, $t(14) = 2.26$, $p < .05$. The significant main effect for the liking measure was contributed to primarily by the epilepsy subjects, who perceived that they were liked less well by the confederate than did the allergy subjects, $t(14) = 3.19$, $P < .01$. As the means in Table 1 show, the scar group perceived a level of liking by the confederates that was midway between the epilepsy and allergy subjects' perception, though not significantly different from either group.

The univariate analyses revealed no significant effects for the remaining four measures. An inspection of Table 1 does show, however, that the pattern of means for these other measures is generally consistent with the conclusion that scar and epilepsy subjects perceived their conditions as having a more negative impact on the confederates' behavior and disposition toward them as people than did allergy subjects.

Discussion

The general pattern of results is consistent with our hypothesis that a negatively valued physical characteristic is perceived by its possessor as having a greater impact on the behavior of an interactant than one that is not negatively connoted. Further, there is some evidence suggesting that the type of physically stigmatizing condition involved will affect the aspects of the other individual's behavior that are scrutinized for evidence that the physical deviance is being responded to. In the present case, for example, individuals who thought that they had

TABLE 1 Mean Ratings of the Confederates on the Dependent Measures in Study 1

	Type of disability		
Dimension	Allergy	Epilepsy	Scar
Eye contact	12.00	10.37	11.75
Tenseness	2.37	7.12	8.00
Talking	9.37	9.37	10.37
Distance	7.37	7.87	8.62

Note. Ratings were made on 14-point scales; the higher the number, the higher the attributed level of the characteristic.

Again this is like the earlier result. Why do you suppose that scar and epilepsy subjects are reacting similarly and differently from those in the allergy condition?

This makes sense, in that the scar condition people would tend to think of themselves as less attractive than other people (like those in the epilepsy condition).

This seems to be intuitive: those with a hidden stigmatized condition (like epilepsy) would think that they are less likeable than someone with a hidden non-stigmatized condition (like allergy).

a scar were more likely to focus on the gaze behavior of their interactants, whereas those who thought that the other attributed epilepsy to them were sensitive to behaviors indicating tenseness and anxiety.

These results are obviously consistent with an expectancy notion. Subjects presumably entered the experiment anticipating how others might respond to various forms of physical deviance and, when placed in interaction with a peer, readily found evidence consistent with these expectations. A questionnaire study (Kleck & Strenta, Note 1), using subjects drawn from the same population as the experiment reported above, confirms that physically normal individuals do have clear expectations concerning the impact of various physical conditions on dyadic social interaction. Parallel to the findings reported here, individuals thought that a physically normal individual, when interacting with either a facially scarred person or a paraplegic in a wheelchair, would (a) be more patronizing, (b) find the individual less attractive, (c) be more tense during the interaction, and (d) tend to prefer relatively large interaction distances. When the physical condition was an allergy, perceivers expected it to have little if any impact on social interaction.

Although an expectancy explanation thus appears reasonable, we do not know whether the perceptions of the other individual's behavior were a direct function of what our subjects thought they would find or whether such thoughts served to modify the subjects' behavior, which in turn altered that of the confederates, with the modification being accurately reported by the perceiver. That interpersonal expectancies can have an impact on the behavior of others is now well documented (e.g., Snyder & Swan, 1978), and in the light of this robust phenomenon, we made a strong effort to control our confederates' behavior and kept them blind to the experimental hypotheses and conditions.

To further assess the possibility of confederate behavior differences as a function of subject expectancy, two independent female judges, age peers of our subjects, viewed the confederate's portion of the videotape for each of her interactions separately and rated her behavior on the dimensions that had been used as dependent measures for the subjects. Since inter-judge reliabilities were quite low (.52 for the tenseness dimension being the highest), separate multivariate analyses of variance were conducted for each judge to determine if either could successfully discriminate the experimental conditions. Though the overall multivariate tests were far short of significance in both cases, univariate analyses were nevertheless conducted to see if either judge was successfully discriminating experimental conditions on any measure. Consistent with the multivariate findings, none of the individual tests approached significance.

As noted earlier, the scar and allergy manipulations of Study 1 were selected in part because questionnaire data (Kleck & Strenta, Note 1) suggested that persons expected the former to have important effects on interaction, whereas the latter was viewed as relatively trivial. Epilepsy was chosen as the third condition, because it, like facial deformity, is a negatively valued form of deviance (e.g., Kleck et al., 1968) but is nonobvious in much the same way as an allergy. Further, the allergy and epilepsy manipulations could be accomplished by the substitution of either term in otherwise equivalent instructions given to subjects. The scar manipulation on the other hand, involved the complex process of applying makeup to the subject's face, giving her an opportunity to view the scar in a mirror, and then removing it without her awareness. To some extent, therefore, the epilepsy condition provided a helpful control for the various conceptually irrelevant differences that of necessity existed between the scar and allergy conditions.

Confused yet? ☺ This is the tricky thing about doing experiments like these—how to break down the component interaction slices in such a way to account for what is influencing, and what is influenced by, the subject's and the confederate's behavior.

TABLE 2 Perceived Impact of Experimental Manipulations on the Behavior of Others in Study 2

Hypothesis	Experimental condition		
	Allergy[a]	Allergy demand[b]	Epilepsy[b]
Experimenter's	4.64	5.69	5.56
Own	3.17	3.38	5.06

Note. Ratings were made on a 7-point scale; high numbers denote perceived high impact.

[a]$n = 18$. [b]$n = 16$.

Given the direct parallels between the allergy and epilepsy manipulations, it appears reasonable to interpret the results as being a function of differential expectations that subjects had regarding the impact of these conditions on social interaction. The possibility exists, however, that the subjects themselves did not have clearly articulated differential expectations but attributed such expectations to the experimenter and were, therefore, simply acting consistently with perceived experimenter "demand." The fact that the study utilized a between-subjects design in which individuals were not aware of the other cells (physical conditions being manipulated) undermines such an interpretation, though not completely. In Study 2, we attempted to provide more direct data on experimenter demand by having individuals read the instructions that had been given to subjects in the allergy and epilepsy conditions in Study 1 and then respond to questions concerning their perceptions of the experimenter's hypothesis, as well as stating their own expectations regarding the likely outcome of the study. For comparison purposes, a third set of instructions was prepared, which was intended to more explicitly and unambiguously communicate the experimenter's hypothesis.

STUDY 2

Method

Subjects and procedure. Fifty male and female college students from an introductory psychology course were randomly assigned to one of three experimental conditions. In each of these, subjects were given written instructions that they were told had been employed in a previous experiment that sought to explore the effects of a physical health condition on social interaction outcomes. These instructions placed them in the subject role of Study 1; they thought that the person they were to interact with had information regarding a health problem that they were experiencing (i.e., an allergy or epilepsy). The point of Study 1 as conveyed in these instructions was to have the subjects in that study assess the extent to which the imputed physical condition affected the other individual's behavior toward them.

When they had finished reading the instructions, subjects in Study 2 were asked to rate on a 7-point scale (a) the degree of impact that they thought the experimenter anticipated the imputed physical condition would have on the other individual's behavior and (b) the degree of impact that they personally felt such a physical state would have.

Experimental materials. The same instructions that had been used in Study 1 for the allergy and epilepsy manipulations constituted two cells of the present design. In both sets of instructions, the sentence most likely to affect perception of the experimenter's hypothesis was, "The question as to whether or not the other subject will behave differently toward you because he/she thinks you have an allergy (epilepsy) is an interesting but unstudied one." To provide a condition that would be less ambiguous regarding the experimenter's hypothesis and against which responses to these two sets of instructions could be compared, the above sentence was modified to read, "The question as to whether or not the other subject will behave differently toward you because he/she thinks you have an allergy is an interesting one and recent data we have collected suggest that the other subject's behavior will be different." This will subsequently be referred to as the allergy demand condition.

Results and Discussion

Table 2 shows the means for the subjects' rating of what they thought the experimenter expected regarding the impact of independent variable (physical condition) and what they personally expected the study to find. Consistent with our findings in Study 1, persons reading the epilepsy instructions reported that they expected a greater impact on another's behavior than did subjects reading either version of the allergy instructions, $t(32) = 3.8$, $p < .001$, for allergy. versus epilepsy; $t(30) = 3.54$, $p = .001$, for allergy demand versus epilepsy. At the same time, however, persons in the allergy condition perceived that the experimenter expected this variable to have less of an impact than did persons in the epilepsy condition, $t(32) = 2.04$, $p < .05$. Subjects in the allergy demand group did not differ from epilepsy subjects in their attributions of experimenter expectation.

These data, rather than resolving the issue, leave open the possibility that the results of Study 1 are amenable to either an expectation or experimenter demand explanation, or perhaps some combination of the two. The data are helpful, however, in that they serendipitously provide the materials for a more definitive test of the two alternative explanations. The allergy demand instructions had been written to provide a condition for which subjects would have little difficulty inferring that the experimenter expected his manipulation to have an impact. The means in Table 2 reveal that this was indeed the outcome and that subjects perceived that the experimenter in the allergy demand condition expected as robust an effect as did the experimenter in the epilepsy condition. What is important, however, is that subjects in the allergy demand cell projected a hypothesis upon the experimenter (he was perceived as expecting high impact), which they themselves did not share (they expected relatively little impact), $t(15) = 5.57$, $p < .0001$. Thus, the allergy demand condition and the epilepsy condition were equivalent in terms of perceived experimenter demand but very different in terms of subjects' expectations. If individuals' responses in the paradigm of Study 1 were a function of the inferred experimenter's hypothesis, then the allergy demand instructions should have generated results parallel to those found for the epilepsy condition of that study. If, on the other hand, subjects' own expectations were the important variable, the allergy demand instructions should have resulted in data parallel to the original allergy condition in Study 1. In Study 3, the allergy and epilepsy manipulations of Study 1 were replicated precisely, and the allergy demand instructions were included as a third condition.

Unfortunately, the data do not allow the researchers to make any determination about a differential effect between the subjects' own expectations about how the confederates should act, and the subjects' views of how experimenters think the confederates should act.

See Table 2. Subjects thought that the experimenter would view the allergy demand and epilepsy condition as equivalent in their effects on the confederate. But, subjects' own view of the influence of those two conditions on the confederate were different: they believed the epilepsy condition would be much more influential on the confederate's behavior compared to the allergy demand condition.

STUDY 3

Method

Subjects. Subjects were 30 females from the same population as those used for Study 1. Fifteen were unpaid volunteers from an introductory psychology course, and 15 were paid subjects recruited from campus dormitories.

Confederates. Two college-age females served as confederates, and each was randomly paired with half of the subjects in each of the three cells of the design. The confederates were unacquainted with the subjects with whom they interacted and were blind to the purposes of the study, the experimental manipulations, and the dependent measures.

Procedure. When the subject arrived at the laboratory, she was given a set of written instructions that randomly assigned her to one of three conditions: allergy, allergy demand, or epilepsy. Throughout the experimental session, the experimenter was kept blind to the particular cell assignment of each subject, though he was familiar with the general nature of the research. The instructions informed the subject that she would be placed in a conversational encounter with another female student and that the experimenter's interest was in whether that person's behavior would be affected by a physical condition that was to be imputed to the subject.

Biographical information was exchanged as in Study 1, to lead the subject to believe that the other person perceived her as having an allergy or epilepsy. After the exchange, the experimenter brought the two persons together in the experimental room and told them that additional instructions would be played over a speaker in the corner of the room. This speaker concealed a video camera focused on the confederate and a microphone that was used to record the verbal exchange. The experimenter moved to the adjoining control room from which he played the tape-recorded instructions and videotaped the confederate. As before, the instructions specified "strategies people use in making friends" as the discussion topic.

Following approximately 6 minutes of interaction, both individuals were asked to go to separate rooms to complete a questionnaire. When the subject had completed this form, she was given the opportunity to view and comment on the videotape of the confederate's behavior. As in Study 1, she was asked to comment on any aspect of the other person's behavior that she felt was responsive to the medical information that had supposedly been given prior to the start of the interaction. At the conclusion of the commentary, which was tape-recorded, the subject was asked to summarize her observations in writing and make any additional comments. When she had finished writing, the experimenter consulted the subject's instruction sheet to determine which condition she had been assigned to. He then gave her the appropriate form containing the two questions that had been the focus of Study 2, that is, (a) what degree of impact she thought he anticipated the allergy (epilepsy) would have on the other person and (b) what her expectations had been regarding the degree of impact of the imputed condition. The rationale for the study was then explained to her, and any questions she had concerning the procedures were answered in detail.

Results

As in Study 1, the tape-recorded verbal commentaries were transcribed and appended to the written comments of the subject. Two judges, unfamiliar with the previous research and the general purposes of the present study, rated each description on the extent to which the person giving it felt that the physical condition attributed to her had affected the other person's (confederate's) behavior. As before, these judgments were made on 14-point bipolar scales, and the reliability between judges across the entire sample of 30 protocols reached an acceptable level, .73.

An overall analysis of variance based on the average judge rating assigned to each subject in each of the three conditions was highly significant, $F(2, 27) = 6.73$, $p < .005$. The mean ratings for each condition were 2.2, 2.45, and 5.0 for allergy, allergy demand, and epilepsy, respectively. As might be expected given this array of means, both allergy conditions were significantly different from the epilepsy cell, $t(18) = 3.37$, $p < .005$, and $t(18) = 2.52$, $p < .05$, for allergy versus epilepsy and allergy demand versus epilepsy, respectively.

A content analysis of the commentaries similar to that conducted for Study 1 revealed that references to tenseness and gaze behavior occurred with sufficient frequency across protocols to justify statistical analysis. Frequency counts conducted by one judge and the experimenter for each of these categories were highly reliable: .96 for tenseness and .98 for gaze behavior. An overall analysis of variance of the frequency of tenseness references was significant, $F(2, 27) = 3.7$, $p < .05$, and separate comparisons revealed that as with the perceived impact data, the two allergy conditions differed from the epilepsy cell but not from each other, $t(18) = 2.61$, $p < .05$, for allergy demand versus epilepsy; $t = .0$, ns, for allergy versus allergy demand. An overall analysis of the frequency of gaze behavior references revealed that these did not discriminate the experimental conditions, just as they did not in Study 1.

As in Study 1, subjects completed a questionnaire that asked them to rate the confederate's behavior on seven dimensions: amount of eye contact, tenseness, patronization, amount of talking, liking, how attractive the confederate found them to be, and whether the confederate would have preferred a closer or more distant seating arrangement. All ratings were made on 14-point bipolar scales. A multivariate analysis of variance involving all seven measures, collapsed across confederates, did not yield a significant main effect for experimental groups, thus precluding univariate analyses of the dimensions separately.

Prior to debriefing, subjects were asked to rate the expectations which they had had and which they thought that the experimenter had had at the start of the session regarding the possible impact of the manipulation (allergy or epilepsy) on the other individual's behavior. This was done on the same 7-point scale used in Study 2. Unlike the subjects in Study 2, persons who had actually gone through the procedures did not project differential experimenter expectations as a function of conditions, $F(2, 27) = .48$, ns. This appears reasonable in that once one has experienced the relatively elaborate arrangements of the experiment, it is difficult to believe that the experimenter is expending all this effort for a manipulation that he believes will not have an effect. These responses could also be seen to further obviate an experimenter demand interpretation of the results, though since they were taken at the end of the experiment rather than prior to any interaction, they are somewhat problematic in this regard.

Subjects' own expectations regarding the impact of the manipulation were precisely parallel to those of subjects in Study 2. That is, allergy compared to allergy demand subjects did not anticipate a differential impact, $t(18) = 1.04$, ns, whereas both allergy groups differed from the epilepsy cell, $t(18) = 1.81$, $p < .10$, and $t(18) = 3.04$, $p < .01$, for allergy versus epilepsy and allergy demand versus epilepsy, respectively. As in Study 2, persons in the allergy conditions

Judge ratings of the written verbal commentaries show that both allergy conditions were seen as not having a major influence on the confederate's behavior. But, the epilepsy condition was seen as having a strong influence on the confederate's behavior.

Well this is interesting. There were no significant differences between allergy, allergy demand, and epilepsy conditions in terms of how subject's rated the confederate's behavior on these 7 dimensions. Why do you think that happened? What would you have predicted should have happened?

This experiment, compared to the results of experiment 2 (where subjects didn't interact with a confederate), showed that subjects didn't believe that the experimenter would have different expectations than the subject.

also perceived that the experimenter expected a greater impact for the manipulations than they did, $t(18) = 3.58$, $p < .01$, and $t(18) = 4.64$, $p = .001$, for allergy and allergy demand, respectively, whereas for the epilepsy condition, this was not the case, $t(18) = 1.54$, ns.

The results of Study 3 replicate those of Study 1 in that a negatively valued physical characteristic (epilepsy) is perceived by the person to whom it is imputed as having a greater impact on the behavior of an interactant than is one that is not negatively connoted (allergy). Further, these results, in conjunction with those of Study 2, strongly undermine the plausibility of a demand interpretation of the results and offer additional support for the expectancy notion advanced earlier.

As noted when the expectancy hypothesis was first advanced to account for the results of Study 1, there are two plausible mechanisms by which an expectancy might function in this paradigm. If a person to whom a negative characteristic has been imputed thinks it will have an impact on others, then he/she may modify his/her behavior in such a way as to directly affect the behavior of the other. From this perspective, the discrimination that our subjects were making between the allergy and epilepsy conditions could reflect real differences in confederate behavior created by a self-fulfilling prophecy dynamic. On the other hand, confederates may have been behaving in much the same manner across conditions, but subjects' expectations caused them to differentially perceive or interpret this behavior.

A preliminary assessment of these two possibilities was conducted as part of Study 1 by having naive judges view all of the videotapes of the confederates in each of the three conditions in that study and rate their behavior on a number of dimensions. Though these judges were unable to discriminate the conditions, thus arguing against a self-fulfilling prophecy mechanism, it should be noted that the judges were uninformed regarding the experimental conditions or arrangements. It could be argued that one is less likely to detect true behavioral differences, particularly if they are relatively subtle, without knowledge of the situational constraints that have created the differences. Since our original subjects had direct knowledge of those constraints, they may have been better able to detect the impact of the variables on confederate behavior than were our naive judges. The fourth study has as part of its purpose an examination of this possibility, using correctly informed and misinformed observers as subjects.

The primary purpose of Study 4 was to assess whether observers of an interaction perceive the impact of a deviant physical condition on an interactant in a manner similar to actors who think that they possess that characteristic. It would be reasonable to expect, given the observers' more objective perspective on the interaction, that they would be less inclined to see an impact where none exists. At the same time, consistent with the results of both Study 1 and our questionnaire expectancy data, it was anticipated that observers would be less inclined to find behavioral responses to an allergy condition than to a facial scar.

STUDY 4

Method

Subjects. Subjects were 32 females drawn from the same population used in the previous studies. Twenty were volunteers from an introductory psychology course, and 12 were paid subjects recruited from dormitories.

Results replicate the data of experiment 1. Generally researchers do not need to attempt to replicate their own results (in a multi-experiment paper), but when they do obtain such replication data, it is great to put in a paper, because it gives the reviewers (and readers) more confidence in the findings, and is more likely to be published as a result.

If I have a negative stigma, and I think it may affect your behavior toward me, I may act pre-emptively to sway your perceptions of me.

Here, in this experiment, the authors want to see if observers (or trained behavior raters) see any effect of the subject's condition on the confederates' behavior, in a way that is similar to how the subject him/herself perceives the impact of his/her condition on the confederate.

Procedure. Subjects, who were tested individually, were told that their participation required that they be informed regarding a previous interaction between persons of their own age. They were then handed a description of this interaction, which randomly assigned them to either the allergy or scar condition. (The epilepsy manipulation was not used.) This description detailed the physical arrangements of the interaction, specified the true topic of conversation, and indicated how the experimental manipulation of physical condition had been achieved (i.e., biographical questionnaire in the case of allergy and cosmetic material in the case of facial scar). The subject was not told that the scar had been removed prior to the start of the interaction or that the allergy information had been deleted from the biographical sketch shown to the confederate.

Subjects were told that they would be looking at the videotape of one pair of subjects who had participated in the previous study. As in the first study, one half of the television monitor was masked so that the subject could see only the confederate. The subject was informed that this was being done to reduce the distraction that might otherwise be created and to allow her to concentrate on the "normal" interactant.

The videotapes in the present study were those made of the two confederates in the allergy and scar conditions of Study 1. All of the tapes from both of these Study 1 conditions were paired with a scar description for one half of the subjects and with an allergy description for the other half. Thus, one half of our observers had an expectancy consistent with those of the subjects in Study 1, and the other half had expectancies inconsistent with them.

When they had finished viewing the tape segment, subjects completed a set of self-report measures identical to those used in the first study. They also reviewed the videotape and verbally pointed out specific aspects of the confederates' behavior, if any, that were responsive to the manipulation of the physical state of their interactant. As with the subjects in Study 1, they summarized these observations in writing. Finally, they were asked to respond to two questions: (a) "If you were interacting with someone who was facially scarred (had an allergy), how would you act so as to make the person think the scar (allergy) did not affect your behavior?" and (b) "In that interaction would you acknowledge or mention the scar (allergy)? Why or why not?"

As soon as the subject had completed her answers, the experimenter questioned her on her perceptions of the study and informed her of the deceptions involved. Any questions that she had regarding the procedures or the general research issues were answered in detail.

Results

The design of the study was a simple 2×2 analysis of variance in which observers were led to believe that they were viewing tapes of interactions involving someone with either a facial scar or an allergy (tape description), and this was crossed with whether the tape actually involved a subject who thought she had a facial scar or an allergy attributed to her by an interactant (type of tape shown). Main effects for tape description thus indicate that observer expectancies are important, whereas main effects for the type of tape shown suggest that there are actual behavior differences in the tapes that the observers were detecting independent of their expectations. The presence of these perceived behavioral differences would obviously support the notion that a self-fulfilling prophecy mechanism had been at work in Study 1 and that the scar and allergy condition subjects in that study were behaving differentially and thus eliciting different patterns of behavior from the confederates.

TABLE 3   Mean Ratings of the Confederates on the Dependent Measures in Study 4

	Scar description		Allergy description	
	Scar tape	Allergy tape	Scar tape	Allergy tape
Eye contact	7.25	8.62	8.00	6.62
Tenseness	7.62	7.87	6.87	5.50
Talking	10.62	11.75	10.00	10.50
Distance	8.37	9.00	7.25	8.75
Attraction	6.50	6.25	7.75	7.87
Liking	8.00	9.50	8.37	7.75
Patronization	6.12	5.75	4.87	5.12

Note. Ratings were made on 14-point scales; the higher the number, the higher the attributed level of the characteristic.

We discussed this earlier, but just to refresh your memory . . . when the statistical analyses reveal that the p-value is greater that .05 but equal to or less than .10, many researchers refer to such a p-value as "marginally significant." It doesn't meet our .05 cutoff for significance, but we will refer to such results as "marginally significant" to denote our interest in the data (usually that the data are in the predicted direction). So here, the prediction that the judges would perceive the scar condition as having more of an impact on the confederate than the allergy condition is in the predicted direction, but the difference between the judgments is not statistically significant.

The verbal and written commentaries were used to derive the same measures as in Studies 1 and 3. Again, two judges unfamiliar with the design of the study independently rated each description on the extent to which it revealed (in the observers' eyes) some impact of the allergy or scar on the confederates' behavior. The interrater reliability was .79, and the average of the two judges' ratings was entered into an analysis of variance. Though judges tended to perceive the scar-described tapes as resulting in greater impact than allergy described tapes, this tendency was only marginally significant, $F(1, 28) = 3.15, p < .10$. As in Studies 1 and 3, the observers' commentaries were content analyzed for all references to gaze behavior and tenseness by the experimenter and an independent judge, with respective interrater reliabilities of .97 and .99. The only significant effect for these two measures was that observers who thought that they were watching interactions involving a facially scarred person made more references to the confederates' gaze behavior as a probable outcome of the condition than did observers viewing persons with an allergy, $F(1, 28) = 30.94, p < .001$. There were no significant main effects or interactions involving type of tape shown to the observer.

The observers rated the confederate and her behavior on the same dimensions used by the subjects in Studies 1 and 3, that is, amount of perceived eye contact, tenseness, amount of talking, degree of perceived patronization, her apparent liking for her interactant, whether she would have preferred a closer or more distant seating arrangement, and how attractive she found her interactant to be. A multivariate analysis of variance of these ratings revealed that whether the interaction had been described to the observers as involving a scar or an allergy made a difference, $F(7, 22) = 3.94, P < .01$. In this analysis, there were no main effects for type of tape shown and no significant interaction between the description of the tape provided to the observer and the cell of the previous study (scar or allergy) from which the tape had been drawn.

Univariate analyses for each of the seven dependent measures revealed several effects of borderline significance. For example, subjects receiving the scar description rated the confederate as more tense than did those receiving the allergy description, $F(1, 28) = 2.88$, $P < .10$. As can be seen from the means for these measures, given in Table 3, the general pattern is for the scar to be perceived as having a more negative impact on an interactant's behavior and interpersonal disposition than an allergy has.

This is fitting with the results of their previous experiments. But note that this overall trend is still not statistically significant.

Finally, responses to the questions (a) "How would you act so as to make the person think the scar (allergy) did not affect your behavior?" and (b) "Would you acknowledge or mention the scar (allergy)?" were examined. Consistent with the other findings, 13 out of 16 subjects in the scar condition responded to Question a by suggesting that they would carefully monitor their gaze behavior, apparently because it was the most likely behavior to be perceived by the disfigured individual as linked to the scar. Comments such as, "I would try to look at her frequently, as if there were nothing wrong," "I would try to keep eye contact, not avoiding her face but at the same time not staring at it," and "I would attempt to meet her gaze and not avert my eyes from either it or the scar" are representative of this concern. Only two persons in the allergy condition mentioned the need to monitor gaze behavior and, in general, unlike the scar condition subjects, persons in this condition disavowed the need for a conscious behavioral strategy. Comments such as, "It (the allergy) wouldn't affect my behavior, and I think I would feel perfectly relaxed around her and just be myself " or "I don't think that if a person did have an allergy I would act any differently toward her" are representative of this group.

Subjects in both conditions agreed (scar = 81%; allergy = 75%) that they would not *explicitly* mention the other person's physical failing unless that person brought it up. As might be expected, the reasons given for not initiating acknowledgment were quite different across the allergy and scar conditions. Of those persons in the allergy condition who stated that they would avoid mentioning the issue, six (50%) indicated that it was primarily because the condition was "uninteresting" or "irrelevant to the interaction." Only one individual felt that explicit mention of the allergy might generate embarrassment in the conversation. Of the 13 persons who said that they would avoid mention of a scar, on the other hand, 8 (62%) alluded to the embarrassment and anxiety that would probably follow from explicit acknowledgment.

DISCUSSION

As expected, observers of a dyadic interaction perceived that if one member of the dyad was facially scarred, this would have a greater impact on the behavior of the other than if that person had an allergy. Though the general pattern of attributions made to the "normal" interactant by the observers in Study 4 was similar to that made by the actors in Study 1, the differences were clearly less robust. Perhaps the most striking similarity between the results of the two studies is that persons who think one member of a dyad has a facial scar (Study 4) or who think they themselves have that scar (Study 1) are very prone to see the gaze behavior of the normal interactant as reflective of responsiveness to the physical defect. It should be kept in mind that subjects in both studies were female and that there is some evidence that women are more responsive to the gaze behavior of an interactant than men are (e.g., Exline, 1963; Kleck & Nuessle, 1968). Further, gaze behavior appears to be an aspect of the behavior of others that we do not consciously attend to in most situations and, therefore, have little awareness as to what would constitute a normal level and style of looking (Ellsworth & Ludwig, 1972). If for some reason our attention is drawn to that behavior, we may conclude, quite erroneously, that it is linked to a specific aspect of our own person (as in Studies 1 and 3) or to a physical characteristic of one member of a social interaction (as in Study 4).

The results of Study 4 provide support for the notion that we are working with a perceptual bias rather than a self-fulfilling prophecy. That is, the different expectations that the actors brought to their interactions with the confederates in Study 1 did not appear to have a direct impact on the confederates' behavior. This conclusion is supported by the lack of a main effect for type of tape in Study 4. Observers in this study saw no more evidence for an impact of a facial scar on social interaction when they were seeing a tape of an interaction involving a person who thought that she had a scar than when they saw a tape of an interaction involving a person who thought that an allergy had been attributed to her. This is indirect evidence at best but is consistent with the data reported in Study 1 suggesting that judges could not discriminate differences in confederate behavior as a function of the nature of the expectancy that the confederate's interactant brought to the conversational interaction.

We have focused attention on this issue because it has been repeatedly demonstrated that how we expect others to behave can directly affect their behavior (Snyder & Swan, 1978). From this perspective, the causal chain would include these four links: (a) an expectancy or hypothesis for how an interactant will behave, (b) which leads to a change in own behavior, (c) whereupon the change in own behavior modifies the behavior of the interactant, and finally (d) the change in the interactant's behavior is perceived as confirming the expectancy rather than being linked to the change in own behavior. We had created a paradigm that we hoped would rule out such a mediating mechanism, primarily by keeping our confederates blind to the experimental manipulations and by stressing the need for constancy in their behavior. It is obviously necessary to provide independent evidence for the success of this strategy, and this has been done in part through Study 4 and in the independent judge assessment of confederate behavior in Study 1.

One could question the importance of ruling out the self-fulfilling prophecy explanation for the present results. Whether the tendency to perceive a salient physical characteristic as affecting the behavior of those who interact with us is mediated by our own change in behavior, which in turn has an effect on those interactants, or is mediated by perceptual bias on our part, the result is essentially the same, that is, as physically deviant individuals we find evidence that our deviance is important to our social outcomes. Viewed from the perspective of the physically normal individual, however, which process is at work clearly could have quite different implications. If the interactive outcomes I experience with physically deviant individuals are largely a function of expectation-linked behaviors on their part, I can consciously not respond to those behaviors or strive to disabuse the deviant individual of his or her expectations and thus break the expectation-behavior interactive outcome cycle. If, on the other hand, it is simply a case of perceptual bias, then no matter what I choose to do, my behavior can be causally linked to the physical defects of the persons with whom I interact. Indeed, subjects in the fourth study who suggested that acting naturally was the best strategy to avoid having one's behavior linked to the physical failing of another nevertheless saw evidence of responses to a physically deviant characteristic in the "natural" responses of our confederates.

It should be kept in mind that the paradigm used in the first study is one in which persons are led to believe that they are temporarily deviant, and only in the eyes of one other person. The leap from these results, therefore, to the conclusion that they support Wright's (1960) assertion that physically handicapped persons are often prone to articulate their social reality entirely in terms of their handicap, even when the objective facts do not support such a construction, is tenuous at best. It is now necessary to demonstrate that persons who are permanently physically deviant make the same kinds of disability-linked attributions to a natural

---

This is counter-intuitive and quite interesting. One would think that someone with an obvious stigma would have expectations about the confederate behavior toward themselves, and thus they would be more likely to act in a way that would bring about expectancy-confirming behavior from the confederate.

This is the self-fulfilling prophecy explanation for how people with physical stigmas would approach an interaction with another.

The authors are answering potential critics here, who might ask "why does it matter what the explanation is for how those with physical stigmas interact with others? Whether it is self-fulfilling prophecy or perceptual bias, the result is the same: those with stigmas believe that their condition has an effect on their social interactions."

On the other hand, if the interaction between a physically normal person and one with a stigma was due to the expectations of the stigmatized person, the normal person can simply choose to not respond to those expectations, or even actively work to refute such expectations. But if the interaction is largely influenced by perceptual biases of the normal individual, then the normal person's behavior is always going to be determined by the presence of physical stigmas of their partners. The results of experiments 4 and 1 partially indicate that such interactions tend to be driven by the perceptual biases of the normal interaction partner.

stream of behavior as did the subjects in the present studies. It is entirely plausible that with some history of interaction with others, a physically deviant individual develops strategies for testing and evaluating whether a specific behavior or social outcome can be correctly attributed to a physical failing. Research directed toward this goal is now underway.

NOTE

1. Kleck, R. E., & Strenta, A. *Expectations regarding the impact of negatively valued physical characteristics on social interaction*. Unpublished manuscript, Dartmouth College, 1979.

REFERENCES

Davis, F. Deviance disavowal: The management of strained interaction by the visibly handicapped. *Social Problems*, 1961, *9*, 120–132.

Ellsworth, P. C., & Ludwig, L. M. Visual behavior in social interaction. *Journal of Communication*, 1972, *22*, 375–403.

Exline, R. V. Explorations in the process of person perception: Visual interaction in relation to competition, sex, and the need for affiliation. *Journal of Personality*, 1963, *31*, 1–20.

Goffman, E. *Stigma: Notes on the management of spoiled identity*. Englewood Cliffs, N.J.: Prentice-Hall, 1963.

Kelley, H. H. *Attribution in social interaction*. Morristown, N.J.: General Learning Press, 1971.

Kleck, R. E. Physical stigma and nonverbal cues emitted in face-to-face interaction. *Human Relations*, 1968, *21*, 19–28.

Kleck, R. E. Physical stigma and task oriented inter actions. *Human Relations*, 1969, *22*, 53–60.

Kleck, R. E., et al. The effect of stigmatizing conditions on the use of personal space. *Psychological Reports*, 1968, *23*, 111–118.

Kleck, R. E., & Nuessle, W. Congruence between indicative and communicative functions of eye contact in interpersonal relations. *British Journal of Social and Clinical Psychology*, 1968, *7*, 241–246.

Kleck, R. E., Ono, H., & Hastorf, A. H. The effect of physical deviance upon face-to-face interaction. *Human Relations*, 1966, *19*, 425–436.

Kleinke, C. L. *First impressions: The psychology of encountering others*. Englewood Cliffs, N.J.: Prentice Hall, 1975.

MacGregor, F. C. *Transformation and identity*. New York: New York Times Book Company, 1974.

Maddox, G. L., Back, R. W., & Liederman, V. T. Overweight as social deviance and disability. *Journal of Health and Social Behavior*, 1968, *9*, 287–298.

McArthur, L. Z., & Solomon, L. K. Perceptions of an aggressive encounter as a function of the victim's salience and the perceiver's arousal. *Journal of Personality and Social Psychology*, 1978, *36*, 1278–1290.

Snyder, M. L., Kleck, R. E., Strenta, A., & Mentzer, S. J. Avoidance of the handicapped: An attributional ambiguity analysis. *Journal of Personality and Social Psychology*, 1979, *37*, 2297–2306.

Snyder, M., & Swan, W. B., Jr. Behavioral confirmation in social interaction: From social perception to social reality. *Journal of Experimental Social Psychology*, 1978, *14*, 148–162.

Wright, B. *Physical disability: A psychological approach*. New York: Harper & Row, 1960.

POST-ARTICLE DISCUSSION

I hope you found the paper as fascinating as I did! Let's talk about the experiments. Kleck and Strenta investigated how people with potentially stigmatizing conditions are perceived by others and how those with the conditions think that the others perceive them. They further wanted to specifically look at those with physical stigmas (in this case, a physical scar on the face) compared to those with a nonphysical "condition" that wasn't visible but still may be perceived adversely by others (in this case, epilepsy). One of the basic questions that members of stereotyped groups (or those with stigmas) ask is, To what do I attribute other people's positive or negative behavior toward me? Is it due to my stigmatized group (e.g., stereotypes), or is it something about me and my own character? This is known as an attributional ambiguity. Kleck and Strenta were interested in understanding how those with stigmatizing conditions address the attributional ambiguity concerning their stigma.

Put yourself in the researchers' shoes and think now how you would experimentally manipulate subjects having either an unseen stigma or a visible physical stigma. The former might be easier, as one could just indicate to the subject that their interaction partner believes that they have epilepsy (but not to discuss it with the partner). Recall the experimenters' excellent solution: They had subjects complete a two-page demographics questionnaire where they were to write on the second page about having either allergies (unseen nonstigma) or epilepsy (unseen stigma). This was to be shown to the interaction partner, but unbeknown to the subject, the second page was torn off and not shown to the partner. So here we can get an idea of how stigmatized persons perceive the behavior of others with regard to their stigma. That is, will the stigmatized subjects perceive staring where none exists? Will they perceive condescension where it is not presented or intended? The data will also indicate any differences in the perception of others' behavior between those subjects with stigmatized conditions (epilepsy) and those with nonstigmatized conditions (allergy).

The physical stigma condition is more difficult. We can't actually harm the subjects (e.g., chop off their leg), so what would be a physical condition that we could manipulate on the subject that would still be a stigmatized condition? Kleck and Strenta's clever answer to this question is perhaps my favorite part of the study: They applied a fake scar to the face of subjects. Subjects then viewed it in a mirror, and afterward, the experimenter had to "apply a moisturizer" to the scar and secretly removed the scar without the subject knowing it. The subject then went into their interaction with another subject. Again, doing this allows the researchers to ask the "stigmatized" subjects questions about how they thought their partner was reacting to their scar (although no scar was present). Data indicated that those with stigmatized conditions (scar and epilepsy) perceived their partners as being more anxious and liking them less than those in the nonstigmatized (allergy) condition. We're not going to go over all the results, but the point of this discussion is to highlight the brilliant solutions these researchers came up with in the design of their experiments to address these rather complex social interaction questions. Through careful thought, researchers can create powerful experiments that give us insight into how we think of others, how others think of us, and how we think others are thinking of us.

THINGS TO THINK ABOUT

1. We all would like to know how other people perceive us and if their perceptions are affected by any particular aspect of our outward appearance. For example, if you wear glasses, do you assume others perceive you in a certain way (as intelligent or socially awkward, depending on the stereotypes you associate with wearing glasses)? If you were a researcher, how would you design an experiment to randomly assign people to various stigmatizing conditions, and how would you elicit those subjects' views of their interaction partner's thoughts about the subject?

2. Do you have any critiques about the particular stigma conditions the authors used for this research (scar, epilepsy, allergy)? Are there pros and cons to these particular stigmas? If you think they should have used other stigmas, explain why.

3. Why do you suppose that subjects perceived the confederates in the epilepsy and scar conditions equally tense? Why would one believe that a hidden condition like epilepsy would make an interaction partner as tense as does an obvious physical stigma like a scar?

4. Regarding Experiment 4, do you think there are any limitations to how the researchers were trying to determine whether there was an effect of the stigma (i.e., the dependent variable [DV] was eye gaze)? What are the pros and cons of using eye gaze as a DV?

5. Are there other physically stigmatizing conditions about which people might be self-conscious and toward which other nonstigmatized people might react? Can you think of some that would arouse a greater reaction (or less of a reaction) than the scar used in this study? If yes, why would the reaction be different?

6. As the researchers suggest, it is quite likely that people with permanent physical stigmas develop a different interaction style with nonstigmatized people compared to those in the temporary physical stigma condition in the experiment. How do you think the style would manifest in those with permanent stigmas? What would their "default interaction rules" (or assumptions) be?

INTRODUCTION TO READING 6.2

Willis and Todorov (2006)

When you form an impression of another person, you consider the person's attributes, characteristics, and other information you know about that person (e.g., her occupation). Then after that information is processed, you come up with an overall impression or evaluation of the person, and you refer to that henceforth when thinking about or interacting with the person. This all seems quite reasonable, but research has indicated that it is not altogether accurate. Specifically, impression formation tends to happen a lot faster than we might think, and often, it doesn't even require conscious thought (Ambady, Bernieri, & Richeson, 2000; Bar, Neta, & Linz, 2006). For example, research shows that we tend to rather automatically categorize people along three "primitive" categories: age, race, and gender (Fiske & Neuberg, 1990; Gilbert, 1989). But, once we make those instant judgments, what about all the other dimensions on which we form impressions of others? That is, are those judgments (e.g., of honesty, attractiveness, friendliness, compassion) equally automatic, or do some require more deliberate, conscious consideration?

The paper you will read now, by Willis and Todorov, examines whether we process certain information about others (specifically, trait judgments) in different ways depending on the nature of the trait. For example, do we assess whether someone is trustworthy faster than we assess their attractiveness? The other main focus of their experiment was to determine whether such initial quick judgments are modified with the passage of more time, or whether we tend to verify or strengthen our initial judgments with more time. Do we trust our snap judgments (sometimes people refer to this as "trusting your gut"), or do we require further information about the person and modify our first impressions based on that later information? As always, when thinking about the research questions, as you start to read the paper, think about how you would design an experiment to address those research questions. Enjoy the paper!

Reading 6.2

First Impressions

Making Up Your Mind After a 100-Ms Exposure to a Face

Janine Willis and Alexander Todorov

ABSTRACT—*People often draw trait inferences from the facial appearance of other people. We investigated the minimal conditions under which people make such inferences. In five experiments, each focusing on a specific trait judgment, we manipulated the exposure time of unfamiliar faces. Judgments made after a 100-ms exposure correlated highly with judgments made in the absence of time constraints, suggesting that this exposure time was sufficient for participants to form an impression. In fact, for all judgments—attractiveness, likeability, trustworthiness, competence, and aggressiveness—increased exposure time did not significantly increase the correlations. When exposure time increased from 100 to 500 ms, participants' judgments became more negative, response times for judgments decreased, and confidence in judgments increased. When exposure time increased from 500 to 1,000 ms, trait judgments and response times did not change significantly (with one exception), but confidence increased for some of the judgments; this result suggests that additional time may simply boost confidence in judgments. However, increased exposure time led to more differentiated person impressions.*

Lavater's (1772/1880) *Essays on Physiognomy*, which was written in 1772 and reprinted in more than 150 editions by 1940, described in minute detail how to relate facial features to personality traits (e.g., "the nearer the eyebrows are to the eyes, the more earnest, deep, and firm the character," p. 59). Although these ideas strike most people today as ludicrous and bring to mind phrenology, empirical evidence shows that the effects of facial appearance on social outcomes are pervasive. In almost every significant domain of life, attractive people get better outcomes than unattractive people (Hamermesh & Biddle, 1994; Zebrowitz, 1999). The effects of baby-faced appearance are as pervasive as are the effects of attractiveness (Montepare & Zebrowitz, 1998; Zebrowitz, 1999). For example, baby-faced individuals are less likely to receive severe judicial outcomes than mature-faced individuals (Zebrowitz & McDonald, 1991).

From the structure of the face, people form not only global impressions, but also specific trait impressions (Hassin & Trope, 2000). For example, we showed that inferences of competence, based solely on facial appearance, predicted the outcomes of U.S. congressional elections in 2000, 2002, and 2004 (Todorov, Mandisodza, Goren, & Hall, 2005). Although we measured impressions on a variety of traits, including attractiveness, trustworthiness, and likeability, the trait inference that predicted the election outcomes was competence. Competence was also rated as the most important attribute for a person running for a public office. This finding suggests that person attributes that are important for specific decisions are inferred from facial appearance and influence these decisions.

> Seems strange, right? Why would we assume that a person's personality can be assessed based on their facial structure?

> Interesting. Another physical characteristic that has accurately predicted presidential election results is height of the candidate. In approximately 2/3 of the past elections, the taller candidate was elected (Murray & Schmitz, 2011).

From both the standard-intuition and the rational-actor points of view, trait inferences from facial appearance should not influence important deliberate decisions. However, to the extent that these inferences occur rapidly and effortlessly, their effects on decisions may be subtle and not subjectively recognized. Using the terms of dual-process theories (Chaiken & Trope, 1999; Kahneman, 2003), we have argued that trait inferences from faces can be characterized as fast, intuitive, unreflective System 1 processes that contrast with slow, effortful, and deliberate System 2 processes (Todorov et al., 2005). We provided preliminary evidence for this proposal by showing that inferences of competence based on 1-s exposure to the faces of the winners and the runners-up for the Senate races sufficed to predict the election outcomes.

In this article, we report a series of studies in which we systematically manipulated the exposure time of faces to further explore the minimal conditions under which people make trait inferences from facial appearance. Research on visual processing has shown that high-level object representations can be constructed very rapidly from visual scenes (Grill-Spector &

> Basic summary of what is being studied.

Address correspondence to Alexander Todorov, Department of Psychology, Green Hall, Princeton University, Princeton, NJ 08544-1010, e-mail: atodorov@princeton.edu.

Kanwisher, 2005; Rousselet, Fabre-Thorpe, & Thorpe, 2002; Thorpe, Fize, & Marlot, 1996). It is possible that inferences about socially significant attributes are also rapidly extracted from facial appearance. We conducted five experiments, each focusing on a different judgment from facial appearance: attractiveness, likeability, competence, trustworthiness, and aggressiveness. Among the studied traits, attractiveness is the only one that is unambiguously related to facial appearance; that is, it is a property of facial appearance. In this respect, judgments of attractiveness provide a benchmark for judgments of character traits. Liking is a global affective response that may require minimal inferential activity (Zajonc, 1980). In contrast to attractiveness and liking, trustworthiness, competence, and aggressiveness are specific traits that have clear behavioral manifestations. These traits are also important for both social and economic interactions.

In all the experiments, faces unfamiliar to the participants were presented for 100 ms, 500 ms, or 1,000 ms. For each face, participants were asked to make a trait judgment and then to express their confidence in that judgment. We tested three hypotheses: (a) that a 100-ms exposure to a face is sufficient for making a trait judgment, (b) that additional exposure time increases confidence in trait judgments without necessarily changing the judgments, and (c) that additional exposure time allows for more differentiated trait impressions.

If trait inferences from faces can be characterized as System 1 inferences, minimal exposure time should be sufficient for trait inferences to occur. In order to obtain criterion judgments, we asked a large group of participants to make trait judgments of the faces in the absence of time constraints. If a 100-ms exposure to a face is sufficient for making a trait inference, then trait judgments made after 100-ms exposure should correlate with judgments made in the absence of time constraints. In contrast, if 100 ms is insufficient, these judgments should be uncorrelated, and only judgments made after longer exposures should correlate with judgments made in the absence of time constraints.

We were also interested in how additional exposure time affects trait judgments and confidence in these judgments. If people commit to a judgment early in time, additional time can serve only as a justification of this judgment. If this is the case, confidence should increase as a function of exposure time, but there should be no corresponding change in judgment. For example, if 500-ms exposure is sufficient for participants to form stable trait judgments, little change in judgments should be observed with additional exposure time. However, additional exposure time may boost confidence in judgments.

Even if trait impressions can be formed after minimal exposure time, additional time may allow for more differentiated impressions. For example, it is possible that after 100-ms exposure, people perform a coarse affective discrimination of faces, such that judgments of different traits are highly correlated. Additional time may allow for more fine-grained impressions based on specific trait attributions, in which case judgments of different traits would be less correlated. We tested these predictions using factor analysis.

METHOD

Participants

A total of 245 undergraduate students from Princeton University participated in the studies either for payment or for partial course credit. One hundred twenty-eight participated in a preliminary study in which we obtained measures of trait inferences from facial appearance in

---

This makes sense, because if 100-ms exposure is sufficient to form an impression, then that would correlate with later trait judgments. But if that time frame was not sufficient to form a trait judgment, then the researcher would obtain random trait judgment information, and these, by definition, would be much less correlated with subsequent trait judgments.

Seems logical, right?

This type of preliminary study (sometimes called a pre-test) is often necessary when dealing with subjective information like ratings of attractiveness, or in this case, trait inferences based on facial appearance. The researcher wants to have data that support their baseline assumptions about the stimuli presented to the subjects in the main experiments. For example, if I said I was showing a photo of a very attractive male and an unattractive male, a critic of my study might ask "how do you know that people find the photo attractive (or unattractive)?" and if I did a preliminary study, I could point to those data that support that most people find the person in the photo very attractive (or unattractive).

the absence of time constraints. One hundred seventeen participated in the five main experiments; 20 were asked to make attractiveness judgments, 25 to make liking judgments, 23 to make competence judgments, 24 to make trustworthiness judgments, and 25 to make aggressiveness judgments.

What kind of experimental design would this be? (Hint: it is a between-subjects design).

Stimuli

In all the studies, we used a database of photographs of 70 amateur actors, 35 females and 35 males between 20 and 30 years of age (Lundqvist, Flykt, & Öhman, 1998). In the pictures, all actors wore gray T-shirts, and there were no beards, mustaches, earrings, eyeglasses, or visible makeup. We used frontal head-shot photographs of individuals with neutral expressions. Of the 70 photographs, 2 photographs of males were excluded because of poor quality; we also excluded 2 photographs of females in order to have equal numbers of male and female photographs.

To obtain reliable measures of trait inferences from facial appearance, we presented participants in the preliminary study with the photographs and asked them to judge the degree to which the person in each picture was attractive, likeable, competent, honest or trustworthy, aggressive, extraverted or enthusiastic, sympathetic or warm, dependable or self-disciplined, calm or emotionally stable, open to new experiences or complex, and ambitious. The judgments on the first five dimensions provided the criterion judgments for the five experiments. In the preliminary study, each face was presented on a separate questionnaire page, and the order of the trait judgments was fixed. All judgments were made on a 9-point scale ranging from 1 (*not at all*) to 9 (*extremely*). The photographs were randomly divided into three groups, each one containing the same number of males and females, and for each group of photographs, we generated two random orders. Participants were randomly assigned to one of the six sets of photographs (3 groups × 2 orders) and completed the task at their own pace. Each photograph was rated by 42 or 43 participants. The trait judgments were highly reliable. For the three groups of photographs, the Cronbach alphas were .97, .96, and .95 for attractiveness; .94, .91, and .89 for likeability; .92, .92, and .92 for trustworthiness; .85, .91, and .96 for competence; and .87, .75, and .89 for aggressiveness.

The mean trait judgments across participants served as the criterion judgments for the experiments. To the extent that limited exposure time is sufficient for people to form trait impressions from faces, the experimental judgments made under time constraints would be expected to correlate with the criterion judgments. It should be noted that, for two reasons, this procedure underestimated the true correlation between judgments made in the absence of time constraints and judgments made with time constraints: The two sets of judgments were measured on different scales (see Procedure) and were made under different conditions (paper-and-pencil questionnaire vs. computer-controlled presentation).

Remember the researcher always strives to give as much detail in the method, so that other researchers who try to replicate the study will have the best chance to re-create the experiment procedures. Here, the description is good. A researcher could also opt to put his or her stimuli into a publicly-accessible "cloud-based" place on the Internet where people can view the stimuli. In this case, it would be the actual 70 photos used.

Procedure

All five experiments followed the same procedure. Participants were told that this was a study about first impressions and that they should make their decisions as quickly as possible. The instructions emphasized that photographs would be presented for very brief periods of time and that we, the experimenters, were primarily interested in participants' first impressions, or gut feelings. Each experiment started with three practice trials in order to familiarize participants with the task.

For the experimental trials, the 66 faces (33 males and 33 females) were randomly divided into three sets of 22 such that each group had the same number of male and female faces. We created three experimental versions of the stimuli by counterbalancing the exposure time assigned to each set (100, 500, or 1,000 ms). For example, each face from the first set was presented for 100 ms in the first version, for 500 ms in the second version, and for 1,000 ms in the third version. Participants were randomly assigned to one of the three experimental versions. For each participant, 22 of the faces were presented for 100 ms, 22 were presented for 500 ms, and 22 were presented for 1,000 ms. Because we were interested in first impressions, each face was presented only once. Thus, the total number of trials was 66 per participant. The order of trials was randomized for each participant by the computer (i.e., the levels of exposure time were randomly intermixed).

Each trial started with a fixation point (1) presented for 500 ms at the center of the screen. Then a photograph was presented for 100 ms, 500 ms, or 1,000 ms. Immediately afterward, a question appeared in the location of the photograph (e.g., "Is this person competent?"). The only difference among the studies was the trait judgment that participants were asked to make. Participants responded using the computer keyboard, pressing the "/" (slash) key, which was labeled "yes," or pressing the "Z" key, which was labeled "no." Given the limited exposure times, we decided to use dichotomous trait judgments because they are simpler than continuous trait judgments. Further, in the correlation analyses (see the next paragraph), the criterion judgments were correlated with the proportions of trait attributions across participants (i.e., continuous scores; the probability of trait attribution). Following this yes/no judgment, the next screen asked participants to rate how confident they were in their judgment. This rating was made on a 7-point scale, ranging from 1 (*least confident*) to 7 (*most confident*). Participants responded by using the number keys at the top of the keyboard. The intertrial interval was 1,500 ms.

To test whether judgments made under limited exposure time correlate with judgments made in the absence of time constraints, we correlated the proportions of trait attributions for each face (at each exposure time) with the mean criterion judgments for that face. Further, for each experiment, we analyzed the proportions of trait attributions, the response times for the trait judgments, and the mean confidence in judgments as a function of exposure time. We removed response time outliers by deleting response times that were 3 standard deviations above the participant's mean. In all experiments, less than 2% of the trials were excluded.

RESULTS AND DISCUSSION

Correlation of Time-Constrained With Time-Unconstrained Judgments

As shown in Table 1, even after 100-ms exposure to a face, trait judgments were highly correlated with judgments made in the absence of time constraints. Although the correlations for all judgments but attractiveness increased with the increase in exposure from 100 to 1,000 ms, none of these changes was significant. We compared the correlations at 100 and 500 ms, at 500 and 1,000 ms, and at 100 and 1,000 ms using Williams's test for dependent correlations (Steiger, 1980). None of these tests reached significance.

We expected that we would find the highest correlation for judgments of attractiveness. Attractiveness, after all, is a property of facial appearance. However, the correlations for judgments of trustworthiness were slightly higher. We also conducted partial correlation analyses, controlling for judgments of attractiveness, to rule out the possibility that the judgments made

When presenting stimuli (e.g., faces to rate), it is crucial that the stimuli be presented in varying order from subject to subject, so that the order of presentation doesn't become a confound that would adversely influence the results. This is also important to remember for dependent variable measures, such as questionnaires, surveys, etc.

TABLE 1 Correlations Between Time-Constrained Trait Judgments From Facial Appearance and Judgments Made in the Absence of Time Constraints

| | Exposure time | | | | | |
| | 100 ms | | 500 ms | | 1,000 ms | |
Trait judgment	Zero-order correlation	Partial correlation	Zero-order correlation	Partial correlation	Zero-order correlation	Partial correlation
Trustworthiness	.73	.63	.66	.59	.74	.69
Competence	.52	.39	.67	.58	.59	.50
Likeability	.59	.40	.57	.46	.63	.50
Aggressiveness	.52	.52	.56	.58	.59	.61
Attractiveness	.69	—	.57	—	.66	—

Note. The partial correlations control for judgments of attractiveness made after the same exposure time. All correlations were significant, $p < .001$, $p_{rep} > .98$.

FIG. 1. Percentage of variance in judgments made in the absence of time constraints accounted for by time-constrained trait judgments.

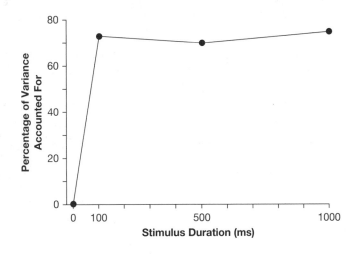

> Just as the authors predicted, when there are no time constraints, people's ratings of the traits associated with a face changes little with increasing time that they are exposed to the face.

after limited exposure time simply reflected an attractiveness halo effect. Although the correlations were reduced (Table 1), they remained highly reliable for all judgments. Comparing the difference between the zero-order and the partial correlations at the different levels of exposure time suggests that the effect of attractiveness on trait judgments was reduced with increased exposure to the faces. The partial correlations increased with increased exposure time, but as in the case of the zero-order correlations, none of the changes reached significance.

How much of the variance in time-unconstrained judgments can be accounted for by time-constrained judgments? To answer this question, we conducted three regression analyses (one for each level of exposure time) in which time-unconstrained judgments (5 types of judgment × 66 faces) were regressed on time-constrained judgments and dummy variables controlling for the type of judgments (4) and the face stimuli (65). As shown in Figure 1, with the increase in exposure from 100 to 1,000 ms, the variance accounted for increased only 2.2%. Although we did not include conditions in which participants were exposed to faces for more than 1,000 ms, it is reasonable to assume that the explained variance could not be improved with longer exposures. Assuming that the average reliability of the judgments is .90, the ceiling of the explained variance should be, on average, 81.0%. Given that the procedures for collecting the time-constrained judgments and the time-unconstrained (criterion) judgments were different and that these differences could have increased the error variance, the accounted-for variance at 1,000-ms exposure (74.9%) seems very close to the possible ceiling.

Analysis Within Experiments

All judgments showed the same pattern as a function of exposure time. As shown in the top panel of Figure 2,[1] when exposure time increased from 100 to 500 ms, judgments became more negative (for all judgments, $p < .05$ $p_{rep} > .91$, $d > 0.85$). Faces were perceived as less attractive, less likeable, less trustworthy, less competent, and more aggressive. The mean level of judgments stabilized at the 500-ms exposure, and no significant changes were observed for the increase to 1,000-ms exposure. As shown in the middle panel of Figure 2, when exposure time increased from 100 to 500 ms, response times for all five judgments decreased (for all judgments, $p < .05$, $p_{rep} > .93$, $d > 0.91$). As with the trait judgments, little change was observed when exposure time increased from 500 to 1,000 ms; although response times continued to decrease, the only significant effect was for trustworthiness judgments, $t(23) = 4.14$, $p_{rep} = .99$, $d = 1.73$.

As shown in the bottom panel of Figure 2, when exposure time increased from 100 to 500 ms, confidence in all five judgments increased. The only effect that did not reach significance was for judgments of aggressiveness, $t(24) = 1.47$, $p_{rep} = .84$, $d = 0.60$ (for the other four judgments, $p < .05$, $p_{rep} > .93$, $d > 0.94$). When exposure time increased from 500 to 1,000 ms, confidence in judgments, except judgments of competence, increased again. Although this increase in confidence was significant only for attractiveness judgments, $t(19) = 2.59$, $p_{rep} = .95$, $d = 1.19$, and approached significance for trustworthiness judgments, $t(23) = 1.94$, $p_{rep} = .90$, $d = 0.81$, the combined p value from all five experiments was .028 ($z = 2.20$), and the average effect size d was 0.41.

Relations Between Trait Inferences

We conducted principal-components analyses with Varimax rotation to test whether person impressions became more differentiated as a function of increased exposure to the faces. As shown in Table 2, the analyses for both the 100-ms and the 500-ms exposure times identified only one factor, suggesting a coarse positive/negative discrimination. All positive traits had high positive loadings on the factor, and aggressiveness had a high negative loading. This factor accounted for 62.5% of the variance in judgments made after 100-ms exposure and 58.3%

---

[1] The analyses we report here were conducted at the level of participants (i.e., analyzed the mean judgments across faces). We conducted the same analyses at the level of faces (i.e., analyzed the mean judgments across participants) and obtained identical results.

Margin notes:

This is weird! Why do you suppose this happened?

Factor analysis is often done on items in a questionnaire, to determine which items conceptually "hang" together. That is, which items seem to be measuring the same thing, and which items seem to be measuring something else. As you can see in Table 2, the traits "trustworthiness", "competence", "likeability", and "attractiveness" all denote a positive characteristic (if the person is judged to possess those qualities). The trait "aggressiveness" denotes an undesirable quality (if the target is judged to possess that characteristic). So, roughly there are two mini-scales here (positive and negative).

FIG. 2.

Probability of trait attribution (top panel), response time (middle panel), and confidence in trait judgment (bottom panel) as a function of the trait being judged and exposure time. The probability of trait attribution of aggressiveness is reversed (i.e., higher probability means fewer attributions of aggressiveness) so that for all traits, higher probabilities reflect more positive valence. Confidence judgments were made on a 7-point scale, ranging from 1 (*least confident*) to 7 (*most confident*). Error bars show within-subjects standard errors.

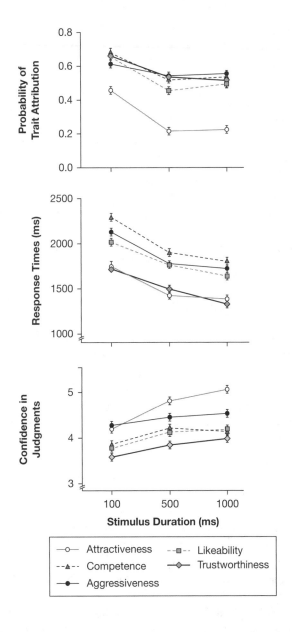

TABLE 2   Factor Loadings of Trait Judgments on Factors Identified in the Principal Components Analysis With Varimax Rotation

	Exposure time			
	100 ms:	500 ms:	1,000 ms:	
Trait judgment	Factor 1	Factor 1	Factor 1	Factor 2
Trustworthiness	.85	.83	.61	.61
Competence	.81	.84	.91	.06
Likeability	.81	.81	.79	.33
Attractiveness	.81	.72	.84	.00
Aggressiveness	−.66	−.58	−.01	−.96

Note. For each exposure time, factor analyses were performed on the aggregated judgments for each face. Only factors with eigenvalues greater than 1 were extracted.

of the variance in judgments made after 500-ms exposure. The difference in the explained variance suggests that judgments made after 100-ms exposure were more correlated than judgments made after 500-ms exposure. In contrast to the analyses for the 100- and 500-ms exposure times, the analysis for the 1,000-ms exposure time identified two orthogonal factors, suggesting a more differentiated person impression. The first factor accounted for 50.5% of the variance, and the second accounted for 27.8%. The first factor comprised all positive traits, and the second factor contrasted aggressiveness and trustworthiness. Attractiveness and competence were practically unrelated to aggressiveness in this factor solution.

GENERAL DISCUSSION

> There is a lot of evidence that suggests that we make judgments quite quickly, and these data further bolster that notion, in that trait judgments after only 100 ms exposure were highly correlated with judgments made with no time constraints.

Our findings suggest that as minimal an exposure as 100 ms is sufficient for people to make a specific trait inference from a stranger's face. For all five traits, judgments made after 100-ms exposure to a face were highly correlated with judgments made in the absence of time constraints. In fact, additional exposure time did not increase these correlations. In this context, revisiting the response times for the judgments is informative. Response times decreased when exposure time increased from 100 to 500 ms. However, response times were measured from the offset of the face to the response. Thus, in the 500-ms condition, participants had an extra 400 ms to compute their judgments. If participants computed the judgments faster in the 500-ms condition than in the 100-ms condition, the response times should have decreased by more than 400 ms in the former condition. However, for all five judgments, the response times in the 500-ms condition decreased by less than 400 ms, suggesting that the judgments were computed as fast, if not faster, in the 100-ms condition as in the 500-ms condition.

Although judgments were formed after 100-ms exposure to the faces, participants' trait judgments shifted systematically as a function of increased exposure time. When exposure time increased from 100 to 500 ms, judgments became more negative. The positivity in judgments made after 100-ms exposure shows that the person positivity bias (Sears, 1983) may be particularly pronounced under conditions of minimal information in a safe experimental environment. When exposure time increased from 500 to 1,000 ms, none of the judgments shifted significantly, which suggests that a 500-ms exposure was sufficient for participants to create a subjectively satisfying trait impression. This interpretation is consistent with the findings for confidence. The increase in confidence was larger when exposure time increased from 100 to 500 ms than when it increased from 500 ms to 1,000 ms. Although judgments did not change when exposure time increased from 500 to 1,000 ms, confidence in judgments did increase for four of the five judgments. These findings suggest that minimal exposure to faces is sufficient for people to form trait impressions, and that additional exposure time can simply boost confidence in these impressions. That is, additional encounters with a person may serve only to justify quick, initial, on-line judgments.

We expected that the highest correlation between judgments made after 100-ms exposure and judgments made in the absence of time constraints would be for judgments of attractiveness. However, trustworthiness judgments showed the highest correlation. In hindsight, this finding is not surprising. Evolutionary psychologists have argued that detection of trustworthiness is essential for human survival (Cosmides & Tooby, 1992). Further, functional neuroimaging studies show that detection of trustworthiness in a face may be a spontaneous, automatic process linked to activity in the amygdala (Winston, Strange, O'Doherty, & Dolan, 2002), a subcortical brain structure implicated in the detection of potentially dangerous stimuli (Amaral, 2002). Work with patients with bilateral amygdala damage shows impaired ability to discriminate between trustworthy and untrustworthy faces (Adolphs, Tranel, & Damasio, 1998). These findings are consistent with the idea that people can be especially efficient in making inferences of trustworthiness, as shown by our findings. In fact, only judgments of attractiveness were as fast as judgments of trustworthiness in the present study.

We showed that a 100-ms exposure to a face suffices for people to make a trait inference, but we did not show that this is the minimum exposure that allows such inferences. Grill-Spector and Kanwisher (2005) showed that object categorization decisions were as fast as object detection decisions, concluding that "as soon as you know it is there, you know what it is." In fact, the accuracy of decisions was above chance for durations as short as 33 ms in their study. Identifying the lower limit of exposure time for inferring socially significant attributes from faces is an important task. Maybe, as soon as a face is there, you know whether to trust it. One implication of the current findings is that different trait judgments can have different time thresholds. For example, trustworthiness in a face may be inferred earlier than competence in a face.

To the extent that people form differentiated person impressions from facial appearance, additional exposure to a face can facilitate the formation of such impressions. The data from the factor analysis are consistent with this hypothesis. With increased exposure time, trait judgments became less correlated, suggesting a more fine-grained discrimination. For example, after 1,000-ms exposure, judgments of aggressiveness were independent of judgments of attractiveness and competence. The partial correlation analysis, showing that the effect of attractiveness on trait judgments decreased with increased exposure time, is also consistent with this hypothesis.

CONCLUSIONS

As minimal an exposure time as a tenth of a second is sufficient for people to make a specific trait inference from facial appearance. Additional exposure time increases confidence in judgments and allows for more differentiated trait impressions. However, the judgments are

The longer we are exposed to a person, the more confident we are in our initial trait impression made after only 100 ms exposure.

Fascinating suggestion, and the authors make a compelling case that the present data support previous data that point to an especially adept ability in humans to detect trustworthiness in others, because such a perception is important to one's survival. As such, it would make sense that such an ability would be found in a primitive structure like the amygdala (which is most commonly associated with a fear response, and detection of threat—see Bar, Neta, & Linz (2006)).

Do you think this would be the case? If yes, why do you suppose it would be that way?

So, the data suggest that we make really fast trait judgments about others and that we tend to be more confident in those judgments as time progresses.

already anchored on the initial inference. Coupled with findings suggesting that inferences from facial appearance may be uncontrollable (Hassin & Trope, 2000, Experiment 4), our findings suggest that trait inferences from facial appearance can be characterized as fast, intuitive, System 1 processes. Lavater (1772/1880) might have been right about one thing: "Whether they are or are not sensible of it, all men [and women] are daily influenced by physiognomy" (p. 9). Not only trait inferences from facial appearance, but more generally inferences about other people may be effortless (e.g., Todorov & Uleman, 2003; Uleman, Blader, & Todorov, 2005). Person impressions are created effortlessly on-line from minimal information.

Acknowledgments—We thank Andy Conway and Ran Hassin for comments on an earlier version of this article and Manish Pakrashi for his help in running the experiments. This research was supported by National Science Foundation Grant BCS-0446846 to Alexander Todorov.

REFERENCES

Adolphs, R., Tranel, D., & Damasio, A.R. (1998). The human amygdala in social judgment. *Nature, 393,* 470–474.

Amaral, D.G. (2002). The primate amygdala and the neurobiology of social behavior: Implications for understanding social anxiety. *Biological Psychiatry, 51,* 11–17.

Chaiken, S., & Trope, Y. (Eds.). (1999). *Dual process theories in social psychology.* New York: Guilford Press.

Cosmides, L., & Tooby, J. (1992). Cognitive adaptations for social exchange. In J.H. Barkow, L. Cosmides, & J. Tooby (Eds.), *The adapted mind: Evolutionary psychology and the generation of culture* (pp. 163–228). London: Oxford University Press.

Grill-Spector, K., & Kanwisher, N. (2005). Visual recognition: As soon as you know it is there, you know what it is. *Psychological Science, 16,* 152–160.

Hamermesh, D., & Biddle, J. (1994). Beauty and the labor market. *The American Economic Review, 84,* 1174–1194.

Hassin, R., & Trope, Y. (2000). Facing faces: Studies on the cognitive aspects of physiognomy. *Journal of Personality and Social Psychology, 78,* 837–852.

Kahneman, D. (2003). A perspective on judgment and choice. *American Psychologist, 58,* 697–720.

Lavater, J.C. (1880). *Essays on physiognomy; for the promotion of the knowledge and the love of mankind* (Gale Document Number CW114125313). Retrieved May 15, 2005, from Gale Group, Eighteenth Century Collections Online. (Original work published 1772)

Lundqvist, D., Flykt, A., & Öhman, A. (1998). *The Karolinska directed emotional faces* [Database of standardized facial images]. (Available from Psychology Section, Department of Clinical Neuroscience, Karolinska Hospital, S-171 76 Stockholm, Sweden)

Montepare, J.M., & Zebrowitz, L.A. (1998). Person perception comes of age: The salience and significance of age in social judgments. In M.P. Zanna (Ed.), *Advances in experimental social psychology* (Vol. 30, pp. 93–161). San Diego, CA: Academic Press.

Rousselet, G.A., Fabre-Thorpe, M., & Thorpe, S.J. (2002). Parallel processing in high-level categorization of natural images. *Nature Neuroscience, 5,* 629–630.

Sears, D.O. (1983). The person-positivity bias. *Journal of Personality and Social Psychology, 44,* 233–250.

Steiger, J.H. (1980). Tests for comparing elements of a correlation matrix. *Psychological Bulletin, 87,* 245–251.

Thorpe, S., Fize, D., & Marlot, C. (1996). Speed of processing in the human visual system. *Nature, 381,* 520–522.

Todorov, A., Mandisodza, A.N., Goren, A., & Hall, C.C. (2005). Inferences of competence from faces predict election outcomes. *Science, 308,* 1623–1626.

Todorov, A., & Uleman, J.S. (2003). The efficiency of binding spontaneous trait inferences to actors' faces. *Journal of Experimental Social Psychology, 39,* 549–562.

Uleman, J.S., Blader, S., & Todorov, A. (2005). Implicit impressions. In R. Hassin, J.S. Uleman, & J.A. Bargh (Eds.), *The new unconscious* (pp. 362–392). New York: Oxford University Press.

Winston, J., Strange, B., O'Doherty, J., & Dolan, R. (2002). Automatic and intentional brain responses during evaluation of trustworthiness of faces. *Nature Neuroscience, 5*, 277–283.

Zajonc, R.B. (1980). Feeling and thinking: Preferences need no inferences. *American Psychologist, 35*, 151–175.

Zebrowitz, L.A. (1999). *Reading faces: Window to the soul?* Boulder, CO: Westview Press.

Zebrowitz, L.A., & McDonald, S.M. (1991). The impact of litigants' babyfaceness and attractiveness on adjudications in small claims courts. *Law and Behavior, 15*, 603–623.

POST-ARTICLE DISCUSSION

Chuck Darwin (I call him Chuck, because we're so close) once theorized (1904) that it would make evolutionary sense for animals (and humans) to have developed a more acute detection system for signs of threat from others compared to signs of friendliness or even affection. The reason is that a threat indicator may signal a threat to one's survival, and, as you know, Darwin's theory says that the universe is all about survival of the fittest and passing on one's genes. We obviously need to survive if we are to pass on our genes. In 1988, this idea was tested empirically by Hansen and Hansen at Oakland University in Michigan. They showed subjects one of two photos of a crowd, all of whom had their faces looking up to the camera. In one photo, everyone had a happy expression except for one person, who had an angry expression. In the other photo, it was the opposite: all angry faces except for one happy face. People were randomly assigned to one of the photos and asked to find the one face that was different, and they were timed. Results showed, as Darwin predicted, that people were significantly faster at finding the one angry face in a sea of happy faces than they were at finding the one happy face in a sea of angry faces.

If we were to extend this evolutionary logic to how we process information about other people, we might reasonably come to the broad conclusion that when thinking about other persons, there are some trait judgments that would be more important to process than others, and thus, we would consider those first, and faster, than we would think about other traits. Although more research is needed to ascertain the details surrounding potential latency differences in trait judgments, the data obtained by Willis and Todorov suggest tentative support for the idea that the fastest judgments are made for determinations of trustworthiness and, interestingly, attractiveness. Trustworthiness makes sense from an evolutionary view. As we discussed earlier, it is especially important to determine whether another individual is a threat to one's existence, and trust is a critical element in such a determination. However, the ability to figure out whether another individual is attractive is not crucial to our survival. From an evolutionary view, it might be helpful for mating (Buss, 1989), but not for our immediate survival. Finally, the studies reported on in this article show us that although we make our judgments about others very quickly, those initial snap judgments don't seem to be modified later; on the contrary, with increased time to consider those judgments, we become more confident in those initial quick assessments.

THINGS TO THINK ABOUT

1. What sorts of impressions of other people do you suppose people make based only on the face of the target individual? How long do you suppose it takes people to form those impressions?

2. Are first impressions about a person (based on his face) largely guided by the perceiver's stereotypes about facial characteristics? Or, are such impressions based mostly on the perceiver's own experience with people of similar facial characteristics, and thus they draw their own conclusions about similarities among people sharing a similar facial feature?

3. When doing an experiment similar to those that Willis and Todorov (2006) conducted—in which you are trying to ascertain how people respond to photographs of target individuals' faces—how would you obtain the photos, and how would you hold the photos constant (standardized, and as free from potential confounds as possible)?

4. Why did the authors do a pretest with a separate group of subjects to have them rate the photos (with unhindered exposure to the photos)?

5. In that preliminary study, why did the researchers make sure there were an equal number of male and female photographs? Why did they have two orders of photo presentation?

6. How can the researchers tell what the minimum amount of time is for a subject to form an impression of the target individual?

7. When people form an impression of someone, do you think that people tend to process certain traits first and other traits later (if even only a few seconds later)? If yes, would there be an evolutionary explanation for this?

8. What are the limitations to this experiment? How would you have done the study differently, and why?

7

Attribution

One of the constant questions we ask ourselves while navigating our social world is "Why did he (or she) say (or do) that?" We ask this in order to get information about other people, which will help us better predict how those people will behave with us in the future. The more we think we have a handle on our social world (i.e., the more we believe we are able to predict what others will say or do), the less anxious we will feel in our social interactions with those persons and the greater ease we will have in obtaining our goals (by avoiding difficult people and gravitating toward those who will enhance our lives). The question of how we explain others' behavior is a question of **attribution.** There are two broad explanations for others' behavior: internal versus external, or, phrased differently, personality versus situation (Heider, 1958). Which explanation one decides best explains another's behavior can have significant consequences for the perceiver's thoughts, feelings, and behavior.

For example, suppose you are driving and merging onto a highway. You are driving along in the right lane, and on the left, a slightly faster car moves past you and suddenly moves into your lane, causing you to hit your brakes. If you attributed the driver's behavior to the situation, you might say, "The person didn't see me, and it was an accident. We all have made accidents like

that. No worries." And with that attribution, you'd likely not give it a further thought. But, if you attributed the driver's behavior to her personality, you might say, "She saw me and didn't care that I was here. She thought she'd disrespect me and bully her way into my lane, because she is a jerk." That explanation would likely make you angry. Perhaps even angry enough to get into a confrontation with the person, which could be dangerous! In this introduction to the articles in this chapter, we discuss some of the major theories and empirical findings concerning attribution. However, it is not an exhaustive review. Those seeking a more complete exposition of the landscape of attribution research should consult other sources (see, e.g., Heider, 1958; Jones & Davis, 1965; Jones et al., 1972; Kelley, 1967).

KELLEY'S COVARIATION THEORY

Let's say your friend saw a movie recently and raved to you how great it was. You want to know, is your friend's behavior due to something about your friend (internal attribution) or something about the movie (external attribution)? According to Kelley (1967), when people are trying to figure out the cause of someone else's behavior, they consider a number of factors. First, how do other people feel about the movie? Do they also rave about it, or is your friend alone in his praise? This is the issue of **consensus**. To the degree it is the latter, you might be inclined to think that the movie is terrible (because everyone else agrees it is terrible) and that the reason your friend raved about it had more to do with your friend (maybe he loves all movies in that genre) than the qualities of the movie. Second, how often did your friend rave about the movie? Every time the movie comes up in conversation, does your friend rave about it? This is the issue of **consistency**. If your friend constantly raves about the movie each time it comes up in conversation, we actually can't make an attribution yet, because we need to consider it in light of consensus information as well as **distinctiveness** information. This third piece of information asks how unique that behavior is by your friend. Does he rave about virtually every movie he sees, or is he very picky and will rarely shower praise on a movie? Kelley says that people take into consideration all three pieces of information when attempting to make either an internal or external attribution to the person's behavior. So, back to your movie-loving friend. Let's say he always raves about the movie (high consistency), he doesn't rave about other movies (high distinctiveness), and other people seem to also love the movie (high consensus). In this case, we would likely attribute your friend's positive review of the movie to something about the movie and not about your friend. Subsequent research supports Kelley's theory and the idea that people make attributions in this way (Hilton, Smith, & Kim, 1995; White, 2002).

CORRESPONDENT INFERENCE THEORY

Another approach to understanding how we attempt to interpret the behavior of others was put forth by Jones and Davis (1965). In their theory of correspondent inference, Jones and Davis propose that people consider three different factors before making their attributional judgment: expectedness, choice, and effects. First, how typical or expected is the behavior? A behavior that is unusual from the person is more informative to us. Second, a behavior that is freely chosen by the other person is more informative about her than a behavior she is forced to do. Third, behaviors that are done to produce a non-common effect are more informative about the person. For example, if a friend says he is excited to go hiking with his family on a beautiful sunny day, it might be difficult to discern exactly why he is going hiking. Suppose, however, your friend is going hiking on a cloudy windy day, alone. That latter situation is more informative in explaining your friend's behavior, because he is still doing the behavior (hiking) but there seems to be only one reason (he loves to go hiking).

CORRESPONDENCE BIAS: FUNDAMENTAL ATTRIBUTION ERROR

Research on attribution has found that people have a curious tendency to disregard clear evidence of situational causes on others' behavior, and they instead believe that the cause of other people's behavior is their personality. This is such a pervasive bias that Jones (1979) called it a correspondence bias. It also goes by a more common name: the fundamental attribution error. This is the tendency to attribute other people's behavior to their personality and disregard situational influences on their behavior.

To demonstrate this, Ross (1977) had a large group of people come to a room to participate in an experiment. He explained that the study involved playing a game much like the TV game show *Jeopardy*.

He randomly chose four people from the group to come to the front of the room, where three would be contestants and one would be the host. The remaining subjects were the audience. After a few rounds of questions, the experimenter gave the audience, contestants, and host a questionnaire. One of the key questions asked how the respondent would rate the intelligence of the contestants compared to the intelligence of the host. The host rated her intelligence the same as the contestants. She had no reason to think that she was smarter merely because she had all the answers on the podium in front of her (which is why she knew all the answers to the questions). The other two groups (the contestants and audience) rated the intelligence of the host as far and above that of the contestants! Why would that be? They both disregarded the situational explanation for the host knowing all the answers (that she had the answers in front of her on the podium) and just remembered that she knew all the answers and the contestants didn't know all the answers. They therefore surmised that the host must be super smart relative to the contestants. This of course is the fundamental attribution error. The audience and contestants attributed the behavior of the host (always knowing the answers) to her, rather than considering the situation (answers in front of her on podium). Gilbert (1989, 2002) says that the attribution process is a two-step process. First, we automatically attribute others' behavior to their personality. Second, we "error-correct" and search for any situational factors that might change that initial impression. The problem is, most of the time we either miss the situational factors or we are not motivated (or too lazy) to search for them. The fundamental attribution error isn't the only attributional failure. We also engage in a self-serving attribution process called "the actor-observer effect" (Jones & Nisbett, 1972). This is the process whereby we attribute our own behavior to the situation, and we attribute others' behavior to their personality.

INTRODUCTION TO READING 7.1

Schwarz and Clore (1983)

The concept of attribution, like attitudes, has long been a core area of research in social psychology. The reason is that it helps a perceiver understand his social world. When we are trying to figure out the reason why someone did or said something, the explanation is one of two possibilities: She did it because of her personality (internal attribution), or she did it because of some external force causing her to do it (situational attribution). We also do this with trying to understand our own behavior. To what do we attribute our own behavior? Usually, we say our behavior depends on the situation, whereas we attribute others' behavior to their personality (a bias referred to as the "actor-observer effect").

Sometimes, our attributional process can get misdirected. Dutton and Aron (1974) showed that men on a high suspension bridge (a 230-foot high, wooden plank, swaying bridge) who were met by an attractive research assistant were more likely to misattribute their nervousness (from the bridge) as attraction and were more likely to call her later than men who were approached on a solid bridge (and who were therefore not nervous) by the same attractive woman. In the study you are about to read, Schwarz and Clore wondered whether our answers to broad questions about our life—such as our feelings about our current well-being and our thoughts about our future—would be influenced by the misattribution of our current moods. In other words, suppose you were in a negative mood because, say, the person you were excited to see on a date this Friday cancelled the date (and didn't reschedule). Would that negative mood be used (misattributed) as information to guide how you see your future and how you feel about your whole life? That doesn't seem to make much sense, does it? Enjoy the paper, and we'll talk more afterward!

Reading 7.1

Mood, Misattribution, and Judgments of Well-Being: Informative and Directive Functions of Affective States

Norbert Schwarz

Gerald L. Clore

Two experiments investigated whether judgments of happiness and satisfaction with one's life are influenced by mood at the time of judgment. In Experiment 1, moods were induced by asking for vivid descriptions of a recent happy or sad event in respondents' lives; in Experiment 2, moods were induced by interviewing participants on sunny or rainy days. In both experiments, subjects reported more happiness and satisfaction with their life as a whole when in a good mood than when in a bad mood. However, the negative impact of bad moods was eliminated when subjects were induced to attribute their present feelings to transient external sources, irrelevant to the evaluation of their lives. Subjects who were in a good mood, on the other hand, were not affected by misattribution manipulations. The data suggest (a) that people use their momentary affective states as information in making judgments of how happy and satisfied they are with their lives in general and (b) that people in unpleasant affective states are more likely to search for and use information to explain their state than are people in pleasant affective states. Thus the data demonstrate informative and directive functions of affective states.

The role of affect in information processing has recently received some attention, and at least three possible influences of affect have been suggested. Two of these influences, suggested by Wyer and Carlston (1979), are that affective states may serve both informational and directive functions. An example of the informational function is that people may use their momentary affective state as information relevant to making various kinds of judgments, including evaluations of the quality of their lives or their attraction to another person. In addition, moods may serve a directive function in that they direct one's attention to specific classes of information in an attempt to sort out the plausible causes for such feelings. Finally, moods may also increase the availability of mood-congruent thoughts or information (Bower, 1981; Isen, Shalker, Clark, & Karp, 1978).

The present studies investigate the role of mood-related factors in judgments of general well-being, that is, judgments of happiness and satisfaction with one's life. Pilot work suggested that thinking about a single happy or sad event in one's life affects the evaluation of that life as a whole. Why is this the case? Thinking about a happy or sad event not only may change a person's mood but also may increase the availability of this and similarly valenced events in memory (Tversky & Kahneman, 1973). Either of these factors could influence the person's judgments of general well-being.

In Experiment 1, we attempted to separate these processes. To do this, we used a procedure conceptually similar to that developed by Zanna and Cooper (1974) to isolate the role of arousal in cognitive-dissonance phenomena. Specifically, we held constant the activity of thinking about positive and negative life events while varying the apparent relevance of any feelings resulting from this activity to judgments about one's life. This was accomplished by offering some subjects the suggestion that their feelings might be due to a situational factor that was irrelevant to the evaluation of their lives. If respondents attribute their feelings to such factors, they should be less likely to use them as an informational basis for evaluating

---

The research reported in this article was conducted during the first author's postdoctoral year at the University of Illinois and was partially supported by a fellowship from the Deutsche Forschungsgemeinschaft to Norbert.Schwarz and National Science Foundation Grant BNS 76-24001 to Robert S. Wyer, Jr.

The authors wish to thank Bob Wyer and Fritz Strack for their helpful comments at various stages of this research and Peggy Clark for her provocative critique of an earlier draft of this article. Experiment 1 was presented at the 1981 meeting of the Midwestern Psychological Association, Michigan, May 1981.

Requests for reprints should be sent to Norbert Schwarz, Psychologisches Institut, Universitaet Heidelberg, Hauptstrasse 47-51, D-6900 Heidelberg, Federal Republic of Germany.

This is the key idea that is being tested in this paper. The authors suggest that when people make judgments, in addition to considering various relevant facts, one piece of information they use is their current mood (or affect) state. Their mood tells them "how do I feel about it?" and a piece of information thus is weighed along with the other information in forming a final judgment.

Mood-congruent cognition has been supported in numerous studies. Essentially, when we are in a particular mood, we are more likely to access mood-congruent memories and information. For example, when you are in a negative mood, and you remember your past failed romantic relationship, you may disproportionately remember the negative times and the negative aspects of your ex-partner. But when you are in a good mood, and thinking of the same relationship, you may tend to remember only the good times.

This is an intriguing idea: can our current mood (whatever put us in that mood is irrelevant) influence judgments of broad, sweeping questions, such as "what do you think of your life? Will you be a success in the future?" You might think that our current mood has nothing to do with our judgments about those big questions. Logically, they are not connected. But, as we have seen in other papers, and broad work in social cognition, people are not very logical!

This is known as "misattribution". Essentially it is the belief that the cause of some feeling or behavior is due to one thing, when in fact it is due to something else. People do this all the time naturally. Researchers make use of misattribution as well. A famous example is the Schacter and Singer (1962) experiment on the two-factor theory of emotion. Subjects were injected with a saline solution (control condition) or epinephrine (increases heart rate and blood pressure temporarily) and were told to wait for a short period with another person (a confederate) who ostensibly had the same injection earlier. The confederate either acted very happy or very angry. When subjects in the experimental condition were told in advance that the injection would cause them to become physiologically aroused, they didn't misattribute their arousal to anything else but the drug. But when they weren't so informed, they misattributed their arousal to the mood of the confederate, and they too believed they were feeling the same mood.

Feeling good may be a signal to stop searching for more information. Positive affect may be a signal that "all is well." Negative affect, however, may motivate us to search for more information, to explain why we are feeling that way and how to change it so that we feel better. Searching for more information may make us susceptible to misdirection or misattribution about the source of our negative feelings.

their lives. To the extent that such misattributions of mood or feelings reduce the relationship between thinking about happy or sad events and judgments of general well-being, one can conclude that respondents used these momentary feelings as a basis for judgment. An alternative hypothesis is that writing about a happy or a sad event increases the availability of other similarly valenced life events from memory, leading subjects to overestimate the frequency of such events in their life. If the availability of these mood-congruent memories rather than present feelings is the basis of subjects' happiness and satisfaction judgments, then they should be influenced in all conditions regardless of the attribution manipulation, because the impact of these memories should not depend on the explanation of an individual's present mood.

Additional considerations are raised by recent theorizing about the directive effects of affective states. Wyer and Carlston (1979, p. 198ff.) argue, with reference to a study by Arkin, Gleason, and Johnston (1976), that only unpleasant affective states may motivate persons to seek explanations, whereas persons in pleasant affective states may not be motivated to do so. Different processes may contribute to this effect. On the one hand, as suggested by Wyer and Carlston (1979), persons in unpleasant affective states may try to seek explanations that reduce their unpleasantness. On the other hand, a variety of studies showed that people generally report that they are "happier than most" and "feel pretty good" (Goldings, 1954; Wessman & Ricks, 1966; see Matlin & Stang, 1978, for a review). Kerber and Clore (Note 1) also suggested that when processing social information, the assumption by default (at least among college students) is that people are happy. If this is the case, positive moods simply do not demand explanation either to oneself or others. If this is so, unpleasant states may be perceived as an unexpected deviation from individuals' usual feelings and might generate more attempts at explanation for this reason. Finally, aversive (but not pleasant) states need to be altered by appropriate action, for which, again, reasonable explanations of the state seem to be a prerequisite.

If affective states have a directive effect on reasoning, as suggested by these considerations, the misattribution manipulations in the present studies should affect subjects who described negative life events but not subjects who described positive life events.

Experiment 2 was a field study rather than a laboratory study in which mood was governed by whether subjects were interviewed on sunny or rainy spring days. The same set of hypotheses were tested, but in some respects this study is the reverse of the first. In Experiment 1, we induced subjects to attend to a situational factor that did not actually produce their mood, but in Experiment 2, they were induced to attend to a situational factor that did produce their mood. In both studies, attributions to situational factors were expected to reduce the likelihood that subjects would attribute their moods to more personally relevant aspects of their lives.

Thus the present studies attempted to explore the contributions of salience of life events and of informational and directional effects of subjects' affective states on reports of general well-being. Moreover, we were interested in whether those processes might affect, to different degrees, different measures of well-being. In this regard, Andrews and McKennel (1980) suggested that judgments of happiness might be "affective," whereas judgments of satisfaction might be "cognitive." Using Bradburn's (1969) affect-balance scale, these authors reported that past affective experiences in a respondent's life (e.g., being praised or being criticized) were good predictors of happiness ratings but not of satisfaction ratings. More generally, ratings of satisfaction may reflect the outcome of social comparison processes, whereas ratings of happiness may reflect the respondent's internal state.

EXPERIMENT 1

In the first experiment, we asked subjects to give vivid descriptions of either a happy or a sad event in their recent past. On the one hand, this task should increase the cognitive availability of positive or negative events, and on the other hand, it should change subjects' mood. To isolate the effect of mood, we ran the experiment in an unusual soundproof room and suggested to some subjects that the room might make them feel good and to others that it might make them feel bad (adapted from Fazio, Zanna, & Cooper, 1977). A third group of subjects was not given any expectations concerning the effects of the room.

We expected that subjects who described negative life events would report being less happy and less satisfied than control subjects, who did not describe any past life events, whereas subjects who described positive life events would report being more happy and more satisfied than control subjects. However, if persons use their affective state as a basis for evaluating the quality of their life, both discounting and augmentation effects (Kelley, 1971) should result from the room manipulation.

Specifically, subjects who described negative life events should discount the bad feelings resulting from thinking about negative life events when the bad feelings can be misattributed to the room, that is, to a transient source, irrelevant to the evaluation of their lives. These subjects should report less unhappiness and dissatisfaction than those with no room expectations. On the other hand, when they expect the room to make them feel elated, they should report more unhappiness and dissatisfaction than the no-expectation group. That is, we expect augmentation effects when subjects realize they feel badly in spite of conditions presumably fostering good feelings.

Similarly, subjects who described positive life events should report lower well-being when they attribute their positive feelings to the room (discounting) and higher well-being when they expect the room to make them feel bad (augmentation) compared to those who have no room expectations.

The occurrence of these discounting and augmentation effects would indicate that subjects use their feelings as relevant information at the time of judgment in assessing the quality of their lives; thus demonstrating the informational value of affective states. If, however, persons are only motivated to explain their affective state if they feel bad—as suggested by the directive functions hypothesis—discounting and augmentation effects should only be obtained when subjects describe negative life events. Subjects who describe positive events should not be influenced by the misattribution manipulations. In contrast, if mood is irrelevant to that type of judgment, or if mood affects it only via the increased availability of mood-congruent cognitions (Bower, 1981; Isen et al., 1978), we should simply find a main effect of the quality of the life events described, because the impact of salient cognitions should not depend on the explanation of a person's mood.

Finally, if judgments of happiness are more "affective" than are judgments of satisfaction, the former should be more influenced by the misattribution manipulations than the latter.

Method

Participants. Sixty-one introductory psychology students who were randomly assigned to experimental conditions received course credit for their participation. They were run in groups of three or four persons each.

This is a common mood manipulation technique in research: have participants write in detail about an event in their lives that made them feel the ____ (happiest, saddest, angriest, etc.). Research indicates that this activity puts people back in the mood they are vividly describing, at least for a brief period (less than an hour, usually).

Ok, why do you think
participants were told this?

Overview. To set up the misattribution possibilities, the experiment was conducted in an odd-looking soundproof room. Participants were first told that the room might make them feel either tense or elated, or they were given no expectation concerning the room's effect. They then heard a series of three-note piano progressions on tape as part of a bogus "sound-memory task" (intended to legitimize the soundproof room). Next they wrote about a life event that had made them feel good or bad. The dependent variables were then assessed using questions about life satisfaction and happiness, present mood, and some causal-attribution scales. The design was therefore a 2 X 3 factorial involving two types of life-event descriptions (positive or negative) and three types of expectations about room effects (tense, elated, or no effect). In addition, a control condition was run in which subjects reported their life satisfaction without having previously described a life event and without having been in the soundproof room.

Expectation. Participants were given one of the three expectations about the soundproof room. Those given a *bad-mood expectation* were told that participants in an earlier study had complained about feeling "tense" and "depressed" in the room. Those given a *good-mood expectation* were told that earlier participants felt "elated" and "kind of high" in the room, perhaps because of its soundproof quality. Subjects in these conditions were then told the Department of Psychology wanted to find out what caused these feelings. They were given a one page questionnaire on which to rate the room for comfort, lighting, ventilation, and so on. Participants with *no mood expectation* sat in the same room but were not told about the reactions of earlier participants and were not given a questionnaire.

All subjects received the questionnaire at the beginning of the experiment, but it was desirable to suggest that the room might have its effects later (during the period when life events were described). To accomplish this, the cover page of the questionnaire for the expectation groups contained an instruction to the experimenter from the Department of Psychology to hand the questionnaire to some subjects at the beginning, to some subjects during, and to some subjects at the end of the experiment. It explained that the impact of the room might depend on the amount of time spent in it. In addition, subjects were asked to indicate at which of these times they received the questionnaire. This instruction was intended to convey the impression that subjects' moods might change over the course of the experiment.

Here is the mood manipulation
check. The IV (a manipulation),
in this case, assigning people to
feel either good or bad, is then
immediately measured to make
sure that it has had the intended
effect on the subject.

Mood. Following the ratings of the experimental room, subjects were exposed to a series of three-note tonal progressions as part of the bogus sound-memory task and were then asked to collaborate on a 25-minute filler task prior to the sound-recognition test. The sound memory task simply provided an excuse for running the experiment in a soundproof room. The filler task actually constituted the main part of the study. Specifically, subjects were asked to collaborate on the development of a "life-event inventory," purportedly a test instrument to assess events in people's lives. Printed instructions asked them to describe "as vividly and in as much detail as possible" a recent event that made them feel "really good" or one that made them feel "really bad." They were told that these descriptions would provide the basis for the generation of items for the life-event inventory. Subjects were given 20 minutes to complete the task. To ensure that they attended to the emotional aspects of the event, they were asked to indicate how the experience made them feel, what aspects made them feel that way, what the experiences made them think about, and so on. Positive and negative mood conditions were run in each experimental session, and the experimenter was blind to the condition.

Half of the essays from each experimental condition were randomly selected and rated for the pleasantness of the described event. No differences, according to room expectations, emerged either for the positive ($F < 1$) or the negative descriptions, $F(2, 12) = 1.32$, *ns*, which indicated that the descriptions were equally positive or negative across the three expectation conditions.

This is to ensure that there are no differences in the descriptions of the rooms across the three expectation conditions. If there <u>were</u> differences, that would have introduced a potential confound to the experiment.

Measures. Following these descriptions, participants were asked to answer some general questions, purportedly to help in the selection of appropriate response scales for the life-event inventory being developed. The questions, which were answered along either 7- or 11-point rating scales, included two measures of general well-being. One of these pertained to general happiness (How happy do you feel about your life as a whole?) and the other to life satisfaction (How satisfied are you with your life as a whole these days?). Both of these questions had previously been used in other surveys of well-being (cf. Andrews & McKennel, 1980). Following these measures, subjects' present affective states were assessed by the questions "How happy (unhappy) do you feel right now, at this moment?" and "How good (bad) do you feel at this moment?"

Finally, to assess causal attributions for their momentary moods, participants were asked two questions, one about how much their present feelings were due to what they thought about (an internal attribution) and one about how much their feelings were due to the room (an external attribution).

Participants in a non-factorial control group, run concurrently with the experimental conditions, responded to the same dependent measures without first describing events from their lives.

Results

Temporary mood. The task of describing pleasant and unpleasant life events influenced mood, as expected. Compared to participants who described positive life events, those who described negative life events reported feeling significantly less happy at this moment ($Ms = 3.7$ vs. 5.5 on a 7-point scale) and less good ($Ms = 5.8$ vs. 8.4 on an 11-point scale), $Fs(2, 54) = 22.7$ and 20.7, respectively, $ps < .001$. Moreover, compared to control group subjects ($Ms = 5.1$ and 7.9), subjects who described negative events felt only less happy and less good at this moment, $ts(54) = 2.97$ and 3.06, $ps < .004$, whereas subjects who described positive events felt only somewhat happier and better, $ts(54) = 1.32$ and 1.30, respectively, $ps < .20$. That is, compared to the control group, the instruction to think about negative events had a more pronounced effect on subjects' mood than did the instruction to think about positive events. This finding, however, seems to be due primarily to the preexisting positive mood of the control group.

As expected, the manipulation of subjects' expectations for how the room would make them feel did not affect their reported mood ($Fs \leq 1$). In other words, opportunities to explain the source of the mood did not change the level of the mood itself.

General well-being. Table 1 shows the effects of event descriptions and room expectancies on ratings of both general happiness and life satisfaction. The pattern of results was similar in each case and consistent with the hypotheses. That is, subjects who had described positive life events reported being happy and satisfied with their lives regardless of their expectations about the effects of the room they were in. However, when subjects had described negative experiences, their ratings depended on the extent to which the room could potentially account for their negative

Expectations about the room had no effect on ratings of life satisfaction among those in a good mood.

feelings. That is, they reported less happiness and less life satisfaction when the room was described as likely to make them elated and reported more happiness and satisfaction when it was described as likely to make them sad than when no expectations about the room's effects were given. These conclusions are confirmed statistically for both happiness and life satisfaction by main effects for the type of event described, $Fs(2, 54) = 59.2$ and 32.8, respectively, $ps < .001$, and by an Event Description X Room Expectations interaction, $Fs(2, 54) = 10.6$ and 5.6, respectively, $ps < .01$.

Thus the data are consistent with both informative and directive effects hypotheses. That is, subjects who were in a bad mood tried to explain their feelings in terms of transitory situational factors and therefore discounted them as reasonable sources of information about their life situation when they could attribute their feelings to the room they were in. Indeed, the discounting was sufficiently complete that the bad-mood-expectation condition no longer differed from the good-mood condition. On the other hand, participants who felt bad but who expected the room to make them feel "elated" or "kind of high" reported non-significantly less happiness than did those who expected no side effects and much less happiness than did participants with the same expectations who were in the good-mood condition.

In contrast, subjects who were in good mood were not influenced by possible situational explanations of their mood. This fact may indicate that subjects were not motivated to search for factors that could account for positive affective states.

Attributions. In general, we expected attributions for mood states to be consistent with the information provided. For example, compared to subjects without expectations about the room, those expecting the room to make them feel tense should attribute bad moods externally to the room and good moods internally to their thoughts. Data relevant to this hypothesis are summarized in Table 2. Because within-cell variability in responses to these attribution scales was high, the expected effects were not significant. However, three of the four comparisons between means for subjects expecting elation versus tension were in the predicted direction (although the mean for the no-expectation group was often misplaced). The pattern of the data supports the misattribution reasoning, the only deviation being that participants in the bad-mood condition who expected the room to make them feel "elated" still attributed their bad mood more to the room and less to their thoughts than did the no-expectation group. This pattern of attribution may account for the weakness of the augmentation effect found in this condition.

TABLE 1 General Happiness and Life-Satisfaction Ratings: Experiment 1

Description of event	Expectation about room				
	Tense	No mood	Elated	Total	Control
General happiness (7-point scale)					
Positive	6.5$_{a,b}$	6.4$_{a,b}$	6.7$_a$	6.5	5.5$_b$
Negative	6.1$_{a,b}$	4.1$_c$	3.6c	4.5	
Life satisfaction (I I-point scale)					
Positive	9.6$_a$	8.6$_a$	9.7$_a$	9.3	8.9$_a$
Negative	8.6$_a$	5.7$_b$	4.4$_b$	6.2	

Note. Means that do not share a common subscript differ at $p < .05$ (Newman-Keuls test).

TABLE 2   Causal Attributions of Subjects' Present Affective State

Description of event	Expectation about room			
	Tense	Neutral	Elated	Control
Attribution to thoughts				
Positive	9.8$_b$	7.9$_{a,b}$	7.3$_a$	5.4$_a$
Negative	8.9$_{a,b}$	9.3$_b$	8.0$_{ab}$	
Attribution to the room				
Positive	2.8$_{ab}$	1.5$_a$	3.5$_{a,b}$	2.4$_{a,b}$
Negative	5.6$_b$	2.4$_{a,b}$	3.5$_{a,b}$	

Note. Scales range from 1 to 11. Within each variable, means that do not share a common subscript differ at $p < .05$ (Newman-Keuls test).

Correlational analyses. Additional support for the hypothesis that subjects based their assessment of general well-being on their affective state at the time of judgment is provided by correlational analyses. Specifically, subjects' reports of momentary mood were generally correlated significantly. with their reports of both general happiness and satisfaction with their lives; this was true for control subjects ($rs = .74$ and $.79$, respectively, $p < .002$). It was also true for subjects in the no-misattribution conditions after describing positive events ($r = .57$, $p < .07$ and $r = .67$, $p < .04$) and after describing negative events ($r = .81$, $p < .01$ and $r = .58$, $p < .07$). None of the correlations in the misattribution conditions, on the other hand, reached significance at the .10 level. Contrary to expectations, the correlation of mood with happiness was not significantly higher in any of the conditions than was its correlation with satisfaction.

Discussion

Writing vivid and detailed descriptions of pleasant and unpleasant life experiences appears to influence not only subjects' momentary mood states but also their judgments of how happy and satisfying their lives are in general. Considered in isolation, this could occur for two reasons. First, writing about a happy or a sad life event may increase the availability of similarly valenced events in memory. This, in turn, could lead subjects to overestimate the prevalence of such events in their lives (Tversky & Kahneman, 1973) and bias their judgments. Second, people may use their mood at the time of judgment as information in evaluating the quality of their lives. The results favor the second interpretation. That is, when subjects were given a chance to attribute their *bad* mood to a transient source, irrelevant to the quality of their lives, the description task no longer influenced their judgment of general well being. In the terminology of attribution research, this is referred to as a "discounting effect" (Kelley, 1971), because subjects discounted aspects of their own lives as a cause of their bad moods when another external cause (the soundproof room) was made salient. Thus, these data demonstrate informational functions of affective states.

Discounting occurs when alternative plausible causes for an effect are made salient. Augmentation effects have also been reported (e.g., Schwarz, Servay, & Kumpf, 1981) when

Results supported the author's "feelings as information" hypotheses. When people were able to attribute their negative mood to an external source (like the room), they didn't use their negative affect as a piece of information in judging their overall life satisfaction or predictions about their future.

aspects of a situation are made salient that could reasonably produce a state opposite to that of the subject. Augmentation effects were anticipated primarily in the condition in which subjects were in a bad mood but had expected to be made giddy and elated. The results showed only a trend toward augmentation effects. Judging from the pattern of attribution results, subjects may have found it less credible that the soundproof room could produce elation than that it would produce tension, making augmentation effects in the bad-mood condition unlikely.

On the other hand, subjects who thought about positive events and reported being in a good mood were not influenced by the misattribution manipulations and reported high well-being regardless of experimental condition. This result is in line with the hypothesis that affect has a directive influence and that persons are more likely to seek explanations for negative than for positive feelings. It should be noted, however, that the momentary mood of subjects who described positive events was only insignificantly better than was the mood of control subjects, whereas the mood of subjects who described negative life events was significantly worse. That is, the mood of subjects who described negative events deviated more from what might be considered "normal" than did the mood of subjects who described positive events, a finding that seems to reflect the well-known tendency of people to report positive resting moods (see Matlin & Stang, 1978, for a review).

EXPERIMENT 2

The results of Experiment 1 support the hypothesis that people use their momentary mood state as information in evaluating the quality of their lives. The evidence came, however, from a relatively complex laboratory experiment involving some extraordinary stage managing. We decided, therefore, to test the hypothesis again in a more naturalistic way.

In this second study, well-being was assessed as part of a telephone interview conducted either on warm and sunny days or on rainy spring days: Cunningham (1979) had previously shown that weather had a reliable effect on mood. If people use their affective states as information to evaluate their lives, they should report greater well-being and life satisfaction on sunny days than on rainy days. This effect should be attenuated, however, when respondents are led to attribute their mood to the weather, that is, to a transitory source irrelevant to the evaluation of their lives. In this case, their mood should be discredited as reliable information concerning their general well-being. In addition, if only negative affective states lead respondents to seek explanations, then this attenuation of the effect of weather on well-being should occur only when the weather is bad and not when the weather is good.

Method

In a 2 × 3 factorial design, subjects were called either on sunny or on rainy spring days and were asked to answer questions on life satisfaction as part of a telephone survey. The salience of the weather as a plausible explanation for mood was varied. Weather either was not mentioned at all, was mentioned in passing as small talk, or was mentioned as a primary focus of the experiment.

Respondents. Ninety-three telephone numbers randomly selected from the student directory of the University of Illinois at Urbana-Champaign were called, and the persons answering the

---

In all psychological research, it is best to approach studying a concept or problem using multiple methods, and multiple measures. To the degree that you obtain the same outcomes using different ways of looking at the problem, you can say that the finding is robust and we can have that much more confidence in the data. Here, the authors tested their predictions in the lab, and now in the second experiment, they want to replicate their findings in a more real-world setting.

When reminded about the weather (sunny or cloudy), people shouldn't use their mood (from the weather) as a source of information in judging their future well being. In the conditions where people are not reminded about the weather, they should use their mood as information in predicting their future well being.

As in experiment 1, if only negative mood triggers a search for explanations, then the influence of misattribution to weather should only happen in bad moods (in cloudy weather conditions).

Why do you think they had two weather-salient manipulation conditions?

Is there any problem using only college students for this experiment? Would they have to do anything different to the design to use people from the community (non-students)?

phone served as respondents. They were called by a female interviewer on either sunny or rainy weekdays during April and May. Nine respondents refused to participate in the interview, five on rainy days and four on sunny days, which left 84 subjects in the analysis.

Procedure. The interviewer always opened the conversation with "Hello, I'm __, we're doing research for the psychology department at Circle Campus in Chicago." This university was selected as the interviewer's alleged affiliation under the pretense that the interviewer was calling from out of town.

In *indirect-priming conditions* the interviewer continued with an irrelevant aside: "By the way, how's the weather down there?" After the subject's response the interviewer continued, "Well, let's get back to our research. What we are interested in is people's moods. We randomly dial numbers to get a representative sample. Could you just answer four brief questions?"

In *direct-priming conditions* the interviewer continued after saying hello and indicating that she was calling from Chicago Circle with the words, "We are interested in how the weather affects person's mood. We randomly dial numbers. . . ."

In *no-priming conditions* the interview continued after the standard opening as in the indirect-priming condition without the aside about the weather.

Following one of these introductions, the interview continued with the assessment of the respondent's perceived quality of life and present feeling state:

1. First, on a scale of l to 10, with 10 being the happiest, how happy do you feel about your life as a whole?

2. Thinking of how your life is going now, how much would you like to change your life from what it is now? This is also on a scale of l to 10. Ten means "change a very great deal" and one "means not at all."

3. All things considered, how satisfied or dissatisfied are you with your life as a whole these days? (with number 10 being the most satisfied).

4. And, how happy do you feel at this moment? Again, 10 is the happiest. That's all the questions I have. Thank you for your time and cooperation.

On any given rainy or sunny day the same number of calls were made in each priming condition. Thus a confounding of weather and priming was avoided. Finally, it should be noted that the interviewer was blind to the experimental hypothesis and did not expect an interaction effect of weather and priming but did expect a main effect of weather.

Results

Mood. An analysis of "momentary happiness" ratings showed that subjects called on sunny days felt happier ($M = 7.5$) than did subjects called on rainy days ($M = 5.4$), $F(1, 78) = 39.90$, $p < .001$, and that this mood measure was not affected by the priming manipulation, $F(2, 78) = 1.58$, *ns*.

Well-being. The effects of weather and priming manipulations on each dependent variable are shown in Table 3. In each case, the pattern of results is similar and consistent with predictions. That is, respondents on sunny days reported themselves to be generally happy and satisfied with their lives, and they had little desire to change. This tendency was similar

---

In the subject section of an experiment report, you need to state how many subjects you contacted or ran through the experiment, and how many were dropped and why they were dropped from the experiment, and how many total subjects you were left with.

Wow! That is a very significant difference in moods between sunny days and cloudy days. Cunningham (1979) was right about the influence of weather on mood!

This follows in line with predictions about positive mood.

under all conditions and planned comparisons of the no-priming condition with both priming conditions revealed no significant differences, $ts(78) = .20, .75,$ and $.80$, respectively. In
contrast, respondents on rainy days reported themselves to be generally less happy, $t(78) = 3.68$,
$p < .001$, and less satisfied, $t(78) = 3.56$, $p < .001$, and desiring more change, $t(78) = 1.96$,
$p < .06$, in the no-priming condition than in either the direct- or the indirect-priming condition. In other words, the influence of the weather on these life judgments was appreciable only
under no-priming conditions. Moreover, as shown in Table 3, respondents' appraisals of their
lives on rainy days under no-priming conditions generally differed from their responses in the
other five conditions, which did not differ from each other. However, the results for the "desire
to change" measure were not as strong as for the happiness and the satisfaction measures.

In summary, the data of this study replicated both the informational and the directive
effects of subjects' affective states found in Experiment 1.

Correlational analyses. As in Experiment 1, there was a tendency for the correlation of subjects'
reported present affective state with their reported happiness to be higher under no-priming
conditions ($r = .79$) than under both priming conditions ($r = .63$, $z = 1.36$, *ns*). The correlation
with satisfaction, on the other hand, was the same in the no priming ($r = .49$) and the priming
conditions ($r = .48$) and was lower than the correlation with happiness in both the no-priming
($z = 1.89$, $p < .06$) and the priming conditions ($z = 1.11$, *ns*).

GENERAL DISCUSSION

Informative Functions of Affective States

The two experiments reported here, one in the laboratory and one involving telephone
interviews, both provide evidence that respondents use their momentary moods to make

TABLE 3 Mean Ratings of General Happiness, Desire to Change, and Life Satisfaction: Experiment 2

Dependent variable	Priming		
	None	Indirect	Direct
General happiness			
Sunny	7.43a	7.29a	7.79a
Rainy	5.00b	7.00a	6.93a
Desire to change			
Sunny	3.93a	3.43a	3.57a
Rainy	5.79b	4.57a,b	4.93a,b
Life satisfaction			
Sunny	6.57a	6.79a	7.21a
Rainy	4.86b	6.71a	7.07a

Note. $n = 14$ per cell. Means that do not share a common subscript differ at $p < .05$ (Newman-Keuls test).

In conditions where the subjects were not reminded about the weather, the weather had a huge effect on life judgments.

The data from experiment 2 replicated the overall findings of experiment 1.

judgments about their general happiness and life satisfaction. Both thinking about good versus bad experiences and being in sunny versus rainy weather influenced subjects' reports of general well-being. However, this influence was not direct. Instead, it appeared to occur only insofar as these factors affected subjects' moods, and these moods were considered to provide reliable information about well-being. Subjects appear to seek personally irrelevant explanations for an unpleasant mood state when such explanations are available. As a consequence, they then do not use their mood as information about their well-being. When in a good mood, however, subjects do use their mood as a basis for judging the quality of their life regardless of the availability of alternative explanations for the mood.

The impact of (mis)attribution manipulations on subjects' judgments, under bad mood conditions make the results difficult to interpret in terms of the effect of mood on the availability of mood-consistent ideas (Bower, 1981; Isen et al., 1978). According to this reasoning, mood-congruent events should be more available in memory, leading subjects to overestimate the prevalence of positive or negative events in their lives. To the extent that subjects base their evaluations on this recalled evidence, they should report higher well-being under positive than under negative mood. Note, however, that the implications of the recalled events should not be altered by the attribution manipulations. That is, the mood-congruent-availability notion should predict a main effect of mood but not an interaction of mood and attribution. On the other hand, the attribution manipulation should affect the diagnostic value of subjects' present affective state, resulting in the interaction effect found in both studies. Therefore, the data provide evidence that moods themselves have an informational function.

Directive Effects of Affective States

Although opportunities for attribution and misattribution had strong effects on the reported well-being of participants in negative moods, those in positive moods reported high well-being regardless of experimental conditions, as predicted by the directive-effects hypothesis. This evidence is consistent with the results reported by Williams, Ryckman, Gold, and Lenny (1982), who used misattribution procedures to study the role of affect in the attitude-similarity-attraction paradigm. As in the present study, they found that subjects took the opportunity to attribute away negative but not positive affect. Also, Arkin et al. (1976) reported that subjects who received positive feedback about their performance (presumably putting them in a good mood) were insensitive to situational factors that could account for this feedback.

In this regard, we have favored the hypothesis that people are more motivated to seek explanations for negative than for positive moods, and we suggested that this might be primarily due to the fact that most people experience negative moods as deviating from their usually positive feelings. By the same logic depressed persons for whom bad moods are usual, and persons in social situations in which bad moods are expected (e.g., funerals), should show attempts to explain any good feelings they might experience. Similarly, persons in unusually positive mood states might attempt to find out the causes of their feelings. Unfortunately, the present studies do not allow an evaluation of these issues because the positive mood induced through thinking about positive life events was not significantly better than was the to make mood of control group subjects. Also, rainy and sunny weather, used as a mood manipulation in the second study, does not lend itself easily to the creation of a "neutral" control group.

Overall finding from both studies. Think about this for a moment. . . isn't it rather astounding that when people are making a judgment about their overall life satisfaction, and future well-being, that they use their current mood (which could be based on any number of irrelevant things) as a piece of information to help them answer those questions?

This is a fascinating extension of their predictions and would make for an intriguing future study!

Thus it seems reasonable to assume that extreme positive moods might produce effects similar to the ones we found for negative moods. We would like to suggest, however, that for most people most of the time unpleasant states are more likely to trigger explanations than pleasant states are.

Motivational Bias

By itself, the tendency to attribute bad moods but not good moods to external sources may indicate the operation of a motivational self-serving bias. Two pieces of data from Experiment 1, however, lead us to suggest that some factors, in addition to motivational bias, are at work. Both pieces of data are instances in which subjects did not take opportunities to increase the perceived quality of their lives. They suggest a two-stage branching system in which subjects must first seek explanations before available explanations are adopted. At the first stage, bad moods but not good moods are problematic and tend to activate explanation-searching activity. This stage, in which subjects do or do not seek explanations, could be motivated by a desire to maintain or reinstate feelings of well-being. Results at the next stage, however, are not always consistent with such a motivation. Thus, for example, subjects who felt good subsequent to describing positive life-events but who expected the room to make them feel bad could have augmented their feelings of well-being, but like other good-mood subjects, did not take the explanation-seeking branch. As a result, the opportunity to augment their good mood through attributional enhancement was foreclosed. There was no evidence of such augmentation effects in the good-mood condition. Conversely, bad-mood subjects, who generally did take the explanation-search branch, sometimes opened themselves to explanations that worsened their already negative level of well-being. Thus, for example, subjects who felt bad as a result of describing negative life events but who expected the room to make them feel elated, further decreased their sense of well-being. Though this effect was not significant, the pattern of means was nevertheless inconsistent with an unembellished motivational interpretation. Thus, although the present data are certainly not strong enough to allow a straightforward rejection of a self-serving bias explanation, they nevertheless seem to favor an informational interpretation: It appears that once subjects are in an explanation-search mode, processing of the information available is not motivationally biased even if the original decision to search might have involved such factors.

Preparatory Information

In the first experiment, one might argue that the reason mood did not influence life appraisals for subjects expecting to be in a bad mood was that the expectation manipulation had forewarned them, leading to more efficient coping with their mood changes. This argument has been advanced by Calvert-Boyanowsky and Leventhal (1975) as a general critique of studies of the misattribution of arousal. They point out that subjects under misattribution conditions usually receive a list of arousal symptoms that subjects under control conditions do not get and that research on the effect of preparatory information (e.g., Staub & Kellett, 1972) suggests that this alone might account for differences in emotional response. Note, however, that this reasoning implies that subjects expecting a bad mood should be less affected by the negative mood induction. As indicated by the mood data, however, this was not the case. Only the description task and not the mood-expectation manipulation influenced subjects' present affective state. Also, of course, there was no advance warning in Experiment 2 when

When trying to explain why people use affect as information, the authors explore the notion that the person is motivated by a self-serving bias. Those in a good mood do not seek explanations for their mood. Those in a negative mood may seek explanations with the goal of bringing their mood back up to its normal good state. However, the authors here note that this explanation (the self-serving bias) doesn't quite fit with their data, which indicated that those in a negative mood sometimes felt worse as a result of seeking explanations (e.g., when they expected the room to make them feel better).

weather was used to induce mood, so the explanation would not fit those results. Thus, we may conclude that our results are not due to a differential induction of mood, as suggested by Calvert-Boyanowsky and Leventhal (1975). Rather, they seem to be due to differential implications of one's present affective state for the judgment to be made, under different experimental conditions.

HAPPINESS VERSUS SATISFACTION

Although the effect of subjects' mood on judgments of happiness was somewhat more pronounced than its effect on judgment of satisfaction (as was indicated by a repeated measures analyses of variance not reported here), both measures were influenced by subjects' affective state in much the same way. That is, we found little evidence that happiness might be "affective," whereas satisfaction might be "cognitive" (cf. Andrews & McKennel, 1980). Thus, although the data reported by Andrews and McKennel (1980) suggest that happiness is more a function of past affective experiences than is satisfaction, our data suggest that persons use their affective state at the time of judgment to make both judgments in a similar way. Note, however, that in both studies judgments of happiness were obtained prior to judgments of satisfaction, which might account for some of the consistency between these measures. Thus, additional research will be needed to clarify potential differences in the impact of affect on different measures of well-being.

NOTE

1. Kerber, K. W., & Clore, G. L. *Causal relationships in the affect-cognition cycle: Interpersonal implications, intentionality and liking.* Unpublished manuscript, College of the Holy Cross, 1982.

REFERENCES

Andrews, F. M., & McKennell, A. C. Measures of self reported well-being: Their affective, cognitive, and other components. *Social Indicators Research,* 1980, *8,* 127–155.

Arkin, R. M., Gleason, J. M., & Johnston, S. Effect of perceived choice, expected outcome, and observed outcome of an action on the causal attributions of actors. *Journal of Experimental Social Psychology,* 1976, *12,* 151–158.

Bower, G. H. Mood and memory. *American Psychologist,* 1981, *36,* 129–148.

Bradburn, N. M. *The structure of psychological well being.* Chicago: Aldine, 1969.

Calvert-Boyanowsky, J., & Leventhal, H. The role of information in attenuating behavioral responses to stress: A reinterpretation of the misattribution phenomenon. *Journal of Personality and Social Psychology,* 1975, *32,* 214–221.

Cunningham, M. R. Weather, mood, and helping behavior: Quasi experiments with the sunshine samaritan. *Journal of Personality and Social Psychology,* 1979, *37,* 1947–1956.

Fazio, R.H., Zanna, M. P., & Cooper, J. Dissonance and self-perception: An integrative view of each theory's proper domain of application. *Journal of Experimental Social Psychology,* 1977, *13,* 464–479.

Goldings, M. J. On the avowal and projection of happiness. *Journal of Personality,* 1954, *23,* 30–47.

Isen, A. M., Shalker, T. E., Clark, M., & Karp, L. Affect, accessibility of material in memory, and behavior: A cognitive loop? *Journal of Personality and Social Psychology,* 1978, *36,* 1–12.

Kelley, H. H. Causal schemas and the attribution process. In E. E. Jones et al. (Eds.), *Attribution: Perceiving the causes of behavior.* Morristown, N.J.: General Learning Press, 1971.

Matlin, M. W., & Stang, D. J. The *Pollyanna principle: Selectivity in language, memory, and thought.* Cambridge, Mass.: Schenkman, 1978.

Schwarz, N., Servay, W., & Kumpf, M. *Attribution of arousal as a mediator of the effectiveness of fear-arousing communications.* Paper presented at the meeting of the Eastern Psychological Association, New York, April 1981. (ERIC Document Reproduction Service No. ED 205 867)

Staub, E., & Kellett, D. S. Increasing pain tolerance by information about aversive stimuli. *Journal of Personality and Social Psychology.* 1972, *21,* 198–203.

Tversky, A., & Kahneman, D. Availability: A heuristic for judging frequency and probability. *Cognitive Psychology,* 1973, *5,* 207–232.

Wessman, A. E., Ricks, D. F. *Mood and personality.* New York: Holt, Rinehart & Winston, 1966.

Williams, S., Ryckman, R. M., Gold, J. A., & Lenny, E. The effects of sensation seeking and misattribution of arousal on attraction. *Journal of Research on Personality,* 1982, *16,* 217–226.

Wyer, R. S., & Carlston, D. *Social cognition, inference, and attribution.* Hillsdale, N.J.: Erlbaum, 1979.

Zanna, M. P., & Cooper, J. Dissonance and the attribution process. In J. Harvey et al. (Eds.), *New directions in attribution research* (Vol. I). Hillsdale, N.J.: Erlbaum, 1976.

Received June 23, 1982

Revision received November 19, 1982 ▪

THIRD EDITION OF THE *PUBLICATION MANUAL*

APA has just published the third edition of the *Publication Manual.* This new edition replaces the 1974 second edition of the *Manual.* The new *Manual* updates APA policies and procedures and incorporates changes in editorial style and practice since 1974. It amplifies and refines some parts of the second edition, reorganizes other parts, and presents new material. (See the March issue of the *American Psychologist* for more on the third edition.)

All manuscripts to be published in the 1984 volumes of APA's journals will be copy edited according to the third edition of the *Manual.* Therefore, manuscripts being prepared now should be prepared according to the third edition. Beginning in 1984, submitted manuscripts that depart significantly from third edition style will be returned to authors for correction.

The third edition of the *Publication Manual* is available for $12 for members of APA and $15 for nonmembers. Orders of $25 or less must be prepaid. A charge of $1.50 per order is required for shipping and handling. To order the third edition, write to the Order Department, APA, 1400 N. Uhle Street, Arlington, VA 22201.

POST-ARTICLE DISCUSSION

The results of these studies (and others; see Schwarz, 1990) indicate that people tend to use their moods as pieces of information when they are making social judgments or judgments about their own self, even when those questions have nothing to do with those moods. I've mentioned it several times throughout this volume, so you might be sensing a theme here: Over and over, people demonstrate that they are not logical or rational in their judgments. We are prone to all manner of biases, heuristics, and flaws in the ways that we think about ourselves and our social world (Kahneman, Slovic, & Tversky, 1982; Nisbett & Ross, 1980).

I wanted to highlight a couple things about this article. First, it uses two different approaches (lab setting vs. real-world setting) to examine the same phenomenon. This is good because to the degree that similar results are obtained with different approaches, we can have that much more confidence in the findings. Second, the authors examine an interesting question (one that is easily relatable) and obtain somewhat counterintuitive results. Finally, I wanted to briefly touch on the discussion section of this paper.

Most research papers examine competing theories for a given predicted outcome. This paper is no exception. The authors consider the possibility that the misattribution effects might be explained by a mood-congruent recall effect, which makes a plethora of positive-mood memories available when one is in a good mood, and similarly, when one is in a bad mood, one's mind has greater access to related negative memories. The pattern of the data showed support for the "feelings as information" explanation over the mood-congruent recall effect. A good research paper (and this is an excellent example) will always test competing theories and then make a compelling, data-supported case for why one theory is best at explaining the results compared to other theories. Finally, in the discussion section, it is good to bring up possible limitations of the experiment and suggest ways future researchers might improve on the experiment. I've had students write up their research and spend one paragraph discussing their results and then several paragraphs on a litany of self-flagellating experiment flaws. That's a bit overboard!

In summary, good researchers always want to anticipate their critics in terms of the design of the experiment, the theories tested (in the design phase), and potential alternative explanations for the obtained data (in the post–data collection and analysis phase). This makes for the best experiment you can construct, and for a more thorough and scientifically sound paper. This paper does all those things, which is another reason it is a classic in the field and is included in this text-reader.

THINGS TO THINK ABOUT

1. Why do you think that the difference between the mood of those in the control condition and those who were told to think about a positive event in their life was so small, but the difference between the control mood condition and those told to describe a bad event in their life was so large?

2. How might our positive affect also bias the way we think or process information? How would negative affect bias our cognitive processes? Are there similarities in each mood state's effect on our cognition?

3. Could seasonal affective disorder (where some people become depressed in the winter as a result of the lack of sunlight) be treated with a therapeutic program utilizing misattribution?

4. Do you think that, once the subjects state their views of their overall well-being and life satisfaction (whether positive or negative), they might continue to adhere to that conclusion even when asked the same questions during a different (opposite) misattribution scenario (e.g., cloudy day, asked later on a sunny day, and vice versa)? Would they maintain that original conclusion because it was publicly stated and they want to remain cognitively consistent?

5. The authors speculate that depressed persons and people who expect to feel negatively in a given situation (e.g., a funeral) would be likely to search for explanations for any positive mood they are feeling. Do you agree, and what do you think would happen in that situation?

INTRODUCTION TO READING 7.2

Winkielman et al. (1998)

How do you know if your memory is good? It depends how you define *good*. Is a good memory one where you can remember a lot of things? Or is it judged to be good if you recall memories quickly (it is easy for you to recall)? This fundamental question by which we assess an important part of our cognitive life is at the heart of the study you are about to read. We like to think that the way by which we make our assessments about the strength and quality of our memory is an objective ruler that remains constant throughout our life, so that when we detect differences from one assessment at a particular time, to another later assessment, we then conclude the memory has shifted, and not the criteria by which we measure the two assessments. But, as you have been reading throughout this volume, social psychologists have experimentally demonstrated over and over again that human cognitive processes and judgments are not logical.

Can our judgments about our memory be influenced by external forces? For example, if someone tells me that I am doing a memory task that most people find easy, but when I do it, I find it to be difficult, do I then view my memory recall as poor compared to the average person? If I recall a lot of information, I wouldn't think of my memory as poor, right? You might be surprised! Here is another great example of how powerful misattribution can be in our cognitive processes. Enjoy the paper!

Reading 7.2

Research Report

The Role of Ease of Retrieval and Attribution in Memory Judgments:

Judging Your Memory as Worse Despite Recalling More Events

Piotr Winkielman, Norbert Schwarz, and Robert F. Belli

Abstract—*Participants who had to recall 12 childhood events (a difficult task) were more likely to infer that they could not remember large parts of their childhood than participants who had to recall 4 events (an easy task), although the former recalled three times as many events. This pattern of results suggests that memory judgments are based on the experienced ease or difficulty of recall. Accordingly, the negative impact of recalling 12 events was attenuated when participants were led to attribute the experienced difficulty to the task rather than to the poor quality of their memory. The findings emphasize the role of subjective experiences and attribution in metamemory judgments.*

People's beliefs about memory have been assessed across a wide range of domains (see Dixon, 1989, and Herrmann, 1982, for reviews). The present research focuses on a topic that has received less research attention—the strategies that people use in assessing the quality of their memory. For example, suppose you are asked, "Are there large parts of your childhood after age 5 that you cannot remember?" and are offered the response alternatives "yes," "unsure," and "no" (Ross, 1989). How would you arrive at an answer? How do people evaluate their own memory for a specified time period? One possibility is that they focus on how much information they can retrieve about the specified time period. The more information is retrieved, the better their memory presumably is. An alternative possibility is based on the notion of the availability heuristic (Tversky & Kahneman, 1973). When judging their memory, individuals may rely on the subjective experience of ease or difficulty of recall. If so, they may judge their memory as good when recall is experienced as easy, but as poor when recall is experienced as difficult.

Note, however, that the more events people attempt to recall, the more likely it is that they experience the task as difficult. Individuals who attempt to recall many events may not realize that the experienced difficulty is due to task demands and may instead attribute it to the poor quality of their memory. Hence, individuals who attempt to recall many events may infer poorer memory than individuals who attempt to recall only a few events, despite the fact that the former are likely to recall more material. The present research tested this paradoxical possibility, which is compatible with previous observations in other domains of judgment.

For example, Schwarz et al. (1991, Experiment 1) asked some participants to recall 6 examples of their own assertive behaviors (easy task) and others to recall 12 examples (difficult task). The latter participants subsequently evaluated themselves as less assertive than the former, despite the fact that they had just recalled twice as many assertive behaviors. Confirming the causal role of the phenomenal experience of difficulty of recall, this finding was not obtained when participants were led to attribute the experienced difficulty to an irrelevant source, such as distracting music played to them (Schwarz et al., 1991, Experiment 3). In this case, individuals relied on the amount of recall and reported higher assertiveness after recalling 12 rather than 6 examples. As this example illustrates, recall tasks render two distinct sources of information accessible: the recalled content and the ease with which this content can be brought to mind. Depending on which of these sources individuals draw on, they may arrive at opposite conclusions (see Schwarz, in press, and Schwarz & Clore, 1996, for a discussion of phenomenal experiences in judgment).

The present research extends previous work on the experience of remembering (for reviews, see Jacoby, Kelley, & Dywan, 1989; Kelley & Jacoby, 1996). This work has typically manipulated the ease of retrieval for specific items by some version of a priming procedure and addressed, for example, how retrieval fluency contributes to the subjective experience of remembering the item (e.g., Lindsay & Kelley, 1996; Whittlesea, 1993) and to judgments of truth (e.g., Begg, Armour, & Kerr, 1985) or confidence (e.g., Kelley & Lindsay, 1993). Extending this work, the present study explores how the ease or difficulty with which material can be brought to mind in a free recall task influences more general metamemory judgments, such as "How good is my memory for my childhood?" Moreover, in the present study, we did not employ a priming procedure, but manipulated recall difficulty by asking participants to recall either a few or many memories from a specified time period, thus pitching the implications of the amount of recall against the implications of the subjective experience of ease or difficulty of recall.

Specifically, participants were asked to recall either 4 or 12 childhood events. Whereas the former task is experienced as easy, the latter is experienced as difficult. Subsequently, they

Quantity vs. speed. Which do YOU think is the way most people judge whether they believe their memory is good?

One of the main ideas this paper is going to explore. Sounds counterintuitive, doesn't it, that those who recall more events might rate their memory as poorer than those who recall fewer events? So the researchers are suggesting that people may misattribute the difficulty of retrieving memories with the quality of their memory as a whole.

rated the completeness of their childhood memory. We predicted that participants would rate their memory as worse after successfully retrieving many childhood events than after retrieving a few childhood events, in contrast to what the actual number of recalled events would seem to imply.

Hypotheses.

If obtained, this finding would indicate that participants misattribute the difficulty of the task to the poor quality of their memory. To provide a direct test of this interpretation, we informed some of the participants who had to recall 12 events that most people find this task rather difficult. We predicted that these participants would rate their childhood memory as more complete than participants who completed the same recall task without information about the task's difficulty. Conversely, we tried to inhibit task attributions by informing other participants that most people find it easy to recall 12 events. We expected these participants to be particularly likely to rate their childhood memory as incomplete. Such a differential impact of the same recall experience would further support the informative role of recall experiences in memory judgments by demonstrating that the impact of these experiences depends on their perceived diagnosticity (see Schwarz & Clore, 1996, for a review of related findings in other domains).

So if one thinks most people find recalling 12 events from their past as difficult, then when they finish that (actual difficult) task, they will blame the difficulty on the TASK and not their memory, and they will believe their memory is better than those who did NOT have any external thing (like task difficulty) on which to blame their feelings about the task difficulty.

Finally, we included a condition in which participants rated the completeness of their childhood memory before they retrieved 12 childhood events. The judgments obtained in this condition presumably reflected participants' default assumptions about their memory, thus providing a baseline against which the impact of recalling 4 versus 12 events could be assessed.

On the other hand, if people are told that most people find recalling 12 items as easy, then when the subject inevitably finds the task to be difficult, he/she will blame his/her difficult time on his/her poor memory.

Following their memory judgments, participants asked to recall 4 events were asked to recall an additional 8 events. This procedure allowed us to ensure that all participants could recall 12 events and that any differences in their memory judgments did not reflect differences in the amount of information that could be retrieved.

In many (but not all) experiments, it is good to have a control condition to compare how subjects perform on the DV compared to those in the different experimental conditions.

METHODS

Participants

The participants were 142 undergraduates at the University of Michigan (61% women, 39% men; mean age = 19.9 years).

Materials and Procedure

In various settings (before a lecture, in a library), participants were randomly given one of five versions of a "memory questionnaire." In the *0-events* condition, participants were first asked about the completeness of their childhood memory: "Regarding childhood memory, are there large parts of your childhood after age 5 which you can't remember?" Response options were "yes," "no," and "unsure" (modeled after Ross, 1989). Next, participants were asked to report 12 events that they experienced while they were 5 to 7 years old and 8 to 10 years old. They had to report 6 specific events on six numbered lines for each age period. Finally, participants rated their recall experience: "Now we want you to think back to the task where you had to write down several different childhood events. How difficult was this task for you?" They responded on a scale ranging from 1 (*very easy*) to 7 (*very difficult*).

Address correspondence to Piotr Winkielman, Department of Psychology, Ohio State University, 1885 Neil Ave., Columbus, OH 43210-1222; e-mail: winkielman.1@osu.edu.

In the *4-events* condition, participants were first asked to report 4 childhood events (2 for each age period). Next, they were asked about the completeness of their childhood memory and the difficulty of their recall experience. Finally, the participants were asked to report an additional 8 events.

There were three 12-events versions of the questionnaire. In each version, participants were asked to report 12 childhood events (6 for each age period). Before the recall task, participants assigned to the *12-events/difficult* condition were informed that "most people find recalling childhood events difficult." Participants assigned to the *12-events/easy* condition were informed that "most people find recalling childhood events easy." Participants assigned to the *12-events/control* condition received no information about task difficulty. After the recall task, participants were asked about the completeness of their childhood memory and the difficulty of their recall experience.

RESULTS

Manipulation Checks

Our manipulation of recall difficulty was successful. Participants who had to recall 12 events and received no information about task difficulty rated the recall task as more difficult ($M = 3.98$) than participants who had to recall only 4 events initially ($M = 3.00$), $t(46) = 2.24$, $p < .05$. As expected, the compliance with experimental instructions was very good, with 91.5% of the participants retrieving all requested events. To ensure that our analyses were based on responses of participants who did not experience any failures to retrieve requested events, we excluded from further analyses the 8.5% (12) participants who did not report all 12 events. However, the results of all critical tests are similar when all participants are left in the sample.

Judgments of Childhood Memory

Table 1 shows participants' responses to the memory question. The reports of poor childhood memory increased with the number of events recalled: Whereas only 19% of the participants who had to recall 4 events reported that they could not remember large parts of their childhood, 46% of the participants who had to recall 12 events (and received no information about task difficulty) did so. The judgments of participants who answered the memory question before they retrieved childhood events (0-events condition) fell in between these extremes (37% "yes" responses).

The proportions of "yes" responses in the 4-events and 12-events/control conditions were compared using contrast analysis on proportions (Rosenthal & Rosnow, 1985). The analyses were set up in two ways. One analysis compared "yes" responses with "unsure" and "no" responses combined ($z = 2.05$, $p = .04$). The other analysis compared only "yes" and "no" responses ($z = 2.43$, $p = .02$).

To assess the relative contribution of experienced ease and difficulty, we constructed a logistic regression model that treated the responses to the memory question as an ordinal level dependent variable ("yes" = −1, "unsure" = 0, "no" = 1), using the 0-events condition as the referent group. Results confirmed the prediction that participants in the 0-events condition would provide significantly more "yes" responses and significantly fewer "no" responses than those in the 4-events condition ($\beta = -0.85$, $p = .05$). Moreover, they also provided significantly fewer "yes" responses and significantly more "no" responses than those in the

Interesting data that support their hypotheses. The more information they are asked to recall, the poorer they perceive their memory to be.

12-events/control condition ($\beta = 0.78$, $p < .05$). These findings indicate that experienced ease of recall leads to judgments of better childhood memory, whereas experienced difficulty of recall leads to judgments of poorer childhood memory, relative to a condition in which no experiential information is available.

We further hypothesized that the impact of a given recall experience depends on its perceived diagnosticity for the judgment at hand.

Judging Your Memory

Accordingly, we predicted that participants who attributed the difficulty they encountered in recalling 12 events to the nature of the task would not use this difficulty as diagnostic information in assessing the completeness of their childhood memory. The pattern of results confirmed this prediction. Without information about task difficulty, 46% of the participants who had to recall 12 events responded with "yes" when asked if their childhood memory was incomplete. In contrast, this was true for only 27% of the participants who were informed that most people find the task difficult. Again, two contrast analyses on proportions were performed. One analysis compared "yes" responses with "unsure" and "no" responses combined ($z = 1.52$, $p < .12$). The other analysis compared only "yes" and "no" responses ($z = 2.13$, $p < .04$). Moreover, when participants were informed about the task difficulty, their memory judgments did not differ from the judgments provided by participants who had to recall either 4 events or no event at all ($ps > .30$, irrespective of response combination).

Finally, we predicted that informing participants that most people find the task easy would enhance the impact of the difficulty they experienced in recalling 12 events. Contrary to this prediction, however, the responses obtained in this condition did not differ from the responses provided by participants who received no information about task difficulty ($p > .3$, for both response combinations). Informing participants that other people find the task easy may not have added much to the interpretation of their phenomenal experience. In fact, most people are likely to expect that they can retrieve a dozen childhood events without much difficulty, thus rendering the task information redundant. Hence, participants in the 12-events/easy condition and the 12-events/control condition may have found the experienced difficulty equally surprising and diagnostic.

Hypothesis was confirmed: in the 12 events condition, those who were not told about the task being difficult for most people tended to blame their performance on their poor memory (46%). But significantly fewer of those in the 12-events condition, when told the task was perceived as difficult to most people, rated their own memory as incomplete (27%).

Interestingly, this prediction was not supported. The authors speculate that it is likely that most people find the task easy anyway, and so telling them that others find it easy doesn't significantly influence their own perceptions of the task difficulty.

TABLE 1

Number and percentage of participants endorsing each response category when asked, "Regarding childhood memory, are there large parts of your childhood after age 5 which you can't remember?"

	Response category		
Condition	Yes	Unsure	No
0 events	11 (37%)	7 (23%)	12 (40%)
4 events	4 (19%)	6 (29%)	11 (52%)
12 events/control	13 (46%)	8 (29%)	7 (25%)
12 events/difficult	7 (27%)	5 (19%)	14 (54%)
12 events/easy	11 (44%)	5 (20%)	9 (36%)

DISCUSSION

Our results suggest that one's judgments of memory are influenced by the number of events one is asked to retrieve. Paradoxically, asking people to recall more events results in lower estimates of memory completeness, contrary to what would be expected if people based their judgments on the number of recalled events. We suggest that this effect reflects the fact that a recall task makes accessible two distinct sources of information: the recalled content and the ease with which this content comes to mind. Depending on which of these sources individuals draw on, they may arrive at opposite conclusions (Schwarz et al., 1991; Wänke, Schwarz, & Bless, 1995). Recalling many events is generally experienced as more difficult than recalling a few events. If people focus on the experienced difficulty, and do not take the task demands sufficiently into account, they may misattribute the experienced difficulty to the poor quality of their memory. Consistent with this interpretation, the impact of recall difficulty was attenuated when participants were led to attribute it to the nature of the task.

These results are consistent with related research that highlighted the role of phenomenal experiences in memory judgments (see Jacoby et al., 1989; Kelley & Jacoby, 1996, for reviews). This research focused on the ease or difficulty with which a specific item comes to mind. Extending this work, the present findings demonstrate that recall experiences not only may influence judgments pertaining to specific items, but also may influence assessments of the quality of one's memory in general. Moreover, the present manipulations illustrate that the sheer attempt to recall a large amount of material may result in inferences of poor memory, even when the recall attempt is successful, as was the case in the present study.

At a general level, our findings contribute to the research on the judgmental processes that underlie respondents' answers to questions about their memories (see Dixon, 1989, and Herrmann, 1982, for reviews). They draw attention to the questions that have gone largely unnoticed in this literature: What are the strategies that people use in assessing the quality of their memory? Do they rely on the number of events that can be retrieved or on the subjective experience accompanying the recall? What is the role of attribution in this process? Our findings also have important implications for clinicians and researchers interested in the validity of self-reported amnesia for childhood events following memory work (Belli & Loftus, 1994; Belli, Winkielman, Read, Schwarz, & Lynn, in press; Ceci & Loftus, 1994; Lindsay & Read, 1994). Our findings highlight that reports of poor childhood memory may simply reflect the fact that recalling childhood events is more difficult than people think—leading them to infer poorer memory the more events they (successfully) try to recall.

Acknowledgments—The authors would like to thank Kent Harber, Tim Ketelaar, Barbel Knauper, Magdalena Ponurska, Don Read, Uli Schimmack, Bob Wyer, and two anonymous reviewers for their help with this article.

REFERENCES

Begg, I., Armour, V., & Kerr, T. (1985). On believing what we remember. *Canadian Journal of Behavioral Science, 17,* 199–214.

Belli, R.F., & Loftus, E.F. (1994). Recovered memories of childhood abuse: A source monitoring perspective. In S.J. Lynn & J. Rhue (Eds.), *Dissociation: Theory, clinical, and research perspectives* (pp. 415–433). New York: Guilford Press.

Main—and non-intuitive!— finding.

Questions the researchers tried to address in the present study.

Belli, R.F., Winkielman, P., Read, J.D., Schwarz, N., & Lynn, S.J. (in press). Recalling more childhood events leads to judgments of poorer memory: Implications for the recovered/false memory debate. *Psychonomic Bulletin & Review.*

Ceci, S.J., & Loftus, E.F. (1994). 'Memory work': A royal road to false memories? *Applied Cognitive Psychology, 8,* 351–364.

Dixon, R.A. (1989). Questionnaire research on metamemory and aging. In L.W. Poon, D.C. Rubin, & B.A. Wilson (Eds.), *Everyday cognition in adulthood and late life* (pp. 394–415). New York: Cambridge University Press.

Herrmann, D.J. (1982). Know thy memory: The use of questionnaires to assess and study memory. *Psychological Bulletin, 92,* 434–452.

Jacoby, L.L., Kelley, C.M., & Dywan, J. (1989). Memory attributions. In H.L. Roediger, III, & F.I.M. Craik (Eds.), *Varieties of memory and consciousness: Essays in honor of Endel Tulving* (pp. 391–422). Hillsdale, NJ: Erlbaum.

Kelley, C.M., & Jacoby, L.L. (1996). Memory attributions: Remembering, knowing, and feeling of knowing. In L.M. Reder (Ed.), *Implicit memory and metacognition* (pp. 287–308). Mahwah, NJ: Erlbaum.

Kelley, C.M., & Lindsay, D.S. (1993). Remembering mistaken for knowing: Ease of retrieval as a basis for confidence in answers to general knowledge questions. *Journal of Memory and Language, 32,* 1–24.

Lindsay, D.S., & Kelley, C.M. (1996). Creating illusions of familiarity in a cued recall remember/know paradigm. *Journal of Memory and Language, 35,* 197–211.

Lindsay, D.S., & Read, J.D. (1994). Psychotherapy and memories of childhood sexual abuse: A cognitive perspective. *Applied Cognitive Psychology, 8,* 281–338.

Rosenthal, R., & Rosnow, R.L. (1985). *Contrast analysis: Focused comparisons in the analysis of variance.* Cambridge, England: Cambridge University Press.

Ross, C.A. (1989). *Multiple personality disorder: Diagnosis, clinical features, and treatment.* New York: Wiley.

Schwarz, N. (in press). Accessible content and accessibility experiences: The interplay of declarative and experiential information in judgment. In J. Metcalfe & F. Strack (Eds.), Metacognition [Special issue]. *Personality and Social Psychology Review.*

Schwarz, N., Bless, H., Strack, F., Klumpp, G., Rittenauer-Schatka, H., & Simons, A. (1991). Ease of retrieval as information: Another look at the availability heuristic. *Journal of Personality and Social Psychology, 61,* 195–202.

Schwarz, N., & Clore, G.L. (1996). Feelings and phenomenal experiences. In E.T. Higgins & A. Kruglanski (Eds.), *Social psychology: A handbook of basic principles* (pp. 433–465). New York: Guilford Press.

Tversky, A., & Kahneman, D. (1973). Availability: A heuristic for judging frequency and probability. *Cognitive Psychology, 5,* 207–232.

Wänke, M., Schwarz, N., & Bless, H. (1995). The availability heuristic revisited: Experienced ease of retrieval in mundane frequency estimates. *Acta Psychologica, 89,* 83–90.

Whittlesea, B.W.A. (1993). Illusions of familiarity. *Journal of Experimental Psychology: Learning, Memory, and Cognition, 19,* 1235–1253.

POST-ARTICLE DISCUSSION

Let's talk about some elements of an excellent scientific paper. The paper should address an interesting topic, ideally one that most people can relate to. A good paper should consider the problem by testing multiple theories and should clearly explain those theories and their differing predictions in the introduction. The paper should clearly explain the design, and the design should be solid, such that readers are confident in its ability to test the theories regarding the problem at hand. The paper should clearly explain, using an economy of words, why the data support one theory and other competing theories are not supported. Finally, the paper should

(Continued)

(Continued)

give an honest evaluation of the experiment limitations and suggest avenues for future researchers who want to address unanswered questions that the present study did not address.

The paper by Winkielman, Schwarz, and Belli (1998) you just read does all those things very well. Good science tells a story of the problem, why it is important, how the researchers designed their study to address the problem, why the data either did or did not support the predictions, and what the unanswered questions are for future researchers. Good research should not be written in a flowery, jargonistic, or pretentious way. The story the researcher tells should be interesting, be compelling, flow logically, and argue its point convincingly and concisely. The papers throughout this book were chosen for their excellence in hitting most if not all of these points. Some papers, mostly the ones written long ago, are a bit unusual in terms of their structure and writing, but they make up for that in their importance and pioneering contributions to social psychology. Overall, you should develop a good sense from this book about good scientific writing, as the researchers in these papers set a high bar by which you should measure all future research papers.

THINGS TO THINK ABOUT

1. Is there a different way the researchers could have conveyed to the subjects that the memory task was easy or difficult? A way that was stronger and had more of an impact on subjects?

2. The authors didn't find any differences in the difficulty people experienced in the recall of 12 events when they were told to expect it was easy compared to those who were given no information about task difficulty. Do you think this result was due to the fact that they didn't specify what memories subjects should try to retrieve?

3. How do you think most people rate the completeness of their memory: by amount of memories retrieved or by the ease with which they can retrieve their memories?

4. What constituted a retrieved memory in this study? Did the authors specify if and how they measured the retrieved memories? If not, should they have done so? How detailed does a retrieved memory need to be to be counted in this study?

5. Do you think people are more invested in knowing that their memory for personal events is good or that their immediate overall short-term memory is good? That is, does the type of memory used or accessed matter in an experiment like this?

8

Social Influence

Our world is a social world, full of people we interact with daily or just occasionally. Those people have varying levels of influence on our own behavior. Of course, we will never interact with the vast majority of people on the planet, but even some of those can have an impact on our behavior. The overall mission of social psychologists is to understand how we interact with others and how others influence our behavior. Specifically, research on social influence focuses on how the real or imagined pressure from others causes us to change our behavior. Let us focus on this definition for a moment. In social psychology, research has shown that the best way to understand and to predict how an individual will behave is to find out how he perceives or construes the situation. Contrary to the behaviorists who imbue the environment (and stimuli in it) with all the power to elicit behavior, social psychologists say that the better predictor of behavior is an understanding of how the person perceives that environment (and stimulus).

For example, let's take the situation of getting a speeding ticket. For some people, that is a horrible event, and it will really make them upset for weeks or even longer. On the other hand, for some people, it is no big deal, and as soon as the officer drives away, these people may throw the ticket in their back seat and forget about it seconds later. It is the same event, but the two different ways of perceiving it result in two vastly different moods and behaviors. Another example is a piece of art. Suppose we have 10 people all looking at Renoir's famous painting "Luncheon of the Boating Party" at the Phillips Collection in Washington, D.C. It is the same painting, but it will have 10 different effects on the thoughts, feelings, and behaviors of each of these people, because each approaches the painting with his or her own unique learning history and personality. Coming back to our definition then, we see that equally important to our behavior is not only the direct influence that someone has on us (e.g., asking us to change our behavior) but the *imagined pressure* that we think others are putting on us to change our behavior. In this introduction, we explore three major types of social influence: conformity, compliance, and obedience. As is the case with all of the brief introductions to each chapter in this book, this is not intended to be an exhaustive review (see Guadagno, 2018; Hogg, 2010, for more extensive reviews) but a general overview of major themes in social influence research.

CONFORMITY

On a continuum of social influence, the mildest type of social pressure occurs when we perceive that there are social norms to which we must adhere. Remember a social norm is an unwritten rule. So when we are conforming, what we are doing is changing our behavior in response to what we think is a social norm governing our behavior in that context. For example, what is the main social norm operating in an elevator? That's right: Stand still, be quiet, and stare forward at the door. That is inevitably what most people do. There is no law saying we HAVE to behave that way on an elevator, but it is one of those unwritten rules (social norms) that cause us to modify our behavior on the elevator. Similarly, when you are entering a public building and there is someone several steps behind you also intending to enter the building, what do you do? Exactly: You hold the door open for the person. Again, there is no formal law saying we should behave that way, but we do it because we have learned that is the polite, civil thing to do in society. A final example: What you wear each day is a reflection of your generally conforming to unwritten norms or standards for how people in our society clothe themselves. Unless you are Lady Gaga, you cannot get by with wearing a dress made out of meat to the supermarket without drawing a lot of ridicule, scorn, and unwanted attention.

One of the first experiments to examine the power of conformity was conducted by Solomon Asch (1951, 1956). Each subject came to the lab, where there were five other subjects seated in a half-circle of numbered desks, with Desk 6 open, where the subject sat. (By the way, the other "subjects" were confederates working with the experimenter, pretending to be subjects.) The experimenter explained that their job was to look at a series of cards and indicate which line (in a group of lines) matched the main, standard line. They had a choice of three lines per card. They went around the table for each card, and each subject said aloud what line he or she believed was the match.

After a few uneventful cards where the lines were all fairly obvious and everyone was in agreement, the confederates then identified a clearly wrong line as the match. They were all in agreement. By the time the real subject must give her answer, there were five other people who had said the wrong line was the right line. It is sort of like someone asking, "What color is the sky?" and five people in front of you all saying it is green, and you're thinking, "Huh? It is blue. Everyone knows that. But, what are the odds that they are all wrong and I am right? Maybe it IS green." This tremendous pressure leads to self-doubt, and in this condition of a unanimous majority, 37% of subjects conformed to the majority and gave the same answer. In another variation, one confederate disagreed with the majority and said the obvious correct answer. When this happened (i.e., when the subject now saw someone disagreeing with the majority), the subject felt less pressure to conform, and in those instances, only 10% of the subjects still conformed to the majority.

Why do people conform? Two main motives: the desire to be correct (what researchers call "informational influence") and the desire to be liked (called "normative influence"). When there is a presidential election in the United States, one problem used to occur on election night. The polls would close at 8 p.m. on the East Coast, and television stations there would report exit polling and returns and would begin making predictions about which candidate was in the lead or who would win. Why is that a problem? The West Coast voters still had 3 hours of voting left to go (and voters in Hawaii had 6 more hours!). These East Coast projections would influence a lot of voters on the West Coast, and that, critics argued, was a negative influence on the whole voting process. West Coast voters who wanted to be right would listen to the projections and vote for who was leading or projected to win, so they could say they voted for the winner and were on the "winning team." Seems silly, but that was such a concern that now most stations have a blackout on election night so that East Coast information doesn't get announced until after polls close on the West Coast.

From the time we were children, we have known what it is like to be left out of a group. It doesn't feel good. So most people "go along to get along." That is, they tend to conform to the group because they know that in doing so, the other group members will like them. If a bunch of your friends want to play kickball and you don't and you say, "Let's ride bikes instead," the group is likely to get irritated with you and go ahead with their plans to play kickball without you. Why do people get irritated at others who don't conform to the group? We don't like someone who doesn't play by the rules. We think, "Who do they think they are? Do they think they are special? We are all playing this, so why ruin things by not going along?" This thinking continues into adulthood and in the workplace. People don't like those who upset the system or aren't team players, and they are often shunned, passed over for promotion, transferred, or fired. Other studies have found that people are more likely to conform when the size of the group is three or more (Bond & Smith, 1996), when the group is cohesive (Crandall, 1988), and when one has not already publicly committed to a position (Robertson, 2006).

COMPLIANCE

Whereas conformity is the mildest form of social influence and is an essentially self-originated, self-initiated, and imagined pressure, compliance represents a more direct pressure whereby the individual is asked directly to change his behavior. This can take various forms from passive advertisements ("Buy our product!") and bumper stickers asking you to vote for a particular candidate to people directly asking you in person to change your behavior.

If I want you to comply with my request, I can exert pressure on you in a number of ways. French and Raven (1959) suggested six ways in particular, which they refer to as "social power." I can promise you a **reward** if you comply, or I can promise that something negative (**coercion**) will happen for you if you do not comply with my request. I can make a persuasive argument why you should comply (**information**), or I can suggest you comply because I have special knowledge and **expertise** in this area. I could ask that you comply because I know you want to be like me (**referent**) or because I have the **legitimate authority** to ask you to do something.

Other studies have found that there are certain cognitive "tricks" one can employ to enhance the likelihood that the requestee will comply with your request. For example, using the **"foot in the door"** method, I will ask you to commit to a small behavior (e.g., to donate 25 cents a week to a charity), and if you agree, then I might soon ask you to commit to a larger request (e.g., donate $25 a month to a charity). Because you have already shown a positive attitude toward donating to charity, you will be more likely to also agree to the larger request. One reason for this is that people have a strong desire to be consistent (Festinger, 1957) in their thoughts and behaviors. If I have shown a positive attitude toward the charity by saying yes to the small request, I will look like a hypocrite if I later refuse to support that charity with a bigger donation. Using the **"door in the face"** technique, I will ask you for an outrageously large request. When you refuse, I will then follow up with a smaller request (which, of course, is what I wanted from you all along). When it looks like I am compromising, you'll feel more compelled to comply with my smaller request, as a way of rewarding my compromise. This technique significantly enhances compliance rates. Some data suggest about 17% of the time, when a respondent is asked for the small request by itself, the respondent will comply with the request. But when the door in the face technique is used, that compliance rate (to the small request) goes up to 50% (Cialdini et al., 1975)! In the **"lowballing"** method, the requester gets the other person to comply with a request on the basis of incomplete information. The requester then later increases the request by revealing hidden conditions (e.g., "the fine print," or extra fees, costs, work, etc.). This is a tactic stereotypically associated with unscrupulous car salespersons. They get the person to agree to buy the car, then reveal extra charges as they are writing up the contract ("Oh, you wanted a steering wheel? That will be another $200."). Again, the motive for consistency is a strong reason why this technique works. Finally, retailers are very familiar with the **"that's not all"** method of inducing compliance in customers. In this approach, the requester starts with a large request but then appears to decrease the size of the request with sales, discounts, or bonuses. We all like to feel like we're getting a good deal when we buy something. We like to get the biggest value for our money. So what some retailers do is have a price tag on a product that includes the "suggested retail" price (which is always the highest) and then a big red slash through it and a much smaller price for a short time only. A simple experiment (that I always discuss in lectures) illustrates this. Burger (1986) went to a college campus, set up tables with signs that said "Cupcakes for Sale" but no price. When people came up and asked how much they cost, he would tell half of them "75 cents." To the other half, he would say, "$1, but because we are closing soon, you can have them for 75 cents." Results showed that people were more likely to buy a cupcake

in the "that's not all" condition (73%) compared to the 75 cent only condition (44%). Those numbers mean big money to retailers.

OBEDIENCE

At the far end of the spectrum of social influence, furthest away from the imagined pressure of conformity, is obedience. In obedience, one person is telling another to change her behavior. There is no request; it is an order, and the person ordering expects the other individual to obey and change her behavior accordingly. Under what conditions are people more or less likely to obey another person? This question formed the centerpiece of one of the most famous (and critics say *in*famous) programs of experiments in social psychology, and perhaps in all of psychology. I am referring to the obedience experiments conducted by Stanley Milgram in the 1960s. Normally I'd discuss the experiments in detail here, but one of the papers you are about to read is the classic paper by Milgram explaining the results of his obedience experiments, so here we'll just discuss some of the other findings on obedience that Milgram and others discovered.

Bickman (1974) had a man walk around in the city wearing either normal clothes (jeans and a T-shirt) or a security guard uniform. The man would then walk up to people and order them to do something (e.g., "Give that man change for the pay phone!" or "Pick up that bag!"). In the normal clothes condition, essentially no one obeyed the order. When told to do something by the man wearing a security guard uniform, nearly all of the respondents did as they were ordered. People didn't stop to analyze in detail his uniform or the legitimacy of his order. Milgram's research confirms what Bickman found: People tend to obey even the most minimal sign of authority. When Milgram did variations of his experiment, he found that certain factors made a big difference in contributing to obedience rates. For example, the prestige of Yale University (where Milgram did his research) made a difference in the subjects' mind (they likely thought that Yale wouldn't let any harm come to subjects in any research). Obedience dropped to 48% from its original level (I won't reveal that here, but you will read that in the Milgram paper in this chapter) when he ran the experiment in an office building off campus. When he had the learner receive electrical shots in the same room as the subject (called the "teacher," who was administering the shocks to the learner [a confederate]), obedience dropped to 40%. When the subject had to push the learner's hand down on a metal shock plate to get shocked, obedience dropped to 30%.

When an ordinary person was put in charge of the experiment, obedience dropped to 20%. When the experimenter was not in the lab room but was phoning in his orders, obedience dropped to 19%. When subjects saw two previous subjects disobey the experimenter, only 10% of those subjects obeyed the experimenter orders. So, the authority of the person making the order to obey, the proximity of the person ordering to the target of the order, and the context in which the order is issued all contribute to influence obedience in everyday life. Milgram's research was pioneering, illuminating, and controversial. Most would say that the contribution of his obedience research to our scientific knowledge in psychology is difficult to overestimate, and that outweighs concerns that critics level at the research.

INTRODUCTION TO READING 8.1

Milgram (1963)*

Ever since he was a young boy growing up in New York City, Stanley Milgram was aware of the suffering of his fellow Jews at the hands of the Nazis in the Holocaust. At the end of World War II, Milgram and his family listened closely to the radio broadcast of the Nuremberg war crime trials of the Nazis, and he remembered hearing the defendants saying they were not responsible for their war crimes because they were just doing what they were told. This outrageous denial of responsibility for their crimes may have planted the seed in Milgram's mind to try to further understand how people respond to pressure to obey authority figures. While a graduate student in psychology, Milgram was interested in extending the famous conformity research of his advisor, Solomon Asch (1951), to look at how people would respond to group pressure to do something they normally wouldn't do. He thought he might look at cross-cultural differences in this conformity pressure, but he never got the funding or logistics or full approval of his advisor to do that. After he received his PhD, Milgram took a position as a professor at Yale University. When thinking about his extension of Asch's study, he thought he wanted something more compelling than having subjects match lines on a board. He wanted to look at a "phenomenon of great consequence" (Blass, 2004, pp. 61–62). He thought he would have a group administer increas-ing amounts of shock to another person, and then he would examine the extent to which a subject would conform to the group's behavior in shocking another person. But, to do this, he needed to know the baseline level of the extent to which the individual would shock that other person without group pressure. At this thought, Milgram realized he had his experiment idea. The question became this: How far will the average person go to hurt someone else (with increasingly higher electric shocks) when ordered to do so by the experimenter?

This paper is probably the most famous (and infamous) experiment in all of social psychology and had a tremendous influence on our understanding of obedience. It also had the unforeseen effect of sparking controversy about its ethics, which led to the creation of institutional research boards (IRBs) in colleges and universities around the world to ensure all research done on campus would conform to specific ethical conditions. This research also made Stanley Milgram a household name. Sadly, he died at a rather young age (51). Had he lived longer, who knows what other great contributions he could have made to social psychology with his unique, clever analysis of human behavior. Enjoy the paper, and we'll talk afterward!

---

*Most of the material from this introduction was adapted from Russell (2011).

Reading 8.1

Behavioral Study Of Obedience[1]

STANLEY MILGRAM[2]

This article describes a procedure for the study of destructive obedience in the laboratory. It consists of ordering a naive S to administer increasingly more severe punishment to a victim in the context of a learning experiment. Punishment is administered by means of a shock generator with 30 graded switches ranging from Slight Shock to Danger: Severe Shock. The victim is a confederate of the E. The primary dependent variable is the maximum shock the S is willing to administer before he refuses to continue further. 26 Ss obeyed the experimental commands fully, and administered the highest shock on the generator. 14 Ss broke off the experiment at some point after the victim protested and refused to provide further answers. The procedure created extreme levels of nervous tension in some Ss. Profuse sweating, trembling, and stuttering were typical expressions of this emotional disturbance. One unexpected sign of tension—yet to be explained— was the regular occurrence of nervous laughter, which in some Ss developed into uncontrollable seizures. The variety of interesting behavioral dynamics observed in the experiment, the reality of the situation for the S, and the possibility of parametric variation within the framework of the procedure, point to the fruitfulness of further study.

Obedience is as basic an element in the structure of social life as one can point to. Some system of authority is a requirement of all communal living, and it is only the man dwelling in isolation who is not forced to respond, through defiance or submission, to the commands of others. Obedience, as a determinant of behavior, is of particular relevance to our time. It has been reliably established that from 1933–45 millions of innocent persons were systematically slaughtered on command. Gas chambers were built, death camps were guarded, daily quotas of corpses were produced with the same efficiency as the manufacture of appliances. These inhumane policies may have originated in the mind of a single person, but they could only be carried out on a massive scale if a very large number of persons obeyed orders.

Obedience is the psychological mechanism that links individual action to political purpose. It is the dispositional cement that binds men to systems of authority. Facts of recent history and observation in daily life suggest that for many persons obedience may be a deeply ingrained behavior tendency, indeed, a prepotent impulse overriding training in ethics, sympathy, and moral conduct. C. P. Snow (1961) points to its importance when he writes:

> This is one of the key questions that motivated Milgram to conduct his studies of obedience: do humans have a default tendency to obey?

[1] This research was supported by a grant (NSF G-17916) from the National Science Foundation. Exploratory studies conducted in 1960 were supported by a grant from the Higgins Fund at Yale University. The research assistance of Alan C. Elms and Jon Wayland is gratefully acknowledged.
[2] Now at Harvard University.

When you think of the long and gloomy history of man, you will find more hideous crimes have been committed in the name of obedience than have ever been committed in the name of rebellion. If you doubt that, read William Shirer's "Rise and Fall of the Third Reich." The German Officer Corps were brought up in the most rigorous code of obedience . . . in the name of obedience they were party to, and assisted in, the most wicked large scale actions in the history of the world [p. 24].

While the particular form of obedience dealt with in the present study has its antecedents in these episodes, it must not be thought all obedience entails acts of aggression against others. Obedience serves numerous productive functions. Indeed, the very life of society is predicated on its existence. Obedience may be ennobling and educative and refer to acts of charity and kindness, as well as to destruction.

General Procedure

A procedure was devised which seems useful as a tool for studying obedience (Milgram, 1961). It consists of ordering a naive subject to administer electric shock to a victim. A simulated shock generator is used, with 30 clearly marked voltage levels that range from 15 to 450 volts. The instrument bears verbal designations that range from Slight Shock to Danger: Severe Shock. The responses of the victim, who is a trained confederate of the experimenter, are standardized. The orders to administer shocks are given to the naive subject in the context of a "learning experiment" ostensibly set up to study the effects of punishment on memory. As the experiment proceeds the naive subject is commanded to administer increasingly more intense shocks to the victim, even to the point of reaching the level marked Danger: Severe Shock. Internal resistances become stronger, and at a certain point the subject refuses to go on with the experiment. Behavior prior to this rupture is considered "obedience," in that the subject complies with the commands of the experimenter. The point of rupture is the act of disobedience. A quantitative value is assigned to the subject's performance based on the maximum intensity shock he is willing to administer before he refuses to participate further. Thus for any particular subject and for any particular experimental condition the degree of obedience may be specified with a numerical value. The crux of the study is to systematically vary the factors believed to alter the degree of obedience to the experimental commands.

The technique allows important variables to be manipulated at several points in the experiment. One may vary aspects of the source of command, content and form of command, instrumentalities for its execution, target object, general social setting, etc. The problem, therefore, is not one of designing increasingly more numerous experimental conditions, but of selecting those that best illuminate the *process* of obedience from the socio psychological standpoint.

Related Studies

The inquiry bears an important relation to philosophic analyses of obedience and authority (Arendt, 1958; Friedrich, 1958; Weber, 1947), an early experimental study of obedience by Frank (1944), studies in "authoritarianism" (Adorno, Frenkel-Brunswik, Levinson, & Sanford, 1950; Rokeach, 1961), and a recent series of analytic and empirical studies in social power (Cartwright, 1959). It owes much to the long concern with *suggestion* in social psychology, both in its normal forms (e.g., Binet, 1900) and in its clinical manifestations (Charcot, 1881). But it derives, in the first instance, from direct observation of a social fact; the individual who is commanded by a legitimate authority ordinarily obeys. Obedience comes easily and often. It is a ubiquitous and indispensable feature of social life.

METHOD

Subjects

The subjects were 40 males between the ages of 20 and 50, drawn from New Haven and the surrounding communities. Subjects were obtained by a newspaper advertisement and direct mail solicitation. Those who responded to the appeal believed they were to participate in a study of memory and learning at Yale University. A wide range of occupations is represented in the sample. Typical subjects were postal clerks, high school teachers, salesmen, engineers, and laborers. Subjects ranged in educational level from one who had not finished elementary school, to those who had doctorate and other professional degrees. They were paid $4.50 for their participation in the experiment. However, subjects were told that payment was simply for coming to the laboratory, and that the money was theirs no matter what happened after they arrived. Table 1 shows the proportion of age and occupational types assigned to the experimental condition.

Personnel and Locale

The experiment was conducted on the grounds of Yale University in the elegant interaction laboratory. (This detail is relevant to the perceived legitimacy of the experiment. In further variations, the experiment was dissociated from the university, with consequences for performance.) The role of experimenter was played by a 31-year-old high school teacher of biology. His manner was impassive, and his appearance somewhat stern throughout the experiment. He was dressed in a gray technician's coat. The victim was played by a 47-year-old accountant, trained for the role; he was of Irish American stock, whom most observers found mild mannered and likable.

Procedure

One naive subject and one victim (an accomplice) performed in each experiment. A pretext had to be devised that would justify the administration of electric shock by the naive subject. This was effectively accomplished by the cover story. After a general introduction on the presumed relation between punishment and learning, subjects were told:

Today's researchers refer to an accomplice like this as a "confederate"—someone who works with the experimenter, pretending to be another subject in the study, but who is acting a specific way to influence the real subject.

TABLE 1   Distribution of Age and Occupational Types in the Experiment

Occupations	20–29 years n	30–39 years n	40–50 years n	Percentage of total (Occupations)
Workers, skilled and unskilled	4	5	6	37.5
Sales, business and white-collar	3	6	7	40.0
Professional	1	5	3	22.5
Percentage of total (Age)	20	40	40	

Note. Total $N = 40$.

But actually, we know *very little* about the effect of punishment on learning, because almost no truly scientific studies have been made of it in human beings.

For instance, we don't know how *much* punishment is best for learning—and we don't know how much difference it makes as to who is giving the punishment, whether an adult learns best from a younger or an older person than himself—or many things of that sort.

So in this study we are bringing together a number of adults of different occupations and ages. And we're asking some of them to be teachers and some of them to be learners.

We want to find out just what effect different people have on each other as teachers and learners, and also what effect *punishment* will have on learning in this situation.

Therefore, I'm going to ask one of you to be the teacher here tonight and the other one to be the learner.

Does either of you have a preference?

Subjects then drew slips of paper from a hat to determine who would be the teacher and who would be the learner in the experiment. The drawing was rigged so that the naive subject was always the teacher and the accomplice always the learner. (Both slips contained the word "Teacher.") Immediately after the drawing, the teacher and learner were taken to an adjacent room and the learner was strapped into an "electric chair" apparatus.

The experimenter explained that the straps were to prevent excessive movement while the learner was being shocked. The effect was to make it impossible for him to escape from the situation. An electrode was attached to the learner's wrist, and electrode paste was applied "to avoid blisters and burns." Subjects were told that the electrode was attached to the shock generator in the adjoining room.

In order to improve credibility the experimenter declared, in response to a question by the learner: "Although the shocks can be extremely painful, they cause no permanent tissue damage."

Learning task. The lesson administered by the subject was a paired-associate learning task. The subject read a series of word pairs to the learner, and then read the first word of the pair along with four terms. The learner was to indicate which of the four terms had originally been paired with the first word. He communicated his answer by pressing one of four switches in front of him, which in turn lit up one of four numbered quadrants in an answerbox located atop the shock generator.

Shock generator. The instrument panel consists of 30 lever switches set in a horizontal line. Each switch is clearly labeled with a voltage designation that ranges from 15 to 450 volts. There is a 15-volt increment from one switch to the next going from left to right. In addition, the following verbal designations are clearly indicated for groups of four switches going from left to right: Slight Shock, Moderate Shock, Strong Shock, Very Strong Shock, Intense Shock, Extreme Intensity Shock, Danger: Severe Shock. (Two switches after this last designation are simply marked XXX.)

The question that the learner asks is (this is not a precise quote, but pretty close) "a few years ago I was diagnosed with a heart condition at the VA. Nothing too serious, but I was wondering, um, how strong are these shocks? How painful are they?" The real subject is standing there at the doorway to the lab room where the confederate is being strapped to his chair and hears this conversation. This establishes that this middle-aged man has a heart condition.

I always thought this was kind of funny. Like, "these shocks are SO intense, we can't even think of a label for them!"

Upon depressing a switch: a pilot light corresponding to each switch is illuminated in bright red; an electric buzzing is heard; an electric blue light, labeled "voltage energizer," flashes; the dial on the voltage meter swings to the right; various relay clicks are sounded.

The upper left-hand corner of the generator is labeled Shock Generator, Type ZLB, Dyson Instrument Company, Waltham, Mass. Output 15 Volts–450 Volts.

Details of the instrument were carefully handled to insure an appearance of authenticity. The panel was engraved by precision industrial engravers, and all components were of high quality. No subject in the experiment suspected that the instrument was merely a simulated shock generator.[3]

Sample shock. Each naive subject is given a sample shock on the shock generator, prior to beginning his run as teacher. This shock is always 45 volts, and is applied by pressing the third switch of the generator. The shock is applied to the wrist of the naive subject, and has its source in a 45-volt battery wired into the generator. This further convinces the subject of the authenticity of the generator.

Shock instructions. The subject is told to administer a shock to the learner each time he gives a wrong response. Moreover—and this is the key command—the subject is instructed to "move one level higher on the shock generator each time the learner flashes a wrong answer." He is also instructed to announce the voltage level before administering a shock. This serves to continually remind subjects of the increasing intensity of shocks administered to the learner.

Preliminary and regular run. Pretests revealed that the procedure of reading words and administering shocks requires some practice before it can be handled smoothly. Therefore, immediately preceding the regular run, the teacher is given a preliminary series of 10 words to read to the learner. There are 3 neutral words in the practice series (i.e., words that the learner answers correctly), so that shocks are administered for 7 of the words, with the maximum shock at 105 volts (moderate shock). Almost all subjects master the procedure by the time the preliminary run is over.

Subjects are then presented with a second list, and are told that the procedure is the same as for the first list; the experimenter adds, however:

> When you get to the bottom of the list, repeat it over again, and continue giving shocks, until the learner has learned all the pairs correctly.

The experimenter instructs the subject to,

> start from 15 volts and increase the shock level one step each time the learner gives a wrong answer.

One of the great aspects of Milgram's obedience experiments is that he goes through a lot of effort to convey to the subject that what subjects think is happening (delivering a sample shock to the subject, shocking a middle-aged guy with a heart condition, etc.) is really happening. It all seems very authentic, and few if any subjects were suspicious.

[3]A related technique, making use of a shock generator, was reported by Buss (1961) for the study of aggression in the laboratory. Despite the considerable similarity of technical detail in the experimental procedures, both investigators proceeded in ignorance of the other's work. Milgram provided plans and photographs of his shock generator, experimental procedure, and first results in a report to the National Science Foundation in January 1961. This report received only limited circulation. Buss reported his procedure 6 months later, but to a wider audience. Subsequently, technical information and reports were exchanged. The present article was first received in the Editor's office on December 27, 1961; it was resubmitted with deletions on July 27, 1962.

In the famous documentary Milgram made of his experiments, this isn't the case. The learner makes little sounds like "ouch!" or "ow!" or "oooh!" when they receive shocks lower than about 75 volts. Then at that point, the learner starts saying things like "I've changed my mind, this hurts and I don't want to do this anymore. Let me out!" (this is a paraphrasing). The calls and pleadings to be let out grow more fervent as shocks near 250 volts. Then they turn to screams and saying his heart is bothering him and begging to be let out. Then after 315, he stops responding. Naturally, what is the subject thinking?

Feedback from the victim. In all conditions the learner gives a predetermined set of responses to the word pair test, based on a schedule of approximately three wrong answers to one correct answer. In the present experimental condition no vocal response or other sign of protest is heard from the learner until Shock Level 300 is reached. When the 300-volt shock is administered, the learner pounds on the wall of the room in which he is bound to the electric chair. The pounding can be heard by the subject. From this point on, the learner's answers no longer appear on the four-way panel.

At this juncture, subjects ordinarily turn to the experimenter for guidance. The experimenter instructs the subject to treat the absence of a response as a wrong answer, and to shock the subject according to the usual schedule. He advises the subjects to allow 5–10 seconds before considering no response as a wrong answer, and to increase the shock level one step each time the learner fails to respond correctly. The learner's pounding is repeated after the 315-volt shock is administered; afterwards he is not heard from, nor do his answers reappear on the four-way signal box.

"Treat a non-response as a wrong response." Holy cow, really? That is a cold experimenter, right? The experimenter calmly appears to be unconcerned about the learner who was just a few seconds ago yelling about his heart, begging to be let out and now is silent. You would think that nearly all subjects at this point are thinking "this is ridiculous, I am not going to keep shocking that guy, he could be passed out or worse. I am going to stop." But you'd be wrong.

Experimenter feedback. At various points in the experiment the subject may turn to the experimenter for advice on whether he should continue to administer shocks. Or he may indicate that he does not wish to go on. It was important to standardize the experimenter's responses to these inquiries and reactions.

If the subject indicated his unwillingness to go on, the experimenter responded with a sequence of "prods," using as many as necessary to bring the subject into line.

Prod 1: Please continue *or* Please go on.

Prod 2: The experiment requires that you continue.

Prod 3: It is absolutely essential that you continue.

Prod 4: You have no other choice, you *must* go on.

The prods were always made in sequence: Only if Prod 1 had been unsuccessful, could Prod 2 be used. If the subject refused to obey the experimenter after Prod 4, the experiment was terminated. The experimenter's tone of voice was at all times firm, but not impolite. The sequence was begun anew on each occasion that the subject balked or showed reluctance to follow orders.

Notice these are fairly benign, calm commands. They aren't hostile or abusive. Subjects also know they are free to leave at any point in the experiment and they will still be compensated for their participation. The point with these commands is that they are the mildest types of orders, because Milgram is seeking to learn whether such minimal orders (or demands for obedience) can have an effect on the subjects' behavior.

Special prods. If the subject asked if the learner was liable to suffer permanent physical injury, the experimenter said:

Although the shocks may be painful, there is no permanent tissue damage, so please go on. [Followed by Prods 2, 3, and 4 if necessary.]

If the subject said that the learner did not want to go on, the experimenter replied:

Whether the learner likes it or not, you must go on until he has learned all the word pairs correctly. So please go on. [Followed by Prods 2, 3, and 4 if necessary.]

Dependent Measures

The primary dependent measure for any subject is the maximum shock he administers before he refuses to go any further. In principle this may vary from 0 (for a subject who refuses to administer even the first shock) to 30 (for a subject who administers the highest shock on the generator). A subject who breaks off the experiment at any point prior to administering the thirtieth shock level is termed a *defiant* subject. One who complies with experimental commands fully, and proceeds to administer all shock levels commanded, is termed an *obedient* subject.

Further records. With few exceptions, experimental sessions were recorded on magnetic tape. Occasional photographs were taken through one-way mirrors. Notes were kept on any unusual behavior occurring during the course of the experiments. On occasion, additional observers were directed to write objective descriptions of the subjects' behavior. The latency and duration of shocks were measured by accurate timing devices.

Interview and dehoax. Following the experiment, subjects were interviewed; open-ended questions, projective measures, and attitude scales were employed. After the interview, procedures were undertaken to assure that the subject would leave the laboratory in a state of well being. A friendly reconciliation was arranged between the subject and the victim, and an effort was made to reduce any tensions that arose as a result of the experiment.

Preliminary Notions

Before giving an account of the experimental results, it is instructive to consider how persons predict others will perform when commanded to administer powerful shocks to another person. Fourteen Yale seniors, all psychology majors, were provided with a detailed description of the experimental situation. They were asked to reflect carefully on it, and to predict the behavior of 100 hypothetical subjects. More specifically, they were instructed to plot the distribution of obedience of "100 Americans of diverse occupations, and ranging in age from 20 to 50 years," who were placed in the experimental situation.

There was considerable agreement among the respondents on the expected behavior of hypothetical subjects. All respondents predicted that only an insignificant minority would go through to the end of the shock series. (The estimates ranged from 0 to 3%; i.e., the most "pessimistic" member of the class predicted that of 100 persons, 3 would continue through to the most potent shock available on the shock generator—450 volts.) The class mean was 1.2%. The question was also posed informally to colleagues of the author, and the most general feeling was that few if any subjects would go beyond the designation Very Strong Shock.

Result of Experiment 1

Subjects accept situation. With few exceptions subjects were convinced of the reality of the experimental situation, that they were administering shocks to another person, and the most potent shocks were extremely painful. In the post-experimental interview subjects were asked: "How painful to the learner were the last few shocks that you administered to him?" Subjects were instructed to indicate their answers on a printed 14-point scale ranging from "Not at all painful" to "Extremely painful." The modal response was 14 (Extremely painful) with the mean at 13.42.

Signs of extreme tension. Many subjects showed signs of nervousness in the experimental situation, and especially upon administering the more powerful shocks. In a large number of cases

This is very important. Subjects need to know that they really were not shocking the middle-aged man, and their meeting him at the end likely was a great relief to the great many subjects who naturally thought that the man was either unconscious or even dead! I should also briefly mention that in experiments like this where a lot of deception is used, it is crucial that the experimenter carefully debrief the subject, in such a way to ensure that it is important that the subject (and all subjects) believe the cover story and the deception or else the experiment wouldn't work. It is important that they avoid making the subject feel gullible or unintelligent for believing the cover story, and that, as Milgram says here, the experimenter should work to ensure that the subject leaves the lab no worse off than he entered it.

the degree of tension reached extremes that are rarely seen in socio-psychological laboratory studies. Subjects were observed to sweat, tremble, stutter, bite their lips, groan, and dig their fingernails into their flesh. These were characteristic rather than exceptional responses to the experiment.

One sign of tension was the regular occurrence of nervous laughing fits. Fourteen of the 40 subjects showed definite signs of nervous laughter and smiling. The laughter seemed entirely out of place, even bizarre. Full-blown, uncontrollable seizures were observed for 3 subjects. On one occasion we observed a seizure so violently convulsive that it was necessary to call a halt to the experiment. The subject, a 46-year-old encyclopedia salesman, was seriously embarrassed by his untoward and uncontrollable behavior. In the post-experimental interviews subjects took pains to point out that they were not sadistic types, and that the laughter did not mean they enjoyed shocking the victim.

Distribution of scores. It had been conjectured that persons would not, in general, agree to administer shocks beyond the level designated as Very Strong Shock. The distribution of maximum shocks for this experiment is shown in Table 2. The obtained distribution of scores deviates radically from the prediction.

Upon command of the experimenter, each of the 40 subjects went beyond the expected breakoff point. No subject stopped prior to administering Shock Level 20. (At this level —300 volts—the victim kicks on the wall and no longer provides answers to the teacher's multiple-choice questions.)

Of the 40 subjects, 5 refused to obey the experimental commands beyond the 300-volt level. Four more subjects administered one further shock, and then refused to go on. Two broke off at the 330-volt level, and 1 each at 345, 360, and 375 volts. Thus a total of 14 subjects defied the experimenter. It is instructive to reprint their remarks at the point of defiance, as transcribed from the tape recordings:

[0124] I think he's trying to communicate, he's knocking. . . . Well it's not fair to shock the guy . . . these are terrific volts. I don't think this is very humane. . . . Oh, I can't go on with this; no, this isn't right. It's a hell of an experiment. The guy is suffering in there. No, I don't want to go on. This is crazy. [Subject refused to administer more shocks.]

[0123] He's banging in there. I'm gonna chicken out. I'd like to continue, but I can't do that to a man. . . . I'm sorry I can't do that to a man. I'll hurt his heart. You take your check. . . . No really, I couldn't do it.

These subjects were frequently in a highly agitated and even angered state. Sometimes, verbal protest was at a minimum, and the subject simply got up from his chair in front of the shock generator, and indicated that he wished to leave the laboratory.

Of the 40 subjects, 26 obeyed the orders of the experimenter to the end, proceeding to punish the victim until they reached the most potent shock available on the shock generator. At that point, the experimenter called a halt to the session. (The maximum shock is labeled 450 volts, and is two steps beyond the designation: Danger: Severe Shock.) Although obedient subjects continued to administer shocks, they often did so under extreme stress. Some expressed reluctance to administer shocks beyond the 300-volt level, and displayed fears similar to those who defied the experimenter; yet they obeyed.

After the maximum shocks had been delivered, and the experimenter called a halt to the proceedings, many obedient subjects heaved sighs of relief, mopped their brows, rubbed their fingers over their eyes, or nervously fumbled cigarettes. Some shook their heads, apparently

---

Margin notes:

You can see this in Milgram's documentary. Most of those who did the nervous laughter quit the laughing around 75 volts, when the subject started complaining of pain and asking to be let out.

Wow! Scary. Of course, Milgram didn't expect this would happen, and his goal wasn't to cause harm to the subjects. From an objective, scientific perspective, however, it might be said that this was evidence (along with other self-reported responses from the subjects in post-experimental questionnaires and interviews) that the subjects were really immersed into the reality of the experiment. They all thought they were really giving dangerous, even life-threatening, shocks to this man, and even that he might be hurt in the next room as a result. Such full psychological and emotional involvement (without the seizures!) in the experiment is ideal (what we call "psychological realism"), because the subjects' behavior is much more likely to be natural and true (as opposed to them thinking about the artificiality of the lab and that this is just an experiment, in which case their behavior may not be natural, but rather a reaction to the lab artificiality).

65% of all subjects shocked the learner all the way to the 450-volt mark (full obedience)! Astonishing and counterintuitive result, since Milgram asked experts before he ran the experiment their predictions, and they said maybe 1% of subjects would fully obey. By the way, if you were wondering if women would be more compassionate than men, nope: both genders shocked the victim equally.

TABLE 2 Distribution of Breakoff Points

Verbal designation and voltage indication	Number of subjects for whom this was maximum shock
Slight Shock	
15	0
30	0
45	0
60	0
Moderate Shock	
75	0
90	0
105	0
120	0
Strong Shock	
135	0
150	0
165	0
180	0
Very Strong Shock	
195	0
210	0
225	0
240	0
Intense Shock	
255	0
270	0
285	0
300	5
Extreme Intensity Shock	
315	4
330	2
345	1
360	1
Danger: Severe Shock	
375	1

(Continued)

TABLE 2 (Continued)

Verbal designation and voltage indication	Number of subjects for whom this was maximum shock
390	0
405	0
420	0
XXX	
435	0
450	26

in regret. Some subjects had remained calm throughout the experiment, and displayed only minimal signs of tension from beginning to end.

DISCUSSION

The experiment yielded two findings that were surprising. The first finding concerns the sheer strength of obedient tendencies manifested in this situation. Subjects have learned from childhood that it is a fundamental breach of moral conduct to hurt another person against his will. Yet, 26 subjects abandon this tenet in following the instructions of an authority who has no special powers to enforce his commands. To disobey would bring no material loss to the subject; no punishment would ensue. It is clear from the remarks and outward behavior of many participants that in punishing the victim they are often acting against their own values. Subjects often expressed deep disapproval of shocking a man in the face of his objections, and others denounced it as stupid and senseless. Yet the majority complied with the experimental commands. This outcome was surprising from two perspectives: first, from the standpoint of predictions made in the questionnaire described earlier. (Here, however, it is possible that the remoteness of the respondents from the actual situation, and the difficulty of conveying to them the concrete details of the experiment, could account for the serious underestimation of obedience.)

But the results were also unexpected to persons who observed the experiment in progress, through one-way mirrors. Observers often uttered expressions of disbelief upon seeing a subject administer more powerful shocks to the victim. These persons had a full acquaintance with the details of the situation, and yet systematically underestimated the amount of obedience that subjects would display.

The second unanticipated effect was the extraordinary tension generated by the procedures. One might suppose that a subject would simply break off or continue as his conscience dictated. Yet, this is very far from what happened. There were striking reactions of tension and emotional strain. One observer related:

> I observed a mature and initially poised businessman enter the laboratory smiling and confident. Within 20 minutes he was reduced to a twitching, stuttering wreck, who was rapidly approaching a point of nervous collapse. He constantly pulled on

This illustrates a fundamental question in social psychology: what is the relative contribution of the person (personality) vs. the environment (situation) in influencing the individual's behavior. We tend to assume that people act according to their personality, and we rarely consider external factors that might be influencing another's behavior. This is known as the "fundamental attribution error." But one of the reasons Milgram's experiments on obedience are so interesting is that they show that the situation can overwhelm personality in its influence on behavior.

his earlobe, and twisted his hands. At one point he pushed his fist into his fore-head and muttered: "Oh God, let's stop it." And yet he continued to respond to every word of the experimenter, and obeyed to the end.

Any understanding of the phenomenon of obedience must rest on an analysis of the partic-ular conditions in which it occurs. The following features of the experiment go some distance in explaining the high amount of obedience observed in the situation.

1. The experiment is sponsored by and takes place on the grounds of an institution of unimpeachable reputation, Yale University. It may be reasonably presumed that the personnel are competent and reputable. The importance of this background authority is now being studied by conducting a series of experiments outside of New Haven, and without any visible ties to the university.

2. The experiment is, on the face of it, designed to attain a worthy purpose—advancement of knowledge about learning and memory. Obedience occurs not as an end in itself, but as an instrumental element in a situation that the subject construes as significant, and meaningful. He may not be able to see its full significance, but he may properly assume that the experimenter does.

3. The subject perceives that the victim has voluntarily submitted to the authority system of the experimenter. He is not (at first) an unwilling captive impressed for involuntary service. He has taken the trouble to come to the laboratory presumably to aid the experimental research. That he later becomes an involuntary subject does not alter the fact that, initially, he consented to participate without qualification. Thus he has in some degree incurred an obligation toward the experimenter.

4. The subject, too, has entered the experiment voluntarily, and perceives himself under obligation to aid the experimenter. He has made a commitment, and to disrupt the experiment is a repudiation of this initial promise of aid.

5. Certain features of the procedure strengthen the subject's sense of obligation to the experimenter. For one, he has been paid for coming to the laboratory. In part this is canceled out by the experimenter's statement that: "Of course, as in all experiments, the money is yours simply for coming to the laboratory. From this point on, no matter what happens, the money is yours."[4]

6. From the subject's standpoint, the fact that he is the teacher and the other man the learner is purely a chance consequence (it is determined by drawing lots) and he, the subject, ran the same risk as the other man in being assigned the role of learner. Since the assignment of positions in the experiment was achieved by fair means, the learner is deprived of any basis of complaint on this count. (A similar situation obtains in Army units, in which—in the absence of volunteers—a particularly dangerous mission may be assigned by drawing lots, and the unlucky soldier is expected to bear his misfortune with sportsmanship.)

---

[4]Forty-three subjects, undergraduates at Yale University, were run in the experiment without payment. The results are very similar to those obtained with paid subjects.

7. There is, at best, ambiguity with regard to the prerogatives of a psychologist and the corresponding rights of his subject. There is a vagueness of expectation concerning what a psychologist may require of his subject, and when he is overstepping acceptable limits.

Moreover, the experiment occurs in a closed setting, and thus provides no opportunity for the subject to remove these ambiguities by discussion with others. There are few standards that seem directly applicable to the situation, which is a novel one for most subjects.

8. The subjects are assured that the shocks administered to the subject are "painful but not dangerous." Thus they assume that the discomfort caused the victim is momentary, while the scientific gains resulting from the experiment are enduring.

9. Through Shock Level 20 the victim continues to provide answers on the signal box. The subject may construe this as a sign that the victim is still willing to "play the game." It is only after Shock Level 20 that the victim repudiates the rules completely, refusing to answer further.

These features help to explain the high amount of obedience obtained in this experiment. Many of the arguments raised need not remain matters of speculation, but can be reduced to testable propositions to be confirmed or disproved by further experiments.[5]

The following features of the experiment concern the nature of the conflict which the subject faces.

10. The subject is placed in a position in which he must respond to the competing demands of two persons: the experimenter and the victim. The conflict must be resolved by meeting the demands of one or the other; satisfaction of the victim and the experimenter are mutually exclusive. Moreover, the resolution must take the form of a highly visible action, that of continuing to shock the victim or breaking off the experiment. Thus the subject is forced into a public conflict that does not permit any completely satisfactory solution.

11. While the demands of the experimenter carry the weight of scientific authority, the demands of the victim spring from his personal experience of pain and suffering. The two claims need not be regarded as equally pressing and legitimate. The experimenter seeks an abstract scientific datum; the victim cries out for relief from physical suffering caused by the subject's actions.

12. The experiment gives the subject little time for reflection. The conflict comes on rapidly. It is only minutes after the subject has been seated before the shock generator that the victim begins his protests. Moreover, the subject perceives that he has gone through but two-thirds of the shock levels at the time the subject's first protests are heard. Thus he understands that the conflict will have a persistent aspect to it, and may well become more intense as increasingly more powerful shocks are required. The rapidity with which the conflict descends on the subject, and his realization that it is predictably recurrent may well be sources of tension to him.

13. At a more general level, the conflict stems from the opposition of two deeply ingrained behavior dispositions: first, the disposition not to harm other people, and second, the tendency to obey those whom we perceive to be legitimate authorities.

---

[5] A series of recently completed experiments employing the obedience paradigm is reported in Milgram (1964).

REFERENCES

ADORNO, T., FRENKEL-BRUNSWIK, ELSE, LEVINSON, D. J., & SANFORD, R. N. *The authoritarian personality.* New York: Harper, 1950.

ARENDT, H. What was authority ? In C. J. Friedrich (Ed.), *Authority.* Cambridge: Harvard Univer. Press, 1958. Pp. 81–112.

BINET, A. *La suggestibilite.* Paris: Schleicher, 1900. Buss, A. H. *The psychology of aggression.* New York: Wiley, 1961.

CARTWRIGHT, S. (Ed.) *Studies in social power.* Ann Arbor: University of Michigan Institute for Social Research, 1959.

CHARCOT, J. M. *Oeuvres completes.* Paris: Bureaux du Progres Medical, 1881.

FRANK, J. D. Experimental studies of personal pressure and resistance. *J. gen. Psychol.,* 1944, 30, 23–64.

FRIEDRICH, C. J. (Ed.) *Authority.* Cambridge: Harvard Univer. Press, 1958.

MILGRAM, S. Dynamics of obedience. Washington: National Science Foundation, 25 January 1961. (Mimeo)

MILGRAM, S. Some conditions of obedience and disobedience to authority. *Hum. Relat.,* 1964, in press.

ROKEACH, M. Authority, authoritarianism, and conformity. In I. A. Berg & B. M. Bass (Eds.), *Conformity and deviation.* New York: Harper, 1961. Pp. 230–257.

SNOW, C. P. Either-or. *Progressive,* 1961(Feb.), 24.

WEBER, M. *The theory of social and economic organization.* Oxford: Oxford Univer. Press, 1947.

(Received July 27, 1962)

POST-ARTICLE DISCUSSION

There is a lot we learned from this important program of research. The study shows that people tend to obey even the slightest form of authority (more on this in a moment). A second finding is that when you put people in an "evil situation" (telling them to hurt another person), you get evil behavior. Now this phrasing is mine only, and Milgram might not phrase it that way. I describe it that way because it nicely covers what is happening here. In most subjects (65%), the situation overwhelms the personality and drives their behavior, causing them to fully obey and continue increasing shocks until they reach the end and deliver the full 450 volts. This override of personality by the situation is similar to what happened in Zimbardo's famous prison study (Haney, Banks, & Zimbardo, 1973). Zimbardo explained, "If you put good apples into a bad situation, you get bad apples" (Xidias, 2016).

As discussed elsewhere, this research was controversial. Critics said that it was unethical for a number of reasons, including revealing to people that they have the capacity to hurt (or kill) someone, that they have this dark side. Subjects may not want to know that, but they didn't have a choice. The experiment was extremely stressful for most subjects (they really believed they were greatly injuring the learner), and critics say that any scientific benefit was not greater than the harm to the subject. On the whole, however, most researchers regard Milgram's obedience research as an outstanding program of experiments that taught us a lot about the power and limits of obedience (Blass, 2004, 2009). Could these findings be obtained with today's more sophisticated subjects? Absolutely. Burger (2009) reported that he replicated Milgram's main findings in his research.

THINGS TO THINK ABOUT

1. When this paper was published, a lot of people had concerns about the ethics of the experimenter subjecting the participants to something they really didn't sign up for (i.e., learning that they have the capacity to hurt someone else). Do you think the benefit to science outweighed what the subjects experienced?

2. Do you think that certain personality types or people who are more religious would be less susceptible to the orders of the experimenter to deliver painful shocks to the learner?

3. Would it have made a difference in obedience levels if the learner had been a healthy 20-year-old? Why?

4. Do you think that humans are genetically predisposed to obey authority? Is it a tendency or instinct that has been evolutionarily adaptive? Or is it learned? Or some combination thereof?

5. Why do you think that 14 out of 40 subjects showed definite "signs of nervous laughter" when they were hurting the learner?

INTRODUCTION TO READING 8.2

Langer et al. (1978)

For a time, in the early 1970s researchers in social psychology were exploring the thesis that humans logically and rationally considered all available information before coming to a reasoned conclusion, which would influence their cognitive goals (such as forming an attitude). For example, Fishbein and Ajzen (1975) put forth their "theory of reasoned action," which stated that when people determine their attitudes toward an attitude object, they consider the attributes of the object and their beliefs about the degree to which it is good or bad to have that attribute. Then they do a simple calculation in their minds as to how the person's desirable attributes versus undesirable attitudes combine to form either an overall positive attitude toward the attitude object or a negative attitude. Although the model is interesting and has intuitive value, the data didn't really support the model. Rather, social cognition research shows that we tend to be messy in our thinking, and our decisions are often based on all manner of errors and shortcuts (Kahneman & Tversky, 1982; Nisbett & Ross, 1980).

Ellen Langer and her colleagues wondered whether this heuristic thinking influences our social interactions and social decisions. Specifically, how are our decision-making processes influenced by the novelty of the situation or surroundings? If we've been in the situation before (or many times), do we still pay careful attention to the other person, what the person is saying, and the environment in making our decisions? It makes sense that we might be more attuned to a novel environment or new people. Langer et al. designed a clever experiment to test what Langer calls "mindlessness" (heuristic cognitive processes) in our social interactions and social judgments. We like to think we are always in control of our thoughts and that we know from where our social judgments originate. But, as you will read, that is not always the case! Enjoy!

Reading 8.2

The Mindlessness of Ostensibly Thoughtful Action: The Role of "Placebic" Information in Interpersonal Interaction

Ellen Langer

Arthur Blank and Benzion Chanowitz

Three field experiments were conducted to test the hypothesis that complex social behavior that appears to be enacted mindfully instead may be performed without conscious attention to relevant semantics. Subjects in compliance paradigms received communications that either were or were not semantically sensible, were or were not structurally consistent with their previous experience, and did or did not request an effortful response. It was hypothesized that unless the communication occasioned an effortful response or was structurally (rather than semantically) novel, responding that suggests ignorance of relevant information would occur. The predictions were confirmed for both oral and written communications. Social psychological theories that rely on humans actively processing incoming information are questioned in light of these results.

Consider the image of man or woman as a creature who, for the most part, attends to the world about him or her and behaves on the basis of reasonable inference drawn from such attention. The view is flattering, perhaps, but is it an accurate accounting of covert human behavior?

Social psychology is replete with theories that take for granted the "fact" that people think. Consistency theories (cf. Abelson et al., 1968), social comparison theory (Festinger, 1954; Schachter, 1959), and attribution theory (Heider, 1958; Jones et al., 1972; Kelley, 1967), for example, as well as generally accepted explanations for phenomena like bystander (non) intervention (Darley & Latane, 1968), all start out with the underlying assumption that people attend to their world and derive behavioral strategies based on *current* incoming information. The question raised here is not whether these formulations are correct, nor is it whether people are capable of thoughtful action. Instead, we question how often people outside of the laboratory are actually mindful of the variables that are relevant for the subject and for the experimenter in the laboratory, and by implication, then, how adequate our theories of social psychology really are.

This article questions whether, in fact, behavior is actually accomplished much of the time without paying attention to the substantive details of the "informative" environment. This idea is obviously not new. Discussions of mind/body dualism by philosophers and the consequences that different versions of this relation have on its status as an isomorphic, deterministic, or necessary relationship between the two are part of psychology's heritage. However, the extent of the implications of this idea has not been fully appreciated nor researched. How much behavior can go on without full awareness? Clearly, simple motor acts may be overlearned and performed automatically, but what about complex social interactions?

The class of behavior of greatest interest here is not that which is commonly understood to be automatic, such as walking or typewriting, but rather that which is commonly assumed to be mindful but may be, in fact, rather automatic. We shall refer to it here as mindless behavior—mindless in the sense that attention is not paid precisely to those substantive elements that are relevant for the successful resolution of the situation. It has all the external earmarks of mindful action, but new information actually is not being processed. Instead, prior scripts, written when similar information really was once new, are stereotypically reenacted. Berne (1964) discussed the idea of *scripts* in a popularized way, and Abelson (1976) rigorously elaborated the concept in generating a computer simulation of belief systems. To Abelson, a script is a "highly stylized sequence of typical events in a well-understood situation, . . . a coherent sequence of events expected by the

---

The authors are grateful to Robert Abelson for his comments on an earlier draft of this manuscript and to Cynthia Weinman for conducting Experiment 1.

Requests for reprints should be sent to Ellen Langer, Department of Psychology and Social Relations, 1318 William James Hall, Harvard University, Cambridge, Massachusetts 02138.

Sidebar notes:

In other words, the main question the authors are asking is, "do people really consider all the environmental information available to them at a given moment when making a decision about others?" Or is it the case that people act, as the authors term it, "mindlessly" and instead make social decisions based on non-cognitive factors like emotions, habit, or some other cognitive heuristic/default?

The authors are making an analogy between mindless behavior and behavior that results from a "script." A cognitive script is usually defined by social psychologists as "knowledge of a situation and the ways that events in that situation typically unfold." An example of this is your "restaurant script" that you have learned over your lifetime resulting from dozens of restaurants you've visited. You learn to expect a sequence of events that are the same in essentially any restaurant you visit. It helps you anticipate how to act, and your actions may be rather automatic.

individual, involving him either as a participant or as an observer" (p. 33). (See Author's note, p. 642.)

The notion of a script was used to describe a study by Langer and Abelson (1972), where it was argued that asking a favor had certain script dimensions and that the success of getting compliance depended on the specific syntax of the request rather than on the specific content of the statement. In that study, the words making up the request were held constant, while the order of the words spoken was varied. The opening words determined which script was followed, and compliance varied accordingly. Similar to the notion of script is Goffman's (1974) concept of *frames,* Harre and Secord's (1973) idea of *episode,* Thorngate's (1976) idea of *caricature,* Miller, Galanter, and Pribram's (1960) notion of *plans,* and Neisser's (1967) concept of *preattentive processing.* Each of these formulations speaks to the individual's ability to abide by the particulars of the situation without mindful reference to those particulars.

However, while Abelson has come closest to delineating the structure of scripts, no one has yet experimentally determined the minimum requirements necessary to invoke a particular script, nor has scripted behavior really been demonstrated to be mindless. While the former issue is not addressed in the present article, the latter is the article's main concern, and we may shed some light on the requirements for script learning and enactment once the mindlessness of ostensibly thoughtful actions has been demonstrated. This suggests that the essence of a script may not lie in recurring semantics but rather in more general paralinguistic features of the message. When we speak of people *organizing* incoming information, it is as important to take into account what they systematically ignore as it is to take into account what they systematically process. And when we speak of people ignoring information, it is important to distinguish between information that is ignored because it is irrelevant and information that is ignored because it is already known. It is known because it has been seen many times in the past, and aspects of its structure that *regularly* appear indicate that this time is just like the last. Thus, what is meant by mindlessness here is this specific ignorance of relevant substance.

This article reports three field experiments undertaken to test the mindlessness of ostensibly thoughtful action in the domains of spoken and written communication. It was hypothesized that when habit is inadequate, thoughtful behavior will result and that this will be the case when either of two conditions is met: (a) when the message transmittal is structurally (rather than semantically) novel or (b) when the interaction requires an effortful response.

EXPERIMENT 1

Method

The first experiment was conducted in the context of a competence paradigm, where people about to use a copying machine were asked to let another person use it first. The study utilized a 3 × 2 factorial design in which the variables of interest were the type of information presented (request; request plus "placebic" information; request plus real information) and the amount of effort compliance entailed (small or large).

Subjects. The subjects were 120 adults (68 males and 62 females) who used the copying machine at the Graduate Center of the City University of New York. Each person who approached the machine on the days of the experiment was used as a subject unless there

(margin notes)

A central rationale for the present experiments: can the researchers demonstrate that scripts are mindlessly enacted?

Specifically, mindlessness refers to ignoring potentially relevant information.

Hypothesis for the first experiment: when there is an inadequate "habit" (or script, or cognitive heuristic), the individual will process the social information in their environment thoughtfully. This thoughtful processing will result when the information is new or when the interaction requires a thoughtful response.

Recall that this means two variables, with 3 levels of one variable (type of request: request, request + placebo information, and request + real information), and 2 levels of the other variable (amount of compliance effort: small vs. large).

was a line at the machine when the experimenter arrived or a person came to use the machine immediately after a subject had been approached. (There was a minimum wait of 5 minutes between subjects.) Half of the experimental sessions were conducted by a female who was blind to the experimental hypotheses, and the remaining sessions were run by a male experimenter who knew the hypotheses.

Procedure. Subjects were randomly assigned into one of the groups described below. The experimenter was seated at a table in the library that permitted a view of the copier. When a subject approached the copier and placed the material to be copied on the machine, the subject was approached by the experimenter just before he or she deposited the money necessary to begin copying. The subject was then asked to let the experimenter use the machine first to copy either 5 or 20 pages. (The number of pages the experimenter had, in combination with the number of pages the subject had, determined whether the request was small or large. If the subject had more pages to copy than the experimenter, the favor was considered small, and if the subject had fewer pages to copy, the favor was taken to be large). The experimenter's request to use the machine was made in one of the following ways:

1. *Request only.* "Excuse me, I have 5 (20) pages. May I use the xerox machine?"
2. *Placebic information.* "Excuse me, I have 5 (20) pages. May I use the xerox machine, because I have to make copies?"
3. *Real information.* "Excuse me, I have 5 (20) pages. May I use the xerox machine, because I'm in a rush?"

Once the request was made and either complied or not complied with, the experimenter returned to the table and counted the number of copies the subject made. The dependent measure was whether subjects complied with the experimenter's request.

If subjects were processing the information communicated by the experimenter, then the rate of compliance should be equivalent for Groups 1 and 2, since the amount of information conveyed is the same for both of these groups, but it might be different for Group 3, since this group received additional information. If, however, subjects are responding to the situation on the basis of a prior script that reads something like "Favor X + Reason Y =... Comply," then the rate of compliance should be the same for Groups 2 and 3 (placebic and real information) and greater than for Group 1 (request only). It was predicted that the latter result would obtain.

TABLE 1   **Proportion of Subjects Who Agreed to Let the Experimenter Use the Copying Machine**

Favor	Reason		
	No info	Placebic info	Sufficient info.
Small	.60	.93	.94
n	15	15	16
Big	.24	.24	.42
n	25	25	24

Thus, while the information given to Group 2 was redundant in an information theory sense (Shannon & Weaver, 1949), it was predicted to be necessary, and thus not redundant, in a script sense.

As stated earlier, it was assumed that people would not behave in this pseudothinking way when responding was potentially effortful. Then, there is sufficient motivation for attention to shift from simple physical characteristics of the message to the semantic factors, resulting in processing of current information. Thus, it was predicted that as the favor became more demanding, the placebic-information group would behave more like the request-only group and differently (yielding a lower rate of compliance) from the real-information group.

Results and Discussion

The proportion of subjects who complied in each group was computed, and a 3 × 2 × 2 (Request × Effort × Experimenter) analysis of variance was performed using 0 and 1 as scores (complied vs. did not comply). This analysis yielded three main effects: communication, $F(2, 108) = 3.02$, $p < .05$; effort, $F(1, 108) = 43.40$, $p < .001$; and experimenter, $F(1, 108) = 6.67$, $p < .01$. The proportions of subjects who complied with the different requests are presented in Table 1. Not surprisingly, the female experimenter had a higher rate of compliance than the male experimenter, but since there were no interactions between this variable and the others, the data are combined in the table for ease of reading. A contrast analysis using planned, orthogonal comparisons was performed. The contrast analyses that were performed set the small effort/placebic-information group and the small effort/sufficient-information group as equal to each other but distinct from the small effort/no-information group; the large effort/sufficient-information group was contrasted with the large effort/placebic-information group and the large effort/no-information group. These contrasts reflect the hypothesis that when there was small effort involved, the placebic-information group would be similar to the sufficient-information group but that when effort was large, the placebic-information group would be similar to the no-information condition. It was found that for the small-effort contrast, the means of the placebic and sufficient-information conditions were virtually identical and significantly different from the no-information condition, $F(1, 114) = 6.35$, $p < .05$. For the contrast comparing the more effortful favor, the no-information and placebic-information groups were identical and tended to be different from the sufficient-information group, $F(1, 114) = 2.83$, $.10 < p > .05$.

Also, and not surprisingly, for requests of the same type, small requests result in greater compliance than larger requests.

The results support the hypothesis that an interaction that appears to be mindful, between two people who are strangers to each other and thus have no history that would enable precise prediction of each other's behavior, and in which there are no formal roles to fall back on to replace that history, can, nevertheless, proceed rather automatically. If a reason was presented to the subject, he or she was more likely to comply than if no reason was presented, even if the reason conveyed no information. Once compliance with the request required a modicum of effort on the subject's part, thoughtful responding seemed to take the place of mindlessness, and the reason now seemed to matter. Under these circumstances, subjects were more likely to comply with the request based on the adequacy of the reason presented.

Let's just focus on the small favor request condition (where the experimenter says "I have 5 pages"). In the basic request, only 60% of the subjects agree. But look at the high and nearly identical compliance rates for questions 2 and 3: for 2 (the non-reason reason), 93% agreed! For question 3 (the real and legitimate reason), 94% agreed. You might be shaking you head and rubbing your eyes now. No you read that right. Nearly 100% agree when you present a real request reason. But, you also nearly get 100% compliance when you present the requestee with a completely ridiculous reason. How does that happen? We'll discuss it shortly.

No significant differences in compliance when using a female vs. male experimenter, and no interaction of experimenter gender with other variables, so the data for each gender of experimenter are combined. This is commonly done in analyses.

In the small request conditions, the authors argue, the subject processes the request mindlessly, and searches for something to help them process the request. In this case, the word "because" is the word that is key. The subject uses it as a guide, thinking that anything after that word is a legitimate reason. That simple heuristic guides their decision making, which is why they obtained nearly identical and very high compliance rates for questions 2 and 3 (non-reason, and legitimate reasons, each following the word "because"). Again, this is all taking place rather automatically and in fractions of a second, with little to no effortful cognition going on.

EXPERIMENT 2

The next two experiments attempted to extend the results of Experiment 1 to the domain of written communications, since it is our contention that pseudothinking behavior is more the rule than the exception for practically all verbal behavior as well as nonverbal behavior. The more one participates in any activity, the more likely it is that scriptlike qualities will emerge. Through repeated exposure to a situation and its variations, the individual learns to ignore and remain ignorant of the peculiar semantics of the situation. Rather, one pays attention to the scripted cue points that invite participation by the individual in regular ways.

In Experiments 2 and 3, we sought to engage subjects in an activity that would have for them scripted qualities. Specifically, the activity we chose involved receiving and responding to letters and memoranda that were sent through either the U.S. Mail or interoffice mail, depending on the study. As in Experiment 1, it was assumed that ostensibly thoughtful action would proceed mindlessly as long as the structure of the activity involved remained consistent with its scripted character.

Following this assumption, we expected that individuals who received mail that asked for a response would return what was requested if the communication was structurally phrased so as to follow the commonly expected script for mail. The return of the response would serve as evidence of the fact that the person had read the material and engaged in the activity of correspondence through the mail. If the communications to the subject were semantically senseless and yet fulfilled the script requirements for written communication, we could safely assume that the return of the mail signified that we had engaged the subject in mindless behavior—that he or she had not "thought about" the material but had returned it merely because it satisfied the structural requisites for a habitual behavior. To make the case more strongly, we sent to the subjects communications that were equally senseless semantically but which varied in their adherence to the structural requirements of communications. If the responses varied directly with the adherence to structural consistency expected in communications, we could infer that the behavior that led to the subjects' returns was of a scripted character—entirely habitual, despite the fact that, on the face of it, if we observed the behavior we would assume it was thoughtfully processed in character.

In Experiment 2, subjects were mailed a meaningless, five-item questionnaire. The cover letter either demanded or requested the return of the questionnaire and was either signed (e.g., "Thank you for your help, George L. Lewis") or unsigned. It was assumed that signed requests and unsigned demands were more congruent with the structure of most written communications than unsigned requests and signed demands and therefore would be more conducive to sustaining mindless behavior. The cover letter had no letterhead and could not possibly, with thought, be construed as representing a legitimate authority. Therefore, "thoughtful" processing of the cover letter would not uncover any rational reasons for returning the questionnaire.

In order to test whether habitual responding was taking place, rather than merely polite compliance, two groups of subjects were selected who were assumed to vary in their experience with written communications. It was predicted that the more experienced subjects (who were also the more educated subjects) would be more likely to return the questionnaire when the structure of the request/demand was consistent with their past than the less experienced subjects, for whom congruency was not expected to matter.

On the other hand, in the large request conditions, the subjects are more likely to engage in effortful cognition to help them decide how to react to the request. In this case, you'll notice that subjects respond to each request based on the actual merits of each request. For questions 1 and 2, there was no good reason presented to the subject for why the subject should let the experimenter cut in front of them at the Xerox machine. So you get very low compliance rates (each at 24%). But, when presented with a legitimate reason, as in question 3, subjects were much more likely to comply (42% agreed to the request).

I am going to do something a bit unusual compared to most articles in this volume, and not comment on experiments two and three. Of course the reader is free to read them, but the primary reason I wanted to include this paper is the very interesting results of experiment 1, which make an important point about mindlessness, and which have been discussed in textbooks since this article was published. I will make some further comments at the end of the paper.

Method

Subjects. Forty subjects were selected randomly from the Manhattan telephone directory and constituted the random-status group. Another 40 subjects were chosen randomly from the "Physicians" section of the Manhattan Yellow Pages and constituted the high-status group.

Procedure. Each subject received a questionnaire in the U.S. Mail consisting of the five following questions:

1. The subway or bus is the more enjoyable mode of public transportation?
2. Movies or plays are the more enjoyable form of public entertainment?
3. Libraries or parks are the more enjoyable form of free public entertainment?
4. Forests or playgrounds are the more enjoyable public places to spend time?
5. Cash or credit cards is the more efficient form of public exchange of goods?

All subjects received the questionnaire at their residence. Along with the questionnaire, the subjects received a stamped envelope addressed to a post office box, as well as a cover sheet that varied in one of the following four ways:

1. *Congruent conditions.* (a) *Request / personal*— "I would appreciate it if you would fill out the attached questionnaire and return it in the enclosed envelope to me by September 10. Thank you for your help, George L. Lewis." (b) *Demand/impersonal*— "The attached questionnaire is to be filled out and re turned by September 10."

2. *Incongruent conditions.* (a) *Request/impersonal*—"I would appreciate it if you would fill out the attached questionnaire and return it in the enclosed envelope to me by September 10." (b) *Demand/personal*—"The attached questionnaire is to be filled out and returned in the enclosed envelope by September 10. Thank you for your help, George L. Lewis."

Thus, the study was a 2 (random vs. high status) × 2 (request vs. demand) × 2 (personal vs. impersonal) factorial design. Again, it was predicted that high-status subjects who received congruent communications would be more likely to comply than the other groups.

TABLE 2   Proportion of Subjects Who Returned the Questionnaire

	Status	
Condition	High	Random
Congruent	.55	.20
n	20	20
Incongruent	.32	.37
n	19	19

Results and Discussion

Table 2 presents the proportion of subjects who returned the questionnaire, by congruence and status. An analysis of variance was performed using 0 and 1 scores. Although there were no main effects, a contrast that set the high-status congruent group as different from the remaining groups, which in turn were equal to each other, was significant at $p < .05$, $F(1, 74) = 5.91$. The congruent and incongruent cells of Table 2 are broken down for examination in Table 3. The analyses of variance of these data were not significant. However, there was a trend for a three-way interaction, $F(1, 70) = 3.48$, $p < .08$, which indicates again that the congruency effect tends to be modified by status. It appears that our notion of what is congruent was correct only for people like ourselves, who have had an abundance of certain kinds of written communications and not others. That is, instead of there being a general script for written communications, there are probably several scripts peculiar to individuals in their relation to social institutions. In fact, on second thought, it seems that communiques sent from employer to employee, or from manager to office worker (the latter two probably comprised much of the random-status group), would more than likely be either of the demand/personal or request/impersonal sort, since these forms allow the sender to maintain his or her status while still observing a modicum of civility.

Experiment 3 was undertaken to test again, more rigorously, the mindlessness of ostensibly thoughtful actions in regard to written communications. However, for this study, the script was first determined empirically and then tested.

EXPERIMENT 3

Method

Eighty-three memoranda were collected from the wastepaper baskets of 20 secretaries of various departments at the Graduate Center of the City University of New York. Sixty-eight percent of these had the request/impersonal form described earlier. While varying in content, each of these communications requested rather than demanded that the secretary do something (e.g., "Please make 20 copies of this"), and none were signed at the bottom of the request. Thus, for this group of people, the communication most congruent with

TABLE 3 Proportion of Subjects Who Returned the Questionnaire

Condition	High status Personal	High status Impersonal	Random status Personal	Random status Impersonal
Demand	.33	.40	.44	.20
n	9	10	9	10
Request	.70	.30	.20	.30
n	10	10	10	10

[1]Two of the original letters were returned with the notice that the addressee no longer lived at the address. Hence, there were 78 subjects in the study.

their experience would be request/impersonal. Even though in these instances the receiver in all likelihood knew who the sender was, this kind of communication is still considered impersonal, since it stands in contrast to those communications where the sender also is known but where the memo is signed just the same. The distinction between signed and unsigned memos is being drawn, in spite of the fact that in both cases the sender is known, because small structural differences of this kind are predicted to either cue in a script or not, depending upon one's past experience. The remaining 32% of the memos were virtually equally distributed among the other categories. With this in mind, 40 secretaries at the Graduate Center were sent, through interoffice mail, a senseless memorandum that was either congruent with their experience or incongruent. In order to allow for comparisons with Experiment 2, the same four forms of written communication that were used previously were randomly sent to these subjects. However, now there were one congruent form (request/impersonal) and three incongruent forms (request/personal, demand/personal, demand/impersonal).

Request. "I would appreciate it if you would return this paper immediately to Room 238 through interoffice mail."

Demand. "This paper is to be returned immediately to Room 238 through interoffice mail."

Half of each of these messages were signed ("Sincerely, John Lewis"), and half were unsigned and merely had a number (IU 74021-A) at the bottom of the message.

Nothing more was written on the memo. Subjects were simply asked to return l piece of paper that asked them only to return that paper to Room 238. The designated room did not exist in the building. The mailroom attendants put the returned letters aside for us.

Thus, the study utilized a 2 (request vs. demand) × 2 (personal vs. impersonal) factorial design, with 10 subjects in each cell.

Results and Discussion

Table 4 presents the proportion of subjects who returned the letters as a function of the various conditions. To test the hypothesis that mindless behavior will result when script requirements are met, the proportions of subjects who returned the memo in the congruent condition (.90) and the incongruent conditions (.60) were compared. Using O and 1 scores, the analysis showed them to be significantly different from each other, $t(38) = 1.78$, $p < .05$. It should be noted that what we are calling congruent was determined by sampling a fraction of the secretaries' past experience with written communications. Sixty-eight percent of the memos fell into the request/impersonal condition. Quite possibly, if we had mapped out first what was congruent for each secretary and then sent the appropriately structured-for-congruence memo to her or him, the compliance might have reached 100%.

Experiments 2 and 3 provide support for the mindlessness hypothesis in regard to written communications. It would seem that thoughtful processing of the information communicated to these subjects would have resulted in a nonresponse from them. Nevertheless, when the script was congruent with subjects' experience, 55% of the physicians and 90% of the secretaries complied with the meaningless communication.

Conclusions

These studies taken together support the contention that when the structure of a communication, be it oral or written, semantically sound or senseless, is congruent with one's past experience, it may occasion behavior mindless of relevant details. Clearly, some information from the situation must be processed in order for a script to be cued. However, what is being suggested here is that only a minimal amount of structural information may be attended to and that this information may not be the most useful part of the information available. While the authors do in fact believe that people very often negotiate their interpersonal environments mindlessly, studies like these may simply demonstrate that subjects are not thinking about what one thinks they are thinking about (i.e., what is relevant), rather than demonstrating that their minds are relatively blank. If we knew all of the things subjects could be thinking about, we could use the present experimental paradigm to at least test this alternative. However, since there are an infinite number of thoughts subjects may be thinking, this strong hypothesis will have to remain at the level of conjecture until other experimental methods are devised. The difficulty of inventing such a methodology should not preclude efforts in that direction, since if mindlessness is the rule rather than the exception, many of the findings in social psychology would have to be reformulated (see Langer, 1978, for a more detailed discussion of this point).

While these studies may be open to alternative interpretations, they suggest that perhaps there has been misdirected emphasis on people as rational information processors. Instead of viewing people as either rational or irrational, it would seem wise to at least consider the possibility that their behavior may be rational and yet in some way systematic. These studies then raise questions about the inferential processes traditionally assumed by cognitive social psychology. This has been alluded to by Bern (1972) and more recently by Dweck and Gilliard (1975). It may not be that a person weighs information and then proceeds but that he or she more often just proceeds on the basis of structural cues that occasion further *regular* participation in the interaction. To the extent that this script domination is typical of daily interaction, corrections must be made in our accounts of how individuals behave.

When does this mindless activity take place? If the interpretation offered for these studies is correct, then it would suggest that the occurrence may not be infrequent nor restricted to overlearned motoric behavior like typewriting. Instead, if complex verbal interactions can be overlearned, mindlessness may indeed be the most common mode of social interaction. While such mindlessness may at times be troublesome, this degree of selective attention, of tuning the external world out, may be an achievement (cf. Langer, 1978) and perhaps should be studied as such. At least it would seem that both the advantages and disadvantages should be investigated, as the boundaries of the phenomenon are delimited. At present, however, we may

TABLE 4 Proportion of Subjects Who Returned the Memo

Condition	Memo type	
	Personal	Impersonal
Demand	.60	.50
Request	.70	.90

Note. n = 10/cell.

be in the uncomfortable position of overgeneralizing our laboratory findings for reasons not yet mentioned by laboratory-research critics. Once an individual is brought into the laboratory he or she is likely to be self-conscious. This self-consciousness may be thought provoking and habit inhibiting. Thus, we may be left with the situation where we are studying the responses of thinking subjects and then generalizing to successfully nonthinking people.

REFERENCES

Abelson, R. P. Script processing in attitude formation and decision-making. In J. S. Carroll & J. W. Payne (Eds.), *Cognition and social behavior*. Hillsdale, N.J.: Erlbaum, 1976.

Abelson, R. P , Aronson, E., McGuire, W. L., Newcomb, T. M., Rosenberg, M. J., & Tannenbaum, P. H. (Eds.). *Theories of cognitive consistency: A sourcebook* . Chicago: Rand McNally, 1968.

Bern, D. J. Self-perception theory. In L. Berkowitz (Ed.), *Advances in experimental social psychology* (Vol. 6). New York: Academic Press, 1972.

Berne, E. *Games people play*. New York: Grove Press, 1964.

Darley, J. M., & Latané, B. Bystander intervention in emergencies: Diffusion of responsibility. *Journal of Personality and Social Psychology,* 1968, *8,* 377–383.

Dweck, C., & Gilliard, D. Expectancy statements as determinant of reactions to failure: Sex differences in persistence and expectancy change. *Journal of Personality and Social Psychology, 1975, 32,* 1077–1084.

Festinger, L. A theory of social communication processes. *Human Relations,* 1954, *7,* 117–140.

Goffman, E. *Frame analysis: An essay on the organization of experience*. New York: Harper & Row, 1974.

Heider, F. *The psychology of interpersonal relations*. New York: Wiley, 1958.

Harre, H., & Secord, P. F. *The explanation of social behavior*. Totowa, N.J.: Littlefield, Adams, 1973.

Jones, E. E., Kanouse, D. E., Kelley, H. II, Nisbett, R. E., Valins, S., & Weiner, B. *Attribution: Perceiving the causes of behavior*. Morristown, N.J.: General Learning Press, 1972.

Kelley, H. H. Attribution theory in social psychology. In D. Levine (Ed.), *Nebraska Symposium on Motivation* (Vol. 15). Lincoln: University of Nebraska Press, 1967.

Langer, E. J. Rethinking the role of thought in social interaction. In J. Harvey, W. Ickes, & R. Kidd (Eds.), *New directions in attribution theory* (Vol. 2). Hillsdale, N.J.: Erlbaum, 1978.

Langer, E , & Abelson, R. P. The semantics of asking a favor: How to succeed in getting help without really dying. *Journal of Personality and Social Psychology,* 1972, *24,* 26–32.

Miller, G. A., Galanter, E., & Pribram, K. H. *Plans and the structure of behavior*. New York: Holt, Rinehart & Winston, 1960.

Neisser, U. *Cognitive psychology*. New York: Appleton-Century-Crofts, 1967.

Schachter, S. *The psychology of affiliation*. Stanford, Calif.: Stanford University Press, 1959.

Shannon, C. E., & Weaver, W. *The mathematical theory of communication*. Urbana: University of Illinois Press, 1949.

Thorngate, V. Must we always think before we act? *Personality and Social Psychology Bulletin,* 1976, *2,* 31–35.

Author's note. Since the Langer and Abelson (1972) paper was published, there have been diverging uses of the term *script* which did not become apparent until after this manuscript was prepared. The clarification of the present distinction lies in the degree of active information processing implied by the word *script* . Abelson's use of the term *script* seems to allow a range of cognitive activity. In our formulation, the use of *script* signifies only relative cognitive inactivity. To avoid confusion, the word *script* as it appears in this article should be read as **"mindlessness."**

POST-ARTICLE DISCUSSION

When you were reading the results of this experiment, were you thinking about all the ways your daily behaviors might be enacted in a "mindless" fashion? The analogy that Langer makes between mindlessness and a cognitive "script" is a good one. When we encounter similar situations over time, we develop a generic script that tells us the order in which things happen and what to expect in those situations. Think of it like an overlearned behavior, such as riding a bicycle or driving. After a while, the behavior becomes automatic, and little if any cognitive effort is expended in that chain or sequence of behaviors. That frees up our brain to be on the lookout for novel information, because such information requires more attention and cognitive effort.

In that familiar line at the Xerox machine, subjects were asked to let someone else cut in front of them to make their copies. Subjects have placed themselves in this line (a familiar situation), and thus it should be the case that they likely aren't paying much attention to others or the immediate. Then, someone comes up to them and asks for their help to cut in line. Now, is this an unusual situation? Not entirely, but it is still awkward. So how do subjects respond? If they think carefully (treat it like a novel situation), they should be paying special careful attention, and they should be able to differentiate the three different requests (and there should be different levels of compliance). But if the request is treated like one that is commonplace, then they may fall back on cognitive heuristics to help them make a fast decision about the request. Most people have a "be nice to others" default heuristic, in which case you might get a "ceiling effect" of high compliance across all three conditions. Results were interesting: The default kicked in, and in the baseline request (with no reason given), 80% complied. But when they hear a reason provided for the request to cut in line, the subjects gave a high rate of compliance both in the legitimate reason condition (90%) and the non-reason condition (93%). The higher percentage of compliance in the reason condition is due to the subjects using a heuristic to help them decide whether to comply. In this case, the heuristic may be something like "If the request has a reason, then it is a legitimate request and say yes."

Thus, as we see, the subjects heard the word *because*, and that was all they needed to decide it was a legitimate request. We know they mindlessly processed those because the non-reason ("Because I have to make some copies") was treated essentially the same as the real reason ("Because I am in a rush"). In other words, we could have put "Because purple money dinosaur" as our reason and still obtained a 93% compliance! The results of this research suggests that when people are in familiar situations, they act mindlessly and make their social judgments based on heuristics or other cognitive shortcuts.

THINGS TO THINK ABOUT

1. What are some other ways the questions might have been designed, such that information of different types, importance, or salience might have influenced the subject's response to the interrupting question?

2. Do you think that the male experimenter who knew the hypotheses might have introduced experimenter expectancy effects?

3. The researchers found that female experimenters had a higher compliance rate than male experimenters and said this "was not surprising." Why would that be unsurprising?

4. The authors suggest that the results of Experiment 1 show that when we encounter situations that look familiar, we sort of cognitively "tune out" and are less aware of our surroundings (because we think we know what to expect). Do you agree?

5. Is being mindless adaptive? Is it a good thing? How would it be helpful from an evolutionary standpoint?

9

Prejudice

One of the biggest advances that early humans made was forming groups. By themselves, the chances for survival dropped, due to predators, elements, or lack of survival skills (e.g., hunting). Groups of humans traded valuable survival information and taught each other skills that helped them live longer (e.g., which plants to avoid eating). However, along with all the survival benefits with group membership came a cost to the creation of these groups: the formation of negative intergroup attitudes. These early humans learned something that modern psychologists have demonstrated time and time again in the lab: People seem prone to rather automatically consider their group in a favorable way and to consider all other outside groups negatively (Fiske, 2002). This "us versus them" mentality is the basis for the formation of **prejudice**. Prejudice can be defined as a biased evaluation of a group, based on real or imagined characteristics of the group members (Nelson, 2006). While we can prejudge a group in a positive way, prejudice is much more likely to be a negative prejudgment and to carry with it negative feelings about those in other groups. In fact, it may be argued that prejudice between groups was at the heart of most (or even all) wars in human history (Duckitt, 1992; Rowatt, Carpenter, & Haggard, 2014).

Research on prejudice began right about the same time that the field of social psychology came into being, in the early 20th century, with the publication of two seminal textbooks defining the field, by Allport (1924) and McDougall (1908). It was during this time that one of the core concepts of prejudice research was popularized: the **stereotype**. The term was adopted in social science from a journalist, Walter Lippmann (1922), who used the word *stereotype* (which was used in printing processes to denote a process whereby fixed casts of material are reproduced) to describe the tendency of people to think of someone or something in similar terms. A good definition of stereotype, consistent with the way that most prejudice researchers today would define it, is by Ashmore and Del Boca (1981), who wrote that a stereotype is "a belief about the personal attributes of a group of people" (p. 16). In contrast with prejudice, which normally entails negative feelings about a group, stereotypes can describe positive or negative beliefs about a group. Given the important effects of prejudice on thinking and behavior, and its implications for intergroup peace, it is important that we make every effort to really understand what gives rise to prejudice, why it persists, and how we can reduce and eliminate it. In this introduction, we discuss what prejudice researchers have learned over the past century of theory and experimentation. As is the case with all of the introductory chapters in this book, this is not meant to be an exhaustive review (for comprehensive reviews, see Dovidio, Hewstone, Glick, & Esses, 2013; Fiske & Tablante, 2015; Jackson, 2015; Nelson, 2016), but it should provide the reader with a solid understanding of where the field has been and currently is.

EARLY VIEWS ON PREJUDICE

When research on prejudice began, the focus was to understand prejudice and stereotyping as originating in the perceiver in a social interaction. Prejudiced people were thought to have a number of moral and cognitive deficits, such as laziness and irrationality (Jones, 1997), and they were believed to be rigid and nonanalytic in their thinking (Stroebe & Insko, 1989). Some research suggested that prejudice emerges in people when they become frustrated (Dollard, Doob, Miller, Mowrer, & Sears, 1939). In the **frustration-aggression hypothesis**, Dollard et al. (1939) proposed that when people become frustrated, they become aggressive. One kind of aggression is prejudice, which can emerge in those who feel thwarted from a goal by others (who become the targets of the perceiver's prejudice). As an example of this, Hovland and Sears (1940) found that some whites who felt hit hard by an economic downturn in the 1930s took out their anger and frustration on African Americans in myriad ways, including lynching. The researchers found a negative correlation between the price of cotton and the number of lynchings of African Americans in the southern states of the United States between 1882 and 1930. Specifically, they found that as the price of cotton dropped, the number of lynchings

increased (Hepworth & West, 1988). One problem (and it is a fatal one) with the frustration-aggression hypothesis is that it says that all frustration always leads to aggression. Instead of one specific negative mood (e.g., frustration), could it be the case that any negative mood would increase the likelihood of aggression? This is the basis of Berkowitz's (1989) reformulation of the frustration-aggression hypothesis. Berkowitz suggests that any negative event leads one to experience negative feelings, which, in turn, increases the likelihood of aggressive behavior. This view has been supported by many subsequent studies (Bushman & Huesmann, 2010).

Some research suggested that prejudice was more likely to occur in a perceiver who had a prejudiced personality (Adorno, Frenkel-Brunswick, Levinson, & Sanford, 1950). The idea was that perhaps there is a constellation of personality characteristics that, together, would indicate a lower tolerance for people who are different from the perceiver. Adorno and his colleagues interviewed hundreds of men and found what they called an **authoritarian personality**. People with an authoritarian personality were reared by a parent who used domineering, strict disciplinary measures. Authoritarians are submissive to authority, cynical, and sexually inhibited, and they dislike or distrust people who are different from them. Critics found a few problems with this approach to prejudice, however. First, although it could account for some prejudice, it couldn't explain why there were regional differences in prejudice (Pettigrew, 1959). It couldn't explain why people who were not authoritarians also showed prejudice. It had a heavy psychodynamic component, and researchers in the 1950s were moving away from Freudian explanations for behavior.

So it was clear that another approach was needed. There was a sea change in prejudice research with the publication of

Allport's landmark book, *The Nature of Prejudice* (1954). In this work, Allport said that prejudice was not a product of moral or other characterological deficits but rather of normal cognitive functioning. Allport was saying that prejudice can and does happen in everyone, as a function of the normal way our brains perceive the world (Brown, 1965; Fishman, 1956). So rather than focus on the personality or character defects in the perceiver, Allport (and others also made this argument) was saying that it would be more informative to examine the factors that enhance or inhibit the likelihood of the development, maintenance, expression, and reduction of prejudice.

ORIGIN AND MAINTENANCE OF PREJUDICE AND STEREOTYPES

Through the 1960s and the early 1970s, social psychologists focused on the cognitive *processes* that lead to stereotyping and prejudice (Fiske & Taylor, 1991; Hamilton & Sherman, 1994). Researchers started with the proposition that our brains, through evolutionary processes, are hard-wired to categorize objects (and people; Fiske & Neuberg, 1990). This makes adaptive sense in that we can view an object and, by its features or similar function, group it with similar objects into a category. Thereafter, when we perceive an object, we can instantly know what to call it and what it is, and move on to more immediate or important cognitive functions. Consider the tedium if, for everything we perceived, we had to stop what we were doing and analyze its component features to try to figure out what it is. We'd never get anything done!

A problem arises when we apply this ability to categorizing people. Assuming that everyone who has the same skin color, or age, or gender (for example) is the same in terms of personality, behaviors,

interests, and so forth, is, of course, absurd. But that is the nature of stereotypes. We assume that everyone in a category has the same characteristics. Our tendency to categorize people is something that develops in early childhood and becomes so well learned that we rather automatically categorize people according to a few basic (or sometimes called "primitive") categories: race, age, and gender (Brewer, 1988; Fiske & Neuberg, 1990). These categorizations are important because they have great influence over how the perceiver thinks, feels, and acts toward the target person.

Ingroups Versus Outgroups

One of the most basic ways we categorize other people is whether they are part of groups to which we belong. Those groups are called **ingroups.** Groups to which we do not belong are termed **outgroups** (Allport, 1954). Typically, we assume people in our ingroups share the same values, beliefs, and attitudes as we do. We also assume that everyone in an outgroup is the same. This is known as the **outgroup homogeneity bias** (Hamilton, 1976). There are virtually unlimited dimensions on which we can make this ingroup versus outgroup distinction: gender, race, religion, political attitudes, whether one wears glasses, height, you get the idea. Interestingly, the dimension doesn't even need to be a meaningful one. Research shows that when people are randomly assigned to Group A versus Group B, they tend to favor people in their own group over the other group (Brown, 1995; Tajfel, Flament, Billig, & Bundy, 1971). This concept of "**minimal groups**" further illustrates the strong tendency we have to break the world into "us versus them" categorizations and how that tendency can impact how we differentially interact with others, depending on the group to which we have assigned them.

Sources of Prejudice in Children

One of the primary early influences on the attitudes a child develops toward the world is the child's parents. Freud theorized that around age 5 or 6, children internalize the attitudes and beliefs of their parents. Allport (1954) suggested that children "catch" their parent's negative racial attitudes by observing how their parents behave and what they say with regard to outgroups, specifically toward stereotyped outgroups (Rohan & Zanna, 1996). But there is evidence that suggests that before age 10, children don't really internalize those attitudes, but rather they are parroting their parents' beliefs (Aboud, 1988).

Maintenance of Stereotypes and Prejudice

Once one has learned stereotypes and endorses them, the stereotypes become a filter through which the individual perceives the world. Much research suggests support for the idea that stereotypes bias the cognitive processing of stereotype-relevant information such that we tend to pay attention to and remember information that is consistent with our stereotypes, and we disregard and do not remember stereotype-inconsistent information (Bodenhausen & Lichtenstein, 1987; Doosje, Spears, de Redelijkheid, & van Onna, 2007; Wigboldus, Dijksterhuis, & Van Knippenberg, 2003). As a result of this biased filter, our stereotypes not only are maintained but they grow stronger. Does that mean we are doomed to always perceive others in terms of stereotypes, and once we get the stereotypes we can never get rid of them? Not necessarily. Research indicates that when people are motivated to not be prejudiced and to perceive others on their own merits (without prejudice), they can do it, but it requires consistent motivation and cognitive effort (Dovidio & Gaertner, 2010; Hilton & Darley, 1991; Pendry & Macrae, 1996).

Another cognitive tendency tends to keep stereotypes alive. When we see a member of a stereotyped outgroup who violates the stereotype, we are confronted with a problem: Do we change our stereotype to include the possibility of those from the outgroup confirming and disconfirming the group stereotype? Or do we treat the unusual individual as an anomaly (a fluke)? By the way, this decision usually isn't as conscious as one might hope. Most of the time, we choose to maintain our stereotype and treat the individual as an exception to the stereotype rule. When we do that, we put that individual in her own category and keep her separate from the main stereotype outgroup. This is known as **subcategorization** (Kunda & Oleson, 1995). This allows the perceiver to have it both ways, so to speak. He can still maintain his stereotype (and prejudice against the outgroup) and yet have positive attitudes toward individual members of the outgroup. In so doing, he can convince himself and others that he is not prejudiced toward the outgroup because he has positive attitudes toward those individual, subcategorized members of the outgroup. This is the "I am not prejudiced; some of my best friends are _____" rationale.

Recall earlier the discussion of how stereotypes bias what we perceive and remember (we notice and remember stereotype-consistent information and disregard and don't remember stereotype-inconsistent information). As a result of this, we remember only examples that confirm our stereotypes. For example, suppose someone asked me, "What are the chances that an old person is going to be grumpy?" I am being asked to make a probability estimate (based on a common stereotype that older people are grumpy). I consult my "database" about what characteristics tend to go with what groups (i.e., my stereotypes), and I find that for the group "old people," all my examples of older people in my memory are "grumpy," so I will estimate a high probability that any given older person will be grumpy (say, 89%). From then on, I will remember that estimate and use it for my own justification for the veracity of my stereotypes about older people. These faulty correlations are known as **illusory correlations** (Fiedler, 2017; Hamilton & Rose, 1980). The illusory correlations form further "data" supporting the stereotypes, thus maintaining the stereotypes.

REDUCING PREJUDICE

As you might imagine, there have been a number of ideas put forth on how people might reduce or eliminate the influence of prejudice on their social judgments. Some have been more successful than the others, and we briefly discuss some of the more prominent approaches. One early approach was called the **contact hypothesis** (Williams, 1947; Wilner, Walkley, & Cook, 1955). The idea behind the contact hypothesis is that prejudice emerges as a result of two groups not knowing each other (fear of the unknown), and if we want to reduce that prejudice, the two groups should be brought into contact. The members of the two groups will then talk to the other group members and, in so doing, start to learn more about the other group, individuate members, and think of them as individuals rather than outgroup members. Despite the appeal of this hypothesis, research shows that prejudice reduction via contact hypothesis is not quite that simple. Researchers showed that mere contact was insufficient and that other conditions must be present in order for the contact hypothesis to reduce prejudice (Allport, 1954; Amir, 1969; Pettigrew, 1998). One study suggested that 13 conditions (!) need to be present in order for prejudice to be reduced through contact (Stephan, 1985).

Current research on the issue affirms the importance of Allport's (1954) suggestion to pay attention to the types and quality of contact (e.g., sometimes increased contact leads to increased negative attitudes, not more positive attitudes) and says that we need better methodological tools to assess the nature of the contact and prejudice reduction (if any occurred; McKeown & Dixon, 2017).

It might seem logical that if one wanted to reduce animosity between groups, one way to do that would be to try to eliminate distinctions between the groups. One way to try to accomplish this has been the "color-blind" approach (Nelson, 2006). Using this approach, the perceiver makes a conscious effort to not perceive people according to their category memberships but rather to evaluate them according to their personal, individual characteristics. It sounds reasonable, but this approach has been widely criticized in the literature (Jones, 1997; Neville, Gallardo, & Sue, 2016). The primary problem is that by saying that race doesn't matter when it does matter does nothing to really deal with the racial disparities, and it relegates the stereotyped group to a permanent lesser position, relative to the majority. Instead, researchers have advocated that people should embrace, not ignore, our differences. The "multicultural" approach asks perceivers to notice and appreciate the differences between the groups. In so doing, the individual realizes that each group holds its strengths and each group is equally important in our society. There is evidence that this approach is successful in reducing prejudice (Wolsko, Park, Judd, & Wittenbrink, 2000; Zarate & Garza, 2002).

A final approach (this is by no means an exhaustive coverage of all prejudice reduction approaches; for a more comprehensive discussion, see Nelson, 2016) to reducing prejudice is known as the **common ingroup identity model** (Dovidio, Gaertner, Isen, & Lowrance, 1995; Gaertner &

Dovidio, 2000; Gaertner, Dovidio, Guerra, Hehman, & Saguy, 2016). According to this view, prejudice can be reduced by encouraging people of different groups to reconceptualize themselves as members of a larger, unified group. So individuals need to cognitively decategorize themselves from their current group and recategorize themselves as members of a broader, common ingroup. Research shows that this also has the effect of promoting positive attitudes toward and interactions with members of the outgroup (Gaertner et al., 2016). The basis for the common ingroup identity model has a long history in psychology. In the late 1950s, Muzafer Sherif conducted a famous experiment in which he had two groups of boys at a summer camp compete for a scarce resource (Sherif, Harvey, White, Hood, & Sherif, 1961). As a result, prejudice emerged between the groups. Then, he introduced some tasks that required the cooperation of all boys together. This superordinate goal had the effect of causing the boys to conceptualize themselves not as "us versus them" but as members of the same "team." In so doing, their prejudice toward each other vanished. These various approaches, along with several others we haven't discussed, are all effective ways to help reduce or eliminate prejudice. One of the best things that can help ensure the success of these methods is the motive of the individual to perceive others accurately rather than to rely on stereotypes (Hilton & Darley, 1991; Pendry & Macrae, 1996).

INTRODUCTION TO READING 9.1
Devine (1989)

For decades, essentially from the beginning of the field of social psychology in the early 1900s, one of the ongoing questions among prejudice researchers is how to explain the differences between the prejudiced person and the nonprejudiced person. What is it that makes the prejudiced person prejudiced? Most of these early attempts to answer this question dealt with racial prejudice in particular. Is it a problem with their moral character? Is it the case that they have a prejudiced personality? (Adorno et al., 1950; Altemeyer, 1981). Is racial prejudice a reflection of a particular view that African Americans do not share the same values as Caucasians (Gaertner & Dovidio, 1986; Kinder & Sears, 1981)?

While there is evidence for each of these explanations, researchers have also been interested in a more fundamental, cognitive view of how prejudice or stereotypes influence our perceptions (or don't, in the case of low-prejudiced persons; Nelson, 2006). One landmark paper in this line of inquiry was the paper you are about to read, by Patricia Devine. Devine hypothesized that high- and low-prejudiced persons are the same in terms of their knowledge of the cultural stereotypes about African Americans, but they differ in that one group (the high-prejudiced group) allow those stereotypes to influence their social judgments of African Americans, whereas the other group (low-prejudiced) actively suppress the stereotypes, regard African Americans as individuals, and consider each person according to her own individual merits. This marked a significant change in how we view high-prejudiced and low-prejudiced persons. Maybe high-prejudiced persons aren't defective morally or possessed of heinous personality characteristics, but rather, they are just like their low-prejudiced counterparts, and the only difference is that high-prejudiced people believe in the truth of the stereotype, so they have no problem letting that stereotype guide their social perception. When you read, pay special attention to the creative way Devine gets at these different cognitive processes in high- versus low-prejudiced persons, and think about the design. Put on your critic hat (make it a jaunty beret) and consider whether you think there are ways to fine-tune the method or do it differently. Enjoy the paper!

Reading 9.1

Attitudes and Social Cognition

Stereotypes and Prejudice: Their Automatic and Controlled Components

Patricia G. Devine

Three studies tested basic assumptions derived from a theoretical model based on the dissociation of automatic and controlled processes involved in prejudice. Study 1 supported the model's assumption that high- and low-prejudice persons are equally knowledgeable of the cultural stereotype. The model suggests that the stereotype is automatically activated in the presence of a member (or some symbolic equivalent) of the stereotyped group and that low-prejudice responses require controlled inhibition of the automatically activated stereotype. Study 2, which examined the effects of automatic stereotype activation on the evaluation of ambiguous stereotype-relevant behaviors performed by a race-unspecified person, suggested that when subjects' ability to consciously monitor stereotype activation is precluded, both high- and low-prejudice subjects produce stereotype-congruent evaluations of ambiguous behaviors. Study 3 examined high- and low-prejudice subjects' responses in a consciously directed thought-listing task. Consistent with the model, only low-prejudice subjects inhibited the automatically activated stereotype-congruent thoughts and replaced them with thoughts reflecting equality and negations of the stereotype. The relation between stereotypes and prejudice and implications for prejudice reduction are discussed.

Social psychologists have long been interested in stereotypes and prejudice, concepts that are typically viewed as being very much interrelated. For example, those who subscribe to the tripartite model of attitudes hold that a stereotype is the cognitive component of prejudiced attitudes (Harding, Proshansky, Kutner,& Chein, 1969; Secord & Backman, 1974). Other theorists suggest that stereotypes are functional for the individual, allowing rationalization of his or her prejudice against a group (Allport, 1954; LaViolette & Silvert, 1951; Saenger, 1953; Simpson & Yinger, 1965).

In fact, many classic and contemporary theorists have suggested that prejudice is an inevitable consequence of ordinary categorization (stereotyping) processes (Allport, 1954; Billig, 1985; Ehrlich, 1973; Hamilton, 1981; Tajfel, 1981). The basic argument of the *inevitability of prejudice* perspective is that as long as stereotypes exist, prejudice will follow. This approach suggests that stereotypes are automatically (or heuristically) applied to members of the stereotyped group. In essence, of a stereotype is equated with prejudice toward the group. This perspective has serious implications because, as Ehrlich (1973) argued, ethnic attitudes and stereotypes are part of the social heritage of a society and no one can escape learning the prevailing attitudes and stereotypes assigned to the major ethnic groups.

The inevitability of prejudice approach, however, overlooks an important distinction between knowledge of a cultural stereotype and acceptance or endorsement of the stereotype (Ashmore & Del Boca, 1981; Billig, 1985). That is, although one may have *knowledge of a stereotype,* his or her *personal beliefs* may or may not be congruent with the stereotype. Moreover, there is no good evidence that knowledge of a stereotype of a group implies prejudice toward that group. For example, in an in-depth interview study of prejudice in war veterans, Bettleheim and Janowitz (1964) found no significant relation between

This idea coincides with a basic view in cognitive psychology that says that the brain has evolved (or is naturally predisposed) to categorize objects in our world. It allows us to process a stimulus quickly (e.g., group things according to similar features and functions) and then move on to more important information processing. The problem with this automatic categorization arises when we apply it to social categorization of people. This is where stereotypes emerge.

This is an interesting and not altogether settled idea: the idea that once you think of a stereotype, a prejudice emerges. Thinking of someone in stereotyped terms may or may not necessarily lead one to perceive that person with negative affect (prejudice).

This is a key point for this whole paper, and it is the basis for all three experiments. Does knowing about a stereotype equate to belief in or endorsement of the truth of that stereotype? For example, is it the case that your knowledge of the stereotype that older people are afraid of technology mean that you believe that stereotype is true for all older people?

Another important point.

This article is based on a dissertation submitted by Patricia G. Devine to the Ohio State University Graduate School in partial fulfillment of the requirement for the doctoral degree. This research was supported by a Presidential Fellowship and by a Graduate Student Alumni Research Award both awarded by the Ohio State University Graduate School.

Thanks are extended to Thomas M.Ostrom, chair of the dissertation committee, and to the other members of the committee, Anthony G. Greenwald and Gifford Weary.

Correspondence concerning this article should be addressed to Patricia G. Devine, Department of Psychology, 1202 West Johnson Street, University of Wisconsin, Madison, Wisconsin 53706.

stereotypes reported about Blacks and Jews and the degree of prejudice the veterans displayed toward these groups (see also Brigham, 1972; Devine, 1988; Karlins, Coffman, & Walters, 1969).

Although they may have some overlapping features, it is argued that stereotypes and personal beliefs are conceptually distinct cognitive structures. Each structure represents part of one's entire knowledge base of a particular group (see Pratkanis, in press, for a supporting argument in the attitude domain). Beliefs are propositions that are endorsed and accepted as being true. Beliefs can differ from one's knowledge about an object or group or one's affective reaction toward the object or group (Pratkanis, in press). To the extent that stereotypes and personal beliefs represent different and only potentially overlapping subsets of information about ethnic or racial groups, they may have different implications for evaluation of and behavior toward members of the ethnic and racial groups. Previous theorists have not adequately captured this distinction and explored its implications for responding to stereotyped group members. The primary goal of the three studies reported here was to examine how stereotypes and personal beliefs are involved in responses toward stereotyped groups.

This work challenges the inevitability of prejudice framework and offers a model of responses to members of stereotyped groups that is derived largely from work in information processing that distinguishes between automatic (mostly involuntary) and controlled (mostly voluntary) processes (e.g., Posner & Snyder, 1975; Schneider & Shiffrin, 1977; Shiffrin & Schneider, 1977). Automatic processes involve the unintentional or spontaneous activation of some well-learned set of associations or responses that have been developed through repeated activation in memory. They do not require conscious effort and appear to be initiated by the presence of stimulus cues in the environment (Shiffrin & Dumais, 1981). A crucial component of automatic processes is their inescapability; they occur despite deliberate attempts to bypass or ignore them (Neely, 1977; Shiffrin & Dumais, 1981). In contrast, controlled processes are intentional and require the active attention of the individual. Controlled processes, although limited by capacity, are more flexible than automatic processes. Their intentionality and flexibility makes them particularly useful for decision making, problem solving, and the initiation of new behaviors.

Previous theoretical and empirical work on automatic and controlled processes suggests that they can operate independently of each other (Logan, 1980; Logan & Cowan, 1984; Neely, 1977; Posner & Snyder, 1975). For example, by using a semantic priming task, Neely demonstrated that when automatic processing would produce a response that conflicted with conscious expectancies (induced through experimenter instructions), subjects inhibited the automatic response and intentionally replaced it with one consistent with their conscious expectancy.

For example, Neely (1977) examined the influence of a single-word prime on the processing of a single-word target in a lexical decision task (i.e., whether the target was a word). The prime was either semantically related to the target (e.g., *body*-arm) or related to the target through experimenter instructions (e.g., subjects were told that *body* would be followed by a bird name such as sparrow). In this latter condition, subjects had a conscious expectancy for a bird name when they saw the *body* prime, but *body* should also have automatically primed its semantic category of body parts.

Neely (1977) found that with brief intervals between the prime and target (i.e., 250 ms), the prime facilitated decisions for semantically related targets regardless of experimenter instructions. Neely argued that this facilitation was a function of automatic processes. At longer delays (i.e., 2,000 ms), however, experimenter-induced expectancies produced both facilitation for expected targets and inhibition for unexpected targets regardless of their semantic relation to the prime. Before such inhibition of automatically activated responses can occur, there has to be enough *time* and *cognitive capacity* available for the conscious expectancy to develop and inhibit the automatic processes.

AUTOMATIC AND CONTROLLED PROCESSES: IMPLICATIONS FOR ACTIVATION OF STEREOTYPES AND PERSONAL BELIEFS

The dissociation of automatic and controlled processes may provide some theoretical leverage for understanding the role of stereotypes and personal beliefs in responses to members of racial or ethnic groups. In the model proposed, interest centers on the conditions under which stereotypes and personal beliefs are activated and the likelihood that personal beliefs overlap with the cultural stereotype. There is strong evidence that stereotypes are well established in children's memories before children develop the cognitive ability and flexibility to question or critically evaluate the stereotype's validity or acceptability (Allport, 1954; P. Katz, 1976; Porter, 1971; Proshansky, 1966). As a result, personal beliefs (i.e., decisions about the appropriateness of stereotypic ascriptions) are necessarily newer cognitive structures (Higgins & King, 1981). An additional consequence of this developmental sequence is that stereotypes have a longer history of activation and are therefore likely to be more accessible than are personal beliefs. To the extent that an individual rejects the stereotype, he or she experiences a fundamental conflict between the already established stereotype and the more recently established personal beliefs.

The present model assumes that primarily because of common socialization experiences (Brigham, 1972; Ehrlich, 1973; P. Katz, 1976; Proshansky, 1966), high- and low-prejudice persons are equally knowledgeable of the cultural stereotype of Blacks. In addition, because the stereotype has been frequently activated in the past, it is a well-learned set of associations (Dovidio, Evans, & Tyler, 1986) that is automatically activated in the presence of a member (or symbolic equivalent) of the target group (Smith & Branscombe, 1985). The model holds that this unintentional activation of the stereotype is equally strong and equally inescapable for high- and low-prejudice persons.

A major assumption of the model is that high- and low-prejudice persons differ with respect to their personal beliefs about Blacks (Greeley & Sheatsley, 1971; Taylor, Sheatsley, & Greeley, 1978). Whereas high-prejudice persons are likely to have personal beliefs that overlap substantially with the cultural stereotype, low-prejudice persons have decided that the stereotype is an inappropriate basis for behavior or evaluation and experience a conflict between the automatically activated stereotype and their personal beliefs. The stereotype conflicts with their non-prejudiced, egalitarian values. The model assumes that the low-prejudice person must create a cognitive structure that represents his or her newer beliefs (e.g., belief in equality between the races, rejection of the stereotype, etc.). Because the stereotype has a longer history of activation (and thus greater frequency of activation) than the newly acquired personal beliefs, overt non-prejudiced responses require intentional inhibition of the automatically activated stereotype and activation of the newer personal belief structure. Such inhibition and initiation of new responses involves controlled processes.

One of the assumptions tested in this paper is whether stereotypes are automatically activated. Also, do we have automatically activated efforts to suppress those stereotypes? Or are stereotype suppression efforts a much more effortful cognitive process?

This analysis suggests that whereas stereotypes are automatically activated, activation of personal beliefs require conscious attention. In addition, non-prejudiced responses require both the inhibition of the automatically activated stereotype and the intentional activation of non-prejudiced beliefs (see also Higgins & King, 1981). This should not be surprising because an individual must overcome a lifetime of socialization experiences. The present model, which suggests that automatic and controlled processes involved in stereotypes and prejudice can be dissociated, posits that the inevitability of prejudice arguments follow from tasks that are likely to engage automatic processes on which those high and low in prejudice are presumed not to differ (i.e., activation of a negative stereotype in the absence of controlled stereotype-inhibiting processes). Interestingly, the model implies that if a stereotype is automatically activated in the presence of a member of the target group and those who reject the cultural stereotype do not (or perhaps cannot) monitor consciously this activation, information activated in the stereotype could influence subsequent information processing. A particular strength of the model, then, is that it suggests how knowledge of a stereotype can influence responses even for those who do not endorse the stereotype or have changed their beliefs about the stereotyped group.

Higgins and King (1981) presented a similar analysis with respect to the effect of gender stereotypes on memory. They demonstrated that when gender was not salient, subjects' descriptions of self and others reflected traditional views of gender-linked attributes. They suggested that under such conditions traditional gender stereotypes, with their longer history (i.e., greater frequency) of activation, are passively (automatically) activated and influence recall. When gender was made salient, however, subjects apparently inhibited the traditional stereotype and descriptions were more consistent with their more recently developed, modern views of gender-linked attributes.

In summary, the present model suggests that a target's group membership activates, or primes, the stereotype in the perceiver's memory (Smith, 1984; Wyer & Srull, 1981), making other traits or attributes associated with the stereotype highly accessible for future processing (Dovidio et al., 1986; Gaertner & McLaughlin, 1983; Smith & Branscombe, 1985). The implications of this automatic stereotype activation may be serious, particularly when the content of the stereotype is predominately negative, as is the case with racial stereotypes. For example, Duncan (1976) found that Whites interpreted the same ambiguous shove as hostile or violent when the actor was Black and as playing around or dramatizing when the actor was White. Duncan assumed that the presence of the Black actor automatically primed the stereotype of Blacks and because the stereotype associates Blacks with violence, the violent behavior category was more accessible when viewing a Black compared with a White actor. Sager and Schofield (1980) replicated these findings with schoolchildren. Both Black and White children rated ambiguously aggressive behaviors (e.g., bumping in the hallway) of Black actors as being more mean or threatening than the same behaviors of White actors.

In only one of these studies (Gaertner & McLaughlin, 1983) was prejudice assessed and responses of high- and low-prejudice subjects compared. Thus, the extent to which high- and low-prejudice persons differ or are similar in their automatic and controlled responses to target group members remains unclear.

The present studies were designed to test implications of the dissociation of automatic and controlled processes in prejudice. Study 1 examined the validity of the assumption that high- and low-prejudice subjects are equally knowledgeable of the cultural stereotype.

The category that is activated automatically will determine the lens through which the perceiver sees all subsequent information about that person. For example, if a perceiver primarily sees a black woman as a woman first, they will perceive information about her through the lens of gender stereotypes.

Description of studies 1 and 2.

Study 2 explored the implications of automatic racial stereotype priming on the evaluation of ambiguous stereotype-relevant behaviors. This task permitted examination of the effects of automatic stereotype activation independently of controlled processes relevant to the stereotype. Finally, Study 3 examined the likelihood that high- and low-prejudice subjects will engage in controlled processes to inhibit prejudiced responses in a consciously directed thought-listing task.

STUDY 1: STEREOTYPE CONTENT AND PREJUDICE LEVEL

Historically, little attention has focused on individual differences in prejudice when assessing the content of stereotypes. Although implicit in the stereotype assessment literature (Brigham, 1971), the assumption that high- and low-prejudice subjects are equally knowledgeable of the cultural stereotype has not been documented. The first step in validating the present model was to examine directly high- and low-prejudice subjects' knowledge of the content of the cultural stereotype of Blacks.

In contrast to the typical adjective checklist assessment of stereotype content (Gilbert, 1951; Karlins et al., 1969; D. Katz & Braly, 1933), a free response task was used in the present study. This task provides a more sensitive test of subjects' knowledge of the stereotype because no cues (e.g., a list of possible characteristics) regarding possible content are provided. Thus, high- and low-prejudice subjects were asked to list the content of the cultural stereotype of Blacks regardless of their personal beliefs.

Method

Subjects and procedure. Forty White introductory psychology students participated in groups of 4–6 for course credit. To ensure anonymity, subjects were isolated from each other and the experimenter left the room after giving general instructions. Written instructions told subjects that the questionnaire was designed to help researchers better understand social stereotypes and that interest centered on the cultural stereotype of Blacks. The experimenter informed them that she was not interested in their personal beliefs but in their knowledge of the content of the cultural stereotype. Subjects were provided with a page with several blank lines on which to list the components of the stereotype and were asked not to write any identifying marks on the booklet.

After listing the components of the stereotype, subjects completed the seven-item Modem Racism Scale (McConahay, Hardee, & Batts, 1981). The Modem Racism Scale is designed to measure subjects' anti-Black attitudes in a nonreactive fashion. The Modem Racism Scale has proven to be useful in predicting a variety of behaviors including voting patterns and reactions to busing (Kinder & Sears, 1981; Sears & Kinder, 1971; Sears & McConahay, 1973). Subjects indicated their agreement with each of the items on the 5-point rating scale that ranged from –2 *(disagree strongly)* to +2 *(agree strongly)*. Subjects put the completed booklet into an unmarked envelope and dropped it into a large box containing several envelopes. Finally, subjects were debriefed and thanked for their participation. The Modem Racism Scale ranges from –14 *(low prejudice)* to +14 *(high prejudice)*. The scale had good reliability (Cronbach's alpha = .83). Subjects were assigned to a high-prejudice ($N = 21$) or a low-prejudice ($N = 19$) group on the basis of a median split of scores on the scale.

Study 3 description.

An assumption of this research (and many other researchers) is that the content of the stereotypes that Whites have about Blacks is the same. Experiment 1 will assess whether that is true.

Remember that truism about social research that we mentioned earlier in the book? If you want to know how someone thinks about something, you simply ASK them.

We discussed this elsewhere in this book, but it is important to reiterate. When a researcher gives a measure to subjects and then seeks to break them into groups based on their scores on the assessment, (most commonly, high vs. low scores) there are usually two ways to do so. First, as is done here, one can do a median split, and split the groups along the 50% median score in the distribution of obtained scores. The second way is to take the top third or quarter and the bottom third or quarter of the scores, and have those be your experiment groups. The best option, in this author's opinion, is to do the latter (the top and bottom third) because it yields groups that are conceptually more distinct, and that will enable the researcher to have a better chance of discovering an effect, if one is present. The problem with median splits is that the people in the middle are essentially identical to those one or two points away from those in the other group. Thus, including them in the analyses muddies the water. One common reason median splits are done is when the sample size is small (as in this case) and doing a top/bottom third or quarter split would cut out too many in the middle, leaving too few subjects for the top and bottom groups to have enough statistical power for the analyses. [Note: I'm not sure if this is why Devine did the median split; I'm just saying that is why some researchers may elect to do it.]

TABLE 1 Proportion of Thoughts Listed in Each of the Coding Categories as a Function of Prejudice Level

Category	High prejudice	Low prejudice
Poor	.80	.75
Aggressive/tough	.60	.60
Criminal	.65	.80
Low intelligence	.50	.65
Uneducated	.50	.50
Lazy	.55	.75
Sexually perverse	.50	.70
Athletic	.75	.50
Rhythmic	.50	.40
Ostentatious	.50	.40
Inferior	.20	.30
Food preferences	.25	.35
Family characteristic	.25	.30
Dirty/smelly	.20	.30
Descriptive terms	.55	.50

Note. None of these differences is significant.

Results and Discussion

The coding scheme, based primarily on the previous stereotype assessment literature, included traits such as lazy, poor, athletic, rhythmic, ostentatious, and so on. In addition, a category was included for themes related to hostility, violence, or aggressiveness. Although these terms have not been included in the traditional assessment literature, the assumption that Blacks are hostile or aggressive has guided much of the research on the effect of racial stereotypes on perception and behavior (Donnerstein & Donnerstein, 1972; Donnerstein, Donnerstein, Simon, & Ditrichs, 1972; Duncan, 1976; Sager & Schofield, 1980). Trait listings, however, do not completely capture the components of cultural stereotypes. For example, subjects also listed descriptive features (e.g., afro, brown eyes) and family characteristics (e.g., many children, single-parent homes). Coding categories for these components and a miscellaneous category for components listed that did not clearly fit into the existing categories were included. In all, there were 16 coding categories (see Table 1).

Two judges, blind to subjects' prejudice level, were provided with the coding instructions and the 40 protocols in different random orders. Each characteristic listed received one classification by each judge; the judges agreed on 88% of their classifications.

Excellent inter-rater reliability.

Table 1 shows coding categories and the proportion of high- and low-prejudice subjects who used the coding category in describing the stereotype. There are several noteworthy aspects of these data. First, the most striking aspect of these data is that the most common theme in subjects' protocols was that Blacks are aggressive, hostile, or criminal-like (see Table 1). All subjects listed either the aggressive or criminal categories and many listed both categories. This finding is important because, as was suggested earlier, much of the intergroup perception literature has been predicated on the assumption that Blacks are hostile and aggressive. Second, consistent with the stereotype assessment literature, the protocols were dominated by trait listings and were predominately negative. Third, there appeared to be few differences in the content reported by high- and low-prejudice subjects.

The prediction of no difference between the high- and low-prejudice subjects' knowledge of the cultural stereotype was tested in two different ways. First, none of the differences in Table 1 was statistically reliable. Second, two separate judges were given subjects' protocols and were instructed to read the content listed and to separate the protocols into high- and low-prejudice groups. The judges could not reliably predict the subjects' prejudice level from the content of their protocols. These data validate Ehrlich's (1973) assumption as well as the first assumption of the present model: High- and low-prejudice persons are indeed equally knowledgeable of the cultural stereotype.

STUDY 2: AUTOMATIC PRIMING, PREJUDICE LEVEL, AND SOCIAL JUDGMENT

Study 1 showed that prejudice has little effect on direct reports of stereotype content. However, the free response task directly involved controlled processes. Subjects were explicitly instructed to be bias-free when making these reports. These data, then, are not necessarily informative regarding the implicit cognitive structures that are accessed during automatic processing. What is needed is a task in which the controlled processes do not provide an alternative explanation for the automatic processes. Thus, the goal of the Study 2 was to examine automatic stereotype priming effects for both high- and low-prejudice subjects.

Several studies have demonstrated that increasing the temporary accessibility of trait categories available in memory influences subsequent evaluations of a target person who performs ambiguous trait-relevant behaviors. These findings have been produced with conscious processing of the primes (Carver, Ganellin, Froming, & Chambers, 1983; Srull & Wyer, 1979, 1980) and with priming that is reported to be nonconscious (Bargh, Bond, Lombardi, & Tota, 1986; Bargh & Pietromonaco, 1982). That is, Bargh and Pietromonaco (1982) demonstrated that even when subjects were unaware of the content of the primes, priming increased the likelihood that the primed category was used to interpret subsequently presented ambiguous category related information.

Nonconscious priming was of particular interest in this research because it is this type of processing that would allow the clearest dissociation of automatic and controlled processes involved in responses to members of a stereotyped group. Thus, the priming technique developed by Bargh and Pietromonaco (1982) was used in this study to automatically or passively prime the racial stereotype. Because the priming task activates the stereotype without conscious identification of the primes, the effects of stereotype activation can be studied independently of controlled stereotype-related processes. Specifically, interest centered on the effect of

Most of the time, when one does an experiment or assesses two groups, one predicts differences between the two groups on the IV as due to differing levels of the IV between the two groups. But here, we are "predicting the null hypothesis"—that there are NO differences between the groups.

Results support that high- and low-prejudiced persons are equally knowledgeable about the stereotypes about Blacks.

automatic racial stereotype activation on the interpretation of ambiguous stereotype-related behaviors performed by a race-unspecified target person.

In this study, evaluation of ambiguously hostile behaviors was examined because the assumption that Blacks are hostile is part of the racial stereotype (Brigham, 1971; Study I) and because it has guided research in intergroup perception (Duncan, 1976; Sager & Schofield, 1980; Stephan, 1985). Because interest centered on the effects of activation of the stereotype on the ratings of a target person's hostility, no words directly related to hostility were used in the priming task. This study explicitly examined Duncan's (1976) hypothesis that the activation of the racial stereotype, which presumably activates a link between Blacks and hostility, explains why ambiguously aggressive behaviors were judged as being more aggressive when performed by a Black than a White actor.

According to the assumptions of the present model, priming will automatically activate the cultural stereotype for both those high and low in prejudice. Because hostility is part of the racial stereotype, increased priming should lead to more extreme ratings on the hostility-related scales for both high- and low-prejudice subjects.

Thus, following Bargh and Pietromonaco (1982), during an initial perceptual vigilance task, subjects were asked to identify the location of stimuli, which were actually words, presented rapidly in subjects' parafoveal visual field. These strategies were used to prevent subjects from consciously identifying the content of the primes. During the vigilance task either 20% or 80% of the words presented were related to the racial stereotype. Then, during an ostensibly unrelated impression-formation task, subjects read a paragraph describing a race-unspecified target person's ambiguously hostile behaviors and rated the target person on several trait scales. Half of the trait scales were related to hostility and thus allowed a test of the effect of stereotype activation on ratings of the target person's hostility. The remaining trait scales were not related to hostility and provided the opportunity to examine the possibility that stereotype activation led to a global negative evaluation that generalized beyond hostility ratings.

The data from this study could have important theoretical implications regarding the role of controlled processes and automatic processes involved in prejudice. However, the criteria required to establish automatic activation have been debated (see Holender, 1986, and Marcel, 1983b, for reviews). Greenwald, Klinger, and Liu (in press) recently suggested that automatic activation can be achieved through either *detectionless processing* or *attentionless processing,* both of which have been shown to produce reliable priming effects. Detectionless processing involves presenting stimuli below subjects' threshold level for reliable detection (Bolota, 1983; Fowler, Wolford, Slade, & Tassinary, 1981; Greenwald et al., in press; Marcel, 1983a). Attentionless processing involves processing stimuli that, although detectable, cannot be recalled or recognized (Klatzky, 1984).

In this study attentionless processing was accomplished by presenting the primes parafoveally (Bargh & Pietromonaco, 1982) followed immediately with a pattern mask. With phenomenal awareness of the semantic content of the primes as the criterion for conscious processing (Marcel, 1983a, 1983b), any effects of priming in this study without immediate conscious identification of the primes or recognition for them will be taken as evidence of attentionless automatic processing effects.

Method

Subjects and selection criteria: Data were collected over two academic quarters. Introductory psychology students were pretested on the seven-item Modern Racism Scale embedded in a

This is a common method in psychological research: if you only present a single-themed questionnaire, it is apparent to the subject what you're measuring, and that can bias their responses. To "throw the subject off the scent," so to speak, researchers often include many other "filler" items in the questionnaire that measure related topics, so the subject can't be sure what the researcher is really measuring, and their responses are less likely to be skewed by subjects answering according to social desirability concerns.

number of political, gender, and racial items. This was done to minimize the likelihood that subjects would identify the scale as a measure of prejudice. The experimenter told subjects that completion of the questionnaire was voluntary and that responses would be kept confidential. Subjects were also provided with a form concerning participation in subsequent experiments and provided their names and phone numbers if they were willing to be contacted for a second study for which they could earn extra credit.

Over the two quarters a total of 483 students filled out the Modern Racism Scale. Participants from the upper and lower third of the distribution of scores were identified as potential subjects ($N = 323$). When contacted by phone, potential subjects were asked about their vision, and only subjects with perfect vision or corrected perfect vision were considered eligible. High-prejudice subjects' scores on the Modern Racism Scale fell within the upper third of scores (between +2 and + 14), and low-prejudice subjects' scores fell within the lower third of scores (between –9 and –14). The scale had good reliability (Cronbach's alpha = .81). From this sample of 323 subjects, 129 who agreed and had good vision participated in the experiment. After replacing 3 Black subjects, 1 subject who reported having dyslexia following the vigilance task, and 3 subjects who failed to follow instructions, the sample consisted of 78 White subjects in the judgment condition, 32 White subjects in the recognition condition, and 12 White subjects in the guess condition.

The experimenter remained blind to subjects' prejudice level, priming condition, and stimulus replication condition. Subjects were telephoned by one experimenter, who prepared the materials (with no treatment information) for the second experimenter, who conducted the experiment.

The method and procedure for this study were modeled after Bargh and Pietromonaco (1982). The only difference between their procedure and the one in this study was that in this study, stimuli were presented tachistoscopically rather than on a computer monitor. The experimental room contained a Scientific Prototype two-channel tachistoscope connected to an experimenter-controlled panel for presenting stimuli. Subjects placed their heads against the eyepiece such that the distance from subjects' eyes to the central fixation point was constant. The presentation of a stimulus activated a Hunter Model 120 Klockounter on which the interval between stimulus onset and the response was recorded to the nearest millisecond. Subjects indicated their responses by pushing one of two buttons (labeled *left* or *right*) on a response box. The experimenter recorded each response and its latency.

The stimuli were black and presented on a white background. Each stimulus was presented for 80 ms. and was immediately followed by a mask (a jumbled series of letters). In addition, following Bargh and Pietromonaco (1982), the interstimulus interval was 2–7 s. The stimuli (words) were centered in each quadrant, with the center of each word being approximately 2.3 in. (0.06 m) from the central fixation point. The eye-to-dot distance was 31 in. (0.79 m) for the Scientific Prototype tachistoscope. As a result, to keep the stimulus within the parafoveal visual field (from 2° to 6° of visual angle), words could not be presented closer than 1.08 in. (0.03 m) or farther than 3.25 in. (0.08 m) from the fixation point. Twenty-five of the 100 trials within each replication were randomly assigned to each quadrant.

Stimulus materials. Words that are labels for the social category *Blacks* (e.g., Blacks, Negroes, niggers) or are stereotypic associates (e.g., poor, lazy, athletic) were the priming stimuli. Twenty-four primes were used to generate two stimulus replications. Efforts were made to produce roughly equivalent content in the two replications. Replication 1 primes included the following: nigger, poor, afro, jazz, slavery, musical, Harlem, busing, minority, oppressed, athletic, and prejudice. Replication 2 primes included the following: Negroes, lazy, Blacks, blues, rhythm, Africa, stereotype, ghetto, welfare, basketball, unemployed, and plantation. Twelve neutral words (unrelated to the stereotype) were included in each replication. All neutral words were high-frequency words (Carrol, Davies, & Richman, 1971) and were matched in length to the stereotype-related words. Neutral words for Replication 1 included the following: number, considered, what, that, however, remember, example, called, said, animal, sentences, and important. Replication 2 neutral words included the following: water, then, would, about, things, completely, people, difference, television, experience, something, and thought. Ten additional neutral words were selected and used during practice trials.

Within each stimulus replication, the stereotype-related and neutral words were used to generate two separate 100-word lists. One list contained 80 stereotype-related words (the rest were neutral words) and the other contained 20 stereotype-related words (the rest were neutral words). The lists were organized into blocks of 20 words. In the 80% stereotype-priming condition, each block contained 16 stereotype-related words and 4 neutral words. Within each block, to make 16 stereotype-related words, 4 of the 12 stereotype-related words were randomly selected and presented twice.

For both stimulus replications, the words within each block were randomly ordered with the restriction that the first stereotype-related word was a label for the group (e.g., Negro or nigger). The positions of the minority items (stereotype-related words in the 20% priming list and neutral words in the 80% priming list) were the same for the 20% and 80% priming lists. Each of the 12 stereotype-related and the 12 control words appeared approximately the same number of times as the other stereotype-related and neutral words, respectively.

Judgment condition. The experimenter told subjects that they would participate in two separate tasks. First, they were seated at the tachistoscope and then provided with a description of the vigilance task. The experimenter told subjects that the vigilance task involved identifying the location of stimuli presented for brief intervals. Subjects also learned that stimuli could appear in one of the four quadrants around the dot in the center of the screen. They were to identify as quickly and as accurately as possible whether the stimulus was presented to the left or the right of the central dot. Subjects indicated their responses by pressing the button labeled *left* or *right* on the response panel. The experimenter informed subjects that the timing and the location of the stimuli were unpredictable. Because both speed and accuracy were emphasized, subjects were encouraged to concentrate on the dot, as this strategy would facilitate detection performance. All subjects first completed 10 practice trials and then 100 experimental trials. Overall, the vigilance task took 11–13 min to complete.

Following the vigilance task, the second task was introduced. Subjects were told that the experimenter was interested in how people form impressions of others. They were asked to read a paragraph describing the events in the day of the person about whom they were to form an impression. This paragraph is the now familiar "Donald" paragraph developed by Srull and Wyer (1979, 1980; see also Bargh & Pietromonaco, 1982, and Carver et al., 1983). This 12-sentence paragraph portrays Donald engaging in a series of empirically established ambiguously hostile behaviors. For example, Donald demands his money back from a store clerk immediately after a purchase and refuses to pay his rent until his apartment is repainted.

After reading the paragraph, subjects were asked to make a series of evaluative judgments about Donald. Subjects rated Donald on each of 12 randomly ordered trait scales that ranged from 0 *(not at all)* to 10 *(extremely)*. Six of the scales were descriptively related to hostility; 3 of these scales were evaluatively negative (hostile, dislikeable, and unfriendly) and

Let's stop a moment to make sure we're all on the same page with what's going on so far. Devine cites previous research that shows that a negative stereotype about African Americans is that they are more hostile than other racial groups. Thus, subjects will be primed with words that either evoke the category of African Americans or not (neutral words). Once the African American category is primed, Devine predicts, subjects who then are asked to read about a person's ambiguously hostile behaviors are more likely to interpret the behaviors as hostile.

3 were evaluatively positive (thoughtful, kind, and considerate). The remaining 6 scales were not related to hostility; 3 of these scales were evaluatively negative (boring, narrow-minded, and conceited) and 3 were evaluatively positive (intelligent, dependable, and interesting).

After completing the rating scales, the experimenter questioned subjects about whether they believed that the vigilance task and the impression-formation task were related. No subject reported thinking the tasks were related or indicated any knowledge of why the vigilance task would have affected impression ratings. The experimenter then explained the nature of priming effects to the subjects. During this debriefing, however, the fact that subjects had been selected for participation on the basis of their Modern Racism Scale scores was not revealed. Subjects were then thanked for their participation.

Recognition test condition. Up through completion of the vigilance task, recognition test subjects were treated exactly the same as the judgment subjects. Subjects in this condition were exposed to either the 80% or 20% priming lists of Replication 1 or Replication 2. Following the vigilance task, however, the experimenter explained that the stimuli were actually words and that subjects would be asked to try to recognize the words previously presented. The recognition test was distributed and subjects were instructed to check off the items that they believed had been presented. The experimenter told them that only half of the words on the list had been presented during the vigilance task.

The 48 items of this test consisted of the 24 words in Replication 1 (12 stereotype-related and 12 neutral words) and the 24 words in Replication 2 (12 stereotype-related and 12 neutral words). Words in Replication 2 served as distractors (words not presented) for Replication 1 targets (words actually presented), and Replication 1 words were used as distractors for Replication 2 targets during the recognition test. The recognition test items were randomly ordered.

Guess condition. The experimenter told subjects in this condition that the words would be presented quickly in one of four locations around the central fixation point. Their task was to guess each word immediately following its presentation. The experimenter instructed subjects to maintain their gaze on the fixation point, as this was the best strategy for guessing words given their unpredictable location and timing. Subjects saw either the 80% list of Replication 1 or the 80% list of Replication 2. Subjects were to make a guess for each word presented, even making blind guesses if necessary, and were prompted to guess if they failed to do so spontaneously. This requirement was introduced to lower subjects' guessing criterion so as to provide a fair test of their immediate awareness of the stimuli (Bargh & Pietromonaco, 1982).

Results

Several checks on subjects' awareness of the content of primes were included in this study. Attentionless processing should allow detection but not immediate or delayed recognition of the stimuli.

Guess condition: A check on immediate awareness. Six high- and 6 low-prejudice subjects were run in this condition. Half of each group were presented with the 80% list of Replication 1 and half with the 80% list of Replication 2. If word content were truly not available to consciousness under the viewing conditions of this study, then subjects should not have been able to guess the content of the stereotype-related or neutral words. Subjects reported that this was a difficult task and that they had no idea of the content of the stimuli. Overall, they made few accurate guesses.

Of the 1,200 guesses, subjects guessed 20 words accurately, a hit rate of 1.67%. Overall, subjects guessed 1.4% of the stereotype-related words and 3.33% of the neutral words. Replicating Bargh and Pietromonaco (1982), the neutral word hit rate was appreciably higher than that for stereotype-related words. The neutral words were high-frequency words and thus would presumably be more easily detectable under the viewing conditions in this study.

Incorrect guesses were examined for their relatedness to the racial stereotype. Only three of the incorrect guesses could be interpreted as being related to the stereotype. Twice *Black* appeared as a guess, once from a high-prejudice subject and once from a low-prejudice subject. These data suggest that neither high- nor low-prejudice subjects were able to identify the content of the priming words at the point of encoding, thus satisfying one criterion for attentionless processing.

Recognition condition: A check on memory for primes. Although subjects could not guess the content of the words at the point of stimulus presentation, it is possible that a recognition test would provide a more sensitive test of subjects' awareness of the content primes. On the basis of their performance on the recognition test, subjects were assigned a hit (correct recognition of presented items) and a false alarm (incorrect recognition of new items) score for both stereotype-related and neutral words.

The hits and false alarms were used to generate d' scores for both stereotype-related and neutral words, which corresponded to subjects' ability to correctly identify previously presented information. Green and Swets (1966) have tabled d' scores for all possible combinations of hits and false alarms. The primary analysis concerned whether subjects performed the recognition task better than would be expected by chance. Over all subjects, neither d' for stereotype-related words ($M = .01$) nor for neutral words ($M = .07$) differed significantly from zero ($ps > .42$). These same comparisons were also done separately for high- and low-prejudice subjects. These analyses, like the overall analysis, suggest that subjects could not reliably recognize the primes. High-prejudice subjects' mean d' scores for stereotyped-related and neutral words were .02 and .12, respectively ($ps > .40$). Low-prejudice subjects' mean d' scores for stereotype-related and neutral words were .01 and .02, respectively ($ps > .84$).

In addition, the d' scores were submitted to a four-way mixed model analysis of variance (ANOVA)-Prejudice Level × Priming × Replication × Word Type-with word type (stereotype-related vs. neutral) as a repeated measure.[1] Interest centered on whether (a) high- and low-prejudice subjects were differentially sensitive to stereotype-related and neutral words on the recognition test and (b) priming affected recognition performance. The analysis revealed that prejudice level did not affect subjects' overall performance, $F(1, 24) = 0.07$, $p = .78$, and that it did not interact with word type, $F(1, 24) = 0.04$, $p = .84$.

The second crucial test concerned whether increasing the number of primes interacted with recognition of the word type or subjects' prejudice level to affect performance on the recognition test. None of these tests was significant. Priming did not interact with word type, $F(1, 24) = 0.47$, $p = .50$, or affect the Prejudice × Word Type interaction, $F(1, 24) = 0.32$, $p < .56$. The analysis revealed no other significant main effects or interactions. Subjects were not able to reliably recognize either stereotype-related or neutral words, suggesting that subjects did

---

[1] The overall hit and false alarm rates for stereotype-related and neutral words were also examined as a function of prejudice level, priming, and replication. These data were submitted to a five-way mixed-model analysis of variance. Prejudice level, priming, and replication were between-subjects variables; word type (stereotype-related vs. neutral) and response type (hits vs. false alarms) were within-subject variables. This analysis, like the d' analysis, revealed no significant main effects or interactions.

not have conscious access to the content of the primes, thus establishing the second criterion for attentionless processing.

Automatic stereotype activation and hostility ratings. The major issue concerned the effect of automatic stereotype activation on the interpretation of ambiguous stereotype-congruent (i.e., hostile) behaviors performed by a race-unspecified target person. Following Srull and Wyer (1979) and Bargh and Pietromonaco (1982), two subscores were computed for each subject. A hostility-related subscore was computed by taking the mean of the six traits denotatively related to hostility (hostile, dislikeable, unfriendly, kind, thoughtful, and considerate). The positively valenced scales (thoughtful, considerate, and kind) were reverse scored so that higher mean ratings indicated higher levels of hostility. Similarly, an overall hostility-unrelated subscore was computed by taking the mean of the six hostility-unrelated scales. Again, the positive scales were reverse scored.

The mean ratings were submitted to a mixed-model ANOVA, with prejudice level (high vs. low), priming (20% vs. 80%), and replication (1 vs. 2) as between-subjects variables and scale (hostility related vs. hostility unrelated) as a within-subjects variable. The analysis revealed that the Priming × Scale interaction was significant, $F(1, 70) = 5.04, p < .03$. Ratings on the hostility-related scales were more extreme in the 80% ($M = 7.52$) than in the 20% ($M = 6.87$) priming condition.[2] The hostility-unrelated scales, however, were unaffected by priming ($Ms = 5.89$ and 6.00 for the 20% and 80% priming conditions, respectively). Moreover, the three-way Prejudice Level × Priming × Scale interaction was not significant, $F(1, 70) = 1.19, p = .27$. These results were consistent with the present model and suggest that the effects of automatic stereotype priming were equally strong for high- and low-prejudice subjects. Activating the stereotype did not, however, produce a global negative evaluation of the stimulus person, as only trait scales related to the behaviors in the ambiguous passage were affected by priming.

These analyses suggest that the automatic activation of the racial stereotype affects the encoding and interpretation of ambiguously hostile behaviors for both high- and low-prejudice subjects. To examine this more closely, separate tests on the hostility-related and hostility-unrelated scales were conducted. If high- and low-prejudice subjects are equally affected by the priming manipulation, then prejudice level should not interact with priming in either analysis. The analysis on hostility-related scales revealed only a significant priming main effect, $F(1, 70) = 7.59, p < .008$. The Prejudice Level × Priming interaction was nonsignificant, $F(1, 70) = 1.19, p = .28$. None of the other main effects or interactions was significant. In the analysis of the hostility-unrelated scales, neither the priming main effect, $F(1, 70) = 0.23, p = .63$, nor the Prejudice Level × Priming interaction, $F(1, 70) = 0.02$, $p = .88$, reached significance.

Subjects' prejudice level did enter into several higher order interactions. The Prejudice Level × Priming × Replication interaction, $F(1, 70) = 4.69, p < .03$, indicated that the priming effect was slightly reversed for low-prejudice subjects exposed to Replication 1. A Prejudice Level × Scale Relatedness × Replication interaction, $F(1, 70) = 4.42, p < .04$, suggested that the difference between scores on hostility-related and hostility unrelated scales was greater for low-prejudice subjects in Replication 1 and high-prejudice subjects in Replication 2.

Results supported Devine's automatic vs. controlled stereotyping model (that high and low prejudice persons automatically activate stereotypes). The next question is . . . do low-prejudice people actively suppress that stereotype when thinking about others?

[2] The primary analysis was repeated for high- and low-prejudice subjects separately. The two-way Priming × Scale Related interaction was obtained for both high- and low-prejudice subjects (both $ps < .05$), thus supporting the primary analysis.

Discussion

Study 2 examined the effects of prejudice and automatic stereotype priming on subjects' evaluations of ambiguous stereotype-related behaviors performed by a race-unspecified target person under conditions that precluded the possibility that controlled processes could explain the priming effect. The judgment data of this study suggest that when subjects' ability to consciously monitor stereotype activation is precluded, both high- and low-prejudice subjects produce stereotype-congruent or prejudice-like responses (i.e., stereotype-congruent evaluations of ambiguous behaviors).

As predicted, when people cannot consciously evaluate or suppress the prime words (but they DO perceive them), the stereotype is automatically activated in high- and low-prejudiced persons.

These findings extend those of Srull and Wyer (1979, 1980), Bargh and Pietromonaco (1982), Bargh et al. (1986), and Carver et al. (1983) in demonstrating that in addition to trait categories, stereotypes can be primed and can affect the interpretation of subsequently encoded social information. Moreover, it appears that stereotypes can be primed automatically by using procedures that produce attentionless processing of primes (Bargh & Pietromonaco, 1982). The effects of stereotype priming on subjects' evaluation of the target person's hostility are especially interesting because no hostility-related traits were used as primes. The data are consistent with Duncan's (1976) hypothesis that priming the racial stereotype activates a link between Blacks and hostility. Unlike Duncan's research, however, stereotype activation was achieved through attentionless priming with stereotype-related words and not by the race of the target person.

In summary, the data from Studies 1 and 2 suggest that both those high and low in prejudice have cognitive structures (i.e., stereotypes) that can support prejudiced responses. These data, however, should not be interpreted as suggesting that all people are prejudiced. It could be argued that neither task allowed for the possibility of nonprejudiced responses. Study 1 encouraged subjects not to inhibit prejudiced responses. Study 2 suggested that when the racial category is activated and subjects' ability to consciously monitor this activation is bypassed, their responses reflect the activation of cognitive structures with a longer history (i.e., greater frequency) of activation. As previously indicated, it appears that these structures are the culturally defined stereotypes (Higgins & King, 1981), which are part of people's social heritage, rather than necessarily part of subjects' personal beliefs.

This is a really important point to take from Devine's experiments: the data indicate that high- and low-prejudiced people are equally aware of, and equally activate stereotypes of others. But—and this is what will be tested in experiment 4—once activated, low- prejudiced people are distinct from high-prejudiced people in that they actively try to suppress the stereotype when thinking about a member of the stereotyped outgroup (i.e., they try to individuate the person, and think of them on their own merits, rather than based on stereotypes). High prejudiced persons do no such suppression, and let the stereotypes apply to their evaluation of the target.

This analysis suggests that the effect of automatic stereotype activation may be an inappropriate criterion for prejudice because to use it as such equates knowledge of a stereotype with prejudice. People have knowledge of a lot of information they may not endorse. Feminists, for example, may be knowledgeable of the stereotype of women. Blacks and Jews may have knowledge of the Black or Jewish stereotype.[3] In none of these cases does knowledge of the stereotype imply acceptance of it (see also Bettleheim & Janowitz, 1964). In fact, members of these groups are likely to be motivated to reject the stereotype corresponding to their own group. In each of these cases, however, the stereotypes can likely be intentionally or automatically accessed from memory.

Exactly. There is a big difference between knowledge of a stereotype, and endorsement of a stereotype. You know all the stereotypes about other groups. So does that make you a prejudiced person? No, unless you believe in the truth of the stereotype.

[3] Data from 4 Black subjects who participated in Study 1, but who were not included in the analyses, suggest that Blacks are at least knowledgeable of the cultural stereotype. That is, there was considerable overlap between the content reported by the Black and White subjects. Two independent raters could not reliably predict the race of subjects from the protocols. In addition, Sager and Schofield (1980) found that Black and White children interpreted the same ambiguously hostile behaviors as being more aggressive or hostile when performed by a Black than a White actor. Sager and Schofield argued that subjects were making stereotype-congruent judgments of the Black actor.

The present data suggest that when automatically accessed the stereotype may have effects that are inaccessible to the subject (Nisbett & Wilson, 1977). Thus, even for subjects who honestly report having no negative prejudices against Blacks, activation of stereotypes can have automatic effects that if not consciously monitored produce effects that resemble prejudiced responses. Study 3 examined the responses of high- and low-prejudice subjects to a task designed to focus attention on and thus activate subjects' personal beliefs about Blacks (in addition to the automatically activated stereotype).

STUDY 3: CONTROLLED PROCESSES AND PREJUDICE LEVEL

The present model suggests that one feature that differentiates low- from high-prejudice persons is the effort that they will put into stereotype-inhibition processes. When their non-prejudiced identity is threatened, low-prejudice persons are motivated to reaffirm their nonprejudiced self-concepts (Dutton, 1976; Dutton & Lake, 1973). Thus, when the conflict between their nonprejudiced personal beliefs and the stereotype of Blacks is made salient, low-prejudiced persons are likely to resolve the conflict by denouncing the stereotype and express-ing their nonprejudiced beliefs. To express stereotype-congruent ideas would be inconsistent with and perhaps threaten their nonprejudiced identities.

Study 3 tested this hypothesis by asking high- and low-prejudice subjects to list their thoughts about the racial group *Blacks* under anonymous conditions. This type of task is likely to make the stereotype-personal belief conflict salient for low-prejudice subjects. The model suggests that under these conditions, high- and low-prejudice subjects will write dif-ferent thoughts about Blacks. High-prejudice subjects, because their beliefs overlap with the stereotype, are expected to list stereotype-congruent thoughts. Low-prejudice subjects, it is argued, will take this opportunity to demonstrate that they do not endorse the cultural stereo-type; they are likely to inhibit stereotype-congruent thoughts and intentionally replace them with thoughts consistent with their nonprejudiced personal beliefs. According to the model, resolution of the conflict between personal beliefs and the cultural stereotype in the form of nonprejudiced responses requires controlled inhibition (Logan & Cowan, 1984; Neely, 1977) of the automatically activated stereotype.

Method

Subjects. Subjects were 67 White introductory psychology students who participated for course credit.[4] Subjects were run in groups of 3–6 and were seated at partitioned tables so that subjects were isolated from each other. These procedures were used to enhance anonymity so that subjects would not feel inhibited and would write whatever came to mind.

An additional precaution was taken to ensure anonymity. Before subjects were given instructions regarding the thought-listing task, their experimental participation cards were collected, signed, and left in a pile in the front of the room for subjects to pick up after the study. The experimenter asked subjects not to put any identifying information on their

---

[4] Four Black students signed up to participate. These students did not fill out the thought-listing or Modern Racism measure but were given credit for showing up to participate. The nature of the study was described to them, and they were told why interest centered on the responses of White subjects.

booklets. These procedures were followed so that it would be clear that subjects' names could not be associated with their booklets and that they would receive credit regardless of whether they completed the booklet. No subject refused to complete the measures.

Procedure. After subjects' cards were signed the experimenter asked them to turn over and read the general instructions on the first page of the booklet. Subjects' first task was to list as many alternate labels as they were aware of for the social group *Black Americans*. They were told that the experimenter was interested in how people think about and talk informally about social groups. As such, the experimenter told them that slang or other unconventional group labels were acceptable. Subjects were allowed 1 min to complete this task. The purpose of this task was to encourage activation of subjects' cognitive representation of Blacks. If, for example, high- and low-prejudice persons refer to the social group with different labels (i.e., pejorative vs. nonpejorative) and the labels have different associates, this could provide a basis for explaining any potential differences in content between high- and low-prejudice subjects.

Following the label-generation task, subjects read the thought-listing instructions that asked them to list all of their thoughts in response to the social group *Black Americans* and to the alternate labels they generated. The experimenter told them that any and all of their thoughts (e.g., beliefs, feelings, expectations), flattering or unflattering, were acceptable. Subjects were encouraged to be honest and forthright. The experimenter provided them with two pages of 10 thought-listing boxes in which to record their thoughts and asked them to put only one thought in each box. They were allowed 10 min to complete the task. Finally, subjects completed the seven-item Modern Racism Scale and read through a debriefing document that described the goals of the research and thanked them for their participation.

> Notice they completed just the 7- item scale, no other filler items! Do you think that might be a problem? Why or why not?

Results

Coding scheme. On the basis of a pilot study[5] a scheme for coding the types of thoughts generated was developed. Two judges, blind to subjects' prejudice level, were provided with the coding scheme instructions. A statement or set of statements listed in a box was considered one thought and was assigned one classification by each judge. Each judge rated the 67 protocols in different random orders. The judges agreed on 92% of their classifications. A third judge resolved discrepancies in scoring.

----

[5] The coding scheme was developed and pretested in a pilot study, the goal of which was to demonstrate that subjects' cognitive representations of social groups are richer and more complex than simple trait based structures. The coding scheme was developed on the basis of considerations of the stereotype assessment, prejudice, attitude, and cognitive organization literature. The stereotype literature, for example, led to an examination of the types of traits (i.e., positive or negative) listed in response to the category label. The prejudice and attitude measurement literature, however, led to examination of whether positive (e.g., statements of equality, recognition of Blacks' plight historically, etc.) or negative (resentment of affirmative action, avoid interactions with Blacks) belief thoughts would be elicited by the label.

The cognitive organization literature (Collins & Quillian, 1969; Rips, Shoben, & Smith, 1973) suggested that both criteria! (e.g., physical descriptors) as well as noncriterial (e.g., associated terms) should be examined. On the basis of Rosch's (1978) categorization model, the coding scheme included a category for basic (e.g., athletes) and subordinate (e.g., Richard Pryor) level exemplars of the social category. Superordinate labels were not included because subjects had been asked to generate alternate labels prior to the thought-listing task. Strong support for the coding scheme was found in the pilot study. The pilot study did not examine the complexity of thought listings as a function of subjects' prejudice level. That was the goal of this study.

The major interest in this study was in whether the content of thoughts generated would differ as a function of prejudice level.[6] Before examining those data, however, the alternate labels subjects generated for Black Americans were examined. If high-prejudice subjects generate more negative labels (e.g., nigger, jigaboo, etc.) than low-prejudice subjects and pejorative labels are more strongly associated with stereotype-congruent information, this could explain possible differences between high- and low-prejudice subjects. Subjects were divided into high-prejudice ($N = 34$) and low-prejudice ($N = 33$) groups on the basis of a median split of scores on the Modern Racism Scale.

The proportion of pejorative and nonpejorative labels generated was calculated for each subject. Pejorative labels included terms such as the following: niggers, coons, spades, spearchuckers, jungle bunnies, and jigs. Nonpejorative labels included the following: Blacks, Afro Americans, Brothers, and colored people. One high-prejudice subject was eliminated from this comparison because she failed to generate any alternate labels. The comparison indicated that the proportion of pejorative alternate labels did not differ between high-prejudice ($M = .53$) and low-prejudice ($M = .44$) subjects, $t(64) = .68$, $p > .10$. It appears, then, that high- and low-prejudice subjects were aware of the various pejorative labels.

Examination of the thought-listing protocols, however, revealed important differences between high- and low-prejudice subjects. The important differences appeared to be associated with the belief and trait categories.[7] Negative beliefs included thoughts such as "Blacks are free loaders"; "Blacks cause problems (e.g., mugging, fights)"; "Affirmative action sucks"; and so on. Positive-belief thoughts included "Blacks and Whites are equal"; "Affirmative action will restore historical inequities"; "My father says all Blacks are lazy, I think he is wrong" (e.g., negation of the cultural stereotype); "It's unfair to judge people by their color—they are individuals"; and so on. The positive and negative traits were typically listed as single words rather than being written in complete sentences. Negative traits included hostile, lazy, stupid, poor, dirty, and so on. The positive traits included musical, friendly, athletic, and so on.

The frequency of these positive-belief, negative-belief, and trait thoughts listed in subjects' protocols were submitted to a Prejudice Level (high vs. low) × Valence (positive vs. negative) × Thought Type (trait vs. belief) mixed-model ANOVA. Prejudice level was a between-subjects variable, and valence and thought type were within-subjects variables. The analysis revealed the expected Prejudice Level × Valence interaction, $F(1, 65) = 28.82$, $p < .0001$. High-prejudice subjects listed more negative ($M = 2.06$) than positive ($M = 1.48$) thoughts, and

Because that would mean that high-prejudiced persons have access to more stereotype-related information than do low-prejudiced persons, and that would be a major contributor to why we would observe differences between the groups in their behavior and attitudes toward the stereotyped outgroup.

Interesting, showing that high and low prejudiced subjects are aware of and have access to the very negative stereotype labels for the outgroup.

---

[6] As a prerequisite to examining the content of the protocols, an analysis on the number of thoughts and the number of alternate labels generated by high- and low-prejudice subjects was performed to examine whether prejudice level affected these tasks. Although it was expected that subjects would generate more thoughts than alternate labels, the key tests of interest were provided by the prejudice-level main effect (whether one group listed more items than the other) and the Prejudice Level × Task interaction (whether prejudice level differentially affected the tasks). These data were submitted to a Prejudice Level (high vs. low) × Task (label generation vs. thought generation) mixed-model analysis of variance. The analysis revealed that subjects generated a greater number of thoughts ($M = 12.67$) than labels ($M = 4.72$), $F(1, 65) = 156.83$, $p < .0001$. However, neither the prejudice main effect, $F(1, 65) = 0.66$, $p < .42$, nor the Prejudice Level × Task interaction, $F(1, 65) = 0.01$, $p < .94$, was significant.

[7] A canonical discriminant function analysis in which subjects' prejudice level was predicted as a function of the best linear combination of the 10 coding categories revealed a single canonical variable (Wilks's lambda 0.63), $F(10, 56) = 3.25$, $p < .002$. The canonical squared multiple correlation was 0.37. Positive-belief thoughts were located at one extreme of the canonical structure (-0.88) and negative trait thoughts at the other (0.78). None of the other categories discriminated significantly between high- and low-prejudice groups.

low-prejudice subjects listed more positive ($M = 2.28$) than negative ($M = 1.10$) thoughts. In addition, there was a Prejudice Level × Type interaction, $F(1, 65) = 18.04$, $p < .0001$. This interaction suggested that high-prejudice subjects were more likely to list trait ($M = 2.56$) than belief ($M = 1.52$) thoughts. In contrast, low-prejudice subjects were more likely to list belief ($M = 2.86$) than trait ($M = 1.12$) thoughts. These interactions are important because the Black stereotype traditionally has been largely negative and composed of traits (Brigham, 1971). Ascription of negative components of the stereotype was verified in these data only for high-prejudice subjects.

These two-way interactions were qualified, however, by a significant Prejudice Level × Valence × Thought Type interaction, $F(1, 65) = 4.88$, $p < .03$. High-prejudice subjects most often listed negative traits ($M = 3.32$). A post hoc Duncan test ($p = .05$) revealed that for high-prejudice subjects, the frequency of negative trait thoughts differed significantly from each of the other three thought types but that the frequency of positive belief ($M = 1.17$), negative-belief ($M = 1.18$), and positive trait ($M = 1.79$) thoughts did not differ from each other. In contrast, low-prejudice subjects most frequently listed positive-belief thoughts ($M = 4.52$). This mean differed significantly (Duncan test, $p = .05$) from the negative-belief ($M = 1.21$), positive trait ($M = 1.24$), and negative trait ($M = 1.00$) means, but the latter three means did not differ from each other.

It was argued earlier that this type of task would encourage subjects to intentionally access and report thoughts consistent with their personal beliefs. Trait ascriptions are part of high prejudice, but not low-prejudice, subjects' beliefs according to the present model. It appears that in this task, both high- and low-prejudice subjects' thoughts reflected their beliefs. High-prejudice subjects reported primarily traits and low-prejudice subjects reported beliefs that contradicted the cultural stereotype and emphasized equality between the races.

To follow up implications from the previous studies, subjects' protocols were examined to determine whether the themes of hostility, aggressiveness, or violence were present. Statements such as "They are hostile," "Blacks are violent," "Blacks are aggressive," and so on were considered to reflect this theme. Non-trait-based thoughts such as "They rape women" or "I'm scared of them" were less frequent but were also considered to reflect the general theme. Sixty percent of the high-prejudice subjects directly included such themes in their thought-listing protocols. In contrast, only 9% of the subjects scoring low in prejudice included hostility themes in their protocols. A z test on proportions indicated that this difference was reliable ($z = 4.41$, $p < .01$).

Discussion

Taken together, these sets of analyses indicate that high- and low-prejudice subjects were willing to report different thoughts about Blacks. In addition, these analyses suggested that there were sufficient levels of variability in prejudice levels among the subjects to detect the effects of prejudice in the previous studies should those effects exist. The thought-listing task was one in which subjects were likely to think carefully about what their responses implied about their prejudice-relevant self-concepts. For those who valued a nonprejudiced identity, writing stereotype-congruent thoughts would have been inconsistent with and perhaps would have threatened their nonprejudiced identity.

Thus, even under anonymous conditions, low-prejudice subjects apparently censored and inhibited (Neely, 1977) the automatically activated negative stereotype-congruent information and consciously replaced it with thoughts that expressed their nonprejudiced values.

The thought-listing protocol revealed that high-prejudiced persons believe in the truth of the prejudiced statements, and ascribed more negative traits to the stereotyped outgroup. The low-prejudiced subjects, however, personally endorsed beliefs opposite to those negative stereotypes, and endorsed equality between racial groups.

This is one of the key findings of Devine's seminal paper. That high- and low-prejudiced persons have equal access to and knowledge about the cultural stereotypes about a given group, but once activated, only the low-prejudiced persons actively work to inhibit and override those stereotypes, and instead they supplant them with egalitarian thoughts and cognitive efforts to individuate the outgroup member (to regard them on their own merits as a person, not a category member).

Low-prejudice subjects wrote few perjorative thoughts. Their thoughts were more likely to have reflected the importance of equality or the negation of the cultural stereotype. Moreover, low-prejudice subjects appeared reluctant to ascribe traits to the group as a whole. In contrast, the protocols of high-prejudice subjects seemed much more consistent with the cultural stereotype of Blacks. Their thoughts were primarily negative, and they seemed willing to ascribe traits to the group (especially negative traits).

A most important comparison for the present three studies, and for the intergroup perception literature more generally, concerns the likelihood of subjects reporting thoughts reflecting the theme of hostility. Much of the intergroup perception literature has assumed that the hostility component of the stereotype influences perceptions of Blacks (Donnerstein et al., 1972; Duncan, 1976; Sager & Schofield, 1980), and Studies 1 and 2 suggested that hostility is strongly associated with Blacks for both high- and low-prejudice subjects. Study 2 in particular suggested that hostility is automatically activated when the category label and associates are presented. The present data, however, suggest that high- and low-prejudice subjects differ in their willingness to attribute this characteristic to the entire group. High-prejudice subjects included thoughts suggesting that Blacks are hostile and aggressive much more frequently than did low-prejudice subjects. The present framework suggests that this difference likely reflects low-prejudice subjects engaging in controlled, stereotype-inhibiting processes. Low-prejudice subjects apparently censored negative, what they considered inappropriate, thoughts that came to mind.

GENERAL DISCUSSION

The model examined in these studies makes a clear distinction between knowledge of the racial stereotype, which Study 1 suggested both high- and low-prejudice persons possess, and personal beliefs about the stereotyped group. Study 2 suggested that automatic stereotype activation is equally strong and equally inescapable for high- and low-prejudice subjects. In the absence of controlled stereotype-related processes, automatic stereotype activation leads to stereotype-congruent or prejudice-like responses for both those high and low in prejudice. Study 3, however, provided evidence that controlled processes can inhibit the effects of automatic processing when the implications of such processing compete with goals to establish or maintain a nonprejudiced identity.

This is another major conclusion to be taken from this paper. There is a big difference between knowledge of stereotypes and whether one personally believes in the truth of those stereotypes.

The present model suggests that a change in one's beliefs or attitude toward a stereotyped group may or may not be reflected in a change in the corresponding evaluations of or behaviors toward members of that group. Consider the following quote by Pettigrew (1987):

> Many southerners have confessed to me, for instance, that even though in their minds they no longer feel prejudice toward blacks, they still feel squeamish when they shake hands with a black. These feelings are left over from what they learned in their families as children. (p. 20)

It would appear that the automatically activated stereotype congruent or prejudice-like responses have become independent of one's current attitudes or beliefs. Crosby, Bromley, and Saxe (1980) argued that the inconsistency sometimes observed between expressed attitudes and behaviors that are less consciously mediated is evidence that (all) White Americans are prejudiced against Blacks and that non-prejudiced responses are attempts at impression management (i.e., efforts to cover up truly believed but socially undesirable attitudes). (See also Baxter, 1973; Gaertner, 1976; Gaertner & Dovidio, 1977; Linn, 1965; Weitz, 1972.) Crosby et al. argued that nonconsciously monitored responses are more trustworthy than are consciously mediated responses.

In the context of the present model in which automatic processes and controlled processes can be dissociated, I disagree fundamentally with this premise. Such an argument denies the possibility for change in one's attitudes and beliefs, and I view this as a severe limitation of the Crosby et al. (1980) analysis. Crosby and her colleagues seem to identify the flexibility of controlled processes as a limitation. In contrast, the present framework considers such processes as the key to escaping prejudice. This statement does not imply that change is likely to be easy *or* speedy (and it is certainly not all or nothing). Non-prejudiced responses are, according to the dissociation model, a function of intentional, controlled processes and require a conscious decision to behave in a non-prejudiced fashion. In addition, new responses must be learned and well-practiced before they can serve as competitive responses to the automatically activated stereotype-congruent responses. What is needed now is a fully articulated model of controlled processes that delineates the cognitive mechanisms involved in inhibition. Logan and Cowan (1984; see also Bargh, 1984) have developed a model of controlled processes that may provide valuable insights into the inhibition process.

Thus, in contrast to the pessimistic analysis by Crosby et al. (1980), the present framework suggests that rather than all people being prejudiced, all are victims of being limited capacity processors. Perceivers cannot attend to all aspects of a situation or their behavior. In situations in which controlled processes are precluded or interfered with, automatic processing effects may exert the greatest influence on responses. In the context of racial stereotypes and attitudes, automatic processing effects appear to have negative implications.

Inhibiting stereotype-congruent or prejudice-like responses and intentionally replacing them with nonprejudiced responses can be likened to the breaking of a bad habit. Its consequences are spontaneous and undesirable, at least for the low-prejudice person. For those who have integrated egalitarian ideals into their value system, a conflict would exist between these ideals and expressions of racial prejudice. The conflict experienced is likely to be involved in the initiation of controlled stereotype-inhibiting processes that are required to eliminate the habitual response (activation). Ronis, Yates, and Kirscht (in press) argued that elimination of a bad habit requires essentially the same steps as the formation of a habit. The individual must (a) initially decide to stop the old behavior, (b) remember the resolution, and (c) try repeatedly and decide repeatedly to eliminate the habit before the habit can be eliminated. In addition, the individual must develop a new cognitive (attitudinal and belief) structure that is consistent with the newly determined pattern of responses.

An important assumption to keep in mind in the change process, however, is that neither the formation of an attitude from beliefs nor the formation of a decision from attitudes or beliefs entails the elimination of earlier established attitudinal or stereotype representations. The dissociation model holds that although low-prejudiced persons have changed their beliefs concerning stereotyped group members, the stereotype has not been eliminated from the memory system. In fact, it remains a well-organized, frequently activated knowledge structure. During the change process the new pattern of ideas and behaviors must be consciously activated and serve as the basis for responses or the individual is likely to fall into old habits (e.g., stereotype-congruent or prejudice-like responses).

Great analogy. Breaking the influence of the automatically activated stereotypes on one's perception of the outgroup member requires a lot of motivation and cognitive effort to replace such thoughts (once activated) with more egalitarian and individuating cognitions.

The model suggests that the change process involves developing associations between the stereotype structure and the personal belief structure. For change to be successful, each time the stereotype is activated the person must activate and think about his or her personal beliefs. That is, the individual must increase the frequency with which the personal belief structure is activated when responding to members of the stereotyped group. To the extent that the personal belief structure becomes increasingly accessible, it will better provide a rival response to the responses that would likely follow from automatic stereotype activation. In cognitive terms, before the newer beliefs and attitudes can serve as a rival, the strong association between the previously learned negative attitude and Blacks will have to be weakened and the association of Blacks to the new nonprejudiced attitudes and beliefs will have to be made stronger and conscious.

In summary, at minimum, the attitude and belief change process requires intention, attention, and time. During the change process an individual must not only inhibit automatically activated information but also intentionally replace such activation with nonprejudiced ideas and responses. It is likely that these variables contribute to the difficulty of changing one's responses to members of stereotyped groups. In addition, these variables probably contribute to the often observed inconsistency between expressed attitudes and behavior. The nonprejudiced responses take time, attention, and effort. To the extent that any (or all) of these are limited, the outcome is likely to be stereotype-congruent or prejudice-like responses.

In conclusion, it is argued that prejudice need not be the consequence of ordinary thought processes. Although stereotypes still exist and can influence the responses of both high- and low-prejudice subjects, particularly when those responses are not subject to close conscious scrutiny, there are individuals who actively reject the negative stereotype and make efforts to respond in nonprejudiced ways. At least in situations involving consciously controlled stereotype-related processes, those who score low in prejudice on an attitude scale, are attempting to inhibit stereotypic responses (e.g., Study 3, Greeley & Sheatsley, 1971; Taylor, et al., 1978; see also Higgins & King, 1981). The present framework, because of its emphasis on the possible dissociation of automatic and controlled processes, *allows for the possibility* that those who report being non-prejudiced are in reality low in prejudice.

This analysis is not meant to imply that prejudice has disappeared or to give people an excuse for their prejudices. In addition, it does not imply that only low-prejudice persons are capable of controlled stereotype inhibition. High-prejudice persons could also consciously censor their responses to present a nonprejudiced identity (probably for different reasons than low-prejudice persons, however). What this analysis requires is that theoreticians be more precise on the criteria established for labeling behavior as prejudiced or nonprejudiced. The present model and set of empirical studies certainly does not resolve this issue. However, the present framework highlights the potential for non-prejudiced behaviors when social desirability concerns are minimal (Study 3) and invites researchers to explore the variables that are likely to engage controlled stereotype-inhibiting processes in intergroup settings. At present, it seems productive to entertain and systematically explore the possibility that being low in prejudice reflects more than impression management efforts and to explore the conditions under which controlled stereotype-inhibition processes are engaged.

REFERENCES

Allport, G. W. (1954). *The nature of prejudice*. Reading, MA: Addison Wesley.

Ashmore, R. D., & Del Boca, F. K. (1981). Conceptual approaches to stereotypes and stereotyping. In D. L. Hamilton (Ed.), *Cognitive processes in stereotyping and intergroup behavior* (pp. 1–35). Hillsdale, NJ: Erlbaum.

Bargh, J. A. (1984). Automatic and conscious processing of social information. In R. S. Wyer Jr., & T. K. Srull (Eds.), *The handbook of social cognition* (Vol. 3, pp. 1–43). Hillsdale, NJ: Erlbaum.

Bargh, J. A., Bond, R. N., Lombardi, W. J., & Tota, M. E. (1986). The additive nature of chronic and temporary sources of construct accessibility. *Journal of Personality and Social Psychology 50*, 869–878.

Bargh, J. A., & Pietromonaco, P. (1982). Automatic information processing and social perception: The influence of trait information presented outside of conscious awareness on impression formation. *Journal of Personality and Social Psychology, 43*, 437–449.

Baxter, G. W. (1973). Prejudiced liberals? Race and information effects in a two person game. *Journal of Conflict Resolution. 17*, 131–161.

Bettleheim, B., & Janowitz, M. (1964). *Social change and prejudice*. New York: Free Press of Glencoe.

Bolota, D. A. (1983). Automatic semantic activation and episodic memory encoding. *Journal of Verbal Learning and Verbal Behavior, 22*, 88–104.

Billig, M. (1985). Prejudice, categorization, and particularization: From a perceptual to a rhetorical approach. *European Journal of Social Psychology, 15*, 79–103.

Brigham, J. C. (1971). Ethnic stereotypes. *Psychological Bulletin, 76*, 15–33.

Brigham, J. C. (1972). Racial stereotypes: Measurement variables and the stereotype-attitude relationship. *Journal of Applied Social Psychology, 2*, 63–76.

Carrol, J. B., Davies, P., & Richman, B. (1971). *The American Heritage word frequency book*. New York: Houghton Mifflin.

Carver, C. S., Ganellin, R. J., Froming, W. J., & Chambers, W. (1983). Modeling: An analysis in terms of category accessibility. *Journal of Experimental Social Psychology, 19*, 403–421.

Collins, A. M., & Quillian, M. R. (1969). Retrieval time from semantic memory. *Journal of Verbal Learning and Verbal Behavior, 8*, 240–247.

Crosby, F., Bromley, S., & Saxe, L. (1980). Recent unobtrusive studies of black and white discrimination and prejudice: A literature review. *Psychological Bulletin, 87*, 546–563.

Devine, P. G. (1988). *Stereotype assessment: Theoretical and methodological issues*. Unpublished manuscript, University of Wisconsin Madison.

Donnerstein, E., & Donnerstein, M. (1972). White rewarding behavior as a function of the potential for black retaliation. *Journal of Personality and Social Psychology, 24*, 327–333.

Donnerstein, E., Donnerstein, M., Simon, S., & Ditrichs, R. (1972). Variables in interracial aggression: Anonymity, expected retaliation, and a riot. *Journal of Personality and Social Psychology, 22*, 236–245.

Dovidio, J. F., Evans, N. E., & Tyler, R. B. (1986). Racial stereotypes: The contents of their cognitive representations. *Journal of Experimental Social Psychology, 22*, 22–37.

Duncan, B. L. (1976). Differential social perception and attribution of intergroup violence: Testing the lower limits of stereotyping of blacks. *Journal of Personality and Social Psychology, 34*, 590–598.

Dutton, D. G. (1976). Tokenism, reverse discrimination, and egalitarianism in interracial behavior. *Journal of Social Issues, 32*, 93–107.

Dutton, D. G., & Lake, R. A. (1973). Threat of own prejudice and reverse discrimination in interracial situations. *Journal of Personality and Social Psychology, 28*, 94–100.

Ehrlich, H. J. (1973). *The social psychology of prejudice*. New York: Wiley.

Fowler, C. A., Wolford, G., Slade, R., & Tassinary, L. (1981). Lexical access with and without awareness. *Journal of Experimental Psychology: General, 110*, 341–362.

Gaertner, S. L. (1976). Nonreactive measures in racial attitude research: A focus on "liberals." In P. A. Katz (Ed.), *Towards the elimination of racism* (pp. 183–211). New York: Pergamon Press.

Gaertner, S. L., & Dovidio, J. F. (1977). The subtlety of white racism, arousal, and helping. *Journal of Personality and Social Psychology, 35*, 691–707.

Gaertner, S. L., & McLaughlin, J. P.(1983). Racial stereotypes: Associations and ascriptions of positive and negative characteristics. *Social Psychology Quarterly, 46*, 23–30.

Gilbert, G. M. (1951). Stereotype persistence and change among college students. *Journal of Abnormal and Social Psychology, 46,* 245–254.

Greeley, A., & Sheatsley, P. (1971). Attitudes toward racial integration. *Scientific American, 222,* 13–19.

Green, D. M., & Swets, J. A. (1966). *Signal detection theory and psycho physics.* New York: Wiley.

Greenwald, A. G., Klinger, M., & Liu, T. J. (in press). Unconscious processing of word meaning. *Memory & Cognition.*

Hamilton, D. L. (1981). Stereotyping and intergroup behavior: Some thoughts on the cognitive approach. In D. L. Hamilton (Ed.), *Cognitive processes in stereotyping and intergroup behavior* (pp. 333–353). Hillsdale, NJ: Erlbaum.

Harding, J., Proshansky, H., Kutner, B., &. Chein, I. (1969). Prejudice and ethnic relations. In G. Lindzey (Ed.), *Handbook of social psychology* (Vol. 5). Reading, MA: Addison-Wesley.

Higgins, E. T., & King, G. (1981). Accessibility of social constructs: Information-processing consequences of individual and contextual variability. In N. Cantor & J. F. Kihlstrom (Eds.), *Personality and social interaction* (pp. 69–121). Hillsdale, NJ: Erlbaum.

Holender, D. (1986). Semantic activation without conscious identification in dichotic listening, parafoveal vision, and visual masking: A survey and appraisal. *Behavioral and Brain Sciences, 9,* 1–66.

Karlins, M., Coffman, T. L., & Walters, G. (1969). On the fading of social stereotypes: Studies in three generations of college students. *Journal of Personality and Social Psychology, 13,* 1–16.

Katz, D., & Braly, K. (1933). Racial stereotypes in one hundred college students. *Journal of Abnormal and Social Psychology, 28,* 280–290. Katz, P. A. (1976). The acquisition of racial attitudes in children. In P. A. Katz (Ed.), *Towards the elimination of racism* (pp. 125–154). New York: Pergamon Press.

Kinder, D. R., & Sears, D. O. (1981). Prejudice and politics: Symbolic racism versus racial threats to the good life. *Journal of Personality and Social Psychology, 40,* 414–431.

Klatzky, R. L. (1984). *Memory and awareness.* San Francisco: Freeman.

LaViolette, F., & Silvert, K. H. (1951). A theory of stereotypes. *Social Forces. 29,* 237–257.

Linn, L. S. (1965). Verbal attitudes and overt behavior: A study of racial discrimination. *Social Forces, 43,* 353–364.

Logan, G. D. (1980). Attention and automaticity in Stroop and priming tasks: Theory and data. *Cognitive Psychology, 12,* 523–553.

Logan, G. D., & Cowan, W. B. (1984). On the ability to inhibit thought and action: A theory of act control. *Psychological Review, 91,* 295–327.

Marcel, A. J. (1983a). Conscious and unconscious perception: Experiments on visual masking and word recognition. *Cognitive Psychology, 15,* 197–237.

Marcel, A. J. (1983b). Conscious and unconscious perception: An approach to the relations between phenomenal experience and perceptual processes. *Cognitive Psychology, 15,* 238–300.

McConahay, J. B., Hardee, B. B., & Batts, V. (1981). Has racism declined? It depends upon who's asking and what is asked. *Journal of Conflict Resolution, 25,* 563–579.

Neely, J. H. (1977). Semantic priming and retrieval from lexical memory: Roles of inhibitionless spreading activation and limited-capacity attention. *Journal of Experimental Psychology, 106,* 226–254.

Nisbett, R. E., & Wilson, T. D. (1977). Telling more than we can know: Verbal reports on mental processes. *Psychological Review, 84,* 231–259.

Pettigrew, T. (1987, May 12). "Useful" modes of thought contribute to prejudice. *New York Times,* pp. 17, 20.

Porter, J. D. R. (1971). *Black child, white child: The development of racial attitudes.* Cambridge, MA: Harvard University Press.

Posner, M. I., & Snyder, C. R. R. (1975). Attention and cognitive control. In R. L. Solso (Ed.), *Information processing and cognition: The Loyola Symposium.* Hillsdale, NJ: Erlbaum.

Pratkanis, A. R. (in press). The cognitive representation of attitudes. In A. R. Pratkanis, S. J. Breckler, & A. G. Greenwald (Eds.), *Attitude structure and function.* Hillsdale, NJ: Erlbaum.

Proshansky, H. M. (1966). The development of intergroup attitudes. In L. W. Hoffman & M. L. Hoffman (Eds.), *Review of child development research* (Vol. 2, pp. 311–371). New York: Russell Sage Foundation.

Rips, L. J., Shoben, E. J., & Smith, E. E. (1973). Semantic distance and the verification of semantic relations. *Journal of Verbal Learning and Verbal Behavior, 12,* 1–20.

Ronis, D. L., Yates, J. F., & Kirscht, J. P.(in press). Attitudes, decisions, and habits as determinants of repeated behavior. In A. R. Pratkanis, S. J. Breckler, & A. G. Greenwald (Eds.), *Attitude structure and function*. Hillsdale, NJ: Erlbaum.

Rosch, E. (1978). Principles of categorization. In E. Rosch and B. B. Lloyd (Eds.), *Cognition and categorization* (pp. 28–48). Hillsdale, NJ: Erlbaum.

Saenger, G. (1953). *The social psychology of prejudice*. New York: Harper.

Sager, H. A., & Schofield, J. W. (1980). Racial and behavioral cues in black and white children's perceptions of ambiguously aggressive acts. *Journal of Personality and Social Psychology, 39,* 590–598.

Schneider, W., & Shiffrin, R. M. (1977). Controlled and automatic human information processing: I. Detection, search, and attention. *Psychological Review, 84,* 1–66.

Sears, D. O., & Kinder, D. R. (1971). Racial tensions and voting in Los Angeles. In W. Z. Hirsch (Ed.), *Los Angeles: Viability and prospects for metropolitan leadership* (pp. 51–88). New York: Praeger.

Sears, D. O., & McConahay, J. B. (1973). *The politics of violence: The new urban blacks and the Watts riot.* Boston: Houghton Mifflin.

Secord, P. F., & Backman, C. W. (1974). *Social psychology*. New York: McGraw-Hill.

Shiffrin, R. M., & Dumais, S. T. (1981). The development of automatism. In J. R. Anderson (Ed.), *Cognitive skills and their acquisition* (pp. 111–140). Hillsdale, NJ: Erlbaum.

Shiffrin, R. M., & Schneider, W. (1977). Controlled and automatic human information processing: II. Perceptual learning, automatic attending, and a general theory. *Psychological Review, 84,* 127–190.

Simpson, G. E., & Yinger, J. M. (1965). *Racial and cultural minorities* (rev. ed.) New York: Harper & Row.

Smith, E. R. (1984). Model of social inference processes. *Psychological Review, 91,* 392–413.

Smith, E. R., & Branscombe, N. R. (1985). *Stereotype traits can be processed automatically.* Unpublished manuscript, Purdue University, West Lafayette, IN.

Srull, T. K., & Wyer, R. S., Jr. (1979). The role of category accessibility in the interpretation of information about persons: Some determinants and implications. *Journal of Personality and Social Psychology, 37,* 1660–1672.

Srull, T. K., & Wyer, R. S., Jr. (1980). Category accessibility and social perception: Some implications for the study of person memory and interpersonal judgments. *Journal of Personality and Social Psychology, 38,* 841–856.

Stephan, W. G. (1985). Intergroup relations. In G. Lindzey & E. Aronson (Eds.), *The handbook of social psychology* (3rd ed., Vol. 2, pp. 559–658). Hillsdale, NJ: Erlbaum.

Tajfel, H. (1981). *Human groups and social categories: Studies in social psychology*. Cambridge, England: Cambridge University Press.

Taylor, D. G., Sheatsley, P. B., & Greeley, A. M. (1978). Attitudes toward racial integration. *Scientific American, 238,* 42–49.

Weitz, S. (1972). Attitude, voice, and behavior: A repressed affect model of interracial interaction. *Journal of Personality and Social Psychology, 24,* 14–21.

Wyer, R. S., Jr., & Srull, T. K. (1981). Category accessibility: Some theoretical and empirical issues concerning the processing of social stimulus information. In E. T. Higgins, C. P. Herman, & M. P. Zanna (Eds.), *Social cognition: The Ontario Symposium* (Vol. I, pp. 161–197). Hillsdale, NJ: Erlbaum.

POST-ARTICLE DISCUSSION

Devine's paper is one of the most-cited articles in the study of prejudice because it showed compelling evidence that demonstrates that both high- and low-prejudiced persons automatically access their shared cultural stereotype information when they think of the stereotype category, but only the low-prejudiced persons are motivated to actively not use that stereotypic information when thinking about people in that stereotype category. That is, when the stereotype is automatically activated in low-prejudiced persons, they engage in controlled, effortful cognition to blunt or inhibit the influence of that stereotype on their subsequent cognition. Devine further said that these results show that there is no correlation between explicit measures of prejudice (such as the Modern Racism Scale; McConahay, 1986) and the automatic activation of the stereotype in the low-prejudiced person, whereas there is a high correlation between those two things in high-prejudiced persons (because they are not motivated to suppress the stereotype). As we discussed earlier, this shows that although we all know the stereotypes in our culture for many stigmatized groups, it doesn't mean that we are powerless to stop their influence on our daily thought. Rather, if one is sufficiently motivated, one can suppress the influence of automatically activated stereotypes on one's cognition, thereby helping the perceiver to treat the target person according to his or her own merits as an individual and, in so doing, also help to reduce prejudice in society.

THINGS TO THINK ABOUT

1. One of the basic assumptions that Devine tested is the idea that high- and low-prejudiced people equally know the stereotypes in their culture about stereotyped outgroups. Do you think this is true? Do you think that high-prejudiced people have more stereotypes in their mind than do low-prejudiced persons?

2. Do you think that low-prejudiced persons are just better able to hide their prejudices and that the difference between low-prejudiced persons and high-prejudiced persons is that high-prejudiced people don't care about openly showing their stereotypes and prejudices?

3. Why do you think it was important for Devine to establish the content of the stereotypes that Whites have about African Americans in Study 1?

4. In Study 2, why do you think that the prejudice × priming interaction was not significant?

5. Why do you think that, for some experiments, Devine separated high- and low-prejudiced subjects on the basis of the top third and bottom third of the scores on the Modern Racism Scale (MRS) and other times made the two groups (high- vs. low-prejudiced subjects) based on a median split?

INTRODUCTION TO READING 9.2
Bodenhausen (1990)

One of the axioms of psychology is that people like to think that their personality guides their behavior across all situations. In fact, that is the way that current personality researchers think of the concept of traits: as stable characteristics of one's self that consistently guide behavior across situations. But one thing that social psychologists have learned over the past century is that sometimes our behavior is influenced not by our personality but by the situation. Infamous examples of this are the Zimbardo prison study (Haney et al., 1973), Milgram's (1963) obedience research, and the Good Samaritan study by Darley and Batson (1973). In studies like these, research reveals the power of the situation to drive behavior. The paper you are about to read is another example of this. Bodenhausen (1990) showed, with a clever, simple design, how the time of day can be the deciding factor for whether or not one thinks about others in terms of a stereotype. You would think that being low-prejudiced is something that is stable within a person, like a personality trait. If you are low-prejudiced in one situation, you are in all situations. But, what if you get tired? Does that affect your ability to individuate others and think about them according to their individual merits? The answer may surprise you!

Reading 9.2

Research Report

Stereotypes As Judgmental Heuristics: Evidence of Circadian Variations In Discrimination

Galen V. Bodenhausen

Abstract—The *question of when people rely on stereotypic preconceptions in judging others was investigated in two studies. As a person's motivation or ability to process information systematically is diminished, the person may rely to an increasing extent on stereotypes, when available, as a way of simplifying the task of generating a response. It was hypothesized that circadian variations in arousal levels would be related to social perceivers' propensity to stereotype others by virtue of their effects on motivation and processing capacity. In support of this hypothesis, subjects exhibited stereotypic biases in their judgments to a much greater extent when the judgments were rendered at a nonoptimal time of day (i.e., in the morning for "night people" and in the evening for "morning people"). In Study One, this pattern was found in probability judgments concerning personal characteristics; in Study Two, the pattern was obtained in perceptions of guilt in allegations of student misbehavior. Results generalized over a range of different types of social stereotypes and suggest that* *biological processes should be considered in attempts to conceptualize the determinants of stereotyping.*

When do people rely on their stereotypic beliefs in forming impressions of and making judgments about other people? This question is at the heart of many recent investigations of stereotyping and discrimination. Bodenhausen and Wyer (1985) proposed that stereotypes can be viewed as judgmental heuristics that are sometimes used to simplify the cognitive tasks confronted by the social perceiver. Whether we respond to others based on general beliefs about their group or a thoughtful analysis of each person's unique attributes depends to a large extent on whether stereotypic beliefs provide an easy, seemingly relevant basis for responding and whether a quick and less effortful response is necessary or desirable (Chaiken, Liberman, & Eagly, 1989). Stereotypic responses may predominate unless the social perceiver has sufficient momentary ability and motivation to engage in effortful, systematic thought. Motivational factors include personal involvement (Erber & Fiske, 1984) and incentives for accuracy (Neuberg & Fiske, 1987). Factors that limit ability to process information systematically include distraction (Petty, Wells, & Brock, 1976), information overload (Rothbart, Fulero, Jensen, Howard, & Birrell, 1978), and task complexity (Bodenhausen & Lichtenstein, 1987).

The present research examined the intriguing possibility that there are regular patterns of variation in the social perceiver's motivation and information processing capacities that produce what might be characterized as circadian rhythms in social perception. It has been well established that there are significant time-of-day effects in many types of human performance (Blake, 1967; Colquhoun, 1971; Freeman & Hovland, 1934). These effects have been attributed to variations in circadian arousal levels affecting the capacity and efficiency of working memory (Folkard, Wever, & Wildgruber, 1983) as well as to more general notions of fatigue or alertness. For many tasks, performance peaks at a certain level of circadian arousal, and this peak occurs at a fairly regular point in the day.

Several studies suggest that there are considerable inter-individual differences in the time of day at which one reaches one's peak, or acrophase (Horne & Ostberg, 1977; Patkai, 1971). The notion of "morning people" and "night people" suggests that there are two clusters of individuals who tend to reach their functional peak either earlier or later in the day. In order to explore this possibility, Horne and Ostberg (1976) devised a self-assessment questionnaire to measure this individual difference. The measure, called the Morningness Eveningness Questionnaire (MEQ), has since been utilized fairly extensively and has been shown to have predictive validity and other desirable psychometric properties (Smith, Reilly, & Midkiff, 1989).

If people are more likely to rely on stereotypic preconceptions in making judgments when they are not particularly motivated or are less cognitively able to consider carefully the relevant evidence at hand, and if cognitive capabilities and motivation fluctuate as a function of time of day, it follows that reliance on stereotypes in the judgment process should also vary as a function of time of day, other things being equal. Stereotypic responses should be least likely during acrophase. Because some people show a pattern of matutinal acrophase, they should be least likely to exhibit symptoms of stereotyping during the morning. Others characteristically show a vespertine acrophase, so they should be least likely to show stereotype-based discrimination during the evening. These predictions were investigated in two studies, using two different judgment tasks and several different social stereotypes.

Correspondence and reprint requests to Galen V. Bodenhausen, Department of Psychology, Psychology Research Building, Michigan State University, East Lansing, MI 48824-1117.

Margin notes:

The answer may seem deceptively simple . . . wouldn't people always use their stereotypes when making impressions about others? Bodenhausen wants to examine the conditions under which people are more or less likely to utilize stereotypes when thinking about others.

Research shows that in order to NOT stereotype others, we need two things to happen: we have to be motivated to not think about the other person in terms of stereotypes, and we need to have the cognitive capacity to think carefully about the other individual (i.e., not be distracted or doing other cognitive tasks at the same time).

So what Bodenhausen is investigating in this research is whether our motivation and cognitive capacity varies as a function of physiological arousal related to our circadian rhythms. That is, does our ability to disregard stereotypes when making social judgments fluctuate with the rise and fall of our daily physiological arousal?

Hypotheses. Morning people, who are most alert in the morning, should be least likely to use stereotypes when making social judgments in the morning and most likely to rely on stereotypes when their arousal level is lowest (mid- to late afternoon). Evening people should be most likely to rely on stereotypes in social judgments in the morning, when their arousal level is lowest, and least likely to use stereotypes in the late afternoon and early evening, when their arousal level is highest.

STUDY 1

The first study examined the impact of common social stereotypes on performance in a probability estimation task. Specifically, materials used by Tversky and Kahneman (1983) to demonstrate the conjunction fallacy in probability judgment were adopted. The conjunction fallacy refers to the erroneous belief that the joint probability of two events is greater than the probability of either of the constituent events separately. It is theoretically linked to the operation of the representativeness heuristic (Kahneman & Tversky, 1972). When people use this heuristic, they make probability estimates based on the apparent similarity of the event or entity being judged to a representative stereotype. People show a strong tendency to believe that the conjunction of a representative (stereotypic) and an unrepresentative element is more probable than the probability of the unrepresentative element in isolation.

In this study. I tested students on a probability estimation task at either 9 a.m. or 8 p.m. It was expected that morning people would be more prone to rely on simple stereotypes and commit the conjunction fallacy in the evening. whereas evening people would be more likely to commit the conjunction fallacy in the morning.

Method

Subjects and design

Fifty-nine undergraduate psychology students were recruited for a study of human judgment. They received course credit. Subjects were randomly assigned to report to the testing location at either 9 a.m. or 8 p.m. in groups of approximately 15. Show-up rates were in excess of 80% for all sessions and did not differ as a function of time of day.

Subjects completed the MEQ and were categorized as either morning types or evening-types on the basis of a median split of their scores. Thus, the research design was a 2 (time of day: 9 a.m. vs. 8 p.m.) × 2 (personality type: morning vs. evening) between-subjects factorial design.

Materials and procedure

Subjects were given a booklet in which they were asked to read a description of one of two people, Bill or Linda, and make judgments about the person's characteristics. The descriptions were taken verbatim from Tversky and Kahneman (1983). Bill was described in terms representative of common stereotypes about accountants. Linda was described as possessing traits stereotypically ascribed to feminists. After reading the description, subjects were asked to choose which of two statements about the target was more likely to be true. One of these statements consisted of a conjunction of a representative (stereotypic) label and an unrepresentative characteristic (e.g., "Bill is an accountant who plays jazz for a hobby") while the other was the unrepresentative characteristic in isolation. Choice of the conjunction constitutes the conjunction fallacy.

Having completed the probability judgment task, subjects were given the MEQ as part of an ostensibly unrelated study and then were debriefed.

Results and Discussion

The results were collapsed across the two target cases (i.e., Bill and Linda). The conjunction fallacy occurred with high probability under all of the experimental conditions.

However, the expected pattern was obtained: 94% of subjects with "morning" personalities committed the conjunction fallacy during an evening experimental session ($n = 16$), while only 71% did so in the morning ($n = 14$). Conversely, subjects with "evening" personalities were more likely to commit this fallacy during a morning experimental session (92%, $n = 12$) than during the evening (70%, $n = 17$). In an analysis of error rates, the interaction of personality type and time of testing was significant, $F(1, 55) = 4.55$, $p < .05$. There were no other significant effects.

These results support the idea that people process information in a more heuristic fashion during times of the day at which they are not at their "peak" level of circadian arousal. Specifically, subjects relied more on representative stereotypes about feminists and accountants (rather than applying a straightforward rule of logic) when there was a mismatch between their acrophase and the time of testing.

STUDY 2

In the second study, subjects were asked to consider cases of alleged misbehavior by college students and to determine the probability of the accused students' guilt. Sometimes the students were identified as members of particular social groups, and they were accused of committing offenses that were consistent with stereotypes of these groups. In other conditions, the cases involved students who had been accused of involvement in the exact same offenses but who had not been identified as members of a stereotyped group. Subjects were expected to rely more on guilt-implying stereotypic beliefs when asked to make guilt judgments at nonoptimal times of day.

Method

Subjects and design

Subjects were 189 undergraduate students recruited from psychology classes; they received course credit. Subjects were randomly assigned to experimental sessions held at 9 a.m., 3 p.m., or 8 p.m. They were classified as morning or evening types by a median split of MEQ scores. Participants considered a case involving either a stereotyped or a nonstereotyped student defendant, also randomly determined. Thus, the basic design of the experiment was a 3 (time of testing: 9 a.m., 3 p.m., or 8 p.m.) × 2 (personality type: morning vs. evening) × 2 (stereotype activation: present vs. absent) between-subjects factorial design.

Materials and procedure

The study was presented as an investigation of legal socialization in the college environment. Specifically, subjects were told that they would read about the alleged misconduct of other college students and would be asked to "provide feedback" about these cases. Three different cases were constructed. One involved a student accused of cheating on an exam, one a student who allegedly physically attacked his roommate, and one a student who allegedly sold drugs. Each of these offenses matched to a stereotyped group that had been shown (via pretesting in the same subject population) to be associated, however unfairly, with these offenses. Specifically, athletes were seen as more likely to be cheaters, Hispanics as more likely to be physically aggressive, and African Americans as more likely to sell drugs.

Interestingly, the differences, while reliable in each personality condition (morning vs. evening person) are not really that huge (94 vs. 71 for morning, and 92 vs. 70 for evening types), the analyses indicate that was enough to support the predictions ($p < .05$).

Just a refresher: remember the p-value refers to the statistical significance of the differences between IV conditions on their influence on the DV. Our threshold for significance is high: .05 or less. That means we are saying that there is only a 5% (or less) chance that the differences we observed between IV conditions on the DV are due to random error, and that there is a 95% chance (or greater) that the differences are due to the real differential influence of the IV levels on the DV.

Even though the results of the experiment supported the hypotheses, it is always a good idea for a researcher to replicate the study using different methods. To the extent the results again support the predictions, we can be even more confident in the results.

Why 3? Because the researcher wants to make sure that if there was an effect, it is due to what he or she thinks is causing the effect (use of a stereotype) and not something specific about an irrelevant factor (type of crime). What happens if we obtain the predicted finding only for one crime, or just two? Then we have a differential effect of the crime on judgment of guilt and that is not something we want (it is a confound). But if the researcher obtains similar findings regardless of type of crime, we can have more confidence the type of crime is not a confound.

Similarly, the use of different stereotyped groups is crucial here because we want to show that the effect (using a stereotype as a judgmental heuristic when at a low physiological point) occurs despite the particular stereotyped group in question. Not only did Bodenhausen examine two stereotyped racial groups, but also a group stereotyped about its intelligence (athletes). The cue for each stereotype is something about the individual that will bring up the suspect's group in the suspect's mind. How to activate that stereotype in an innocuous but noticeable way? For the two racial groups, it is the name of the suspect. Bodenhausen pretested the names to make sure that people tend to perceive the suspect as a member of the intended racial group (either Hispanic or Black). He also found that a prominent stereotype about athletes is that they are more likely to cheat on exams because they are less intellectual.

It is not enough for an experimenter to assume that a given stimulus will have a desired effect on a subject, he/she must have objective data to support the contention that a particular stimulus has a given effect on subjects. So in this case, we cannot assume a particular name will tend to cause subjects to activate a particular stereotype about an ethnic group. So researchers use pre-testing to obtain objective data that will hopefully support the idea that the stimulus (name) has its intended effect (consider the stereotypes about that group).

A small set of evidence was provided about each case (approximately 4 to 5 relevant pieces of information) in the form of a written prose summary. This evidence was identical for stereotypic and nonstereotypic offenders. Some evidence pointed toward guilt, but no conclusive proof was forthcoming. Stereotype activation was accomplished in two different ways. For the cheating case, a sentence identifying the defendant as a "well-known athletic star on campus" was either included or was not. In the other two cases, stereotypes were activated by manipulating the defendant's drug dealing case, the student defendant was named either "Mark Washburn" or "Marcus Washington." Pretesting confirmed that students inferred Garcia, but not Garner, to be Hispanic, and Washington, but not Washburn, to be African-American.

Following presentation of the case evidence, subjects were asked to indicate the likelihood of the student's guilt on an 11-point scale (0 = extremely unlikely to 10 = extremely likely). They were also asked to rate the seriousness of the alleged offense on an 11-point scale ranging from 0 (completely trivial) to 10 (extremely serious). Then they were asked some filler questions that reflected the alleged purpose of the study. Finally, subjects were debriefed.

Results and Discussion

An initial analysis of subjects' guilt judgments included the three case replications as a factor in the analytic model. There was a theoretically uninteresting main effect such that guilt was seen as most likely in the cheating case ($M = 7.14$), moderately likely in the assault case ($M = 5.65$), and least likely in the drug dealing case ($M = 4.61$). As there were no interactions of this replication factor with the other independent variables (all $ps > .35$), the results were collapsed across this variable for ease of presentation.

Mean ratings of the defendant's likelihood of guilt as a function of stereotype activation, time of testing, and personality type are presented in Table 1. The expected interaction of stereotype activation, time of testing, and personality type was significant, $F(2, 177) = 3.49$, $p < .05$. No other effects were significant in the overall analysis. Supplementary analyses confirmed that, as expected, morning types perceived stereotyped targets to be more likely to be guilty in the afternoon and evening than the morning. $F(1, 44) = 5.16$, $p < .05$. For evening

TABLE 1   Mean ratings of perceived guilt likelihood of student defendants as a function of time of day, personality type, and stereotype activation

	Time of Day		
	9 a.m.	3 p.m.	8 p.m.
Morning Types Stereotype	4.92 (13)	6.67 (18)	6.50 (16)
No Stereotype	5.39 (13)	5.61 (18)	5.79 (14)
Evening Types Stereotype	6.79 (19)	5.13 (16)	5.60 (15)
No Stereotype	5.05 (19)	5.67 (15)	6.45 (13)

Note. Cell sizes are indicated in parentheses.

types, perceptions of the stereotyped targets' guilt were significantly greater in the morning than in the afternoon or evening, $F(1, 47) = 4.39$, $p < .05$. Perceptions of the nonstereotyped defendants were not affected by time of testing, $ps > .25$.[8]

These results bolster our confidence in the proposition that stereotypes are more likely to be relied on in judgmental tasks that occur at nonoptimal times of day. Using a different type of task and three different social stereotypes the implications of the first study were supported quite nicely.

GENERAL DISCUSSION

The results obtained in these studies have a number of interesting implications. First and foremost, they support the view that stereotypes function as judgmental heuristics and, as such, are likely to be more influential under circumstances in which people are less motivated or less able to engage in more systematic and careful judgment strategies (Bodenhausen & Lichtenstein, 1987; Chaiken et al., 1989). Morning people, who reach their functional peak early in the day, were more likely to fall back on stereotypic responses in the afternoon and evening, while evening people, who reach their functional peak later in the day, showed a greater tendency toward stereotypic responses in the morning. These results suggest that regular variations in arousal levels may play a role in determining the types of information processing strategies that are adopted by social perceivers. These results also highlight the potential value that may accrue from considering the role of time and temporal cycles in studies of social cognition. McGrath and Kelly (1986) have argued that time has been a neglected variable in social psychological research, one that might be exploited in numerous ways. One way, exemplified in the present research, is to use temporal cycles as a methodological tool to examine basic theoretical issues. Broadbent, Broadbent, and Jones (1989) also employed this strategy. They were able to resolve some conflicting results in research on basic attentional processes by examining the impact of time of day on task performance. Although circadian variations were explored in the present research primarily as a way of testing specific theoretical claims about the effects of processing resources on social judgment strategies, the more general possibility of regular circadian variations in social perception is an intriguing issue that deserves further exploration.

Consideration of the role of circadian variations in arousal levels on social judgment is particularly interesting because it represents a conflux of biological, cognitive, and social processes. As such, it may provide one small step toward an integrated theoretical account of human thought and action that exploits important developments in several subdisciplines. As the motivational and ability factors that affect social information processing strategies become more well specified, the role of basic psychological processes will doubtlessly become increasingly recognized.

Acknowledgments—I am grateful to Norbert Kerr and Joseph McGrath for their helpful comments on a previous version of this article.

---

[8]A similar pattern of results obtained for the seriousness judgment. Details are available from the author.

Main finding. People use stereotypes as mental shortcuts (heuristics) when they have to do a cognitive task (e.g., make a social judgment) and they do not have the required physiological arousal to allow them to engage in the cognition-intense task of thinking carefully about a person ("individuating").

The sound-bite headline: whether people stereotype others depends on the time of day.

REFERENCES

Blake, M.J.F. (1967). Time of day effects on performance in a range of tasks. *Psychonomic Science, 9,* 349–350.

Bodenhausen, G.V., & Lichtenstein, M. (1987). Social stereotypes and information-processing strategies: The impact of task complexity. *Journal of Personality and Social Psychology, 52,* 871–880.

Bodenhausen, G.V., & Wyer, R.S. (1985). Effects of stereotypes on decision making and information-processing strategies. *Journal of Personality and Social Psychology, 48,* 267–282.

Broadbent, D.E., Broadbent, M.H.P., & Jones, J.L. (1989). Time of day as an instrument for the analysis of attention. *European Journal of Cognitive Psychology, 1,* 69–94.

Chaiken, S., Liberman, A., & Eagly, A. (1989). Heuristic and systematic information processing within and beyond the persuasion context. In J. Uleman & J. Bargh (Eds.), *Unintended thought* (pp. 212–252). New York: Guilford.

Colquhoun, W.P. (1971). Circadian variations in mental efficiency. In W.P. Colquhoun (Ed.), *Biological rhythms and human performance.* London: Academic Press.

Erber, R., & Fiske, S.T. (1984). Outcome dependency and attention to inconsistent information. *Journal of Personality and Social Psychology, 47,* 709–726.

Folkard, S., Wever, R.A., & Wildgruber, C.M. (1983). Multi-oscillatory control of circadian rhythms in human performance. *Nature, 305,* 223–226.

Freeman, G., & Hovland, C. (1934). Diurnal variation in performance and related physiological processes. *Psychological Bulletin, 31,* 777–799.

Horne, J.A., & Ostberg. O. (1976). A self-assessment questionnaire to determine morningness eveningness in human circadian rhythms. *International Journal of Chronobiology, 4,* 97–110.

Horne, J.A., & Ostberg, O. (1977). Individual differences in human circadian rhythms. *Biological Psychology, 5,* 179–190.

Kahneman. D., & Tversky, A. (1972). Subjective probability: A judgment of representativeness. *Cognitive Psychology, 3,* 430–454.

McGrath. J.E., & Kelly, J.R. (1986). *Time and human interaction: Toward a social psychology of time.* New York: Guilford.

Neuberg, S.L., & Fiske, S.T. (1987). Motivational influences on impression formation: Outcome dependency, accuracy-driven attention, and individuating processes. *Journal of Personality and Social Psychology, 53,* 431–444.

Patkai, P. (1971). Interindividual differences in diurnal variation in alertness, performance, and adrenaline excretion. *Acta Physiologica Scandinavica, 81,* 35–46.

Petty, R.E., Wells, G.L., & Brock, T.C. (1976). Distraction can enhance or reduce yielding to propaganda: Thought disruption versus effort justification. *Journal of Personality and Social Psychology, 34,* 874–884.

Rothbart, M., Fulero, S., Jensen, C., Howard, J., & Birrell, P. (1978). From individual to group impressions: Availability heuristics in stereotype formation. *Journal of Experimental Social Psychology, 14,* 237–255,

Smith, C.S., Reilly, C., & Midkiff, K. (1989). Evaluation of three circadian rhythm questionnaires with suggestions for an improved measure of morningness. *Journal of Applied Psychology, 74,* 728–738.

Tversky, A., & Kahneman, D. (1983). Extensional versus intuitive reasoning: The conjunction fallacy in probability judgment. *Psychological Review, 90,* 293–315.

POST-ARTICLE DISCUSSION

The results of Experiment 1 showed that the time of day, combined with where one was in one's particular circadian cycle, had a significant effect on whether the subject fell prey to the conjunction fallacy in making judgments about the target persons in the written materials. Bodenhausen wondered whether our cognitive processes would be impaired significantly during those times of the day when we are at our low level of physiological arousal. That is, when people who normally wake up early and have the most energy in the morning ("morning people") and get the most done during that time are asked to do cognitive work in the late afternoon or early evening, they may be more likely to make cognitive mistakes or use mental shortcuts in their judgments. The same thing happens to the judgments of people who wake up late and do their best work and highest activity late afternoon or early evening ("evening people") and are asked to make cognitive judgments in the morning.

In Experiment 2, Bodenhausen wanted to find out if time of day would influence another type of cognitive activity: social judgments about others. In this case, he wondered if people would use a stereotype to help them come to a decision about the guilt or innocence of a suspect accused of a crime. In all cases, the evidence presented made it ambiguous as to the guilt of the accused. So, if one were thinking carefully about the issue, it would be difficult to come to a definitive conclusion one way or the other.

However, Bodenhausen predicted that when people are physiologically at their low arousal point, they would be too tired or unmotivated to do careful cognitive thought, and instead, they would rely on any cognitive heuristic (perhaps a stereotype?) to help them come to a decision. This is indeed what he found. Subjects were more likely to use a stereotype about the accused to decide the person's guilt when they were doing the experiment at a time when they should be feeling very low physiological arousal (e.g., morning people doing the study in the mid- to late afternoon).

It is a truism in psychology that people assume that the reason they behave the way they do is due to their personality traits, which are supposed to guide our behavior across situations. We like to think that about ourselves, and we think that about others, too. In the latter case, that tendency is so strong we have a term for it: *fundamental attribution error* (Ross, 1977). This is the notion that we assume other people's behavior is due to their personality, and we rarely, if ever, correct that impression according to situational influences. That is one reason this paper is important: It reminds us that something as profound as whether we stereotype others can be guided less by our personality and more by something as seemingly innocuous as whether we are sufficiently physiologically aroused at the time we are making the social judgment. It is a lesson to all social psychologists about the importance of considering the possible situational influences when attempting to explain and predict behavior.

THINGS TO THINK ABOUT

1. Can you think of other ways, besides a survey, to measure whether one is a "morning" versus "evening" person?

2. Why did the researcher run two experiments? What did each reveal about the co-influence of physiological arousal and time of day on cognitive processes?

3. Do you think the researcher should have run the experiment using only low-prejudiced persons? Why or why not?

4. Do you think that this effect might be different depending on stereotype? The researcher found the same result for stereotypes about race and athletes. But would we find the same effect with stereotypes about other groups (e.g., women, older persons, gays and lesbians, different religions, handicapped, mentally ill, etc.). Why or why not?

5. Why do stereotypes persist? What advantage do they give, and is it more than the costs for using them in social judgments?

10

Prosocial Behavior

Humans are very social creatures, and we naturally seek out the company of others (Fiske, 1991). In so doing, we reap psychological and emotional benefits, we find companionship, and we develop romantic relationships. The groups (e.g., police, doctors, teachers, merchants) we form can create new things for society and can perform functions necessary for the well-being of those in the larger group (the town or city). Indeed, it is this feeling of connectedness that seems to facilitate the inclination toward prosocial behavior. Research by Twenge, Baumeister, DeWall, Ciarocco, and Bartels (2007) showed that when people are made to feel socially excluded from a group, they cooperate less, donate less money toward the group, and are less likely to volunteer to help in further lab experiments. Twenge and colleagues suggested that social exclusion impairs the capacity for empathic connection with others, and that is what accounts for the drop in prosocial behavior toward the group.

Not everyone seems to work for the common good, however. Some people are more self-focused than others. Clearly, there are benefits to helping others, such as the good feelings we receive when we have improved the situation of another person, the social approval and praise from others at our behavior, and even the knowledge that the recipient of our help will likely help us in the future when we need assistance. Thus, it would seem logical that most (or nearly all) people would help other people and organizations. Yet, we know that isn't the case.

What makes some people help others, while other people ignore opportunities to help and instead focus on their own goals? Much research in social psychology has been devoted to understanding the situational and personality variables that inhibit and enhance the likelihood that a person will help someone in need. Once we know the influences that affect whether and how helping behavior occurs in a given context, we can change the environment and people (through education about helping) to increase the amount of helping in society. Note that this brief review is not exhaustive, and the interested reader can get a more comprehensive understanding of the research on prosocial behavior from other sources (e.g., Penner, Dovidio, Piliavin, & Schroeder, 2005).

WHY WE HELP: MOTIVATION FOR PROSOCIAL BEHAVIOR

Even if we understand situational and personality variables that make a person more likely to offer help, we may still be at a loss to explain why people who should help (given the requisite personality characteristics and contextual pressures are present) don't help. Another way to examine questions we have about predicting helping is to attempt to understand the motivations that tend to give rise to helping behavior (Piliavin & Charng, 1990). That is, "Why do people help?" If we can understand the cognitive or affective engines behind why people initiate helping in a certain situation, we might be even more accurate in predicting helping behavior. We may even be able to identify ways to encourage helping. In this introduction, we explore the various theories that researchers have put forth in an attempt to explain why people sometimes help and why they sometimes don't respond to others in need.

Evolutionary Theories of Helping

As with any behavior, psychologists seek to determine the relative contribution of genetics and environment (the nature vs. nurture debate) to a particular behavior. Altruism has been a bit of a thorn in the side of evolutionary theory. According to Darwin (1859), the main goal of evolution is "survival of the fittest." Through the process of "natural selection," organisms that are able to successfully adapt to changes in the environment survive and pass on their genes, and those who cannot adapt die (along with their maladaptive genes). The main force that propels life, according to evolutionary theory, is to survive and produce offspring, so that one may pass on one's genes. Any characteristic or behavior that jeopardizes the life of the organism is not adaptive, and those factors would lead that organism (and those maladaptive genes) to die out. The reason why altruism poses a problem for evolutionary theorists is that altruism does not benefit the helper and, in some instances, can actually place the helper in dangerous, life-threatening situations. Such a tendency

should have been selected out eons ago, since many of those tendencies to help ended in the death of the helper. Yet, prosocial altruistic behaviors remain with us today. How is this possible?

Evolutionary psychologists have attempted to explain this in a couple of different ways. Research has shown that people are somewhat more likely to make sacrifices for blood relatives than they are for complete strangers (Kruger, 2003; Rushton, 1989). According to the concept of **kin selection**, we should be more likely to help those who share our genes than complete strangers, because in so doing, we increase the chances that some of the family's genes will survive (in the event of the death of the helper) and be passed on in the relative's offspring. In light of this, altruism and prosocial behavior don't contradict evolutionary theory, because, although they don't necessarily increase the survival of the helper, they promote the genes that the helper shares with her genetic relatives.

Before we proceed further, let us review a basic aspect of Darwinian evolutionary theory. According to the notion of **classical fitness**, a person's reproductive success is determined by how successful he is in passing on genes to the next generation (Buss, 1996). But Hamilton (1964) suggested that we also consider the influence of the person on her relatives, when ascertaining that person's reproductive success. He termed this **inclusive fitness**. This idea of Hamilton's was a breakthrough in evolutionary psychology, because it allows the consideration of the impact of complex social behavior on reproductive success, and we then can begin to understand which behaviors have the greatest impact in the process of natural selection.

Burnstein, Crandall, and Kitayama (1994) applied the inclusive fitness theory to helping behavior in their experiments, to try to find evidence that would support an evolutionary interpretation of prosocial behavior. They hypothesized that natural selection should favor those who are more likely to help those in their groups (i.e., those with whom the person shares genetic material). They presented participants with various scenarios, asking them how they would respond to a crisis and who they would help (and who they would let die) in emergency situations. The researchers also asked participants how they would respond in nonemergency helping situations. Results indicated support for the inclusive fitness theory in emergency situations: People were most likely to help those who shared the most genetic material with them. The amount of helping decreased in a linear fashion as a function of the decreasing genetic relatedness. Wealthy, healthy, and younger people were also more likely to be helped than poor, sick, and old people in emergency situations. On the other hand, when the scenario was a nonemergency situation, the inclusive fitness predictions were not supported. Older adults and poor people were more likely to be helped than the young and wealthy.

Another approach that has been proposed is known as **reciprocity**. Recall that reciprocity is simply the idea that "if you scratch my back, I'll scratch yours." According to this explanation, altruism fits with evolutionary theory because by helping someone else, we are really helping enhance our own genetic fitness. That is, helping someone, even if it is a stranger, indirectly ultimately helps promote our own genetic fitness because that other person "owes" us a favor. So, if in the future we ever find ourselves in need of help, we can rely on the principle of reciprocity and "call in" our favor, and that person will give us the help we need, thereby ensuring our continued survival (and chances for passing on our genes). Now, that might be a bit of a stretch, saying that altruism is really helping oneself in the long run, but it is an interesting

idea. As an interesting side note, reciprocal altruism has also been demonstrated experimentally and observed in the field among monkeys and chimpanzees (Brosnan & de Waal, 2002).

Social Exchange

Some have speculated that before people help another person, they weigh the costs and benefits of both helping and not helping (Enzle & Lowe, 1976; Thibaut & Kelley, 1959). According to this idea, when we are confronted with a decision (sometimes a split-second decision, such as in an emergency, when lives are at stake) about whether to help another person, we do a quick calculation (usually lasting only fractions of a second) of our subjective assessment of the salient costs and benefits to us for either choosing to help or not help. Social exchange theory says that we are motivated to stay in a relationship if we perceive that the rewards we receive for being in the relationship exceed the costs we incur. The motivation to maximize our rewards and minimize our costs in relationships is referred to as the **minimax principle**.

According to the minimax principle, we will render aid only when we believe that there are more benefits than costs to helping the victim. Notice I used the term *subjective assessment* and the word *salient* when referring to this calculation of costs versus rewards. This is because our "calculation" is anything but a careful, rational, logical analysis of all the costs and rewards. Rather, it is a decision that takes place in the span of a fraction of a second or a few seconds, and it is one that is based on what costs and rewards are available (salient) in our consciousness at that moment of helping. The decision is also greatly influenced by the emotions we're feeling at that moment.

There are a number of rewards for helping, but there are also a number of good outcomes for NOT offering help. We may help because we know there is a reward (social or financial) for helping, we are promoting helping as a valued behavior, and we can avoid feeling guilty for not helping. On the other hand, when deciding whether to help, the rewards for not helping (no loss of time, no legal liability, no danger to one's life, no involvement in court, no obligation to the victim, generally avoiding a number of hassles or inconveniences) can sometimes be greater and as a result, we don't render assistance. You may be saying to yourself, "Self, that sounds awfully cold and calculating, and that can't be how most people decide whether to help another." Well, yes, it does appear rather emotionless, but in fact, emotion plays a strong role in guiding our helping behavior. As Cialdini's research on the **negative state relief model** suggests, sometimes we may help because the personal distress we are experiencing at seeing the victim in need of help can be alleviated by helping the person (Cialdini, Darby, & Vincent, 1973). We may help because our strong religious values tell us we should help in all instances and that if we do not help, we'll feel terribly guilty (Batson, 1991).

Schwarz (1990) suggested another way emotions may influence our decision to help. In their **feelings as information theory**, Schwarz and Clore (1983, 1988) suggested that people use their current affective state as a piece of information to tell them how to evaluate a given situation. For example, suppose you just heard a very funny joke. Then, seconds later, you meet a friend of your friend's. After 30 seconds of small talk, you all part ways. Later, when someone asks you what you thought of that person you met, you are likely to express a positive opinion of him, because when you met him, part of the process of forming an attitude about him entailed using your current mood as indicator of how you feel about that person. Because your mood was good, you formed

a positive attitude. Now if you happened to be in a very negative mood and then met the individual, your impression of the man would likely not have been as positive.

EMPATHY, EGOISM, AND "PURE ALTRUISM"

In Season 5 of the NBC show *Friends*, in an episode titled "The One Where Phoebe Hates PBS," Joey declares to Phoebe that there is no such thing as a "selfless act" and challenges her to prove him wrong. The challenge makes for amusing television, and it is also a fun thought problem I pose to my students when we start discussing prosocial behavior. The problem with the responses that we come up with to this problem is that they inevitably contain some kernel of reward or positive feeling for the helper, and thus the act cannot be considered purely altruistic. By that strict definition of *selfless* (or altruistic, the definition of *selfless* that Joey was using), it is very difficult to think of a selfless act.

The question of whether pure altruism exists has intrigued philosophers and psychologists for a long time. Compte (1875/1973) believed that pure altruism existed. Those who disagreed contended, as Joey did with Phoebe, that any time you feel good or obtain a reinforcement for helping, the act is not altruistic. This is known as **psychological hedonism** (or **egoism**), and it has been discussed by philosophers ranging from Epicurus (trans. 1993) to Hume (1888/1960) and Mill (1863/1971). There are two ways to view this hedonism. The "strong form" says that all human behavior is directed at the goal of obtaining pleasure. The "weak form" says that goal attainment will always bring pleasure (Batson, 1991). According to Batson (1991), altruism is not incompatible with the weak form of psychological hedonism. With that definition of altruism, the goal of the helper isn't to obtain a good feeling for herself but rather to help someone else. The act of helping may produce a by-product of feeling good, but that doesn't make the motivation egoistic.

When we see another person in need, typically two emotional responses are evoked in us (Batson, Fultz, & Schoenrade, 1987). The first, called **personal distress,** is a feeling of alarm, anxiety, being upset, or feeling disturbed. This feeling typically leads to an egoistic (selfish) motivation to relieve our distress. The second emotion, termed **empathy,** involves feelings of compassion, caring, and sympathy, and it triggers an altruistic motivation to help the victim and increase the victim's welfare. According to Batson (1987, 1991; Batson & Coke, 1981, 1983; Coke, Batson, & McDavis, 1978), when we first witness another person in need, we automatically experience some amount of personal distress. Additionally, if we are able to take the person's perspective (Krebs & Russell, 1981) and have the ability to imagine how that person is affected by need (Stotland, 1969), we will soon feel empathy for the victim (Batson, 1991). To the degree that the victim is similar to us, that will increase the ease with which we can imagine ourselves in the victim's situation. The easier it is to imagine ourselves in that situation, the more likely we will experience feelings of empathy for the victim.

It is important to distinguish **prosocial behavior** from **altruism** here, because Batson is only talking about the latter. Prosocial behavior is any behavior that promotes the welfare of the other person. With prosocial behavior, the motivation of the helper can be selfish (e.g., I help someone because I know it will make me feel good to help her, or it will make me look good to my friends who see me help). Altruism is behavior that is done to promote the welfare of the other person, and the helper is not motivated by a desire to increase his own welfare. This last component is crucial. In this definition, then, if the goal or motive to help includes any improvement to the helper's welfare, then the behavior cannot be considered purely altruistic. So, according to Batson (1991), the key distinguishing difference between an egoistic act of helping and an altruistic act is the helper's motive or goal.

According to Batson's **empathy-altruism hypothesis**, when people feel personal distress but no empathy, they will help the victim only when they believe that the benefits for doing so outweigh the costs for helping (Batson & Coke, 1981; Coke et al., 1978). This is prosocial but not altruistically motivated behavior. However, according to this hypothesis, when people feel empathy for the victim, they will help even if the costs for helping outweigh the benefits, and their helping will be purely altruistically motivated. No other emotions, besides empathy, will evoke the same pure altruistic motivation, according to the model. In over a dozen experiments over the past few decades, Batson and others have found evidence that supports the idea that when people feel empathy for someone, they are more likely to help that individual, and the help they offer is more likely to arise from a purely altruistic motive and not be driven by self-interest (Batson, 1987, 1998; Batson et al., 1987; Batson, Lishner, & Stocks, 2015).

Negative Mood

Maybe the reason we help others is to feel better ourselves. We know that helping feels good. So, when we find that we are feeling bad, we should be especially likely to initiate helping toward another person, because we know that in so doing, we'll feel better. This is the essential thesis behind one of the chief theoretical rivals to the empathy-altruism hypothesis, the **negative state relief model** (Cialdini, Darby, & Vincent, 1973).

In one study, Manucia, Baumann, and Cialdini (1984) asked male and female participants to do a study on "perceptual memory." Participants were told about a fast-acting memory-enhancing drug (which really was a placebo) that they would take during the experiment.

Half of the subjects read a letter attesting to the drug's safety but which also said that the drug causes side effects that result in changes in the participant's mood (which dissipate after 45 minutes of ingestion). This is the "fixed mood" condition. In the "labile" (changeable) mood condition, participants read the safety letter, but it was different from the fixed condition in that it had the information about the mood side effects deleted.

Those in the fixed mood condition were further told that the drug takes whatever mood the participant was in and prolongs it for 30 minutes, no matter what happens. Those in the labile mood condition were told that the drug doesn't have any mood-related side effects.

As a memory exercise, all participants were then asked to imagine a time when they either felt angriest or saddest or to describe their route to school (neutral mood). They were asked to describe these events in as much detail as possible. In so doing, the researchers wanted to induce in the participants those moods (happy, sad, or neutral). The researchers suggested that the main reason people help is a selfish one, to feel better (to enhance one's mood). So, one should see more helping among the sad participants (who want to feel better) compared to the happy participants. Neutral-mood participants should help slightly more than happy individuals. To show that this impetus is driven primarily by the participants' need to enhance their own mood (egoistic, selfish motive), one should only see these helping differences among those who think that helping will result in the change in mood they expect (i.e., only in the labile mood condition). In those who believe their mood is unchangeable (the fixed mood condition), there should be little motive to help, even among the negative mood condition persons, because helping won't change their mood.

Helping in this study was measured by participants' willingness to volunteer to make phone calls (and how many phone calls they said they would make). Results revealed support for these predictions. There was no difference in helping between happy labile and happy fixed participants. It was the same for the neutral condition participants. However, there was a significant difference in helping among the sad labile and sad fixed conditions. Those in the first condition, who believed that their mood could be enhanced (changed), volunteered to make significantly more phone calls. This is consistent with Cialdini's negative state relief model. These findings were supported in a later study by Cialdini and colleagues (1987).

Positive Moods

Much research shows that when people feel good, they are more inclined to help another person (Batson, 1979; Carlson, Charlin, & Miller, 1988; Isen, Clark, & Schwartz, 1976; Rosenhan, Salovey, & Hargis, 1981; Weyant, 1978). On sunny days, people are in a better mood and thus are more willing to help another (Cunningham, 1979). Good weather is beneficial for persons on the street asking for money. Lockard, McDonald, Clifford, and Martinez (1976) found that people gave more money to homeless persons in the spring and less in the fall. Research by Keller and his colleagues explained why this may be so. They found that people reported better mood, memory, and broadened cognitive style (open to new information) in the pleasant weather occurring in the spring; a weaker relationship was found between mood and pleasant weather during the rest of the year. Keller and colleagues suggested that the pleasantness of the good weather is novel and more impactful following winter. However, over the summer, we get used to the pleasant weather conditions, and its effect on our mood isn't as strong in the late summer or early fall. It should be noted that the association between good weather and increased helping behavior has been demonstrated by numerous studies. The strongest aspect of the good weather in this association—sunshine—accounts for only approximately 13% of the variance in accounting for helping behavior (Cunningham, 1979). That means that most of a person's willingness to help is driven by social and personality factors. Helping has also been consistently correlated with increased well-being, happiness, health, and longevity in those helpers who are not overwhelmed or burned out by their helping behavior (Brown, Consedine, & Maqai, 2005; Post, 2005).

The existence of pure altruism has been a hotly debated issue for over 40 years in social psychology. Batson and his colleagues have published numerous, compelling experiments that suggest support for the idea that when people feel empathy for another person, they are more likely to help out of a purely altruistic motive. But ascertaining the motive for helping has always been a tricky undertaking. The central question (when trying to identify a behavior that purportedly is driven by pure altruism) is "Can we ever really know whether all the underlying motives for a helping behavior are free of egoistic influence?" Think of the motives for a behavior like an onion. If we peel back the first layer, we find the motive for the behavior, but we know we're not done (there are other layers we haven't uncovered). So we peel back the next layer, and we now think we've identified another motive. Even if these motives are purely altruistic, the problem is that we don't know how big the onion is, how many layers or motives

remain undiscovered, and we don't know whether any of those are egoistic.

Most people aren't really concerned if the motive behind someone helping them is purely altruistic or if the helper is doing it for selfish reasons. The main thing of interest is whether the person helps or not. The debate about the existence of pure altruism is interesting in that, if it does exist, then we might be able to better predict when people will help. If they feel this pure altruism toward another person, they will likely help the victim no matter what circumstances are present. But many questions would present themselves in the event that pure altruism was shown to exist. Is it akin to a personality trait? Is it more of a feeling? Under what conditions will a person experience pure altruism? Are there situational variables that enhance or inhibit the influence of pure altruism on the likelihood of someone offering help? Until researchers come up with a way to accurately measure the true motives for a given act, so that we can know whether they are egoistic or altruistic, the search for pure altruism will continue, along with the debate.

WHEN HELP IS GIVEN: SITUATIONAL FACTORS INFLUENCING PROSOCIAL BEHAVIOR

Let's examine some of the situational factors that influence helping. One of the important points to remember about this research is that in many instances, the situation, not the person's own convictions, beliefs, or values, is what dictates whether someone helps another person or whether someone remains a passive bystander.

Similarity

Just as we tend to hang out with and make friends with people who are similar to us on a number of different demographic variables (e.g., age, religion, values, political attitudes, etc.), research also indicates that the similarity of the victim to the potential helper has a strong influence on whether the helper will offer assistance. Many experiments have demonstrated that people are more willing to help others who are similar to them, compared to victims who are dissimilar (Dovidio, 1984; Feldman, 1968). Sole, Marton, and Hornstein (1975) found that people are more willing to help another person who has attitudes that are most similar to those of the helper's. Even something as a sport jersey can determine whether you get assistance. Levine, Prosser, Evans, and Reicher (2005) found that an injured stranger wearing an ingroup team jersey was significantly more likely to be given assistance than an injured person wearing a jersey of a rival team. One reason we help similar others is that it makes us feel good to help those who are like us, who (we assume) share the same views, beliefs, and values. In helping a similar other, we may be trying to preserve those elements of ourselves that we like in others.

The Number of People at the Scene

Suppose you are walking in the city, doing some shopping. Suddenly, you feel light-headed, and collapse on the sidewalk, banging your head on the concrete. Your head is bleeding and in pain, your right ribs hurt, and you're dazed. You need assistance, and you need to get to a hospital right away to get evaluated. In a big metropolitan area like this, many people witness your fall. You should have a small crowd around you, with lots of people offering to help. Unfortunately, most onlookers do NOT help. But that doesn't make sense. Surely, in a crowd, there must be some compassionate, kind, helpful person(s) who will offer help to someone

who needs help, right? Well, not quite. Let's back up for a minute, to the early 1960s.

On the evening of March 13, 1964, 19-year-old Catherine "Kitty" Genovese arrived home at 3:15 a.m. from her job as a bar manager in Queens. Unbeknownst to her, 29-year-old Winston Moseley decided that he wanted to kill a woman. He did not know Genovese. He saw her and began to chase her. He caught up to her and stabbed her twice in the back. Over the next 35 minutes, he would stab her, be frightened away from someone at a window yelling at him to "let that girl alone!" (Gansberg, 1964), then return again to continue attacking her. After she was dead (about 40 minutes after the attack started), someone called the police. The attacker was convicted of murder and sent to prison. What made this murder stand out from many other violent crimes and murders is that police and reporters later learned that at least 38 people witnessed or heard at least part of Kitty's attack, but none of them did anything to try to help her. When they went to their windows to try to see the attack, witnesses reported seeing many other people in their windows also looking at the attack. But no one even called the police. Why? Many witnesses thought others had likely already called the police and said that they "didn't want to get involved" (Gansberg, 1964).

John Darley and Bibb Latané read the newspaper accounts of this brutal murder and wanted to know more about why all of these witnesses didn't help Genovese. In one experiment, Latané and Darley (1968) asked male participants to come to a lab to "discuss some of the problems involved in life at an urban university" (p. 217). Participants were randomly assigned to one of three groups: completing questionnaires in a small lab room alone, with two other confederates pretending to be real participants, or with two other real participants like themselves. In the condition with the confederates, the confederates were to avoid talking as much as possible. The goal of the experiment was to see how long it took for people to recognize a situation as an emergency and to go for help. The researchers wanted to examine the influence of group size and nonresponding bystanders on the help-seeking behavior in the real participant.

Participants were told to fill out some questionnaires at the start of the session, while the experimenter was in another lab room. After a few minutes in the room, the experimenters introduced a continuous stream of thick white smoke into the room via a small vent. What percentage of participants in each condition would interpret this as an emergency, and how soon would they leave the room to seek help?

When by themselves, most participants immediately noticed the smoke and reported it within 2 minutes of noticing it. After 3½ minutes, 75% of them went for help. In the condition with two other actual participants in the waiting room, the situation changed drastically. Of all the persons who participated in this condition ($n = 24$), only 10% went for help within the first 4 minutes, and even after 6 minutes, only 38% of the participants had gone for help. Finally, Latané and Darley found that two passive confederates had a dramatic effect on the real participant's likelihood to interpret the smoke as an emergency and to go for help. Even after 6 minutes had elapsed, only 10% of the participants in this condition went for help.

This experiment highlights the powerful influence of other bystanders in a helping situation on whether a witness is likely to recognize the situation as a helping situation and to either offer help or implement a search for help. Let's get a few terms out of the way and then we'll discuss each further. Research by Darley and Latané and others over the decades has found that the more people who witness an emergency situation, the less likely that victim is going to get help. This is known as the **bystander effect** (Latané & Darley, 1970). Why would the likelihood that the victim receives help drop when more people are present? That doesn't seem to make sense. Surely, by the principles of probability, as one adds more people, it seems that the chances for help would increase, because you'd be increasing the chances that those bystanders are a doctor, or a religious person, or a very compassionate person (someone who routinely helps others), and so on.

One of the fascinating aspects of this research is that although as the bystander audience increases in size, it is indeed more likely to be comprised of people who are more likely to help "by nature," the situation they are in has a stronger effect on their helping (or not helping, in this case) behavior. When bystanders notice the other witnesses, they tend to think that, as the size of the group of bystanders increases, it is more likely that someone else either has already gone for help, will help, or is better equipped to render assistance to the victim. As a result, they tend to think, as many of the Kitty Genovese witnesses did, that it is not their responsibility to help the victim. In other words, the more people who are witnessing an emergency situation, the less personally responsible each person feels for helping the victim. This is known as **diffusion of responsibility**. If you are thinking to yourself, "Self, those two concepts sound awfully similar," you're right, they are similar, and it is easy to get them confused. One way to keep them straight is to think of bystander effect as a probability statement about the likelihood that any help will be given by anyone. Diffusion of responsibility, as the term implies, refers to each witness's perception that it is his or her responsibility to help. Think back to the Kitty Genovese murder. We know that both the bystander effect and diffusion of responsibility were at play in accounting for the

38 nonresponding witnesses. Crucial to this tragedy is the fact that when the bystanders went to their windows to see what was the matter, they also saw across the street to the other apartment building and saw many other people at their windows also looking at the commotion. Seeing all the other witnesses had a powerful inhibiting effect on their likelihood to help, just as it did in Latané and Darley's (1968) "smoke" experiment. It is interesting to wonder what might have happened if there was no other apartment building across the street, making it so they saw no other witnesses. Would more people have been inclined to help? Research suggests the answer is yes.

Another fascinating dynamic going on in many helping situations, and which is exemplified nicely in Latané and Darley's (1968) "smoke study," is something called **pluralistic ignorance**. This is the idea that, when we are confused about whether there is an emergency, or someone in need of help, we look to the reactions of other people around us to help us determine the answer. If many people around us are rushing to the aid of the "victim" and administering first aid, or calling 911, or even if most of their facial expressions and body language indicates alarm, it seems clear it is a helping situation. But what happens if it looks like it could be a helping situation, but no one is acting that way? What if they are just walking around the person (who is lying face down on the sidewalk), stone-faced, as if nothing is wrong? In these situations, you are most likely to feel the same way that participants in the smoke study felt when they were with the nonresponding confederates. Something tells you that something is wrong (person lying face down on the sidewalk, or smoke pouring in the lab room), but the reactions of others (no response, no alarm) are telling you there is no trouble here. In these cases, most people go along with the nonresponding bystanders and do nothing, because they may think to themselves, "Well, they must all know something I don't know." Interestingly, the similarity of the nonresponsive bystander to the potential helper can have a strong influence on whether the perceiver will offer help. Smith, Smythe, and Lien (1972) found that when the nonresponding bystander was similar to the participant (the perceiver), only 5% of the participants tried to help the victim. However, when the nonresponding bystander was very dissimilar to the perceiver, 35% of the participants offered help to the victim.

INTRODUCTION TO READING 10.1
Darley and Latané (1968)

You may remember from your intro to psychology course the sad story of Kitty Genovese, a 28-year-old woman living in New York City who was savagely murdered in 1964. Her death gained widespread attention because newspapers reported that the police found at least 38 witnesses who saw her being killed over a span of at least 30 minutes, and no one helped her or even bothered to call police. This story also captured the attention of John Darley, a professor of psychology and his graduate student, Bibb Latané. They began their pioneering research on why people help and why some do not help others (and not just in emergency situations). One of the fascinating things their research revealed is that a victim is more likely to get help if there is just one witness, compared to if there is a crowd of witnesses. They referred to this as the "bystander effect." The more people who witness someone needing help, the less likely the victim will get help. A close corollary to this is something they called "diffusion of responsibility." This says that the more people who witness a victim needing help, the less personally responsible each person feels to help the victim. Darley and Latané tested both of these phenomena (with a particular focus on diffusion of responsibility). This famous study manipulates the number of "bystanders" (in addition to the subject) to a victim who suddenly appears to have a serious medical emergency. The question they investigated is "Will the addition of more witnesses inhibit the likelihood that the subject will seek help for the victim?" Another interesting factor the researchers thought to examine is whether the subject believes that the bystanders also had medical expertise, as that would possibly inhibit the subject's inclination to seek help (assuming the medically knowledgeable bystander would be better suited to help first). Finally, they wondered whether the gender of the subject or the bystanders have an effect on helping. Are women or men more likely to help the victim? Enjoy reading this classic paper, and we'll chat more afterward!

Reading 10.1

Bystander intervention in emergencies:

Diffusion of Responsibility[1]

John M. Darley and Bibb Latané

Ss overheard an epileptic seizure. They believed either that they alone heard the emergency, or that 1 or 4 unseen others were also present. As predicted the presence of other bystanders reduced the individual's feelings of personal responsibility

[1]This research was supported in part by National Science Foundation Grants GS1238 and GS1239. Susan Darley contributed materially to the design of the experiment and ran the subjects, and she and Thomas Moriarty analyzed the data. Richard Nisbett, Susan Millman, Andrew Gordon, and Norma Neiman helped in preparing the tape recordings.

and lowered his speed of reporting ($p < .01$). In groups of size 3, males reported no faster than females, and females reported no slower when the l other bystander was a male rather than a female. In general, personality and background measures were not predictive of helping. Bystander inaction in real-life emergencies is often explained by "apathy," "alienation," and "anomie." This experiment suggests that the explanation may lie more in the bystander's response to other observers than in his indifference to the victim.

Several years ago, a young woman was stabbed to death in the middle of a street in a residential section of New York City. Although such murders are not entirely routine, the incident received little public attention until several weeks later when the *New York Times* disclosed another side to the case: at least 38 witnesses had observed the attack and none had even attempted to intervene. Although the attacker took more than half an hour to kill Kitty Genovese, not one of the 38 people who watched from the safety of their own apartments came out to assist her. Not one even lifted the telephone to call the police (Rosenthal, 1964).

Preachers, professors, and news commentators sought the reasons for such apparently conscienceless and inhumane lack of intervention. Their conclusions ranged from "moral decay," to "dehumanization produced by the urban environment," to "alienation," "anomie," and "existential despair." An analysis of the situation, however, suggests that factors other than apathy and indifference were involved.

A person witnessing an emergency situation, particularly such a frightening and dangerous one as a stabbing, is in conflict. There are obvious humanitarian norms about helping the victim, but there are also rational and irrational fears about what might happen to a person who does intervene (Milgram & Hollander, 1964) . "I didn't want to get involved," is a familiar comment, and behind it lies fears of physical harm, public embarrassment, involvement with police procedures, lost work days and jobs, and other unknown dangers.

In certain circumstances, the norms favoring intervention may be weakened, leading bystanders to resolve the conflict in the direction of nonintervention. One of these circumstances may be the presence of other on-lookers. For example, in the case above, each observer, by seeing lights and figures in other apartment house windows, knew that others were also watching. However, there was no way to tell how the other observers were reacting. These two facts provide several reasons why any individual may have delayed or failed to help. The responsibility for helping was diffused among the observers; there was also diffusion of any potential blame for not taking action; and finally, it was possible that somebody, unperceived, had already initiated helping action.

When only one bystander is present in an emergency, if help is to come, it must come from him. Although he may choose to ignore it (out of concern for his personal safety, or desires "not to get involved"), any pressure to intervene focuses uniquely on him.

When there are several observers present, however, the pressures to intervene do not focus on any one of the observers; instead the responsibility for intervention is shared among all the onlookers and is not unique to any one. As a result, no one helps.

A second possibility is that potential blame may be diffused. However much we may wish to think that an individual's moral behavior is divorced from considerations of personal punishment or reward, there is both theory and evidence to the contrary (Aronfreed, 1964; Miller & Dollard, 1941, Whiting & Child, 1953). It is perfectly reasonable to assume that, under

---

This is the infamous case of the murder of Kitty Genovese, which you may recall from the lecture on helping in your introductory psychology class. This real-life event is one of the things that spurred Darley and Latané to initiate their pioneering work on bystander apathy in helping.

circumstances of group responsibility for a punishable act, the punishment or blame that accrues to any one individual is often slight or nonexistent.

Finally, if others are known to be present, but their behavior cannot be closely observed, any one bystander can assume that one of the other observers is already taking action to end the emergency. Therefore, his own intervention would be only redundant—perhaps harmfully or confusingly so. Thus, given the presence of other onlookers whose behavior cannot be observed, any given bystander can rationalize his own inaction by convincing himself that "somebody else must be doing something."

These considerations lead to the hypothesis that the more bystanders to an emergency, the less likely, or the more slowly, any one bystander will intervene to provide aid. To test this proposition it would be necessary to create a situation in which a realistic "emergency" could plausibly occur. Each subject should also be blocked from communicating with others to prevent his getting information about their behavior during the emergency. Finally, the experimental situation should allow for the assessment of the speed and frequency of the subjects' reaction to the emergency. The experiment reported below attempted to fulfill these conditions.

PROCEDURE

Overview. A college student arrived in the laboratory and was ushered into an individual room from which a communication system would enable him to talk to the other participants. It was explained to him that he was to take part in a discussion about personal problems associated with college life and that the discussion would be held over the intercom system, rather than face-to-face, in order to avoid embarrassment by preserving the anonymity of the subjects. During the course of the discussion, one of the other subjects underwent what appeared to be a very serious nervous seizure similar to epilepsy. During the fit it was impossible for the subject to talk to the other discussants or to find out what, if anything, they were doing about the emergency. The dependent variable was the speed with which the subjects reported the emergency to the experimenter. The major independent variable was the number of people the subject thought to be in the discussion group.

Subjects. Fifty-nine female and thirteen male students in introductory psychology courses at New York University were contacted to take part in an unspecified experiment as part of a class requirement.

Method. Upon arriving for the experiment, the subject found himself in a long corridor with doors opening off it to several small rooms. An experimental assistant met him, took him to one of the rooms, and seated him at a table. After filling out a background information form, the subject was given a pair of headphones with an attached microphone and was told to listen for instructions.

Over the intercom, the experimenter explained that he was interested in learning about the kinds of personal problems faced by normal college students in a high pressure, urban environment. He said that to avoid possible embarrassment about discussing personal problems with strangers several precautions had been taken. First, subjects would remain anonymous, which was why they had been placed in individual rooms rather than face-to-face. (The actual reason for this was to allow tape recorder simulation of the other subjects and the emergency.)

Second, since the discussion might be inhibited by the presence of outside listeners, the experimenter would not listen to the initial discussion, but would get the subject's reactions later, by questionnaire. (The real purpose of this was to remove the obviously responsible experimenter from the scene of the emergency.)

The subjects were told that since the experimenter was not present, it was necessary to impose some organization. Each person would talk in turn, presenting his problems to the group. Next, each person in turn would comment on what the others had said, and finally, there would be a free discussion. A mechanical switching device would regulate this discussion sequence and each subject's microphone would be on for about 2 minutes. While any microphone was on, all other microphones would be off. Only one subject, therefore, could be heard over the network at any given time. The subjects were thus led to realize when they later heard the seizure that only the victim's microphone was on and that there was no way of determining what any of the other witnesses were doing, nor of discussing the event and its possible solution with the others. When these instructions had been given, the discussion began.

In the discussion, the future victim spoke first, saying that he found it difficult to get adjusted to New York City and to his studies. Very hesitantly, and with obvious embarrassment, he mentioned that he was prone to seizures, particularly when studying hard or taking exams. The other people, including the real subject, took their turns and discussed similar problems (minus, of course, the proneness to seizures). The naive subject talked last in the series, after the last pre-recorded voice was played.[2]

When it was again the victim's turn to talk, he made a few relatively calm comments, and then, growing increasingly louder and incoherent, he continued:

> I-er-um-I think I-I need-er-if-if could-er-er-some body er-er-er-er-er-er-er give me a little-er-give me a little help here because-er-I-er-I'm-er-er h-h-having a-a-a real problem-er-right now and I-er-if somebody could help me out it would-it would-er-er s-s-sure be-sure be good . . . because er-here-er-er-a cause I-er-I-uh-I've got a-a one of the-er-sei-----er-er-things coming on and-and-and I could really-er-use some help so if somebody would-er-give me a little h-help-uh-er-er-er-er-er c-could somebody-er-er-help-er-uh-uh-uh (choking sounds). . . . I'm gonna die-er-er-I'm . . . gonna die-er-help-er-er-seizure-er- [chokes, then quiet].

The experimenter began timing the speed of the real subject's response at the beginning of the victim's speech. Informed judges listening to the tape have estimated that the victim's increasingly louder and more disconnected ramblings clearly represented a breakdown about 70 seconds after the signal for the victim's second speech. The victim's speech was abruptly cut off 125 seconds after this signal, which could be interpreted by the subject as indicating that the time allotted for that speaker had elapsed and the switching circuits had switched away from him. Times reported in the results are measured from the start of the fit.

Group size variable. The major independent variable of the study was the number of other people that the subject believed also heard the fit. By the assistant's comments before the

---

[2]To test whether the order in which the subjects spoke in the first discussion round significantly affected the subjects' speed of report, the order in which the subjects spoke was varied (in the six person group). This had no significant or noticeable effect on the speed of the subjects' reports.

Explains for the subject why he/she won't be able to hear anyone else when one person is talking. And why no one else is heard when the "victim" is talking and then has a seizure.

experiment, and also by the number of voices heard to speak in the first round of the group discussion, the subject was led to believe that the discussion group was one of three sizes: either a two-person group (consisting of a person who would later have a fit and the real subject), a three-person group (consisting of the victim, the real subject, and one confederate voice), or a six-person group (consisting of the victim, the real subject, and four confederate voices). All the confederates' voices were tape-recorded.

Variations in group composition. Varying the kind as well as the number of bystanders present at an emergency should also vary the amount of responsibility felt by any single bystander. To test this, several variations of the three-person group were run. In one three-person condition, the taped bystander voice was that of a female, in another a male, and in the third a male who said that he was a premedical student who occasionally worked in the emergency wards at Bellevue hospital.

In the above conditions, the subjects were female college students. In a final condition males drawn from the same introductory psychology subject pool were tested in a three-person female-bystander condition.

Time to help. The major dependent variable was the time elapsed from the start of the victim's fit until the subject left her experimental cubicle. When the subject left her room, she saw the experimental assistant seated at the end of the hall, and invariably went to the assistant. If 6 minutes elapsed without the subject having emerged from her room, the experiment was terminated.

As soon as the subject reported the emergency, or after 6 minutes had elapsed, the experimental assistant disclosed the true nature of the experiment, and dealt with any emotions aroused in the subject. Finally the subject filled out a questionnaire concerning her thoughts and feelings during the emergency, and completed scales of Machiavellianism, anomie, and authoritarianism (Christie, 1964), a social desirability scale (Crowne & Marlowe, 1964), a social responsibility scale (Daniels & Berkowitz, 1964) , and reported vital statistics and socioeconomic data.

RESULTS

Plausibility of Manipulation

Judging by the subjects' nervousness when they reported the fit to the experimenter, by their surprise when they discovered that the fit was simulated, and by comments they made during the fit (when they thought their microphones were off), one can conclude that almost all of the subjects perceived the fit as real. There were two exceptions in different experimental conditions, and the data for these subjects were dropped from the analysis.

Effect of Group Size on Helping

The number of bystanders that the subject perceived to be present had a major effect on the likelihood with which she would report the emergency (Table 1). Eighty-five percent of the subjects who thought they alone knew of the victim's plight reported the seizure before the victim was cut off, only 31% of those who thought four other bystanders were present did so.

Seems like a long enough time to allow for a subject to decide whether to seek help. It is important to specify details like this—the outer time limit for the subject to intervene—so that those who wish to replicate the study at a later time, have all the details needed to reconstruct the experiment properly.

A note here about debriefing. Whenever one does an experiment that involves deception, it is important to do an oral, face-to-face debriefing (as opposed to just giving the subject a sheet on the way out that explains the true nature of the experiment). The primary reason for doing this is that it is important that subjects don't feel gullible, embarrassed, or otherwise negatively about having been deceived. The experimenter should take time to clearly explain the experiment and why deception is necessary, and that it is important that every subject believes the cover story, and that they shouldn't feel upset if they did believe it. For more on this point, see our discussion of the Aronson chapter in the Methods section of this book.

This is a subjective judgment on the part of the researchers. It is always best to have some sort of objective indicator of whether the subject was suspicious.

This is a standard procedure, to drop participants who are suspicious. A good practice when one is about to start an experiment is to run a "pilot study." This entails running the experiment normally for about a week, and making sure to do a thorough oral debriefing at the end, to ask subjects detailed questions about their thoughts or suspicions about any aspect of the experiment. The researcher then uses that information to make adjustments to the method, and then sets aside the pilot data before starting to run the experiment. This is a great help in "debugging" the experiment.

These results nicely support the concept of diffusion of responsibility. When the subject believes that he/she is the only one hearing the victim have his/her seizure, the subject knows he/she is the only one who can get help, and in those cases, you see 85% going for help within 52 seconds. But as we add other "subjects" who are bystanders, the perceived responsibility of the real subject to help diminishes. You can see this in condition 2, where the subject believed it was him/her self, the victim, and one other bystander. Now the subject perceives their responsibility to help is cut by 50%, and that shows up in a longer response time (93 seconds) and fewer going for help (62%). This response rate is cut in half (down to 31%) when the subject believes there are 4 other bystanders (thus, his/her perceived responsibility drops to 20%), and it takes a whopping 166 seconds for the subject to go get help (if he/she gets help).

TABLE 1   Effects of Groups Size on Likelihood and Speed of Response

Group size	N	% responding by end of fit	Time in sec.	Speed score
2 (S & victim)	13	85	52	.87
3 (S, victim, & 1 other)	26	62	93	.72
6 (S, victim, & 4 others)	13	31	166	.51

Note. p value of differences: $x^2 = 7.91$, $p < .02$; $F = 8.09$, $p < .01$, for specific scores.

Every one of the subjects in the two person groups, but only 62% of the subjects in the six-person groups, ever reported the emergency. The cumulative distributions of response times for groups of different perceived size (Figure 1) indicates that, by any point in time, more subjects from the two-person groups had responded than from the three-person groups, and more from the three-person groups than from the six-person groups.

Ninety-five percent of all the subjects whoever responded did so within the first half of the time available to them. No subject who had not reported within 3 minutes after the fit ever did so. The shape of these distributions suggest that had the experiment been allowed to run for a considerably longer time, few additional subjects would have responded.

Speed of Response

To achieve a more detailed analysis of the results, each subject's time score was transformed into a "speed" score by taking the reciprocal of the response time in seconds and multiplying by 100. The effect of this transformation was to deemphasize differences between longer time scores, thus reducing the contribution to the results of the arbitrary 6-minute limit on scores. A high speed score indicates a fast response.

An analysis of variance indicates that the effect of group size is highly significant $(p < .01)$. Duncan multiple-range tests indicate that all but the two- and three-person groups differ significantly from one another $(p < .05)$.

Victim's Likelihood of Being Helped

This point is supported in study after study on the bystander effect and diffusion of responsibility. A victim is more likely to be helped if there is only one bystander (witness) than if the victim is surrounded by 10, 50, or even 100 witnesses!

An individual subject is less likely to respond if he thinks that others are present. But what of the victim? Is the inhibition of the response of each individual strong enough to counteract the fact that with five onlookers there are five times as many people available to help? From the data of this experiment, it is possible mathematically to create hypothetical groups with one, two, or five observers.[3] The calculations indicate that the victim is about equally likely to get help from one bystander as from two. The victim is considerably more likely to have gotten help from one or two observers than from five during the first minute of the fit. For instance, by 45 seconds after the start of the fit, the victim's chances of having been helped by the single

---

[3]The formula for the probability that at least one person will help by a given time is $1 - (1 - P)^n$ where n is the number of observers and n is the probability of a single individual (who thinks he is one of n observers) helping by that time.

FIG. 1   Cumulative distributions of helping responses.

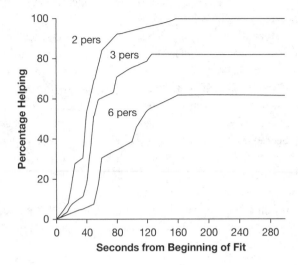

bystanders were about 50%, compared to none in the five observer condition. After the first minute, the likelihood of getting help from at least one person is high in all three conditions.

Effect of Group Composition on Helping the Victim

Several variations of the three-person group were run. In one pair of variations, the female subject thought the other bystander was either male or female; in another, she thought the other bystander was a premedical student who worked in an emergency ward at Bellevue hospital. As Table 2 shows, the variations in sex and medical competence of the other bystander had no important or detectable effect on speed of response. Subjects responded equally frequently and fast whether the other bystander was female, male, or medically experienced.

Sex of the Subject and Speed of Response

Coping with emergencies is often thought to be the duty of males, especially when females are present, but there was no evidence that this was the case in this study. Male subjects responded to the emergency with almost exactly the same speed as did females (Table 2).

TABLE 2   Effects of a group composition on response and speed of response[a]

Group composition	N	% responding by end of fit	Time in sec.	Speed score
Female S, male other	13	62	94	74
Female S, female other	13	62	92	71
Female S, male medic other	5	100	60	77
Male S, female other	13	69	110	68

[a] Three-person group, male victim.

Interesting variation right? Do you think that a subject would be more or less likely to help if he/she thought that the other bystander was the same or opposite gender, or if he/she were told that the other subject had medical training?

The answer to the previous question is: no. Neither gender of the other bystander, nor the medical expertise of the other bystander, had any influence on the likelihood of the real subject to help.

Reasons for Intervention or Nonintervention

After the debriefing at the end of the experiment each subject was given a 15-item checklist and asked to check those thoughts which had "crossed your mind when you heard Subject 1 calling for help." Whatever the condition, each subject checked very few thoughts, and there were no significant differences in number or kind of thoughts in the different experimental groups. The only thoughts checked by more than a few subjects were "I didn't know what to do" (18 out of 65 subjects), "I thought it must be some sort of fake" (20 out of 65), and "I didn't know exactly what was happening" (26 out of 65).

It is possible that subjects were ashamed to report socially undesirable rationalizations, or, since the subjects checked the list *after* the true nature of the experiment had been explained to them, their memories might have been blurred. It is our impression, however, that most subjects checked few reasons because they had few coherent thoughts during the fit.

We asked all subjects whether the presence or absence of other bystanders had entered their minds during the time that they were hearing the fit. Subjects in the three- and six-person groups reported that they were aware that other people were present, but they felt that this made no difference to their own behavior.

Individual Difference Correlates of Speed of Report

The correlations between speed of report and various individual differences on the personality and background measures were obtained by normalizing the distribution of report speeds within each experimental condition and pooling these scores across all conditions $(n = 62-65)$. Personality measures showed no important or significant correlations with speed of reporting the emergency. In fact, only one of the 16 individual difference measures, the size of the community in which the subject grew up, correlated $(r = -.26, p < .05)$ with the speed of helping.

DISCUSSION

Subjects, whether or not they intervened, believed the fit to be genuine and serious. "My God, he's having a fit," many subjects said to themselves (and were overheard via their microphones) at the onset of the fit. Others gasped or simply said "Oh." Several of the male subjects swore. One subject said to herself , "It's just my kind of luck, something has to happen to me!" Several subjects spoke aloud of their confusion about what course of action to take, "Oh God, what should I do?"

When those subjects who intervened stepped out of their rooms, they found the experimental assistant down the hall. With some uncertainty, but without panic, they reported the situation. "Hey, I think Number l is very sick. He's having a fit or something." After ostensibly checking on the situation, the experimenter returned to report that "everything is under control." The subjects accepted these assurances with obvious relief.

Subjects who failed to report the emergency showed few signs of the apathy and indifference thought to characterize "unresponsive bystanders." When the experimenter entered her room to terminate the situation, the subject often asked if the victim was "all right." "Is he being taken care of ?" "He's all right isn't he?" Many of these subjects showed physical signs of nervousness; they often had trembling hands and sweating palms. If anything, they seemed more emotionally aroused than did the subjects who reported the emergency.

Wow, that is a lot of suspicious subjects! Recall earlier the researchers said they believed that nearly all the subjects seemed to believe the manipulation. That may be true, but one-third of the subjects are now saying they were suspicious. One likely possibility is that these subjects, upon hearing the true nature of the study (and that the seizure was faked), might want to say they knew it all along, so they won't feel embarrassed for believing the cover story. Can you think of a way to better assess whether subjects are truly suspicious?

Hey, that's what I just said. ☺

Interesting! Personality types appear to have no influence on subjects' responses in this helping experiment. We usually think of personality influencing our behavior across situations, but this is an interesting demonstration of how situational factors (number of bystanders) can be more influential on our behavior than our personality.

Why, then, didn't they respond? It is our impression that non-intervening subjects had not decided *not* to respond. Rather they were still in a state of indecision and conflict concerning whether to respond or not. The emotional behavior of these non-responding subjects was a sign of their continuing conflict, a conflict that other subjects resolved by responding.

The fit created a conflict situation of the avoidance-avoidance type. On the one hand, subjects worried about the guilt and shame they would feel if they did not help the person in distress. On the other hand, they were concerned not to make fools of themselves by overreacting, not to ruin the ongoing experiment by leaving their intercom, and not to destroy the anonymous nature of the situation which the experimenter had earlier stressed as important. For subjects in the two-person condition, the obvious distress of the victim and his need for help were so important that their conflict was easily resolved. For the subjects who knew there were other bystanders present, the cost of not helping was reduced and the conflict they were in more acute. Caught between the two negative alternatives of letting the victim continue to suffer or the costs of rushing in to help, the non-responding bystanders vacillated between them rather than choosing not to respond. This distinction may be academic for the victim, since he got no help in either case, but it is an extremely important one for arriving at an understanding of the causes of bystanders' failures to help.

Although the subjects experienced stress and conflict during the experiment, their general reactions to it were highly positive. On a questionnaire administered after the experimenter had discussed the nature and purpose of the experiment, every single subject found the experiment either "interesting" or "very interesting" and was willing to participate in similar experiments in the future. All subjects felt they understood what the experiment was about and indicated that they thought the deceptions were necessary and justified. All but one felt they were better informed about the nature of psychological research in general.

Male subjects reported the emergency no faster than did females. These results (or lack of them) seem to conflict with the Berkowitz, Klanclerman, and Harris (1964) finding that males tend to assume more responsibility and take more initiative than females in giving help to dependent others. Also, females reacted equally fast when the other bystander was another female, a male, or even a person practiced in dealing with medical emergencies. The ineffectiveness of these manipulations of group composition cannot be explained by general insensitivity of the speed measure, since the group-size variable had a marked effect on report speed.

It might be helpful in understanding this lack of difference to distinguish two general classes of intervention in emergency situations: direct and reportorial. Direct intervention (breaking up a fight, extinguishing a fire, swimming out to save a drowner) often requires skill, knowledge, or physical power. It may involve danger. American cultural norms and Berkowitz's results seem to suggest that males are more responsible than females for this kind of direct intervention.

A second way of dealing with an emergency is to report it to someone qualified to handle it, such as the police. For this kind of intervention, there seem to be no norms requiring male action. In the present study, subjects clearly intended to report the emergency rather than take direct action. For such indirect intervention, sex or medical competence does not appear to affect one's qualifications or responsibilities. Anybody, male or female, medically trained or not, can find the experimenter.

In this study, no subject was able to tell how the other subjects reacted to the fit. (Indeed, there were no other subjects actually present.) The effects of group size on speed of helping, therefore, are due simply to the perceived presence of others rather than to the influence of their actions. This means that the experimental situation is unlike emergencies, such as a fire, in which bystanders interact with each other. It is, however, similar to emergencies, such as the Genovese murder, in which spectators knew others were also watching but were prevented by walls between them from communication that might have counteracted the diffusion of responsibility.

The present results create serious difficulties for one class of commonly given explanations for the failure of bystanders to intervene in actual emergencies, those involving apathy or indifference. These explanations generally assert that people who fail to intervene are somehow different in kind from the rest of us, that they are "alienated by industrialization," "dehumanized by urbanization," "depersonalized by living in the cold society," or "psychopaths." These explanations serve a dual function for people who adopt them. First, they explain (if only in a nominal way) the puzzling and frightening problem of why people watch others die. Second, they give individuals reason to deny that they too might fail to help in a similar situation.

The results of this experiment seem to indicate that such personality variables may not be as important as these explanations suggest. Alienation, Machiavellianism, acceptance of social responsibility, need for approval, and authoritarianism are often cited in these explanations. Yet they did not predict the speed or likelihood of help. In sharp contrast, the perceived number of bystanders did. The explanation of bystander "apathy" may lie more in the bystander's response to other observers than in presumed personality deficiencies of "apathetic" individuals. Although this realization may force us to face the guilt-provoking possibility that we too might fail to intervene, it also suggests that individuals are not, of necessity, "noninterveners" because of their personalities. If people understand the situational forces that can make them hesitate to intervene, they may better overcome them.

> The authors make an important point here. Their research shows that the reason people don't help when there are other witnesses is not because they have a deficiency in their moral character, but rather, the situation overrides any personality characteristics they have, and causes them to not intervene.

REFERENCES

ARONFREED, J. The origin of self-criticism. *Psychological Review,* 1964, 71, 193–219.

BERKOWITZ, L., KLANDERMAN, S., & HARRIS, R. Effects of experimenter awareness and sex of subject on reactions to dependency relationships. *Sociometry,* 1964, 27, 327–329.

CHRISTIE, R. The prevalence of Machiavellian orientations. Paper presented at the meeting of the American Psychological Association, Los Angeles, 1964.

CROWNE, D., & MARLOWE, D. *The approval motive.* New York: Wiley, 1964.

DANIELS, L., & BERKOWITZ, L. Liking and response to dependency relationships. *Human Relations,* 1963, 16, 141–148.

MILGRAM, S., & HOLLANDER, P. Murder they heard. *Nation,* 1964, 198, 602–604.

MILLER, N., & DOLLARD, J. *Social learning and imitation.* New Haven: Yale University Press, 1941.

ROSENTHAL, A. M. *Thirty-eight witnesses.* New York: McGraw-Hill, 1964.

WHITING, J. W. M., & CHILD, I. *Child training and personality.* New Haven: Yale University Press, 1953.

POST-ARTICLE DISCUSSION

Now, if I had asked you before you read this paper to predict the outcome, you'd likely make the assumption that most people would: that is, the more people who see a victim, the greater the chance that victim will be helped. But something happens when we add bystanders (witnesses) to the scene. Each assumes the other is better qualified to help or that someone has already sought help. No matter the assumption, the end result is a lower likelihood of help from anyone. This study nicely demonstrated this diffusion of responsibility on the part of the witnesses. Recall our discussion of the fundamental attribution error. This study shows that personality does not drive behavior in this situation. Helping, although intuitively personality driven, is also sometimes subject to more powerful situational forces. When thinking about the causes of other people's behavior, we are well advised to consider all the possible situational forces that may be acting on the subject, that might drive behavior over any personality trait forces.

THINGS TO THINK ABOUT

1. Why do you think that the perceived gender of other coactors or their perceived medical expertise had no effect on the subject's tendency to go for assistance?

2. Why do you think they had so many subjects (about 33%) who reported being suspicious of some aspects of the experiment?

3. Do you think another type of emergency (e.g., fire or other type of medical emergency) would have had a different effect on subjects' willingness to go for help?

4. The authors measured authoritarianism, Machiavellianism, social desirability, and social responsibility, and found that these personality variables had no effect on the tendency to help. Can you think of other personality characteristics that might have an effect that the authors could have considered?

5. What is the design of this study? (List all IVs.) Additionally, what is being measured?

INTRODUCTION TO READING 10.2
Darley and Batson (1973)

One of the enduring issues in psychology is how to determine the relative contribution of one's personality traits versus situational factors in determining our behavior. In other words, under what conditions is our behavior solely or mostly determined by our personality, and when is our behavior driven by outside, situational influences? People like to think that their behavior is stable across situations, because it is based on a stable aspect of ourselves: our personality. Thinking this makes us feel comfortable because it allows us to understand ourselves and predict how we will act. We are especially likely to explain others' behavior as due to their personality, and rarely do we consider the possible influence of situational factors on their behavior. This is such a pervasive tendency that we refer to it as the fundamental attribution error (Sabini, Siepmann, & Stein, 2001).

So, when it comes to helping others, it seems logical that researchers would assume that such behavior would be driven by the individual's "helpful personality characteristics" such as compassion, empathy, thoughtfulness, and so on. But mostly because we are "cognitive misers" (we generally don't like to do extra cognitive work), we rarely consider the situational forces on other people's behavior. To illustrate this, consider the following experiment on helping behavior: You tell subjects that you would like them to give a speech to a group of people on the other end of campus on job opportunities for graduates. Half are told they have plenty of time to get there; others are told they are running late and they need to really rush to get there. This is the situational variable (time pressure). Along the way, an assistant to the researcher (pretending to be an average student) is slumped over in a doorway and coughing, mumbling about a respiratory condition. Nearly everyone would help, right? Seems reasonable. What if we go overboard and we make all the subjects be seminary students? These are people whose personality is all about compassion, caring, and helping others. So now we should really expect ALL subjects to help the victim. Right?

As you will see in this landmark paper, the results were quite surprising to most people, but they shouldn't be a surprise to social psychologists. Enjoy!

Reading 10.2

"From Jerusalem to Jericho":

A Study of Situational and Dispositional Variables In Helping Behavior[1]

John M. Darley [2] and C. Daniel Batson

The influence of several situational and personality variables on helping behavior was examined in an emergency situation suggested by the parable of the Good Samaritan. People going between two buildings encountered a shabbily dressed person slumped by the side of the road. Subjects in a hurry to reach their destination were more likely to pass by without stopping. Some subjects were going to give a short talk on the parable of the Good Samaritan, others on a non-helping relevant topic; this made no significant difference in the likelihood of their giving the victim help. Religious personality variables did not predict whether an individual would help the victim or not. However, if a subject did stop to offer help, the character of the helping response was related to his type of religiosity.

Helping other people in distress is, among other things, an ethical act. That is, it is an act governed by ethical norms and precepts taught to children at home, in school, and in church. From Freudian and other personality theories, one would expect individual differences in internalization of these standards that would lead to differences between individuals in the likelihood with which they would help others. But recent research on bystander intervention in emergency situations (Bickman, 1969; Darley & Latane, 1968; Korte, 1969; but see also Schwartz & Clausen, 1970) has had bad luck in finding personality determinants of helping behavior. Although personality variables that one might expect to correlate with helping behavior have been measured (Machiavellianism, authoritarianism, social desirability, alienation, and social responsibility), these were not predictive of helping. Nor was this due to a generalized lack of predictability in the helping situation examined, since variations in the experimental situation, such as the availability of other people who might also help, produced marked changes in rates of helping behavior.

These findings are reminiscent of Hartshorne and May's (1928) discovery that resistance to temptation, another ethically relevant act, did not seem to be a fixed characteristic of an individual. That is, a person who was likely to be honest in one situation was not particularly likely to be honest in the next (but see also Burton, 1963).

The rather disappointing correlation between the social psychologist's traditional set of personality variables and helping behavior in emergency situations suggests the need for a fresh perspective on possible predictors of helping and possible situations in which to test

[1]For assistance in conducting this research thanks are due Robert Wells, Beverly Fisher, Mike Shafto, Peter Sheras, Richard Detweiler, and Karen Glasser. The research was funded by National Science Foundation Grant GS-2293.
[2]Requests for reprints should be sent to John Darley, Department of Psychology, Princeton University, Princeton, New Jersey 08540.

them. Therefore, for inspiration we turned to the Bible, to what is perhaps the classical helping story in the Judeo-Christian tradition, the parable of the Good Samaritan. The parable proved of value in suggesting both personality and situational variables relevant to helping.

> "And who is my neighbor?" Jesus replied, "A man was going down from Jerusalem to Jericho, and he fell among robbers, who stripped him and beat him, and departed, leaving him half dead. Now by chance a priest was going down the road; and when he saw him he passed by on the other side. So likewise a Levite, when he came to the place and saw him, passed by on the other side. But a Samaritan, as he journeyed, came to where he was; and when he saw him, he had compassion, and went to him and bound his wounds, pouring on oil and wine; then he set him on his own beast and brought him to an inn, and took care of him. And the next day he took out two dennarii and gave them to the innkeeper, saying, "Take care of him; and whatever more you spend, I will repay you when I come back." Which of these three, do you think, proved neighbor to him who fell among the robbers?" He said, "The one who showed mercy on him." And Jesus said to him, "Go and do likewise." [Luke 10: 29-37 RSV]

From this biblical parable, Darley and Batson had the idea for the first IV for their study: time pressure: rushed vs. no time pressure.

To psychologists who reflect on the parable, it seems to suggest situational and personality differences between the non-helpful priest and Levite and the helpful Samaritan. What might each have been thinking and doing when he came upon the robbery victim on that desolate road? What sort of persons were they?

One can speculate on differences in thought. Both the priest and the Levite were religious functionaries who could be expected to have their minds occupied with religious matters. The priest's role in religious activities is obvious. The Levite's role, although less obvious, is equally important: The Levites were necessary participants in temple ceremonies. Much less can be said with any confidence about what the Samaritan might have been thinking, but, in contrast to the others, it was most likely not of a religious nature, for Samaritans were religious outcasts.

Here, Darley and Batson are talking about motives for helping, and contrasting a more egoistic (selfish) motive that gets one admiration from others, or favor with God, compared to a more altruistic motive, where the aim of the helper is solely to relieve the victim's suffering. This is a fundamental question that Batson asks throughout most of his subsequent research on what he calls the "Empathy-Altruism Hypothesis" (which suggests that when people feel empathy, they will be more likely to help, and that helping will be more likely to be purely altruistic).

Not only was the Samaritan most likely thinking about more mundane matters than the priest and Levite, but, because he was socially less important, it seems likely that he was operating on a quite different time schedule. One can imagine the priest and Levite, prominent public figures, hurrying along with little black books full of meetings and appointments, glancing furtively at their sundials. In contrast, the Samaritan would likely have far fewer and less important people counting on him to be at a particular place at a particular time, and therefore might be expected to be in less of a hurry than the prominent priest or Levite.

In addition to these situational variables, one finds personality factors suggested as well. Central among these, and apparently basic to the point that Jesus was trying to make, is a distinction between types of religiosity. Both the priest and Levite are extremely "religious." But it seems to be precisely their type of religiosity that the parable challenges. At issue is the motivation for one's religion and ethical behavior. Jesus seems to feel that the religious leaders of his time, though certainly respected and upstanding citizens, may be "virtuous" for what it will get them, both in terms of the admiration of their fellowmen and in the eyes of God. New Testament scholar R. W. Funk (1966) noted that the Samaritan is at the other end of the spectrum:

> The Samaritan does not love with side glances at God. The need of neighbor alone is made self-evident, and the Samaritan responds without other motivation [pp. 218–219].

That is, the Samaritan is interpreted as responding spontaneously to the situation, not as being preoccupied with the abstract ethical or organizational do's and don'ts of religion as the priest and Levite would seem to be. This is not to say that the Samaritan is portrayed as irreligious. A major intent of the parable would seem to be to present the Samaritan as a religious and ethical example, but at the same time to contrast his type of religiosity with the more common conception of religiosity that the priest and Levite represent.

To summarize the variables suggested as affecting helping behavior by the parable, the situational variables include the content of one's thinking and the amount of hurry in one's journey. The major dispositional variable seems to be differing types of religiosity. Certainly these variables do not exhaust the list that could be elicited from the parable, but they do suggest several research hypotheses.

Hypothesis 1. The parable implies that people who encounter a situation possibly calling for a helping response while thinking religious and ethical thoughts will be no more likely to offer aid than persons thinking about something else. Such a hypothesis seems to run counter to a theory that focuses on norms as determining helping behavior because a normative account would predict that the increased salience of helping norms produced by thinking about religious and ethical examples would increase helping behavior.

Hypothesis 2. Persons encountering a possible helping situation when they are in a hurry will be less likely to offer aid than persons not in a hurry.

Hypothesis 3. Concerning types of religiosity, persons who are religious in a Samaritan like fashion will help more frequently than those religious in a priest or Levite fashion.

Obviously, this last hypothesis is hardly operationalized as stated. Prior research by one of the investigators on types of religiosity (Batson, 1971), however, led us to differentiate three distinct ways of being religious: (*a*) for what it will gain one (cf. Freud, 1927, and perhaps the priest and Levite), (*b*) for its own intrinsic value (cf. Allport & Ross, 1967), and (*c*) as a response to and quest for meaning in one's everyday life (cf. Batson, 1971). Both of the latter conceptions would be proposed by their exponents as related to the more Samaritanlike "true" religiosity. Therefore, depending on the theorist one follows, the third hypothesis may be stated like this: People (*a*) who are religious for intrinsic reasons (Allport & Ross, 1967) or (*b*) whose religion emerges out of questioning the meaning of their everyday lives (Batson, 1971) will be more likely to stop to offer help to the victim.

The parable of the Good Samaritan also suggested how we would measure people's helping behavior—their response to a stranger slumped by the side of one's path. The victim should appear somewhat ambiguous—ill dressed, possibly in need of help, but also possibly drunk or even potentially dangerous.

Further, the parable suggests a means by which the incident could be perceived as a real one rather than part of a psychological experiment in which one's behavior was under surveillance and might be shaped by demand characteristics (Orne, 1962), evaluation apprehension (Rosenberg, 1965), or other potentially artifactual determinants of helping behavior.

The authors are proposing that those who are thinking about religious/ethical thoughts are no more likely to help a victim than those who are not thinking about religious thoughts. So, they are predicting a null effect (no difference on the DV between the two experimental conditions).

This is an intriguing question: is it really the case that our willingness to offer help to a victim depends on something as situationally driven and sort of random as whether we are in a hurry at that particular moment? Wouldn't common sense say that if you are the kind of person who helps others, then you're going to help all the time, regardless of whether you are in a rush to get somewhere or not?

Those who are wanting to help solely to benefit the other will be more likely to help compared to those for whom the motive to help is driven by selfish motives, such as public acclaim and gaining favor from God.

One of the most interesting facets of this experiment, and why it makes for a compelling study, is the use of seminary students as subjects. Here we have a helping study, and they're using seminary students, whose whole being, personality, job, and motives are all about helping others. So you might worry that no matter what IVs the subjects are faced with, the results will indicate helping behavior across the board. In other words, a ceiling effect (high helping in all conditions). So why use seminary students? Because if we find situational influences (the IV) that influence helping, that overwhelm the influence of personality characteristics, and that would be powerful evidence for the interactionist perspective in social psychology, the idea that behavior is determined by a combination of situational and personality influences. This is also the basic idea underlying Kurt Lewin's famous Field Theory formula: B = f(P×E)— Behavior is a function of the person and the environment.

A 2 × 2 design. Time pressure: rushed vs. no rush. And type of thoughts the subject has before encountering the victim: religious (parable of Good Samaritan) vs. nonreligious. DV is whether and how help is administered.

The victim should be encountered not in the experimental context but on the road between various tasks.

METHOD

In order to examine the influence of these variables on helping behavior, seminary students were asked to participate in a study on religious education and vocations. In the first testing session, personality questionnaires concerning types of religiosity were administered. In a second individual session, the subject began experimental procedures in one building and was asked to report to another building for later procedures. While in transit, the subject passed a slumped "victim" planted in an alleyway. The dependent variable was whether and how the subject helped the victim. The independent variables were the degree to which the subject was told to hurry in reaching the other building and the talk he was to give when he arrived there. Some subjects were to give a talk on the jobs in which seminary students would be most effective, others, on the parable of the Good Samaritan.

Subjects

The subjects for the questionnaire administration were 67 students at Princeton Theological Seminary. Forty-seven of them, those who could be reached by telephone, were scheduled for the experiment. Of the 47, 7 subjects' data were not included in the analyses—3 because of contamination of the experimental procedures during their testing and 4 due to suspicion of the experimental situation. Each subject was paid $1 for the questionnaire session and $1.50 for the experimental session.

Personality Measures

Detailed discussion of the personality scales used may be found elsewhere (Batson, 1971), so the present discussion will be brief. The general personality construct under examination was religiosity. Various conceptions of religiosity have been offered in recent years based on different psychometric scales. The conception seeming to generate the most interest is the Allport and Ross (1967) distinction between "intrinsic" versus "extrinsic" religiosity (cf. also Allen & Spilka, 1967, on "committed" versus "consensual" religion). This bipolar conception of religiosity has been questioned by Brown (1964) and Batson (1971), who suggested three-dimensional analyses instead. Therefore, in the present research, types of religiosity were measured with three instruments which together provided six separate scales: (a) a *doctrinal orthodoxy* (D-o) scale patterned after that used by Glock and Stark (1966), scaling agreement with classic doctrines of Protestant theology; (b) the Allport-Ross *extrinsic* (AR-E) scale, measuring the use of religion as a means to an end rather than as an end in itself; (c) the Allport-Ross *intrinsic* (AR-I) scale, measuring the use of religion as an end in itself; (d) the *extrinsic external* scale of Batson's Religious Life Inventory (RELI-EE), designed to measure the influence of significant others and situations in generating one's religiosity; (e) the *extrinsic internal* scale of the Religious Life Inventory (RELI-EI), designed to measure the degree of "driveness" in one's religiosity; and (f) the *intrinsic* scale of the Religious Life Inventory (RELI-I), designed to measure the degree to which one's religiosity involves a questioning of the meaning of life arising out of one's interactions with his social environment. The order of presentation of the scales in the questionnaire was RELI, AR, D-o.

Consistent with prior research (Batson, 1971), a principal-component analysis of the total scale scores and individual items for the 67 seminarians produced a theoretically meaningful, orthogonally rotated three-component structure with the following loadings:

Religion as means received a single very high loading from AR-E (.903) and therefore was defined by Allport and Ross's (1967) conception of this scale as measuring religiosity as a means to other ends. This component also received moderate negative loadings from D-o (−.400) and AR-I (−.372) and a moderate positive loading from RELI-EE (.301).

Religion as end received high loadings from RELI-EI (.874), RELI-EE (.725), AR-I (.768), and D-o (.704). Given this configuration, and again following Allport and Ross's conceptualization, this component seemed to involve religiosity as an end in itself with some intrinsic value.

Religion as quest received a single very high loading from RELI-I (.945) and a moderate loading from RELI-EE (.75). Following Batson, this component was conceived to involve religiosity emerging out of an individual's search for meaning in his personal and social world.

The three religious personality scales examined in the experimental research were constructed through the use of complete-estimation factor score coefficients from these three components.

Scheduling of Experimental Study

Since the incident requiring a helping response was staged outdoors, the entire experimental study was run in 3 days, December 14–16, 1970, between 10 A.M. and 4 P.M. A tight schedule was used in an attempt to maintain reasonably consistent weather and light conditions. Temperature fluctuation according to the *New York Times* for the 3 days during these hours was not more than 5 degrees Fahrenheit. No rain or snow fell, although the third day was cloudy, whereas the first two were sunny. Within days the subjects were randomly assigned to experimental conditions.[3]

It is important to state in detail, all efforts taken to maintain standardization of conditions for all subjects. Here, the authors explain how they did this by running the study in a short period of time, during the same time period, and that the weather also didn't fluctuate between subjects.

Procedure

When a subject appeared for the experiment, an assistant (who was blind with respect to the personality scores) asked him to read a brief statement which explained that he was participating *in* a study of the vocational careers of seminary students. After developing the rationale for the study, the statement read:

> What we have called you in for today is to provide us with some additional material which will give us a clearer picture of how you think than does the questionnaire material we have gathered thus far. Questionnaires are helpful, but tend to be somewhat oversimplified. Therefore, we would like to record a 3–5-minute talk you give based on the following passage . . .

---

[3]An error was made in randomizing that increased the number of subjects in the intermediate-hurry conditions. This worked against the prediction that was most highly confirmed (the hurry prediction) and made no difference to the message variable tests.

In Variable 1: **Message the task-relevant condition the passage read,**

> With increasing frequency the question is being asked: What jobs or professions do seminary students subsequently enjoy most, and in what jobs are they most effective? The answer to this question used to be so obvious that the question was not even asked. Seminary students were being trained for the ministry, and since both society at large and the seminary student himself had a relatively clear understanding of what made a "good" minister, there was no need even to raise the question of for what other jobs seminary experience seems to be an asset. Today, however, neither society nor many seminaries have a very clearly defined conception of what a "good" minister *is* or of what sorts of jobs and professions are the best context in which to minister. Many seminary students, apparently genuinely concerned with "ministering," seem to feel that it is impossible to minister in the professional clergy. Other students, no less concerned, find the clergy the most viable profession for ministry. But are there other jobs and/or professions for which seminary experience is an asset? And, indeed, how much of an asset is it for the professional ministry? Or, even more broadly, can one minister through an "establishment" job at all?

In the helping-relevant condition, the subject was given the parable of the Good Samaritan exactly as printed earlier in this article. Next, regardless of condition, all subjects were told,

> You can say whatever you wish based on the passage. Because we are interested in how you think on your feet, you will not be allowed to use notes in giving the talk. Do you understand what you are to do? If not, the assistant will be glad to answer questions.

After a few minutes the assistant returned, asked if there were any questions, and then said:

> Since they're rather tight on space in this building, we're using a free office in the building next door for recording the talks. Let me show you how to get there [draws and explains map on 3×5 card]. This is where Professor Steiner's laboratory is. If you go in this door [points at map], there's a secretary right here, and she'll direct you to the office we're using for recording. Another of Professor Steiner's assistants will set you up for recording your talk. Is the map clear?

Variable 2: Hurry. In the high-hurry condition the assistant then looked at his watch and said, "Oh, you're late. They were expecting you a few minutes ago. We'd better get moving. The assistant should be waiting for you so you'd better hurry. It shouldn't take but just a minute." In the intermediate-hurry condition he said, "The assistant is ready for you, so please go right over." In the low-hurry condition he said, "It'll be a few minutes before they're ready for you, but you might as well head on over. If you have to wait over there, it shouldn't be long."

The incident. When the subject passed through the alley, the victim was sitting slumped in a doorway, head down, eyes closed, not moving. As the subject went by, the victim coughed

---

First IV is message (the topic of the talk they will ostensibly give to the other group): task-relevant vs. helping-related.

Second IV is time pressure on the subject to get to the other end of campus to deliver the speech: Hurried vs. not hurried.

twice and groaned, keeping his head down. If the subject stopped and asked if something was wrong or offered to help, the victim, startled and somewhat groggy, said, "Oh, thank you [cough]. . . . No, it's all right. [Pause] I've got this respiratory condition [cough]. . . . The doctor's given me these pills to take, and I just took one. . . . If I just sit and rest for a few minutes I'll be O.K. . . . Thanks very much for stopping though [smiles weakly]." If the subject persisted, insisting on taking the victim inside the building, the victim allowed him to do so and thanked him.

Helping ratings. The victim rated each subject on a scale of helping behavior as follows:

0 = failed to notice the victim as possibly in need at all; 1 = perceived the victim as possibly in need but did not offer aid; 2 = did not stop but helped indirectly (e.g., by telling Steiner's assistant about the victim); 3- stopped and asked if victim needed help; 4- after stopping, insisted on taking the victim inside and then left him.

The victim was blind to the personality scale scores and experimental conditions of all subjects. At the suggestion of the victim, another category was added to the rating scales, based on his observations of pilot subjects' behavior:

5 = after stopping, refused to leave the victim (after 3–5 minutes) and/or insisted on taking him somewhere outside experimental context (e.g., for coffee or to the infirmary).

(In some cases it was necessary to distinguish Category 0 from Category 1 by the post-experimental questionnaire and Category 2 from Category 1 on the report of the experimental assistant.)

This 6-point scale of helping behavior and a description of the victim were given to a panel of 10 judges (unacquainted with the research) who were asked to rank order the (unnumbered) categories in terms of "the amount of helping behavior displayed toward the person in the doorway." Of the 10, 1 judge reversed the order of Categories 0 and 1. Otherwise there was complete agreement with the ranking implied in the presentation of the scale above.

The speech. After passing through the alley and entering the door marked on the map, the subject entered a secretary's office. She introduced him to the assistant who gave the subject time to prepare and privately record his talk.

Helping behavior questionnaire. After recording the talk, the subject was sent to another experimenter, who administered "an exploratory questionnaire on personal and social ethics." The questionnaire contained several initial questions about the interrelationship between social and personal ethics, and then asked three key questions: (*a*) "When was the last time you saw a person who seemed to be in need of help?" (*b*) "When was the last time you stopped to help someone in need?" (*c*) "Have you had experience helping persons in need? If so, outline briefly." These data were collected as a check on the victim's ratings of whether subjects who did not stop perceived the situation in the alley as one possibly involving need or not.

When he returned, the experimenter reviewed the subject's questionnaire, and, if no mention was made of the situation in the alley, probed for reactions to it and then phased into an elaborate debriefing and discussion session.

This is done to prevent experimenter expectancy effects. If we are getting ratings from the "victim," we need to be sure that nothing is biasing the victim's ratings of the subject's helpfulness. One big potential bias would be if the victim knew what experimental condition the subject was in, because that knowledge might skew the way the victim rates the subject's helpfulness.

This questionnaire of the subject provides a way to confirm whether the victim's subjective ratings of the helpfulness of the subject was accurate (e.g., if the victim perceived that the subject didn't even notice him, but then the subject later wrote on the questionnaire that he did notice the subject and possibly was about to help). These are generically referred to as "manipulation check" questionnaires, and are put at the end of the experiment session so they don't bias the subject's responses on key DVs. Another common manipulation check would be a "how are you feeling now" type of questionnaire for experiments that induce subjects to feel a particular mood.

Debriefing

In the debriefing, the subject was told the exact nature of the study, including the deception involved, and the reasons for the deception were explained. The subject's reactions to the victim and to the study in general were discussed. The role of situational determinants of helping behavior was explained in relation to this particular incident and to other experiences of the subject. All subjects seemed readily to understand the necessity for the deception, and none indicated any resentment of it, After debriefing, the subject was thanked for his time and paid, then he left.

RESULTS AND DISCUSSION

Overall Helping Behavior

One of the main findings: Time pressure was a major influence on whether people helped. Those who felt like they had more time to get to the speech were more likely to stop and help the victim. This is independent of the effects of type of message and any other personality characteristics of the subject.

The average amount of help that a subject offered the victim, by condition, is shown in Table 1. The unequal-N analysis of variance indicates that while the hurry variable was significantly ($F = 3.56$, $df = 2,34$, $p < .05$) related to helping behavior, the message variable was not. Subjects in a hurry were likely to offer less help than were subjects not in a hurry. Whether the subject was going to give a speech on the parable of the Good Samaritan or not did not significantly affect his helping behavior on this analysis.

Other studies have focused on the question of whether a person initiates helping action or not, rather than on scaled kinds of helping. The data from the present study can also be analyzed on the following terms: Of the 40 subjects, 16 (40%) offered some form of direct or indirect aid to the victim (Coding Categories 2–5), 24 (60%) did not (Coding Categories 0 and 1).

TABLE 1　Means and Analysis of Variance of Graded Helping Responses

	M			
	Hurry			
Message	Low	Medium	High	Summary
Helping relevant	3.800	2.000	1.000	2.263
Task relevant	1.667	1.667	.500	1.333
Summary	3.000	1.818	.700	
Analysis of variance				
Source	S.S	df	MS	F
Message (A)	7.766	1	7.766	2.65
Hurry (B)	20.884	2	10.442	3.56*
A x B	5.237	2	2.619	.89
Error	99.633	34	2.930	

Note. $N = 40$.

*$p < .05$

The percentages of subjects who offered aid by situational variable were, for low hurry, 63% offered help, intermediate hurry 45%, and high hurry 10%; for helping-relevant message 53%, task-relevant message 29%. With regard to this more general question of whether help was offered or not, an unequal-N analysis of variance (arc sine transformation of percentages of helpers, with low- and intermediate-hurry conditions pooled) indicated that again only the hurry main effect was significantly ($F = 5.22$, $p < .05$ related to helping behavior; the subjects in a hurry were more likely to pass by the victim than were those in less of a hurry.

Reviewing the predictions in the light of these results, the second hypothesis, that the degree of hurry a person is in determines his helping behavior, was supported. The prediction involved in the first hypothesis concerning the message content was based on the parable. The parable itself seemed to suggest that thinking pious thoughts would not in crease helping. Another and conflicting prediction might be produced by a norm salience theory. Thinking about the parable should make norms for helping salient and therefore produce more helping. The data, as hypothesized, are more congruent with the prediction drawn from the parable. A person going to speak on the parable of the Good Samaritan is not significantly more likely to stop to help a person by the side of the road than is a person going to talk about possible occupations for seminary graduates.

Since both situational hypotheses are confirmed, it is tempting to stop the analysis of these variables at this point. However, multiple regression analysis procedures were also used to analyze the relationship of all of the independent variables of the study and the helping behavior. In addition to often being more statistically powerful due to the use of more data information, multiple regression analysis has an advantage over analysis of variance in that it allows for a comparison of the relative effect of the various independent variables in account-ing for variance in the dependent variable. Also, multiple regression analysis can compare the effects of continuous as well as nominal independent variables on both continuous and nominal dependent variables (through the use of point biserial correlations, r_{pb}) and shows considerable robustness to violation of normality assumptions (Cohen, 1965, 1968). Table 2 reports the results of the multiple regression analysis using both help versus no help and the graded helping scale as dependent measures. In this table the overall equation Fs show the F value of the entire regression equation as a particular row variable enters the equa-tion. Individual variable Fs were computed with all five independent variables in the equation. Although the two situational variables, hurry and message condition, correlated more highly with the dependent measure than any of the religious dispositional variables, only hurry was a significant predictor of whether one will help or not (column 1) or of the overall amount of help given (column 2). These results corroborate the findings of the analysis of variance.[4]

Notice also that neither form of the third hypothesis, that types of religiosity will predict helping, received support from these data. No correlation between the various measures of religiosity and any form of the dependent measure ever came near statistical significance, even though the multiple regression analysis procedure is a powerful and not particularly conserva-tive statistical test.

This is counterintuitive. It would seem reasonable to believe that if one was about to give a speech about the Good Samaritan (about helping others) that the message of helping others would be foremost in one's mind, and therefore that person would be more inclined to help a stranger who obviously appears to be having trouble, compared to one who was about to give a speech about job prospects for seminary students (and who, presumably, did not have the message of helping salient on their minds when encountering a person needing help). BUT, that is not what the results indicated. The content of the message had no effect on the likelihood that the subject would offer help.

So the results indicated that the third hypothesis was not supported. The type of religiosity (helping to gain something for oneself vs. for its intrinsic value vs. response to and quest for meaning) had no effect on the likelihood that the subject would offer help. In other words, the selfish motive for helping (to gain something for oneself) had no more influence on helping than did the more "Samaritan-like" type of helping (the intrinsic value and quest). Again, it is counterintuitive: one would expect those who are motivated more by "purely altruistic" helping goals would be more inclined to help a stranger than those motivated for more egoistic reasons.

---

[4]To check the legitimacy of the use of both analysis of variance and multiple regression analysis, para-metric analyses, on this ordinal data, Kendall rank correlation coefficients were calculated between the helping scale and the five independent variables. As expected r approximated the correlation quite closely in each case and was significant for hurry only (hurry, r –.38, $p < .001$).

TABLE 2 Stepwise Multiple Regression Analysis

	Help vs. no help					Graded helping			
	Individual variable		Overall equation			Individual variable		Variable equation	
Step	r^a	F	R	F	Step	r	F	R	F
1. Hurry[b]	−.37	4.537*	.37	5.884*	1. Hurry	−.42	6.665*	.42	8.196**
2. Message[c]	.25	1.495	.41	3.834*	2. Message	.25	1.719	.46	5.083*
3. Religion as quest	−.03	.081	.42	2.521	3. Religion as quest	−.16	1.297	.50	3.897*
4. Religion as means	−.03	.03	.42	1.838*	4. Religion as means	−.08	.018	.50	2.848*
5. Religion as end	.06	.000	.42	1.430	5. Religion as end	−.07	.001	.50	2.213

Note. $N = 40$. Helping is the dependent variable. $df = 1/34$.

[a] Individual variable correlation coefficienut is a point biserial where appropriate.

[b] Variables are listed in order of entry into stepwise regression equations.

[c] Helping-relevant message is positive.

*$p < .05$.

**$p < .05$.

Personality Difference among Subjects Who Helped

To further investigate the possible influence of personality variables, analyses were carried out using only the data from subjects who offered some kind of help to the victim. Surprisingly (since the number of these subjects was small, only 16) when this was done, one religiosity variable seemed to be significantly related to the kind of helping behavior offered. (The situational variables had no significant effect.) Subjects high on the religion as quest dimension appear likely, when they stop for the victim, to offer help of a more tentative or incomplete nature than are subjects scoring low on this dimension ($r = -.53$, $p < .05$).

This result seemed unsettling for the thinking behind either form of Hypothesis 3. Not only do the data suggest that the Allport/Ross-based conception of religion as *end* does not predict the degree of helping, but the religion as quest component is a significant predictor of offering less help. This latter result seems counterintuitive and out of keeping with previous research (Batson, 1971), which found that this type of religiosity correlated positively with other socially valued characteristics. Further data analysis, however, seemed to suggest a different interpretation of this result.

It will be remembered that one helping coding category was added at the suggestion of the victim after his observation of pilot subjects. The correlation of religious personality variables with helping behavior dichotomized between the added category (1) and all of the others (0) was examined. The correlation between religion as quest and this dichotomous helping scale was essentially unchanged ($r_{pb} = -.54$, $p < .05$). Thus, the previously found correlation

Interestingly, the Religion As Quest personality variable is also associated with more tolerance toward people who have different beliefs and values, and with less prejudice toward others (Batson & Burris, 1994).

between the helping scale and religion as quest seems to reflect the tendency of those who score low on the quest dimension to offer help in the added helping category.

What does help in this added category represent? Within the context of the experiment, it represented an embarrassment. The victim's response to persistent offers of help was to assure the helper he was all right, had taken his medicine, just needed to rest for a minute or so, and, if ultimately necessary, to request the helper to leave. But the *super* helpers in this added category often would not leave until the final appeal was repeated several times by the victim (who was growing increasingly panicky at the possibility of the arrival of the next subject). Since it usually involved the subject's attempting to carry through a present plan (e.g., taking the subject for a cup of coffee or revealing to him the strength to be found in Christ), and did not allow information from the victim to change that plan, we originally labelled this kind of helping as rigid—an interpretation supported by its increased likelihood among highly doctrinal orthodox subjects ($r = .63$, $p < .01$). It also seemed to have an inappropriate character. If this more extreme form of helping behavior is indeed effectively less helpful, then the second form of Hypothesis 3 does seem to gain support.

But perhaps it is the experimenters rather than the super helpers who are doing the inappropriate thing; perhaps the best characterization of this kind of helping is as different rather than as inappropriate. This kind of helper seems quickly to place a particular interpretation on the situation, and the helping response seems to follow naturally from this interpretation. All that can safely be said is that one style of helping that emerged in this experiment was directed toward the presumed underlying needs of the victim and was little modified by the victim's comments about his own needs. In contrast, another style was more tentative and seemed more responsive to the victim's statements of his need.

The former kind of helping was likely to be displayed by subjects who expressed strong doctrinal orthodoxy. Conversely, this fixed kind of helping was unlikely among subjects high on the religion as quest dimension. These latter subjects, who conceived their religion as involving an ongoing search for meaning in their personal and social world, seemed more responsive to the victim's immediate needs and more open to the victim's definitions of his own needs.

CONCLUSION AND IMPLICATIONS

A person not in a hurry may stop and offer help to a person in distress. A person in a hurry is likely to keep going. Ironically, he is likely to keep going even if he is hurrying to speak on the parable of the Good Samaritan, thus inadvertently confirming the point of the parable. (Indeed, on several occasions, a seminary student going to give his talk on the parable of the Good Samaritan literally stepped over the victim as he hurried on his way!)

Although the degree to which a person was in a hurry had a clearly significant effect on his likelihood of offering the victim help, whether he was going to give a sermon on the parable or on possible vocational roles of ministers did not. This lack of effect of sermon topic raises certain difficulties for an explanation of helping behavior involving helping norms and their salience. It is hard to think of a context in which norms concerning helping those in distress are more salient than for a person thinking about the Good Samaritan, and yet it did not significantly increase helping behavior. The results were in the direction suggested by the norm salience hypothesis, but they were not significant. The most accurate conclusion seems to be that salience of helping norms is a less strong determinant of helping behavior in the present situation than many, including the present authors, would expect.

So the seemingly counter-intuitive finding that the religion as quest orientation was associated with lower and more tentative helping can be interpreted as described here by Darley and Batson: that those who helped according to their own script (and was little or not at all modified by information from the victim) were more orthodox in their religious orientation. Conversely, those who seemed to offer tentative helping were actually *more* responsive to the victim's comments, and this was more likely to be found in those high in religion as question orientation.

Wow! Rude! ☺

Thinking about the Good Samaritan did not increase helping behavior, but being in a hurry decreased it. It is difficult not to conclude from this that the frequently cited explanation that ethics becomes a luxury as the speed of our daily lives increases is at least an accurate description. The picture that this explanation conveys is of a person seeing another, consciously noting his distress, and consciously choosing to leave him in distress. But perhaps this is not entirely accurate, for, when a person is in a hurry, something seems to happen that is akin to Tolman's (1948) concept of the "narrowing of the cognitive map." Our seminarians in a ·hurry noticed the victim in that in the post-experiment interview almost all mentioned him as, on reflection, possibly in need of help. But it seems that they often had not worked this out when they were near the victim. Either the interpretation of their visual picture as a person in distress or the empathic reactions usually associated with that interpretation had been deferred because they were hurrying. According to the reflections of some of the subjects, it would be inaccurate to say that they realized the victim's possible distress, then chose to ignore it; instead, because of the time pressures, they did not perceive the scene in the alley as an occasion for an ethical decision.

For other subjects it seems more accurate to conclude that they decided not to stop. They appeared aroused and anxious after the encounter in the alley. For these subjects, what were the elements of the choice that they were making? Why were the seminarians hurrying? Because the experimenter, *whom the subject was helping,* was depending on him to get to a particular place quickly. In other words, he was in conflict between stop ping to help the victim and continuing on his way to help the experimenter. And this is often true of people in a hurry; they hurry because somebody depends on their being somewhere. Conflict, rather than callousness, can explain their failure to stop.

Finally, as in other studies, personality variables were not useful in predicting whether a person helped or not. But in this study, unlike many previous ones, considerable variations were possible in the kinds of help given, and these variations did relate to personality measures-specifically to religiosity of the quest sort. The clear light of hindsight suggests that the dimension of kinds of helping would have been the appropriate place to look for personality differences all along; *whether* a person helps or not is an instant decision likely to be situationally controlled. How a person helps involves a more complex and considered number of decisions, including the time and scope to permit personality characteristics to shape them.

REFERENCES

ALLEN, R. O., & SPILKA, B. Committed and consensual religion. A specification of religion-prejudice relationships. *Journal for the Scientific Study of Religion,* 1967, 6, 191–206.

ALLPORT, G. W., & Ross, J. M. Personal religious orientation and prejudice. *Journal of Personality and Social Psychology,* 1967, 5, 432–443.

BATSON, C. D. Creativity and religious development: Toward a structural-functional psychology of religion. Unpublished doctoral dissertation, Princeton Theological Seminary, 1971.

BICKMAN, L. B. The effect of the presence of others on bystander intervention in an emergency. Unpublished doctoral dissertation, City College of the City University of New York, 1969.

BROWN, L. B. Classifications of religious orientation. *Journal for the Scientific Study of Religion,* 1964, 4, 91–99.

BURTON, R. V. The generality of honesty reconsidered. *Psychological Review,* 1963, 70, 481–499.

COHEN, J. Multiple regression as a general data analytic system. *Psychological Bulletin,* 1968, 70, 426–443.

Darley and Batson explain the non-helping of those in a hurry as due to this conflict: between helping the experimenter, and stopping to help the victim. They weren't being uncaring or cold, according to the authors, they were just distracted by their preoccupation with carrying out their responsibility to the experimenter.

COHEN, J. Some statistical issues in psychological research. In B. B. Wolman (Ed.), *Handbook of clinical psychology*. New York: McGraw-Hill, 1965.

DARLEY, J. M., & LATANE, B. Bystander intervention in emergencies: Diffusion of responsibility. *Journal of Personality and Social Psychology,* 1968, 8, 377–383.

FREUD, S. *The future of an illusion*. New York: Liveright, 1953.

FUNK, R. W. *Language, hermeneutic, and word of God*. New York: Harper & Row, 1966.

GLOCK, C. Y., & STARK, R. *Christian beliefs and anti-Semitism*. New York: Harper & Row, 1966.

HARTSHORNE, H., & MAY, M. A. *Studies in the nature of character*. Vol. 1. *Studies in deceit*. New York: Macmillan, 1928.

KORTE, C. Group effects on help-giving in an emergency. *Proceedings of the 77th Annual Convention of the American Psychological Association,* 1969, 4, 383–384. (Summary)

ORNE, M. T. On the social psychology of the psychological experiment: With particular reference to demand characteristics and their implications. *American Psychologist,* 1962, 17, 776–783.

ROSENBERG, M. J. When dissonance fails: On eliminating evaluation apprehension from attitude measurement, *Journal of Personality and Social Psychology,* 1965, 1, 28–42.

SCHWARTZ, S. H., & CLAUSEN, G. T. Responsibility, norms, and helping in an emergency. *Journal of Personality and Social Psychology,* 1970, 16, 299–310.

TOLMAN, E. C. Cognitive maps in rats and men. *Psychological Review,* 1948, 55, 189–208.

POST-ARTICLE DISCUSSION

This experiment has become famous in the literature on helping research because of its surprising, counterintuitive results. No one would have predicted that, in a group of all seminary students as subjects, some would be more likely to offer help than others. This is because we are used to thinking of personality as consistently driving behavior across situations. So if one is a seminary student, a core part of her personality must be that she is the sort of person who wants to help others. That is what her religion and faith call her to do, and that is the kind of person who is drawn to enter the seminary. As we discussed before the article, people rarely consider the situational forces that might also be acting on someone's behavior. We assume that the reason someone did or said something is due to his personality. But as we learned from the famous (or infamous?) experiments by Milgram (1963) and Zimbardo (Haney et al., 1973), sometimes the situation overwhelms personality and it is those situational forces that drive behavior, not our personal characteristics. The job of social psychologists is to help us understand those conditions under which personality or the situation is most influential in our behavior. The Darley and Batson paper you just read is another example of the situation overwhelming personality for some subjects. When seminary students were in a hurry, they either didn't offer help or they offered more superficial assistance compared with those not in a hurry. In addition to this paper illustrating clever research design and methodology, these findings illustrate the importance of the situation when we are making attributions about other people's behavior. Rather than rely on our default fundamental attribution error in explaining other people's behavior, we should engage in the second step of error correction and ask how personality attributions might be modified by any existing situational forces on behavior (Gilbert, 2002; Gilbert & Malone, 1995). Often that is easier said than done, especially given that we are cognitively lazy and there is little incentive for error correction like this in daily life. But important research like this shows us how wrong our social judgments can be when we don't do that error correction.

THINGS TO THINK ABOUT

1. Do you agree with the researchers' explanation for why those in a hurry didn't help? If no, why do you think they didn't help?

2. Why do you think that Darley and Batson would predict a null effect of the parable on helping?

3. Why do you suppose the authors think that those who are religious for what it will gain them (i.e., priest, Levite) will be less likely to help than those who are religious for intrinsic reasons or those who use religion as a quest for meaning in their lives?

4. Did the use of seminary students have an effect on the results? Would the results have been different if the subjects were average college students?

5. Consider the design: Were there any other aspects of the experiment that the experimenters failed to standardize between conditions? What other limitations to the design are there, and how would you set up the experiment differently?

6. What do you think about the post hoc description of "type of helping" (super helping/rigid vs. tentative) as explaining different amounts of helping among different religious orientations?

11

Aggression

As long as philosophers have contemplated the human condition, they have also wondered about the nature of aggression in humans. What is its purpose? Where does it come from? What makes people more or less aggressive? Is it innate, or is it caused by outside, situational forces? Like those early philosophers, social psychologists have sought to understand aggression, because of its social nature: It assumes at least two people, an aggressor and a target (Allport, 1924; Geen, 1995; McDougall, 1926). Before we proceed further, let us define aggression as the motive and behavior involved in harming someone else. In this introduction, we very briefly cover some of the major theories and approaches to understanding aggression that researchers in social psychology have considered. This short review is not exhaustive, and there are other places an interested reader can find a more encyclopedic coverage of aggression (e.g., Bushman & Huesmann, 2010).

INSTINCT THEORIES

One popular early view of the origin of aggression suggested that aggression is caused by an "animal instinct" we have in our brains, stemming from the primitive group of structures in the center of our brains known as the **limbic system** (Scott et al., 1997; Yang, Raine, & Colletti, 2010). This notion was popularized by Freud following a famous correspondence with Albert Einstein, in which the physicist asked Freud about the nature of aggression, specifically, his thoughts on how humans could be so cruel to each other (in reference to World War I; Freud, 1920/1959, 1930). Prior to this, Freud had written about a "life instinct," or *eros*, which was the driving force in preserving our lives and our positive (love) relationships with others. After considering Einstein's query further, Freud then suggested that there is an opposite "death instinct," or *thanatos*, which operates to bring the individual to an ultimate state of nonstress (Freud, 1932/1963). The ultimate state of stresslessness would be death. But, Freud said, most of the time the *eros* is stronger, and the death instinct energy is deflected outward toward others, in the form of aggression (and, in the extreme, war). Others, notably Lorenz (1966), also supported the instinct theory of aggression. However, it soon fell by the wayside among most researchers because of a lack of empirical evidence for such an instinctual cause of aggression.

FRUSTRATION

Another early influential theory about the causes of aggression was proposed by Dollard and colleagues (1939) in their frustration-aggression hypothesis. Dollard and his colleagues suggested that being thwarted from a goal (being frustrated) always causes a person to become aggressive. All aggression, therefore, was always caused by frustration. You may have already noticed a problem with this theory. Yes, it is the words *all* and *always*. Nothing in psychology is ever 100%, because people are messy. There will always be outliers for any explanation of any behavior. So those words doomed the theory from the outset. Later, Berkowitz (1993) reformulated the frustration-aggression hypothesis to say that frustration, or any unpleasant experience, will increase the likelihood of negative feelings, and these in turn will increase the likelihood of being aggressive. That parsimonious revision nicely accounts for most types of aggression.

EVOLUTIONARY VIEWS

Perhaps aggression is part of being human because it is adaptive to be aggressive. This is the essential argument put forth by evolutionary psychologists in explaining aggression. Recall that Darwin's theory of evolution (Darwin, 1859) and natural selection states that the main goal for all organisms is to pass on their genes (primarily via offspring). Behaviors that help the organism survive will be passed on to the next generation, whereas behaviors that make one vulnerable or weak will lead to death, and those genes will not be passed down through future generations. So, the idea is that, because aggression is still present today, it must therefore have been adaptive evolutionarily; it also means that being aggressive is hardwired into our genes as humans. But research has shown wide variations cross-culturally in the amount of aggression and, even within a particular culture, a difference in the frequency and types of violence (Buller, 2005; Ruback & Weiner, 1995). In light of this variation, how can we say that aggression is hardwired into us through evolution? Evolutionary psychologists respond by saying that such cultural variations in aggression may be due to different evolutionary pressures requiring different adaptations (Buss, 1995; Buss & Malamuth, 1996). Although the evolutionary approach to explaining social behavior has garnered popularity in recent years in social psychology (Neuberg, Kenrick, & Schaller, 2010), it remains for some critics a speculative explanation (Rose & Rose, 2000).

HORMONES, GENDER, AND AGGRESSION

The male hormone testosterone has been associated with increased aggression in animals (Moyer, 1983; Muller, Moe, & Groothuis, 2014) and humans (Dabbs, Carr, Frady, & Riad, 1995; Montoya, Terburg, Bos, & von Honk, 2012). Animals injected with testosterone become more aggressive, and male prisoners convicted of violent crimes show higher levels of testosterone compared with those convicted of nonviolent crimes. A problem with this research in humans is the chicken and the egg conundrum: Are men more aggressive because they have higher levels of testosterone, or does being more aggressive cause an increase in testosterone levels? The research on the relationship is thus correlational and doesn't point to a solid cause-and-effect relationship.

If testosterone, a male hormone, is linked with aggression, that should mean that men are more aggressive than women, right? Research supports this assertion (Bettencourt & Miller, 1996; Maccoby & Jacklin, 1974). But the issue is not as cut and dry as it might appear. Is there another idea, besides testosterone, that can account for these gender differences in aggression? Yes, and it suggests that the differences between men and women in aggression are due to differences in the way that we socialize them, from the time they are babies through adulthood. According to social roles theory (Eagly, 1987), all else being equal, socialization differences explain gender differences in behavior better than do theories about differences in brain structures, brain chemicals, hormones, sex chromosomes, or other explanations. In other words, males are more aggressive than females because parents and society teach males to be aggressive. Females are discouraged from being aggressive. Social roles theory has been supported by subsequent research and is a parsimonious theory that makes a compelling case for the origin of sex differences in a wide variety of behaviors (Eagly & Wood, 2012).

SOCIAL LEARNING

According to social learning theory, we acquire aggressive behaviors by watching others (called "models") perform those behaviors (Bandura, 1978). Aggression is not necessarily innate but rather is a learned behavior in a social context. Beginning with his famous "Bobo doll" experiment (Bandura, Ross, & Ross, 1961), Bandura and his colleagues showed that children imitate aggressive behavior they see in adult models. This basic finding has been supported by hundreds of subsequent studies, and it also pointed to the strong influence that violent media has on children (Eron, 1982; Eron, Huesmann, Lefkowitz, & Walder, 1996). Interestingly, exposure to violent media has been shown to also have a significant effect on adults. Adults also demonstrate an increased likelihood toward violent behavior after they view violent media (Paik & Comstock, 1994; Phillips, 1983).

Viewing violent media has another pervasive effect on adults: It tends to numb their sensitivity to witnessing or committing violent behaviors (Krahe et al., 2011; Thomas, Horton, Lippincott, & Drabman, 1977). This is a key finding that is being tested in one of the articles you will read in this chapter. Bushman and Anderson (2009) reasoned that if watching violent movies or playing violent video games numbs our sensitivity to future incidents of violence, then it may impair our sensitivity to recognizing when others need help. The authors designed two clever studies, one in the field and one lab experiment, to test this idea. There's a lot to discuss about the Bushman and Anderson article, but we'll wait for a moment while we finish our overview of aggression research. Let us turn now to understanding how violence and aggression can differ even within a culture.

REGIONAL DIFFERENCES IN AGGRESSION

Although it should be no surprise that attitudes toward aggression and what is considered aggressive behavior differ tremendously between cultures (Barber, 2006; Douglas & Strauss, 2006), very little attention has been directed at the question of regional differences in aggression within a culture. In the early 1990s, Nisbett and Cohen introduced a fascinating theory that could account for differences in attitudes toward aggression (and aggressive behavior) between those who live in the southern United States and those in the northern states (Cohen & Nisbett, 1994; Nisbett, 1993). Nisbett (1993) noted that there has long been a big regional difference between the North and the South in attitudes toward aggression, going back to the early colonists. Nisbett suggested this difference is due to a difference in agricultural economies, whereby Northerners were cooperative with each other, helping each other for the common good, whereas the Southerners were independent and isolated. This isolation made Southerners (and their livestock) vulnerable to poachers and thieves. Thus, they needed to be more violent, in order to fend off the constant threat to their livelihood. A man's reputation (as fearsome) was extremely important, and any threat to that was a threat to his honor, his family, and his livelihood. Thus, aggression was seen as not only acceptable in the South but encouraged. These values and attitudes perpetuated themselves in the North and South even long past their necessity (i.e., urbanization, other ways to secure livestock) and to the present day. This brings us to our second paper in this chapter, the article by

Cohen and colleagues (1996). In it, you will read more about this "**culture of honor**" and discover the fascinating and clever ways the researchers empirically examined the differences between the North and the South in their views of aggressive behavior.

This brief introduction to the major empirical and theoretical approaches to understanding aggression in social psychology should give you a sense of how researchers have tried to identify the many causes of aggression and how the two articles you are about to read illustrate outstanding science and clever ways researchers have opened our eyes and minds to new ways of looking at aggression. Now, have fun reading the papers, and we'll talk further after each one.

INTRODUCTION TO READING 11.1

Bushman and Anderson (2009)

One of the enduring questions in psychology has been the following: Does watching aggression or behaving aggressively make one more relaxed and therefore less likely to be aggressive? Those who say yes include Freud (1932/1963) and Dollard and colleagues (1939). This classic idea derives from Freud's version of catharsis, which says that when one performs or watches others engage in aggressive behaviors (or even fantasizes about aggression), one is relieved of aggressive energy and is therefore less likely to further aggress. Decades of research since Freud has shown just the *opposite* about his catharsis hypothesis. It turns out that watching aggression and acting aggressively don't make one less likely to be aggressive; rather, they *enhance* one's aggressive tendencies (Branscombe & Wann, 1992; Patterson, 1974). Another consistent finding about the effects of watching aggression is that the viewer becomes desensitized to subsequent acts of aggression by others (Molitor & Hirsch, 1994) and against others (Mullin & Linz, 1995).

In the following paper by Brad Bushman and Craig Anderson, you will read how they demonstrate the effects of this desensitization on a person's perception of various helping situations. Bushman and Anderson theorized that if exposure to violence makes one desensitized to future violence, might that desensitization also dampen the individual's sensitivity to the plight of another person needing help? In other words, people who were just exposed to violence should be less likely to notice, or slower to notice, that someone needs help, and they should be therefore slower to offer help, compared to people who haven't just watched violence. It is a fascinating question, and the way that the researchers address it in their two studies is quite interesting and clever. More on that in a moment.

Let's take an aside here to compare this paper with the second reprinted article in this chapter, the article by Cohen, Nisbett, Bowdle, and Schwarz.

One thing you'll notice in the Cohen et al. paper is the leisurely pace and the detailed introduction. The authors have plenty of page space to go into great detail about the background to their study, and they have the luxury of explaining in detail all of the decisions they made all along the way throughout the paper. That paper length is fairly typical of a multistudy article in a top journal like *Personality and Social Psychology*. Other top journals have less space, and therefore require authors to be much more concise in their research report. This is the case with the Bushman and Anderson paper in *Psychological Science*. When you read the Bushman paper, you'll see the introduction is very brief, and the authors get immediately to their premise, rationale, and hypotheses. There are pros and cons to this type of article for the reader. On the pro side, it makes the article more readable, a faster read, and clear. On the con side, some of the assumptions or decisions on design are not explained and that might frustrate some readers. See for yourself which type of article (each with its own pros and cons) you prefer.

When looking at the two studies by Bushman and Anderson, put yourself in the researcher's position. If you were doing a lab study examining the influence of viewing aggression (or behaving aggressively) on one's tendency to notice someone needing help (and to offer help), how would you set up your design? Two big problems off the top: How are you going to manipulate aggression, and how will you construct a believable situation wherein someone needs help (that doesn't make subjects suspicious that it is fake or part of the study)? Now, if you were to examine the same issue (violence desensitizing one to a victim needing help) in the real world, how would you do that? You need to design a field experiment to examine people who just watched (or participated in) violence and then stage a realistic victim needing help. When you read how the researchers addressed these challenges, ask yourself this: Does this seem to work, or are there confounds that I see that the authors don't seem to address? Do you see ways that you could improve their design? One last intriguing question for you to consider: If watching violence or behaving violently makes a person more likely to behave violently and at the same time desensitized to violence, what is the mechanism by which the desensitization should decrease sensitivity to the plight of someone who needs help? That is, what is it about being more likely to be aggressive that cuts off our sensitivity to others? Some sort of psychological tunnel vision? Is compassion inhibited when we are in a state of aggression arousal? Without further delay, enjoy the paper, and we'll chat afterward!

Reading 11.1

Research Report

Comfortably Numb

Desensitizing Effects of Violent Media on Helping Others

Brad J. Bushman[1,2] and Craig A. Anderson[3]

ABSTRACT—*Two studies tested the hypothesis that exposure to violent media reduces aid offered to people in pain. In Study 1, participants played a violent or nonviolent video game for 20 min. After game play, while completing a lengthy questionnaire, they heard a loud fight, in which one person was injured, outside the lab. Participants who played violent games took longer to help the injured victim, rated the fight as less serious, and were less likely to "hear" the fight in comparison to participants who played nonviolent games. In Study 2, violent and nonviolent movie attendees witnessed a young woman with an injured ankle struggle to pick up her crutches outside the theater either before or after the movie. Participants who had just watched a violent movie took longer to help than participants in the other three conditions. The findings from both studies suggest that violent media make people numb to the pain and suffering of others.*

> Film is a powerful medium, film is a drug, film is a potential hallucinogen—it goes into your eye, it goes into your brain, it stimulates and it's a dangerous thing—it can be a very subversive thing.
>
> — Oliver Stone (quoted in Dworkin, 1996)

This study shows that you don't need to have a huge introduction to communicate clearly the background and rationale for a study. Here in this first paragraph, the authors have already told us the whole premise for the study.

If film is a drug, then violent film content might make people "comfortably numb" (borrowing the words of Pink Floyd). Specifically, exposure to blood and gore in the media might make people numb to the pain and suffering of others—a process called *desensitization*.

One negative consequence of such physiological desensitization is that it may cause people to be less helpful to those in need.

The link between desensitization and helping behavior is provided by a recent model that integrates the pioneering work on helping by Latané and Darley (1968) with our work on physiological desensitization to aggression, illustrated in Figure 1. Several factors must be in place before someone decides to help a victim (Latané & Darley, 1970; see Fig. 2). Three of these factors are particularly relevant here. First, the individual must notice or attend to the violent incident. However, decreased attention to violent events is likely to be one consequence of desensitization. Second, the individual must recognize the event as an emergency. However, desensitization can reduce the perceived seriousness of injury and the perception that an emergency exists. Third, the individual must feel a personal responsibility to help. However, decreased sympathy for the victim, increased belief that violence is normative, and decreased negative attitudes toward violence all decrease feelings of personal responsibility.

Although previous research has shown that violence in the media can produce desensitization related outcomes (e.g., Linz, Donnerstein, & Adams, 1989; Molitor & Hirsch, 1994; Mullin & Linz, 1995; Thomas, Horton, Lippincott, & Drabman, 1977), this model illuminates two gaps in the desensitization literature. First, there are no published studies testing the hypothesis that violent media stimuli known to produce physiological desensitization also reduce helping behavior. Second, there are no field experiments testing the effect of violent-entertainment media on helping an injured person. We recently found that playing a violent video game for just 20 min decreased skin conductance and heart rate while watching real scenes of violence (Carnagey, Anderson, & Bushman, 2007). We conducted two studies to help fill these gaps: a lab experiment using violent video games (Study 1) and a field study using violent movies (Study 2).

STUDY 1

Participants played a violent or a nonviolent video game. Later, they overheard a staged fight leading to injury. We predicted that playing a violent video game, in comparison to playing a nonviolent game, would decrease the likelihood of help, delay helping, decrease the likelihood of noticing an emergency (the first step in the helping process), and decrease the judged severity of the emergency (the second step in the helping process).

Method

Participants

Participants were 320 college students (160 men, 160 women) who received extra course credit in exchange for voluntary participation.

Procedure

Participants were tested individually. They were told that the researchers were studying what types of people liked various types of video games. After giving consent, participants played a randomly assigned violent (*Carmageddon, Duke Nukem, Mortal Kombat, Future Cop*) or nonviolent (*Glider Pro, 3D Pinball, Austin Powers, Tetra Madness*) video game.

Desensitization—*the reduction of a natural sensitivity to a stimulus*

All good experiments are grounded in a theory. Here Bushman and Anderson ground theirs in past helping models by Latané and Darley, and they explain how that early work connects with their current study.

Here, Bushman and Anderson lay out the rationale for their study. They explain why this study is new and necessary.

All experiment reports in psychology list the author's hypotheses at the end of the introduction, just before the description of the method.

Though they make no predictions about gender differences, it is a good idea to examine men and women in the study to determine if men and women respond differently to this desensitization.

As a critical reader, you might ask yourself how they know these games are violent (and non-violent)? How did they operationally define violent? Also, are each of the games equally violent (or equally nonviolent)?

FIG. 1. Model of the effects of exposure to media violence. Such exposure serves as a desensitization procedure leading to increases in aggression and decreases in helping. Adapted from Carnagey, Anderson, and Bushman (2007).

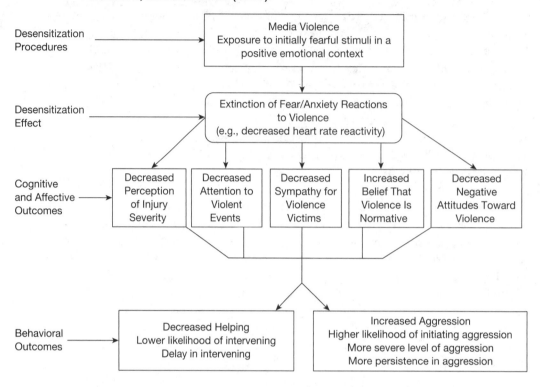

We used the same violent and nonviolent video games and the same participant pool that Carnagey et al. (2007) used to demonstrate physiological desensitization to violence.

The experimenter set a timer for 20 min, handed the participant a lengthy questionnaire, and said,

> After the timer goes off, please complete this questionnaire. I need to code some data for another study, but I promise to be back in about 40 min. Please don't leave the building until I get back. I have to ask you some questions about the video game before you leave. Okay?

The experimenter then departed.

After playing the video game for 20 min, participants rated on a 10-point scale (1 = *not at all*, 10 = *extremely*) how action-packed, enjoyable, fun, absorbing, arousing, boring, entertaining, exciting, involving, stimulating, addicting, and violent the video game was. The violence rating was used as a manipulation check. The other ratings were used as possible covariates in the analyses to control for differences in video games other than violent content. After reverse-scoring boring ratings, principal components factor analysis showed that the covariates loaded on a single factor (eigenvalue = 7.21), and were therefore combined (Cronbach α = .94). Because the results were virtually identical with and without the covariates, we only report the simpler analyses that excluded the covariates.

"manipulation check"—This is a common way to determine if a manipulation (the IV) was indeed effective, and if the subject perceived the IV accurately.

FIG. 2.   Five steps to helping. Adapted from Latané and Darley (1970).

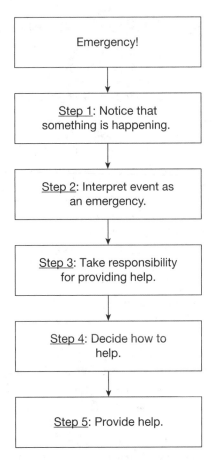

Next, participants indicated their favorite type of video game (i.e., education, fantasy, fighting with hands or weapons, skill, or sports). They also completed a lengthy bogus questionnaire (over 200 items), ostensibly to determine what types of people prefer various types of video games. The real purpose of the questionnaire was to keep participants busy while a recording of a staged fight was played outside the lab.

Three minutes after the participant finished playing the video game, the experimenter, who was outside of the lab, played an audio recording of a staged fight between two actors. The 6-min fight was professionally recorded using experienced actors. Two parallel versions of the fight involved male actors (used for male participants) or female actors (used for female participants). In the recording, the two actors were presumably waiting to do an experiment. They began by talking about how one stole the other's girlfriend (male version) or boyfriend (female version). The discussion quickly deteriorated into a shouting match (as indicated in the following script from the male version):

First actor: You stole her from me. I'm right, and you know it, you loser.

Second actor: Loser? If I'm a loser, why am I dating your ex-girlfriend?

First actor: Okay, that's it, I don't have to put up with this shit any longer.

Consider the design: you've just exposed the subject to the desensitizing violence. Next you want to see if it inhibits the subject's perception of a helping situation and makes him or her less likely to help another. Do you just have the subject sit there while the helping manipulation occurs? Seems too contrived, right? So let's have the subject do some task (here, a 200-item questionnaire) to make the "fight" next door seem unrelated to our study.

To keep things standardized for all participants, the "fight" is just a recording of people fighting, rather than having actors really yelling in the next room. That way, potential differences in live performances of the fight is not a confound.

How long should the fight be? This is an unknown, and one that can only be answered by testing out different durations on small samples before we start the actual study. These are called "pre-tests" or "pilot testing." It helps researchers work out the finer points like duration of the fight, or if something is making a participant unduly suspicious. Then we can make changes to the method before we start the main data collection.

When the recording reached this point, the experimenter threw a chair onto the floor, making a loud crash, and kicked the door to the participant's room twice.

> Second actor: [groans in pain] First actor: Ohhhh, did I hurt you?
>
> Second actor: It's my ankle, you bastard. It's twisted or something. First actor: Isn't that just too bad?
>
> Second actor: I can't even stand up! First actor: Don't look to me for pity.
>
> Second actor: You could at least help me get off the floor.
>
> First actor: You've gotta be kidding me. Help you? I'm outta here. [slams the door and leaves]

At this point, the experimenter pressed the start button on the stopwatch to time how long it would <u>take</u> for participants to help the second actor—the violence victim. On the recording, the victim groaned in pain for about 1.5 min. Because the first actor had "left," there was no perceived danger to the participant in helping the second actor.

The experimenter waited 3 min after the groans of pain stopped to give participants ample time to help. If the participant left the room to help the victim, the experimenter pressed the stop button on the stopwatch and then debriefed the participant.

If the participant did not help after 3 min, the experimenter entered the room and said, "Hi, I'm back. Is everything going all right in here? I just saw someone limping down the hallway. Did something happen here?" The experimenter recorded whether the participant mentioned hearing the fight outside the room. Those who reported hearing the fight rated how serious it was on a 10-point scale (1 = *not at all serious*, 10 = *extremely serious*). As justification for rating the severity of the fight, the experimenter explained the rating was required for a formal report that needed to be filed with the campus police. Finally, the participant was fully debriefed.

We conducted a pilot study involving 50 college students (25 men, 25 women) to test whether they thought the fight was real. Only 5 of the first 10 participants in the pilot study thought the fight was real. We therefore increased the realism of the fight (e.g., knocked over a chair and pounded on the door). After making these changes, all of the remaining 40 participants thought the fight was real.

Results

Preliminary Analyses

As expected, violence ratings were higher for the violent games ($M = 7.89$) than for the nonviolent games ($M = 1.51$), $F(1, 316) = 823.13$, $p < .0001$, $P_{rep} > .99$, $d = 3.22$. We used four violent games and four nonviolent games to improve generalizability (Wells & Windschitl, 1999). Within each type of video game, we tested whether the four games produced different effects on any of the dependent variables. No significant differences were found among the four violent or the four nonviolent games. Thus, data were collapsed across exemplars of video game types for subsequent analyses.

Main Analyses

Helping. Although in the predicted direction, there was no significant difference in helping rates between violent and nonviolent video game players, 21% and 25%, respectively,

---

This rating is a great indicator of the participant's view of the fight and how severe the helping situation appeared to be. Now, if most participants didn't help, and then we find that most perceived the fight to not be serious, well that may be a good reason why no one offered help to the victim.

And here is a perfect reason why it is important to pilot test one's experiments: here, only 50% of the subjects believed in the authenticity of the fight. So, the authors modified aspects of the fight, and retested it, and got 100% of the pilot test subjects to believe that the fight was real.

No difference in helping rates between nonviolent video game participants vs. nonviolent video game participants. Interesting!

$z = 0.88$, $p = .38$, $P_{rep} > .59$, $\Phi = -.05$. Participants who said their favorite type of video game involved "fighting with hands or weapons" were less likely to help than those who said their favorite video game was nonviolent, 11% and 26%, respectively, $z = 2.46$, $p < .02$, $P_{rep} > .92$, $\Phi = -.14$.

Time to Help. When people who played a violent game did decide to help, they took significantly longer ($M = 73.3$ s) to help the victim than those who played a nonviolent game ($M = 16.2$ s), $F(1, 70) = 6.70$, $p < .02$, $P_{rep} > .92$, $d = 0.61$.

Heard Fight. The first step to helping is to notice the emergency. As expected, people who played a violent game were less likely to report that they heard the fight than those who played a nonviolent game, 94% and 99%, respectively, $z = 2.00$, $p < .05$, $P_{rep} > .87$, $\Phi = -.11$.

Severity of Fight. The second step to helping is to judge the event as an emergency. As expected, people who played a violent game thought the fight was less serious ($M = 5.91$) than did those who played a nonviolent game ($M = 6.44$), $F(1, 239) = 4.44$, $p < .04$, $P_{rep} > .89$, $d = 0.27$. Men also thought the fight was less serious ($M = 5.92$) than did women ($M = 6.49$), $F(1, 239) = 5$ 5.43, $p < .03$, $P_{rep} > .90$, $d = 0.29$.

Discussion

Violent video games known to produce physiological desensitization in a previous study (Carnagey et al., 2006) influenced helping behavior and related perceptual and cognitive variables in theoretically expected ways in Study 1. Participants who played a violent game took significantly longer to help, over 450% longer, than participants who played a nonviolent game. Furthermore, compared to participants who played a nonviolent game, those who played a violent game were less likely to notice the fight and rated it as less serious, which are two obstacles to helping.

STUDY 2

Participants in Study 2 were adult moviegoers. Our confederate, a young woman with a wrapped ankle and crutches, "accidentally" dropped her crutches outside a movie theater and struggled to retrieve them. A researcher hidden from view timed how long it took moviegoers to retrieve the crutches for the confederate. We expected that participants who had just watched a violent movie would take longer to help the confederate than would participants who had just watched a nonviolent movie or participants who had not yet seen a movie.

Method

Participants

Participants were 162 adult moviegoers.

Procedure

A minor emergency was staged just outside theaters that were showing either a violent movie (e.g., *The Ruins*, 2008) or a nonviolent movie (e.g., *Nim's Island*, 2008). The violent movies were

---

Even though the data indicated no differences in helping rates between the two conditions, the researchers DID find expected significant differences between the conditions in terms of perceptions of the victim, time elapsed before offering help, and the severity of the fight, which support their overall prediction that violent media desensitizes one to subsequent helping situations.

In lab vs. field research there are pros and cons to each. Generally speaking, however, it is best to attempt to test one hypotheses with different methods. To the degree that one obtains support for one's hypotheses using different research approaches, we can be that much more confident in the results and conclusions we make. Here, the researchers are testing their predictions experimentally (Study 1, in the lab) and out in a field setting (Study 2, at the movie theater).

It would be ideal for the researchers to explain further why they chose these two films for their "violent" and "nonviolent" conditions. The authors say that they simply chose the non-violent movie based on its PG rating, and the violent due to its R rating. But the MPAA (movie rating board) says that violence can be found even in PG and G movies. So it would be good to know that this particular nonviolent movie truly was devoid of all violence. Moreover, it would be good to know what type of violence is present in the "violent movie" in this experiment.

rated "R"; the nonviolent movies were rated "PG." Participants had the opportunity to help a young woman with a wrapped ankle who dropped her crutches just outside the theater and was struggling to retrieve them. The confederate was told to pick up her crutches after 2 min if nobody offered help, but she always received help in less than 11 s. After receiving help, she thanked the helper and then hobbled away from the theater. A researcher hidden from view timed with a stopwatch how long it took participants to help the confederate. The researcher also recorded the gender of the person offering help and the number of potential helpers in the vicinity.

The researcher flipped a coin in advance to determine whether the emergency was staged before or after the showing of a violent or nonviolent movie. Staging the emergency before the movie allowed us to test (and control) the helpfulness of people attending violent versus nonviolent movies. Staging the emergency after the movie allowed us to test the hypothesis that viewing violence inhibits helping. The confederate dropped her crutch 36 times, 9 times in each of the four experimental conditions.

Results and Discussion

Although the helping delay increased as the number of bystanders increased, and women helped less often than men, these effects were not statistically significant and were not analyzed further. The data were analyzed using a model testing approach, in which a specific contrast representing our theoretical model and the residual between-groups variance are both tested for significance. If the theoretical model adequately accounts for differences among observed means, then the specific contrast should be significant and the residual between-groups variance should be nonsignificant. As predicted, participants who had just viewed a violent movie took over 26% longer to help ($M = 6.89$ s) than participants in the other three conditions ($M = 5.46$ s), $F(1, 32) = 6.20$, $p < .01$, $P_{rep} > .95$, $d = 0.88$ (see Fig. 3). Furthermore, the residual between-groups variance was not significant, $F < 1.0$, indicating that the theoretical model adequately accounted for the pattern of means. Indeed, the model accounted for 98% of the between-groups variance. The lack of a difference in helping before watching the movie rules out the possibility that less-helpful people were more likely to attend the violent movies.

GENERAL DISCUSSION

These two studies support the desensitization hypothesis linking media violence to decreased helping behavior. In Study 1, violent video games known to desensitize people caused decreases in helping-related behavior, perceptions, and cognitions. In Study 2, violent movies delayed helping in a wholly naturalistic setting. The person in need of help had an injured ankle in both studies. In Study 1, the injury resulted from interpersonal violence, whereas in Study 2, the cause of injury was unknown. The similar results across very different studies suggest that desensitization caused by media violence generalizes beyond failure to help victims of violence. Theoretically, we expect such generalization; one factor influencing helping behavior is judged severity of injury, and that judgment is influenced by one's own emotional and physiological reaction to the injury.

In sum, the present studies clearly demonstrate that violent media exposure can reduce helping behavior in precisely the way predicted by major models of helping and desensitization theory. People exposed to media violence become "comfortably numb" to the pain and suffering of others and are consequently less helpful.

The researchers measured this because Latané & Darley found, in their classic research on bystander apathy, that eyewitnesses are less likely to help a victim as the number of other witnesses increases.

The researcher's hypotheses were supported!

FIG. 3.

Mean time elapsed before adults helped a confederate pick up her crutches as a function of whether they watched a violent or nonviolent movie before or after the staged emergency.

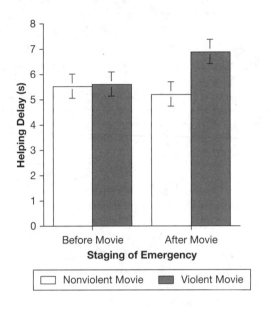

You might say to yourself: why would they measure helping BEFORE the movie exposure? The reason is to assess whether there is a difference in types of people who attend each movie. Maybe people already desensitized to violence like violent movies, in which case, you would find the predicted difference even before they were exposed to violent media (the movie). As it turns out, that was not the case, and the researchers are able to say that the difference in helping was due to the different types of movies each group had seen.

ACKNOWLEDGMENTS

We thank Colleen Phillips for her help with Study 1 and Elizabeth Henley and Brad Gamache for their help with Study 2.

REFERENCES

Carnagey, N.L., Anderson, C.A., & Bushman, B.J. (2007). The effect of video game violence on physiological desensitization to real-life violence. *Journal of Experimental Social Psychology, 43,* 489–496.

Dworkin, A. (1996). *Slicing the baby in half.* Retrieved December 12, 2008, from the Times Higher Education Web site: http://www.timeshighereducation.co.uk/story.asp?storyCode=162012&sectioncode=6

Latané, B., & Darley, J.M. (1968). Group inhibition of bystander intervention in emergencies. *Journal of Personality and Social Psychology, 10,* 215–221.

Latané, B., & Darley, J.M. (1970). *The unresponsive bystander: Why doesn't he help?* New York: Appleton-Century-Crofts.

Linz, D., Donnerstein, E., & Adams, S.M. (1989). Physiological desensitization and judgments about female victims of violence. *Human Communication Research, 15,* 509–522.

Molitor, F., & Hirsch, K.W. (1994). Children's toleration of real-life aggression after exposure to media violence: A replication of the Drabman and Thomas studies. *Child Study Journal, 24,* 191–207.

Mullin, C.R., & Linz, D. (1995). Desensitization and resensitization to violence against women: Effects of exposure to sexually violent films on judgments of domestic violence victims. *Journal of Personality and Social Psychology, 69,* 449–459.

Thomas, M.H., Horton, R.W., Lippincott, E.C., & Drabman, R.S. (1977). Desensitization to portrayals of real life aggression as a function of television violence. *Journal of Personality and Social Psychology, 35,* 450–458.

Wells, G.L., & Windschitl, P.D. (1999). Stimulus sampling and social psychological experimentation. *Personality and Social Psychology Bulletin, 25,* 1115–1125.

POST-ARTICLE DISCUSSION

Two of the many great characteristics of this paper are its simplicity and clarity. It is a study in wonderful scientific writing, sophisticated but understandable to the lay person. It is also an interesting and fast read. We immediately understand the basic premise in the opening paragraph. By the third paragraph (and that is the extent of the whole introduction!), we have the hypotheses for the two studies. Bushman and Anderson nicely show us the rationale for their studies in paragraph 3, and then they tie it to classic research by Latané and Darley on helping behavior and bystander apathy. They say that if viewing violence decreases sensitivity, it may make one less likely to notice that another person needs help. Specifically, in their famous five steps to helping model, Latané and Darley (1970) say that to help, one must (1) notice the event, (2) interpret it as an emergency (or that someone needs help), (3) accept responsibility to help, (4) know how to help, and (5) help. Bushman and Anderson say that viewing violence interferes with the first three steps.

How does one design a study to address this? Bushman and Anderson's first experiment is fascinating and presents an interesting design. In this lab study, they have to first come up with a way for people to behave aggressively but in such a way that they don't get hurt or hurt others. Their solution: Play violent video games. Yes, that would work. Next, what do you mean by "violent video games"? And what is considered a "nonviolent" video game?

The next big problem Bushman and Anderson had to address was how to stage an emergency or helping situation. Do you want it IN the lab (e.g., experimenter fainting) or near/outside the lab room, within hearing range? What sort of emergency is it? Is it believable? When will you start timing the participant to see if she notices or goes to help? While we are on this point, remember from the margin notes an important part of this experiment: the pilot testing. The authors found that, initially, few participants (5 out of 10) believed the helping emergency was real. After changing some things, their subsequent participants all reported that they believed the emergency was real. Pilot testing is an essential part of all experimentation.

Now, keeping yourself in the shoes of the researcher for a few more moments, how would you test your hypotheses about viewing violence and desensitization to the plight of others outside of the lab? You first need to find a place where violence is occurring (and a similar place where it isn't occurring). Then you need to stage a helping situation (with a confederate) right outside and then determine how long it takes people to notice and help the victim. Perhaps outside a boxing match? Or outside Wal-Mart on Black Friday (watch out!)? Bushman and Anderson chose violent and nonviolent movies and then had a confederate on crutches drop her crutches and struggle to pick them up. Recall an earlier point I brought up: How do the researchers define violence (in these movies)? Do you think it was random that the researchers had a female confederate for this study? Not at all. People are likely to think that a male on crutches is less in need of help than a female on crutches.

Bushman and Anderson created a theoretical model (on p. 2 of their paper) describing how they believe that viewing violence desensitizes an individual and how that desensitization manifests itself in terms of one's perception of the need of another person (for help). So according to the researchers, the mechanism by which viewing violence influences helping is via desensitization. However, recall our discussion of catharsis and how it energizes the person to be even more likely to commit subsequent acts of aggression. An unanswered question (for future research) is, Does viewing violence (or acting violently) make one more likely to be violent (as suggested by catharsis research)? If so, how does that influence the desensitization process? Does it go like this?

Viewing violence → increased likelihood to be aggressive → decreased sensitivity → decreased sensitivity to the plight of others

Or something like the following?

Viewing violence → increased likelihood to be violent → decreased sensitivity to the plight of others

Viewing violence → decreased sensitivity → decreased sensitivity to the plight of others

Or is it something else entirely? That is a question for another study. One of the main criteria by which papers were chosen for inclusion in this volume is that they had to demonstrate clever and creative, clear, sophisticated yet understandable experimental design solutions to not-so-intuitive theoretical and conceptual problems. The Bushman and Anderson studies do just that and also teach us much about good design, clever problem solving, outstanding writing, and good science.

THINGS TO THINK ABOUT

1. Let's start with the rationale for the experiment: the idea that exposure to violence in the media would make one desensitized to the plight of others and therefore one would be less likely to be helpful to those in need. Although there is a lot of empirical support for the desensitizing effects of violence in reaction to viewing other violence or even committing violence oneself, does that type of desensitization translate to a complete desensitization across the board (and therefore to making one less likely to perceive others in need), or did the authors make too big of a leap in suggesting that?

2. As you may know, there are certain limitations to conducting experiments outside of the controlled setting of the lab (i.e., "in the field"). One is the lack of control over confounding variables. Can you think of possible confounds that may account for the differences between experimental conditions in the movie study?

3. When critically examining an experiment's method, one important question to ask is how are the researchers operationally defining their IVs? In the video game study, the researchers have subjects either play a nonviolent or violent video game. What data do the researchers present to show that people perceive these two groups distinctly different in terms of violence? Also, within each group, are all of the video games perceived as equally violent (for the violent group) or nonviolent

(in the nonviolent group)? Do you think that, for example, today's violent games (e.g., Call of Duty) might be significantly more violent than the games used by the researchers in this 6-year-old study?

4. In addition to self-report measures by participants in the video game study, should the researchers also have gathered physiological measurements of arousal before and during the video game? What would the benefits and limitations of such measures be in this experiment?

5. In the video game study, do you think that it would be better for the researchers to have the participants to react to an overheard (but tape recorded) "fight" (and a victim who needs help) between two other subjects in the adjacent lab room (as they did for this study), or have participants react to a written plea for help (e.g., charity, request for time/money)? Why?

6. In the movie experiment, the researchers found that when they assessed helping among moviegoers before the movie, there were no differences in helping rates between the nonviolent and violent moviegoers. The authors used that finding to support the idea that the two groups did not differ in their sensitivity to the need of others before the movie. Now, suppose they DID find differences between groups in helping before the movie. Would the only reason be that that helping difference is due to personality (or sensitivity) differences? Can you think of any other possible confounds that could account for differences?

7. Let's revisit a point made in the margins of the article regarding the movie study. The researchers staged the helping situation outside of nonviolent movies or violent movies. They gave a sample movie and said only that the violent movies were rated R and nonviolent ones were rated PG. How did they determine violence (and how did they define violence) in the violent movies? Are all PG movies nonviolent? (Short answer: no.) So, we clearly need more information here. Suppose you are an experimenter who wants to re-create this study. What are your questions about this issue?

8. Do you think the "woman dropping her crutches" manipulation in the movie experiment represented a good helping scenario (believable, important enough to require assistance immediately)? If not, what are your ideas for alternate helping situations, and why would they be an improvement?

9. What are the unanswered questions that you have about the study and the conclusions (that exposure to violent media does indeed suppress one's perception of a victim's plight and, once one perceives that someone needs help, makes one less likely to offer help)? What are the mechanisms by which violent media make one less sensitive to the plight of others and cause one to be less likely to offer help?

INTRODUCTION TO READING 11.2

Cohen et al. (1996)

In all of my courses, I always do a review of psychological research methods at the outset to make sure we're all on the same page going forward in terms of understanding the studies we'll discuss. You may remember from your intro research methods class a discussion about external validity (also known as generalizability) of research findings from the lab. When discussing this concept, I tell students that researchers ideally want to generalize their lab findings to the whole world, to all of humanity. Unfortunately, because of cultural differences, we cannot do that, so we must restrict it to people within the borders of the United States. We assume that everyone in the U.S. population is generally the same and has the same "American" set of political, cultural, economic, and spiritual values.

However, the fascinating research in this paper by Cohen, Nisbett, Bowdle, and Schwarz (1996) reminds researchers that such an assumption is not necessarily accurate. Cohen and colleagues' outstanding work shows us that, in this case, there are regional differences within the United States that can have important, large influences on behavior, depending of course, on what one is studying. In the area of aggression, Cohen et al. highlight the interesting and strange fact that an old "culture of honor" that arose long ago in the early days of the country as a result of practical reasons still has a strong hold on behavior and values hundreds of years after the reasons for that culture have faded away.

This study of the culture of honor reminds psychological researchers of the importance of not assuming that one's research will generalize to an entire country. We see citizens of a country as homogeneous, but there are important differences within a culture or country that researchers need to remember. Another reason this paper was selected for this volume is the authors' examination of the phenomenon via field research and the inventive and clever ways the researchers solved the empirical challenges in doing so. Two thirds of all research in social psychology is done in the lab, because it allows us to make clear cause-and-effect statements about behavior and because we have control over the environment, and therefore observed differences between groups on the dependent variable are likely due to the differences in the levels of the independent variables and not due to confounds.

Although Cohen and Nisbett have, in other papers, reported experiments on the culture of honor in the lab, these field studies by Cohen et al. are important because they allow us to examine the phenomenon with a better ability to say that the observed results are generalizable to the real world, either because participants are unaware they are being observed or their behavior in their natural setting is not intruded on by the experimenter in such a way as to affect it or change it. When you read the following paper, pay special attention to how the researchers explain the design of their experiment, how they operationalize their variables, and the rationale they give for the experimental choices they make. Ask yourself if there are any pitfalls in the direction the authors went and if you can think of potential confounds in their design. How would you do things differently? Or would you do anything differently? Enjoy the paper, and we'll recap afterward!

Reading 11.2

Field Experiments Examining the Culture of Honor: The Role of Institutions in Perpetuating Norms About Violence

Dov Cohen

Richard E. Nisbett

Two field experiments illustrate how institutions of the U.S. South and West can help per-petuate violence related to a culture of honor. In Study 1, employers across the United States were sent letters from job applicants who had allegedly killed someone in an honor-related conflict. Southern and western companies were more likely than their northern counterparts to respond in an understanding and cooperative way. In Study 2, newspapers were sent facts for a story concerning a stabbing in response to a family insult. Southern and western papers created stories that were more sympathetic toward the perpetrator and presented his actions as more justified than northern papers did. Control conditions in both studies showed that the greater sympathy of southern and western institutions involves honor-related vio-lence, not all violence or crime in general. Findings highlight the importance of examining the role of institutional behavior in perpetuating culture.

A mark of a well-written paper is that the researchers present the main rationale for the experiment right away, succinctly, and clearly, as they do here.

The standard view of the Old South and West is that these regions accepted, and even glorified, certain types of violence. In these frontier areas where the law was weak, where one's wealth could be rustled away instantly, and where citizens had to depend on themselves for protec-tion, violence—or at least the threat of it—became a powerful force in social interaction. Insults or any challenge indicating that a person could be pushed around had to be met with harsh retaliation so that a man would not be branded an "easy mark."

Anthropologists call societies that hold such violent norms *cultures of honor*. Such cultures have been created independently many times and in many places the world over (Gilmore, 1990; Nisbett & Cohen, 1996; Schneider, 1971). And the conditions that can give rise to cultures of honor—weak or absent law enforcement, portable (and, therefore, steal-able) wealth, economic uncertainty, and high variability of economic outcomes—are present today in pockets all over the world, from the inner cities of the United States to sparsely populated regions of Asia, Europe, and Micronesia. In such societies, in which one is vulner-able to predation, it becomes adaptive for one to adopt a tough, don't-mess-with-me stance.

Many subcultures within the United States can be characterized as possessing some ver-sion of a culture of honor, undoubtedly contributing to the high rate of violence in this country. What is striking, however, is not that cultures of honor exist where the conditions that created them are still in place but that some of these cultures continue to persist, even after there may be no functional reason for individuals to behave that way.

The regional cultures of honor in the South and West are good examples of this persis-tence. For the most part, the South and West are no longer frontier, herding regions where social and economic circumstances make the culture of honor a functional adaptation. Yet, the cultures in these regions remain strong. In this article, we use two field experiments to demonstrate that the culture of honor continues to exist in the South and the West at an institutional (as well as individual) level. Institutional supports for violence may well "feed back" and help to perpetuate that culture.

Examining Culture

Psychologists are used to studying culture at the level of individual attitudes and behaviors. But as Miller and Prentice (1994) showed, collective norms exist that cannot be derived by simply aggregating individual attitudes. Understanding the collective is not just a matter of assessing the individuals in it and then summing their scores on some dimension (see also Kuran, 1995; Schelling, 1978; Sunstein, 1995). To examine culture, one needs to go beyond the level of the individual and examine public representations (Sperber, 1990). To say that one culture is more violent than another does not mean simply that there are more violent individuals in one culture; it normally means that there are more institutional, social, and collective supports for violence in that culture. Culture exists, and can be studied, at the collective, public level as well as the individual, private level.

Although behaviors are ultimately performed by individuals or groups of individuals, such behaviors can carry profound cultural consequences when they affect institutional policies or public representations. Behavior takes on the imprimatur of cultural approval as people act in their "official" roles. In this way, public representations can feed back and influence what is defined as culturally acceptable, worthy of reward or punishment. In this article, we try to demonstrate two mechanisms by which this happens: (a) the social stigma or lack of stigma for violent acts and (b) media representations of violence as heinous and unacceptable or as justified and understandable.

Persistence of a Culture of Honor in the South and West

There is evidence from a number of different methods that a culture of honor does indeed persist in the modern South and West. Such evidence comes from analyses of homicide records, attitude surveys, laboratory experiments, aggregate behavioral data, and laws and social policies.

The white homicide rates of the South and West far surpass those of the North (see discussions by Baron & Straus, 1988, 1989; Gastil, 1971; Hackney, 1969; Huff-Corzine, Corzine, & Moore, 1986, 1991; Kowalski & Peete, 1991; Land, McCall, & Cohen, 1990; Lee, 1995a; Nisbett & Cohen, 1996, chap. 2; Nisbett, Polly, & Lang, 1995; Reaves & Nisbett, 1995). The differences

The researchers are making an important point here. Normally, psychologists study individual behavior (we leave examinations of societal-level behavior— e. g. poverty, justice—to the sociologists). However, here the researchers are proposing to examine a phenomenon— regional differences in aggression—by examining differences at the cultural level. Before you read further, think about how you might design experiments to address that challenge.

Authors' Note: This work was supported in part by grants to Nisbett from the Russell Sage Foundation and the National Science Foundation (DBS-9121346) and by a grant to Cohen and Nisbett from the Office of the Vice President for Research at the University of Michigan. We are indebted to the following people for their help with the development and execution of the experiments: Eli Cohen, Lisa Cohen, Ronna Cohen, David Dulio, Amie Eigner, Becky Gastman, Kent Harber, David Howell, Andrea Kozak, Kerrie Johnson, Sheri Levy, Karla Metzger, Kristen Nimelli, Andrew Reaves, Dave Rodriguez, Jeremy Shook, Cassie Slisher, Pamela Smith, Kent Talcott, Van Talcott, Kevin Taylor, Ken Visser, and Phil Wills. David Budescu, Larry Hubert, and Ulrich Schimmack provided help with statistical issues. Norbert Schwarz made helpful comments on an earlier draft. Address correspondence to Dov Cohen, 233 Psychology, University of Illinois, 603 E. Daniel, Champaign, IL 61820, e-mail dcohen@s.psych.uiuc.edu.

PSPB, Vol. 23 No. 11, November 1997 1188-1199

can be quite dramatic. For example, Nisbett and his colleagues (Nisbett & Cohen, 1996, chap. 2; Nisbett et al., 1995; Reaves & Nisbett, 1995) showed that homicide rates in small towns in the South are triple those of small towns in the North. Importantly, the effect is limited to differences between southern and northern Whites. Regional differences do not exist for Black homicide rates, suggesting that it is something about White southern culture (rather than just living below the Mason-Dixon Line) that elevates southern White homicide rates.

Further, in a more detailed analysis, Nisbett and colleagues (Nisbett, 1993; Nisbett & Cohen, 1996; Nisbett et al., 1995) showed that it is only conflict-, argument-, or brawl-related homicides—not homicides committed in the context of other felonies such as robbery—that are elevated in the South and West. This pattern was also confirmed by Rice and Goldman (1994), who found not only that southerners were more likely to kill over arguments but also that they were more likely to kill people they knew. "Both of these findings," Rice and Goldman argued, "are consistent with common cultural explanations for southern violence" (p. 381).

In attitude surveys, White southern (and, to a lesser extent, western) respondents are more likely to endorse violence consistent with culture-of-honor norms (Cohen & Nisbett, 1994; Nisbett & Cohen, 1996). Although they are not more likely to endorse violence of all sorts, they are more likely to endorse it when used for self-protection, to answer an affront, or to socialize children. Ellison (1991) also found that "native southerners are disproportionately inclined to condone defensive or retaliatory forms of violence" (p. 1223). Thus, there seems to be a coherent ideology of violence for southern Whites revolving around culture-of-honor concerns (see also work by Baron & Straus, 1989, pp. 165–169; Ellison & Sherkat, 1993; Reed, 1981).

In laboratory experiments, southern White males respond differently to an insult than do their northern White male counterparts. After they are insulted, southern subjects become more (a) angry, (b) convinced that their masculine reputation has been damaged, (c) cognitively primed for aggression, (d) physiologically stressed and aroused, (e) physiologically prepared for aggression (as indicated by increases in testosterone level), (f) domineering in subsequent encounters with other people, and (g) physically aggressive in their behavior in subsequent challenge situations (Cohen, Nisbett, Bowdle, & Schwarz, 1996).

The cultures of the South and (especially) the West are also more likely to approve of violence as shown by subscriptions to violent magazines, viewership of violent television programs, production of college football players, hunting license applications, national guard enrollments, and a number of other indicators in Baron and Straus's (1989) Legitimate Violence Index. Lee (1995a, 1995b) came to a similar conclusion in his analysis of magazine subscription rates, arguing that the West (and, to a lesser extent, the South) was higher in its machismo interests. It was these regions where people were most likely to read magazines "in which physical strength, self-defense, weapons, combat, and sex are prominent themes" (Lee, 1995b, p. 91).

Finally, the laws of the South and West are more likely to endorse violence consistent with a strong ethic of self-protection and honor. Southern and western states are more likely than their northern counterparts to have (a) looser gun control laws, (b) laws allowing people to use violence in defense of self and property (including laws allowing people to stand their ground and kill instead of retreating), and (c) legislators who are more likely to vote hawkishly on national defense issues (Cohen, 1996). The present work supplements this body of research by adding another method—field experiments—to supply more converging, real-world evidence that the South and West possess a culture of honor and, moreover, that this culture has self-sustaining aspects.

Cohen and Nisbett make the point that southerners are not more likely to endorse any violence, but they are more likely to support violent responses to those who have offended their personal or family's honor.

STUDY 1: SANCTIONS BY EMPLOYERS FOR AN HONOR-RELATED KILLING

If violence is less stigmatized in the South and West than in the North, then we should see this in institutional practices, such as the hiring of employees. People who have committed crimes of violence in defense of their honor should be seen less as undesirable criminals and more as decent citizens who deserve a break. Thus, if a letter inquiring about employment were sent to companies describing a person who had good credentials but who also had been convicted for honor-related violence, then the letter should receive a warmer, more promising response from companies in the South and West. To provide a tighter test of the hypothesis, organizations in the North, South, and West that were part of the same company chain were compared. Some employers were sent a letter describing an honor-related crime (the homicide condition), and others were sent a control letter describing a crime not involving personal honor (the theft condition).

Method

Materials

Letters inquiring about employment were sent to companies across the United States. The applicant described himself as a qualified, hard-working 27-year-old man who was relocating to the area. In the homicide condition, the third paragraph read as follows:

> There is one thing I must explain, because I feel I must be honest and I want no misunderstandings. I have been convicted of a felony, namely manslaughter. You will probably want an explanation for this before you send me an application, so I will provide it. I got into a fight with someone who was having an affair with my fiancee. I lived in a small town, and one night this person confronted me in front of my friends at the bar. He told everyone that he and my fiancee were sleeping together. He laughed at me to my face and asked me to step outside if I was man enough. I was young and didn't want to back down from a challenge in front of everyone. As we went into the alley, he started to attack me. He knocked me down, and he picked up a bottle. I could have run away and the judge said I should have, but my pride wouldn't let me. Instead I picked up a pipe that was laying in the alley and hit him with it. I didn't mean to kill him, but he died a few hours later at the hospital. I realize that what I did was wrong.

In the theft condition, the third paragraph read as follows:

> There is one thing I must explain, because I feel I must be honest and I want no misunderstandings. I have been convicted of a felony, namely motor vehicle theft. You will probably want an explanation for this before you send me an application, so I will provide it. I have no excuse for my behavior. I was young and I needed money. I had a wife and kids and by stealing a couple of expensive cars, I was able to give them what I always needed to give them and pay off the bills I owed. I never intended to cause the car owners any serious trouble. I was sentenced for grand theft auto and am very sorry for my crime. I was desperate but now I realize this is no excuse. I realize that what I did was wrong.

All letters continued and requested an application for employment, the name and phone number of a contact person, and hours when the applicant might stop by for an interview.

Sample

Procedure for sampling. A letter (of either the honor or theft type) was mailed to 921 organizations. These organizations were businesses that were part of five national chains: a general merchandise store chain, a low-end motel chain, a high-end hotel chain, a family restaurant chain, and a motorcycle dealership chain. The chains were chosen because they represented a diverse cross section of the economy, operated nationwide, and accepted applications by mail. And importantly, we could find listings for the locations of all their outlets in the United States.

The particular businesses were selected by figuring out how many outlets would represent the state (based on its population) and then sampling every nth outlet within that state. Businesses from the South were over-sampled so that this region could be broken out if necessary in the analysis stage. Thus, for each chain, approximately 100 letters were sent to southern companies in that chain, and 100 letters were sent to non-southern companies in that chain. (Because not all states had enough stores to fill their quota of letters, there were somewhat less than 1,000 letters sent.)

Following census categorization, we defined the South as Census Divisions 5, 6, and 7: Delaware, Maryland, Virginia, West Virginia, North Carolina, South Carolina, Georgia, Florida, Kentucky, Tennessee, Alabama, Mississippi, Arkansas, Louisiana, Oklahoma, and Texas. Washington, D.C., is also defined as the South by the census but was excluded for the studies of this article because it is probably not representative of either northern or southern culture.

The West was defined as Census Divisions 8 and 9, excluding Alaska and Hawaii. (This includes New Mexico, Arizona, Colorado, Utah, Nevada, Wyoming, Idaho, Montana, California, Oregon, and Washington.) Alaska and Hawaii were excluded from the West because they do not share the common historical heritage of the region. All other states not in the South or West are obviously in the third category of states. In this article, these states are referred to as *northern* merely as a shorthand way of referring to nonsouthern and nonwestern states. The definitions of these regions are consistent with other work on regional differences and violence (see Baron & Straus, 1988, 1989; Cohen, 1996; Cohen & Nisbett, 1994; Nisbett, 1993; Nisbett & Cohen, 1996; Nisbett et al., 1995).

After the study was completed, debriefing letters were sent to all organizations, whether they responded to the original letter or not. The debriefing letter contained a brief summary of the study and its purposes. The few employers who contacted us after receiving our debriefing letter were very positive about the study and found the topic quite important.

Response rates. Of the 921 letters sent, 9 were returned as undeliverable. A total of 112 responses were received, for an overall response rate of 12%. Northern companies were more likely to respond to the letters than were southern and western companies, as indicated by logistic regression analysis, $f(908) = 2.93$, $p < .01$. The response rate for the northern-homicide condition was 16% of 149 letters; for northern-theft condition, 17.5% of 154 letters; for southern- and western-homicide condition, 11% of 308 letters; and for southern- and western-theft condition, 9% of 301 letters. One might have expected northern companies to respond more often to a theft letter than to an honor letter, whereas southern and western companies might respond more often to an honor letter than to a theft letter. This was indeed the pattern, but the interaction was far from significant. This lack of interaction, however, aids us in interpreting the content of the letters. Differential response rates (for which there was no interaction) cannot account for the interaction effects on the compliance and tone indexes that follow.

Measures

What is crucial for our purposes is the content of the response letters. An entirely unsympathetic letter basically shuts the door on the applicant, ends communication, and may be worse than no response at all. In contrast, a letter that is cooperative, fills the person's requests, and is generally sympathetic would clearly be positive and an invitation to further communication. This was why we analyzed the responses we received for (a) compliance with requests and (b) the tone of the letter or note (if enclosed).

Compliance, tone, and job availability items. We noted whether each organization complied with the requests of the letter by sending an application, the name of a contact person, the phone number for the contact, and hours or days to stop by. Some potential employers sent back a business card and a note or a letter, and these responses were noted as well. For each of the above items, the organizations received a score of 1 if the response included the item and a 0 if it did not. The scores were then summed over the six items to compute a compliance index.

When a letter was received from an organization, its tone was evaluated by two judges who were blind to condition. The tone items were scored for how encouraging the letter was (4-point scale), how understanding it was (4-point scale), how personal it was (3-point scale), and whether it mentioned an appreciation for the applicant's candor (dichotomous scale). All scores were turned into dichotomous variables (for example, encouraging or not, understanding or not, etc.) and then summed. (Variables were dichotomized because a 0–1 scale was the simplest meaningful metric that could be common to all four items of the tone index.)

On one question, raters also coded how available the note indicated that jobs were in that organization. The codes for this question were as follows: 0 = we cannot hire felons, 1 = there are no jobs now, 2 = there are no jobs now but we will keep your materials on file or no mention about jobs, and 3 = there are jobs available.

Coding. Codes for the items of the compliance index (the presence of a note or letter, an application form, etc.) were obvious from inspection. The various measures used to create the compliance index were moderately correlated with each other. Ruder-Richardson formula 20 was used to compute an internal consistency score (analogous to Cronbach's alpha) for the compliance index ($r = .48$) (Carmines & Zeller, 1979, p. 48; Rosenthal & Rosnow, 1991, p. 49).

For the tone index, we examined interrater agreement by computing Cohen's Kappas for the dichotomous ratings of how encouraging, understanding, and personal the letters were (Cohen, 1960). Cohen's Kappas were .58, .81, and .79, respectively (all significant at $p < .001$). Coder scores were averaged together before being combined into a scale. The reliability coefficient for the scale was .76, using Ruder-Richardson formula 20.

For the codings of job availability, nine categories were originally used, but then we collapsed this down to the four ordinal categories indicated above for greater reliability. Because of the objective nature of these categories, an interrater agreement score was not computed, and coder ratings were not averaged together. Rather, any discrepancies in coding (of which there were only five) were resolved by a third coder who was blind to condition.

> When one has non-numeric information to transform into numbers (that make it easier to statistically analyze), we often will use raters to code behavior. Here, different researchers rate the same subject behavior based on pre-set criteria. The degree to which they agree is known as "inter-rater reliability."

Results

The prediction was that southern and western companies would be more accepting than northern companies of the homicide letter applicant but that the regions would not differ in their treatment of the theft applicant.[1]

Compliance scores. As may be seen in Table 1, the mean compliance scores differed significantly as a function of region and condition in the way predicted.[2] Compliance scores were approximately equal for both regions (or even slightly higher in the North) for the theft letter. But for the homicide letter, compliance scores were higher for companies in the South and West than for companies in the North. The contrast was significant at $p < .06$, $t(WS) = 1.91$. The effect size ($r = .18$) was in the small-to-moderate-size range.[3]

Tone index. Letters or notes were enclosed for 78 responses. As may be seen in Table 1, the predicted pattern for the index of the tone items again held. Control letters were responded to with about the same degree of warmth and understanding in all regions. But honor letters were responded to more warmly in the South and West than in the North. The contrast was significant, $t(74) = 2.02$, $p < .05$. The effect size ($r = .23$) was in the small to moderate range.

Job availability. As predicted, there was little difference between northern versus southern and western companies for the theft letter (northern control = 2.0, southern control = 2.05). And as predicted, northern companies were less welcoming for the homicide letter than southern and western companies were (northern honor = 1.71, southern honor = 1.96). However, the standard contrast was not significant (p level = .11), $t(74) = 1.62$. The effect size ($r = .19$) was in the small to moderate range.

Interactions between region, letter type, and organization. The interactions of interest were obviously the Region x Type of Letter interactions. But one might also wonder whether these interactions would be strengthened or weakened, depending on the type of organization that was responding. They were not. The p levels for the three-way interaction between region, letter type, and organization type were all non-significant ($p > .80$ for the compliance index, $p > .65$ for the tone index, and $p > .20$ for the job availability item). There were, however, some effects for type of organization (not involving the region variable). Perhaps, these reflect the effects of organizational culture on the employment process and workplace environment (for research on organizational or small-group culture, see, for example, Levine & Moreland, 1991; Lewis, 1989; Martin, 1992; Pratt, 1994; Pratt & Rafaeli, 1996; Schein, 1990; Tichy & Cohen, 1996). Without greater ethnographic information on the organizations in our study, however, speculation about effects involving organization type would have little meaning.

Summary and discussion. In sum, for our measures of tone and compliance, control letters were treated about equally everywhere, whereas the honor letters were responded to more positively in the South and West than in the North. The only item for which the standard contrast did not achieve significance was the job availability item. Perhaps the job availability item was different because it was the response that was most constrained by reality. That is, managers are relatively free to write response letters with any tone that they feel is appropriate, but it would take an outright lie to say that there is no job when jobs are available. Still, it is probably worth noting that

TABLE 1   Compliance With Requests, Warmth of Response, and Indication of Job Availability for Honor Applicants and Control Applicants to Companies in the North, South, and West, Study 1

	Honor Letter	Control Letter
Compliance index		
North	2.83 (1.27)	3.15 (1.35)
South and West	3.52 (1.39)	2.93 (1.27)
Interaction $p < .06$		
Tone of response		
North	0.75 (0.83)	1.39 (1.30)
South and West	1.69 (1.59)	1.43 (1.47)
Interaction $p < .05$		
Job availability item		
North	1.71 (0.61)	2.00 (0.49)
South and West	1.96 (0.36)	2.05 (0.38)
Interaction $p < .11$		

Note: Standard deviations are in parentheses.

the northern-homicide condition was the only condition in which a manager wrote back that he could not hire felons and in which not a single manager wrote back that jobs were available.

Consistent with this, we might note that perhaps the greatest signs of cultural difference involved the more extreme responses to the letters. In response to the homicide letter, no northern manager sent back a complete package of items, and none received the highest scores on the tone index. In contrast, southern and western employers could be quite warm toward the applicant in the homicide condition: One quarter of all southern and western employers responded to the homicide letter in a way that earned the highest score on the tone index.

A qualitative example may help make this point more vividly. In response to the applicant who had killed the man who provoked him, one southern store owner wrote back that although she had no jobs, she was sympathetic to the man's plight:

> As for your problem of the past, anyone could probably be in the situation you were in. It was just an unfortunate incident that shouldn't be held against you. Your honesty shows that you are sincere. . . .

> I wish you the best of luck for your future. You have a positive attitude and a willingness to work. Those are the qualities that businesses look for in an employee. Once you get settled, if you are near here, please stop in and see us.

No letter from a northern employer was anywhere near as sympathetic toward this man who killed in defense of his honor.

STUDY 2: PORTRAYALS OF HONOR-RELATED VIOLENCE IN THE MEDIA

In a classic study, Bartlett (1950) showed that as stories are remembered and retold, they are distorted in ways that make sense according to the culture of the listener. We propose that the same phenomenon should occur for northern and southern listeners who are told about an incident involving honor-related violence. Specifically, in retelling a story, southern and western story tellers should be more likely than their northern counterparts to mention provocations and explain the violence in a fashion that is more sympathetic to the perpetrator.

One could examine this phenomenon at the individual level by giving a story to northerners, southerners, and westerners and seeing how they organize and retell it. But one can also examine this phenomenon in a context in which it has potential collective consequences. A reporter working for a newspaper is not just an individual but—acting in an institutional role—also creates a public representation for mass consumption.

The reporter's retelling of the story obviously reaches more people than any given individual's retelling, and by virtue of the paper's status, the story becomes a public representation of the way things are (or should be). News stories are not just objective statements of facts; they are statements of values about what a culture views as relevant, appropriate, and acceptable (see, for example, Binder, 1993; Faludi, 1991; Lee, Hallahan, & Herzog, 1996; Meyers, 1994; Morris & Peng, 1994). Thus, through the power of the reporter's role, private representations become public representations that can feed back on and influence the private representations of others (see Kuran, 1995).

One cannot just compare actual news stories about violence in defense of honor in these regions, because differences in the articles could be due to differences in "objective" facts or in "subjective" interpretations. The present study controlled for this problem by sending out a fact sheet describing a fictional honor-related stabbing to newspapers in the North, West, and South. The papers were asked to turn these events into a story (for pay) as it would appear in the paper. The prediction was that newspapers in the South and West would treat the honor-related violence more sympathetically, portray the violence as more justified, describe the assaulting person as being less blameworthy, and downplay any aggravating circumstances. For this story, we described events revolving around a central culture-of-honor concern—namely, insults or attacks against female family members (Fiske, Markus, Kitayama, & Nisbett, in press). Wyatt-Brown (1982, p. 53) described how insults against female members of the family were treated with utmost seriousness in the Old South, and Cohen and Nisbett (1994) showed that this is still true today.

A control story giving facts for a violent crime that was not honor related allowed for a tighter test of the hypothesis. We expected that stories written by southerners, westerners, and northerners would not differ in the degree of sympathy expressed for such a crime.

College newspapers were used because we assumed compliance rates would be higher for them than for professional newspapers. This probably provides for a conservative test of our hypothesis, because college newspapers (relative to rural papers, for example) are written by and produced for a more liberal segment of the population. There was also another advantage to using college newspapers, as these papers were overwhelmingly staffed by reporters who grew up in the same region where they went to school.

Sidebar notes:

In this study, the authors ask: Do portrayals of violence differ in northern vs. southern (and western) states?

Again, the researchers are attempting to examine cultural differences in perceptions of honor violence by making the argument that news stories represent the voice of the culture, not just one reporter (or anchor).

Is it a problem or confound that the researchers used college newspapers for their experiment? If the intent was to say that newspapers reflect their regional culture, is that more true for mass media (major city newspapers) than for college papers?

Method

Materials

We created a set of facts to be used as the basis for two news stories and sent them to college newspapers across the country. A cover letter explained that the research concerned how newspapers turn a collection of facts into a news story. The letter said it would probably take about 1 hr to turn the facts into news stories and offered the reporter or the general fund of the paper $25 for the help. Thus, reporters knew they were participating in a study (although they were blind to its purpose and hypotheses). The stories had to include a headline and be no longer than 250 words each. A brief questionnaire also asked how much space the paper would allot each story and for demographic information about the reporter.

The fact sheets contained many miscellaneous facts, as well as some that were highly relevant for a culture-of-honor interpretation. Some of the salient facts from the stories are summarized here:[4]

Honor story. Victor Jensen stabbed Martin Shell. Jensen is a 28-year-old Caucasian who works as a janitor at Warren High School, and Shell is a 27-year-old Caucasian who works as a mechanic at the Bradley GM car dealership. Shell is currently in stable condition at Mercy Hospital after last night's incident.

Shell dated Jensen's sister, Ann, for about a month, but they broke up a few weeks before the party. Ann was present at the party, but she was not involved in the stabbing.

Witnesses told police that Shell and Jensen talked to each other throughout the evening. Around 1:30 a.m., Shell spilled a glass of beer on Jensen's pants. The two began arguing and had to be separated by others at the party. Shell shouted that Jensen's sister, Ann, was "a slut." Jensen then started to walk toward Shell but was restrained by three other people at the party. Several men at the party were heard to make comments about what they would do if someone said that about their sister.

Around 1:45 a.m., Jensen left the party. As Jensen was leaving, Shell and his friends laughed at Jensen. Shell then shouted that both Jensen's sister and mother were "sluts." When Jensen returned to the party around 1:55 a.m., he demanded that Shell take back his comments "or else." Shell laughed at Jensen and said, "Or else what, Rambo?" Jensen then pulled a 4-in. knife out of his jacket and stabbed Shell twice. Shell was unarmed at the time of the stabbing.

Several quotes expressing opinions about the incident from both Jensen's and Shell's statements to police were also included.

Control story. Robert Hansen pistol-whipped John Seger. Seger was working at a 7-11 convenience store when Hansen robbed the store and pistol-whipped Seger. Hansen took the $75 that was in the cash register and a carton of cigarettes. Seger is a 22-year-old Caucasian and is in stable condition at Mercy Hospital. Hansen is a 19-year-old Caucasian and is in custody at the Washtenaw County Jail. Hansen was convicted on a charge of simple assault 6 months ago and served 2 days in jail.

According to the police report about the robbery, Hansen showed the pistol and demanded that Seger open the store's safe. The pistol was not loaded, according to police. Seger told

Hansen that he did not know the combination to the safe, and he offered Hansen the $75 in the cash register.

Seger tried to open the safe but kept insisting he did not know the combination. Hansen then pistol-whipped Seger, striking him five times in the head with the butt of his weapon. When Seger fell to the ground, Hansen spit on him, swore at him, and kicked him in the stomach.

Several quotes from Hansen's and Seger's statements to the police were given, including a few from Hansen stating that money was stolen from him earlier in the evening and he was mad about that.

Sample

Sampling was done from a list of colleges in the *1994 World Almanac* (Famighetti, 1993). Once a college was selected, its student newspaper was found through a listing in the *1994 Editor and Publisher Yearbook* (I. Anderson, 1994). To be eligible for selection, a college had to be a 4-year school and have a student enrollment of at least 5,000.

A total of 303 letters were sent out to colleges across the country. No region of the country was oversampled; 154 letters went to colleges in the North, 53 went to colleges in the West, and 96 went to colleges in the South. Responses were received from 47 schools in the North (31%), 15 schools in the West (28%), and 32 schools in the South (33%). Of the 94 responses that were received, 83 were written by White reporters. It is only the White responses that are reported below, because previous research indicates that the relevant regional differences may exist only among Whites (Nisbett & Cohen, 1996; Nisbett et al., 1995).

Consistent with previous research focusing on White non-Jewish populations, we excluded predominantly Jewish and historically Black schools from our sample (Cohen, Nisbett, et al., 1996; Nisbett & Cohen, 1996). We also excluded schools located in Washington, D.C. (because this region is representative of neither northern nor southern culture) and University of Michigan schools (because of the remote possibility that a reporter might be familiar with our hypotheses).

Measures

Three coders rated the honor and control stories for tone and content. The coders were not blind to the experimental hypotheses or, obviously, to the type of story—honor versus control—but they were blind to what region the story came from.

We computed a justification index, examining whether writers reported or ignored nine key facts relevant to determining how justified the attack was. We constructed the index by giving papers a point for mentioning each act Shell took to provoke Jensen and a point for ignoring each act that aggravated the nature of Jensen's crime. The six actions that Shell took to provoke Jensen were spilling beer on him, insulting his sister once, insulting her again, laughing at him, insulting his mother, and laughing at him or insulting him when he asked for a retraction. The three aggravating circumstances to Jensen's crime were that Jensen returned to the party 10 min, or some time later, with a knife (suggesting premeditation); that Jensen stabbed Shell twice (or multiple times); and that Shell was unarmed at the time he was attacked. The items in the justification index were dichotomously scored, and the index had an internal consistency score of $r = .49$, using Ruder-Richardson formula 20. (Because of the

Your next problem as a researcher: How do you select which colleges you will contact? What do you think of the way the researchers approached this? Any problems in their method?

objective nature of the items—a fact was either mentioned or it was not—an interjudge reliability score was not computed.)

We also computed a blameworthiness index. Coders rated the tone of the article on several dimensions: whether the most important factor leading to the stabbing seemed to be an insult from Shell to Jensen (vs. an argument between the two), whether the incident that started the whole conflict seemed to be a provocation from Shell to Jensen (vs. an argument between the two), whether Shell or Jensen seemed to be more at fault, whether the focus of the story was on the person doing the provoking or the person who did the stabbing (thus emphasizing either the situational or the dispositional causes of the attack), whether Shell could be characterized as an innocent victim or someone who got what he deserved, whether Jensen could be characterized as a hothead or a man defending his honor, and whether the story in general could be characterized as being about a psycho or a hothead or a man defending his honor. The intraclass correlation for judges' ratings was .77, as given by Shrout and Fleiss's (1979) formula (3,1). Judges' ratings were averaged together to form the final index. The alpha coefficient for this index, reflecting how well the individual items held together, was .89. Higher numbers on the index indicated more blameworthiness.

Also, there was one question for both the honor and the control story that asked judges to rate (on a 4-point scale) how sympathetically each story portrayed the offender. We analyzed these data using a 2 x 2 ANOVA with region as one factor and type of crime as the other. (Justification and blameworthiness indexes were not analyzed using an interaction strategy because there were no justification or blameworthiness items in the control story that were directly analogous to those in the honor story. The control story was, after all, a classic felony assault.) Based on the difference scores of sympathy for the honor offender minus sympathy for the control offender, we also categorized newspapers into those that treated the honor-related offender more sympathetically than the control offender and those that did not. For the categorizations, the associated pairwise Kappas for the three judges were .56, .26, and .21, all significant at $p < .05$.

Finally, in addition to rating the actual story, judges also rated just the lead and headline of the story. Thus, they scored whether insult, argument, or honor were mentioned in the headline or first sentence. And they rated whether the headline or first sentence seemed to indicate that the story was about a psycho or a hothead or a man defending his honor. Judges also examined the use of quotes by Shell and Jensen (some of which related to an honor theme and some of which did not).

For the control story, judges rated the content and tone of the story on a number of dimensions—for example, whether the robbery or the beating seemed to be the focus of the

TABLE 2 Justification and Blameworthiness Indexes for the Honor Story for Papers in the North, South, and West, Study 2

	North	South and West	$p <$
Justification index	3.37 (1.87)	4.21 (1.43)	.02
Blameworthiness index	0.17 (0.75)	−0.10 (0.68)	.09

Note: Standard deviations are in parentheses.

story, whether different circumstances of the crime were mentioned, whether different aspects of Hansen's background were mentioned, and whether different quotes from Hansen and Seger were used. The regions were not predicted to differ in their treatment of the control story.

Results and Discussion

Justification. As may be seen in the first line of Table 2, southern and western papers were likely to see the crime as more provoked and less aggravated than their northern counterparts did, $t(81) = 2.33$, $p < .02$. This effect was of moderate size, $d = .51$.[5]

Blameworthiness. As may be seen in the second line of Table 2, in the tone of their articles, southern and western papers were less likely to blame Jensen for stabbing Shell than northern papers were, $t(81) = 1.74$, $p < .09$. The effect size ($d = .38$) was in the small to moderate range.

Sympathy. Examining the raw sympathy scores for each story, there was a trend for southern and western papers to treat the honor-related offender more sympathetically and for northern papers to treat the non-honor-related offender more sympathetically, interaction, $F(1, 79) = 2.17$, $p < .15$ (effect size, $r = .16$, was in the small to moderate range). If papers are simply categorized according to which offender they treated most sympathetically, we found that only 19% of southern and western papers treated the nonhonor crime at least as sympathetically as the honor crime, whereas twice as many northern papers (39%) did so, $\chi^2(1, N = 83) = 4.03$, $p < .04$. The effect size measure for the χ^2 statistic, w, was .22, or in the small to moderate range (Cohen, 1977, chap. 7).

Leads, headlines, and quotes. There were no significant differences in the content of the lead sentence and headline or in the use of quotes by Shell and Jensen.

Control story. Although there were several differences in how papers across the country treated the honor-related story, there were virtually no differences in how they treated the control story. Only three items showed even marginally significant differences, and these three indicated that northern papers showed more sympathy than southern and western papers for the man who beat the clerk during the robbery. Thus, the differences found on the story concerning honor-related violence do not reflect an approval of all sorts of violence; rather, they reflect a sympathy among southern and western papers that is specifically focused on honor-related violence.

Demographic items. Demographic information requested at the end of the questionnaire revealed few differences among reporters from the different regions. Their newspapers did not differ in the size of their circulation, nor did the reporters differ in their age, sex, or year in school. Thus, controlling for circulation, gender, age, and year in school using multiple regression equations changed the results very little.

Controlling for demographics also made little difference because the demographic variables were themselves relatively uncorrelated with our dependent variables of justification, blameworthiness, and sympathy. Using multiple regressions, we found only a weak tendency for men to assign less blame than women to the honor-related offender. Effects of age, year in

---

Remember that for an effect to be considered "statistically significant," researchers use a cutoff of $p<.05$. Meaning that there is a 5% or less chance that the observed difference was due to chance. Note here however, the "blameworthiness" effect was $p<.09$. In this case, a better wording for this difference would be to say there is a non-significant "trend in the expected direction." Or some researchers use the term "marginally significant" to refer to p values between .05 and .10.

school, and the paper's circulation on our dependent variables were very slight. Race was also not a confound in these data because we analyzed only the 83 White respondents. Results were similar, however, if the 11 non-White respondents were added to the analysis.

Demographic questions also revealed that most reporters had grown up in the region in which they were currently attending school. Indeed, there were only two cases in which southern and western reporters wrote for northern papers and only three cases in which northern reporters wrote for southern and western papers.

In summary, the papers of the South and West treated honor-related violence more sympathetically in both tone and content than did the papers of the North. The articles from the South and West portrayed the honor-related violence as more justified, less aggravated, and more the fault of the provoker. The control stories indicated that papers of the South and West were not more sympathetic toward violence in general but that sympathy was limited to honor-related violence.

DISCUSSION

The results of these two field experiments indicate that violence related to honor is less stigmatized by institutions of the South and West than by those of the North. In Study 1, southern and western employers responded in a warmer, more sympathetic, and more cooperative way to a person convicted of an honor-related killing than they did to a person convicted of a non-honor-related crime. The reverse was true of northern employers. In Study 2, southern and western newspapers treated a violent crime in defense of honor in a more sympathetic and understanding way than did northern newspapers. As predicted, no differences were found for a story concerning violence not related to honor.

A few issues and concerns should be noted here. One ethical concern is the deception used in Study 1. Although it would have been nice if organizations had known up front that they were involved in a study, one might wonder whether the results of Study 1 would be very convincing if they had been so informed. Deception was used in this field experiment because there is no reason to assume that people are aware of—or would truthfully report—the values guiding their behavior toward job applicants with various histories. Starting with LaPiere's (1934) research, it has been shown that the real behavior of workers within an organization is often poorly reflected by its professed values and that "as if"* questions may provide poor guides to actual practices. In more recent times, Salancik (1979) argued that it is often necessary to use experimentation to "stimulate" an organization and discover its true orientation. Deception in this case was mild and required little effort from experimental participants—sending application forms and, in some cases, a brief note. The costs and benefits must be weighed in deciding whether to use deception, and obviously, reasonable people can and will disagree on whether a study merits its use. In this case, we felt it did.

A more theoretical concern involves the interpretation of the present two studies. Some readers might wonder about the distinction between a culture of honor and a macho culture. Such concerns should be put in context by noting that macho culture is a version of a more general culture of honor (Gilmore, 1990). That is, all cultures of honor emphasize masculinity, toughness, and the ability to protect one's own. Cultures of honor differ from each other, however, in the amount of swagger and attitude they require versus the amount of politeness and gentility they require (E. Anderson, 1994; Cohen, Vandello, Puente, & Rantilla, 1996; Pitt-Rivers, 1965, 1968). Differences between such cultures are interesting and need exploration, but they are all still rightfully considered variations of a general culture of honor.

A note about deception. Recall from our discussion about research methods that, at some level, most experiments require a bit of deception (i.e., a cover story) so that subjects don't know the purpose of the experiment and thus behave or respond differently than they would have otherwise. The general rule is "use deception sparingly, and if used, the benefits should outweigh the costs (of deceiving participants)." Here, the deception was very minor, and the scientific benefit can be argued to be larger, so ethically, the experiment doesn't present a problem.

On a more concrete level, there are some concerns having to do with specific aspects of the studies in this article. One concern involves whether the results can be generalized to real behavior. This certainly is not an issue for Study 1, in which people thought they were responding to real job applicants. It is of some concern for Study 2, in which it is possible that different results would be obtained if reporters were not aware they were participating in a study. (This is obviously the flip side of the ethical issue involving deception discussed above.)

There are plausible hypotheses for why reporters writing a real story might produce stories that muted their own personal bias. However, it is also quite possible that if reporters were writing a real story, the salience of the audience might cause them to be even more sensitive to prevailing cultural norms, and thus regional differences would become even more magnified (see Kuran, 1995). A nice follow-up study might involve examining how actual news stories (of some notoriety) are treated by correspondents from newspapers around the nation. In addition, if one were concerned with editing and presentation issues, then one could examine how wire stories— from the Associated Press, for example—were cut, restructured, and played up or played down by various papers across the country. Such studies might provide details about the process by which news is "distorted."

Another concern has to do with the actual effects in this article. They are not large. In fact, they are almost uniformly in the small to moderate range, using Cohen's (1977) criteria. But it is their consistency—within this package of two studies and together with the results of our lab experiments, archival studies, and attitude surveys— that give us confidence in the results (Nisbett & Cohen, 1996).

Finally, there is the issue of the representativeness of the organizations that responded in both studies. A problem with field experiments is that the response rate can be relatively low. And perhaps this was to be expected given the nature of our requests here. In Study 1, for example, it is possible that the low response rate from this study was due to the applicant in both cases having a criminal record. Although low response rates are problematic, there are two major reasons for why our concerns with this are tempered. First, concerns are allayed to some extent by the comparability of responses in the control conditions of both experiments. The non-honor-related crime was treated equivalently by employers and by newspapers in the North, West, and South, suggesting that any response bias probably affected all regions equally. And also, our concerns are tempered to a larger extent by placing the studies in their broader context. Again, the field experiments presented here give results very consistent with a line of research by Nisbett, Cohen, Reaves, and others, pointing to systematic cultural differences between the South and West versus the North. Through attitude surveys, analyses of laws and social policies, homicide records, and lab experiments, this research has established the existence of regional differences in matters having to do with violence and gender roles. The two field experiments fit well with this line of work, adding to the evidence and suggesting some institutional mechanisms through which the cultures of the South and West are perpetuated.

Study 1 tells us something about the sort of feedback given to men who have committed crimes of violence related to honor. Feedback from northern employers is more likely to convey to such men that they are undesirable, unsympathetic, and unforgiven for their crimes, whereas feedback from southern employers is more likely to convey to these men that they are normal people who got caught in unfortunate situations—situations that "anyone" could have been in—and that their behavior in those situations "shouldn't be held against" them (as one southern letter writer indicated). Thus, Study 1 shows that institutions—as well as individuals— participate in the stigmatization, or lack of stigmatization, of violence.

Our speculation is that Study 1 underestimates regional differences regarding how men who perpetuate culture-of-honor violence are treated. At an early stage of the application process ("please send me an application and information"), most national chains probably have either (a) a policy of treating all applicants equally or (b) a policy of treating convicted felons more harshly than other applicants, regardless of what crime they committed. If so, then the opportunity for differential treatment would have been constrained in this study. Thus, one might expect to see even more differential treatment in institutional and especially in interpersonal situations in which there were not such constraints. Consider, for example, everyday social interactions, personal relationships, less formal organizational settings, or other situations in which association is more voluntary. As one Texas hotel manager called to tell us after receiving the debriefing letter, he had a lot of "empathy" as a person with the man who fought after the "dishonoring of his girlfriend." And he "would not have a problem with this guy being my neighbor, having my kids go over and play in his yard . . . getting to know him. But as an employer, I can't hire him" because of the legal issues involved. We suspect, then, that the feedback and stigmatization (or lack of it) evidenced in Study 1 would be greatly amplified in many less constrained interpersonal and institutional settings in the real world.

Study 2 indicates another way in which institutions can contribute to collective representations that support violence. By treating violence as sympathetic, justified, or legitimately provoked, the media can help feed cultural notions about when such behavior is appropriate. And Study 2 demonstrates that there are clear cultural differences in how papers of the North, West, and South present honor-related violence and explain it to their readers.

Newspapers are just one source of collective story telling, however. It seems remarkable that such differences were found between the stories of the South and West and stories of the North when both sets of newspapers were given the exact same facts. Newspapers are institutions that are supposed to report such stories objectively and according to journalistic formula. One can only imagine what would happen on the next iterations—as readers not bound by a journalist's sense of objectivity and closeness to the facts retell the story to others, who then retell the story to still others, who then retell the story, and so on. As this game of "telephone" continues and stories spread throughout a community, stories would probably stray further and further from the facts and become molded into culturally prescribed myths. These communal myths could both reflect the biases of the culture and serve to perpetuate it—defining some violent actions as sympathetic or even heroic (for discussions of public narratives and communal experiences, see also Bartlett, 1950, p. 173; Faludi, 1991, chap. 1; Gates, 1995).

Researchers in cultural psychology need to examine all sorts of mechanisms by which a culture gets perpetuated—interpersonal interactions, familial socialization, and real or imagined peer enforcement of norms. We also cannot forget that we live our lives constrained by institutions—our media, our workplaces, our legal system, and our economic system. In this light, the mutually reinforcing effects of culture and social structure are extremely important to examine. Just as culture and the individual mind reinforce and strengthen each other (Fiske et al., 1997), so, too, do culture and our social structures.

Presently, we are a long way from understanding the mechanisms through which institutions (or even individuals) perpetuate a culture of honor. However, these field experiments—seen in the context of the laboratory experiments, attitude surveys, policy analyses, and homicide data—suggest that institutions, such as corporations and the media, at least reflect

As with most research reports, at the end of the discussion, the authors suggest directions for future research in this area, and point to unanswered questions. Here, the authors say that there is much we do not yet know about the mechanisms by societal institutions perpetuate a culture.

the norms of their culture. As a consequence, they may produce public representations that perpetuate the culture and keep it strong even after the culture has outlived its original purpose.

NOTES

1. The appropriate contrast to test this prediction is +1, -1, 0, 0 (Rosenthal & Rosnow, 1985). Effect size measures for the interaction contrast follow formulas given by Rosenthal and Rosnow (1991, p. 470), and interpretations of their magnitude follow Cohen's (1977) conventions.

2. All p levels are two-tailed.

3. The contrast reported in the text puts together companies from the South with those of the West. This was done because the small number of responses from the West ($n = 14$) could make estimates unreliable. Nevertheless, analyses that examine the North, West, and South separately—using a contrast of −2, 1, 1, 0, 0, 0—give similar results. This contrast gives significance levels of $p < .02$ for the compliance index and $p < .06$ for the analysis of the tone of the letters.

4. The complete set of facts for the stories—as well as information about means and standard deviations for individual items from Studies 1 and 2—can be obtained by corresponding with the first author.

5. Data in Study 2 were analyzed with t tests between papers of the North versus papers of the South and West. Again, this was done because the small number of western responses ($n = 12$) could make estimates unreliable. However, results look very similar if the papers are separated into three regions—North, West, and South—and a contrast of −2, +1, +1 is used. The p levels for the main variables using this contrast were as follows: justification index, $p < .005$; blameworthiness index, $p < .05$; greater sympathy for the offender in the honor story versus the control story, $p < .03$. In general, responses from the West tended to be even stronger than those from the South.

REFERENCES

Anderson, E. (1994). The code of the streets. *Atlantic Monthly, 5,* 81–94.

Anderson, I. E. (Ed.). (1994). *Editor and publisher international yearbook.* New York: Editor and Publisher.

Baron, L., & Straus, M. A. (1988). Cultural and economic sources of homicide in the United States. *Sociological Quarterly, 29,* 371–392.

Baron, L., & Straus, M. A. (1989). *Four theories of rape in American society: A state-level analysis.* New Haven, CT: Yale University Press.

Bartlett, F. C. (1950). *Remembering: A study in experimental and social psychology.* Cambridge, UK: Cambridge University Press.

Binder, A. (1993). Constructing racial rhetoric: Media depictions of harm in heavy metal and rap music. *American Sociological Review, 58,* 753–767.

Carmines, E. G., & Zeller, R. A. (1979). *Reliability and validity assessment.* Newbury Park, CA: Sage.

Cohen, D. (1996). Law, social policy, and violence: The impact of regional cultures. *Journal of Personality and Social Psychology, 70,* 961–978.

Cohen, D., & Nisbett, R. E. (1994). Self-protection and the culture of honor: Explaining southern violence. *Personality and Social Psychology Bulletin, 20,* 551–567.

Cohen, D., Nisbett, R. E., Bowdle, B. R, & Schwarz, N. (1996). Insult, aggression, and the southern culture of honor: An "experimental ethnography." *Journal of Personality and Social Psychology, 70,* 945–960.

Cohen, D., VandeUo, J., Puente, S., & Rantilla, A. (1996). *"When you call me that, smile!": How norms for politeness and aggression interact in the southern culture of honor.* Unpublished manuscript, University of Illinois.

Cohen, J. (1960). A coefficient of agreement for nominal scales. *Educational and Psychological Measurement, 20,* 37–46.

Cohen, J. (1977). *Statistical power analysis for the behavioral sciences.* New York: Academic Press.

Ellison, G. G. (1991). An eye for an eye? A note on the southern subculture of violence thesis. *Social Forces, 69,* 1223–1239.

Ellison, C. G., & Sherkat, D. E. (1993). Conservative Protestantism and support for corporal punishment. *American Sociological Review, 58,* 131–144,

Faludi, S. (1991). *Backlash: The undeclared war against American women.* New York: Crown.

Famighetti, R. (Ed.). (1993). *The world almanac and book of facts.* Mahwah, NJ: Funk & Wagnalls.

Fiske, A P., Markus, H., Kitayama, S., & Nisbett, R. E. (in press). The cultural matrix of social psychology. In D. T. Gilbert, S. T. Fiske, & G. Lindzey (Eds.), *Handbook of social psychology* (4th ed). Boston: McGraw-Hill.

Gastil, R. D. (1971). Homicide and a regional culture of violence. *American Sociological Review, 36,* 412–427.

Gates, H. L. Jr. (1995, October 23). Thirteen ways of looking at a Black man. *The New Yorker,* pp. 56–65.

Gilmore, D. D. (1990). *Manhood in the making: Cultural concepts of masculinity.* New Haven, CT: Yale University Press.

Hackney, S. (1969). Southern violence. In H. D. Graham & T. R. Gurr (Eds.), *The history of violence in America* (pp. 505–527). New York: Bantam Books.

Huff-Corzine, L., Corzine, J., & Moore, D. C. (1986). Southern exposure: Deciphering the South's influence on homicide rates. *Social Forces, 64,* 906–924.

Huff-Corzine, L., Corzine, J., & Moore, D. C. (1991). Deadly connections: Culture, poverty, and the direction of lethal violence. *Social Forces, 69,* 715–732.

Kowalski, G. S., & Peete, T. A (1991). Sunbelt effects on homicide rates. *Sociology and Social Research, 75,* 73–79.

Kuran, T. (1995). *Private truths, public lies: The social consequences of preference falsification.* Cambridge, MA: Harvard University Press.

Land, K. C., McCall, P. L., & Cohen, L. E. (1990). Structural covariates of homicide rates: Are there any invariances across time and social space. *American Journal of Sociology, 95,* 922–963.

LaPiere, R. T. (1934). Attitudes vs. actions. *SocialForces, 13,* 230–237.

Lee, F., Hallahan, M., & Herzog, T. (1996). Explaining real-life events: How culture and domain shape attributions. *Personality and Social Psychology Bulletin, 22,* 732–741.

Lee, R. S. (1995a). Machismo values and violence in America: An empirical study. In L. L. Adler & F. L. Denmark (Eds.), *Violence and the prevention of violence* (pp. 11–31). Westport, CT: Praeger.

Lee, R. S. (1995b). Regional subcultures as revealed by magazine circulation patterns. *Cross-Cultural Research, 29,* 91–120.

Levine, J. M., & Moreland, R. L. (1991). Culture and socialization in work groups. In L. B. Resnick, J. M. Levine, & S. D. Teasley (Eds.), *Perspectives on socially shared cognition* (pp. 257–279). Washington, DC: American Psychological Association.

Lewis, M. (1989). *Liar's poker.* New York: Norton.

Martin, J. (1992). *Cultures in organizations.* New York: Oxford University Press.

Meyers, M. (1994). News of battering. *Journal of Communication, 44,* 47–63.

Miller, D. T, & Prentice, D. A (1994). Collective errors and errors about the collective. *Personality and Social Psychology Bulletin, 20,* 541–550.

Morris, M. W., & Peng, K. (1994). Culture and cause: American and Chinese attributions for social and physical *events. Journal of Personality and Social Psychology, 67,* 949–971.

Nisbett, R. E. (1993). Violence and U.S. regional culture. *American Psychologist, 48,* 441–449.

Nisbett, R. E., & Cohen, D. (1996). *Culture of honor: The psychology of violence in the South.* Boulder, CO: Westview.

Nisbett, R. E., Polly, G., & Lang, S. (1995). Homicide and regional U.S. culture. In R. B. Ruback & N. A. Weiner (Eds.), *Interpersonal violent behaviors* (pp. 135–151). New York: Springer.

Pitt-Rivers, J. (1965). Honour and social status. In J. G. Peristiany (Ed.), *Honour and shame: The values of Mediterranean society* (pp. 21–77). London: Weidenfeld and Nicolson.

Pitt-Rivers, J. (1968). Honor. In D. Sills (Ed.), *International encyclopedia of the social sciences* (pp. 503–511). New York: Macmillan.

Pratt, M. G. (1994). *The happiest, most dissatisfied people on earth: Ambivalence and commitment among Amway distributors.* Unpublished doctoral dissertation, University of Michigan.

Pratt, M. G., & Rafaeli, A (1996). *Multi-layered identities: Organizational dress as a symbol of complex social identities in organizations.* Manuscript submitted for publication.

Reaves, A. L., & Nisbett, R. E. (1995). *The cultural ecology of rural White homicide in the southern United States*. Unpublished manuscript, University of Michigan.

Reed, J. S. (1981). Below the Smith and Wesson line: Reflections on southern violence. In M. Black & J. S. Reed (Eds.), *Perspectives on the American South: An annual review of society, politics, and culture* (pp. 9–22). New York: Gordon & Breach Science.

Rice, T. W., & Goldman, C. R. (1994). Another look at the subculture of violence thesis: Who murders whom and under what circumstances. *Sociological Spectrum, 14,* 371–384.

Rosenthal, R., & Rosnow, R L. (1985). *Contrast analysis.* Cambridge, UK: Cambridge University Press.

Rosenthal, R., & Rosnow, R. L. (1991). *Essentials of behavioral research.* New York: McGraw-Hill.

Salancik, G. R. (1979). Field stimulations for organizational behavior research. *Administrative Science Quarterly, 24,* 638–649.

Schein, E. H. (1990). Organizational culture. *American Psychologist, 45,* 109–119.

Schelling, T. C. (1978). *Micromotives and macrobehavior.* New York: Norton.

Schneider, J. (1971). Of vigilance and virgins: Honor, shame and access to resources in Mediterranean societies. *Ethnology, 10,* 1–24.

Shrout, P. E., & Fleiss, J. L. (1979). Intraclass correlations: Uses in assessing rater reliability. *Psychological Bulletin, 86,* 420–428.

Sperber, D. (1990). The epidemiology of beliefs. In C. Fraser & G. Gaskell (Eds.), *The social psychological study of widespread beliefs* (pp. 25–44). Oxford, UK: Clarendon.

Sunstein, C. R (1995, December 25). True lies. *The New Republic,* pp. 37–41.

Tichy, N., & Cohen, E. (1996). *The leader driven organization.* Unpublished manuscript, University of Michigan.

Wyatt-Brown, B. (1982). *Southern honor: Ethics and behavior in the Old South.* New York: Oxford University Press.

POST-ARTICLE DISCUSSION

One of the fascinating things about studying behavior is discovering the myriad factors and combinations of factors that can influence behavior in unique, often unforeseen ways. This paper by Cohen and colleagues reminds researchers of a truism in social psychology: What is important in understanding and predicting the behavior of an individual in a particular situation is not the characteristics of the situation (and how they uniformly influence people) but rather the individual's *construal* or *perception* of the situation. For example, it would be absurd to say that Auguste Renoir's painting *The Luncheon of the Boating Party* has a uniform effect on all who view it, causing the same reaction in every viewer. What instead is the case is that a viewer's reaction to the painting depends on his construal of the painting. Some may perceive the painting as a boring impressionist painting. Others, however, may view it with tremendous emotion. And there are infinite reactions in between.

So, in the present paper, we see that people's perception of an aggressive act depends not on the objective facts of the aggressive act, but rather, on their construal of the justification for such an act. Cohen and colleagues found that some people's construal depended on values and attitudes that were prevalent and adaptive long ago, but are no longer necessary, and are still deeply held by people in certain regions of the country (those regions where such attitudes about aggression were adaptive). Thus, what is influencing behavior is not some temporary aspect of the situation but rather an aspect of personality (value-driven construal of a certain type of aggression). This construal is part of who the people are, so it functions like a personality trait. Unlike a trait, however, it is not a part of one's genetic or random learning history (if so, we might find a heterogeneous mixture of people who condone and do not condone honor-related aggression in the North and South). One of the many interesting aspects of this paper is that the authors show that this personality-like characteristic (construal of honor aggression) originates in the history of one's region of the United States, such that a like-minded construal is found concentrated in the North and also among people in the South (and West).

Doing field studies like this has both benefits and drawbacks. I pointed out some of those in the margins to the article and in the introduction to the paper. Now that you've read the paper, you have your own conclusions about things you liked about the paper and things perhaps you would have done differently pertaining to different choices the researchers made. No study is perfect, and there are always things we can change or do another way. The question you, the reader, must ask yourself is this: Did the researchers obtain data that support their predictions, and was the methodology by which they did their study sound? Cohen and colleagues have shown us an outstanding and very creative approach to understanding cultural differences in the construal of honor-related aggression.

THINGS TO THINK ABOUT

1. Both of the studies in this article are done outside of the lab (field studies). If you wanted to experimentally study perceptions of aggression defending one's honor versus non-honor-related aggression, how would you do so in the lab?

2. Can you think of other regional differences that exist in the United States that would still influence behavior (e.g., different standards or values between regions that influence daily behavior, mating choice, etc.)? How about regional differences in other parts of the world that might affect perceptions of aggression?

3. In the newspaper study, do you agree with the researchers' choice to test their predictions using college newspapers versus major city newspapers? Do you suppose the major newspapers would have responded differently to the news accounts of honor-related versus non-honor-related aggression?

4. For the employer survey, the researchers mailed surveys to 921 employers. They got only 12% of their surveys returned. That's a pretty low return rate. Can you think of ways you would improve that return rate (e.g., incentives to respond)?

5. What is it about western and southern regions in the United States and their cultures that make people in those regions much more concerned with defending their honor (and that of their family) and to think that aggression toward the threat agent is not only acceptable but expected? Is there something different about the North and Midwest (or the religions, countries that immigrated to those regions) that leads to less concern with defending family honor through the use of aggression?

(Continued)

(Continued)

6. Do you think that the reporters (asked by the researchers to write a news account of the honor-violence or control story) constructed a story that genuinely reflected how they would treat that material? Was the situation too contrived or artificial to assess how those newspapers would genuinely report those stories? If so, what are other in-the-field (i.e., non-lab) ways you (if you were the researcher) could examine regional differences in perceptions of honor aggression?

CHAPTER

12

Groups

Humans are social creatures. We have a strong need to be with others (Brewer & Miller, 1996). Evolutionary psychologists would argue that doing so is adaptive, because early humans who formed groups were better able to fend off predators, because of their greater numbers, and were able to care for each other, help each other, and teach each other survival skills (Buss, 1995). As a result, it makes sense for psychologists to study how being in groups affects our behavior. Social psychologists focus on "small groups." These are groups that are smaller in scale than, say, a whole population, which would be the focus of sociologists. So we study workplace groups, sports groups, leadership, intergroup conflict, and more. In this introduction, we examine some of the well-known research areas that social psychologists have studied. For a more comprehensive review of this literature, the reader may consult other sources (e.g., Hackman & Katz, 2010; Levine & Moreland, 1998).

ROLES, NORMS, AND GROUP POLARIZATION

We join groups for a number of reasons, but primary among them is that they serve as a vehicle for us to accomplish something that perhaps we could not do by ourselves. For example, you might join a political group to solicit thousands of petition signatures to present to your local government in order to get an issue on the voting ballot during the next election. You might join a charity group in order to bring the most aid to the most people. At work, we might form a task group to come up with a solution to a problem at the workplace.

Research on these small groups shows that when we join a group, we tend to (depending on our personality and learning history) play certain roles. A **role** is a set of expected behaviors. In a group, these can be formally described (e.g., what a "secretary" or "treasurer" does), or they can be informal and not necessarily assigned to one person. Bales (1958) suggested that people tend to lean toward one of two informal roles: expressive or instrumental. Those who are instrumental want to keep the group oriented to the task, and they don't like the group to get distracted or waste time on non-task-related topics. Those who adopt an expressive role want to make sure that the group members are having a good time; they see their job as maintaining morale.

In a group, there are **norms** to which one must adhere (Miller, 1953). Norms are the expectations that group members have for how group members should behave. For example, when the group gets together, how do they decide who speaks, for how long, and in what order? It could be an informal system, or it could be very formal, such as those rules used by the British House of Commons or the U.S. Congress, for example. But most groups need to have some sort of system of norms in place so that members are treated fairly and there is order to the group's progress toward its goals.

Interestingly, research has found something happens to people's group-relevant attitudes once they join the group. Those attitudes become stronger. This is referred to as group polarization (Moscovici & Zavalloni, 1969). For example, let's say you have positive attitudes toward recycling, and then you join a pro-recycling group. If we measure the strength of your attitudes on recycling before joining the group discussion, we'd likely get some strong pro-recycling attitudes. But if we measure your attitudes toward recycling after you leave that group discussion, we're likely to find that you now have VERY strong attitudes in favor of recycling. This occurs because in groups of like-minded people, we learn new reasons to support our position, we hear new evidence in favor of our position, and we start believing that most people in society feel the same as all the people in our group.

SOCIAL FACILITATION

Recall our discussion of the Triplett (1898) study of bicycle race times in Chapter 1. He found that, for some people, their bicycle pace time was faster when they were riding alone compared to riding against a competitor. However, for others, riding against another person made their bicycle time faster than when they were biking alone. These mixed results baffled researchers for over 60 years until Zajonc (1965) published an article on his drive theory of social facilitation. The theory states that the mere presence of an audience (or coactors) will cause

an increase in physiological arousal in the actor. This rise in physiological arousal then sets off the social facilitation effect, whereby one will perform the "dominant response." This dominant response is like a default behavior. The key to how this influences the actor's behavior is the nature of the task for the individual. If this is an easy, well-learned task, the dominant response is usually the correct one, and performance is enhanced. If the task is difficult or not well learned, the dominant response will likely be a random behavior and therefore likely to be incorrect, thereby hurting performance on the task. It is important to note that Zajonc concluded that only the mere presence of the coactors or audience will enhance physiological arousal and thus social facilitation effects. Other researchers had different views about what triggers the elevation in physiological arousal. Those who advocated the distraction-conflict theory said that the presence of others created a split in the attention of the actor between the audience and the task at hand, and this split in attention is what elevated physiological arousal and set off social facilitation (Baron, 1986). Those who advocated the evaluation-apprehension theory said that the presence of others who are judging or evaluating the actor's performance is what elevated the arousal level in the actor and thus initiated social facilitation (Blascovich, Mendes, Hunter, & Salomon, 1999). Which theory best accounts for the data? We'll hold off on this question for now and address it after you read the paper by Zajonc and colleagues in this chapter.

SOCIAL LOAFING

I hate group projects. You probably do, too. Why? Because it is always the same story: Almost everyone in the group slacks off, and it falls to a few people (or one person) to do all the work (Price, Harrison, &

Gavin, 2006). Ugh! Aggravating. It turns out that social psychologists have a name for this: "social loafing" (Latané, Williams, & Harkins, 1979). Social loafing occurs when people are engaged in a task and, believing that their individual contribution to the task cannot be identified, they will then tend to reduce their effort. So the easiest way to avoid social loafing is to make sure that group members know that their individual contributions on the task are identifiable.

DEINDIVIDUATION

Do you ever wonder what causes "mob mentality"? This is the phenomenon whereby people in large groups sometimes do things, deviant or illegal behavior, that they normally would never do by themselves. What is it about being in large crowds that changes our behavior, and often for the worse? Two things happen in such a large crowd: The presence of so many others makes one feel less accountable for one's actions, because it reduces the likelihood that one's own individual behavior can be identified. Second, the presence of the large crowd lowers self-awareness, shifting people's attention away from their moral standards and toward the crowd. When that happens, people are more likely to perform behaviors that are inconsistent with their moral standards (Prentice-Dunn & Rogers, 1980). It should be noted that deindividuation effects can also be achieved by the mere loss of personal identity. One doesn't need to be in a large crowd for deindividuation to occur; one needs only the perception that one cannot be identified (Diener, Fraser, Beaman, & Kelem, 1976; Zimbardo, 1969). An interesting study by Dodd (1985) asked convicted felons and college students to imagine what they would do if they were invisible for 24 hours and couldn't be detected. Results showed that 36% of the responses were antisocial, 19%

nonnormative, 36% neutral, and 9% prosocial. There were no differences in the antisocial rates between groups. College students gave just as many antisocial responses as the felons.

A meta-analysis of more than 60 deindividuation experiments suggested that this past research has it all wrong. The study concluded that being deindividuated doesn't necessarily always lead to deviant behavior (Postmes & Spears, 1998). What happens, the authors suggested, is that being deindividuated leads one to be more likely to follow the norms of the group or crowd. So, if the crowd starts doing deviant behaviors, one will be more likely to do those types of behaviors. But if the crowd is a force for doing positive behavior, one will be more inclined to do those positive behaviors.

GROUPTHINK

In 1961, President John F. Kennedy authorized the Central Intelligence Agency (CIA) to train, fund, and assist Cuban rebels in an attempt to execute a military overthrow of Fidel Castro's government. The invasion landing at the Bay of Pigs was a disaster, with virtually everything going wrong that could go wrong. The rebels were quickly outnumbered and captured, and it became clear to Castro and the world that the United States was behind the failed effort. How could the U.S. government, with all the resources, educated advisors, and second-to-none military power have failed so miserably? Journalists and researchers investigating the decision-making process up to the invasion started noticing a unique set of circumstances that might explain how the decision to invade was given a green light by President Kennedy. The situation and circumstances have come to be known as "groupthink" (Janis, 1972). Groupthink is a flawed group decision-making process that is characterized by an excessive focus on unanimity. Pioneering research by Irving Janis (1972) and others have shown that certain factors, when present, can facilitate the conditions under which poor decision making occurs in the group (Esser, 1998). For example, if the group is under high stress, is a very cohesive group, and is largely isolated from the outside world and non–group member opinions, conditions are present. Moreover, if the group has a directive leader who says what he thinks the group should decide, that only leads the group to acquiesce—because who is going to tell the leader he is wrong? Groups experiencing groupthink tend to have members who discourage disagreement with the group, block dissenting opinions from the leader, believe that God is on their side and they can do no wrong, and believe that they are all in agreement. The good news is that groups can prevent groupthink with a few simple fixes. First, educate group members about groupthink. The more they know about it, the less likely they will succumb to it. Don't let the leader announce her position. Encourage doubts and contrary positions. Assign someone to be the devil's advocate, and point out flaws with whatever position the majority is advocating at that moment. Finally, break the large group into smaller groups and have each small group work toward a solution. Doing these things will help groups prevent groupthink and work efficiently on the task at hand.

INTRODUCTION TO READING 12.1

Zajonc et al. (1969)

For over 60 years, researchers were baffled about the results of Triplett's (1898) study of bicycle race times, which showed that for some people, racing against someone made their own performance improve, whereas for other people, having a competitor made their race time decrease. Triplett speculated that the increase in racing speed with a competitor was due to a release of a competitive instinct. When Zajonc (1965) published his solution to the social facilitation conundrum, he posited that merely having another person around (either a competitor or just watching) would increase the physiological arousal level in the person. Whether what Triplett called a competitive instinct might have also meant physiological arousal increase, we'll never be sure. But Zajonc's drive theory of social facilitation further stated that when this increase in arousal is set in motion, we tend to do the "dominant response," which is akin to a default behavior. Whether that arousal helps or hinders your performance depends on the nature of the task you are engaged in. If it is something well learned or over-learned, the default (or dominant) response will likely be a correct one, and your performance is enhanced. If you are doing something difficult or not well learned, the default response is likely to be random and, as such, incorrect for what you are trying to do, and thus your performance on the task will be impaired.

Other researchers had different ideas about what caused the physiological arousal in this sequence. Some said that the thing that made an actor nervous (physiologically aroused) was the knowledge that the audience (or coactor) was evaluating the actor's performance. This is known as the evaluation-apprehension theory (Blascovich et al., 1999). Others believed that the audience (or coactor) caused the actor's attention to split between himself and the task, and this is what caused the actor to become nervous. This is called the distraction-conflict theory (Baron, 1986). Zajonc believed there was a problem with these two theories. Remember, he said that all that was needed to set off the increased physiological arousal was the mere presence of others. The actor just needed to see the others, not wonder if they were evaluating him. Similarly, Zajonc didn't believe that the actor had to have his attention split to feel that increased physiological arousal. These two theories assume human qualities in the actor (evaluation and attention). Zajonc thought the process was much more primitive and could potentially be found in simpler organisms—hence, the present paper, reporting research wherein he and his colleagues attempted to show social facilitation effects in cockroaches. If he could demonstrate that process in this simple organism, that would be problematic for the other two theories and would be additional support for the drive theory. Let's see how things turn out in this paper, and we'll chat afterward. Enjoy!

Reading 12.1

Social Enhancement and Impairment of Performance in the Cockroach[1]

Robert B. Zajonc,[2] Alexander Heingartner, and Edward M. Herman[3]

Maze and runway performance of cockroaches was observed under solitary and social conditions in an attempt to test the drive theory of social facilitation. In Experiment I cockroaches were observed under two types of social treatments, coaction and audience. In both treatments maze performance was impaired while runway performance was facilitated when compared to performance of subjects in solitary conditions. In Experiment II the effects of reduced presence of conspecifics were investigated. Experiment I generated results that were in support of the hypothesis that the mere presence of conspecifics is a source of general arousal that enhances the emission of dominant responses. The results of Experiment II suggested that partial presence of conspecifics may have distracting effects.

About 35 years ago Gates and Allee (1933) reported a study on the maze learning of isolated and grouped cockroaches in which they observed a clear inferiority of performance of the grouped subjects. Gates and Allee attributed these effects to distraction, saying that cockroaches learning in groups were responding not only to the physical topography of the maze but to the social situation as well, and that the "chemical traces introduced by one of the other roaches simultaneously occupying the maze may have acted to interfere with orientation (Gates & Allee, 1933, p. 357)." Other studies using animal or human subjects also found a deterioration of performance under social conditions (Allee & Masure, 1936; Klopfer, 1958; Pessin & Husband, 1933). In agreement with Gates and Allee, Jones and Gerard (1967) have recently ascribed all these effects to distraction.

However, equally prevalent are data showing improvement in performance as a function of social stimuli. These socially facilitated increments in performance are usually found for behaviors that are either very well learned or instinctive. Thus, for instance, in experiments using human subjects, skilled performance on pursuit rotor (Travis, 1925), accuracy in a vigilance task (Bergum & Lehr, 1963), scores on chain-association, vowel cancellation, and multiplication tasks (Allport, 1924; Dashiell, 1930), and latency of word associations (Matlin & Zajonc, 1968) have all been shown to improve under social conditions. Studies using animal subjects found social increments in eating (Bayer, 1929; Fischel, 1927; Harlow, 1932; Tolman & Wilson, 1965), drinking (Bruce, 1941), bar pressing (Stamm, 1961), copulating

[1]This research was supported by Grant GS-629 from the National Science Foundation. The authors wish to express their gratitude to Susan DeLong, Judith Johnson, and Barbara Moreland for their assistance in various phases of this research.
[2]Requests for reprints should be sent to Robert B. Zajonc, Institute for Social Research, University of Michigan, Ann Arbor, Michigan 48106.
[3]Now at the New School for Social Research, New York, N. Y.

(Larsson, 1956), exploring (Simmel, 1962), nest building (Chen, 1937), and running (Scott & McCray, 1967).

It has recently been suggested (Zajonc, 1965) that these seemingly conflicting results can be reconciled if it is assumed that the presence of others is a source of general drive (D). While the presence of others can certainly be a source of specific cues, of reinforcement, and of rather specific excitation (as in mating or aggression, for example), and it can therefore *direct* behavior, it is also a source of nonspecific arousal, and hence acts as a general *energizer* of all responses that are likely to be emitted in the given situation. The degree of such an arousal need not be intense, of course. Nevertheless, it is assumed that its effects would be those that are predicted by the Spence-Hull drive theory (Spence, 1956). If the animal's dominant responses are appropriate from the point of view of the experimental situation, the presence of others will enhance them; and the resulting performance will appear as being improved. If these dominant responses are largely inappropriate, however, performance in the presence of others will appear as being impaired. Thus, for instance, if the given stimulus situation elicits in the animal dominant responses that are connected with eating, while the experiment "requires" the animal to delay or suppress instrumental responses leading to eating— as is the case in DRL (differential reinforcement of low rates) training—the presence of conspecifics will work against the experimental requirements, and "performance" will appear to suffer. Such an effect has indeed been obtained (Wheeler & Davis, 1967). On the other hand, if the experimenter is interested in establishing high response rates using continuous reinforcement, and if the total experimental situation also elicits dominant responses that are connected with eating, the presence of others will appear to have beneficial consequences. Hence, it is not performance but the emission of dominant responses, whatever they are, that is "facilitated" by the social stimulus.

If information about the subject's response hierarchy were available prior to the tests of social effects, the drive theory of social facilitation could be given a critical test. Such methods have been used with humans (Cottrell, Rittle, & Wack, 1967; Zajonc & Sales, 1966), and the evidence obtained was in substantial agreement with the drive theory of social facilitation. But procedures of this sort have not been employed with animal subjects.

Gates and Allee's (1933) experiment lends itself to some modifications which should generate useful information for the drive theory of social facilitation. In their experiment Gates and Allee (1933) used an Eshaped maze suspended over water. Light served as a noxious stimulus, while an opaque bottle located in the central portion of the maze provided the subjects with the only means of escape. The procedure entailed placing the cockroach (or cockroaches) at one of the terminals of the maze and observing the time required to reach the goal bottle. Because of the many spatial alternatives available—at first all equally inviting—many response tendencies were elicited that were not correct. In fact, of the many ways in which the cockroach could proceed in the Emaze, only one led to escape, and hence to what the experimenter would consider as "appropriate behavior." To the extent that the presence of conspecifics did act as a source of general drive (D), these many "inappropriate" response tendencies were energized, delaying the emission of the appropriate one.

If one could contrive a situation in which the cockroach's response tendencies would be largely "correct" or "appropriate," an increment rather than a decrement in performance should be obtained under social conditions. In comparison with maze performance, this situation would provide a rather stringent test of the drive theory of social facilitation.

Psychologists refer to a Drive as a basic motivational force that initiates behavior, such as hunger, thirst, even sex. Here, Zajonc is making the argument that the presence of other people acts like a fundamental drive in that it initiates physiological arousal in the actor.

This is the key element of Zajonc's Drive Theory of Social Facilitation: the mere presence of others will cause one to feel physiological arousal, and this arousal causes one to do their "dominant response." This rather automatic behavior will either enhance or impede one's performance on their current task, depending on the nature of the task with that individual. Specifically, if the individual has a lot of experience doing the task, and it is therefore well-learned and/or simple, the dominant response will be correct, and therefore the individual's performance will be enhance. If, however, the individual has little or no experience doing the task, and/ or it is a difficult task, then the dominant response will tend to be a random behavior that likely will be incorrect, and thus impede one's performance on the task.

There have been two primary alternate theories about social facilitation effects: distraction-conflict and evaluation-apprehension. In distraction-conflict, the idea is that the presence of others causes a split in one's attention, such that one is simultaneously paying attention to the task and to the other individuals. This split increases physiological arousal, and that triggers social facilitation effects. In evaluation-apprehension, the thinking is that the presence of others who are perceived by the actor as evaluating the actor's performance will make the actor feel physiologically aroused, and this will then trigger social facilitation effects. These both seem like reasonable explanations, but Zajonc thought they had one flaw: they both assume some kind of human-like cognitive or emotional processes to engage social facilitation. Zajonc believed that all you needed to do to initiate social facilitation was have the mere presence of others. No evaluation, no distraction. Just others of the same species need to be present. If you could show social facilitation effects in nonhumans, that would support his drive theory, and not support the other two theories.

The drive theory of social facilitation is as follows: The presence of others causes an increase in physiological arousal (a nonspecific drive), which, in turn, causes one to perform a "dominant response." The dominant response will tend to be correct on tasks that are well-learned or simple, and it will tend to be incorrect on tasks that are not well learned or difficult.

Ewww, right? Why cockroaches? Well, I suppose Zajonc could have chosen a number of different insects or possible animals for his experiments. But the goal was to show that the drive theory applies in even the most simple organisms, so that Zajonc could rule out the need for cognition. If you choose an insect, then what insect would have a baseline, default behavior on which was a reliable behavior on which a researcher could consistently induce a well-learned behavior? What could be more well-learned than an instinctive behavior? Thinking about this further . . . the cockroach is a good choice to fit these parameters, because its default behavior of running away from any light is something the researcher can use.

You might be wondering why we need to know this amount of detail. It is important, when writing a report of any experiment, to describe the method of the experiment in detail so that other researchers who wish to reproduce the experiment in their lab will be able to set up the experiment nearly exactly as you did, so that they can attempt to replicate your results.

The straight runway with the noxious stimulus at the start and the means of escape at the goal can serve this purpose rather well. Such a straight runway, properly constructed, does not prompt the cockroach to turn, for if it turns it must only face the noxious light. The entire stimulus situation is so contrived that the dominant tendencies that are elicited consist of running away from the start box and directly toward the goal box. The present paper reports two experiments in which the performance of cockroaches in a maze and in a runway was compared under various social conditions. In all these experiments socially mediated performance decrements in the maze and socially mediated increments in the straight runway were expected.

EXPERIMENT I

This experiment had two major purposes. The first was to test the drive theory of social facilitation. To accomplish this purpose paired and isolated cockroaches were observed as they performed in a maze and as they performed in a straight runway. As in the experiment carried out by Gates and Allee (1933), the social variable was manipulated by having the subjects traverse the maze or the runway alone or in pairs, that is, in coaction. However, this experimental manipulation, which has been used in nearly all experiments on social facilitation with animals, may lead to a confounding of two possible effects of others' presence: its energizing effects and its directive (or cue) effects. Two animals using the same maze or runway may affect each other's behavior because they act as a source of arousal for each other, or because they emit responses that may be imitated. The second purpose of the present experiment, therefore, was to determine if socially mediated effects obtained in cockroaches when the subjects could not profit from directive cues provided by companions. Hence, while the social variable in one group of subjects was manipulated by means of coaction, in the other group it was manipulated by providing an audience, in order to eliminate all cues connected with the presence of conspecifics that may have been task relevant and may have influenced the subjects' behavioral choices rather than his response vigor. If similar socially mediated effects were obtained with an audience as with coaction, the drive theory of social facilitation would receive more unequivocal support than had these effects been obtained under the conditions of coaction alone.

METHOD

Subjects. Seventy-two adult female cockroaches (*Blatta orientalis*) were used,[4] and for at least 1 week prior to the first experimental trial they were housed in individual mason jars supplied with screened lids. They were maintained in dark quarters with a relatively constant temperature of about 75 degrees Fahrenheit. The insects were fed an ad libitum diet of peeled and sliced apples.

Apparatus. The basic apparatus is shown in Figure 1. It consisted of a 20 × 20 × 20-inch clear plexiglass cube outfitted so as to house either a maze or a runway. A 150-watt floodlight

---

[4]The authors are grateful to Louis M. Roth of the United States Army Natick Laboratory who was kind enough to supply the subjects for the audience treatment. The subjects in the coaction treatment were obtained from the Carolina Biological Supply Company.

FIG. 1.   Diagrams of runways and mazes used in the coaction and in the audience treatments of Experiment I.

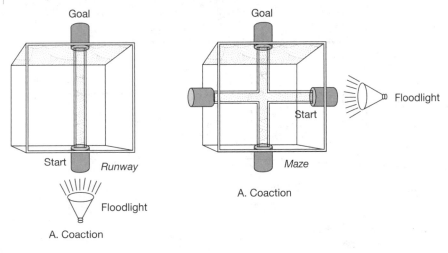

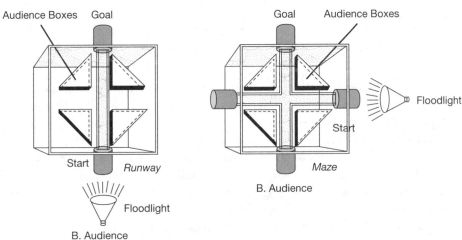

Brilliant design for the easy and difficult tasks: for cockroaches, their well-learned behavior is to run away from light. They would run opposite of where the light is, and likely in a straight line away. Thus, the researcher has a simple behavior that the roach doesn't need to "learn" (run away from light). They should be quite adept at running away in a straight line, hence the runway design works perfectly as an "easy task." However, roaches don't typically run away and then hang a 90 degree angle left or right turn mid-way through their run. So such a maze would be a difficult task for the roach.

served as a source of noxious stimulation. In the center of each vertical wall of the plexiglass housing, 8¼ inches from the top, was a rectangular 1¾ × ¾ inch- opening, which could be closed by means of a guillotine gate made out of sheet metal. A set of tracks on the exterior of each opening served as a shoe for a goal box or a starting box, clamping it firmly in place against the wall opening. Both the goal box and the starting box were made of 4-inch clear plexiglass tubing. A square flange that could slide into the shoe on the vertical wall of the housing was affixed to the opening of the boxes, while the other end of the tubing was sealed with 1-inch clear plexiglass.

The maze and the runway could be suspended in the housing flush with the goal boxes and the starting boxes. Both the runway and the maze were made of black bakelit floor 2 inches wide, with walls made of clear plexiglass, 1 inch high. The runway and the maze were provided with clear plexiglass tops 1-inch thick. The runway consisted of a straight track running between two opposite vertical walls, and was 20 inches long. The maze was made of two runways, placed in the same plane and perpendicular to each other, thus forming a cross with

TABLE 1 Running Time And Starting Latency In Seconds For Subjects Tested Alone, In Coaction, And In The Presence Of An Audience

	Task			
	Runway		Maze	
Treatment	Alone	Social	Alone	Social
Coaction				
Starting latency	8.25 (8)	6.88 (8)	10.56 (8)	11.19 (8)
Running time	40.58 (8)	32.96 (8)	110.45 (8)	129.46 (8)
Audience				
Starting latency	14.80 (10)	9.35 (10)	37.55 (10)	22.75 (10)
Running time	62.65 (10)	39.30 (10)	221.35 (10)	296.64 (10)
Both treatments				
Starting latency	11.89 (18)	8.25 (18)	25.56 (18)	17.61 (18)
Running time	52.84 (18)	36.48 (18)	172.06 (18)	222.34 (18)

Note. Averages of medians. Figures in parentheses indicate the number of roaches in each cell.

the walls of the intersection removed. The lengths of the paths in the runway and in the maze, namely those leading from the starting box to the goal box or to a cul-de-sac, were 20 inches.

The guillotine gates that separated the starting and goal boxes from the runway or maze were made of galvanized sheet metal. To attract the roach to the goal box an opaque cover, painted flat black on the inside, was placed over the box making its interior dark. A flat black posterboard, covering the entire 20 × 20-inch area, was hung on the wall which held the goal box.

For the groups in which the social variable was manipulated by means of a passive audience four 9 × 9 × 1-inch boxes with plexiglass sides and tops and bakelite floors were used. These boxes were placed inside the plexiglass cube housing in such a manner that their floors were flush with the floors of the runway or the maze and their sides directly contiguous with the walls of the runway or the maze. When these boxes were in position almost the entire extent of walls of the runway or maze were in direct contact with the sides of the audience boxes. Air holes in the sides of the boxes lined up with air holes in the walls of the runway and the maze to allow transmission of olfactory cues.

Procedure. Before each trial the runway (or the maze) was swabbed with alcohol which was allowed to evaporate thoroughly. The starting box and the goal box were swabbed in the same manner before each set of 10 trials. The roach was transferred from its home jar to the starting box which had been covered with an opaque container similar to that which also covered the goal box. Each trial began by removing the cover, turning on the flood light, and removing the guillotine door separating the opening in the starting box from the runway or the maze. The floodlight was always in line with the runway or the maze and 10 inches directly behind it. No light other than that provided by the floodlight was present in the experimental room. The trial was terminated when the cockroach (or the pair of cockroaches) entered the goal box and the guillotine gate was lowered behind it (or them), or in 5 minutes—whichever was earlier. The guillotine gate was always lowered immediately after the roach's last leg crossed the entrance of the goal box. In the coaction treatment the starting latencies and the running times were scored for each subject individually, although the gate was not lowered until the last member of the pair entered the goal box.

Thirty-two animals served in the experimental treatment involving coaction[5] and 40 in the treatment involving audience. In each treatment half of the roaches worked in the runway and half in the maze. In addition, within each combination of treatment and task, half of the animals were run in the alone condition and half in the social condition. In the coaction treatment the subjects were placed into starting boxes in pairs. For purposes of identification they were marked with airplane dope, one white and one blue. In the audience treatment 10 adult female *Blatta orientalis,* which were previously housed in common quarters of the laboratory colony, were placed in each of the four audience boxes. The control group of 20 roaches, which was not to be exposed to a passive audience, worked with audience boxes in position, but empty and clean. All roaches run in the audience treatment and in their proper control conditions were run individually. Starting latencies to the nearest second and total running times to the nearest tenth of a second were recorded. Starting latency consisted of the interval beginning with the opening of the guillotine gate of the starting box and ending at the time the last part of the roach's body left the starting box. In all treatments and conditions the subjects were given 10 consecutive trials, all separated by 1-minute inter-trial intervals.

Results

Because starting latencies and running times are generally skewed, the scores subjected to the analysis of variance consisted of median times computed over the 10 trials performed by each subject. The averages reported throughout this paper are averages of these median times. Table 1 shows the entire results of the experiment, and Table 2 shows the analysis of variance of these data. Above all, it is clear that with respect to starting latencies all effects fail to reach acceptable levels of significance. It was considered that leaving the starting box, which, it will be recalled, was the nearest to the floodlight, was a relatively simple task for the roach, comparable to traversing a straight runway. Therefore, under the coaction treatment, starting latencies should be shorter in the social condition than in the alone condition, regardless of whether the subjects are entering the maze or the runway. Under the audience treatment, however, there are no social cues in the starting box in the social as well as in the alone condition and we would, therefore, not expect strong effects associated with either treatments or conditions. While the results are not significant, we note from Table 1 that the task may have affected starting latencies, with the relevant F ratio nearly reaching an acceptable level of significance.

The total running times show patterns that are quite consistent with the drive theory of social facilitation. Relevant here is the significant interaction between the conditions and tasks ($F = 7.57$, $df = 1/64$, $p < .01$) . Roaches running the maze in coaction required longer times than roaches running in isolation. This result replicates the findings of Gates and Allee (1933). However, the effects of coaction are reversed for the runway. Here the coacting roaches perform more quickly than the solitary subjects. And the same pattern of results prevails for the audience treatment. Hence the three-way interaction was not significant.

Support for the drive theory of social facilitation. In the maze (difficult task), presence of others impedes performance (so, cockroaches alone run faster). In the runway (easy task), presence of others enhances performance (those alone run slower).

---

[5]This treatment constitutes a partial replication of a previous experiment, reported elsewhere (Zajonc, 1968).

TABLE 2   Summary Of Analyses Of Variance For Data In Table

Source	df	Starting latency		Running time	
		MS	F	MS	F
Alone vs. social (A)	1	603.78	< 1	5180.48	1.962
Runway vs. maze	1	2386.25	2.650	418826.03	158.639
Coaction vs. audience (C)	1	2514.87	2.793	104373.47	39.533**
A × E	1	83.42	< 1	19977.75	7.567*
A × C	1	422.50	< 1	1823.85	< 1.000
B × C	1	968.58	1.076	69258.45	26.233**
A × B × C	1	143.14	< 1	5764.66	2.183
Error	64	900.36		2640.11	

$^{*}p < .01.$

$^{**}p < .001.$

The analysis of the above results also shows that the running times and the latencies are substantially shorter in the coaction animals than in the audience groups. Unfortunately, because these subjects came from different colonies, we are unable to determine from the data alone whether these differences are due to the diverse origins of the two groups of animals, or whether they have something to do with the experimental treatments. It is a rather plausible conjecture that the differences are attributable to the former factor because of the consistently longer running times of roaches in the control groups of the audience as compared to the coaction treatment.

EXPERIMENT II

Fancy way of saying "peer cockroaches."

In the first experiment it was shown that the presence of an audience of conspecifics is a sufficient condition for the enhancement of dominant responses, such that the performance of the subject in a one-alternative task is improved and the performance of the subject in a multialternative task is impaired. But the variable, "presence of conspecifics," is certainly not precise either from a theoretical or methodological point of view. What are the essential and critical features of "presence of conspecifics" that produce these effects? What is the nature of the social stimulus that elicits these effects and has the capacity of increasing general arousal? Complete answers to these questions must await a great deal of research not only on the nature of the social stimulation involved in social facilitation effects but also on the nature of the arousal that is brought about by the social stimuli. But as a first step we may inquire about the minimal conditions which are sufficient for producing social facilitation effects. Tolman (1965) found that feeding behavior of young chicks was facilitated by the presence of a companion separated from the subject by a plexiglass partition, and also by feeding the subject in front of a mirror. These increments, however, were not as impressive as those obtained with a coacting companion. Tolman (1968) regarded such socially mediated effects primarily in directive (cue) terms. Hence he accepted as more likely the hypothesis that it is the behavior of the companion rather than its mere presence which produces increments and decrements in performance. Animal research, especially on feeding behavior, supports his contention. However, results of Experiment I with audience show that even when the conspecific companion does not emit behavior which can be used by the subject to guide the course of his action, effects which are consistent with the drive theory of social facilitation are obtained.

Experiment II attempted to determine if socially mediated effects such as those obtained in Experiment I would be produced if the immediate presence of conspecifics were somehow curtailed or reduced. Two treatments were employed. In both treatments there were no other roaches besides the subject. Both dealt with some components of the presence of conspecifics, one emphasizing its cue effects, the other emphasizing its energizing (general arousal) effects. Thus, in the former the insects ran in mazes and runways which were outfitted with mirrors alongside their vertical walls. In the second treatment regular runways and mazes were utilized, but the animals were stimulated by the presence of olfactory cues associated with their conspecifics. These treatments were compared with one in which the insects were observed under solitary and socially neutral conditions.

Method

Subjects. One hundred and eighty female *Blattaorientalis* obtained from the Carolina Biological Supply Company were employed in the present experiment. All insects were housed in individual mason jars for 4 days prior to the experiment. One third of the subjects were assigned to the mirror treatment (Mi) , one-third to the odor treatment (Od), and one-third to the alone treatment (Al). In each treatment, half of the subjects (30) were given tests in the straight runway and half in the maze.

Apparatus. The apparatus from Experiment I, in which modifications were made to allow tests under the requirements of the experimental treatments, was employed. In the Mi treatment a runway and a maze were used which were equipped with reflecting half-aluminized film affixed to the entire extent of the walls. Otherwise the apparatus was the same as in the alone treatment of Experiment I. In the Od treatment the regular runway and maze from the audience treatment of Experiment I were used which, it will be recalled, had holes drilled in their walls. An olfactory social stimulus was provided by placing an egg carton impregnated with the odor of conspecifics inside the housing of the apparatus and 4 inches directly beneath the maze or the runway. The egg carton was thoroughly impregnated with the odors of conspecifics by having it in the quarters of the colony for several days prior to the tests. Several cartons were kept in the quarters of the cockroach colony during the course of the experiment, and during each testing session a freshly impregnated carton was always used. The Al treatment was the same as the Od treatment except that a fresh clean egg carton, not impregnated with cockroach odor, was placed 4 inches beneath the runway or the maze. The same procedure was used for scoring latencies and running times as in Experiment I.

Results

Table 3 shows the data from Experiment II. It may at first be noted that under the present experimental treatments the latencies do not differ across tasks ($F < 1$, $df = 1/174$).

TABLE 3 Running Time and Starting Latency in Seconds For Subjects Tested Alone, with Mirror, and in the Presence of Conspecific Odor

Treatment	Task	
	Runway	Maze
Mirror		
Starting latency	27.38	28.88
Running time	77.21	160.71
Odor		
Starting latency	20.00	24.97
Running time	69.53	245.72
Alone		
Starting latency	22.67	18.33
Running time	55.67	219.63

Note. Averages of medians. These means are based on 30 independent observations in each cell.

Such a tendency was present in Experiment I, although it also did not attain an acceptable level of significance. The latencies are also fairly uniform across treatments. The relevant F ratio did not reach an acceptable level of significance ($F = 2.681$, $dj = 2/174$). Similarly, the interaction between treatments and tasks did not attain significance. However, with respect to total running times both main effects and the interaction are significant ($F = 4.197$, $df = 2/174$, $p < .05$ for treatments; $F = 167.925$, $dj = 1/174$, $p <.001$ for tasks; and $F = 7.117$, $df = 2/174$, $p < .001$ for the interaction between them). These effects, it seems, are due primarily to the relatively fast maze running time among the Mi subjects. In contrast to the previous experiment, running times in the straight runway are not improved in the two social treatments. Both the Mi and the Od subjects took longer times to traverse the runway than the Al subjects. Maze running seems to show a relative facilitation for the Mi treatment and an impairment for the Od treatment.

DISCUSSION

The results of Experiment I support the hypothesis that the presence of conspecifics acts as an energizer of dominant responses in the cockroach. There were rather clear indications that enhancement as well as impairment of performance could be obtained with these insects, depending on whether a simple or a complex task was used, and therefore depending on whether the situation was more likely to recruit appropriate or inappropriate response tendencies. While results on starting latencies failed to generate useful information, data on running times unequivocally favored the drive theory of social facilitation.

The fact that performance in the runway was enhanced by the presence of conspecifics does damage to the distraction hypothesis proposed by Gates and Allee (1933) and reintroduced by

Jones and Gerard (1967). It must be noted that the runway and the maze differed only in the number of alternative turns available to the subject at the choice point, that is, 9 inches from the starting box. The runway had only one alternative, while the maze had three. In all other respects the two tasks and the two stimulus situations were nearly identical[6]. It would not be parsimonious, therefore, to maintain that the distraction hypothesis applies to maze performance alone, for we would have to invoke a new psychological process to account for the improvement of running times in the runway.

The results of Experiment I also eliminated the possibility that social facilitation effects depend on the specific behavioral output of the companion. In nearly all previous experiments on social facilitation with animal subjects the coaction paradigm was employed. Data from these studies could therefore be interpreted by assuming that the companion emits behavior which the subject can imitate. The fact that the results in the audience treatment show the same pattern as those in the coaction treatment indicates that specific directive cues need not be involved in socially mediated performance effects. In fact, the effects obtained in the coaction treatment were less pronounced than those found in the audience treatment. Simple effects tests on running time data from Experiment I show a strong interaction between conditions (social versus alone) and tasks (runway versus maze) for the audience treatment ($F = 9.19$, $df = 1/64$, $p < .01$), while the same interaction is only of borderline significance in the coaction treatment ($F = 2.80$, $df = 1/64$, $p < .10$). It should be noted, at the same time, however, that in a previous experiment on coaction in cockroaches (Zajonc, 1968), using subjects as their own controls, this interaction *was* reliable.

Subjects in the coaction treatment did not show tendencies to crowd or to form traffic jams in the runway and in the maze. While they usually did not leave starting boxes or enter goal boxes at the same time, the openings were sufficiently wide to allow them to do so. The fact that maze performance was observed to deteriorate in the audience treatment would lead us to expect that this deterioration was socially mediated in the coaction treatment as well, rather than having been brought about by crowding or traffic jams.

Qualitative observations of the roaches did not reveal specific behaviors by virtue of which such social effects might be produced. Perhaps the only consistent pattern found was that the behavior of the subjects in the coaction treatment was devoid of tendencies to follow or to imitate. The roaches seemed to traverse the alleys of the maze and of the runway in an apparent ignorance of each other. In the audience treatment, too, there was nothing detectable in the subjects' behavior to indicate that they oriented toward the spectator roaches. But, of course, there is today only scanty information on the social significance of the various responses of the cockroach.

Another hypothesis offered to account for the effects associated with the presence of conspecifics assumes that they are not due to an increased arousal but to calming. For instance, Davitz and Mason (1955) have found that rats in an open field test reduce their fear responses when a previously habituated rat is also present. And Liddell (1950) has shown that neurotic symptoms produced in a young goat by means of a continuous noxious stimulation are attenuated when the mother goat is also present. Bovard (1959) proposed that social stimuli elicit a competing response "which inhibits, masks, or screens the stress stimulus, such that the latter has a minimal effect [p. 269]." Because the response of the posterior hypothalamus

---

[6]It is true, however, as the reviewer of this manuscript correctly observed, that the maze did require a right (or a left) turn of the subject, while the runway did not.

initiates pituitary-adrenal cortical and sympathetic-adrenal medullar activity associated with stress reactions, Bovard argued that the presence of another member of the same species must dampen the activity of the posterior hypothalamus, and thereby dampen the stress reactions of the adrenal system. It has been suggested elsewhere (Zajonc, 1965) that the reduced stress reactions may be due simply to the availability for imitation of coping responses. Hence, the experimental data associated with reduction of fear which occurs with the presence of conspecifics might be best accounted for by focusing upon the directive (cue) effects which are provided by the conspecifics. The situation in Experiment I can certainly be considered a stressful one, for the species of the cockroach used in the experiment is rather photophobic. The effects observed in the coaction and in the audience treatment are not consistent with the hypothesis that companions have a calming effect. If this were the case we would expect an increase in the running time in the runway and a decrease in the running time in the maze-results which would be diametrically opposite to those found in Experiment I. But such an effect was found in Experiment II in the Mi treatment. In comparison with the Al treatment, these subjects took longer in the runway and were faster in the maze. The Mi treatment, it will be recalled, stresses the directive (cue) properties associated with the presence of conspecifics. But in Experiment I there also was a treatment (coaction) in which cues were available for imitation but in which an actual companion was present. Yet this experimental situation did not produce a calming effect.

The results of Experiment II are ambiguous. One conclusion to be drawn from these results is that in order for drive effects to take place the presence of conspecifics must be actual. Partial presence, such as the presence of olfactory traces, was not sufficient to produce effects consistent with the drive theory of social facilitation. It seemed, on the contrary, that the Od treatment generated results most consistent with the distraction hypothesis. In comparison with the Al treatment, the subjects running in the presence of the odor of conspecifics had longer times in the maze as well as in the straight runway. The question immediately arises whether social facilitation effects consistent with the drive theory of social facilitation would be obtained in the presence of an immobile audience. For instance, one could observe the runway and maze behavior of cockroaches in the presence of a dead or anaesthetized companion. The danger of such an experiment is that a dead or an immobile cockroach, while leading to an increase in the general arousal level of the subject, might also elicit specific alarm or stress responses that may interfere with task performance. The problem of what are the minimal features of the presence of conspecifics which are sufficient for social facilitation effects which the drive theory predicts is quite difficult from a methodological point of view.

Another problem associated with social facilitation effects is that concerning the nature of the arousal or drive that increases in the presence of others. Social facilitation effects obtained with human subjects can be readily interpreted as caused by a motivation to succeed, a desire to be praised and avoid blame, or in general, by assuming that the presence of others creates in the individual the anticipation of socially positive or negative consequences and thus increases the general arousal level (Cottrell, 1968; Cottrell, Wack, Sekerak, & Rittle, 1968). Had the present been experiments using human subjects one could easily raise questions about self-disclosure, evaluation apprehension, the approval motive, etc. But one finds it rather awkward to attribute this sort of motivation to the cockroach, even though we have no idea if these seemingly spiritless creatures aren't vulnerable to some of the very same passions and weaknesses which beset our sophomore population of subjects.

REFERENCES

ALLEE, W. C., & MASURE, R. H. A comparison of maze behavior in paired and isolated shell parakeets (M*elopsittacas undulatm,* Shaw). *Physiological Zoology,* 1936, 22, 131–156.

ALLPORT, F. H. *Social psychology.* Boston: Houghton Mifflin, 1924.

BAYER, E. Beitrage zur Zweikomponentheorie des Hungers. *Zeitschrijt fur Psychologie,* 1929, 112, 1–54.

BERGUM, B. o., & LEHR, D. J. Effects of authoritarianism on vigilance performance. *Journal of Applied Psychology,* 1963, 47, 75–77.

BOVARD, E. W. The effects of social stimuli on the response to stress. *Psychological Review,* 1959, 66, 267–277.

BRUCE, R. H. An experimental analysis of social factors affecting the performance of while rats. I. Performance in learning in a simple field situation. *Journal of Comparative Psychology,* 1941, 31, 363–377.

CHEN, S. C. Social modification of the activity of ants in nest-building. *Physiological Zoology,* 1937, 10, 420–436.

COTTRELL, N. B. Performance in the presence of other human beings: Mere presence, audience, and affiliation effects. In E. C. Simmel, R. A. Hoppe, & G. A. Milton (Eds.), *Social facilitation and imitative behavior.* Boston: Allyn & Bacon, 1968.

COTTRELL, N. B., RITTLE, R. H., & WACK, D. L. Presence of an audience and list type (competitional or noncompetitional) as joint determinants of performance in paired-associates learning. *Journal of Personality,* 1967, 35, 425–434.

COTTRELL, N. B., WACK, D. L., SEKERAK, G., & RITTLE, R. H. The social facilitation of dominant responses by the presence of an audience and the mere presence of others. *Journal of Personality and Social Psychology,* 1968, 9, 251–256.

DASHIELL, J. F. An experimental analysis of some group effects. *Journal of Abnormal and Social Psychology,* 1930, 25, 190–199.

Dwuz, J. R., & MASON, D. J. Socially facilitated reduction of a fear response in rats. *Journal of Comparative and Physiological Psychology,* 1955, 48, 149–151.

FISCHEL, W. Beitrage zur Soziologie des Haushuhns. *Biologisches Zentralblatt,* 1927, 47, 678–696.

GATES, M. G., & ALLEE, W. C. Conditioned behavior of isolated and grouped cockroaches on a simple maze. *Journal of Comparative Psychology,* 1933, 15, 331–358.

HARLOW, H. F. Social facilitation of feeding in the albino rat. *Journal of Genetic Psychology,* 1932, 41, 211–221.

JONES, E. E., & GERARD, H. B. *Foundations of social psychology.* New York: Wiley, 1967.

KLOPFER, P. H. Influence of social interaction on learning rates in birds. *Science,* 1958, 128, 903–904.

LARSSON, K. *Conditioning and sexual behavior in the male albino rat.* Stockholm: Almquist & Wiksell, 1956.

LIDDELL, H. Some specific factors that modify tolerance for environmental stress. In H. G. Wolff, S. G. Wolf, Jr., & C. C. Hare (Eds.), *Life stress and bodily disease.* Baltimore: Williams & Wilkins, 1950.

MATLIN, M. W., & ZAJONC, R. B. Social facilitation of word associations. *Journal of Personality and Social Psychology,* 1968, 10, 455–460.

PESSIN, J., & HUSBAND, R. W. Effects of social stimulation on human maze learning. *Journal of Abnormal and Social Psychology,* 1933, 28, 148–154.

SCOTT, J. P., & McCRAY, C. Allelomimetic behavior in dogs: Negative effects of competition on social facilitation. *Journal of Comparative and Physiological Psychology,* 1967, 63, 316–319.

SIMMEL, E. C. Social facilitation of exploratory behavior in rats. *Journal of Comparative and Physiological Psychology,* 1962, 55, 831–833.

SPENCE, K. W. *Behavior theory and conditioning.* New Haven: Yale University Press, 1956.

STAMM, J. S. Social facilitation in monkeys. *Psychological Reports,* 1961, 8, 479–484.

TOLMAN, C. W. Emotional behavior and social facilitation of feeding in domestic chicks. *Animal Behaviour,* 1965, 13, *493–502.*

TOLMAN, C. W. The role of the companion in social facilitation of animal behavior. In E. C. Simmel, R. A. Hoppe, & G. A. Tviilton (Eds.), *Social facilitation and imitative behavior.* Boston: Allyn & Bacon, 1968.

TOLMAN, C. W., & WILSON, G. F. Social feeding in domestic chicks. *Animal Behaviour,* 1965, 13, 134–142.

TRAVIS, L. E. The effect of a small audience upon eye-hand coordination. *Journal of Abnormal and Social Psychology,* 1925, 20, 142–146.

WHEELER, L., & DAVIS, H. Social disruption of performance on a DRL schedule. *Psychonomic Science,* 1967, 7, 249–250.

ZAJONC, R. B. Social facilitation. *Science,* 1965, 149, 269–274.

ZAJONC, R. B., & SALES, S. M. Social facilitation of dominant and subordinate responses. *Journal of Experimental Social Psychology,* 1966, 2, 160–168.

ZAJONC, R. B. Social facilitation in the cockroach. In E. C. Simmel, R. A. Hoppe, & G. A. Milton (Eds.), *Social facilitation and imitative behavior.* Boston: Allyn & Bacon, 1968.

POST-ARTICLE DISCUSSION

There are several reasons why this paper is a classic in social psychology. First, it utilizes a clever method to address the research question. Second, the data offer a compelling and strong case to support the drive theory. Third, the support of the theory with this particular group of "subjects" effectively undercuts the other two competing theories that rely on human qualities (evaluation and attention). I think most researchers also really appreciate the creativity that Zajonc and colleagues put into this experiment. Specifically, Zajonc's theory was being challenged, and normally we confine our experiments to using human subjects. But Zajonc and his colleagues realized that the other theories made assumptions about social facilitation that his drive theory did not, and if Zajonc could find a way to obtain social facilitation, perhaps in nonhumans, what would that look like? Could he use dogs? Chimps? Thinking further about his theory, he argued that the process of social facilitation is set in motion (i.e., the heightened physiological arousal) by the mere presence of coactors or an audience of what he called "conspecifics" (peers of the same species). So what if one went really basic in terms of the complexity of the subject, down from humans, past animals, to insects? The rest is history. It is a great lesson on thinking outside the box, on thinking about a problem in new and creative ways. Doing so in this case not only supported his theory but, at the same time, undercut his two main rival theories. A long-standing problem in social psychology (social facilitation), an interesting theory, and a very creative way to support that theory. I hope you enjoyed the paper!

THINGS TO THINK ABOUT

1. Why did Zajonc use cockroaches for this experiment? Why not just use people? Also, why cockroaches and not another type of animal or insect?

2. Why do you suppose that the mere presence of others would cause a rise in physiological arousal? And why would this happen in insects?

3. What is the "dominant response"?

4. Do you think that the researchers would have obtained the same results if they used another insect species as the "audience" for the cockroaches?

INTRODUCTION TO READING 12.2
Ronay et al. (2012)

One of the core areas of social psychology concerns our ongoing goal of gaining a better understanding of how people behave in small groups. How do leaders emerge? Do certain people naturally gravitate toward certain roles in any group, and how is that related to their personality? What is an optimal group size for a given task? How can a group ensure the highest productivity of their members performing their task? There are a lot more questions, but you get the idea. In the paper you are about to read, Ronay and colleagues wondered how productivity is affected when a group is composed of too many members with power, or too many without power, or an equal mix thereof. Another way to look at this is by asking this question: In a group, do people work best in a hierarchy of power among the members, or is it best to have all members on the same level of power?

Another interesting question Ronay et al. asked is how testosterone (and therefore dominance) would influence group harmony and productivity. If you have a group composed of mostly high-testosterone persons, would that lead to increased jockeying for position and therefore more conflict, and (it stands to reason) would that impair productivity? What happens if you have a group mostly composed of low-testosterone persons? Would there be no leader emerging, and would that impair performance as well? If you have a group of "followers," would that increase or decrease the likelihood of within-group conflict? So, again, the main question Ronay et al. investigated in their two experiments is this: Do groups work best when they are hierarchically organized in terms of members' power and dominance, and if so, does that lower the likelihood of conflict among members? When you read the paper, as always, think carefully about the method and whether you would do anything differently to improve it. Enjoy the paper!

Reading 12.2

The Path to Glory Is Paved With Hierarchy: When Hierarchical Differentiation Increases Group Effectiveness

Richard Ronay[1], Katharine Greenaway[2], Eric M. Anicich[1], and Adam D. Galinsky[3]

Abstract

Two experiments examined the psychological and biological antecedents of hierarchical differentiation and the resulting consequences for productivity and conflict within small groups. In Experiment 1, which used a priming manipulation, hierarchically differentiated groups (i.e., groups comprising 1 high-power-primed, 1 low-power-primed, and 1 baseline individual) performed better on a procedurally interdependent task than did groups comprising exclusively

[1]Graduate School of Business, Columbia University; [2]Department of Psychology, University of Queensland; and [3]Kellogg School of Management, Northwestern University

either all high-power-primed or all low-power-primed individuals. There were no effects of hierarchical differentiation on performance on a procedurally independent task. Experiment 2 used a biological marker of dominance motivation (prenatal testosterone exposure as measured by a digit-length ratio) to manipulate hierarchical differentiation. The pattern of results from Experiment 1 was replicated; mixed-testosterone groups achieved greater productivity than did groups comprising all high-testosterone or all low-testosterone individuals. Furthermore, intragroup conflict mediated the productivity decrements for the high-testosterone but not the low-testosterone groups. This research suggests possible directions for future research and the need to further delineate the conditions and types of hierarchy under which hierarchical differentiation enhances rather than undermines group effectiveness.

Keywords

social interaction, neuroendocrinology

Poultry scientists have made a surprising discovery: Ironically, when a chicken colony contains too many high egg producers, overall egg production is reduced. Although breeding for greater egg production works for birds housed separately, when high egg producers are all placed together in a multiple-bird colony, cagewide fertility plummets (Muir, 1996). It turns out the best egg producers are also the most competitive birds, and in a group setting, they quickly begin fighting over food, space, and territory; these intragroup conflicts then drive egg production down and bird mortality up. Chicken farmers take note: If you want to maximize group-level productivity, you need harmony, and it seems that hierarchy provides the key.

There is some evidence that the opposite appears to be the case, however, for humans. Research has found that inequality in groups can impair group functioning and performance. For example, more equality in members' contributions to group discussion leads to better group performance on a variety of tasks (Woolley, Chabris, Pentland, Hashmi, & Malone, 2010). Similarly, wider disparities in pay increase organizational attrition (Wade, O'Reilly, & Pollock, 2006) and predict worse on-field performance in Major League Baseball (Bloom, 1999). Across corporations and baseball diamonds, hierarchical differentiation appears to hurt commitment and performance. Consistent with these data, many political ideologies (e.g., Marx & Engels, 1848/1948), libertarian principles (Hancock et al., 1776), and utopian visions (Bellamy, 1888) have supported the creation of egalitarian social structures.

Despite these compelling data and various attempts to model societies along egalitarian principles, hierarchy appears to be a universal default for human social organization (Fiske, 2010). Hierarchy forms rapidly in human groups, requiring only minimal social interaction to emerge (Anderson & Kilduff, 2009; Van Vugt, 2006). And once formed, hierarchy is self-perpetuating (Magee & Galinsky, 2008). The ubiquity and tenacity of hierarchy as a social structure (Leavitt, 2005) indicate that it has social-evolutionary value (Van Vugt, 2006; Van Vugt, Hogan, & Kaiser, 2008) and provide the basis for functional theories of hierarchy. These theories posit that when a group resolves itself into a clear hierarchy, this enhances

Why do you suppose this would be the case?

Interestingly, people differ in their attitude toward whether society should be hierarchically organized. Sidanius (Sidanius, Liu, Shaw, & Pratto, 1994) calls this "social dominance orientation." Those who believe it is normal and natural for society to be ordered hierarchically are "high SDOs," and those who believe everyone should be equal are called "low SDOs." As a side note, those high in SDO are more likely to be intolerant of those who are different from them (and to be prejudiced).

Corresponding Author:

Richard Ronay, Columbia University, Graduate School of Business, Uris Hall 3022, Broadway, New York, NY 10027

E-mail: r.ronay@columbia.edu

the lot of all group members. The central tenet of these theories is that the unequal distribution of power within groups facilitates the coordination of individuals' efforts and ultimately benefits the groups as wholes (Halevy, Chou, & Galinsky, 2011; Van Vugt et al., 2008). When there is a clear hierarchy, division of labor and patterns of deference reduce conflict, facilitate coordination, and ultimately improve productivity. When a clear hierarchy is absent, competition, conflict, and a lack of clear role differentiation undermine group coordination and performance.

How do you think the unequal distribution of power in a group would actually promote each person's efforts and benefit the group as a whole?

Consistent with the predictions of functional theories, recent work has demonstrated that status conflicts within groups, like those of the chicken colonies containing all high-producing birds, can impair team performance. For instance, status disagreements within small work teams redirect energy and effort toward status contestation and away from group productivity (Bendersky & Hays, 2012). In research examining the group-level performance of Wall Street sell-side equity research analysts, the presence of too many high-achieving individuals within a single team had a negative effect on performance (Groysberg, Polzer, & Elfenbein, in press). These studies suggest that, for humans (as well as chickens) the presence of too many high-status individuals in a group creates all-consuming status contests that disrupt the integration of activities essential for group productivity. It is important to point out that in all of the studies we have cited, the researchers measured but did not manipulate levels of hierarchical differentiation. Here, we present the first studies in which the overall level of hierarchal differentiation was manipulated and effects on group productivity were then measured.

Why do you think this is the case?

Doesn't this seem like "hey, that seems like a fundamental question. How has no one really looked at this before now?"

Recent perspectives have suggested that the benefits of hierarchy are most pronounced in situations of procedural interdependence (Halevy et al., 2011). The various group-level processes that contribute to the advantages of hierarchy—enhanced coordination, reduced conflict, and increased cooperation—are most relevant in contexts involving high, rather than low, levels of procedural interdependence. For instance, although high levels of pay dispersion harm performance when interdependence is low (e.g., professional baseball teams; Bloom, 1999), pay dispersion benefits performance when procedural interdependence is high (e.g., professional basketball teams; Halevy, Chou, Galinsky, & Murnighan, in press).

Building on functional theories of hierarchy, we propose that hierarchical differentiation within groups improves performance especially when procedural interdependence is high. Procedural interdependence requires that a group coordinate individual efforts and integrate them into a group outcome. A high-functioning team needs both its leaders and its followers (Van Vugt et al., 2008), and too many of either is likely to present problems for coordination. Drawing off past research demonstrating that role differentiation and hierarchical differentiation tend to covary (Baron & Pfeffer, 1994; Gruenfeld & Tiedens, 2010), we propose that hierarchy can integrate differentiated roles into a coordinated and productive whole.

Hypothesis.

Good to define your terms.

Although the literature contains correlational evidence for the negative effects of the presence of too many high-power individuals (Groysberg et al., in press), the consequence of having too few high-power individuals remains an open question. A formal test of functional theories of hierarchy requires determining whether productivity goes down both when there are too many and when there are too few high-power individuals within a single group. At one level, the problems of having too few and too many powerful individuals are similar: no clear leader, no role differentiation, and therefore reduced coordination and lower productivity. However, the proximate reason for reduced differentiation, coordination, and productivity may be different in groups that have too few high-power individuals and those that have too many.

An unanswered question that the researchers propose to address in the present paper.

We predicted that a comparison between groups with all high-power individuals and groups with all low-power individuals would reveal greater intergroup conflict in the high-power groups. Given that we expected members of these high-power groups to jostle for control, we predicted that conflict would then undermine group performance. In essence, there would be too many leaders and too few followers in such groups. In contrast, we did not expect intragroup conflict to drive the performance decrements of groups comprising all low-power individuals. Although we did not specifically test the mechanism behind the impaired performance of such groups in the current research, it may be that they have too little hierarchy—too many followers with no leader—to effectively coordinate and integrate behavior or too little agency to drive the group forward.

In the experiments reported here, we manipulated hierarchical differentiation using two different dimensions of hierarchy: power and testosterone. Individual differences in testosterone predict desire for power (e.g., Schultheiss, Dargel, & Rohde, 2003) and dominance (e.g., Mazur & Booth, 1998), and high-testosterone individuals prefer being in high-power roles (Josephs, Sellers, Newman, & Mehta, 2006). In addition, experimental manipulations of power have been shown to increase circulating testosterone (Carney, Cuddy, & Yap, 2010). Thus, power and testosterone feed into and mutually reinforce each other, and lead to the formation of hierarchies via dominance.

In each experiment, we created three types of groups: groups consisting of all high-power or high-testosterone individuals, groups consisting of all low-power or low-testosterone individuals, and groups consisting of a mix of individuals (1 high-power or high testosterone, 1 low-power or low-testosterone, and 1 baseline individual). The groups worked on a task characterized by a high level of procedural interdependence. Experiment 1 included an additional task that required little integration or coordination of individual efforts so that we could explore whether hierarchy facilitates performance on a procedurally independent task.

This research makes a number of important contributions. It is the first in which different levels of hierarchical differentiation were created in small groups whose performance was then measured. Also, we used multiple bases of hierarchy— power and testosterone—to establish the robust advantage of hierarchical differentiation in procedurally interdependent groups. Further, we demonstrated the conditions under which hierarchy matters; we found that there is no effect of hierarchy on performance on a procedurally independent task. Finally, we established that both groups of all high-testosterone individuals and groups of all low-testosterone individuals perform worse than hierarchically differentiated groups, but that the same process does not account for these two effects. Like the chickens discussed at the outset of this article, groups of all high-testosterone members have more conflict than groups of all low-testosterone members and groups whose members have different levels of testosterone; moreover, conflict mediates the lower productivity of the high-testosterone groups but not the lower productivity of the low-testosterone groups.

EXPERIMENT 1

In Experiment 1, we manipulated hierarchical differentiation by priming participants with a high-power, low-power, or baseline prime, and then placing them into 3-person groups of all high-power individuals, all low-power individuals, or a combination of 1 high-power, 1 low-power, and 1 baseline participant. Each group then engaged in two tasks. The first task was characterized by a high level of procedural interdependence: Groups created sentences, each

---

Margin notes:

More hypotheses.

What the researchers are doing here is making the case for why their research question is important, and perhaps why the way they plan to address it has merit. But the wording of the first sentence is a bit unusual. Normally this is the kind of sentence you'd find at the beginning of the discussion, after the results are known. One can't really say their research makes "an important contribution" before one knows the results. What if your results don't pan out? Then your research would not likely see the light of day (wouldn't get accepted for publication, and thus wouldn't make any contribution). So perhaps it might be better to word that first sentence like, "this research aims to address several unanswered questions, and it is designed to do so in the following novel ways."

So . . . what kind of design is this? (Hint: it is a between-subjects design.) How many IVs are there, and how many levels in each IV?

of which had to include at least one word from each group member. The second task was characterized by a low level of procedural inter-dependence: Participants generated novel uses for common household items. We predicted that the hierarchically differentiated groups of 1 high-power participant, 1 low-power participant, and 1 baseline participant would outperform both groups of all high-power individuals and groups of all low-power individuals when procedural interdependence was high. In contrast, we predicted that hierarchy would not enhance performance when procedural interdependence was low.

Method

Participants. Participants were 138 undergraduate students (37 male, 101 female) who were randomly assigned to the high-power, low-power, and baseline priming conditions. Participants were organized into same-sex triads: (a) groups of 3 high-power participants, (b) groups of 3 low-power participants, and (c) groups of 1 high-power participant, 1 low-power participant, and 1 baseline participant. Triads worked together on two tasks under face-to-face conditions; one was a procedurally interdependent task, and the other was a procedurally independent task.

Power manipulation. To manipulate power, we had participants recall and write about an incident in their lives (Galinsky, Gruenfeld, & Magee, 2003). Participants in the high-power condition recalled a time when they had power over another individual. Participants in the low-power condition recalled a time when someone had power over them. Those in the baseline condition recalled their last trip to the supermarket (Rucker & Galinsky, 2008).

High-procedural-interdependence task. To measure group productivity under conditions of high procedural interdependence, we used a modified version of Crown's (2007) letter-word-sentence game. While group members were seated together at a table, each participant was presented with a unique matrix of 16 letters and instructed to find and record on a separate sheet as many words of 3 or more adjoining letters as possible. Letter matrices were matched within and between triads for number of potential words ($M = 142.33$, $SD = 5.51$). Groups then had the shared goal of combining their individual words to create sentences. Each sentence required at least one word from each group member. Thus, to succeed on this task, group members were required to coordinate and integrate their individual efforts and unique information to create sentences. The groups were given 5 min to complete the task. Our measure of group productivity was the total number of sentences created by each group.

Low-procedural-interdependence task. To measure group productivity under conditions of low procedural interdependence, we used a creative generation task that allowed individuals to work independently within their groups (e.g., Markman, Lindberg, Kray, & Galinsky, 2007). Groups were asked to generate as many novel uses for three common items (i.e., newspaper, paper clip, and brick) as they could. They were given 2 min per item to complete the task. Our measure of productivity was the total number of individual suggestions from each group. Thus, unlike in the letter-word-sentence game, success on this task was not contingent on the successful coordination and integration of efforts. Indeed, a single group member could successfully complete the task alone if need be.

This kind of task—high interdependence—also characterizes the type of activity that Aronson (1978) used in his famous Jigsaw Classroom technique designed to reduce prejudice between group members. In that task, each group member has a unique piece of information that is crucial to the completion of the task. The group members must all cooperate or the task won't be completed. Each member is highly interdependent and is crucial to the group. Similarly here, each member has to contribute one (or more) words to the sentences or they fail the task. Interestingly, then, the Jigsaw Classroom procedure works to make everyone equal (and reduce intergroup prejudice), whereas the authors here are predicting that hierarchy (and inequality) and interdependence will result in better group performance.

Restatement of the hypotheses.

One thing a researcher needs to be cognizant of always is any possible gender effects. Will men and women differ in how they react to the IVs and the DVs? One way some researchers solve this is by only using males or only females.

One issue with this: you're going to have many more female triads than males, due to the imbalance of males to females they have recruited for the experiment. This could present a problem, or not. We'll have to see.

This method (writing in detail about a particular event) works to help the subject feel again the main feeling he or she experienced when he or she originally experienced the event. This is done a lot in experiments that need to manipulate the mood of the participants. Here, it is used to

Results

High-procedural-interdependence task. There was a significant effect of group composition on productivity in this task, $F(2, 43) = 3.46$, $p = .04$, $\eta^2 = .14$ (see Fig. 1). As predicted, a planned contrast revealed that the mixed-power groups ($M = 4.50$, $SD = 3.06$) were more productive than the high-power groups ($M = 2.53$, $SD = 1.06$) and the low-power groups ($M = 3.07$, $SD = 1.79$), $t(43) = 2.54$, $p = .02$, $d = 0.75$. Pairwise comparisons revealed that the mixed-power groups were more productive than the high-power groups, $t(43) = 2.53$, $p = .02$, $d = 0.92$, and marginally more productive than the low-power groups, $t(43) = 1.85$, $p = .07$, $d = 0.59$. There was no difference in performance between the high- and low-power groups, $t(43) = 0.68$, $p = .50$, $d = 0.32$.

Low-procedural-interdependence task. As predicted, on the procedurally independent task, no differences emerged between the high-power ($M = 16.58$, $SD = 6.42$), mixed-power ($M = 19.33$, $SD = 6.18$), and low-power ($M = 18.07$, $SD = 2.37$) groups, $F(2, 43) = 1.03$, $p = .37$, $\eta^2 = .05$. When procedural interdependence was low, there was no effect of hierarchical differentiation on productivity.

EXPERIMENT 2

The next experiment had two goals. First, we wanted to examine the biological foundations of hierarchical differentiation, using a measure of individual differences in prenatal testosterone exposure, which has organizing effects on the development of the brain and body (Manning, 2002). Second, we wanted to explore the processes that produce lower productivity in the absence of hierarchical differentiation.

Discussion

Experiment 1 provides the first experimental evidence that hierarchical differentiation facilitates greater productivity. Hierarchically differentiated groups—those that had a mix of

FIG. 1.   Results from Experiment 1: mean number of sentences created as a function of group composition. Error bars indicate ±1 *SEM*.

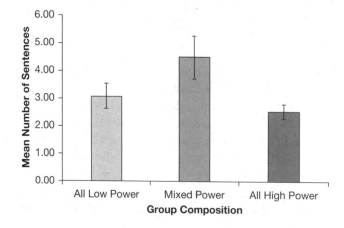

high-power, low-power, and baseline participants—were more productive than groups of all high-power individuals and groups of all low-power individuals. Additionally, Experiment 1 provides support for the hypothesis that hierarchical differentiation is most beneficial in environments characterized by high levels of procedural interdependence (Halevy et al., 2011), as group composition had no effect on performance on the procedurally independent creative generation task.

One marker of in utero testosterone exposure is the ratio between the length of the index finger (2D) and the length of the ring finger (4D); lower ratios indicate exposure to higher levels of androgens during prenatal development (Manning, 2002). Using the 2D:4D ratio as our measure of differences in prenatal testosterone exposure, we created groups consisting of all high-testosterone individuals, all low-testosterone individuals, or a mix of high-, low-, and average-testosterone individuals.

There is a large literature on the relationship between circulating testosterone and dominance-seeking behaviors in humans (e.g., Mazur & Booth, 1998), nonhuman primates (e.g., Beehner, Bergman, Cheney, Seyfarth, & Whitten, 2006), and a range of other animals (e.g., Ruiz-de-la-Torre & Manteca, 1999). The overwhelming finding within this literature is that higher levels of circulating testosterone motivate the pursuit and possession of power and dominance (e.g., Schultheiss et al., 2003) and that experimental manipulations of power increase testosterone levels (Carney et al., 2010). This hormone-fueled drive for power and dominance results in selective attention to potential threats to one's hierarchical status (van Honk, Tuiten, Hermans, et al., 2001; van Honk, Tuiten, Verbaten, et al., 1999), and when placed in low-ranking roles, high-testosterone individuals experience elevated emotional and physiological arousal, increased concerns with their current standing, and diminished cognitive function (Josephs et al., 2006). Thus, it seems likely that individual differences in testosterone play a role in the formation of naturally occurring hierarchies.

Research examining the relationship between prenatal testosterone exposure and dominance-seeking behaviors has produced results that are conceptually consistent with the effects of circulating testosterone (for a review, see Millet, 2011). For instance, in both men and women, 2D:4D ratio has been shown to predict a number of dominance-seeking behaviors (e.g., Millet & Dewitte, 2009; Ronay & Galinsky, 2011), including retributional responding following provocation (Ronay & Galinsky, 2011), sporting ability and within-team performance (Manning, 2002), and the pursuit of status-relevant financial resources following subordination (Millet & Dewitte, 2008). We therefore predicted that limiting within-group variance in this biological marker of dominance seeking would disrupt the development of a clear hierarchy and thereby reduce group productivity.

As noted, our second goal was to understand the processes that produce lower productivity when hierarchical differentiation is compressed. Because high levels of testosterone motivate the pursuit of dominance, we predicted that groups consisting exclusively of high-testosterone individuals would experience elevated competition and conflict as group members jostled for dominance, and that this conflict would impair productivity. In contrast, although we anticipated that groups consisting entirely of low-testosterone individuals would experience similar productivity decrements as a result of low hierarchical differentiation, we did not expect conflict to emerge within these groups or to drive their lower productivity. Specifically, we expected that intragroup conflict would mediate performance decrements when there were too many high-testosterone individuals in a group, but not when there were

This is the classic chicken-and-egg situation with testosterone. It is correlated with power/dominance, but we can't yet state causality. Does having more testosterone cause one to seek more power, or does having more power generate higher levels of testosterone? This pattern has also been found with aggression and testosterone.

First prediction for experiment 2.

That is, having all (or most) of the group be the same in terms of their testosterone (as measured by the 2D:4D ratio).

Second prediction.

Third prediction.

too many low-testosterone individuals. In those groups with broadly distributed levels of prenatal testosterone exposure, we expected to see the benefits of hierarchical differentiation: both higher productivity and less conflict.

Method

Participants and procedure. In Experiment 2, 109 (21 male, 88 female) second-year psychology students were pretested for individual differences in right-hand 2D:4D. We then manipulated hierarchical differentiation by creating (a) groups of high-testosterone participants, (b) groups of low-testosterone participants, and (c) groups of high-testosterone, low-testosterone, and average-testosterone participants. Each group engaged in the high-procedural-interdependence task from Experiment 1. Finally, participants reported on the level of conflict experienced within their group.

Again with the gender imbalance!

Digit ratio and group formation. Each participant's digit ratio was calculated by dividing the length of the fourth digit on the right hand by the length of the second digit on the right hand ($M = 0.97$, $SD = 0.03$; Manning, 2002). A criterion for "high" prenatal testosterone exposure was set at 1 standard deviation below the mean digit ratio, and a criterion for low prenatal testosterone exposure was set at 1 standard deviation above the mean digit ratio. Although the digit ratios of male ($M = 0.94$, $SD = 0.03$) and female ($M = 0.97$, $SD = 0.03$) participants differed significantly, $F(1, 106) = 10.88$, $p < .005$, we did not standardize digit ratios within sex because the influence of digit ratio on behavior has been found to be consistent across the sexes (e.g., Millet & Dewitte, 2009; Ronay & Galinsky, 2011). Using these categorization criteria, we formed groups consisting of all high-testosterone individuals, groups consisting of all low-testosterone individuals, and groups consisting of a mix of high-testosterone, low-testosterone, and average-testosterone individuals. The groups ranged in size from 3 to 5 participants ($M = 3.81$, $SD = 0.47$).

High-procedural-interdependence task. Group productivity was measured using the same modified letter-word-sentence game as in Experiment 1, except that there were two rounds and groups were given 10 min per round to complete the task. To control for the variance in group size, we divided each group's total number of sentences in Rounds 1 ($M = 23.41$, $SD = 9.48$) and 2 ($M = 27.97$, $SD = 13.80$) by the number of participants in that group. Because productivity was not affected by the interaction between round and group composition, $F(1, 23) = 0.16$, $p = .70$, we averaged across the two rounds and used group-size-adjusted productivity as our primary dependent variable ($M = 6.72$, $SD = 2.58$).

If you look at the correlations under column 1 in Table 1 above, you'll see what the authors are talking about. Most of the items conceptually seem to "hang" together due to most of them having decent or higher correlations with the first item (you usually want correlations of .7 or higher).

Intragroup conflict. To determine the level of conflict present within each group, we administered a seven-item measure (response scale from 1, *very true*, to 7, *very untrue*; $\alpha = .93$). Table 1 presents a list of the items along with a statistical summary of the responses (means, standard deviations, and intercorrelations). Although the items were intended to capture a breadth of conflict domains (i.e., process conflict, status conflict, relationship conflict, and task conflict; see Bendersky & Hays, 2012), the obtained reliability value indicated that the scale measured a consistent, unifying construct, so we averaged each participant's responses across all items. We then created a group-level measure of conflict by averaging across individuals' responses within triads.

TABLE 1 Results for the intragroup-conflict items in Experiment 2: Mean responses and interitem correlations

| | | | Correlations | | | | | |
Item	M	SD	1	2	3	4	5	6
1. There was conflict within our group	1.71	0.69	—					
2. There was conflict about task responsibilities within our group	1.76	0.93	.81	—				
3. There was emotional conflict within our group	1.36	0.42	.77	.53	—			
4. I felt comfortable with my role within our group (reverse-scored)	2.34	1.08	.71	.73	.58	—		
5. There was an open and supporting atmosphere within our group (reverse-scored)	2.25	0.74	.60	.60	.55	.58	—	
6. I was listened to within our group (reverse-scored)	2.29	0.03	.72	.72	.70	.84	.71	—
7. During the games I felt connected with one or more other players (reverse-scored)	3.08	1.17	.69	.73	.59	.80	.60	.74

Results

High-procedural-interdependence task. There was a significant effect of group composition on productivity in the letter-word-sentence game, $F(2, 23) = 3.88$, $p = .04$, $\eta^2 = .25$ (see Fig. 2). A planned contrast found that the mixed-testosterone groups ($M = 8.07$, $SD = 2.80$) were more productive than the high-testosterone ($M = 5.01$, $SD = 2.64$) and the low-testosterone ($M = 5.61$, $SD = 1.32$) groups, $t(23) = 2.79$, $p = .01$, $d = 1.12$. Pairwise comparisons revealed that mixed testosterone groups were more productive than both high-testosterone groups, $t(23) = 2.32$, $p = .03$, $d = 1.13$, and low-testosterone groups, $t(23) = 2.16$, $p = .04$, $d = 1.19$. There was no difference in productivity between high- and low-testosterone groups, $t(23) = 0.36$, $p = .72$, $d = 0.30$.

Intragroup conflict. Group composition also had a significant effect on conflict, $F(2, 23) = 3.43$, $p = .05$, $\eta^2 = .30$ (see Fig. 3). A planned contrast found that the high-testosterone groups ($M = 2.29$, $SD = 0.40$) experienced more intragroup conflict than the mixed-testosterone groups ($M = 1.77$, $SD = 0.36$) and the low-testosterone groups ($M = 1.84$, $SD = 0.43$), $t(23) = 2.49$, $p = .02$, $d = 1.27$. Pairwise comparisons revealed that the high-testosterone groups experienced more intragroup conflict than the mixed-testosterone groups, $t(23) = 2.59$, $d = 1.37$, $p = .02$, and marginally more conflict than the low-testosterone groups, $t(23) = 1.98$, $p = .06$, $d = 1.08$. There was no difference in reported conflict between the low-testosterone and mixed-testosterone groups, $t(23) = 0.42$, $p = .68$, $d = 0.12$.

Most productive: mixed-testosterone group.

Same pattern as experiment 1, but this time, the mixed group was significantly more productive than both the high-testosterone AND low-testosterone groups. (See Table 2 below.)

High-testosterone groups had more conflict than the other two groups.

FIG. 2.   Results from Experiment 2: mean number of sentences created as a function of group composition. Error bars indicate ±1 *SEM*.

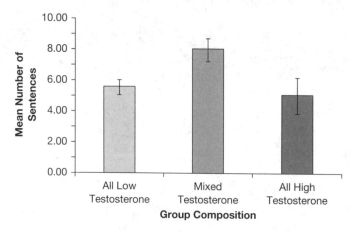

Mediation by conflict. We next tested our hypothesis that conflict would mediate the effect of group composition on productivity in the high-testosterone groups, but not the low-testosterone groups (i.e., moderated mediation; Preacher, Rucker, & Hayes, 2007). A regression analysis comparing the high-testosterone and the mixed-testosterone groups revealed that the productivity decrements in the high-testosterone groups were mediated by intragroup conflict (see Fig. 4). A bootstrapping procedure (Preacher & Hayes, 2004) with 10,000 resamples confirmed that conflict significantly mediated the relationship between the high-testosterone condition and reduced productivity (indirect effect = –1.08, *SE* = 0.79; the 95% bias-corrected confidence interval did not include zero: [–2.99, –0.01]). In contrast, a regression analysis comparing the low-testosterone and the mixed-testosterone groups revealed that intragroup conflict did not mediate the reduction in group productivity in the low-testosterone groups (see Fig. 5). This lack of mediation was confirmed with the same bootstrapping technique (indirect effect = 0.22, *SE* = 0.41; the 95% bias-corrected confidence interval did include zero: [–0.47, 1.23]).

GENERAL DISCUSSION

This research experimentally tested for the first time the central prediction of functional theories of hierarchy: that when power is distributed, intragroup conflicts go down while coordination and productivity go up. We tested these hypotheses by manipulating hierarchical differentiation based on two different dimensions of dominance: a power priming manipulation in Experiment 1 and a biological marker of individual differences in prenatal testosterone exposure in Experiment 2. In Experiment 1, hierarchically differentiated groups—those with a distribution of individuals with high, low, and baseline power—outperformed groups comprising all high-power individuals and groups comprising all low-power individuals. Experiment 1 also demonstrated that the functional benefits of hierarchy are most pronounced under conditions of high procedural interdependence: When group productivity was simply the sum of participants' efforts, hierarchical differentiation did not influence productivity. Consistent with the findings of Experiment 1 is research showing that higher levels of pay dispersion facilitate performance when procedural interdependence is high (e.g., professional basketball;

FIG. 3. Results from Experiment 2: mean level of conflict reported within groups as a function of group composition. Error bars indicate ±1 *SEM*.

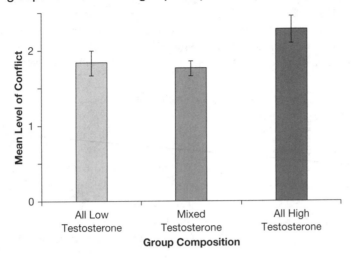

Halevy et al., in press) but can impair performance when interdependence is low (e.g., professional baseball teams; Bloom, 1999).

In Experiment 2, we replicated this pattern of results, using a biological marker of dominance seeking (2D:4D) to manipulate the degree of hierarchical differentiation. Hierarchically differentiated groups (i.e., groups with differential levels of prenatal testosterone exposure) outperformed groups comprising all high-testosterone individuals and groups comprising all low-testosterone individuals.

Experiment 2 also demonstrated that the processes that produced lower productivity differed between the high-testosterone and the low-testosterone groups. The groups consisting exclusively of high-testosterone individuals experienced higher levels of intragroup conflict compared with both the mixed- and the low-testosterone groups. Furthermore, intra-group conflict mediated the performance decrements for the high-testosterone groups, but not the low-testosterone groups. Future research should establish the precise reasons for the poorer performance observed in the groups of all low-power individuals. Whereas groups consisting of all high-power individuals have too many leaders and too few followers,

FIG. 4. Results from Experiment 2: mediation model of the effect of group composition (high-testosterone groups vs. mixed-testosterone groups) on productivity via intragroup conflict. The numbers along the paths are standardized regression coefficients; the numbers in parentheses are simultaneous regression coefficients. Asterisks indicate significant values (*$p < .05$, **$p < .01$).

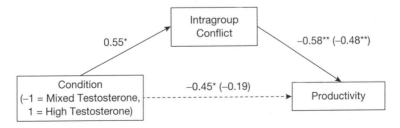

groups consisting of all low-power individuals may have too many followers with no leader. Just as too much conflict can inhibit the ability of high-power groups to coordinate their efforts, ambiguous role differentiation may impair the coordination of low-power groups and hinder their performance. We suspect that a lack of agency may also be at play in groups consisting of all low-power individuals. Future research should videotape groups to gather real-time evidence of the emergence of hierarchy and leadership, role differentiation, and conflict in groups.

This research has practical implications for the composition of groups and the distribution of power and status within groups. Despite the widespread intuition that teams of high performers will outperform their competition, our data contribute to a growing body of literature (Groysberg et al., in press; Halevy et al., 2011) suggesting that this is not always the case. Our findings indicate that such teams are likely to experience elevated levels of conflict, reduced role differentiation, less coordination and integration, and poorer productivity compared with teams that have a broader distribution of power and status.

This research focused on power and dominance motives as the foundation for hierarchy, and future research might examine whether all forms of hierarchy are similarly functional. Recent theories have proposed that hierarchies can be conceptualized as based either in prestige or in dominance (Cheng, Tracy, & Henrich, 2010; Henrich & Gil-White, 2001). Prestige represents influence via respect and reverence and is accorded to people who are believed to possess socially desirable skills or expertise. In contrast, "dominance is typically seen in individuals who control access to resources" (Cheng et al., 2010, p. 335) or who enter every situation "expecting to be in charge or to compete for control" (Fiske, 2010, p. 942). Future research should explore whether and in what ways prestige hierarchies have the same functional consequences as dominance hierarchies.

CONCLUSION

Despite the overt appeal of egalitarian social structures, humans have an enduring implicit preference for hierarchy (Gruenfeld & Tiedens, 2010). Our data suggest that this preference may have its roots in the utilitarian value of distributed power. Pecking orders, it seems, are not just for the birds.

FIG. 5. Results from Experiment 2: mediation model of the effect of group composition (low-testosterone groups vs. mixed-testosterone groups) on productivity via intragroup conflict. The numbers along the paths are standardized regression coefficients; the numbers in parentheses are simultaneous regression coefficients. Asterisks indicate significant values (*p < .05).

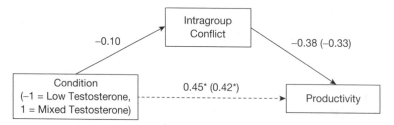

Acknowledgments

We thank Courtney von Hippel for assistance with facilitating data collection for Experiment 2.

Declaration of Conflicting Interests

The authors declared that they had no conflicts of interest with respect to their authorship or the publication of this article.

References

Anderson, C., & Kilduff, G. J. (2009). Why do dominant personalities attain influence in face-to-face groups? The competence-signaling effects of trait dominance. *Journal of Personality and Social Psychology, 96*, 491–503.

Baron, J. N., & Pfeffer, J. (1994). The social psychology of organizations and inequality. *Social Psychology Quarterly, 57*, 190–209.

Beehner, J. C., Bergman, T. J., Cheney, D. L., Seyfarth, R. M., & Whitten, P. L. (2006). Testosterone predicts future dominance rank and mating activity among male chacma baboons. *Behavioral Ecology and Sociobiology, 59*, 469–479.

Bellamy, E. (1888). *Looking backward, 2000–1887*. Boston, MA: Ticknor and Co.

Bendersky, C., & Hays, N. A. (2012). Status conflict in groups. *Organization Science, 23*, 323–340.

Bloom, M. (1999). The performance effects of pay dispersion on individuals and organizations. *Academy of Management Journal, 42*, 25–40.

Carney, D. R., Cuddy, A. J. C., & Yap, A. J. (2010). Power posing: Brief nonverbal displays affect neuroendocrine levels and risk tolerance. *Psychological Science, 21*, 1363–1368.

Cheng, J. T., Tracy, J. L., & Henrich, J. (2010). Pride, personality, and the evolutionary foundations of human social status. *Evolution & Human Behavior, 31*, 334–347.

Crown, D. F. (2007). Effects of structurally competitive multilevel goals for an interdependent task. *Small Group Research, 38*, 265–288.

Fiske, S. T. (2010). Interpersonal stratification: Status, power, and subordination. In S. T. Fiske, D. T. Gilbert, & G. Lindzey (Eds.), *Handbook of social psychology* (5th ed., pp. 941–982). New York, NY: Wiley.

Galinsky, A. D., Gruenfeld, D. H., & Magee, J. C. (2003). From power to action. *Journal of Personality and Social Psychology, 85*, 453–466.

Groysberg, B., Polzer, J., & Elfenbein, H. (in press). Too many cooks spoil the broth: How high status individuals decrease group effectiveness. *Organization Science*.

Gruenfeld, D. H., & Tiedens, L. Z. (2010). Organizational preferences and their consequences. In S. T. Fiske, D. T. Gilbert, & G. Lindzey (Eds.), *Handbook of social psychology* (5th ed., pp. 1252–1287). New York, NY: Wiley.

Halevy, N., Chou, E. Y., & Galinsky, A. D. (2011). A functional model of hierarchy: Why, how, and when vertical differentiation enhances group performance. *Organizational Psychology Review, 1*, 32–52.

Halevy, N., Chou, E. Y., Galinsky, A. D., & Murnighan, K. (in press). When hierarchy wins: Evidence from the National Basketball Association. *Social Psychological & Personality Science*.

Hancock, J., Gwinnett, B., Hall, L., Walton, G., Hooper, W., Hewes, J., . . . Thornton, M. (1776). *The United States Declaration of Independence*. Retrieved from http://www.ushistory.org/declaration/document/

Henrich, J., & Gil-White, F. J. (2001). The evolution of prestige: Freely conferred deference as a mechanism for enhancing the benefits of cultural transmission. *Evolution & Human Behavior, 22*, 165–196.

Josephs, R. A., Sellers, J. G., Newman, M. L., & Mehta, P. H. (2006). The mismatch effect: When testosterone and status are at odds. *Journal of Personality and Social Psychology, 90*, 999–1013.

Leavitt, H. J. (2005). *Top down: Why hierarchies are here to stay and how to manage them more effectively*. Boston, MA: Harvard Business School Press.

Magee, J. C., & Galinsky, A. D. (2008). Social hierarchy: The self-reinforcing nature of power and status. *Academy of Management Annals, 2*, 351–398.

Manning, J. T. (2002). *Digit ratio: A pointer to fertility, behavior, and health*. New Brunswick, NJ: Rutgers University Press.

Markman, K. D., Lindberg, M. J., Kray, L. J., & Galinsky, A. D. (2007). Implications of counterfactual structure for creative generation and analytical problem-solving. *Personality and Social Psychology Bulletin, 33*, 312–324.

Marx, K., & Engels, F. (1948). *The Communist manifesto.* New York, NY: International. (Original work published 1848)

Mazur, A., & Booth, A. (1998). Testosterone and dominance in men. *Brain & Behavioral Sciences, 21*, 353–397.

Millet, K. (2011). An interactionist perspective on the relation between 2D:4D and behavior: An overview of (moderated) relationships between 2D:4D and economic decision making. *Personality and Individual Differences, 51*, 397–401.

Millet, K., & Dewitte, S. (2008). A subordinate status position increases the present value of financial resources for low 2D:4D men. *American Journal of Human Biology, 20*, 110–115.

Millet, K., & Dewitte, S. (2009). The presence of aggression cues inverts the relation between digit ratio (2D:4D) and pro-social behaviour in a dictator game. *British Journal of Psychology, 100*, 151–162.

Muir, W. M. (1996). Group selection for adaptation to multiple-hen cages: Selection program and direct responses. *Poultry Science, 75*, 447–458.

Preacher, K. J., & Hayes, A. F. (2004). SPSS and SAS procedures for estimating indirect effects in simple mediation models. *Behavior Research Methods, Instruments, & Computers, 36*, 717–731.

Preacher, K. J., Rucker, D. D., & Hayes, A. F. (2007). Addressing moderated mediation hypotheses: Theory, methods, and prescriptions. *Multivariate Behavioral Research, 42*, 185–227.

Ronay, R., & Galinsky, A. D. (2011). *Lex talionis*: Testosterone and the law of retaliation. *Journal of Experimental Social Psychology, 47*, 702–705.

Rucker, D. D., & Galinsky, A. D. (2008). Desire to acquire: Powerlessness and compensatory consumption. *Journal of Consumer Research, 35*, 257–267.

Ruiz-de-la-Torre, J., & Manteca, X. (1999). Effects of testosterone on aggressive behavior after social mixing in male lambs. *Physiology & Behavior, 68*, 109–113.

Schultheiss, O. C., Dargel, A., & Rohde, W. (2003). Implicit motives and gonadal steroid hormones: Effects of menstrual cycle phase, oral contraceptive use, and relationship status. *Hormones and Behavior, 43*, 293–301.

van Honk, J., Tuiten, A., Hermans, E., Putman, P., Koppeschaar, H., Thijssen, J., . . . van Doornen, L. (2001). A single administration of testosterone induces cardiac accelerative responses to angry faces in healthy young women. *Behavioral Neuroscience, 115*, 238–242.

van Honk, J., Tuiten, A., Verbaten, R., van den Hout, M., Koppeschaar, H., Thijssen, J., & de Haan, E. (1999). Correlations among salivary testosterone, mood, and selective attention to threat in humans. *Hormones and Behavior, 36*, 17–24.

Van Vugt, M. (2006). Evolutionary origins of leadership and followership. *Personality and Social Psychology Review, 10*, 354–372.

Van Vugt, M., Hogan, R., & Kaiser, R. B. (2008). Leadership, followership, and evolution: Some lessons from the past. *American Psychologist, 63*, 182–196.

Wade, J. B., O'Reilly, C. A. I., & Pollock, T. G. (2006). Overpaid CEOs and underpaid managers: Fairness and executive compensation. *Organization Science, 17*, 527–544.

Woolley, A. W., Chabris, C. F., Pentland, A., Hashmi, N., & Malone, T. W. (2010). Evidence for a collective intelligence factor in the performance of human groups. *Science, 330*, 686–688.

POST-ARTICLE DISCUSSION

There were a number of interesting methodological questions that were raised in the article margin notes that I hope you took some time to contemplate. These questions (e.g., potential effect of gender imbalance of subjects) could be potential sources of error for the experiments. It was also interesting that the method section of both studies didn't have a procedure subsection, similar to how most studies are written. It is not a fatal flaw, but it makes it a lot easier for the reader to conceptualize exactly what is happening to the subject in the session and whether there might be any possible problems (i.e., confounds, or areas where subjects could become suspicious or biased). Another question was the lack of a power manipulation check in Experiment 1. Similarly, do you think there was a way to examine perceived dominance feelings among those in Experiment 2?

Recall elsewhere in this book we discussed the importance of exploring an idea via multiple methods and with multiple measures, in order to have more confidence in the validity of a particular finding. The present two experiments are good examples of this. Experiment 1 looks at the influence of power on group productivity. Experiment 2 does a conceptual replication of this question but uses dominance as an analogue of power, and the immediate index of dominance is the use of a measure of testosterone. To the degree that both approaches converge on the same result, we have that much more confidence in the result. Experiment 1 showed that greater power differentiation enhances group productivity. Experiment 2 showed that dominance differentiation also enhances group productivity. Taken together, the data indicate that people prefer hierarchically organized groups, and they perform best in those structured groups.

THINGS TO THINK ABOUT

1. The authors didn't appear to have a manipulation check for Experiment 1. How would you have designed a check to make sure that subjects responded to your power manipulation in the intended way?

2. What kind of design was Experiment 1 versus Experiment 2?

3. Do you think there were any problems with the imbalance of male and female subjects in both experiments? (The authors never talked about this.)

4. What do you think of the authors' operationalization of high versus low testosterone, in the form of differences in measurement of the fourth finger versus second finger? Is there a better, more accurate measure of testosterone that you can think of? If so, would its use be better than the measure these researchers used?

5. What are the practical applications of these research findings? What are some unanswered questions you have that future researchers might address about power hierarchies in groups?

References

Aboud, F. (1988). *Children and prejudice.* Cambridge, MA: Blackwell.

Adorno, T. W., Frenkel–Brunswik, E., Levinson, D. J., & Sanford, R. N. (1950). *The authoritarian personality.* New York, NY: Harper & Row.

Allport, F. H. (1924). *Social psychology.* Boston, MA: Houghton Mifflin.

Allport, G. W. (1935). Attitudes. In C. Murchison (Ed.), *A handbook of social psychology* (pp. 798–844). Worchester, MA: Clark University Press.

Allport, G. W. (1954). *The nature of prejudice.* Reading, MA: Addison-Wesley.

Allport, G. W. (1985). The historical background of social psychology. In G. Lindzey & E. Aronson (Eds.), *Handbook of social psychology* (3rd ed., Vol. 1, pp. 1–46). New York, NY: Random House.

Allport, G. W., & Postman, L. (1947). *The psychology of rumor.* Oxford, England: Henry Holt.

Altemeyer, B. (1981). *Right-wing authoritarianism.* Winnipeg, Canada: University of Manitoba Press.

Ambady, N., Bernieri, F. J., & Richeson, J. A. (2000). Towards histology of social behavior: Judgmental accuracy from thin slices of the behavioral stream. In M. P. Zanna (Ed.), *Advances in experimental social psychology* (Vol. 32, pp. 201–271). New York, NY: Academic Press.

Amir, Y. (1969). Contact hypothesis in ethnic relations. *Psychological Bulletin, 71*(5), 319–342.

Anderson, C. A., Lepper, M. R., & Ross, L. (1980). Perseverance of social theories: The role of explanation in the persistence of discredited information. *Journal of Personality and Social Psychology, 39*, 1037–1049.

Aronson, E., Brewer, M., & Carlsmith, J. M. (1985). Experimentation in social psychology. In G. Lindzey & E. Aronson (Eds.), *The handbook of social psychology* (3rd ed., Vol. 1, pp. 441–486). New York, NY: Random House.

Aronson, E., Ellsworth, P. C., Carlsmith, J. M., & Gonzales, M. H. (1990). *Methods of research in social psychology* (2nd ed.). New York, NY: McGraw-Hill.

Aronson, E., Fried, C., & Stone, J. (1991). Overcoming denial and increasing intention to use condoms through the induction of hypocrisy. *American Journal of Public Health, 81*(12), 1636–1638.

Asch, S. (1946). Forming impressions of personality. *Journal of Abnormal and Social Psychology, 41*(3), 258–290.

Asch, S. E. (1951). Effects of group pressure upon the modification and distortion of judgment. In H. Guetzkow (Ed.), *Groups, leadership, and men* (pp. 222–236). Pittsburgh, PA: Carnegie.

Asch, S. E. (1956). Studies of independence and conformity: A minority of one against unanimous majority. *Psychological Monographs, 70*(416).

Ashmore, R. D., & Del Boca, F. K. (1981). Conceptual approaches to stereotypes and stereotyping. In D. L. Hamilton (Ed.), *Cognitive processes in stereotyping and intergroup behavior* (pp. 1–35). Hillsdale, NJ: Erlbaum.

Bales, R. F. (1958). Task roles and social roles in problem solving groups. In E. E. Maccoby, T. M. Newcomb, & E. L. Hartley (Eds.), *Readings in social psychology* (3rd ed., pp. 437–447). New York, NY: Holt.

Banaji, M. R., & Heiphetz, L. (2010). Attitudes. In S. T. Fiske, D. T. Gilbert, & G. Lindzey (Eds.), *Handbook of social psychology* (5th ed., Vol. 1, pp. 353–393). New York, NY: Wiley & Sons.

Bandura, A. (1978). Social learning theory of aggression. *Journal of Communication, 28*, 12–29.

Bandura, A., Ross, D., & Ross, S. (1961). Transmission of aggression through imitation of aggressive models. *Journal of Abnormal and Social Psychology, 63*, 575–582.

Bar, M., Neta, M., & Linz, H. (2006). Very first impressions. *Emotion, 6*, 269–278.

Barber, N. (2006). Why is violent crime so common in the Americas? *Aggressive Behavior, 32*, 442–450.

Bargh, J. A., & Thein, R. D. (1985). Individual construct accessibility, person memory, and the recall-judgment link: The case of information overload. *Journal of Personality and Social Psychology, 49*, 1129–1146.

Baron, R. S. (1986). Distraction/conflict theory: Progress and problems. In L. Berkowitz (Ed.), *Advances in experimental social psychology* (Vol. 19, pp. 1–40). Orlando, FL: Academic Press.

Batson, C. D. (1979). Generality of the "glow of goodwill": Effects of mood on helping and information acquisition. *Social Psychology Quarterly, 42*(2), 176–179.

Batson, C. D. (1987). Prosocial motivation: Is it ever truly altruistic? In L. Berkowitz (Ed.), *Advances in experimental social psychology* (Vol. 20, pp. 65–122). New York, NY: Academic Press.

Batson, C. D. (1991). *The altruism question: Toward a social-psychological answer.* Hillsdale, NJ: Erlbaum.

Batson, C. D. (1998). Altruism and prosocial behavior. In D. T. Gilbert, S. T. Fiske, & G. Lindzey (Eds.), *Handbook of social psychology* (4th ed., Vol. 2, pp. 282–316). New York, NY: McGraw-Hill.

Batson, C. D., & Coke, J. S. (1981). Empathy: A source of altruistic motivation for helping? In J. P. Rushton & R. M. Sorrentino (Eds.), *Altruism and helping behavior: Social, personality, and developmental perspectives* (pp. 167–187). Hillsdale, NJ: Erlbaum.

Batson, C. D., & Coke, J. S. (1983). Empathic motivation of helping behavior. In J. T. Cacioppo & R. E. Petty (Eds.), *Social psychophysiology: A sourcebook* (pp. 417–433). New York, NY: Guilford Press.

Batson, C. D., Fultz, J., & Schoenrade, P. A. (1987). Distress and empathy: Two qualitatively distinct vicarious emotions with different motivational consequences. *Journal of Personality, 55,* 19–39.

Batson, C. D., Lishner, D. A., & Stocks, E. L. (2015). The empathy-altruism hypothesis. In D. A. Schroeder & W. G. Graziano (Eds.), *The Oxford handbook of prosocial behavior* (pp. 259–281). New York, NY: Oxford University Press.

Beck, S. R., Robinson, E. J., Carroll, D. J., & Apperly, I. A. (2006). Children's thinking about counterfactuals and future hypotheticals. *Child Development, 77*(2), 413–426.

Berkowitz, L. (1989). Frustration-aggression hypothesis: Examination and reformulation. *Psychological Bulletin, 106,* 59–73.

Berkowitz, L. (1993). *Aggression: Its causes, consequences, and control.* New York, NY: McGraw-Hill.

Bettencourt, B. A., & Miller, N. (1996). Gender differences in aggression as a function of provocation: A meta-analysis. *Psychological Bulletin, 119,* 422–447.

Bickman, L. (1974). The social power of a uniform. *Journal of Applied Social Psychology, 4,* 47–61.

Blascovich, J., Mendes, W. B., Hunter, S. B., & Salomon, K. (1999). Social "facilitation" as challenge and threat. *Journal of Personality and Social Psychology, 77,* 68–77.

Blass, T. (2004). *The man who shocked the world: The life and legacy of Stanley Milgram.* New York, NY: Basic Books.

Blass, T. (2009). From New Haven to Santa Clara: A historical perspective on the Milgram obedience experiments. *American Psychologist, 64,* 37–45.

Bodenhausen, G. V. (1990). Stereotypes as judgmental heuristics: Evidence of circadian variations in discrimination. *Psychological Science, 1*(5), 319–322.

Bodenhausen, G. V., & Lichtenstein, M. (1987). Social stereotypes and information processing strategies: The impact of task complexity. *Journal of Personality and Social Psychology, 52,* 871–880.

Bond, R., & Smith, P. B. (1996). Culture and conformity: A meta-analysis of studies using Asch's line judgment task. *Psychological Bulletin, 119,* 111–137.

Branscombe, N. R., & Wann, D. L. (1992). Role of identification with a group, arousal, categorization process and self-esteem in sports spectator aggression. *Human Relations, 45*(10), 1013–1033.

Branscombe, N. R., Wohl, M. J. A., Owen, S., Allison, J. A, & N'gbala, A. (2003). Counterfactual thinking, blame assignment, and well-being in rape victims. *Basic and Applied Social Psychology, 25,* 265–273.

Brewer, M. B. (1988). A dual-process model of impression formation. In T. K. Srull & R. S. Wyer (Eds.), *Advances in social cognition* (Vol. 1, pp. 1–36). Hillsdale, NJ: Erlbaum.

Brewer, M. B. (2000). Research design and issues of validity. In H. T. Reis & C. M. Judd (Eds.), *Handbook of research methods in social and personality psychology* (pp. 3–16). Cambridge, England: Cambridge University Press.

Brewer, M. B., & Miller, N. (1996). *Intergroup relations.* Pacific Grove, CA: Brooks/Cole.

Brewer, N., & Wells, G. L. (2011). Eyewitness identification. *Current Directions in Psychological Science, 20,* 24–27.

Brosnan, S. F., & de Waal, F. B. M. (2002). A proximate perspective on reciprocal altruism. *Human Nature, 13,* 129–152.

Brown, R. (1965). *Social psychology.* New York, NY: Free Press.

Brown, R. (1995). *Prejudice: Its social psychology.* Cambridge, MA: Blackwell.

Brown, W. M., Consedine, N. S., & Maqai, C. (2005). Altruism relates to health in an ethnically diverse sample of older adults. *Journals of Gerontology: Psychological Sciences and Social Sciences, 60B*(3), 143–152.

Buller, D. J. (2005). Evolutionary psychology: The emperor's new paradigm. *Trends in Cognitive Sciences, 9,* 277–283.

Burger, J. M. (1986). Increasing compliance by improving the deal: The that's-not-all technique. *Journal of Personality and Social Psychology, 51*(2), 277–283.

Burger, J. M. (2009). Replicating Milgram: Would people still obey today? *American Psychologist, 64,* 1–11.

Burnstein, E., Crandall, C., & Kitayama, S. (1994). Some neo-Darwinian decision rules for altruism: Weighting cues for inclusive fitness as a function of the biological importance of the decision. *Journal of Personality and Social Psychology, 67*(5), 773–789.

Bushman, B. J., & Anderson, C. A. (2009). Comfortably numb: Desensitizing effects of violent media on helping others. *Psychological Science, 20*(3), 273–277.

Bushman, B. J., & Huesmann, R. (2010). Aggression. In S. Fiske, D. Gilbert, & G. Lindzey (Eds.), *Handbook of social psychology* (5th ed., Vol. 2, pp. 833–863). Hoboken, NJ: Wiley.

Buss, D. M. (1989). Sex differences in human mate preferences: Evolutionary hypotheses tested in 37 cultures. *Behavioral and Brain Sciences, 12,* 1–49.

Buss, D. M. (1995). Evolutionary psychology: A new paradigm for psychological science. *Psychological Inquiry, 6,* 1–30.

Buss, D. M. (1996). The evolutionary psychology of human social strategies. In E. T. Higgins & A. W. Kruglanski (Eds.), *Social psychology: Handbook of basic principles* (pp. 3–38). New York, NY: Guilford Press.

Buss, D. M., & Malamuth, N. (Eds.). (1996). *Sex, power, conflict: Evolutionary and feminist perspectives.* New York, NY: Oxford University Press.

Cantor, N., & Mischel, W. (1977). Traits as prototypes: Effects on recognition memory. *Journal of Personality and Social Psychology, 35,* 38–48.

Carlson, D. (Ed.). (2013). *The Oxford handbook of social cognition.* New York, NY: Oxford University Press.

Carlson, M., Charlin, V., & Miller, N. (1988). Positive mood and helping behavior: A test of six hypotheses. *Journal of Personality and Social Psychology, 55*(2), 211–229.

Carver, C. S., & Scheier, M. F. (1981). *Action and self-regulation: A control-theory approach to human behavior.* New York, NY: Springer-Verlag.

Chaiken, S. (1980). Heuristic vs. systematic information processing in the use of source versus message cues in persuasion. *Journal of Personality and Social Psychology, 39,* 752–766.

Chaiken, S., Liberman, A., & Eagly, A. (1989). Heuristic and systematic processing within and beyond the persuasion context. In J. Uleman & J. Bargh (Eds.), *Unintended thought* (pp. 212–252). New York, NY: Guilford Press.

Cialdini, R. B., Darby, B. L., & Vincent, J. E. (1973). Transgression and altruism: A case for hedonism. *Journal of Experimental Social Psychology, 9,* 502–516.

Cialdini, R. B., Schaller, M., Houlihan, D., Arps, K., Fultz, J., & Beaman, A. L. (1987). Empathy-based helping: Is it selflessly or selfishly motivated? *Journal of Personality and Social Psychology, 52*(4), 749–758.

Cialdini, R. B., Vincent, J. E., Lewis, S. K., Catalan, J., Wheeler, D., & Darby, B. L. (1975). Reciprocal concessions procedure for inducing compliance: The door in the face technique. *Journal of Personality and Social Psychology, 31,* 206–215.

Cohen, D., & Nisbett, R. E. (1994). Self-protection and the culture of honor: Explaining southern violence. *Personality and Social Psychology Bulletin, 20*(5), 551–567.

Cohen, D., & Nisbett, R. E. (1997). Field experiments examining the culture of honor: The role of institutions in perpetuating norms about violence. *Personality and Social Psychology Bulletin, 23*(11), 1188–1199.

Coke, J. S., Batson, C. D., & McDavis, K. (1978). Empathic mediation of helping: A two-stage model. *Journal of Personality and Social Psychology, 36,* 752–766.

Compte, A. (1973). *A system of positive polity* (Vol. 1). New York, NY: Burt Franklin. (Original work published 1875)

Cooley, C. H. (1902). *Human nature and social order.* New York, NY: Scribner.

Cooper, J. (2007). *Cognitive dissonance: 50 years of a classic theory.* London, England: Sage.

Crandall, C. S. (1988). Social contagion of binge eating. *Journal of Personality and Social Psychology, 55,* 588–598.

Cunningham, M. R. (1979). Weather, mood, and helping behavior: Quasi experiments with the sunshine Samaritan. *Journal of Personality and Social Psychology, 37*(11), 1947–1956.

Dabbs, J. M., Jr., Carr, T. S., Frady, R. L., & Riad, J. K. (1995). Testosterone, crime, and misbehavior among 692 male prison inmates. *Personality and Individual Differences, 18,* 627–633.

Darley, J. M., & Batson, C. D. (1973). From Jerusalem to Jericho: A study of situational and dispositional variables in helping behavior. *Journal of Personality and Social Psychology, 27,* 100–108.

Darley, J. M., & Gross, P. H. (1983). A hypothesis-confirming bias in labeling effects. *Journal of Personality and Social Psychology, 44,* 20–33.

Darwin, C. (1859). *On the origin of the species by means of natural selection, or preservation of favoured races in the struggle for life.* London, England: Murray.

Darwin, C. (1904). *The expression of emotion in man and animals*. London, England: Murray. (Original work published in 1872)

Dasgupta, N. (2009). Mechanisms underlying the malleability of implicit prejudice and stereotypes: The role of automaticity and cognitive control. In T. D. Nelson (Ed.), *Handbook of prejudice, stereotyping, and discrimination* (pp. 267–284). New York, NY: Psychology Press.

Diener, E., Fraser, S. C., Beaman, A. L., Kelem, R. T. (1976). Effects of deindividuation variables on stealing among Halloween trick-or-treaters. *Journal of Personality and Social Psychology, 33*(2), 178–183.

Dodd, D. K. (1985). Robbers in the classroom: A deindividuation exercise. *Teaching of Psychology, 12*(2), 89–91.

Dollard, J., Miller, N. W., Doob, L. W., Mowrer, O. H., & Sears, R. R. (1939). *Frustration and aggression*. New Haven, CT: Yale University Press.

Doosje, B., Spears, R., de Redelijkheid, H., & van Onna, J. (2007). Memory for stereotype (in)consistent information: The role of ingroup identification. *British Journal of Social Psychology, 46*, 115–128.

Dore, B. P., Zerubavel, N., & Ochsner, K. (2015). Social cognitive neuroscience: A review of core systems. In M. Mikulincer & P. Shaver (Eds.), *APA handbook of personality and social psychology* (Vol. 1, pp. 693–720). Washington, DC: American Psychological Association.

Douglas, E. M., & Strauss, M. A. (2006). Assault and injury of dating partners by university students in 19 countries and its relation to corporal punishment experienced as a child. *European Journal of Criminology, 7*, 293–318.

Dovidio, J. F. (1984). Helping behavior and altruism: An empirical and conceptual overview. In L. Berkowitz (Ed.), *Advances in experimental social psychology* (Vol. 17, pp. 361–427). New York, NY: Academic Press.

Dovidio, J. F., & Gaertner, S. L. (2010). Intergroup bias. In S. T. Fiske, D. T. Gilbert, & G. Lindzey (Eds.), *Handbook of social psychology* (5th ed., Vol. 2, pp. 1084–1121). Hoboken, NJ: Wiley.

Dovidio, J. F., Gaertner, S. L., Isen, A. M., & Lowrance, R. (1995). Group representations and intergroup bias: Positive affect, similarity, and group size. *Personality and Social Psychology Bulletin, 21*(8), 856–865.

Dovidio, J. F., Hewstone, M., Glick, P., & Esses, V. M. (Eds.). (2013). *Sage handbook of prejudice, stereotyping, and discrimination*. Thousand Oaks, CA: Sage.

Duckitt, J. H. (1992). *The social psychology of prejudice*. New York, NY: Praeger.

Dunning, D. (2015). Motivated cognition in self and social thought. In M. Mikulincer & P. R. Shaver (Eds.), *APA handbook of personality and social psychology* (Vol. 1, pp. 777–803). Washington, DC: American Psychological Association.

Dutton, D. G., & Aron, A. P. (1974). Some evidence for heightened sexual attraction under conditions of high anxiety. *Journal of Personality and Social Psychology, 30*(4), 510–517.

Eagly, A. H. (1987). *Sex differences in social behavior: A social-role interpretation*. Hillsdale, NJ: Erlbaum.

Eagly, A. H., & Chaiken, S. (1993). *The psychology of attitudes*. New York, NY: Harcourt Brace Jovanovich.

Eagly, A. H., & Wood, W. (2012). Social role theory. In Van Lange, P., Kruglanski, A., & Higgins, E. (Eds.), *Handbook of theories of social psychology* (Vol. 2, pp. 458–476). New York, NY: Sage.

Ekman, P., Friesen, W. V., O'Sullivan, M., Diacoyanni-Tarlatzis, I., Krause, R., Pitcairn, T., . . . Tzavaras, A. (1987). Universals and cultural differences in the judgments of facial expressions of emotion. *Journal of Personality and Social Psychology, 53*(4), 712–717.

Ellsworth, P. C., & Carlsmith, J. M. (1973). Eye contact and gaze aversion in aggressive encounter. *Journal of Personality and Social Psychology, 33*, 117–122.

Enzle, M. E., & Lowe, C. A. (1976). Helping behavior and social exchange. *Social Behavior and Personality, 4*(2), 261–266.

Epicurus. (1993). *The essential Epicurus: Letters, principal doctrines, Vatican sayings, and fragments* (E. O'Connor, Trans.). Buffalo, NY: Prometheus Books.

Eron, L. D. (1982). Parent-child interaction, television violence, and aggression of children. *American Psychologist, 37*, 197–211.

Eron, L. D., Huesmann, L. R., Lefkowitz, M. M., & Walder, L. O. (1996). Does television violence cause aggression? In D. F. Greenberg (Ed.), *Criminal careers* (Vol. 2, pp. 311–321), Aldershot, England: Dartmouth.

Esser, J. K. (1998). Alive and well after 25 years: A review of groupthink research. *Organizational Behavior and Human Decision Processes, 73*(2/3), 116–141.

Feldman, R. (1968). Response to a compatriot and foreigner who seek assistance. *Journal of Personality and Social Psychology, 10*, 202–214.

Festinger, L. (1954). A theory of social comparison processes. *Human Relations, 7*, 117–140.

Festinger, L. (1957). *A theory of cognitive dissonance*. Palo Alto, CA: Stanford University Press.

Fiedler, K. (2017). Illusory correlation. In R. F. Pohl (Ed.), *Cognitive illusions: Intriguing phenomena in thinking, judgment and memory* (pp. 115–133). New York, NY: Routledge.

Fishbein, M., & Ajzen, I. (1974). Attitudes toward objects as predictors of single and multiple behavioral criteria. *Psychological Review, 81,* 59–74.

Fishbein, M., & Ajzen, I. (1975). *Belief, attitude, intention, and behavior: An introduction to theory and research.* Reading, MA: Addison-Wesley.

Fishman, J. A. (1956). An examination of the process and function of social stereotyping. *Journal of Social Psychology, 43,* 26–64.

Fiske, A. P. (1991). The cultural relativity of selfish individualism: Anthropological evidence that humans are inherently sociable. In M. S. Clark (Ed.), *Review of personality and social psychology* (Vol. 12, pp. 176–214). Newbury Park, CA: Sage.

Fiske, S. T. (1993). Social cognition and social perception. *Annual Review of Psychology, 44,* 155–194.

Fiske, S. T. (2002). What we know now about bias and intergroup conflict, the problem of the century. *Current Directions in Psychological Science, 11*(4), 123–128.

Fiske, S. T., & Neuberg, S. L. (1990). A continuum of impression formation, from category-based to individuating processes: Influences of information and motivation on attention and interpretation. In M. P. Zanna (Ed.), *Advances in experimental social psychology* (Vol. 23, pp. 1–74). New York, NY: Academic Press.

Fiske, S. T., & Tablante, C. B. (2015). Stereotyping: Process and content. In M. Mikulincer & P. R. Shaver (Eds.), *APA handbook of social psychology* (Vol. 1, pp. 457–507). Washington, DC: American Psychological Association.

Fiske, S. T., & Taylor, S. E. (1984). *Social cognition.* New York, NY: Longman.

Fiske, S. T., & Taylor, S. E. (1991). *Social cognition* (2nd ed.). New York, NY: McGraw-Hill.

Fiske, S. T., & Taylor, S. E. (2008). *Social cognition: From brains to culture.* New York, NY: McGraw-Hill.

Forbes, C. E., Cox, C. L., Schmader, T., & Ryan, L. (2011). Negative stereotype activation alters interaction between neural correlates of arousal, inhibition and cognitive control. *Social Cognitive and Affective Neuroscience, 7,* 771–781.

French, J. R. P., & Raven, B. (1959). The bases of social power. In D. Cartwright (Ed.), *Studies in social power* (pp. 150–167). Ann Arbor: University of Michigan.

Freud, S. (1930). *Civilization and its discontents* (J. Riviere, Trans.). London: Hogarth Press.

Freud, S. (1959). *Beyond the pleasure principle.* New York, NY: Bantam Books. (Original work published 1920)

Freud, S. (1963). Why war? In P. Rieff (Ed.), *Freud: Character and culture* (pp. 134–147). New York, NY: Collier Books. (Original work published 1932)

Gaertner, S. L., & Dovidio, J. F. (1986). The aversive form of racism. In J. F. Dovidio & S. L. Gaertner (Eds.), *Prejudice, discrimination, and racism* (pp. 61–89). New York, NY: Academic Press.

Gaertner, S. L., & Dovidio, J. F. (2000). *Reducing intergroup bias: The common ingroup identity model.* New York, NY: Psychology Press.

Gaertner, S. L., Dovidio, J. F., Guerra, R., Hehman, E., & Saguy, T. (2016). A common ingroup identity: Categorization, identity, and intergroup relations. In T. D. Nelson (Ed.), *Handbook of prejudice, stereotyping, and discrimination* (2nd ed., pp. 433–454). New York, NY: Psychology Press.

Gansberg, M. (1964, March 27). Thirty-eight who saw murder didn't call the police. *New York Times.*

Gawronski, B., & Payne, B. K. (Eds.). (2010). *Handbook of implicit social cognition: Measurement, theory and applications.* New York, NY: Guilford Press.

Geen, R. (1995). Aggression. In A. Tesser (Ed.), *Advanced social psychology.* New York, NY: McGraw-Hill.

Gilbert, D. T. (1989). Thinking lightly about others: Automatic components of the social inference process. In J. S. Uleman & J. A. Bargh (Eds.), *Unintended thought* (pp. 189–211). New York, NY: Guilford Press.

Gilbert, D. T. (2002). Inferential correction. In T. Gilovich, D. W. Griffin, & D. Kahneman (Eds.), *Heuristics and biases: The psychology of intuitive judgment* (pp. 167–184). New York, NY: Cambridge University Press.

Gilbert, D. T., & Malone, P. (1995). The correspondence bias. *Psychological Bulletin, 117,* 21–38.

Graf, P., & Schacter, D. (1985). Implicit and explicit memory for new associations in normal and amnesic subjects. *Journal of Experimental Psychology: Learning, Memory, and Cognition, 11,* 501–518.

Greenwald, A. G., & Banaji, M. R. (1995). Implicit social cognition: Attitudes, self-esteem, and stereotypes. *Psychological Review, 102,* 4–27.

Guadagno, R. E. (2018). Social influence. In T. D. Nelson (Ed.), *Getting grounded in social psychology* (pp. 171–191). New York, NY: Routledge.

Guastello, S. J., & Guastello, D. D. (2008). Dynamics of attitudes and genetic processes. *Nonlinear Dynamics, Psychology, and Life Sciences, 12,* 75–86.

Hackman, J. R., & Katz, N. (2010). Group behavior and performance. In S. T. Fiske, D. T. Gilbert, & G. Lindzey (Eds.), *Handbook of social psychology* (5th ed., Vol. 2, pp. 1208–1251). New York, NY: Wiley.

Hamilton, D. L. (1976). Cognitive biases in the perception of social groups. In J. S. Carroll & J. W. Payne (Eds.), *Cognition and social behavior* (pp. 81–93). Hillsdale, NJ: Erlbaum.

Hamilton, D. L., & Rose, T. L. (1980). Illusory correlation and the maintenance of stereotypic beliefs. *Journal of Personality and Social Psychology, 39*(5), 832–845.

Hamilton, D. L., & Sherman, J. W. (1994). Stereotypes. In R. S. Wyer & T. K. Srull (Eds.), *Handbook of social cognition* (2nd ed., Vol. 2, pp. 1–68). Hillsdale, NJ: Erlbaum.

Hamilton, W. D. (1964). The genetical evolution of social behaviour: I and II. *Journal of Theoretical Biology, 7*, 1–52.

Haney, C., Banks, C., & Zimbardo, P. (1973). Interpersonal dynamics in a simulated prison. *International Journal of Criminology and Penology, 1*, 69–97.

Hansen, C. H., & Hansen, R. D. (1988). Finding the face in the crowd: An anger superiority effect. *Journal of Personality and Social Psychology, 54*(6), 917–924.

Harris, M. J., & Rosenthal, R. (1985). Mediation of interpersonal expectancy effects: 31 meta-analyses. *Psychological Bulletin, 97*(3), 363–386.

Hastie, R. (1981). Schematic principles in human memory. In E. T. Higgins, C. P. Herman, & M. P. Zanna (Eds.), *Social cognition: The Ontario symposium* (Vol. 1, pp. 39–88). Hillsdale, NJ: Erlbaum.

Heck, P. R., & Krueger, J. I. (2015). Self enhancement diminished. *Journal of Experimental Psychology: General, 144*(5), 1003–1020.

Heider, F. (1946). Attitudes and cognitive organization. *Journal of Psychology, 21*, 107–112.

Heider, F. (1958). *The psychology of interpersonal relations.* Hoboken, NJ: Wiley & Sons.

Hepworth, J. T., & West, S. G. (1988). Lynching and the economy: A time-series reanalysis of Hovland and Sears (1940). *Journal of Personality and Social Psychology, 55*, 239–247.

Hilton, D. J., Smith, R. H., & Kim, S. H. (1995). Process of causal explanation and dispositional attribution. *Journal of Personality and Social Psychology, 68*, 377–387.

Hilton, J. L., & Darley, J. M. (1991). The effects of interaction goals on person perception. In M. P. Zanna (Ed.), *Advances in experimental social psychology* (Vol. 24, pp. 235–267). San Diego, CA: Academic Press.

Hinde, R. A., & Rowell, T. E. (1962). Communication by posture and facial expression in the rhesus monkey. *Proceedings of the Zoological Society of London, 138*, 1–21.

Hogg, M. A. (2010). Influence and leadership. In S. Fiske, D. Gilbert, & G. Lindzey (Eds.), *Handbook of social psychology* (3rd ed., Vol. 2, pp. 1166–1207). Hoboken, NJ: Wiley & Sons.

Hovland, C. I., Janis, I. L., & Kelly, H. H. (1953). *Communication and persuasion: Psychological studies of opinion change.* New Haven, CT: Yale University Press.

Hovland, C. I., & Sears, R. R. (1940). Minor studies in aggression: VI: Correlation of lynchings with economic indices. *Journal of Psychology, 9*, 182–193.

Hume, D. (1960). *A treatise of human nature.* Oxford, England: Clarendon Press. (Original work published 1888)

Isen, A. M., Clark, M., & Schwartz, M. F. (1976). Duration of the effect of good mood on helping: "Footprints on the sands of time." *Journal of Personality and Social Psychology, 15*, 294–301.

Jackson, L. M. (2015). *The psychology of prejudice: From attitudes to social action.* Washington, DC: American Psychological Association.

James, W. (1890). *The principles of psychology.* New York, NY: Henry Holt.

Janis, I. (1972). *Victims of groupthink: A psychological study of foreign-policy decisions and fiascoes.* Oxford, England: Houghton Mifflin.

Jones, E. E. (1979). The rocky road from acts to dispositions. *American Psychologist, 34*, 107–117.

Jones, E. E. (1985). Major developments in social psychology in the past five decades. In G. Lindzey & E. Aronson (Eds.), *Handbook of social psychology* (pp. 47–107). New York, NY: Random House.

Jones, E. E. (1990). *Interpersonal perception.* New York, NY: Freeman.

Jones, E. E., & Davis, K. E. (1965). From acts to dispositions: The attribution process in person perception. In L. Berkowitz (Ed.), *Advances in experimental social psychology* (Vol. 2, pp. 219–266). New York, NY: Academic Press.

Jones, E. E., Kanouse, D. E., Kelley, H. H., Nisbett, R. E., Valins, S., & Weiner, B. (Eds.). (1972). *Attribution: Perceiving the causes of behavior.* Morristown, NJ: General Learning Press.

Jones, E. E., & Nisbett, R. E. (1972). The actor and the observer: Divergent perceptions of the causes of behavior. In E. E. Jones, D. E. Kanouse, H. H. Kelley, R. E. Nisbett, S. Valins, & B. Weiner (Eds.), *Attribution: Perceiving the causes of behavior.* Morristown, NJ: General Learning Press.

Jones, E. E., & Sigall, H. (1971). The bogus pipeline: A new paradigm for measuring affect and attitude. *Psychological Bulletin, 76*(5), 349–364.

Jones, J. M. (1997). *Prejudice and racism* (2nd ed.). New York, NY: McGraw-Hill.

Kahneman, D. (1995). Varieties of counterfactual thinking. In N. J. Roese & J. M. Olson (Eds.), *What might have been: The social psychology of counterfactual thinking* (pp. 375–396). Hillsdale, NJ: Erlbaum.

Kahneman, D., Slovic, P., & Tversky, A. (1982). *Judgment under uncertainty: Heuristics and biases.* New York, NY: Cambridge University Press.

Kahneman, D., & Tversky, A. (1973). On the psychology of prediction. *Psychological Review, 80,* 237–251.

Kahneman, D., & Tversky, A. (1982). Variants of uncertainty. *Cognition, 11*(2), 143–157.

Keller, M. C., Fredrickson, B. L., Ybarra, O., Côté, S., Johnson, K., Mikels, J., Conway, A., & Wager, T. (2005). A warm heart and a clear head: The contingent effects of weather on mood and cognition. *Psychological Science, 16*(9), 724–731.

Kelley, H. H. (1950). The warm-cold variable in first impressions of persons. *Journal of Personality, 18,* 431–439.

Kelley, H. H. (1967). Attribution theory in social psychology. In D. Levine (Ed.), *Nebraska symposium on motivation* (pp. 192–241). Lincoln: University of Nebraska Press.

Kinder, D. R., & Sears, D. O. (1981). Prejudice and politics: Symbolic racism vs. racial threats to the good life. *Journal of Personality and Social Psychology, 40,* 414–431.

Krahe, B., Moller, I., Huesmann, L. R., Kirwil, L., Felber, J., & Berger, A. (2011). Desensitization to media violence: Links with habitual media violence exposure, aggressive cognitions and aggressive behavior. *Journal of Personality and Social Psychology, 100*(4), 630–646.

Krebs, D. (1987). The challenge of altruism in biology and psychology. In C. Crawford, M. Smith, & D. Krebs (Eds.), *Sociobiology and psychology: Ideas, issues, and applications* (pp. 81–118). Hillsdale, NJ: Erlbaum.

Krueger, J. I., Heck, P. R., & Athenstaedt, U. (2018). The search for the self. In T. D. Nelson (Ed.), *Getting grounded in social psychology* (pp. 15–36). New York, NY: Routledge.

Kruger, D. J. (2003). Evolution and altruism: Combining psychological mediators with naturally selected tendencies. *Evolution and Human Behavior, 24*(2), 118–125.

Kruglanski, A., & Stroebe, W. (2012). *Handbook of the history of social psychology.* New York, NY: Psychology Press.

Kubota, J. T., & Phelps, E. A. (2015). Insights from functional magnetic resonance imaging research on race. In T. D. Nelson (Ed.), *Handbook of prejudice, stereotyping,* and discrimination (2nd ed., pp. 299–312). New York, NY: Psychology Press.

Kunda, Z. (1999). *Social cognition: Making sense of people.* Cambridge, MA: MIT Press.

Kunda, Z., & Oleson, K. C. (1995). Maintaining stereotypes in the face of disconfirmation: Constructing grounds for subtyping deviants. *Journal of Personality and Social Psychology, 68*(4), 565–579.

Larson, J. R. (1977). Evidence for a self-serving bias in the attribution of causality. *Journal of Personality, 45*(3), 430–441.

Latané, B., & Darley, J. M. (1968). Group inhibition of bystander intervention in emergencies. *Journal of Personality and Social Psychology, 10*(3), 215–221.

Latané, B., & Darley, J. M. (1970). *The unresponsive bystander: Why doesn't he help?* Englewood Cliffs, NJ: Prentice Hall.

Latané, B., Williams, K., & Harkins, S. (1979). Many hands make light the work: The causes and consequences of social loafing. *Journal of Personality and Social Psychology, 37,* 822–832.

Levine, J. M., & Moreland, R. L. (1998). Small groups. In D. T. Gilbert, S. T. Fiske, & G. Lindzey (Eds.), *Handbook of social psychology* (4th ed., Vol. 2, pp. 415–469). New York, NY: McGraw-Hill.

Levine, M., Prosser, A., Evans, D., & Reicher, S. (2005). Identity and emergency intervention: How social group membership and inclusiveness of group boundaries shape helping behavior. *Personality and Social Psychology Bulletin, 31*(4), 443–453.

Lewin, K. (1951). *Field theory in social science: Selected theoretical papers.* Oxford, England: Harpers.

Lippmann, W. (1922). *Public opinion.* New York, NY: Harcourt, Brace, Jovanovich.

Lockard, J. S., McDonald, L. L., Clifford, D. A., & Martinez, R. (1976). Panhandling: Sharing of resources. *Science, 191,* 406–408.

Lorenz, K. (1966). *On aggression* (M. K. Wilson, Trans.). New York, NY: Harcourt, Brace & World.

Maccoby, E. E., & Jacklin, C. N. (1974). *The psychology of sex differences.* Stanford, CA: Stanford University Press.

Macrae, C. N., Bodenhausen, G. V., Milne, A. B., & Jetten, J. (1994). Out of mind but back in sight: Stereotypes on the rebound. *Journal of Personality and Social Psychology, 67*(5), 808–817.

Macrae, C. N., Milne, A. B., & Bodenhausen, G. V. (1994). Stereotypes as energy-saving devices: A peek inside the cognitive toolbox. *Journal of Personality and Social Psychology, 66*(1), 37–47.

Manucia, G. K., Baumann, D. J., Cialdini, R. B. (1984). Mood influences on helping: Direct effects or side effects? *Journal of Personality and Social Psychology, 46*(2), 357–364.

Markus, H., & Nurius, P. (1986). Possible selves. *American Psychologist, 41*(9), 954–969.

McConahay, J. B. (1986). Modern racism, ambivalence, and the Modern Racism Scale. In J. Dovidio & S. Gaertner (Eds.), *Prejudice, discrimination, and racism* (pp. 91–125). New York: Academic Press.

McDougall, W. (1908). *An introduction to social psychology.* Boston, MA: John Luce.

McDougall, W. (1926). *An introduction to social psychology* (Rev. ed.). Boston, MA: John Luce.

McKeown, S., & Dixon, J. (2017). The "contact hypothesis": Critical reflections and future directions. *Social and Personality Psychology Compass, 11*(1), e12295.

Milgram, S. (1963). Behavioral study of obedience. *Journal of Abnormal and Social Psychology, 67*, 371–378.

Mill, J. S. (1971). *Utilitarianism.* Indianapolis, IN: Bobbs-Merrill. (Original work published 1863)

Miller, D. T., Turnbull, W., & McFarland, C. (1990). Counterfactual thinking and social perception: Thinking about what might have been. In L. Berkowitz (Ed.), *Advances in experimental social psychology* (Vol. 22, pp. 305–331). San Diego, CA: Academic Press.

Miller, G. A. (1956). The magical number seven, plus or minus two: Some limits on our capacity for processing information. *Psychological Review, 63*(2), 81–97.

Miller, H. L. (1953). *Understanding group behavior: A discussion guide.* Chicago, IL: Center for the Study of Liberal Education for Adults.

Molitor, F., & Hirsch, K. W. (1994). Children's toleration of real-life aggression after exposure to media violence: A replication of Drabman and Thomas studies. *Child Study Journal, 24*(3), 191–207.

Montoya, E. R., Terburg, D., Bos, P. A., & van Honk, J. (2012). Testosterone, cortisol, and serotonin as key regulators of social aggression: A review and theoretical perspective. *Motivation and Emotion, 36*, 65–73.

Moscovici, S., & Zavalloni, M. (1969). The group as a polarizer of attitudes. *Journal of Personality and Social Psychology, 12*, 125–135.

Moskowitz, G. (2005). *Social cognition: Understanding self and others.* New York, NY: Guilford Press.

Moyer, K. E. (1983). The physiology of motivation: Aggression as a model. In C. J. Scheier & A. M. Rogers (Eds.), *G. Stanley Hall Lecture Series* (Vol. 3). Washington, DC: American Psychological Association.

Muller, M. S., Moe, B., & Groothuis, T. G. (2014). Testosterone increases siblicidal aggression in black-legged kittiwake chicks. *Behavioral Ecology and Sociobiology, 68*(2), 223–232.

Mullin, C. R., & Linz, D. (1995). Desensitization and resensitization of violence against women: Effects of exposure to sexually violent films on judgments of domestic violence victims. *Journal of Personality and Social Psychology, 69*(3), 449–459.

National Research Council. (2014). *Identifying the culprit: Assessing eyewitness identification.* Washington, DC: National Academies Press.

Nelson, T. D. (1998). A stimulus-response social psychology? *American Psychologist, 53*(9), 1078.

Nelson, T. D. (2006). *The psychology of prejudice* (2nd ed.). New York, NY: Pearson.

Nelson, T. D. (Ed.). (2016). *Handbook of prejudice, stereotyping, and discrimination* (2nd ed.). New York, NY: Psychology Press.

Neville, H. A., Gallardo, M. E., & Sue, D. W. (Eds.). (2016). *The myth of racial color blindness: Manifestations, dynamics and impact.* Washington, DC: American Psychological Association.

Newcomb, T. M. (1943). *Personality and social change: Attitude formation in a student community.* New York, NY: Holt, Rinehart & Winston.

Newcomb, T. M., Koenig, K. E., Flacks, R., & Warwick, D. P. (1967). *Persistence and change: Bennington College and its students after 25 years.* New York, NY: Wiley & Sons.

Niedenthal, P. M., Setterlund, M. B., & Wherry, M. B. (1992). Possible self-complexity and affective reactions to goal-relevant evaluation. *Journal of Personality and Social Psychology, 63*, 5–16.

Nisbett, R. E. (1993). Violence and U.S. regional culture. *American Psychologist, 48*, 441–449.

Nisbett, R. E., Krantz, D. H., Jepson, C., & Kunda, Z. (1983). The use of statistical heuristics in everyday inductive reasoning. *Psychological Review, 90*, 339–363.

Nisbett, R. E., & Ross, L. (1980). *Human inference: Strategies and shortcomings of social judgment.* Englewood Cliffs, NJ: Prentice-Hall.

Ochsner, K., & Lieberman, M. (2001). The emergence of social cognitive neuroscience. *American Psychologist, 56*(9), 717–734.

O'Keefe, D. (2013). The elaboration likelihood model. In J. Dillard & L. Shen (Eds.), *The Sage handbook of persuasion: Developments in theory and practice*. Thousand Oaks, CA: Sage.

Olson, J. M., Roese, N. J., & Zanna, M. P. (1996). Expectancies. In E. T. Higgins & A. W. Kruglanski (Eds.), *Social psychology: Handbook of basic principles* (pp. 211–238). New York, NY: Guilford Press.

Paik, H., & Comstock, G. (1994). The effects of television violence on antisocial behavior: A meta-analysis. *Communication Research, 21,* 516–546.

Patterson, A. H. (1974). Hostility catharsis: A naturalistic quasi-experiment. *Personality and Social Psychology Bulletin, 1,* 195–197.

Pendry, L. F., & Macrae, C. N. (1996). What the disinterested perceiver overlooks: Goal-directed social categorization. *Personality and Social Psychology Bulletin, 22*(3), 249–256.

Pettigrew, T. (1959). Regional differences in anti–negro prejudice. *Journal of Abnormal and Social Psychology, 59,* 28–36.

Pettigrew, T. F. (1998). Intergroup contact theory. *Annual Review of Psychology, 49,* 65–85.

Petty, R. E., & Cacioppo, J. T. (1983). Central and peripheral routes to persuasion: Application to advertising. In L. Percy & A. Woodside (Eds.), *Advertising and consumer psychology* (pp. 3–23). Lexington, MA: Lexington Books.

Petty, R. E., & Cacioppo, J. T. (1986). The elaboration likelihood model of persuasion. In L. Berkowitz (Ed.), *Advances in experimental social psychology* (Vol. 19, pp. 123–205). New York, NY: Academic Press.

Phillips, D. P. (1983). The impact of mass media violence on U.S. homicides. *American Sociological Review, 48,* 560–568.

Piliavin, J. A., & Charng, H. (1990). Altruism: A review of recent theory and research. *Annual Review of Sociology, 16,* 27–65.

Post, S. G. (2005). Altruism, happiness, and health: It's good to be good. *International Journal of Behavioral Medicine, 12*(2), 66–77.

Postmes, T., & Spears, R. (1998). Deindividuation and antinormative behavior: A meta-analysis. *Psychological Bulletin, 123*(3), 238–259.

Prentice-Dunn, S., & Rogers, R. W. (1980). Effects of deindividuating situational cues and aggressive models on subjective deindividuation and aggression. *Journal of Personality and Social Psychology, 39,* 104–113.

Price, K. H., Harrison, D. A., & Gavin, J. H. (2006). Withholding inputs in team contexts: Member composition, interaction processes, evaluation structure, and social loafing. *Journal of Applied Psychology, 91,* 1375–1384.

Ray, W. S. (1951). *A laboratory manual for social psychology*. New York, NY: American Book Company.

Reis, H. T., & Judd, C. M. (2000). *Handbook of research methods in social and personality psychology*. Cambridge, England: Cambridge University Press.

Richeson, J. A., Todd, A. R., Trawalter, S., & Baird, A. A. (2008). Eye-gaze direction modulates race-related amygdala activity. *Group Processes and Intergroup Relations, 11*(2), 23–246.

Robertson, T. (2006). Dissonance effects as conformity to consistency norms: The effect of anonymity and identity salience. *British Journal of Social Psychology, 45*(4), 683–699.

Roediger, H. L. (1990). Implicit memory: Retention without awareness. *American Psychologist, 45,* 1043–1056.

Roese, N. J. (1997). Counterfactual thinking. *Psychological Bulletin, 121,* 133–148.

Roese, N. J., & Jamieson, D. W. (1993). Twenty years of bogus pipeline research: A critical review and meta-analysis. *Psychological Bulletin, 114*(2), 363–375.

Roese, N. J., & Olson, J. M. (1995). *What might have been: The social psychology of counterfactual thinking*. Hillsdale, NJ: Erlbaum.

Rohan, M. J., & Zanna, M. P. (1996). Value transmission in families. In C. Seligman, J. M. Olson, & M. P. Zanna (Eds.), *The psychology of values: The Ontario symposium* (Vol. 8, pp. 253–276). Mahwah, NJ: Erlbaum.

Rose, H., & Rose, S. (2000). *Alas, poor Darwin: Arguments against evolutionary psychology*. London, England: Johnathan Cape.

Rosenhan, D. L. (1973). On being sane in insane places. *Science, 179*(4070), 250–258.

Rosenhan, D. L., Salovey, P., & Hargis, K. (1981). The joys of helping: Focus of attention mediates the impact of positive affect on altruism. *Journal of Personality and Social Psychology, 40,* 899–905.

Rosenthal, R. (1995). Critiquing Pygmalion: A 25-year perspective. *Current Directions in Psychological Science, 4*(6), 171–172.

Rosenthal, R., & Jacobson, L. (1968). *Pygmalion in the classroom: Teacher expectation and pupils' intellectual development*. New York, NY: Holt, Rinehart & Winston.

Ross, E. A. (1908a). The nature and scope of social psychology. *American Journal of Sociology, 13*(5), 577–583.

Ross, E. A. (1908b). *Social psychology*. Oxford, England: Macmillan.

Ross, L. (1977). The intuitive psychologist and his shortcomings: Distortions in the attribution process. In L. Berkowitz (Ed.), *Advances in experimental social psychology* (Vol. 10, pp. 173–220). New York, NY: Academic Press.

Ross, L., Lepper, M. R., & Hubbard, M. (1975). Perseverance in self-perception and social perception: Biased attribution processes in the debriefing paradigm. *Journal of Personality and Social Psychology, 32*, 880–892.

Rothbart, M., Evans, M., & Fulero, S. (1979). Recall for confirming events: Memory processes and the maintenance of social stereotyping. *Journal of Experimental Social Psychology, 15*, 343–355.

Rowatt, W. C., Carpenter, T., & Haggard. M. (2014). Religion, prejudice, and intergroup relations. In V. Saraglou (Ed.), *Religion, personality, and social behavior* (pp. 170–192). New York, NY: Psychology Press.

Ruback, R. B., & Weiner, N. A. (Eds.). (1995). *Interpersonal violent behaviors: Social and cultural aspects*. New York, NY: Springer.

Rushton, J. P. (1989). Genetic similarity, human altruism, and group selection. *Behavioral and Brain Science, 12*, 503–518.

Sabini, J., Siepmann, M., & Stein, J. (2001). The really fundamental attribution error in social psychological research. *Psychological Inquiry, 12*, 1–15.

Sanna, L. J., Chang, E. C., & Meier, S. (2001). Counterfactual thinking and self-motives. *Personality and Social Psychology Bulletin, 27*, 1023–1024.

Schwarz, N. (1990). Feelings as information: Informational and motivational functions of affective states. In R. Sorrentino & E. T. Higgins (Eds.), *Handbook of motivation and cognition* (Vol. 2, pp. 527–561). New York, NY: Guilford Press.

Schwarz, N., & Clore, G. L. (1983). Mood, misattribution, and judgments of well-being: Informative and directive functions of affective states. *Journal of Personality and Social Psychology, 45*(3), 513–523.

Schwarz, N., & Clore, G. L. (1988). Feelings and phenomenal experiences. In A. Kruglanski & E. T. Higgins (Eds.), *Social psychology: Handbook of basic principles* (pp. 385-407). New York, NY: Guilford Press.

Scott, S. K., Young, A. W., Calder, A. J., Hellawell, D. J., Aggleton, J. P., & Johnson, M. (1997). Impaired auditory recognition of fear and anger following bilateral amygdala lesions. *Nature, 385*(6613), 254–257.

Sears, D. O. (1986). College sophomores in the laboratory: Influences of a narrow data base on social psychology's view of human nature. *Journal of Personality and Social Psychology, 51*(3), 515–530.

Sedikedes, C., & Gregg, A. P. (2003). Portraits of the self. In M. A. Hogg & J. Cooper (Eds.), *The Sage handbook of social psychology* (pp. 110–138). Thousand Oaks, CA: Sage.

Sharot, T. (2011). *The optimism bias: A tour of the irrationally positive brain*. New York, NY: Pantheon.

Sherif, M., Harvey, O. J., White, B. J., Hood, W. R., & Sherif, C. W. (1961). *Intergroup contact and cooperation: The robber's cave experiment*. Norman: Oklahoma Book Exchange.

Sigall, H., & Page, R. (1971). Current stereotypes: A little fading, a little faking. *Journal of Personality and Social Psychology, 18*(2), 247–255.

Sinclair, S., Dunn, E., & Lowery, B. S. (2005). The relationship between parental racial attitudes and children's implicit prejudice. *Journal of Experimental Social Psychology, 41*, 283–289.

Smith, R. E., Smythe, L., & Lien, D. (1972). Inhibition of helping behavior by a similar or dissimilar nonreactive fellow bystander. *Journal of Personality and Social Psychology, 23*(3), 414–419.

Snyder, M. (1974). Self-monitoring of expressive behavior. *Journal of Personality and Social Psychology, 30*(4), 526–537.

Sole, K., Marton, J., & Hornstein, H. A. (1975). Opinion similarity and helping: Three field experiments investigating the bases of promotive tension. *Journal of Experimental Social Psychology, 11*, 1–13.

Srull, T. K. (1981). Person memory: Some tests of associative storage and retrieval models. *Journal of Experimental Psychology: Human Learning and Memory, 7*, 440–462.

Stephan, W. G. (1985). Intergroup relations. In G. Lindzey & E. Aronson (Eds.), *Handbook of social psychology* (3rd ed., Vol. 2, pp. 599–658). New York, NY: Random House.

Stotland, E. (1969). Exploratory studies of empathy. In L. Berkowitz (Ed.), *Advances in experimental social psychology* (Vol. 4, pp. 271–313). San Diego, CA: Academic Press.

Stroebe, W., & Insko, C. A. (1989). Stereotype, prejudice, and discrimination: Changing conceptions in theory and research. In D. Bar-Tal, C. F. Graumann, A. W. Kruglanski, & W. Stroebe (Eds.), *Stereotyping and prejudice: Changing conceptions* (pp. 3–34). New York, NY: Academic Press.

Swann, W. B., Jr. (2012). Self-verification theory. In P. A. M. Van Lange, A. W. Kruglanski, & E. T. Higgins (Eds.), *Handbook of theories of social psychology* (Vol. 2, pp. 23–42). Thousand Oaks, CA: Sage.

Swann, W. B., Jr., & Bosson, J. K. (2010). Self and identity. In S. T. Fiske, D. T. Gilbert, & G. Lindzey (Eds.), *Handbook of social psychology* (5th ed., Vol. 1, pp. 589–628). Hoboken, NJ: Wiley & Sons.

Swann, W. B., Jr., De La Ronde, C., & Hixon, J. G. (1994). Authenticity and positivity strivings in marriage and courtship. *Journal of Personality and Social Psychology, 66,* 857–869.

Swann, W. B., Jr., & Read, S. J. (1981). Self-verification processes: How we sustain our self-conceptions. *Journal of Experimental Social Psychology, 17*(4), 351–372.

Tajfel, H., Flament, C., Billig, K., & Bundy, R. (1971). Social categorization and intergroup behaviour. *European Journal of Social Psychology, 1,* 149–175.

Taylor, S. E. (1981). The interface of cognitive and social psychology. In J. Harvey (Ed.), *Cognition, social behavior, and the environment* (pp. 189–211). Hillsdale, NJ: Erlbaum.

Taylor, S. E., & Crocker, J. (1981). Schematic bases of social information processing. In E. T. Higgins, C. P. Herman, & M. P. Zanna (Eds.), *Social cognition: The Ontario symposium* (Vol. 1, pp. 89–134). Hillsdale, NJ: Erlbaum.

Thibaut, J. W., & Kelley, H. H. (1959). *The social psychology of groups.* Oxford, England: Wiley.

Thomas, M. H., Horton, R. W., Lippincott, E. C., & Drabman, R. S. (1977). Desensitization to portrayals of real-life aggression as a function of exposure to television violence. *Journal of Personality and Social Psychology, 35*(6), 450–458.

Tversky, A., & Kahneman, D. (1974). Judgment under uncertainty: Heuristics and biases. *Science, 211,* 453–458.

Twenge, J. M., Baumeister, R. F., DeWall, C. N., Ciarocco, N. J., & Bartels, J. M. (2007). Social exclusion decreases prosocial behavior. *Journal of Personality and Social Psychology, 92,* 56–66.

Waller, N. G., Kojetin, B. A., Bouchard, T. J. Jr., Lykken, D. T., & Tellegen, A. (1990). Genetic and environmental influences on religious interests, attitudes, and values: A study of twins reared apart and together. *Psychological Science, 1,* 138–142.

Warrington, E. K., & Weiskrantz, L. (1970). The amnesic syndrome: Consolidation or retrieval? *Nature, 228,* 628–630.

Watson, J. B. (1925). *Behaviorism.* New York, NY: Norton.

Weigel, R. H., & Newman, L. S. (1976). Increasing attitude-behavior correspondence by broadening the scope of the behavioral measure. *Journal of Personality and Social Psychology, 33,* 793–802.

Weyant, J. M. (1978). Effects of mood states, costs, and benefits of helping. *Journal of Personality and Social Psychology, 36*(10), 1169–1176.

White, R. K. (2002). Causal attribution from covariation information: The evidential evaluation model. *European Journal of Social Psychology, 32,* 667–684.

Wicker, A. W. (1969). Attitude versus actions: The relationship of verbal and overt behavioral responses to attitude objects. *Journal of Social Issues, 25*(4), 41–78.

Wicker, A. W. (1971). An examination of the "other variable" explanation of attitude-behavior inconsistency. *Journal of Personality and Social Psychology 19,* 18–30.

Wigboldus, D. H. J., Dijksterhuis, A., & van Knippenberg, A. (2003). When stereotypes get in the way: Stereotypes obstruct stereotype–inconsistent trait inferences. *Journal of Personality and Social Psychology, 84*(3), 470–484.

Williams, R. M. (1947). *Reduction of intergroup tension.* New York, NY: Social Science Research Council.

Wilner, D. M., Walkley, R., & Cook, S. W. (1955). *Human relations in interracial housing: A test of the contact hypothesis.* Minneapolis: University of Minnesota Press.

Wilson, T. D., Lisle, D. J., Kraft, D., & Wetzel, C. G. (1989). Preferences as expectation-driven inferences: Effects of affective expectations on affective experience. *Journal of Personality and Social Psychology, 56,* 519–530.

Wolsko, C., Park, B., Judd, C. M., & Wittenbrink, B. (2000). Framing interethnic ideology: Effects of multicultural and color-blind perspectives on judgments of groups and individuals. *Journal of Personality and Social Psychology, 78*(4), 635–654.

Wundt, W. (1897). *Grundzüge der physiologischen Psychologie.* Leipzig, Germany: Engelmann.

Wyatt, D. F., & Campbell, D. T. (1951). On the liability of stereotype or hypothesis. *Journal of Abnormal and Social Psychology, 46,* 496–500.

Wyer, N. A. (2010). You never get a second chance to make a first (implicit) impression: The role of elaboration in the formation and revision of implicit impressions. *Social Cognition, 28,* 1–19.

Wyer, R. S., & Srull, T. K. (Eds.). (1994). *Handbook of social cognition* (2nd ed., Vol. 1). Hillsdale, NJ: Erlbaum.

Xidias, J. (2016). Are terrorists evil? Philip Zimbardo and the darkness within us all. *MCAT Thinking News.* Retrieved from https://www.macat.com/blog/are-terrorists-evil-zimbardo

Yang, Y., Raine, A., & Colletti, P. (2010). Morphological alterations in the prefrontal cortex and the amygdala in unsuccessful psychopaths. *Journal of Abnormal Psychology, 119,* 546–554.

Zajonc, R. B. (1965). Social facilitation. *Science, 149*, 269–274.

Zajonc, R. B., Heingartner, A., & Herman, E. M. (1969). Social enhancement and impairment of performance in the cockroach. *Journal of Personality and Social Psychology, 13*(2), 83–92.

Zarate, M. A., & Garza, A. A. (2002). In group distinctiveness and self-affirmation as dual components of prejudice reduction. *Self & Identity, 1*, 235–249.

Zimbardo, P. (1969). The human choice: Individuation, reason and order versus deindividuation, impulse and chaos. In *Nebraska symposium on motivation* (Vol. 17, pp. 237–307). Lincoln: University of Nebraska Press.